Rethink
Mahābharata

Rethinking the Mahābhārata

A Reader's Guide to the Education of the Dharma King

Alf Hiltebeitel

The University of Chicago Press
Chicago and London

ALF HILTEBEITEL is professor of religion and director of the Human Sciences Program at The George Washington University. He is the author or editor of numerous books including the two-volume *Cult of Draupadi* and *Rethinking India's Oral and Classical Epics*, both published by the University of Chicago Press.

The University of Chicago Press, Chicago 60637
The University of Chicago Press, Ltd., London

Printed in the United States of America
10 09 08 07 06 05 04 03 02 01 1 2 3 4 5
ISBN: 0-226-34053-8 (cloth)
ISBN: 0-226-34054-6 (paper)

Library of Congress Cataloging-in-Publication Data

Hiltebeitel, Alf.
Rethinking the Mahabharata : a reader's guide to the education of the dharma king / Alf Hiltebeitel.
p. cm
Includes bibliographical references and index.
ISBN 0-226-34053-8 (cloth : alk. paper) — ISBN 0-226-34054-6 (pbk. : alk. paper)
1. Mahābhārata—Criticism, interpretation, etc. I. Title.

BL1138.26 .H45 2001
294.5'923046—dc21 2001027300

To BE

Contents

Acknowledgments

Since 1991, I have known I was headed toward writing a second book about the *Mahābhārata*. It took its twists and turns, but it has been an exciting time to be writing a book about this text. Bookended at the beginning by the ninety-three segments of "Mahābhārata" on Indian national television and at the end by the resumption after over twenty years of the University of Chicago Press's *Mahābhārata* translation, one could almost call it a decade of ferment. It has been a time of deepening awareness of the *Mahābhārata*, for sharpening arguments about it, and for respectful and pleasurable exchange of scholarly views as to its character. With that in mind, I simply wish to thank all those with whom I have been "in conference" reasoning and learning about it during this period: Nick Allen, Marshall Alcorn, Gregory D. Alles, Inés Azar, Greg Bailey, Madeleine Biardeau, Andreas Bigger, John Brockington, Mary Brockington, Johannes Bronkhorst, Yigal Bronner, Alfred Collins, Arti Dhand, Wendy Doniger, Paul Duff, Danielle Feller, James L. Fitzgerald, Norman J. Girardot, David Gitomer, Ariel Glucklich, Robert P. Goldman, Barbara Gombach, Patricia Meridith Grier, Christiano Grottanelli, Don Handelman, Lindsey Harlan, Jack Hawley, Jan Heesterman, Mislav Ježić, Ruth Katz, Randy Kloetzli, Walter O. Koenig, Petteri Koskikallio, James Laine, Mukund Lath, Julia Leslie, Philip Lutgendorf, Thennilapuram Mahadevan, Aditya Malik, J. L. Mehta, Barbara Diane Miller, Barbara Stoller Miller, Robert Minor, Laurie L. Patton, Indira V. Peterson, Sheldon I. Pollock, Edgar Polomé, A. K. Ramanujan, Velcheru Narayana Rao, Tamar Chana Reich, Paula Richman, William Sax, Peter Schreiner, Martha Anne Selby, Arvind Sharma, David Dean Shulman, Doris M. Srinivisan, Ravindran Sriramachandran, Frits Staal, Bruce M. Sullivan, Gary Tubb, Yaraslov Vassilkov, and Michael Witzel.

I would especially like to thank Walter O. Koenig for the stimulating conversation that helped to crystallize the subtitle of this book.

For his editorial acumen, I thank David Brent.

To my sons Adam and Simon and my nephews Conrad and Victor Gould, thanks for the chapters in the mountains.

Conventions

Sanskrit terms generally follow the transcriptions of the standard cited dictionaries. Where terms from other South Asian languages are cited, I generally follow the transcriptions of other translators, though sometimes, perforce, selectively. Translations are my own unless otherwise indicated.

1 Introduction

Western scholarly reception of the *Mahābhārata* is squarely built upon the premise, aired most magisterially by Moriz Winternitz and Hermann Oldenberg, that the *Mahābhārata* is a "literary unthing" (*literarisches Unding*),[1] a "monstrous chaos" (*ungeheuerliches Chaos*).[2] Although our time is now one in which "literary monstrosity" might imply a kind of artistry (one thinks first of Henry James writing on the art of the novel as "such large loose and baggy monsters"),[3] the phrase is simply not adequate to the critical task. Nonetheless, the premise of monstrosity has served a purpose. It has allowed scholars of very different persuasions and interests to design a *Mahābhārata* of convenience through which to nurture—with more bombast than debate, and with scarcely anything that could be called cumulative results—their own contradictory notions of origins and their equally contradictory developmental theories.

Rather than continuing to invest in these assumptions, we might consider how we have come to form them. Much of their underpinnings derive—to carry on with Hans Georg Gadamer—from a concurrence of

[1]Winternitz 1908–22, 1:272; cf. Winternitz 1962, 1:305: "a literary nonsense."

[2]Oldenberg 1922, 1. Cf. Mehta 1971, 69; Proudfoot 1979, 42; Fitzgerald 1980, 30–33; Mangels 1994, 149; Oberlies 1998, 127 and 140; and Reich 1998, 8 and 255 on these passages. Hopkins 1898a, 10, 21, and Kipling (Pinney 1986, 177–78) use similar imagery, as does Mauss saying that "Le Mahabharata est l'histoire d'un gigantesque potlatch" (1950, 243)—something is lost in the translation "a tremendous potlatch" (1967, 54).

[3]James 1922, x. In his Preface to *The Tragic Muse*, written nine years after its first edition, James writes, concurrently with Winternitz and Oldenberg, ". . . again and again, perversely, incurably, the centre of my structure would insist on pacing itself *not*, so to speak, in the middle. . . . [T]he terminational terror was none the less certain to break in and my work threaten to masquerade for me as an active figure condemned to the disgrace of legs too short, ever so much too short, for its body" (xi). Cf. Borges 1964, 26: "Almost instantly, I understood: 'the garden of forking paths' was the chaotic novel" (cf. Hegarty 2000, 11); 23: "I thought of a labyrinth of labyrinths, of one sinuous spreading labyrinth that would encompass the past and the future and in some way involve the stars."

"historically effected consciousnesses."[4] On the one side, Western desires want to straighten out the *Mahābhārata* with the tools of lower and higher criticism, and fault it for not being the *Iliad* (Hiltebeitel 1995b, 25–27; van der Veer 1999, 114–16). On the other, Indian desires wander beyond credibility in attempting to date the *Mahābhārata* war and to find archeological evidence for its "epic period."[5] These desires (or horizons) are not always incompatible, and are all too easy to "fuse."

The epic has been mined for Indo-European myth,[6] Indo-European epic,[7] Indo-European goddesses (Dumézil 1948; Polomé 1988), non-Indo-European goddesses,[8] oral epic,[9] a prior epic cycle,[10] a pre-Brahmanic Kṣatriya tradition,[11] an historical kernel;[12] a textual kernel;[13] the "'old' narrative" beneath the final written "surface";[14] etc. Fed by such varied originary imaginings and notions of growth, strata, interpolation, and prior orality, this excavative scholarship[15] posits an "extant" *Mahābhārata* as the terrain to excavate.[16] It privileges

[4]Pluralizing Gadamer's term (1993, xv, 297–307, 340–79, 396–97); cf. Pollock 1984a, 17.

[5]See van der Veer 1994, 145, 157–62, and below, § B. For impossible datings of the *Mbh* war, too numerous to mention, see Sircar 1969c, who is noteworthy for his contrary view.

[6]See Hiltebeitel [1976] 1990; Wikander 1948; Dumézil 1948, 1968; Dubuisson 1978; Polomé 1988.

[7]As I attempted in Hiltebeitel 1975; [1976] 1990, 28–59, 336–53; and 1982, following the lead of Wikander 1950, 1960a and b, 1978. See also Allen 1996a, 1996b, 1999, 251–52.

[8]Katz 1989, xxi urged that my book be a "retrieval" of such. See Hiltebeitel 1980a, 104.

[9]Advocates of bringing oral theory to the Sanskrit epics include Sen 1966; P. A. Grintser (see de Jong 1975); J. D. Smith 1980, 1987; Ingalls and Ingalls 1991; and, most representatively, M. C. Smith 1972 and 1992, Vassilkov 1995, and J. Brockington 1998. For negative assessments, see Alles 1994, 123; Reich 1998, 26–29.

[10]Katz 1989, 37–38, 50–51, nn. 49 and 50, 57; 1991, 133–35, 146–48 revives the notion that the Pāṇḍava story was "grafted" onto an original Kuru-Pāñcāla cycle; cf. Mazumdar 1906, 225–26; Bhattacharya 1969, 37. For a critique, see Hiltebeitel 1993, 7–9.

[11]J. Brockington 1998, 82, 231; Vassilkov 1999; Salomon 1995b on the epics' "Kṣatriya Sanskrit"; Witzel 1987b, 207, on "non-Brahmanical texts" like the *Mbh*; Oberlies 1998, 141.

[12]It is a particularly baffling fancy (e.g., Brockington 1998, 5; Witzel 1989b, 335) that the Battle of the Ten Kings mentioned in *ṚV* 7.33.3,5 and 83.8 could prefigure the *Mbh*.

[13]See, e.g., M. C. Smith 1972, 1975, 1992; Yardi 1986; Bhattacharji 1992–93, 481, joining Chadwick's notion (1912) of an heroic age to a capacious reading of "Bhārgava interpolations," on which see chap. 3, § C.

[14]Oberlies 1998, 137, sees "the cornerstones of the 'old' narrative" as the dice match, its place in the Kaurava *sabhā*, and the Pāṇḍavas' defeat, banishment, and duration of banishment (138). To this, "ritualized" surface material was added through certain "ground principles" that include framing or "enboxing" *(Enschachtelung)*, which, he thinks, appear to stem from ritual (140).

[15]Alter 1981, 12, characterizes the same "excavative" trend in Biblical scholarship.

[16]On "extant epic," see Proudfoot 1979, 44, 50; Katz 1989, passim, but especially 180 (Yudhiṣṭhira's education is "attached to the story" in the "extant epic") and 219 ("extant *Ramayana*"); Laine 1989, 9, 11, 24, 33; and J. Brockington 1998, 20, 34, 44, 485 (both

a "main story" and puts the text into the service of theories of language, literature,[17] and religion that barely conceal their "higher" ends.[18] Religious adulteration is most typically averred in the notion that Rāma and Kṛṣṇa are "divinized heroes" whose theologies and stories are superimposed on something more originally and authentically "epic" (for John Brockington, "the epic proper"; 1998, 29, 33)—a view whose advocates continue to feel free to overlook counterarguments that Rāma and Kṛṣṇa's divinity is fully structured into the plans of these compositions.[19] To "improve" the text in such fashion is to thoroughly underrate it.

This book, my second on the *Mahābhārata*, was once projected as a "retrospective on the Sanskrit epic from the standpoint of the [South Indian] Draupadī cult, that is, a *Mahābhārata* interpreted from the centrality of the goddess" (Hiltebeitel 1988, xviii). If in this intention, and in my first book and elsewhere, I followed some of these excavative leads, and once called the *Mahābhārata* "a work in progress" ([1976] 1990, 15), it was not without misgivings, since I have always valued the distinction between what *might* lie behind the epic and its *givenness* as a text. In any case, I now think it worth exploring a different tack.

Although much of this "rethinking" book was written in one burst with my *Rethinking India's Oral and Classical Epics* (1999a), a benefit of

Sanskrit epics; cf. ibid., 66: "the received text"). I criticize Katz's and Laine's usages in Hiltebeitel 1993, 2–3, but now realize Proudfoot's precedent, which accompanies his view of the epic as "an intensively interpolated tradition" (1979, 62; repeated 1987, 19, 62).

17 See Winternitz (1962,1: 291–305); Chadwick and Chadwick (1932, 74–78; 1936, 490–91) on the "growth of literature" approach; van Buitenen 1973, xvi–xix; Hiltebeitel 2000a. One appreciates Mangels 1994 for bringing current narrative theory to bear on the *Mbh*, but she remains beholden to the "growth of literature" approach (45), and caught up in the premise of an heroic "main action" (*Haupthandlung*) and oral *Kampfepik* beneath bhakti and dharma overlays (36–38, 44–48, 52, 83–86, 99–100, 144)—which, however, she explains by the somewhat useful notion of an "abstract author" (see below, chap. 2).

18 What Pollock 1984a shows for the *Rām* holds for both epics: their CEs do not support the claims of over a century of "higher criticism" about interpolations. For thoughtful reevaluations, appreciative of the gains made from different perspectives, see Goldman 1995; Goldman and Sutherland 1996, 21–37; and Schreiner 1998, 302–3. On Western biases in applying interpolation theory, see also Hiltebeitel 1993, 17–18, 44–56; 1995b, 24–27; Pisani 1939; Biardeau 1997a, 88; Sutton 2000, xiv.

19 Pollock 1984a (cf. 1991, 15–43, 62–63) is a turning-point in making this latter argument, though J. Brockington 1998 ignores him (see Hiltebeitel 2000a, 164–65). Alles 1994 also remains stuck with Hopkins's false problem of explaining how in India it becomes "inevitable" that Rāma, unlike Achilles, is "divinized" (116–24, esp. 119). On Kṛṣṇa in the *Mbh*, cf. Hiltebeitel [1976] 1990, 1979a, 1989, 1993, and 1995b. One still reads studies that take sarcastic delight in removing Kṛṣṇa wherever possible from *Mbh* passages, telling how he "becomes a god" as part of a late-breaking textual overlay whose plan is to "theocratize Āryāvarta" (Gitomer 1992, 224, 223; cf. Bhattacharji 1992–93, 472); or invoking the "logic of pious Hindus" to explain how "a talkative god manifests himself at the beginning of the battle" (Mangels 1994, 87). Cf. Oberlies 1998, 137; Söhnen-Thieme 1999, 151.

separating them is to make it clear that the two books promote not a single but a double argument about the origins of classical epics on the one hand, and those of India's regional oral martial epics on the other. Rather than positing analogous origins for both in oral epic,[20] I will argue that while the Sanskrit epics do generate a new kind of oral tradition, orality *in* these epics is above all a literary trope that should be understood against a background of redaction and above all writing: the activities that went into the making of these two Sanskrit epics.[21]

This study thus attempts to get at the *Mahābhārata* not only for what it means but how it does what it does.[22] To the extent that there is value in some of the excavative projects mentioned above, it would be in asking less about the text's prehistory, and more about what it does with some of the matters raised, how it makes such things as bards and goddesses and history important. To be sure, bards and goddesses and history existed before the *Mahābhārata*, but we cannot trace them lineally *into* the text, or back *from* the text. Rather, the profitable question to ask is: how has the work presented them? Of what are they its literary figures? In this vein, I now believe my erstwhile goal of tracing the goddess's ascendance through this text would be just one more dig in the dark.

Chapter by chapter, the book takes up a series of enigmas: empire, author, transmission, the stars, noncruelty, love, the wife, and writing. Threaded through them, but especially chapters 2 to 7, is the education of king Yudhiṣṭhira, the eldest of the five Pāṇḍava heroes. For the *Mahābhārata is* Yudhiṣṭhira's education (cf. Klaes 1975; Bailey 1983; Bose 1986). And woven throughout is the question of the author, Vyāsa, the ever-receding figure behind this hero's education and the ultimate enigma of his own text. These topics, laced through this book as they are through the epic itself, serve to invite a reading "against the grain"—and, to be precise, against grains that are as much the product of the *Mahābhārata*'s own craft as they are the results of its learned misreadings.

Indeed, the *Mahābhārata* provides its own "grain" metaphor by which Yudhiṣṭhira is invited to "glean" alternate meanings.[23] I find this

[20]See J. D. Smith 1980 and 1989, followed by Nagy 1996a, 43–46; Blackburn 1989; Vassilkov 1995; Sax 1994, 12 and 1995, 132 (an ongoing view). Cf. Hiltebeitel 1999a, 11–47.

[21]I have found Handelman 1982 provocative on writing, orality, and reading. The *Mbh* justifies a "Rabbinic hermeneutic" of its oral and written "Torah" and the perfection yet indeterminacy of "the law" *(dharma)* it exposits in both legal and narrative form. To recall Dahlmann's nineteenth-century breakdown of the *Mbh*, one may liken *halacha* to what he called "didactic" or *Rechtsbuch* and *aggadah* to "narrative" or *Epos*—though rather than stressing one in service of the other (Dahlmann thought the *Rechtsbuch* more basic and the story designed to illustrate it), one may be attentive to their intertwinement.

[22]Cf. Alles 1994, 104 and 151; Fitzgerald 1991.

[23]I refer to those who adopt the "way of gleaning" *(uñcavṛtti)*; see § C, below, and chaps. 2, § C.19 and 34, and 4, § D.

metaphor of back and forth readings preferable to David Gitomer's notion of "ruptures," "gaps," or "holes" in the text,[24] through which he finds that "various strata of the epic text" (225) reflect opposing views over unnamed centuries of public discourse. No doubt the text does reflect opposing views, including, as Gitomer stresses, at least a conceptual opposition between Kṣatriya institutions emblematized in Yudhiṣṭhira's rival Duryodhana, with his defiance of Kṛṣṇa, and Kṛṣṇaite bhakti or devotion. But in "historicizing" this opposition through "strata," Gitomer makes the Kṣatriya strand older than the Kṛṣṇaite one, and allows that "texts from different ideological eras were simply left to jostle with one another, though such a view implies that epic textual growth and redaction proceeded in an unconscious, mechanical fashion" (225)—the epic is now a *mechanical* monstrosity. On the contrary, I would argue that the passages Gitomer cites to support Duryodhana's defiance encompass Duryodhana in the very bhakti world that he defies.[25] Indeed, Gitomer's conclusion recognizes an opposition between Yudhiṣṭhira and Duryodhana that begs the question of how many strata his method would generate. It also nicely points to the task I have chosen for this book:

> Can we not recognize, in our dialogue with the Indian past, that seeing the problem of Duryodhana does not indicate anything particularly villainous about the dilemma? Yudhiṣṭhira, the *dharmarāja*, also has his differences with Kṛṣṇa (as well as, of course, with Duryodhana). He suffers terrible agonies over the battle expediencies, and finally over the legitimacy of assuming a kingship bought with blood. A study of his predicament in epic and drama would reveal a parallel rupture of meaning, from the side of goodness. (232)

We must ask what it is in the *Mahābhārata* and *Rāmāyaṇa* that their poets made so important not only for their own times, but later ones. The question of the *Mahābhārata*'s own time can thus not be ignored.

A. Empire and Invasion

Regarding scholarly fashions that have sustained the project of dating the Sanskrit epics, it may be that this exercise has at least narrowed its options. Part of the problem has been one of genre (cf. Goldman 1995,

[24]Following Gitomer's use of these terms in the singular (1992, 225, 232).

[25]Even Gitomer has to allow the possibility of "an ironic echo" of bhakti idioms in Duryodhana's final words (9.64.8–29), in which Gitomer finds "the epic authors . . . using Duryodhana's vigorous pursuit of *kṣatradharma* . . . *perhaps* against the incursion of *Vaiṣṇava bhakti*" (1992, 229 and n. 28; my italics).

75–76). With the publication of David Quint's *Epic and Empire: Politics and Generic Form from Virgil to Milton*, which is solely about western epics, scholars of India's epics should find some new challenges: to ask how and why the Sanskrit epics deploy tropes of empire and resistance to it; to reconsider the problem of the two Sanskrit texts' literary dating; and even to consider the anxiety of influence. For according to Plutarch, Alexander the Great, who invaded India in 327–324 B.C., "carried on his campaigns a copy of the *Iliad*, which he kept under his pillow" (Quint 1993, 4) or "'headrest' as he slept" (Nagy 1996b, 202), keeping it "in a precious casket that had been captured from the defeated Persian king Darius."[26] To the extent that the *Mahābhārata* and *Rāmāyaṇa* are "epics," we must raise an overdue question: what prompted Sanskrit poets to develop an epic genre?[27]

As Quint shows, in the West, Alexander was the first to imagine epic as imperial, and Virgil the first to make this imperial vision into "national epic" to celebrate the founding of Rome (1993, 7, 55). In India, shortly after Alexander's invasion, with its highly brutal massacres, including one of a "city of Brahmans" (Bosworth 1996, 95), the Magadha metropolitan state gathered renewed imperial force under the Mauryas. As Romila Thapar observes, this "transition in Magadha remains without an epic to eulogize it. This may be due to the inclination of the rulers of Magadha towards the heterodox sects, where, in the chronicles of early Buddhism, the epic as it were, of the rulers of Magadha is to be found in the *Dīpavamsa* and the *Mahāvamsa* . . . requiring a different form from the epic" (1984, 141). On the contrary, says Thapar, the "transition to a monarchical state in Kośala [Kosala] is reflected not only in the form in which the lineage is recorded in the *Purāṇa*s but also in the *Rāmāyaṇa* itself."[28] Thapar wants to retain some historicity to the *Rāmāyaṇa*'s

[26]Quint 1993, 4. On the possibility of this being a prestigious "edition" (*diórthōsis*) used by Alexander's mentor Aristotle "who read aloud," and even that it was the text upon which Alexander dreamed the founding of Alexandria, supplying the charter myth of the Ptolemaic dynasty in Egypt and the Ptolemies' motivation to obtain this very book for their famous library, see Nagy 1996b, 149–50, 121–22, 149, 176, 186, 198–203. Plutarch, on whom Nagy's reading mainly relies, accompanied Alexander on his campaigns (202).

[27]Sanskrit has no equivalent term, yet the two Sanskrit epics are usually sensed—I think rightly (Hiltebeitel 1999a, 12; but cf. Shulman 1991a, 16–17)—to have a meaningful generic relation as "epic." Interpretative work across them, however, has been dominated by views of the *Rām* as the "first kāvya" (that is, a "first poem" whose core can be excavated) and the *Mbh* as a chaotic encyclopedia (whose many self-described genres—fifth Veda, Upaniṣad, kāvya, itihāsa, purāṇa, ākhyāna, śāstra, etc.—make finding its core a wild goose chase). Sound comparison, however, can begin with their similarity of design (see Pollock 1986, 38–42; Biardeau 1997a, 88–119) and then extend to conventions and themes.

[28]Ibid. Cf. Sircar 1969a, 49–50, on the weakening of Kosala under King Prasenajit by Magadha under King Ajātaśatru through "a protracted war" at the beginning of the fifth

main story, and thus sees this second transition as one in which the poet recalls and embellishes some real events in Kosalan history. But here she follows the risky practice of extracting history out of what seems plausible in epic.[29] Thapar rightly raises the question of empire and epic with regard to the Mauryas and the Buddhists, where it has a negative outcome, but she does not see its implications for the so-called "Hindu epics," in which what interests her are what she calls "reflections" of history.[30] This is not to say that the Sanskrit epics do not recall an historical past. The poets would seem to reflect upon developments in the late Brāhmaṇa period. As Michael Witzel has demonstrated, with the eastward movement of Vedic culture, the "word *mahārājya*—'reign of a great king'—occurs for the first time in Vedic" in one of the "later parts" of the *Aitareya Brāhmaṇa* (7.18), indicating that "the concept of imperial overlordship, based on the *aśvamedha* sacrifice, has gained great importance and will lead, not too late after the Brāhmaṇa period, to the first large empire of Magadha" (1987b, 187). *Śatapatha Brāhmaṇa* 13.5.4.1–22 further describes fourteen kings (several overlapping with those mentioned in the *Mahābhārata*'s "Sixteen Kings Story," plus Janamejaya Pārikṣita) who gained sway by Aśvamedhas. The epic would seem to revisit this Vedic material in the light of Magadha history. But if we resist reading history into the epics' *main* narratives, whose heroes are nowhere mentioned in Vedic literature, it would seem that they are creations of Brahman poets who developed their own variants on the epic genre, centering their stories on kingdoms that had been eclipsed by the time of Magadha's metropolitan states, and celebrating these former kingdoms as empires transposed into a deep and glorious double past that is simply beyond the reach of the historian.[31]

As best I know, Thapar, however obliquely, is the only scholar to have suggested a link between the experience of empire and the adoption by "Hindu" poets of an epic "form" or genre. Although debate could all too easily—as with the debate about Gandharan and Mathuran art[32]—degenerate into renewed scholarly entrenchments over influence

century B.C., followed by Kosala's annexation, and the purāṇic tradition of ending the Ikṣvāku line of Kosala only four rulers after Prasenajit.

[29]See similarly Kulke and Rothermund 1986, 45–47, on the *Mbh*.

[30]See especially Thapar 1978, 1979.

[31]See Sircar 1969c on the *Mbh* war as mythic, and 1965, 14, on tracing Ikṣvāku lineages back to Rāma "who is himself a mythical personage." Cf. Bakker 1986, 3–11, on both epics' treatment of Ayodhyā, in other texts apparently the city called Sāketa and a town not older than the sixth century B.C., as having "basically a fictional character." Cf. Pollock 1998, on the *Shahnāma*, "the first great literary production" of New Persian, which "sought to link the new political formations with an imagined Iranian imperial past."

[32]See Lamotte 1988, 426–42; Alles 1989, 232, 237, implying a correlation between

versus indigenous creation, I believe this link opens serious historical questions about Indian literature and religion. Yet it is not a new issue, but one that has, until fairly recently,[33] largely dropped out of sight since 1947, a year that marks both the independence of India and the end of British imperialism there, and a resurgence of Western scholarly interest in the Indian epics, above all—which should surprise no one, since they provide new ways to reground and even extend Western interests in India—as expressions of Indo-European mythology[34] and Indo-European oral formulaic verse.[35]

Earlier scholars, however, were right to see that the Indian epics reflect on experiences of empire and invasion. The *Mahābhārata* in particular construes the whole episode of Yudhiṣṭhira's assertion of paramountcy through the elimination of his rival, the *Magadha* king Jarāsandha, and his performance of a Rājasūya sacrifice around the issue of empire.[36] This sequence provides in a flurry most of the *Mahābhārata*'s usages of the terms *saṃrāj*, "emperor," and *sāṃrājya*, "empire."[37] Once Yudhiṣṭhira learns from Nārada that he should consider the Rājasūya as a means to empire (*sāṃrājyam*; 2.11.61), Kṛṣṇa says that he has the qualities *(guṇas)* to be emperor *(saṃrāj)* and to make himself emperor of the Kṣatra (*kṣatre saṃrājam ātmānam kartum arhasi*; 2.13.60), but must first defeat Jarāsandha who has obtained empire by birth (*sāṃrājyaṃ jarāsaṃdhaḥ prāpto bhavati yonitaḥ*; 2.13.8). Then, once the Pāṇḍavas win the war and Yudhiṣṭhira considers renouncing the

monumentality (in plastic arts and epic literature) and empire. See also Bronkhorst 1998a on changes in the historical setting for rational debate in Indian philosophy.

[33]See Hiltebeitel 1989; Alles 1989, 1994; Pande 1990; Fitzgerald 1991; Biardeau 1999, xx–xxxv, il-lii. For an earlier view not discussed below, see Hiltebeitel 1979a, 69, on the younger Adolf Holtzmann's "inversion theory," in which the *Mbh* begins as a Buddhist epic celebrating Duryodhana in the image of Aśoka, and in memory of national resistance against the Greeks, and is then subject to Brahmanical inversions.

[34]See Wikander 1948, and Dumézil 1948 for this Indo-Europeanist project's start.

[35]See, e.g., West 1999, 375, arguing that the "institution" behind the Greek Homeridai (singers of "Homer") "would presumably go back to the time of Graeco-Aryan unity sometime before 2000 B.C."—this on the fragile etymological grounds that a reconstructed **omaros* or **omaris*, "assembly," would lie behind *omarion*, a "Place of Union" for assemblies and festivals, and be parallel to Vedic *sam-aryám* as a place of "festive gatherings and, at least in some passages" a place where priest-poets would meet in poetic competition, as at "a sort of eisteddfod." For an alternate etymology of "Joiner" for the Homeridae, with equal claims to Indo-European antiquity, see Nagy 1996a, 89–90; 1996b, 74–75 (note the metaphorical similarity to Vyāsa as "Arranger/Divider").

[36]See Sircar 1969c, 26 and n. 18; Hiltebeitel 1989. Oberlies 1998, 134–41, argues that the whole Rājāsūya episode is late, but relies on shaky arguments about strata; see also Söhnen-Thieme 1999, pointing toward a similar conclusion based on metrics.

[37]Within the Poona CE, there are, between 2.11 and 2.42, eight out of the fourteen such usages in the entire epic (Tokunaga [1991] 1994 is my source for such epic word-counts).

kingdom, Kṛṣṇa urges him to dispel his grief by telling him the "Story of the Sixteen Kings" of old, among whom were seven (including Rāma) who performed the imperial Rājasūya and/or Aśvamedha sacrifices, four who held sway over the whole earth,[38] two who raised the only royal umbrella to signify subjugation of all other kings,[39] and one, Pṛthu Vainya, with whom Kṛṣṇa ends his account, who was consecrated by the great Ṛṣis to be the first king (12.29.129). Indeed, Yudhiṣṭhira might remember from Vyāsa's earlier telling of the "Sixteen Kings" at the death of Abhimanyu that Pṛthu was "consecrated by the great Ṛṣis in an imperial Rājasūya" (*yam abhyaṣiñcan sāmrājye rājasūye maharṣayaḥ*; 7, App. I, No. 8, line 764) to be the first emperor, and that he milked the earth for trees, mountains, gods, Asuras, men, etc. after he was lauded by them all with the words, "You are our emperor. You are a Kṣatriya, our king, protector, and father" (*saṃrāḍ asi kṣatriyo 'si rāja goptā pitāsi naḥ*; ibid., line 784). The corresponding, and also Buddhist and Jain, term *cakravartin*, "turner of the wheel," is not used for Yudhiṣṭhira, but is used in the *Mahābhārata* for "heroic Kṣatriyas who were emperors in the Tretā yuga" (6.11.10), and also for some of the sixteen kings Yudhiṣṭhira hears about in contexts that suggest overlap with the title *saṃrāj*.[40] In the *Rāmāyaṇa*, Rāma inherits the empire of his father Daśaratha, who was a *cakravartin* (5.29.2).

These ideas of empire are thus related to cosmography and the turning of yugas or eras. To understand this, it has been necessary to learn something about archaoastronomy.[41] While I am not persuaded by attempts to date events or read history or allegory from the *Mahābhārata*'s descriptions of stars and planets,[42] the epic poets do project astronomical conjunctions onto the era-turning events they describe. Before the great war, Arjuna lets it be known that the Pāṇḍavas have elderly Brahman "astrologers steeped in the stars who know how to

[38]Said of Śibi Auśīnara, Māndhātṛ Yauvanāśva, Yayāti Nauhuṣa, and Sagara Aikṣvāka (12.29.35; 80–83; 87–90; 124). In the *Droṇaparvan*, the kings are "all *cakravartins*," and the last, rather than Pṛthu who is fifteenth, is incongruously Bhārgava Rāma.

[39]Said of Śibi (12.29.36; cf. 7 Appendix I, No. 8, lines 410–11) and Sagara (12.29.124).

[40]Bharata (1.67.29; 69.47; 3.88.7; 13.75.26; 151.42) and Bhagīratha (3.107.1) are mentioned elsewhere in the *Mbh* as *cakravartins*, as is Marutta (14.4.23).

[41]For the Vedic heavens, an article by Witzel (1984) has been the most reliable. Sullivan 1996 on the Incas is provocative for the theoretical and comparative issues it raises for Indology in relating the stars to an empire of the sun and moon.

[42]Dating the *Mbh* war to the fourth millennium B.C. on the basis of its astronomical allusions, a tradition in Indian scholarship, is simply not convincing. As to Lerner's "astrological key," as an allegory of precessional change and Jungian psychic integration it is far more superimposed on the *Mbh* than elicited from the text. The epic poets not only "introduce" a new "explanation of the Cosmic Order" through "a veil of fiction" (Lerner 1988, xvi), but embed older Vedic astronomical knowledge in their text.

decide on stellar conjunctions *(sāṃvatsarā jyotiṣi cāpi yuktā/ nakṣatrayogeṣu ca niścayajñāḥ)*, the high and low mystery of fate, celestial riddles *(divyāḥ praśnā)*, zodiacs *(mṛgacakrā)*, and hours." The astrologers "predict the great destruction of the Kurus and Sṛñjayas [Pāñcālas], and victory for the Pāṇḍavas," while Janārdana (Kṛṣṇa), who has "knowledge of the invisible" *(aparokṣavidyo)*, sees no doubt, and Arjuna himself, who knows "the shape of the future" *(bhaviṣyarūpam)*, sees with his ancient sight that the sons of Dhṛtarāṣṭra "are not" *(na santi)* to be (5.47.92–95).

Yet if earlier generations of scholars saw a link between Sanskrit epic and empire more clearly than recent generations, they still seriously misconstrued it.

B. Epics and Ages

Conceptions developed around periodizations of the epics arise variously from the need (which is unquestionable) to conceptualize the relationship between historical and literary orders of interpretation—most notably, when scholars address the problems involved in defining periods for the epics' "development." I will discuss two notions: the "epic period" and the "encyclopedic period," each exemplified by one author. But there are many more who could be cited, and more could be said about the overlapping assumptions behind the models. The purpose is to show that forgotten arguments, now as much as a century old, gave closer attention to matters that can provide solutions to questions of dating than most recent scholarship has done.

First, although many have used the term "epic period,"[43] it is best exemplified by C. V. Vaidya, who opens his *Epic India*, the culmination of his trilogy on the epics, with a Preface saying that the "epic period, according to my view, extends roughly speaking, from 3000 to 300 B.C."—although Vaidya also considers 1400–1250 B.C., the "latest dates assigned" to the *Mahābhārata* war, as possible (1907, v; cf. 21, 28; [1905] 1966, 65–110). Suffice it to say just two things: first, this "epic period" begins either way *within* the "Vedic period"[44] and extends just

[43]See most recently Patton 1996 on the *Mbh* as "that most transitional of texts," produced in an "epic period" (410–11, cf. 471), and Sutton 2000, for whom it "arose" (15) in and "reflected" (5) a "transitional" (1, 5) "'epic period' from 400 B.C. to 200 A.D." (15). Yet once Sutton begins (1–9, 15) with this vague chronology and passive text, the term "epic period" largely drops aside (55, 59, 350, 380, 396, 399, 444) in favor of an argument for "the integrity of the *Mahābhārata* as a unitary text" (459; cf. xiv) that "recognizes and explores . . . complexities, contradictions and tensions" (458).

[44]Rāma is from late Ṛg Vedic times (1907, 21 n., 84–85, 175; [1906] 1972, 7–43, 62–67), the Pāṇḍavas from that of the other three Vedas (1907, 11–15, 69–70). Considering only

past the invasion of Alexander; and second, that in order to trace both Sanskrit epics through this chronology, Vaidya supplies several Aryan invasions, a colonizing adventure (the *Rāmāyaṇa*), a civil war (the *Mahābhārata*), and an ethnohistorical *roman à clef*.[45]

Vaidya stresses that, from its founding by the Pāṇḍavas, Indraprastha "figures throughout Indian history as Delhi, the capital of the Empire" (1907, 15). We should not underestimate this association. The Pāṇḍavas' great-grandson Janamejaya is already a great horse sacrificer and universal conqueror in the *Aitareya* and *Śatapatha Brāhmaṇas*.[46] According to Witzel, he and his father Parikṣit consolidated the first Indian state, the Kuru state in the Kurukṣetra region (1995a, 5, 9, 20). For Vaidya, the epic celebrates Janamejaya as "a great sovereign," and empire in India widens with his conquest of "the Punjab or the country of Takshashila" (20). Janamejaya's conquest of Takṣaśilā (1.3.18) has also convinced others[47] that, as O. P. Bharadwaj puts it, Janamejaya held "control over an extensive empire." But Bharadwaj notes that the *Mahābhārata* refers to Takṣaśilā (Taxila) in an anachronistic literary and geographical vacuum; he is thus "inclined to believe that Takṣaśilā did not in reality, form a part of the kingdom of Janamejaya Pārikṣita and its association with him is born out of poetic fancy" (1986, 12). The epic's additional story that Janamejaya heard the epic at Takṣaśilā (18.5.29) could suggest the poets' interest in its borderland reputation in Indian imperial history as a center of Vedic learning from the time of Alexander.[48]

Vaidya thus threads his long "epic period" between three imperial histories: first, a small Pāṇḍava-Kuru empire at a time when Aryan kings fought each other but never engaged in territorial expansion (1907, 180–83), whose "Imperial crown" was Duryodhana's "ambition" (51); second, Janamejaya's extended empire; and third, early Magadha's imperial history down through Alexander. These three imperial

the longer span, Vaidya treats the sixteen thousand-year difference as a trifle (1907, v, 28). Cf. Smith [1958] 1961, 44–60, contrasting "epic period" and "epic India" with the "Vedic period," but shying away from incorporating the terms into his actual discussion.

[45]When the Himalayan-born Pāṇḍavas came to the Kuru capital "they were looked on as intruders" and "invaders," before Dhṛtarāṣṭra gave them half the kingdom in an area dominated by cannibals and Nāgas. Because of "difficulties of the road," they had brought "very few women"; "compelled" to intermarry with Dravidian women, they exhibited a "family custom" of polyandry which showed they could not be from the same family as Duryodhana (Vaidya 1907, 11–15, 69–70). Pusalkar 1970 and Kulke and Rothermund 1986, 45–47 are still refining such notions. In opposition, see Hiltebeitel in press-b.

[46]Bharadwaj 1986, 126; see above, n. 31.

[47]Raychaudhuri 1923, 34; Chatterjee 1930, 164–65.

[48]See Smith [1958] 1961, 85-92. According to Lamotte 1988, 469, in the second century B.C.—to which I assign the writing of the *Mbh*, "for the first time Taxila took on the appearance of a Graeco-Asiatic city."

formations further define Vaidya's three phases of the text's literary history, in which, let us note, the *Mahābhārata* is written from the beginning: Vyāsa, says Vaidya, was "a contemporary of the event" who "wrote his poem some time after the war" in "glorification of Krishna or Narayana as of Arjuna or Nara" (38): he composed it in a "simple and forcible" language that "bears the mark of a spoken language," and is "archaic in appearance and stands on the same level with the language of the Upanishads" (69).[49] During Janamejaya's empire—"roughly 3000 B.C."—Vyāsa's original *Bhārata* swells into the ***Mahā-bhārata*** through additions by Vaiśampāyana, who sings it during intervals at Janamejaya's snake sacrifice. The epic then "assumed its final shape after the rise of Buddhism" and Alexander's invasion (21), upon which Sauti—"the bard," a name for Ugraśravas, son of Lomaharṣaṇa—cast it in its final form during the reign of Candragupta Maurya.

These three periods, however, are no more than a fanciful extraction from what the *Mahābhārata* says of the relations between Vyāsa, Vaiśampāyana (who is only one of Vyāsa's five main disciples), and Ugraśravas. We never hear Vyāsa tell the tale himself; rather it is disseminated to us through two interlaced narrations, each said separately to be of Vyāsa's "thought entire": one by his Brahman disciple Vaiśampāyana at Janamejaya's snake sacrifice, in Vyāsa's presence (1.55.2); and the other by the non-Brahman bard Ugraśravas or Sauti, who claims he heard Vaiśampāyana recite that "thought entire," and travels to repeat it to the Naimiṣa Forest Ṛṣis (1.1.23). Something that takes only as long as Sauti's mysterious journey is allowed by Vaidya, for the sake of this spurious textual history, to take over two thousand five hundred years!—an argument recently but no more convincingly shortened to five hundred years by M. R. Yardi.[50]

Nonetheless, Vaidya's Sauti envisioned "the rules of a well-conducted government as they must have been enforced in the days of Chandragupta" (220–21), when this emperor, tutored by "his Brahmin minister Chanakya"/Kauṭalya, reputed author of the *Arthaśāstra*, brought "the despotic power of kings" to its "highest expression" (266; cf. 175). Vaidya thinks Sauti "recast" the epic at this time out of concern for "the defence of the whole orthodox religion, as it then existed, against Buddhism"—a task he accomplished by making the more Vaiṣṇava work of his predecessors (39–40) "distinctly non-sectarian" through including

[49]Vaidya also considers Vālmīki to have *written* the *Rām* ([1906] 1972, 2, 5, 16, 42).

[50]Yardi proceeds with statistical results to define five authorial styles in the *Mbh*: first a "Vaiśampāyana text" (ca. 955 B.C.), then texts produced by Lomaharṣaṇa and Ugraśravas under the "influence of Śaunaka" (ca. 450 B.C.; xii, 42), and later additions on down to A.D. 100 (1986, 91–147).

stories glorifying Śiva, and with a "unifying spirit which is the charm of this vast work from a philosophic point of view" ([1905] 1966, 44). In making Sauti's "bardic" stage the last of the epic's three strata, Vaidya follows the order of transmission in the text, which gives us no reason to think of the stories going through a *prior* "bardic" transmission.[51]

The notion of "epic period" thus functions for Vaidya as an historiographical device to tell a national mythology of textual growth and cultural decline. After "the beginning of the epic period" when the Indo-Aryans were "like all young and free peoples energetic and active, truthful and outspoken" (1907, 163; cf. [1905] 1966, 56–57), righteous in their fighting, fond of meat as befitting the "imperial dignity" of their horse-sacrifices (1907, 117–20), and "as addicted to drinking as their brethren in Germany" (130), they were transformed during the long "epic period" by racial and caste mixing (22, 48–82), restrictions on women, hypergamy, and marriage by purchase (90–99, 175). But it was only after Alexander's invasion that they "borrowed their evil practices in war from the Greeks." Various *Śāntiparvan* passages, which Vaidya attributes to Sauti, show what "despotic" kings had learned and what dastardly tactics defeated kings could deploy.[52] Sauti sets "vividly before our eyes the idea of a demoralized state of society as conceived by the Aryans about the end of the epic period" which "we feel . . . is not, except in certain broad points, far different from our own" (261–64, 179).

Letting his own historical situation thus speak for itself, Vaidya goes back to the imperial history of Persia beginning with Darius, who "reduced a portion of India to the west of the Indus to a Persian Satrapy." He finds it "not at all strange" that Darius's "autocratic" type of imperium would have "moulded the growth of empires in India," from Magadha on (189). He also observes that neither Sanskrit epic mentions the new Mauryan capital of Pāṭaliputra; both always give Magadha its earlier capitals of either Rajagriha or nearby Girivraja.[53] "The epics do not describe also empires as they came to be" (190). Thus, although

[51]Such as J. Brockington imagines: like many others, he makes bards "the original authors of these epics," which would have passed "from the hands of their traditional reciters, the *sūtas* and *kuśīlavas*, into those of the brāhmans" (1998, 20, 155). Much has to be twisted to make this argument. The *Mbh* bard is only in the text's outer frame (see chap. 2); Kuśa and Lava's recitation turns out to be—according to Brockington—from the late stage that evokes writing (439). Rather, in each Sanskrit epic transmission goes in the reverse, *from* Brahmans *to* bards: a Brahman author creates the new poem, and bards (*kuśīlavas*, *sūtas*) are among those said first to disseminate it. See further Hiltebeitel 2000a, 168–69.

[52]Laying waste the countryside, poisoning water, harassment of the enemy (Vaidya 1907, 261–64).

[53]The latter in the *Mbh* (van Buitenen 1975, 15). Pāṭaliputra was founded about 500 B.C. (Sircar 1969a, 45–49; Alles 1989, 227).

Vaidya never admits it, if his Sauti was writing in the time of Candragupta, he was not only imagining a "Vedic" imperium of the past in current "Hindu" terms, but, while translating the new Mauryan "Machiavellianism" into Bhīṣma's advice to Yudhiṣṭhira, refusing to imagine the historical reality of the new Mauryan capital.[54] Recently, Gregory Alles also remarks on the avoidance of mentioning such imperial cities as Pāṭaliputra and Kausambi in the *Rāmāyaṇa* (1989, 225, 227, 231, 241), while Hans Bakker notes how both epics are the first texts to call Sāketa, which had been absorbed into Magadha, by the name Ayodhyā, "the Invincible."[55] The *Mahābhārata*'s treatment of Takṣaśilā but not Pāṭaliputra could then be an exception, perhaps to assert ancient "Hindu" empire on the boundaries while denying its erosion at the center.

Vaidya also observes that toward the end of his epic period, the tables on invasion are turned. The "Vedic period's" distinction between Ārya and Dāsa was "probably lost sight of during the epic period" to be replaced by that between Ārya and Mleccha (1907, 23). Rather than Āryas invading indigenous Dāsas, the epics tell of Mlecchas who "surrounded their [the Ārya's] country" (25). The *Mahābhārata* "civil war" between the "pure Aryans and the Mixed Aryans" could not have included such peoples: notably the Pāndyas "of the seacoast" who would have had "no existence in those days," and "[o]f course the Yavanas and Shakas [who] are added . . . in an anachronous manner" (1907, 19–20 n.). Their inclusion in the text, says Vaidya, only reflects the "end of the epic period" (26–28). But one cannot so easily dispose of Śakas and Yavanas in the Sanskrit epics. Rather, their presence in them raises interesting questions, as do so many of Vaidya's observations about the tensions between the "end of the epic period" and its stories of old.

The second term, "encyclopedic period," will hold place for theories that ascribe this felt tension to a literary metaphor, and, at their best, try to answer how the text became an "encyclopedia." Representative here is E. W. Hopkins:[56] "for the tale . . . full of the grossest incongruities

[54]Likewise, Vaidya thinks that the usually "incompetent" "last editor" of the *Rām* probably took his exaggerated descriptions of Ayodhyā from what he "actually saw of a great city like Pāṭaliputra" ([1906] 1972, 96; cf. Sircar 1969a, 45–61).

[55]Again, admitting that the identity of the two sites is only probable.

[56]See Fitzgerald 1980, 34–38, 46, tracing the "encyclopedia" idea back to Hopkins and earlier authors (Joseph Dahlmann, Adolph Holtzmann, older and younger). Hopkins's view seems to supply the framework for others' rather unreflective usages of the term: e.g., Bhandarkar [1919-20] 1933b, 523–24; Sukthankar 1936, 68, 72; 1944, 9 (on "the monumental work of preparing the first critical edition of this colossal encyclopedia of ancient India"); Mehta 1971, 68; van Nooten 1971, 2–3; Proudfoot 1979, 41; 1987, 19; Bailey 1983, 109; Goldman 1984, 77; Pollock 1986, 41; Katz 1989, 272; Shulman 1991a, 12; J. Brockington 1998, 484; Sutton 2000, 348, cf. 380. Cf. Puhvel 1987, 70 and Gehrts

. . . to fulfil its encyclopedic character all is fish that comes to the net, and scarcely an attempt is made to smooth away any save the most glaring inconsistencies" ([1901] 1969, 369–70). Hopkins admits there is "no evidence of an epic before 400 B.C." (397), but "imagines" the beginnings of an "original Bhāratī Kathā" in a "circling narration" that "may lie as far back as 700 B.C. or 1700 B.C., for ought we know" (386); but he puts his "facts together" to propose a five-stage development . . . from 400 B.C. to "A.D. 400+." During this time the "Pandu heroes" are consolidated into a story that probably begins without them as "Bhārata (Kuru) lays," Kṛṣṇa rises from a hero to a "demigod" to an "all-god," and "masses of didactic matter" make their way into the text as "intrusion" (397–98). V. S. Sukthankar, summing up his foundational work as chief editor of the *Mahābhārata*'s Poona Critical Edition, comments, "I will say candidly that for all intents and purposes this pretentious table is as good as useless" ([1942] 1957, 9). But such assessments are ignored by textbook writers on Hinduism and Indian civilization, who continue to reproduce the received wisdom,[57] and by others who repeat Hopkins's chronology while working primarily on other texts.[58] It is, however, not persuasive that the *Mahābhārata* is the byproduct of an inchoate "encyclopedic period" of freefall synthesis, or that its poets sought "to fulfill its encyclopedic character," which presumes some centuries of ongoing intent. Rather, both Sanskrit epics seem to serve their authors to ground intertextual projects of their own time in a historical periodization of their own fashioning.[59]

Hopkins, however, says some interesting things about invasions and empires during the period in which he sees the epic being "cast in its present shape" ([1901] 1969, 399, n. 1). Numerous references to Greeks indicate that "the Pandu epic as we have it, or even without its masses of didactic material, was composed or compiled after the Greek invasion" (398; cf. 392–93). And "contemptuous" allusions to Buddhist monuments and references to various Buddhist terms and concepts (391, 475) make it "impossible to suppose that during the triumph of Buddhism such a poem could have been composed for the general public for which it was

1975, 213, on the encyclopedic character of the *Āraṇyakaparvan*. For further discussion, see chap. 4, § C.

[57]Decade by decade, for instance, see Basham 1967, 407–15; T. Hopkins 1971, 88–95; J. Brockington 1981, 54–69; Lipner 1994, 125–26; Flood 1996, 104–8. Brockington 1998, 133–34 still sees himself building upon Hopkins's "outline."

[58]Let me begin with the hope that scholars in three areas—Vedic studies, comparative epic, and South Asian oral epics—will do more to familiarize themselves with the *Mbh*'s Sanskrit text, and current scholarship on it, before repeating these conclusions.

[59]The epics put the solar, lunar, and Magadhan lines into the context of yugas, which, together, the purāṇas carry forward into new "imperial formations" (Inden 2000, 33, 63).

intended" (399). Hopkins sees more favorable conditions for the "casting" of this "anti-Buddhist epic" in the second century with the overthrow of the Mauryan dynasty by Puṣyamitra Śuṅga (399 and n. 1). In calling the *Mahābhārata* "anti-Buddhist," however, Hopkins misleadingly suggests that it confronts one religion head-on. Rather, both epics use the term *nāstika*, "those who teach what is not," to cover all "heresies," probably to deny significance to any one true rival, and to generalize opposing movements into this deontologized category.

Hopkins's "casting" window opens between Puṣyamitra and A.D. 200, but, he says, "handbook writers may safely assign it in general to the second century B.C." (398). As others have observed, most notably Gregory Alles, who assigns composition of the *Rāmāyaṇa* to the Śuṅga period (185–73 B.C.) for similar reasons (1989, 1994), Puṣyamitra, who ruled from ca. 185 to 149, was a Brahman who reasserted sway through the Brahmanical imperial symbolism of sponsoring two Aśvamedha sacrifices (1989, 236). According to B. C. Sinha (who notes other interpretations), Puṣyamitra sponsored the first one to celebrate the departure of the Yavanas (Ionians or "Greeks") after their invasion of Sāketa (Ayodhyā) and occupation of Pāṭaliputra by Demetrius from Bactria. And he undertook the second "more glorious" Aśvamedha during a second Yavana invasion under Menander (King Milinda of Buddhist fame), in which the Śuṅga princes succeeded in protecting the horse even when it strayed onto the Yavana bank of the Indus (1977, 94–98). Yet if we may speak of Śuṅga *imperial*ism (as does Sinha), Śuṅga "*regional*ism" and "decentered"-ness (Alles 1989, 235; 1994, 68, 70) differed markedly from the "repressive" centralization that marked imperial policies of the Mauryas, among whom Aśoka, as Alles observes, "explicitly forbade popular religious assemblies, including those in which poems like the *Rāmāyaṇa* would have been recited" (65).

Both Hopkins and Vaidya thus see Alexander's invasion and the rise of the imperial Mauryas as decisive for the *Mahābhārata*'s recasting. Each also appoints an emperor to situate the text historically: either Candragupta as its heterodox provoker (Candragupta is claimed by the Jains), or Puṣyamitra as its "Hindu" patron. Candragupta is unlikely. But the view of Hopkins and Alles that one or more of the Sanskrit epics was composed—at least in the main—during the Śuṅga period is not without attractions. But I agree with Hopkins, and also Johann Kirste (1902), that one does better to look at least a little later than Puṣyamitra. And I think one should not overemphasize the Śuṅgas themselves as royal patrons. Neither Hopkins nor Alles wrestles with what the epic poets would have made of their Śuṅga benefactors being Brahmans—that is, unsuitable as kings. Given all that is said in both epics about Brahmans making bad kings, it should be difficult to maintain that Brahman kings would patronize epics that disqualified them from ruling. These texts deeply problemetize the "Brahman who would be king," and theorize the exceptional conditions of Kṣatriya default under which Brahman kings might assert a temporary but ultimately unacceptable rule.[60] Perhaps, yes, *during* the Śuṅga period, but not *under* the Śuṅgas, and especially not under the patronage of Puṣyamitra. Not only would the latter's Brahmanhood be a problem, but so would his horse sacrifices, since Yudhiṣṭhira learns the horse sacrifice is very nearly worthless.[61]

Hopkins and Vaidya differ mainly, however, over the nature of the recast text. Whereas Hopkins sees the recasting as only the hugest bulge in "a text that is no text, enlarged and altered in every recension" ([1901] 1969, 400), with further interpolations to accrete encyclopedically thereafter, Vaidya discerns behind it the unifying motivations of the last of the text's three writing authors. Vaidya deems Sauti's "poetical embellishments" and contributions to "moulding a work of such enormous extent into a harmonious and consistent whole" to be estimable ([1905] 1966, 31–36), though not a match for the splendid plot-laying of Vyāsa, of which he says, "It has often occurred to me that if the story of the Mahabharata is not a historical one, it must indeed be the production of an imagination which is higher than that of Shakespeare" (49).[62]

C. Gleaners and Huns

Having worked our way through these old arguments, what can we retain from them? Both Vaidya and Hopkins are no doubt right to view the rise of the imperial Mauryas as a negatively evaluated historical backdrop.[63] From Vaidya we should also retain his appreciation of the epic's literary character, design, *and merit*; his deep intuition of its imperial formations; his insight that in its last (and for us only real) composition, it is written out of concern for "the defence of the whole orthodox religion"; and his sense that it conceals the real imperial history it symbolizes. And from Hopkins we should retain the appreciation of an additional anti-Buddhist posture and a post-Puṣyamitra date. I suggest that

[60]E.g., Rāvaṇa and Droṇa as bad Brahman kings, and the stories about Viśvāmitra and Rāma Jāmadagnya; see Hiltebeitel 1999a, 448–52; in press-c; Fitzgerald forthcoming-b.

[61]*Mbh* 14.93–94; see chap. 2, § C, item 34.

[62]Vaidya credits his authors with literary skills with which to "imagine" not only complex plot and "chaste and powerful" portrayal of character ([1905] 1966, 59).

[63]Sutton 1997 also opts for a Mauryan background, even of the epic's final written redaction (334–35). He argues that the poets could have "modelled" Yudhiṣṭhira after Aśoka (339) or other "heterodox" Mauryas, including Candragupta (334). But I believe he overrates Aśoka's patronage of Brahmans and ascetics as a reason they would have made him a model (340), and does not explain how the epic could have been written this early (see below).

by the time the epic poets give us their carefully concealed perspective on such dynasties as the Nandas, Mauryas, and early Śuṅgas, their rule was "already history."[64] As Walter Ruben says (1968, 114), the five hundred years between 500 B.C. to 30 B.C.,[65] from Bimbisara to the "centuries of war and political trouble caused by foreign invaders from the North-west, . . . were basic for the evolution of Indian civilization, for the growth of epic and Buddhist literature and for the development of Vaiṣṇava and Śaiva mythology and morals."

I suggest, then, that the *Mahābhārata* was composed between the mid-second century B.C. and the year zero. Before this span, only Pāṇini mentions distinctive *Mahābhārata* names, citing Arjuna and Vāsudeva (*Aṣṭādhyāyī* 4.3.98), Mahābhārata (6.2.38), and Yudhiṣṭhira (8.3.95) to exemplify various grammatical rules.[66] A well-considered date for Pāṇini is the mid-fourth century B.C.[67] By "Mahābhārata" he probably refers to a story known in one or more genres,[68] though he could mean an otherwise unknown personal name; and with Arjuna and Vāsudeva he probably alludes to a local cult.[69] One cannot infer from such minimal information that he knew of a pre-second century epic, much less an oral one in ancient Vedic meters.[70] Similarly, if we know anything of a pre-

[64]Cf. Quint 1993, 55, 62–64, on Virgil's rewriting of history as favoring "a collective act of oblivion" to "suppress and rewrite Rome's political memory" after "the national trauma of civil strife." Neither Vālmīki nor Vyāsa, however, had a Hindu Augustus.

[65]30 B.C. marks the end of the last of the Indo-Greek kingdoms in northwest India, that of Śākala founded by Menander, who reigned from 163–150 (Lamotte 1988, 418–25), and also "the collapse of the Śuṅga-Kāṇvas" (445) to the east.

[66]For a good discussion of these sūtras, see Bhandarkar 1871–72, 83–84.

[67]Cardona 1976, 260–68; Hinüber 1990, 34; Falk 1993, 240; Salomon 1998, 12; Bronkhorst 1998a, 25 ("second half of the fourth century B.C.E., or later").

[68]The use of this name in the time of Pāṇini would not support Grünendahl's argument (1997, 237–39) that the term *Mahābhārata* is part of a late package associated with a Nārāyaṇa theology and the *Nārāyanīya*.

[69]Cf. Hopkins [1901] 1969, 390–91; Biardeau 1999, li.

[70]M. C. Smith 1972, 1975, and 1992 sees affinities between irregular *triṣṭubh* stanzas in the *ṚV* and *Mbh* as signs that those in the *Mbh*'s main story (she ignores others) have Vedic antiquity, in contrast to verses in the *śloka* meter; so too Söhnen-Thieme 1999. But the śloka is also a Vedic meter. The *Mbh* poets show a mastery of archaization from the start by having the bard Ugraśravas (who should not know such things) in his first story recite a hymn to the Aśvins in what he calls "Ṛg Vedic verses" (*vāgbhir ṛgbhir;* 1.3.59) with irregular triṣṭubhs (Smith 1992, 45)—whether good or bad imitation, they are mock-Vedic, and set in an Upaniṣadic-type prose tale (Feller 2000, 170, 174, n. 17, 177; cf. Renou 1939; Mishra 1995). Cf. P. L. Vaidya 1954, xxxix: "it is quite easy to show that all the above meters [including irregular triṣṭubhs], found in the constituted text of the Karṇaparvan had been in vogue" in the *Mbh*'s last stage of composition. Belvalkar even thought triṣṭubhs signified late epic (1946, 108). Cf. Lamotte 1988, 581, on "old Mahāyānist" passages with "exact parallels in Pāli. This is because those authors, past masters in the Tripiṭaka, had memories bursting with the old canonical texts and because these texts returned ceaselessly

Vālmīki Rāma story,[71] it is that what we know is not epic. I think the *Rāmāyaṇa* must have been written[72] at about the same time as the *Mahābhārata*, or if anything a little later.[73] With the creation of the *Mahābhārata* and *Rāmāyaṇa*, epic is something new on the Indian scene. Prior *oral epic* versions of these texts are, for now at least, a creation of modern scholarship, and *oral theory* another Western fashion with which to dress them up in the emperor's new clothes.[74] Nowhere has oral epic been found to have emerged in a literary vacuum, such as is now posited for Vedic India. Medieval and later South Asian oral epics, such as we can find them, all presuppose not only surrounding literary worlds, but contemporaneous oral versions of the *Rāmāyaṇa* and *Mahābhārata* themselves as part of the primary cultural work that they carry forward. They are not convincing evidence of preliterate versions of the Sanskrit epics (see Hiltebeitel 1999a, 8, 43–47; in press-a).

I propose further that the *Mahābhārata* was written by "out of sorts" Brahmans who may have had some minor king's or merchant's patronage, but, probably for personal reasons, show a deep appreciation of, and indeed exalt, Brahmans who practice the "way of gleaning": that is, *uñchavṛtti* Brahmans reduced to poverty who live a married life and feed their guests and family by "gleaning" grain. Consider, for example, this richly textured story that is set emphatically (12.340–53) at the end of the

to their lips. For those experts in the teaching, the transposition into mixed Sanskrit or Buddhist Sanskrit of Prākrit was mere child's play"; Lopez 1993, 359–60.

[71]E.g., possibly from the *Jātakas*, or, if earlier, from the *Mbh*, such as the *Rāmopākhyāna* (an *upākhyāna* or "subtale" like *Nala*), or the two versions of the "Sixteen Kings Story" (Kṛṣṇa's at 12.29.46–55, which does not even mention Sītā or Rāvana; Vyāsa's at 7, App. I, No. 8, lines 437–82, which does). These two accounts tell Rāma's story as epitomes of *itihāsa-purāṇa* (*itihāsam purātanam*) attributed originally to Nārada (12.29.12; cf. App. I, No. 8, ll. 330–32), such as we might expect of this bard from his knowledge of these genres already in *ChUp* 7.1.2—a passage that the *Mbh* poets may allude to, but which cannot be taken as referring to the *Mbh* (see Hiltebeitel 2000a, 162). Note also that these representations of Nārada are consistent with his inspiring Vālmīki to tell the story of Rāma, the perfect man (*Rām* 1.1); it takes another *sarga* for the two *krauñca* birds and Brahmā to inspire Vālmīki to compose an "epic" (*Rām* 1.2).

[72]Cf. Proudfoot 1987, 39 and 204, n. 13, in agreement, and above, n. 49, on Vaidya.

[73]Cf. Biardeau 1999, xxxiii, li–lii, dating the *Mbh* to around 200 B.C. (as post-Aśokan) and the *Rām* to around 100 B.C. (after the conversion of Laṅkā to Buddhism).

[74]See p. 8 above. Contrary to Vassilkov, an "archaic stage" of "living oral [*Mbh*] epic" is not "an established fact" (1995, 249, 255). Cf. Jani 1990. Too much has been made of the notion that authentic oral epics and oral poets must be free of the contamination of writing (Lord [1960] 1974, 23–25, 79, 109). Neither Yugoslav nor Indian oral bards have composed oral epics in writing-free cultures. Lord's oral epics turn on the delivery of letters and other written documents (35–95, 224–33)—something Lord fails to theorize, other than as a "theme" (68–98). Cf. Nagy 1992, 44–49; 1996b, 78–80, 196 on "cultures where an oral tradition applies to itself the metaphor of a written text" (78). Cf. nn. 9, 20, 35, 70 above.

Śāntiparvan, where it follows the *Nārāyaṇīya* and concludes Bhīṣma's teachings on emancipation (the *Mokṣadharmaparvan*). Padmanābha, a snake king, returns home to the Naimiṣa Forest (343.2) after a fortnight of pulling the Sūrya's (the Sun's) one-wheeled chariot (350.1). Awaiting him is a Brahman guest, Dharmāraṇya, who has been prompted to make this visit by a Brahman guest he had of his own, and with whom he had shared doubts about the many doors to heaven (342.9; 16)—death in battle and the *uñcha* vow cited jointly among them (13). Dharmāraṇya wants know Padmanābha's "highest dharma." But first he asks what "highest wonder" (350.7) the snake has seen on his solar travels.[75] The greatest "wonder of wonders" (8), says the snake, was seeing a refulgent being attain liberation by entering the "solar disc" *(ravimaṇḍalam)* in a moment (*kṣaṇena*; 13), and learning from Sūrya that this was a perfected Muni who had "gone to heaven vowed to the way of gleaning."[76] Dharmāraṇya says this response answers his other question as well: he now knows his highest dharma will be to take up gleaning (352.9–10). Bhīṣma then rounds off his teachings on mokṣa by telling Yudhiṣṭhira that this story has answered *his* initial question about the "best duty of those in the (four) life-stages" (*dharmamāśramiṇāṃ śreṣṭham*; 340.1). The "highest dharma," says Bhīṣma, is indeed gleaning, and presumably he means by this that it is exemplary for householders, Brahmans or otherwise,[77] who seek emancipation (353.8–9). We are entitled to wonder at the prominence the epic poets give to this practice, which is described to Yudhiṣṭhira at several dramatic moments.[78] I would suggest that it provides an ideal for a time when not only Brahmans would be of sorts, but when kings of a Brahmanical bent might be discomfited as well.

I would also urge that the *Mahābhārata* must have been written over a much shorter period than is usually advanced: as I will argue further in chapter 4, by "committee" (Kirste 1902, 7 and 9) or "team" (Dumézil 1968, 238), and at most through a couple of generations.[79] It has long

[75]Nārada had earlier told the story when asked something similar by Indra (12.340.9-11).

[76]12:351.1cd: *uñchavṛttivrate siddho munir eṣa divaṃgataḥ*.

[77]Gleaning was also practiced by King Yayāti in his latter years (1.81.13), but is mainly practiced by and recommended for Brahmans; see Fitzgerald 1980, 202, n., 246, 271–72, 276, 306; Olivelle 1993, 162–63; *Manu* 7.33; 10.112.

[78]See chap. 2, § C.19 and 34. Yet 12.264 seems a cautionary tale: a severe gleaner-Brahman—his wife wears cast-off peacock feathers and is terrified by his curse (6–7)—is tempered by Dharma, disguised as a deer, into thinking of killing the deer to attain heaven, before Dharma reveals that *ahiṃsā* is the dharma of truth-speakers. Cf. also 12.192.94; 235.22; 13.27.19; *Rām* 2.29.23 (the Brahman Trijaṭa lives in this fashion).

[79]Cf. Inden 2000, 41 and passim on "composite authorship" of the *VDhP* over "two or more generations" or "several decades."

been known that the *Mahābhārata* uses terms for writing.[80] When Bhīṣma tells Yudhiṣṭhira, "Sellers of the Vedas, corrupters of the Vedas, and those who write the Vedas, these surely go to hell,"[81] he registers one of the reasons why a text calling itself a "fifth Veda" would want to make itself appear oral. Another is that the text would promote itself through oral dissemination. As John Kelly puts it, over and against "the emergence of a monastic ecumene devoted to transmission and evaluation of texts" belonging to the heterodoxies, "Sanskrit filled a need for a link language in an expanding social world. In these circumstances, the early development of the *vyākaraṇa* 'grammar' and *nirukta* 'etymology' tools for language self consciousness—combined no doubt with the geographic spread of brāhmaṇas and the spread of Vedic and epic texts themselves—might have made this learnable Sanskrit more capable of solving this ecumenical problem, creating the possibility of writing a text that could combine doctrinal or even dogmatic specificity with the capacity for wide-ranging broadcast and reception."[82]

A sense that the *Mahābhārata*, at least such as we have it, is a written text, is not new. What is new is the sense that its writtenness raises important questions: ones which, it may be said, have slowly shaped themselves around the implications of the Critical Edition. One approach, exemplified by J. Brockington, has been to try to adjust answers to the requirements of oral theory. He sees the *Mahābhārata* as going through four (really five) "stages":[83] (1) a bardic stage, with expansion from within;[84] (2) "mythologization" (I regard the premise of pre-

[80]Dalhmann 1895, 186–88; Falk 1993, 268–69, 304; J. Brockington 1998, 229.

[81]13.24.70: *vedavikrayiṇaś caiva vedānāṃ caiva dūṣakaḥ/ vedānāṃ lekhakāś caiva te vai nirayagāminaḥ.*

[82]1996, 100; Kelly does not specify what text he has in mind.

[83]Brockington's (1998, 20–21) stages bear a rough similarity to those of Nagy 1996b, 109–110, 150–52, 185–86, 205. To reiterate, however, the *Mbh* is not the *Iliad* and Homeric studies (even if Nagy is right, he allows for plenty of controversy; cf. Nagy 1996a, 100–2) are usually poor models for studies of the Sanskrit epics. A similar approach is found in Katz 1989, 11–13. For further discussion, see Hiltebeitel 2000a, 167–68.

[84]Brockington finds that the "core" of the *Mbh* would have "obviously [been] composed after the early Vedic period [ninth and eighth centuries B.C. (26; cf. 133, 159–62)], since the area where the conflict is set lies well east of the Pañjāb, in which the *Ṛgveda* is located" (25)—but a story could be about "somewhere else." For him, oral epic has Vedic antecedents in *gāthā nārāśaṃsī*, "songs in praise of men," which "appear to be the direct precursors of the epics" (5); narrative *(ākhyāna)* and dialogue *(saṃvāda)* hymns; *ākhyāna* narration during the Aśvamedha; Nārada's knowledge of the "fifth Veda composed of tales and stories *(itihāsapurāṇa)*" in *ChUp* 7.1.2; and the war of the ten kings (see above, n. 12). But this is catch-as-catch-can: "a fluid mass of tales must have steadily crystallized into the story of a fratricidal struggle of limited importance, but of great significance for the prestige of the protagonists" (1998, 5); the "first stage . . . of an epic tradition would . . . [be] the progressive clustering of ballads and other material around some central theme. . . ." (19). For a different view, see Hiltebeitel 1993, 10–12, 30–31; 1995a, 25–26; 2000a.

mythologizing bards to be gratuitous); (3) a takeover by the Brahmanical tradition (in which "divinization"—somehow differentiated from "mythologization"—now comes via Brāhmans [see 470]). So far, to put it into Frits Staal's terms (whom I thank for reading this section), "So 2 = 1," and "So (almost) 3 = 2 = 1!" That is, these criteria do not make it possible to distinguish anything. Brockington's next stage, number 4, is then commitment to writing, which is the first for which we have tangible results. And finally, number 5 comes "after the epic was committed to writing," when "the number of manuscripts needed for the purpose seems to have become a virtual library of Indian tradition" open to "new material of all sorts."[85] Brockington sees the "particular character" of both epics as "in part due to their position at a time of transition"[86] that ends with the transition to writing (27). Yet he gets caught in his own designs: Rāma's signet ring and "allusions and a couple of references to arrows marked with names . . . appear to belong to the first stage of growth, for which such dating is implausible" (1998, 439), apparently because it does not fit the requirements of oral theory.[87] Questions can and must be broached around the subject of writing, but they require new answers from those who maintain a prior oral tradition while acknowledging literary effects (115–17) and the encompassment of the oral into the written. Let us also note that Brockington's third stage "displays a certain self-consciousness about the oral nature of the epic" (395). Indeed, by the third stage, "the originally separate traditions of the *Mahābhārata* and the *Rāmāyaṇa* are coalescing, with the attendant effects on their formulaic diction, and even in some instances the likelihood that the borrowing has been from a written text of the other epic, so specific are the details" (396). If so, perhaps we should ask whether, without necessarily positing a *prior* "oral nature," there is any verse in these epics that would *not* show "a certain self-consciousness about orality" if they were written for oral dissemination.

I suggest that one should think of *Mahābhārata* composition occurring along the lines that Narayana Rao attributes to purāṇa composition. It draws on an "originally oral" manner of composition, but what is produced is distinctive for being "a kind of oral literacy" or "a literate orality," with the composition done by "scholars . . . proud of their

[85]1998, 21; cf. 159; I separate a fifth stage from the fourth, following Brockington's use of the word "after."

[86]Cf. above, n. 43; the notion of "transition" can of course be rather too flexible.

[87]True, "names marked" (*nāmāṅkita*) on arrows could describe symbols rather than script (Falk 1993, 304; J. Brockington 1984, 269ff.), but Brockington seems most recently to have abandoned this argument, which looks convenient from more than one angle.

knowledge of grammar and their ability to possess a written text of what they perform orally" (1993, 95). This does not allow us to view the *Mahābhārata* in the light of Lord's position that oral and written composition are "by their very nature mutually exclusive" ([1960] 1974, 129), a point appreciated by P. A. Grintser, whose advocacy (in Russian) of the oral composition of both Sanskrit epics, summarized by de Jong, is the best thought-out argument for oral elements in the Sanskrit epics. In conceding that we receive the Sanskrit epics in a written "transitional" form (de Jong 1975, 28–29, 34), Grintser's position need not be seen as much different from Narayana Rao's. But Grintser is not convincing that, before they were written, "both epics existed already as fully completed poems in the oral stage of their composition" (29). One can only say that the epics' writing poets knew Vedic oral styles (see above, n. 70). Whatever "oral dynamism" may precede the *Mahābhārata*'s written composition and continue after it to prompt modifications in the written text, it is a "written dynamism" (M. M. Mehta 1971, 97) of the type Narayana Rao describes that must explain this epic's composition both in its inception,[88] and in its northern and southern redactorial variations.[89]

While certain other scholars have continued to affirm that some kind of prior core must certainly have existed, but that nothing meaningful can be said about it,[90] rather in contradiction to this sublime but

[88]M. M. Mehta 1971, 81–100. Nagy's discussion (1996b, 9–10) of "*mouvance*" and "*variance*" could enrich these points if we keep our focus on the "incessant vibration" between the "variant manuscript readings reflecting a performance tradition that is still alive in a given culture." But this does mean that a particular text—whether oral or written—must be *from* that older oral tradition kept alive. There are new compositions (as in the troubadour case he discusses). Nagy is so insistent that a high "degree of textual variation is symptomatic of an ongoing oral tradition" (27) that he says it four times in two pages (27–28), trying to universalize an opposition between "mouvance" and "scripture" (25).

[89]Cf. Reich 1998, 24–29, 153, 373, and Inden 2000, 95, on writing and orality, though I disagree that "structuralists cite the orality of the *Mahābhārata* in support of their own position" (Reich, 24). Better "some structuralists," and more caution here: "I introduce history where my predecessors have perceived only system" (Reich, 285). "Structuralist" has become standard labeling (Inden, 98, n. 40; Sutton 2000, xv, 461), but the usages ignore developing work (e.g., Hiltebeitel 1989, 1993; Biardeau 1997a). Reich is instructive on CE-defined insertions, but inflates the likelihood of universal acceptance of late ones (48–50), even of whole parvans (287, 357), despite admitting that "a definite case of universal insertion" is not demonstrable (48), and that "[w]e will never be able to measure quantitatively the depth of this phenomenon, or to reach its bottom in the shape of a truly original archetype" (51).

[90]Typical is M. M. Mehta's attempt at the "depuration of this precious palimpsest" [basically, the text *and* CE apparatus] "to reach our goal of the primal Puruṣa, the Ur-Mahābhārata" (1971, 102); but with nothing to show for it, since he wants mainly to *add* passages to the "archetypal text." Sukthankar is equally vague on the "ideal" of attaining the "original Mahābhārata" (1933, civ; cf. xcvii), positing its oral "fluidity" before anything written (lxxviii–iv). So too van Buitenen 1973, xxiv, xxxi.

unmeaningful object, some of the same scholars have reached the counterintuitive conclusion that the Critical Edition establishes an "archetype," and that this archetype must have been written.[91] Give or take some modifications in phrasing, this argument has persuaded Pisani,[92] Edgerton,[93] M. M. Mehta,[94] Pollock,[95] Proudfoot,[96] Fitzgerald,[97] Oberlies (1998, 141), Bigger (1998, 14–15, 148–49), to some degree Reich,[98] and it persuades me. Yet if there is some tendency to agree that such an archetype must define a synchronic moment (ibid., 16), there is no consensus on its historical implications. Oberlies regards the written form to be a secondary, late, or "surface" phase that involved

[91]See Mehta 1971, 81–100, on Sukthankar, who sometimes seems to reject a written archetype in favor of notions of fluidity (1933, cii), but elsewhere suggests that an "oral dynamism" must have interceded between a written archetype and its recensional variations. I agree with Mehta that a "written dynamism" sufficiently accounts for both. Cf. Mehta 1971, 84, n. 5, and Bhatt 1960, 30, on "the same state of affairs" for the *Rām*.

[92]Pisani (1939, 170–73) speaks of design rather than archetype.

[93]1944, xxxvi–xxxvii: "this text was nothing 'fluid'! To be sure we must at present, and doubtless for ever, remain ignorant about many of its details. But we should not confuse our ignorance with 'fluidity.' . . . It is not an indefinite 'literature' that we are dealing with, but a definite literary composition."

[94]Underscoring the "archetypal redactor's" "ingenuity" (1972, 9, 11), Mehta says, "The author of the written Ur-Archetype, whom we may designate as the First Archetypal Redactor (FAR) is the one (it could have been a whole redactorial syndicate—say, the Bhārgava clan, as suggested by Sukthankar) that put together in written form all the elements we find at present in the Mahābhārata" (1971, 101). He also posits a second "text-critically discernible strat[um] in the Archetype," that of the Last Archetypal Redactor (LAR), who "improves" and "retouches" the FAR's work (ibid.; 1972, 28). But the LAR is rather shadowy, and seems designed to rehabilitate passages that don't make it into the CE (1972, 18, 23, 28, 50, 60–61; see above, nn. 90 and 91).

[95]1984b, 89, n. 201. Pollock is not so persuasive in rejecting the view of Hermann Jacobi, Sylvain Lévi, and others that *Rām*'s Ur-recension would also have been set down in writing (1984b, 87, n. 14); cf. Hiltebeitel 1993, 12, 28.

[96]Proudfoot offers the best discussion of *Mbh* writing versus orality to date (1987, 38–39, 60–61), noting that Sukthankar's emphasis on oral "fluidity" (see above, n. 90) proceeded from a "misunderstanding" based on familiarity with Vedic orality, which, with its emphasis on memory and reciting from memory, "offers no good analogy for the epic tradition" (38). But his effort to justify "higher criticism" on the principle that the text is to be "read in its plain sense" (67, 70) is simply impossible in a text that defies plain sense.

[97]"The amount of unity . . . among the *MBh* manuscripts . . . can be explained only on the assumption of a fixed text antecedent to those manuscripts, an archetype. For the variations which exist can be explained as later, particular innovations" (1991, 153, n. 5); cf. 1980, 56–57, 62, 190; 1991, 152–58.

[98]See n. 89 above. Reich shows that the CE bares an archetype more easily for some parvans than others (33, 85–109), but cannot demonstrate that in the difficult cases, there would not have been one. I do not follow her argument that certain parvans were "evidently never centrally redacted" (34; cf. 79, 165–66).

the epic's "ritualization,"[99] along with which, he thinks, came the added "ground principle" of emboxing or enframing that produced the frame stories.[100] Bigger proposes that the Critical Edition brings to the fore a written "normative redaction"[101] that overgrew all other versions (which he does not insist were oral); like Oberlies, he wants to use "higher text criticism" to continue to excavate "the prehistory of the normative redaction."[102] Both seem to want to accommodate this notion to the idea that if the Critical Edition is evidence of a written archetype, it must include certain features of the epic that look to be late, most notably bhakti components such as the *Nārāyaṇīya*.[103] Thus Oberlies settles on the third century A.D. and the early Gupta period for these developments (1998, 128), while Bigger stays off this "thin ice" and does not commit himself to a Gupta or any other dating.[104] But Fitzgerald lately does. Perhaps in reflection of his earlier view that such a text requires a dynasty behind it,[105] he proposes that "the text approximated

[99]While Oberlies's notion of depth sustains a "redaction-history" of supposedly older "text-layers," his "surface" process works rather mechanically (1998, 140, 138), like Dumézil's notion of myth-to-epic "transposition" (1968; see Hiltebeitel [1976] 1990, 27–33, 359).

[100]1998, 141; see above, n. 14. Circles that gave the epic its theologically motivated "ritualized" text-surface *(Textoberfläche)* produced these features (128, 132, 141; cf. 1995, 179), whose belatedly conceived ritual design is "transposed *(umgesetzt)* into epic events and determines the further course of events" (1998, 139). Oberlies thinks that "framing" could not belong to an early oral phase (1998, 141); but cf. J. Brockington 1998, 115: the "unity of structure would presumably belong to the original oral epic." I do not agree with Oberlies and Bigger's endorsement of Grünendahl's attempt (1997, 238–40) to connect the outer frame (his "first dialogue level" between Ugraśravas and Śaunaka) to a late stage of "Nārāyaṇa theology" (see above, n. 68). The method of using an *Ideenprofil* found in the *Nārānanīya* to identify a stratum throughout the epic is filled with perils, one being that it offers no sense of the relationship between "ideas" and allusions to them. Also, to include Vyāsa's authorship in this package is to ignore his interventions (see chap. 2).

[101]Though preferring "Endredaktion," implying no further redactions (1998, 16; 1999b).

[102]Bigger 1998, 16; cf. 14–15, 19, 150 ("Das MBh dient in gewissen Sinne als Seismograph. . . ."), and 166 ("the MBh is . . . a seismographic instrument that recorded the trends it encountered during its development").

[103]See Oberlies, as cited above in n. 100, and Bigger 1999a, 5, suggesting that Nara and Nārāyaṇa first appear in a Pāñcarātrin textual layer. But the historical scaffolding relating bhakti stories, inscriptions, iconographies, theologies, and sects is very fragile and does not confirm many assertions of "lateness"; see Preciado-Solis 1984, 19–37; Bigger 1998, 1–9.

[104]1998, 15–16; 1999b, 3–4. The weight behind a Gupta dating is not very formidable. A summary by Bigger (1998, 16, and nn. 81 and 85) notes that among the CE editors, only P. L. Vaidya (1954, xxxix) goes out on "this thin *(brüchige)* ice," where he is joined by Agrawala 1956. See also Hopkins [1901] 1969, 397; Bhattacharji 1992-93, 481–82; Dhavalikar 1992-93, 123–24 (the "raging fashion during the Gupta period" of women wearing long upper garments dates Draupadī's disrobing, he thinks); Mukherjee 1994, 13–17; Oberlies, as just noted; Schreiner 1997b, 1; Reich 1998, 287, 357.

[105]"Neither the creation of this text nor the effort to promulgate it could have been casual, and I suspect both were undertaken by some royal house for important symbolic or

for us" in the Critical Edition "was effectively a normative redaction of the MBh produced in or near the Gupta era" (2000, 2). But, he adds, "this Gupta redaction was a reworking of at least one prior written redaction . . . carried out in the wake of the Mauryans and their Śuṅga and Kāṇva successors."[106]

I do not think we need two or more prior written redactions, an erasure by a "normative redaction," or the Guptas to account for the history, diversity, and complexity of what I would rather simply call a single written archetype.[107] Such an archetype would include nearly all the passages and features to be discussed in this book, including the *Mahābhārata*'s double frame with its double telling at double sattras. Indeed, one is challenged to consider the likelihood that it would have included the epic's design of eighteen parvans and a hundred "little books" or *upaparvans*. Current scholarship seems to be settled that at least by the third century B.C., Brahmans in "the heartland of India" were literate (Salomon 1995a, 279). But the only script in evidence at that time is Brāhmī, which was perhaps developed for the Aśokan inscriptions (Falk 1993, 177–239, 339; Salomon 1995a, 273, 276; 1998, 28, 56). The Brāhmī script, lacking features necessary for writing Sanskrit such as certain vowels (*ṛ*, *ṝ*, possibly *au*), markers *(visarga*, *virāma)*, the velar nasal *(ṅa)*, and component characters,[108] could not have been used to write the *Mahābhārata*, unless perhaps in a kind of preliminary shorthand about which it is probably pointless to speculate. But according to Falk, "a thorough reorganization of the northern Brāhmī happened around the turn of the millennium *(der Zeitenwende)*, when an increasing number of authors used this new script for Sanskrit. Then in a few decades the system was so perfected that it survives almost unchanged in many different scripts based on the same system" (1993, 339). Falk, following Dani (1963, 52), relates these innovations to the introduction of broad pen and ink (317–18), which Salomon finds being used slightly earlier in the first century B.C. (1998, 31–34). The *Mahābhārata* could have been one

propagandistic purposes" (1991, 154; cf. 1983, 625). Reich 1998, 287 and 357, also premises a "Vedic revival" patronized by either Puṣyamitra Śuṅga or Samudragupta. But as the *sattra* and hermitage settings of the *Mbh*'s outer and outermost frames will suggest (see chaps. 2–4 and 8), royal patronage should not become a dogma.

[106]Fitzgerald 2000, 2. In Fitzgerald forthcoming-a, 34, he goes on to speak of "the 'Gupta archetype'" and "the 'official' Gupta era redaction." Cf. his forthcoming-b, 1, n. 1, 31–32, 46, and his earlier view (1980, 85) that the *Mokṣadharma* "collection" could be this late.

[107]In 1991, 152, according to Fitzgerald, the CE "revealed that a single Sanskrit version of the '*Mahābhārata*,' fixed in writing, was at the base of the entire manuscript tradition." Now he empasizes "four, or more . . . redactorial efforts" behind it (forthcoming-b, 48).

[108]See Salomon 1998, 30, 37; Falk 1993, 267; Bühler 1904, 53: Chinese Buddhists ascribe the "invention of the signs for the liquid vowels to a South-Indian, either to Sarvavarman, the minister of the Andhra king Sātavāhana, or to the great Buddhist teacher Nāgārjuna."

of the texts composed within such a culturally productive flurry. If so, the turn of the millennium presents a plausible *terminus ante quem.*

But these are conservative dates based on inscriptions. One need not postulate a precise concurrence between inscription writing, which could be the conservative work of tradesmen, and writing developed for texts, which could be innovative, physically ephemeral, the work of an elite,[109] and earlier rather than later than its use on inscriptions.[110] Falk (1988, 109, 117–18) also speaks of 150 B.C. as a time when Brahman authors, after the first decades of Śuṅga rule, may have first developed Sanskrit writing for the transcription of certain Upaniṣads and the *Mahābhāṣya*, Patañjali's commentary on Pāṇini's grammar. Patañjali, who knows *Mahābhārata* names and something of a story,[111] is quite reliably dated to this time, though one cannot be sure whether he *wrote* his commentary, and if not, when this was done. He and the *Mahābhārata* poets have, in any case, the same term, *śiṣṭa*, for what would appear to be a common (even if flexibly oriented) ideal. For Patañjali, the *śiṣṭa* is the "strict" or "learned" Sanskrit-speaking Brahman, culturally and linguistically circumscribed, whose linguistic usage can still be called upon to explain Pāṇini;[112] and for the epic poets, *śiṣṭas* are those whose "strict conduct" *(śiṣṭācāra)*, whether they be Brahmans or others who honor them, defines the "supreme path of the good" *(satām mārgamanuttamam).*[113] When Patañjali describes *śiṣṭas* as "Brāhmaṇas in this abode of the Ārya . . . who possess at a time only as much grain as fits in a small pot *(kumbhīdhānyā)*, are not greedy, act out of duty, not because

[109]Cf. Salomon 1998, 81–84, on "'Epigraphical Hybrid Sanskrit' (EHS)" and its dependency on the competence of scribes.

[110]Cf., however, Pollock 1998, 7, for whom "Sanskrit literature *(kāvya)* is invented at the beginning of the common era," but with inscriptions having priority over other texts (8–9). Yet if Pollock is right about the use of inscriptional Sanskrit to "interpret the world" and "reveal reality" (1996, 212–13; cf. 221–24) while leaving Prakrit and vernacular inscriptions to mundane practicalities, can such a use have been limited to inscriptions?

[111]See Bhandarkar 1871–72, 84–85: "Perhaps the story of the epic was made the subject of new poems in Patanjali's time. . . . But the main story as we now have it, leaving the episodes out of consideration, was current long before Patanjali's time" (85)—the evidence for which, however, is mainly Pāṇini. Cf. Preciado-Solis 1984, 30–32, 36–37.

[112]See Bhandarkar 1929, 581–83; Thieme 1957, 60–62; Cardona 1990, 5–6; Deshpande 1993a, 25–27; 1993b. Thanks to Frits Staal and T. P. Mahadevan on these discussions.

[113]Citing the virtuous hunter who instructs a Brahman repeating the compound *śiṣṭācāra* nine times in one passage (3.198.58–94; see further, chap. 5, § D). Cf. 3.1.29: the Brahmans who follow the Pāṇḍavas into the forest tell Yudhiṣṭhira they do so because he and his brothers have the qualities "approved by the strict" *(śiṣṭasammataḥ)*; 3.32.21: Yudhiṣṭhira tells Draupadī that to cast doubt on "the dharma observed by the strict" *(śiṣṭair ācaritaṃ dharmam)* is among faults that leads to heresy *(nāstikyam*; 32.1); 12.152.16–21: Bhīṣma contrasts the greed-driven "unstrict" *(aśiṣṭān)* who are "beyond the pale of strict conduct" *(śiṣṭācārabahiṣkṛtāḥ)* with those "of pure vows" *(śucivratān)* for whom "strict conduct is dear" *(śiṣṭācāraḥ priyo)*, who are among other things vegetarians. Cf. Biardeau 1997a, 77.

of some obvious motive, and have attained full proficiency in some area of traditional knowledge without the need for anything such as explicit instruction" (Cardona 1990, 5 and 15, n. 18), he evokes something quite similar to the *Mahābhārata*'s *uñchavṛtti* Brahman.[114] Such considerations, and the sense that the *Mahābhārata* gives the feeling of having been authored at a time when cataclysmic political and cultural memories were still vividly recalled, make the mid-second century B.C. more compelling as a *terminus post quem.*

If we can sensibly pull the likely date of *Mahābhārata* composition to one or at most two generations within this period, we can dispense with Hopkins's vision of "a text that is no text" at least up to that point. But must we grant him, Brockington, and others a text that almost *becomes* no text through the five centuries thereafter: that is, from the time of this composition to that of reaching its supposed current dimensions in the time of the Guptas? This question should encourage systematic study of the notes and apparatus of the Critical Edition,[115] and address such matters as manuscript copying and recensional history. One must grant that there are indeed major and minor interpolations into the text, and also probably losses from it.[116] These, however, are only cases of the manuscript history of an already written archetype, and not evidence of what preceded the archetype.[117] The real challenges will continue to come from those who find one or another reason to argue that some portion or passage within the Critical Edition is late, such as the highly devotional *Nārāyaṇīya*[118] portion of the *Śāntiparvan*, or the entire *Anuśāsana Parvan.*[119] Maybe so. But since no one is close to proving anything, let us be all the more cautious about what we try to disprove.

[114]This is said with reference to the *type* of figure *imagined*, and not to the Sanskrit produced, for which the epic poets had no requirement to follow Pāṇini. See Salomon 1995b on the question of "epic Kṣatriya Sanskrit." One would suppose that if a śiṣṭa made *itahāsa-purāṇa* his chosen "branch of learning" in which to articulate "the highest wisdom," he would have some linguistic latitude.

[115]As encouraged by Bigger 1998, 17–18.

[116]See Bigger 1998, 14 and n. 73; Reich 1998, 45.

[117]I do not agree with Proudfoot's view that the "irrefutable evidence that accretion has been rife since the time of the archetype ma[kes] it more difficult to deny the possibility of accretion before the archetype" (1987, 63; cf. 69).

[118]See above at n. 103, and the essays in Schreiner 1997a on the *Nārāyaṇīya*. Although I will refer to the *Nārāyaṇīya* from time to time in reflecting upon other epic components, I am aware that it presents important questions, which I hope to deal with elsewhere.

[119]Arguments that the *Anuśāsana Parvan* may have begun as part of the *Śānti Parvan* rely on its seeming disorderliness and intensified trumpeting for Brahmans, especially around the issue of the obligation of the gift to Brahmans (Hopkins 1898a; Dandekar 1966, xlvii, lxxiv–lxxxiv; Pisani 1968); but these—and especially the latter—are not sufficient reasons to think that this last of the extended segments of the education of Yudhiṣṭhira is late.

I would only argue that even these axiomatically late portions must be looked at with an eye fresh to the possibility that they are not any later—or at least much later: hours, weeks, or months rather than centuries—than the rest, once the rest, and its principles of composition and design, are better understood.[120] Such passages could in any case benefit from some new questions, and must be taken up one at a time.

Yet with that in mind, let me take up one such case and pose a solution that I believe points in the right direction. In thinking about dating the *Mahābhārata*, this book studies how the text itself portrays those who compose, transmit, and receive it as audiences: most notably, Vyāsa who teaches it to his five disciples, including Vaiśampāyana; Vaiśampāyana who recites it before Janamejaya, but also in the presence of Vyāsa and Sauti Ugraśravas; Sauti, who retells it to Śaunaka and the other Ṛṣis of the Naimiṣa Forest; and two additional Ṛṣis, Nārada and Mārkaṇḍeya, who supplement Vyāsa as what we might call primary sources. Some of the most intriguing material comes from the *Nārāyaṇīya* (12.321-39) and a narrative that immediately precedes it: a story I will take up in chapter 8 about Vyāsa's first son Śuka (12.310–20), whom Vyāsa sires before his other sons Dhṛtarāṣṭra, Pāṇḍu, and Vidura.

Now in Śuka's story—and we must note that Śuka means "Parrot"—there comes a time when Vyāsa, aware of Śuka's penchant for liberation *(mokṣa)*, instructs him to leave the hermitage they inhabit on Mount Meru (12.311.12) and go on foot, rather than through the air,[121] to Mithilā to learn from King Janaka of Videha "the meaning of mokṣa in its totality and particulars."[122] Having crossed the varṣas ("continents" or "divisions" of the earth) of Meru, Hari, and Haimavat, Śuka reaches Bhāratavarṣa where he sees "many regions inhabited by

[120]Granted we "know" the *Mbh* as a text that "*grew*, and became what it is by *expansion*" (Reich 1998, 51, with italics), but not that it took eight (32) "centuries of textual production" (26)—a rather burdened term, compounded once as "production/transmission" (270). Reich overworks the "textual battlefield" metaphor, turning the *Mbh* into an eight-hundred-year chain letter (see 301-7 for the metaphor) of "contestatory discourse" governed by an "aesthetic of expansion" (31; cf. n. 25 above on Gitomer 1992). This aesthetic better befits a short period of controlled, consensual "contestation," and also shared conventions, which do not last forever. Reich sometimes points in this direction: e.g., the contestation can be "an argument around the family table" (356), and the "sacrificial contest" a "convention" (321). Cf. Inden 2000, 48, on "the 'metaphysics' . . . at work" in the "process of 'augmentation'" of the *VDhP*. Yet while Inden views most purāṇas and the epics to "have undergone numerous modifications over the centuries" (32; cf. 94), he ignores whether the assumed centuries differ, and leaves the epics to the very vagaries from which he rescues the *VDhP* and the *Nāradīya Purāṇa* (78) by their "composite authorship."

[121]Paraphrasing 12.312.8-9 and 12. The description of the journey, however, gives him every appearance of flying (12-19).

[122]12.312.6: *mokṣārthaṃ nikhilena viśeṣataḥ*.

Chinese and Huns,"[123] and then proceeds to Āryāvarta, the Vedic heartland of northern India, to find Mithilā, Janaka's capital of Videha (15). This passage gave me considerable pause, so long as I was influenced by two prevailing paradigms. First, there is a long debate over whether epic cosmography is geographical or cosmological, as if it were a question of "either/or." But here we have a passage in which the poet seems rather knowingly and whimsically to mix both genres under the "flying feet" of this "parrot-boy." Second is the assumption that if peoples in the Indian epics are referred to, they must be known by contact, and thus by either proximity or invasion, since India, which "has no history," would certainly have no history outside itself. As we have seen, Vaidya and Hopkins made this a linchpin-assumption for dating the epics after Alexander. And the argument would work just as well for the Śakas.[124] But what about the Huns?

If one keeps to the premise that the epic poets would know the Huns from either proximity or invasion, one would first think of the Hephthalite or "White" Huns, who established invasive kingdoms in western India in the second half of the fifth century A.D., challenging the imperial Guptas (Kulke and Rothermund 1986, 94–96). And one would thus have to suspect that all *Mahābhārata* references to Hūṇas, of which there are at least six,[125] including the one in the Śuka story, would either have been interpolated in Gupta times, or be evidence that the passages in which they appear must be late. Hopkins ([1901] 1969, 393–94) and J. Brockington (1998, 210) barely notice the Huns, but Basham and Witzel make this claim.[126] Yet the solution is unnecessary.

[123]12.312.15ab: *sa deśān vividhān paśyaṃś cīnahūnanisevitān.*

[124]See Lamotte 1988: An "old Śaka era" is given as beginning variously in 155 B.C., 150 B.C., and 129 B.C. (453 and n. 6). Śakas or Scythians, "known to history" from the eighth century B.C., were associated by Indians "closely with the Pahlavas (Parthians)" (447), whose empire the Śakas invaded and conquered beginning about 130 B.C. (451–52). After the Śakas had conquered Sindh by about 110 B.C., they advanced to occupy areas of Gandhāra, Gujarāt, western Punjab, Mathurā, and Malwa in the next century (444, 452–56); the *Mbh* and Kāmasūtra agree "with the Greek *Periplus of the Erythraean Sea* in condemning the corruption of morality introduced into the Punjab, Mathurā, and Surāṣṭra by the Śaka customs authorizing prostitution and incestuous unions" (488). Mention of Śakas along with Yavanas in the *Yuga Purāṇa* will bear further investigation for *Mbh* dating and the yuga theory; see Dwivedi 1977, 287–89; Pollock 1996, 204; Mitchiner 1986, 1990.

[125]Relying on Tokunaga [1991] 1994. The five others are 2.29.11 (subdued by Nakula for Yudhiṣthira's Rājasūya); 2.47.19 (two references, one to Hūnas along with Cīnas [with 12 mentions] and Śakas [with 33], and one to Hārahūṇas ["robber Huns" according to van Buitenen], all of whom came to pay tribute at Yudhiṣṭhira's Rājasūya); 3.48.21 (Hārahūṇas along with Cīnas and Tukhāras [with six mentions] came to the Rājasūya); and 6.10.64.

[126]Basham 1989, 70 and 130, n. 3: ". . . there is good reason to believe that the text, even that of the critical edition, was brought up to date as late as about 500 C.E."; to which is footnoted: "In several places the text mentions Hūṇas (Huns), who were hardly known in

The epic poets also know of some distant peoples by their contemporary historical reputations. This is evident in a singular verse which tells that Sahadeva, during his southern (!) "conquest of the regions" before Yudhiṣṭhira's Rājasūya, forced tribute from "Antioch, Rome, and the city of the Greeks."[127] Four of the five other passages that mention Hūnas (or Hūṇas) also recall their tribute to Yudhiṣṭhira's Rājasūya, one claiming that Nakula wrested it on his western digvijaya, and the others saying that some Hūnas came along with the Chinese to give tribute at the Rājasūya itself (see above, n. 125). Not quite as remote as Antioch, Rome, or the city-Greeks, the Hūnas are known not only by reputation but by a certain proximity. But not by invasion. If we consider the *Mahābhārata* to be written sometime between the middle of the second century B.C. and the millennial turn, this would make its earliest possibility contemporary with Seleucid Antioch at the time of the Maccabees[128] and Rome during the Punic Wars, and also a fitting time for its authors to be aware that the Hsiung-Nu Huns were the great northern rivals of the Chinese, whose Sanskrit name "Cīna" must recall the Xin/Ch'in dynasty founded by Shih Huang Ti, who began the great wall in 214 B.C. to defend against them.[129] That the Huns bring tribute to the Rājasūya need not be taken as a sign of *close* proximity, since they are mentioned with the Chinese—although one could imagine them already spreading into the trade routes between China and India, where they have been identified "from the middle of the first century B.C. onwards" (Krishnaswami Aiyangar 1919, 75). But Śuka's route from Meru to Mithilā over the lands of the Hūnas and Cīnas must point only to the Huns' geographical and historical reputation, and, as with Rome and Antioch,[130] to foreign histories with which the epic poets were familiar.

India until about 450, On the other hand another tribe, the Gurjaras, who appeared in India about 550, is not mentioned." The point about the Gurjaras is to be more seriously taken: the *Mbh* indeed does not know about them. Cf. Witzel 1995b, 89; Thakur 1969, 177–78. Biswas, however, takes a view more like mine, for instance with regard to the Hārahūṇas, known despite never having invaded: "Though India did not show very keen interest in the political changes outside its own boundaries there is some evidences (sic) of Indian knowledge of the historico-geographical position of the wider world" (1973, 36; cf. 37–44 on Kālidāsa). She cites some of the epic passages (27, 37), but not the one in the Śuka story.

[127]2.28.49: *antākhīṃ caiva romāṃ ca yavanānām puraṃ tathā.*

[128]Whose revolt against the Seleucids occurred begins in 167 B.C.

[129]A project continued under his successor Hwei-Ti (194–179 B.C.), a contemporary of Puṣyamitra Śunga and Menander (Krishnaswami Aiyangar 1919, 70).

[130]Hopkins [1901] 1969, 383, notes only the Roman reference with the comment, ". . . while the Greek were familiar, the Romans were as yet but a name." Cf. Edgerton 1944, xxviii: not before the first century B.C.; J. Brockington 1998, 134: not before the first century A.D.

2 The Author in the Works

There has been some rough agreement on Vyāsa among sounder scholars: "a mythical personage" (Bhandarkar [1919–20] 1933a, 419), the "mythical author" (Sukthankar 1933, ciii); by name the "arranger" (Shulman 1991a, 11) or "divider" (van Buitenen 1973, 437; B. Sullivan 1990, 1) for his division of the Vedas; "a kind of universal uncle" whose contribution to Vedic, epic, and purāṇic texts is "intended as a symbolic authorship" (van Buitenen 1973, xxiii); the "diffuser (of the Veda)," "primarily the symbol of the authoritativeness of the epic and purāṇic texts" (Biardeau 1999, xxxii; cf. 1968, 119); "the symbolic representation of all the epic poets, the Ṛṣis of the fifth *Veda*, who perceived the correspondences between the epic they were composing and the myths and rituals of their heritage" (B. Sullivan 1990, 24);[1] the "*Wortführer* (spokesman) of the Epiker in the text" (Mangels 1994, 145); the "strange absentee author, whose work carries no signature, worthy of the deconstructive lucubrations of a Derrida!" (J. L. Mehta 1990, 111).[2] Two of these characterizations—Bruce Sullivan's and J. L. Mehta's—come from fine studies of Vyāsa published in 1990, while a third—Annette Mangels's—comes shortly thereafter from a book that draws on narrative theory and features Vyāsa quite prominently.

Mehta, whose essay is a burst of insights, is the first to seriously raise the question of the author's literary "function" in the epic text.[3] He has in mind of course Michel Foucault's "What is an author?" (1979).[4]

[1]Sullivan is quoting and extending my [1976] 1990, 359.

[2]Mehta adds that like Vyāsa, who says his text contains everything, Derrida says, "There is nothing outside the text" ([1976] 1994, 158).

[3]Dandekar (1990, 305) indicates that Mehta, who taught philosophy at Harvard, passed away between the 1987 Sahitya Akademi conference in Delhi that he addressed and the book that resulted from the conference. Mehta sent me a copy of his essay in 1987 with some interesting marginalia, but I then lost touch with him.

[4]See Mehta 1990, 104, and further 111: "the sophisticated analytical tools of current literary

Foucault's applicability is not negligible. First, regarding the ways that the "author function" appropriates discourses (including epic),[5] he sees that these will "vary with each culture" (158) and have a history in any given culture (141). Although Vedic hymns have "family books" and named poets, about whom legends have in many cases formed,[6] and although certain names take on a representative quasi-authorial function for teachings and texts within different oral branches of Vedic learning,[7] for Indian literature, the "individualization" (141) of authors—divine, fictional, or otherwise (147)—first takes on literary proportions in early post- and para-Vedic *smṛti* texts.[8] Among these, the two Sanskrit epics tackle the project of "author-construction" (150) most daringly by portraying *new* authors involved in their own stories[9]—in the *Mahābhārata*, by giving, as Mehta puts it, the "hint" of a "mysterious relationship, like a deep and powerful undercurrent," between the author of the text and the supreme deity as author of the thereby-textualized universe (1990, 111). Second, although Foucault's maxim that "the

theory and the refinement of sensitivity in recent poetics and rhetorics," citing Foucault 1979. B. Sullivan 1990, 115; Miller 1992, 106, n. 2; and Reich 1998, 18–20 nod to Foucault; Mangels notes Vyāsa's authorizing "function" (99–101, 145, 148) but not Foucault.

[5]Foucault 1979, 149. Cf. West 1999, seeing the *Iliad* and *Odyssey* as anonymous until the "invention of Homer" as author by the Homeridai some relatively short time before they were invited to Athens for the Panathenaea in 522 B.C. as a "corporately wealthy" (365) guild of rhapsodes. Be that as it may, West's parallel with the *Mbh* is erroneous: "We have no authors' names for most of the Babylonian epics, or for the works of Ugaritic or Hittite literature, or for the *Mahabharata*. . . ." (ibid.). Homer's identity as oral poet is not invented *in the text*, like Vyāsa's, but (if West is right) *after* it, notably by the Greek *literary* tradition (371, 377)—a point on which there *would be*, then, a significant parallel. The invention here is of a *Mbh* without Vyāsa. Such misinformation would seem to have either its source or purpose in the transmission of oral theory. Cf. chap. 1, n. 35.

[6]See Patton 1996, 165, 212, 215–74, on the Ṛṣis' identification with particular hymns and legends as a long and largely post-*ṚV* process that crystallizes in the *Bṛhaddevatā* (*BD*), a text whose "encyclopedic" and (31–32, 70–71, 465–61) narrative concerns have parallels with the *Mbh* (10, 196–98, 260, 262, 365, 410, 444). Despite Patton's view of the *Mbh*, however (see chap. 1, n. 43), it may be earlier than the *BD*; see her agreement with Tokunaga's dating of the *BD*'s expanded Ṛṣi stories—A.D. 100–600—as younger than those in the *Mbh* (12, 274, 356, 405, 473; Tokunaga 1981). "The insight slowly emerging . . . is that the BD's narratives use the ṛṣi as the template upon which to cast the character of the early classical brahmin—not only in terms of manipulative verbal power, but also in term of his pedigree" (Patton, 274). Thus, whereas the *Mbh* is addressed first to Brahmans (by Vyāsa to his disciples), and thence through them to everyone, the *BD* could be addressed only to Brahmans, since no one else could use their Vedic mantras.

[7]See Witzel 1997, 322, 326; Olivelle 1998, 8–11, on Śākalya, Yājñavalkya, and Janaka.

[8]For the Mīmāṃsā, however, Ṛṣis are disinvested of their author function; see Patton 1996, 405, 421–38.

[9]I see nothing tempting in Witzel's offer of a kind of Vedavyāsa *in nuce* developing, as it were, during the Vedic period (see 1995c, 117; 1997, 326, 328). Cf. Bronkhorst 1998b.

author is the principle of thrift in the proliferation of meaning" must be allowed a certain exorbitance in so extensive a text, it is fair and, as we shall see, quite productive to say that, as "the ideological figure by which one marks the manner in which . . . [post-Vedic Brahmanical culture] fear[ed] the proliferation of meaning," its "author has played the role of the regulator of the fictive."[10] Third, Foucault observes that the "author function" can disperse itself into a plurality of simultaneous selves (1979, 152–53). The *Mahābhārata* poets construct Vyāsa's author function not only in relation to author functions of the deity (mainly the deity known as Viṣṇu, Nārāyaṇa, and Kṛṣṇa); they disperse it through the disciplic narrations of Vyāsa's five disciples (Vaiśampāyana, being one of them, imparts it *only* to humans) and the bardic narration of Ugraśravas; they delegate it for long stretches of narration to two characters caught up in the main action—Saṃjaya (for the war books) and Bhīṣma (through the first two postwar books); and they diffuse it through a rash of often new epic Ṛṣis who serve as the author's colleagues, frequent surrogates, and occasional guarantors.[11] Fourth, as Foucault says of the author's name, "the name seems always to be present, marking off the edges of the text, revealing, or at least characterizing, its mode of being."[12] I will use a terminology of "frames" that befits this point: if the Brahman disciple's narrative defines the epic's inner frame and the bard's its outer frame, there is beyond these an outermost frame that gives the author his openings into the text, and both reveals and conceals its ontology. Finally, in terms of writing, which is where I believe *Mahābhārata* criticism needs to shift its focus from so-called oral epic theory, the *Mahābhārata* gives us an author who leaves signs in the text that cannot be anything but deliberate and are even declared to be subtle. Around the author function exemplified in Vyāsa and his extended "selves," "it is," to quote Foucault, "rather a question of creating a space into which the

[10]Foucault 1979, 159. The point befits Mangels's view of Vyāsa's name, the "*Ordner*" ("Arranger"), among whose duties as "alleged author" is to authorize others' (Vyāsa's Saṃjaya's, Kṛṣṇa's . . .) "fictions" (1, 99–101, 107, 111). For Mangels, however, such features of Vyāsa's "abstract authorship" are an overlay of dharma, bhakti, and smṛti strains upon older epic narration techniques (44–45, 52, 86–88, 148; see chap. 1, n. 17).

[11]Mangels, touching on all these points, is especially illuminating on the interplay between the "author's" omniscience and that of various narrators and hearers (1994, 63–68, 73, 92, 95–97, 107, 110–11, 122–23, 132, 141, 144, 147): among narrators down to the "little Sūta" (107, 143) Saṃjaya as Vyāsa's "protege" *(Schützling)* (110, 123, 126; see further 26, 69–71, 97–129, 140–45); among hearers (primarily Śaunaka, Janamejaya, Dhṛtarāṣṭra, and Yudhiṣṭhira), their possession of a measure of foreknowledge so that they can prompt the various narrators' omniscience (73). But she relegates to overlay and interpolation the correspondence between omniscient author and omniscient deity (52, 86–88, 99–100, 137, 139, 144–45, 148).

[12]Foucault 1979, 147; cf. n. 10 above.

writing subject constantly disappears" (1979, 142). With Vyāsa, we will be able to take this point of Foucault's literally.

A. Epic Fictions

It is not, however, Foucault's powerful essay but rather Mehta's perspective on the *Mahābhārata* that I wish to extend. For Mehta, Vyāsa is not just a myth, or a symbol *of* textual claims or processes. His character presences authorial claims, processes, and literary experiments *in* the text. Jesse Gellrich is worth quoting here on Chaucer and his *House of Fame:* "'Chaucer' remains the 'thing' in question. He is no longer an author recording a dream of being carried off by a bird. 'He' is a fiction, an integer of writing puzzling over how utterly provocative it is to think like a writer."[13]

With such an author we thus raise the matter of fiction.[14] But if we do, we must acknowledge the force of this third term between the usual ones used to argue over epics: are they myth or history? When Vyāsa intervenes in his own story, is it "clearly an afterthought," an "invention" of inept later poets (Winternitz 1897, 721, 736–37), or because he was "a contemporary of the event" (Vaidya 1907, 38)? Interesting work has been done on fiction in prenovelistic works comparable—from different angles, of course—to the *Mahābhārata*: Homer,[15] Plato,[16] Indian Buddhist Mahāyāna literature (see Lopez 1993), Biblical narrative,[17] Chaucer, and Dante (see Gellrich 1985). Frank Kermode suggests some ways we might consider *Mahābhārata* fictions among such works: "We have to distinguish between myths and fictions. Fictions can degenerate into myths whenever they are not consciously held to be fictive. . . . Myth operates within the diagrams of ritual, which presupposes total and adequate explanations of things as they are and were; it is a sequence of radically unchangeable gestures. Fictions are for finding things out, and they change as the needs of sense-making change. Myths are the agents of stability, fictions the agents of change" (1967, 39). In arguing against

[13]Gellrich 1985, 185; cf. Mangels 1994, 145: Vyāsa is the "abstract author as reader/listener" who, among other things, "conceals himself in the narrated figures, in the treatment of narrated time, etc."—as if listening in to his composition.

[14]What follows from here to the end of this section also appears with greater elaboration in Hiltebeitel and Kloetzli forthcoming.

[15]See Richardson 1990; Mangels 1994, 70–71, 110, 127–29; Finkelberg 1998.

[16]See especially Derrida 1998, 248–53 (in his essay "Khōra," originally written in 1987) on "fictional relays" (249) in the *Timaeus*; Gill 1999, xxviii, xxxvi, on the *Symposium*. On other Greek literatures, cf. Gill and Wiseman 1993; Bakhtin 1981.

[17]Cf. Alter 1981, 46, on biblical "writers who, like writers elsewhere, took pleasure in exploring the formal and imaginative resources of their fictional medium, perhaps sometimes unexpectedly capturing the fullness of their subjects in the very play of exploration."

Northrop Frye's "archetypal" or "mythic" readings of literature, Kermode says, "we must avoid the regress into myth which has deceived poet, historian, and critic" (43). To be sure, Indian epic poets made use of history and myth (in Kermode's sense) among their resources, and what they composed has since been taken to be one or the other, or some combination of the two. Perhaps this was even their goal. But what they also did while composing was explore the possibilities of fiction. One must thus be ready to recognize that the *Mahābhārata* poets use fiction, like Dante and Chaucer, as "a new kind of interpreting, one that no longer allows for the straightforward validation of meaning in an 'old book'"[18]—in Indian terms, the Veda rather than the Bible. Indeed, Sukthankar was bold enough to consider the epic "on a level with the greatest works of fiction and drama of all times."[19]

Comparison here is thus above all with the novel, a genre that, according to Paul Ricoeur, has "constituted for at least three centuries now a prodigious workshop for experiments in the domains of composition and the expression of time" (1985, 8). We may say something similar of the genre of "epic" in classical post-Vedic India, for among the many novelties explored by the epic poets, salient among them was a diversity of chronicities. However, whereas in the west, epic was anterior to the novel, and something of an archaic foil to its novelties, in India epic was what was new (we have no evidence to the contrary), and what was old and anterior was Veda. The epic genre thus allowed its poets to construct what Mikhail Bakhtin calls a new chronotope, literally "time space," a "rule-generating force" (1981, 101) by which "spatial and temporal indicators are fused into one carefully thought-out, concrete whole. Time, as it were, thickens, takes on flesh, becomes artistically visible, space becomes charged and responsive to the movements of time, plot, and history" (84). Yet it is ironic that Bakhtin's well-known contrast between epic and novel cannot be well applied to the Sanskrit epics,

[18]Gellrich 1985, 22; cf. 27: fiction as "a discourse that recognizes its own impossibilities and proceeds by locating the authority for making sense no longer in the pages of the past, but in the hands of the reader"; 48: "medieval fictions, in contrast, specialize in doubt."

[19]1957, 19; cf. 1930, 184. Mangels 1994 offers the richest discussion of *Mbh* fiction (18–20, 22–23), fictive authors, narrators, and hearers (32–34, 40, 66–70, 99, 109, 111), omniscience (see above, n. 11) and other fictional "devices" in narrative technique (53, 61, 94–95, 130, 141–44), and of the *Mbh* poets' sense of the limits of fiction (148). Cf. Fitzgerald 1991, 167: by Kumārila's reckoning, since the function of the *Mbh* narrative is rhetorical, it has "no strict obligation to be truthful." Handelman makes a similar point regarding *midrash* (scriptural exegesis) on *aggadah* (narrative): unlike *midrash* on *halacha* (Jewish law), "the Rabbis did not demand belief. . . . aggadah is 'serious play' involving indeterminacy of belief; or perhaps one could use Coleridge's phrase, 'suspension of disbelief'" (1982, 75). Cf. Quint 1993 on "enabling fictions"; Alles 1994, 49–73, 104; Vaidya on the plot-laying of Vyāsa as cited in chap. 1 at n. 62.

which are as much like Bakhtin's "novel" as the western "epic" that defines his contrast:[20] "Outside his destiny, the epic and tragic hero is nothing; he is, therefore, a function of the plot fate assigns him; he cannot become the hero of another destiny or another plot" (1981, 36). Quoting this passage, Gary Morson writes, "By contrast, the life led by a novelistic hero does not exhaust his identity. He could have been different. We sense that, in potential, he has more lives than one" (1994, 112). Indian heroes and heroines' epic lives have other lives both behind and before them, and multiple possibilities for different lives within the lives the epics give them.

I do not mean here the unfolding of new epic-based plots in classical Indian drama and later fiction, in vernacular versions of the epics, or in the ways heroes and heroines of the classical epics work out their "unfinished business" in vernacular regional oral epics.[21] As Bakhtin would point out, Greece has similar unfoldings of epic themes in other genres, which are thus *ipso facto* "not epic." What the Indian epics do, and what the *Mahābhārata* does in particular, is develop devices by which to construct for its audiences an experience of multiple possibilities in its heroes' lives. This is made possible above all by the way they put their authors in the works, and introduce their audiences to the multiple selves of such authors and the nature of their interventions in the text and the lives of their characters. We may characterize this cluster of techniques by Morson's term "sideshadowing." Over and against the more or less linear chronicities and the foreordained worlds implied by foreshadowing and backshadowing, "sideshadowing projects—from the 'side'—the shadow of an alternative present" (Morson 1994, 11) that is filled with possibilities. "Its most fundamental lesson is: to understand a moment is to grasp not only what did happen but also what else might have happened. Hypothetical histories shadow actual ones. . . . Sideshadowing invites us into this peculiar middle realm" (119). Thus the same god who can tell Arjuna that he is Time, and that the heroes gathered for war "are already slain," can precede this by telling him in, the same *Gītā*:

> The beginnings of things are unmanifest;
> Manifest are their middles, son of Bhārata,
> Unmanifest again their ends.
> Why mourn about this? (*BhG* 2.28)

[20]Cf. Reich 1998, 29–30: ". . . there is much 'novel' . . . in the so-called Sanskrit epic. In fact, I doubt whether a pure 'epic' in Bakhtin's sense ever existed" (30).
[21]The latter point is developed extensively in Hiltebeitel 1999a.

I am the beginning and the middle
Of beings, and the very end too. (*BhG* 10.20)

The palpable tension between contingency and determinism opens the field of narrative possibilities. At every point we are given the possibility of many stories. No story is ever the whole story. Every version has another version.[22] Every outcome has multiple fatalities behind it. The stories that heroes and heroines hear are sideshadows of their own. Characters are filled not only with griefs and doubts but haunted by shadows and rumors.[23] Nothing ever really begins (as Duryodhana says of Karṇa, "the origins of rivers and heroes are obscure"; 1.127.11) or ends. "Vortex times" follow one upon another: "As catastrophe approaches, time speeds up. Crises appear more and more rapidly until a moment of apparently infinite temporal density is reached" (Morson 1994, 165). Yet as with Tolstoy's novels, "continuation [is] always possible." There are loose threads left at the end of each crisis, each *Mahābhārata parvan* ("join") or *Rāmāyaṇa kāṇḍa* ("joint" of a reed or cane), and often at the ends of the epics' shorter sections: the *adhyāyas* ("readings") of the *Mahābhārata*, or the *sargas* ("streams," "cantos") of the *Rāmāyaṇa*. Moreover, there is the Vedic convention of the ritual "interval" which the epic poets fictionalize into a narrative convention through which to tell the epics themselves. The *Mahābhārata* is artfully designed as a story about a ritual—a collective *sattra* sacrifice performed by the Ṛṣis of the Naimiṣa Forest—in whose intervals is told the story about another *sattra*—the snake sacrifice of King Janamejaya—in whose intervals is told the story *of* (that is, in both senses, the story *by* and *about*) the author Vyāsa that is also his story about the heroes, a story that embeds many other stories and centers upon an emboxed narrative of a great "sacrifice of battle." Through a design of recurrence and deferral, apocalypses can coincide with the contingent and unfinalizable.

These different types of shadowing involve narrative experiments with time. In this chapter I will bring such temporal dimensions to the fore, reserving spatial ones for subsequent chapters. Both Sanskrit epics have common concerns with time. Rāma leaves the world by entering the Sarayū River with his brothers after he has been visited by Time (Kāla) (*Rām* 7.95). But, as has been appreciated by Yaroslav Vassilkov (1999), it is the *Mahābhārata* that formulates a "doctrine of time," or *kālavāda*. Yet conjuring up notions of "editing" and "blending" to dismiss passages in which *kālavāda*, as I would rather see it, goes part and parcel with the

[22]Thus offering different "perspectives"; see Hiltebeitel [1976] 1990, 127, n. 33, and 140.
[23]Most notably, Vyāsa will always have before him the shadow of his liberated son Śuka, while Rāma lives with rumors in the last book of the *Rām*; on both, see chap. 8.

epic's teachings on bhakti and the law of karma, Vassilkov tries to isolate an earlier *kālavāda* strand from "interpolations" that advance such teachings, and to discover an "heroic fatalism" prior to the text that would come from an archaic phase of the epic's development. More wisely,[24] however, he also says that the *kālavāda* is "constitutive for the epic, being the quintessence of the epic *Weltanschauung*" (26) and not a holdover from some prior "ancient time mythology." The epic's *kālavāda* includes frequent references to the "wheel of time," to time's "revolving" *(paryāya)*. The idea that those about to die are "already slain" and the theme that time "swallows" beings with its "gaping mouth" are not only combined in the *Bhagavad Gītā*, but found elsewhere in the text (22–28). Not only does the *Mahābhārata* make the phrase "time cooks"[25] one of its signatures; there is an "ocean of time" (*kālasāgara*; 12.28.43). The whole world is *kālātmaka* or "has time as its self" (13.1.45). Time is "the supreme Lord" *(parameśvara)*. Caught in "time's noose," always "bewildered" and "impelled by the law of time" *(coditāḥ kāladharmaṇā)*, heroes and heroines should act knowing that although one cannot counter time, fortune does have its favorable moments (Vassilkov 1999, 24), and, I would add, that sometimes, perhaps quite mysteriously, one can also play for time, and that the openings for such play may be *given* by a god who "is time himself" or by an author who calls himself a "preacher of time," a *kālavādin* (18–19). As to the god:

> As if sporting, Janārdana ("Tormentor of Living Beings," Kṛṣṇa), the soul of beings, keeps earth, atmosphere, and heaven running. . . . By his self's yoga, the lord Keśava tirelessly keeps the wheel of time, the wheel of the universe, and the wheel of the yugas revolving *(kālackraṃ jagaccakraṃ yugacakraṃ . . . parivartate)*. I tell you truly, the Lord alone is ruler of time and death, and of the mobile and the immobile. Yet ruling the whole universe, the great yogin Hari

[24]But it would appear also contradictorily. My views on these matters remain the same as those in Hiltebeitel [1976] 1990, 34–35.

[25]The time-as-cooking metaphor, used frequently, also rounds off the epic's end (17.1.3–4). Cf. Heesterman 1993, 175, on the sattra as a form of self-cooking; Malamoud 1996, 48: "This then, is 'cooking the world.' This world, cooked by the Brahman, is the 'created' world which he creates and organizes around himself in the sacrifice." But "the world cooked by sacrificial activity" has no raw natural opposite: "everything is already cooked such that all that remains is to re-cook it. The sacrificial fire fed by the Brahman does nothing other than redouble the activity of the sun . . . ; 'That [sun] cooks everything in this world *(eṣá vā idáṃ sárvam pacati)*, by means of the days and the nights, the fortnights, months, seasons, and year. And this [Agni] cooks what has been cooked by that [sun]: 'he is the cooker of that which has been cooked,' said Bharadvāja" (citing *ŚB* 10.4.2.19). If the sun is the measure of time, and if the year and its units are the means by which the sun cooks, it is but a short step to say that "time cooks" *(kālaḥ pacati)*.

> undertakes to perform acts like a powerless peasant. (*kīnāśa iva durbalaḥ*; 5.66.10–14)[26]

And as to the author, Vyāsa speaks of time's meaning and mysteries throughout, and manages its flows and joins. It is pointless to overlook "devotional" passages, ones in which author and deity are doing precisely the same "work," in favor of a supposedly prior "heroic" *kālavāda*. That the epic occasionally attributes *kālavāda* to demons and condemns it, and makes the Asura Vṛtra, for instance, "a renowned calculator of time" (*kālasaṃkhyana-saṃkhyāta*; 12.270.23), is for the poets but another example of pointing up the dysfunctionality of any teaching truncated from the truths (including the chronicities) of bhakti (see chap. 1, n. 25).

What the epic poets did, then, was construct a new chronotope with which to explore the joins and intersections between different rhythms and images of time and space, including the historical times and spaces in which their tales were told.[27] Like the "workshop" that produced the modern novel, the epic poets achieved this by their "configuration and refiguration" of primarily Vedic images into an "empire of conventions" that would "grow in proportion to the representative ambition" of authors from the epics through the purāṇas (cf. Ricoeur 1985, 13). To describe this new chronotope is to describe its "grid of conventions" (Alter 1981, 47), to get a sense of the chronicities and spatialities it brings to life and the devices used to convey that sense.[28] The important point to keep in mind is the innovative play with which the epic poets explored these temporo-spatial conventions while creating them.

B. Author as Enigma

Mehta, Bruce Sullivan, and Mangels open new ground on Vyāsa, but they leave uncontested certain received ideas that remain staples of

[26]It is Saṃjaya speaking to Dhṛtarāṣṭra here (on their dialogue, see § C.16, 20–21, 25 and 27, below). What he says has its important context in § C.20, and is said *before* Vyāsa gives him the "divine eye" in § C.21. There seem to be "anticipations" of Saṃjaya having the "divine eye," as noted by Belvalkar (1947a, 329–31) and Mangels (1994, 97–98, 107, 113, 142–44). See also Hiltebeitel in press-d and n. 86 below.

[27]Cf. Pollock 1998, 15, on the *Mbh* as the "source, or at least the most articulate forerunner," of medieval texts that "project a meaningful supralocal space of political-cultural reference," "a pure example, thus, of a 'chronotope,' and with the chronotope's politics of space more clearly visible than Bakhtin himself understood."

[28]Cf. Thalmann 1984, xiii-xvii, on the overt, public conventions that sustain Greek "hexameter poetry" from poem to poem, including the *Iliad* and *Odyssey*: "characteristics, ideas, attitudes and concerns" as "means of coming to know and of explaining the world and man's place in it" (xiv; cf. 184). Perhaps because of their Vedic background, *Mbh* conventions are more often covert and enigmatic than overt, but both are made public and both explain the world.

Mahābhārata scholarship. One is that if he is (or represents) the author, he must be (or represent) the author of the epic's kernel: a martial story for which the text itself conveniently gives what some have thought to be an early martial name, *Jaya* or "Victory," and also a length of eight thousand eight hundred verses. This idea, for many axiomatic, ignores two points well made by J. Brockington (1998, 21): "rather than the theory of an independent nucleus called *Jaya*," the term seems to be synonymous with *Bhārata*; moreover, there would seem to be no connection between anything called *Jaya* and the enumeration of eight thousand eight hundred verses that appears in a late passage describing Gaṇeśa as Vyāsa's scribe and "probably refers to the number of obscure verses meant to slow Gaṇeśa down."[29] Nowhere is Vyāsa said to have authored a *Jaya before* the *Mahābhārata*. The other notion is that if Vyāsa is a character in the *Mahābhārata*, most if not all of his interventions must be attributed to a process of textual growth.[30] *Mahābhārata* scholarship has been paralyzed before this gap of its own making and has invented solutions seriatim to avoid closing it.

Sullivan also makes two positive claims about Vyāsa that have been justly questioned by Fitzgerald. One is that Vyāsa personifies features of the creator god Brahmā, that he bears a relation to Brahmā comparable to what Dumézil (1968) has in mind when he speaks of a divine-to-human or myth-to-epic "transposition."[31] I agree with Fitzgerald (1997, 701) that Sullivan succeeds in showing a "parallelism" between Vyāsa and Brahmā but strains to find an incarnational relation between them that would confirm the Dumézilian expectations. Second, Fitzgerald rightly calls "hasty and incomplete" Sullivan's notion that Vyāsa represents "the orthodox ideal which was then being formulated" of the "dharmic brahmin" (702). Indeed, where is Vyāsa's wife? A dharmic Brahman ought to have one. As we shall see, not only does Vyāsa have no wife; given all his stories, he would have been hard pressed to explain one. As we shall see in chapter 4, having wives is not an indifferent matter.

Yet Sullivan detects some intriguing anomalies about Vyāsa. These concern Vyāsa's personal relation to the Veda, the relation of his

[29]The so-called *kūṭaślokas*, "trick verses," to keep Gaṇeśa, who is determined to understand every verse, preoccupied, and giving Vyāsa time to plot his way through his "thought entire," as it were. For a translation of the passage, see B. Sullivan 1990, 118–19; for an interesting discussion, see Kaveeshwar 1972. Fitzgerald (1983) sees this story about writing as one that belatedly "confirms" the text's writtenness.

[30]These arguments (see Winternitz 1897, 721, 736–37, cited on p. 35 above; Hiltebeitel in press-c) parallel those made about the supposed divinization of Kṛṣṇa and the possibility that he was not even part of the original story (see chap. 1, n. 19).

[31]See chap. 1, n. 99. Cf. Mangels 1994, 145, refining the similarity between Vyāsa and Brahmā to the "literary function of *stimulus*."

Mahābhārata to the Veda, and the scene of his literary activities. His insights call for further consideration, sometimes under a different light.

As Sullivan notes, the epic depicts Vyāsa "as heir to the Vedic tradition" (1990, 2), crediting him with dividing the Vedas, calling him Vedavyāsa, regarding him as its foremost Vedic authority, and calling itself the "fifth Veda," yet leaving Vyāsa's relation to the Veda amorphous. The epic mentions hundreds of Vedic Ṛṣis, but Vyāsa is not one of them: "the *Veda* does not attribute any hymns to Vyāsa."[32] How he learned Veda is untold; he is never depicted as having studied it. Once conceived and born on the same day on an island in the Yamunā, he leaves his mother Satyavatī on the same day with the promise that he will come to her instantly whenever she wishes, and has no further dealings with his father Parāśara, who might have taught him the Veda. And if he has innate knowledge of Veda like his son Śuka (12.311.22), the epic never tells us that either.[33] Although Vyāsa teaches Veda *and Mahābhārata* to his four disciples and Śuka (1.57.74–75), along with the rules for proper Veda study and selection of Veda students (12.314–15), the *Mahābhārata* leaves his relation to Veda vague. His "division" of the Veda and his composition of the epic are given only the most obscure narrative connections.

One is thus left with the impression that whatever Vyāsa knows or teaches about Veda, what is important is that he conveys it along with the *Mahābhārata*. Indeed, Vyāsa has a tendency to leave "Vedic stories" to others. At Janamejaya's snake sacrifice, says the bard Ugraśravas, "in the intervals between the rites, the Brahmans told tales based on the Vedas, but Vyāsa told his own tale, the great *Bhārata*."[34] Although this is not precisely true—it is not Vyāsa who recites the *Mahābhārata* here but his disciple Vaiśampāyana, at Vyāsa's bidding—the passage makes an important distinction. Vedic stories are told *along with* the *Mahābhārata*, which is accordingly *not* a Vedic story. If Vedavyāsa makes the *Mahābhārata* a fifth Veda, he does so by way of its imbrication with Vedic stories in a Vedic ritual. More pervasively, he does this by way of his composition's Vedic allusions. We may thus say that Vyāsa imparts what he knows and teaches about Veda not only along with the *Mahābhārata*, but *through* it.

Still more intriguing are the multiple uncertainties—about persons, time, and place—concerning the scene of Vyāsa's literary creation. Vyāsa entrusts the *Mahābhārata* to his five Brahman students (his four disciples and his son) and, as we shall see, there is a hint that the bard

[32]He joins a miniline of "eminent Vedic ṛṣis" (B. Sullivan 1990, 2): Vasiṣṭha-Śakti-Parāśara.
[33]See B. Sullivan 1990, 5, 7, 44, and 52, n. 86, and below, chap. 8.
[34]B. Sullivan 1990, 6, citing 1.53.31.

Lomaharṣaṇa must either have been there too, or else that he must have learned the epic—or at least the *Āstīkaparvan*—from Vyāsa otherwise. But Vyāsa is "not ever depicted reciting his text to an audience," and he "is not the reciter of his own composition as we have it" (B. Sullivan 1990, 9–10). As Mangels says, Vyāsa's irretrievable prior narration is the "missing link" between the actual levels of narration (1994, 111; cf. 42–44, 100). Or as Mehta puts it, "he is never present to the reader, never speaks directly to him, but always as reported, by virtue of his authority, by someone else. Strange absentee author . . . worthy of . . . a Derrida!" (1990, 111). We are also left in the dark as to where Vyāsa did his authoring. Here Sullivan exerts much ingenuity, noting teasers about Vyāsa's "hermitage somewhere," and that, "In the Mbh, wherever Vyāsa is he is not at home" (1990, 40). We shall resume the search, especially in chapter 8.

Nonetheless, we shall even in this chapter find two places called Vyāsa's hermitage *(vyāsāśramam)*: one on the Ganges (see § C.26 below) and one at or near Kurukṣetra (§ C.36 and 41); and it would also seem to be a question of his hermitage(s) when he resorts to "the rocky Himavat" (§ C.6), to Mount Kailāsa (§ C.12), and to Mount Meru (§ C.30 and 33). Also, two tīrthas are "named after Vyāsa." One is Vyāsavana (Vyāsa's Grove), which is at Miśraka where "Vyāsa mixed all the tīrthas for the sake of the Brahmans"; one who goes to Miśraka bathes in all *tīrthas* (sacred water places); by bathing at Manojava at Vyāsa's grove, he attains the fruit of a thousand cows (3.81.76–78). The other is Vyāsasthalī (Vyāsa's Mound, or Land), where, consumed with grief over his son, Vyāsa resolved to give up the body and was resurrected by the gods; there too one gets the fruit of a thousand cows.[35] Vyāsavana and Vyāsasthalī are tīrthas connected with events attributed to Vyāsa's earthly career, events that must have happened before the Pāṇḍavas hear about them in the forest. Whatever it means that Vyāsa "mixed all the tīrthas," which seems to be the opposite of what he does with the Vedas, we should not miss a remarkable incongruity: Vyāsa seems to be mourning his son Śuka here. If this is so, and there is no other good explanation,[36] then by the time of the Pāṇḍavas' forest exile,

[35]3.81.81–82: *tato vyāsasthalī nāma yatra vyāsena dhīmatā/ putraśokābhitaptena dehatyāgārthaniścayaḥ// kṛto devaiśca rajendra punarutthāpitastadā/ abhigamya sthalīṃ tasya gosahasraphalaṃ labhet.*

[36]On Vyāsa's mourning for Śuka, see chap. 8. Pāṇḍu would also be a possibility at this juncture, but we have no reason to think that Vyāsa mourns him any more than any other Kṣatriya descendant, especially with the intensity mentioned. With Nīlakaṇṭha silent, van Buitenen seems alone in noting the passage: "*Grief over his son*: nothing is further known. Possibly there is a conflation with the story of Vasiṣṭha" at 1.166–67 (1975, 824), where Vasiṣṭha fails in five suicide attempts upon the deaths of his hundred sons. Although van

he has also already composed the *Mahābhārata*, most of which is still yet to happen, since Śuka is one of the five disciples to whom he imparts the *Mahābhārata!* If Yudhiṣṭhira doesn't ask whether he is in a time-warp in hearing this, Janamejaya should wonder, as should Śaunaka and, for that matter, Gaṇeśa.[37]

But Vyāsa's earthly career cannot be so easily isolated. Even these two tīrthas are on a route that seems to lead elsewhere. Following the itinerary recommended here by the Ṛṣi Pulastya, if one goes a little further one reaches Naimiṣa Arbor *(kuñja)* on the Sarasvatī River near Kurukṣetra, where formerly, says Pulastya, the Naimiṣeya Ṛṣis once went on pilgrimage and fashioned the arbor so that there "might be a large open space for the Ṛṣis";[38] by bathing there, one also obtains the fruit of a thousand cows (3.81.92–94): that is, in Vedic terms, heaven. In recommending this route amid others, Pulastya repeatedly refers to precise Vedic practices that connect epic pilgrimage with the heavenly world. In following this route, the Pāṇḍavas (minus Arjuna) soon come, with the additional prompting of the Ṛṣi Lomaśa, to Plakṣāvataraṇa tīrtha, which "those of insight call the doorway of the back of the firmament" *(nākapṛṣṭhasya dvāram)*. There, Yudhiṣṭhira is able to see Arjuna in Indra's heaven; and, as Lomaśa confirms, what Yudhiṣṭhira sees is what "the eminent Ṛṣis see" (*paśyanti paramarṣayaḥ*; 3.129.12–20). We shall retrace these signposts in chapters 3 and 4. For now, it is enough to follow Sullivan (1990, 40, n. 54), who follows van Buitenen (1975, 186–87), who himself paraphrases Pulastya, in appreciating that some of these more remote locations "may be accessible [only] by thought" *(manasā)*.[39] These are good interpretative impulses and call for further consideration.

As Sullivan also observes, in the "most complete account of the incarnation of gods and demons"—that is, in the epic's first presentation of its "divine plan," which tells how the goddess Earth enlists the gods to rescue her from sinking into the ocean by incarnating themselves to defeat the demons who have taken birth as kings upon her

Buitenen is wrong that "nothing is further known" of Vyāsa mourning a son, i.e., Śuka, his suggestion has merit if, by analogy with theme-repetition in Bhārgava stories (see chap. 3, § C), one posits such repetition in the Vāsiṣṭha line that runs from Vasiṣṭha to Vyāsa (see n. 32 above). But even granting such "conflation," Vyāsa's son must still be Śuka.

[37]The *BhP* spins from the same time warp the frame story that Śuka recites that purāṇa to Parikṣit, a story that has led Indian commentators to suppose that the two Śukas could not be the same (Ganguli [1884–96] 1970, vol. 10, 530, n. 1; Belvalkar 1966, 2223). Similar inventive arguments have been made that there must be numerous Vyāsas. See chap. 8.

[38]3.81.93cd: *ṛṣīṇāmavakāśaḥ syād yathā tuṣṭakaro mahān.*

[39]3.83.87–88; Pulastya distinguishes "accessible" from "inaccessible" tīrthas, the latter "approached by thought."

(1.58–61)—"Vyāsa is named . . . as if he were one of the gods who sent portions of themselves down to earth! This surprising and anomalous statement is not supported by any other passage" in the epic (1990, 67). Yet had Sullivan considered this passage in connection with his search for Vyāsa's hermitage, which begins to look otherworldly, it might have seemed less anomalous. Sullivan shrewdly observes that Dhṛtarāṣṭra's birth from Vyāsa is described in parallel with the births of so many other heroes and heroines from "particles" or incarnations of divine, other celestial, and demonic beings. It thus places Vyāsa implicitly on a preexisting divine plane. But the siring of Dhṛtarāṣṭra happens *after* Vyāsa has been born on earth. Indeed, one of the anomalies of the passage is that Vyāsa is the only celestial or demonic being mentioned to have been born on earth prior to imparting a celestial or demonic "portion." That he has been born on earth, however, does not mean that he has stayed on earth. Rather, he would seem to have gone to one of those mysterious hermitages "accessible [only] by thought." It is precisely by memory or thought, by "thinking of him," that his mother Satyavatī brings him back into the story to sire Dhṛtarāṣṭra, Pāṇḍu, and Vidura (see § C.2 below). As if to heighten the implication that Vyāsa is considered a *celestial* Ṛṣi in this passage, the next incarnation mentioned is that of Vidura, who is said here (and nowhere else) to have been "born into the world as Atri's son"—Atri being a celestial Vedic Ṛṣi: one of the Seven Sages of the Big Dipper.

Like Mehta, Sullivan thus sees that Vyāsa as author is posed as an enigma. As Mangels observes (see above, n. 13), it is as if the text conceals him. But if that is so, how, and why? These scholars clarify things about Vyāsa as "author" and character in "his own" story. But they say too little about the soteriological design and literary conventions that make these things narratively possible, textually effective, and so deeply mysterious. Yet one of these conventions is already evident. There are time-traveling intergalactic Ṛṣis, among whom Vyāsa makes himself at home. Several such Ṛṣis (Pulastya and Lomaśa being already mentioned) extend the "function" by which the author self-disperses on this plane into a plurality of simultaneous narratological selves. Among these, it is above all Nārada with whom Vyāsa is inextricably intertwined and who shares his mode of action. Nārada—along with Mārkaṇḍeya—exemplifies the epic's new type of bhakti Ṛṣi who ranges even beyond the Vedic Ṛṣis[40] in traversing divine and earthly worlds, and, more than this, in moving in and out of the artifices of the text. A fuller study might

[40]Actually Nārada, unlike Mārkaṇḍeya, is also a Vedic Ṛṣi; see Macdonell and Keith [1912] 1967, 1:445 and chap. 1, n. 84.

trace, as well as seek to differentiate, Vyāsa's interrelations with Nārada.[41] For this one, let us just begin by noting that to keep track of Vyāsa is often to find him where he lets you.

C. Tracking Vyāsa

By "rough count," Mehta "noticed . . . about thirty occasions when [Vyāsa] turns up in the course of the events narrated" (1990, 105). My count is forty-one.[42] Mehta and Sullivan discuss most of these, and Mangels some as well. But except for some beginnings with the latter's notions of Vyāsa as "abstract author" and regulator of the fictive,[43] no one has adequately theorized the relation between Vyāsa's interventions in the main story, which are all that Mehta counts, and passages where he moves around between the epic's inner and outer frames. Indeed, Vyāsa's appearances in the *Mahābhārata* are a problematic category. For along with the obvious cases where he drops into the main narrative, there are numerous instances where he is quoted or his actions recalled. In these, he enters his characters' or narrators' thoughts, with which he has a wonder-provoking relation throughout.

Sticking for the most part to the Critical Edition, the rest of this chapter will trace Vyāsa's interventions in the main story of the epic's inner frame: that is, what Vaiśampāyana tells Janamejeya about Vyāsa's doings in the days of Janamejaya's ancestors. Vyāsa's relation to other frames will be left mainly to chapters 3 and 8. I pay particular attention to Vyāsa's central and recurring interest, amid his varied comings and goings, in the education of Yudhiṣthira. This king has suffered from lack of comparability to Achilles. He cannot be the "real hero"—that Aristotelian cynosure whom an epic or tragedy is supposed to supply; he looks too Brahmanical, etc.[44] But I will argue that he is the real hero,

[41]Oberlies 1998 isolates Nārada from Vyāsa and other Ṛṣis, and singles out just two of Nārada's interventions (prompting Yudhiṣthira to perform the Rājasūya in Book 2, and to go on pilgrimage in Book 3) without considering his other appearances (many of which will be noted below). He also strains to find in "ritual" a common denominator by which to account for the manner in which these two interventions, thus doubly isolated, demonstrate a belated "ritualization" of the "surface" of the whole epic (see chap. 1, n. 14). Oberlies virtually admits that pilgrimage *(tīrthayātrā)* and the Rājasūya are hardly "ritual" in the same sense, putting the term in quotes for the one but not for the other (1998, 129, 131), and trying to explain the Pāṇḍavas' pilgrimage as a kind of Aśvamedha (131–34). I see these as methodological errors. No general connection can be made between Nārada and "ritualization," which is also urged by Vyāsa (e.g., in advising Yudhiṣthira's Aśvamedha).

[42]Mehta misses a few, but the exact number is uncertain since it is not always clear whether Vyāsa has remained on scene or left and returned. Cf. Patni 1995, 26: six appearances.

[43]1994, 52–53, 145. See chap. 1, n. 17; chap. 2, n. 10.

[44]J. Brockington, for instance, says the *Mbh*'s last three books "are all generally regarded

and also the "real king." Arjuna is ultimately a diversion. He forgets what he is taught and doesn't rule a thing.[45] As we shall see, Vyāsa dismisses him by the end of the sixteenth book and saves everything for Yudhiṣṭhira, who remembers everything, at the end. Meanwhile, Vyāsa not only carries his story along. He pops in and out of it like Alfred Hitchcock. Sullivan suggests that his comings and goings have to do with "possession of the powers derived from yoga" (1990, 37). Although that is indeed so, his devices are not only yogic but literary.

1. *Birth.* Having on his day of birth "forced his body to mature that very day by willpower,"[46] Vyāsa leaves, promising his mother Satyavatī-Kālī in these few choice words: "Remembered, I will appear when things are to be done."[47] That is, he will come at her mere thought.

2. *Comes at his mother's summons* (1.99.16–44). Vyāsa appears when Satyavatī summons him to sire sons with Ambikā and Ambālikā, widows of the Kuru king Vicitravīrya. Speaking to Bhīṣma, she quotes Vyāsa's words from the scene of his birth: "'Remember me when things are to be done *(smareḥ kṛtyeṣu māmiti).*' I will remember him *(taṃ smariṣye)* if you wish"; whereupon, with Bhīṣma's permission, "the dark woman *(kālī)* bethought herself *(cintayāmāsa)* of the Muni Kṛṣṇa Dvaipāyana," and the sage, who was then "propounding *(vibruvan)* the Vedas, having understood his mother's thought *(mātur vijñāya cintitam)*, mysteriously appeared that instant."[48] While propounding the Vedas Vyāsa understands his mother's thought and enters the story he also composes. Vedic promulgation is thus his point of entry into the thoughts of his characters, which he can enter in a moment and change forever. Satyavatī tells him to sire sons with the widows, and says he must do it "with non-cruelty":[49] a strange message from a mother to an author about his own

as being late and in any case are extremely short"; he suggests it likely they were "treated as separate books only at a very late date, in order to produce the significant number 18 for the total," and that Yudhiṣṭhira is portrayed as "brāhmaṇical" in book 18 (1998, 155). But every book of the *Mbh* portrays Yudhiṣṭhira as "brāhmaṇical." Cf. Katz 1989, 263–68, and in disagreement, Hiltebeitel 1993, 18. For critical discussion of the "real hero" concept, see Hiltebeitel 1995b, 28; 1999a, 21–29, 110.

[45]I part company here from Biardeau 1978, 87–92, 104–5, 111, and passim; 1997a, 78–80, and also Katz 1989, who sometimes tend to give Arjuna more centrality than he deserves.

[46]So B. Sullivan 1990, 29, for 1.54.3ab: *jātamātraś ca yaḥ sadya iṣṭyā deham avīvṛdhat.* The passage, a quick "biography," continues with his mastery of the Vedas, Vedāṅgas, and *itihāsa*, and his fourfold division of the one Veda (3c-5), but it doesn't say when he did this.

[47]1.57.70cd: *smṛto 'ham darśayiṣyāmi kṛtyeṣviti*, amid 57.68–75 on Vyāsa's birth.

[48]1.99.16–22, ending *prādurbabhūvāviditaḥ kṣaṇena.*

[49]1.99.33c: *ānṛśaṃsyena.* She says he must also do it "out of commiseration for beings" *(anukrośāc ca bhūtānām*; 33a), a combination of qualities we will note again in chap. 5.

characters, and to a soon-to-be expectant father about his own sons. Considering that Vyāsa immediately terrorizes the two women and then curses them to have defective sons, it is easy to appreciate Satyavatī's anxiety. Waiting for the cohabitation, Vyāsa "vanished."[50]

3-4. *Sires Dhṛtarāṣṭra, Pāṇḍu, and Vidura.* Vyāsa comes and goes at least twice to father Dhṛtarāṣṭra, Pāṇḍu, and Vidura. For the initial arrival, Satyavatī tells Ambikā her unknown impregnator will come at midnight (*niśīthe*; 1.100.2d). With lamps still burning, she sees him enter her bedroom ugly, smelly, his eyes ablaze, and she shuts her eyes (5). Having predicted Dhṛtarāṣṭra will be born blind, Vyāsa departs (*niścakrāma*; 13b). Satyavatī "summons" him again to sire Pāṇḍu (14c). He seems to go nowhere until the end of Ambikā's pregnancy, whereupon he fathers Vidura with a servant woman and "vanished."[51]

5. *Favors Gāndharī with a hundred sons.* Once, when Vyāsa "stands before" *(upasthitam)* Gāndhārī hungry and fatigued, she satisfies him. He gives her a boon and she chooses a hundred sons (1.107.7–8b).

6. *Revives the stillborn Kauravas.* When Gāndhārī is about to throw away the ball of hard flesh she has just forced from her womb after a two-year pregnancy, Vyāsa, "having known, came quickly."[52] Where he comes from and whether he knows her thoughts, actions, or both are left vague. He confirms his boon, divides the ball into a hundred thumb-sized embryos, puts them in pots, and leaves instructions for their gestation. Then "the insightful lord Vyāsa went to the rocky Himavat for tapas."[53]

7. *Dispatches the royal widows.* His movements undescribed, after the death of Pāṇḍu, Vyāsa predicts dark times for the Bhāratas and tells Satyavatī, Ambikā, and Ambālikā it is time for them to leave the kingdom for tapas in the forest. Exeunt these three Kaurava widows, who are soon deceased (1.119.5–12).

8. *Present at end of the Pāṇḍavas and Kauravas' training by Droṇa.* His movements unmentioned, Vyāsa joins Droṇa and other preceptors for the heroes' graduation (1.124.1–2).

9. *Predicts the Pāṇḍavas' exile.* Hunting from forest to forest, the banished Pāṇḍavas and Kuntī meet and greet Vyāsa, who tells them, "Long ago I foresaw in my mind"[54] how the Pāṇḍavas would face this

[50]1.99.44b: *antarhito. Antar-dhā* carries a yogic implication of "to place within," as well as the meanings "to hide, conceal, obscure; to hide one's self" (MW 44). B. Sullivan notes that Nārada moves about identically (1990, 37); so do other Ṛṣis, e.g., Pulastya (3.83.96).

[51]1.100.29d: *antar adhīyata.*

[52]1.107.13b: *jñātvā tvaritaḥ samupāgamat.*

[53]1.107.02: *bhagavān vyāsas . . . jagāma tapase dhīmān himavantam śiloccayam.*

[54]1.144.7ab: *mayā idam manasā pūrvaṃ viditam* (van Buitenen 1973, 302).

ordeal, and that now, "knowing it, I have reached you wishing to see to your highest welfare."[55] He tells them to live disguised as Brahmans in the town of Ekacakrā, leads them there, settles them in the house of a Brahman, predicts many of their future successes, and tells them to wait until he returns. Then "he went as he pleased."[56]

10. *Tells the Pāṇḍavas to go to Draupadī's svayaṃvara.* Vyāsa returns[57] to check on the Pāṇḍavas' dharma and narrate the Overanxious Maiden story: Draupadī, in a previous life, asked Śiva for a husband five times; he thus held her accountable to have five husbands at once (1.157.6–13). Cryptically, Vyāsa addresses the Pāṇḍavas in the plural *(mahābalāḥ)* yet tells them that she is destined to marry "you" in the singular *(bhavatā)*. Then he "left" (*prātiṣṭhata*; 14–16).

11. *Sees that the Pāṇḍavas stay on course to Pāñcāla.* While on their path *(pathi)* to Pāñcāla, the Pāṇḍavas "saw" *(dadṛśur)* Vyāsa, who comforts them and, "at the end of a story" *(kathānte)*, gives them leave to continue past delightful forests and ponds (1.176.2–3).

12. *Justifies Draupadī's polyandry, establishes the Pāṇḍavas at Indraprastha.* Yudhiṣṭhira holds that it would be dharma for Draupadī to marry all five brothers. He might infer from having so recently heard Vyāsa's Overanxious Maiden story, but he is mum as to its recollection or meaning—as if it would need more authority than he can impart to it himself. Drupada is dubious. Vyāsa "by chance arrived,"[58] and after asking what others have to say, takes Drupada aside. Knowing the Pāṇḍavas and Draupadī's previous lives, he confirms Yudhiṣṭhira's certainty by telling the Story of the Former Indras (which no one has heard till now). Then, after giving Drupada the "divine eye"[59] to see the truth of it all, he retells the Overanxious Maiden story, which, as noted, probably put the polyandry idea into Yudhiṣṭhira's head.[60] The Story of the Former Indras "authorizes" the polyandry fully and provides a first glimpse, as I will argue in chapter 4, of Vyāsa's Vedic groundplan. Kṛṣṇa is also there to sanction the wedding, having recognized the Pāṇḍavas through their disguises (180.17–21; 191.13–18).

Vyāsa and Kṛṣṇa seem to remain with the newlyweds to help them found their capital of Indraprastha in the "terrible" *(ghora)* Khāṇḍava Forest. Kṛṣṇa leads them *(gatvā kṛṣṇapurogamāḥ)* there, and Vyāsa then leads them in performing the rite of appeasement *(śānti)* and measuring

[55] 1.144.8ab: *tad viditvāsmi samprāptaś cikīrṣuḥ paramaṃ hitam.*
[56] 1.144.20cd: *jagāma bhagavān vyāso yathākāmam ṛṣiḥ prabhuḥ.*
[57] 1.157.1c: *ājagāmātha tān draṣṭum*; "he came to see them."
[58] 1.187.32d: *abhyāgacchad yadṛcchayā* (end of an adhyāya).
[59] 1.189.35–36: *divyaṃ cakṣuḥ, cakṣur divyam.* See Mangels 1994, 138.
[60] The passage keeps Vyāsa present from 1.187.32–190.4.

the city (*nagaraṃ māpayāmāsur dvaipāyanapurogamāḥ*; 1.199.26–28). Note the parallelism: the Pāṇḍavas let both of them "go before" (*purogamāḥ*) them.

After this, Kṛṣṇa leaves for Dvāraka (1.199.50), but nothing is said of Vyāsa, who thus seems to have remained present, yet receded into the background, when the "divine Ṛṣi Nārada by chance arrived"[61]—just as Vyāsa had done shortly before him (see above, n. 58). As if following up Vyāsa's orchestration of the Pāṇḍavas' polyandrous marriage, Nārada prompts them to regulate their privacy with Draupadī by establishing a rule of spousal rotation, and backs this up by telling them the cautionary tale of two brothers, the demons Sunda and Upasunda, who killed each other fighting to possess one woman, Tilottamā, whom the gods had fashioned to defraud them (1.200–4). I will return to this sequence in chapter 7 (§ D), but for the moment its most telling outcome is that Arjuna will break the rule of rotation and be banished to undertake a "celibate" pilgrimage, from which he will return having married three more women, the last of whom, Kṛṣṇa's sister Subhadrā, will assure the Pāṇḍavas' descent as the mother of Abhimanyu (205–13).[62]

Vyāsa also seems to have remained until his next mention among the vast concourse of Ṛṣis and kings who are present when Yudhiṣṭhira, toward the beginning of the *Sabhāparvan*, enters his new hall. Here Vyāsa is joined by his son Śuka and his four disciples, "Sumantu, Jaimini, Paila, and we ourselves"—that is, Vaiśampāyana.[63] There is, however, nothing to indicate whether the five come with Vyāsa, apart from him, or specially for the occasion. Just then, Nārada arrives again "on a tour of all the worlds" (2.5.2) and prompts Yudhiṣṭhira to perform the Rājasūya sacrifice, despite the great dangers it unleashes, since it will gratify his deceased father Pāṇḍu and can make Yudhiṣṭhira an emperor.[64] After Nārada departs for Dvārakā (11.71), Vyāsa is among those consulted about the Rājasūya (12.18) and is present when Kṛṣṇa

[61]1.200.9: *ajagāma yadṛcchayā*.

[62]Oberlies does not mention this first appearance by Nārada, just before his second to advise Yudhiṣṭhira to perform the Rājasūya. Even though Nārada's advice results in Arjuna's pilgrimage and meeting with Kṛṣṇa in connection with his marrying Subhadrā, Oberlies would have had to strain to extend his overworked notion of "ritual" (see above, n. 41) to accommodate Nārada's advice—the new marital rule—that sets these outcomes in motion.

[63]2.4.9: Śuka can count as a disciple, but here *śiṣya* seems to qualify only the other four.

[64]2.11.61–69. See chap. 1 after n. 38. Attributing Nārada's prompting of the Rājasūya to a late "ritualization," Oberlies (1998, 129–39) goes on to argue that the whole Rājasūya narrative is a late re-"surfacing" of a written text over an older, apparently unritualized, heroic narrative that has, among other things, as little as possible to do with Kṛṣṇa (137). As indicated (see chap. 1, n. 14, and above, n. 41), the argument on these points is selective and strained.

arrives for the rite (30.17). Vyāsa brings in the priests and acts as the Brahman while Paila serves as Hotar (30.33–35). Vyāsa is then among those mentioned by Śiśupāla as more deserving of the guest gift than Kṛṣṇa (34.9). Finally, Duryodhana adds that Vyāsa participated in Yudhiṣṭhira's anointing, as did Kṛṣṇa (49.10–15).

In the Critical Edition, Vyāsa never leaves this scene, although we may note that neither he nor Kṛṣṇa is present at the dice match. The author tells us why Kṛṣṇa isn't there,[65] but about his own absence he is silent. But the Southern Recension and a few northern texts, including the Vulgate, do provide Vyāsa with an instructive, though clearly interpolated, exit. It is inserted just after the Rājasūya is completed and Kṛṣṇa has left for Dvārakā (42.55).[66] Surrounded by his disciples, Vyāsa comes before Yudhiṣṭhira to commend him for "having obtained empire so difficult to acquire,"[67] and to request leave. But Yudhiṣṭhira first asks whether the death of Śiśupāla exhausts all the bad omens Nārada had forecast as the result of the Rājasūya. Vyāsa announces that the full destruction of the Kṣatriyas lies ahead, and that Yudhiṣṭhira will be its sole cause.[68] Moreover, he tells Yudhiṣṭhira he will have a dream that night of Śiva facing south toward the land of the dead.[69] Saying that this is not cause for sorrow and that the world is difficult to transcend, Vyāsa bids adieu: "'I will go toward Mount Kailāsa. Vigilant, firm, restrained, protect the earth.' Having so spoken, the lord Kṛṣṇa Dvaipāyana Vyāsa went together with his disciples who followed what they heard" (2, Appendix I, 30, lines 33–37). From here, only the Northern Recension continues, giving Yudhiṣṭhira his first opportunity to wish to end his rule before it begins, and Arjuna his first chance to dissuade him.[70]

Śiṣyaiḥ śrutānugaiḥ, "with disciples who followed what they heard *(śruta)*," is interesting, and could be a pun: "who followed Vyāsa's instructions to leave"; "who followed the Veda"; "who followed the recitation of the fifth Veda." If Vyāsa's disciples follow the Veda of Veda Vyāsa, we may ask whether it means they listen to what we usually call Veda, or follow the *Mahābhārata in medias res*.

13. *Stops the Kauravas from raiding the Pāṇḍavas in the forest.* "Having known with his divine eye" of the Kauravas' fresh plan to attack

[65] See Hiltebeitel [1976] 1990, 86–101; Oberlies 1998, 137.

[66] It breaks the narrative just as it comes into focus on the lingering and bitter Duryodhana. See further Gehrts 1975; Hiltebeitel 1977b; Biardeau 1978, 104–6; Oberlies 1995, 187–92.

[67] Appendix I, 30, line 9: *saṃrājyaṃ prāpya durlabham.*

[68] 2, Appendix I, 30, line 23a: *tvamekaṃ kāraṇaṃ kṛtvā.*

[69] Thus linking Yudhiṣṭhira with Yama, and his rule with Śiva (Biardeau 1978, 105–6).

[70] 2, Appendix I, 30, lines 38–68. Ganguli translates the whole passage ([1884–96] 1970, vol. 2, *Sabha Parva*, 102–4).

the Pāṇḍavas in the forest, "he came"[71] to advise Dhṛtarāṣṭra to restrain his sons, and "went" *(yayau)*. He goes just as the Ṛṣi Maitreya arrives (3.8.21–11.7). Dhṛtarāṣṭra wanted Vyāsa to chastise Duryodhana, but the author, noting that "character" (*śīla*) formed at birth does not glide away until death (9.11), leaves Maitreya to do this, and, further, to curse Duryodhana if he doesn't listen. When Duryodhana rudely slaps his thigh, Maitreya curses him to have it broken (overdetermining Bhīma's prior vow after the dice match to break it). Maitreya then leaves, refusing to continue a story he started, which he passes on to Vidura.[72]

14. *Is among the Brahmans attending the Pāṇḍavas in Dvaita Forest.* While the Pāṇḍavas dwell in Dvaita Forest, the "great wilderness became filled with Brahmans" (3.27.1). There, without details as to his movements, Vyāsa applauds the Ṛṣi Baka Dālbhya's praise of Brahmans to Yudhiṣṭhira (22).

15. *Gives visionary knowledge to Yudhiṣṭhira.* Still early in their exile, the Pāṇḍavas despair. Yudhiṣṭhira tells Bhīma and Draupadī they must prepare for the right time, "but he does not know how."[73] In the middle of the argument, "the great yogin Vyāsa came" (*ājagāma*; 3.37.20c) and says, "Yudhiṣṭhira, I know the thought in your heart *(vedmi te hṛdimānasam)*. With insight, I have come quickly, bull among men" (3.37.22). Vyāsa says he will dispel the fear of his foes that "goes round in Yudhiṣṭhira's heart" (*hṛdi saṃparivartate*; 23) by teaching him a knowledge *(vidyā)* called *pratismṛti;* it will change their fortunes once Yudhiṣṭhira passes it on to Arjuna (27). Giving Yudhiṣṭhira this *vidyā*, which is a "*brahman* or sacred word" (37), Vyāsa reveals that Arjuna is Nara, companion of Nārāyaṇa,[74] who can obtain weapons from the gods (28–30). Then, telling Yudhiṣṭhira to go to another forest and bidding him adieu, Vyāsa "vanished then and there."[75] Yudhiṣṭhira imparts this "*upaniṣad* or secret knowledge which makes visible, . . . illuminates, or makes manifest the entire universe" to Arjuna, and tells him to seek the grace of the gods, starting today with Indra.[76]

[71]3.8.22cd: *ājagāma viśuddhātmā dṛṣṭvā divyena cakṣuṣā*. Vyāsa, who, as noted above (nn. 26 and 59), imparts the divine eye to Saṃjaya and Drupada, has used his own divine eye to compose the *Mbh* (18.5.31–33).

[72]3.11.8–39. See Mangels 1994, 3–5, on the "calmness" *(Gelassenheit)* with which the "Epiker" moves here from narrator to narrator, beginning with Vyāsa as both author and character in his own story, as illustrative of the epic's narrative technique. Maitreya's curse is recalled by Kṛṣṇa at 9.59.15, the scene of Duryodhana's fall.

[73]Paraphrasing and quoting Mehta 1990, 107, who treats the passage (3.37.20–38.12) well.

[74]Which Yudhiṣṭhira later reports to others: 3.84.4.

[75]3.37.35d: *tatraivāntar adhīyata*.

[76]Mehta 1990, 108; *Mbh* 3.38.1–13, with the *upaniṣad* reference and the illumining of the entire universe *(jagat sarvaṃ prakāśate)* at verse 9.

Mehta underscores the terms *vidyā*, *upaniṣad*, and *brahman*:

> [They] all derive from a Vedic context and have the sense of a visionary insight which enables one to penetrate into the true nature of things, and *brahman* specifically points to the power of *Vāk* or language, the Vedic *mantra*, to make things manifest, to disclose their real nature. *Pratismṛti* would then seem to mean a reaching out towards, approaching, gaining access to, a reality by means of the word that reveals it, and at the same time letting this reality approach us and disclose itself. (1990, 108)

Mehta cites a Rākṣasa-destroying mantra (*ṚV* 7.104.7) with the phrase *prati smarethām*, which, following the commentator Sāyaṇa, he takes as a request to Indra and Soma to approach, and argues that the "hymn in which this word occurs reflects exactly the situation in which the Pāṇḍavas find themselves": surrounded by Rākṣasas, with Arjuna about to call down Indra with "the *brahman* he has learnt" from Vyāsa, who is a descendent of Vasiṣṭha, the mantra's Ṛṣi (108–9). *Pratismṛti* thus looks like a precise Ṛg Vedic allusion. The term mantra, however, is not used, perhaps reflecting a brahmanical caution in handing mantras down to Kṣatriyas.[77]

16. *Reports to Dhṛtarāṣṭra*. Vaiśampāyana reports briefly that Vyāsa told Dhṛtarāṣṭra that Arjuna had gone to Indraloka (3.46.2). Saṃjaya then says he has heard that Arjuna also gratified Śiva and the Lokapālas or World Regents, and predicts doom for the Kauravas (3.46.22–31). One can only guess who told Saṃjaya this, but Vyāsa looks like the best candidate. Vyāsa is yet to give Saṃjaya the "divine eye."[78]

17. *Is among the Ṛṣis who welcome the Pāṇḍavas in the forest*. Nārada closes Pulastya's account of tīrthas mentioning Vyāsa—"first of the mutterers of prayers"[79]—as among the great Ṛṣis waiting in the Kāmyaka Forest to greet the Pāṇḍavas and accompany them further. Among others present are the literary vedettes Vālmīki (of the *Rāmāyaṇa*) and Śaunaka (of the *Mahābhārata*); six of the Seven Ṛṣis of the Great Bear (Kāśyapa, Viśvāmitra, Gautama, Bharadvāja, Ātreya, and Vasiṣṭha);[80] Mārkaṇḍeya and Nārada.

[77]Cf. Patton 1996, 213, 290–91, 400, 327–41.

[78]See n. 26 above. This may be an "anticipation" of Saṃjaya receiving the "divine eye" with which to see the war, as with 5.129.12–13 where Kṛṣṇa gives Saṃjaya and others the divine eye *(divyaṃ cakṣur)* to see his theophany.

[79]3.83.104b: *japatāṃ varaḥ*.

[80]Jamadagni it seems has withdrawn in favor of his son Rāma Jāmadagnya, who does not appear in such groups. On traditions of the Seven Ṛṣis, see Mitchiner 1982, passim.

18. *Directs the Pāṇḍavas to go on pilgrimage.* Vyāsa, Nārada, and Parvata "come together" *(samājagmur)* to see the Pāṇḍavas in Kāmyaka Forest; they tell them to tour tīrthas, and that all is well with Arjuna in Indraloka (3.91.17-25).

19. *Counsels Yudhiṣṭhira.* While the Pāṇḍavas bitterly suffer their eleventh year of exile, "after a certain time" Vyāsa "came" *(ājagāma)* to see them (3.245.8). He exalts tapas, yoga, and gifting, mainly by telling the story of Mudgala (246-47). At Kurukṣetra, this sage practiced a vow of gleaning *(uñcavṛtti)* like a pigeon with his wife and sons, gathering rice with which to liberally feed their guests (246.3-11). But when the "mad" sage Durvāsas tested Mudgala and then announced his heavenly reward, a divine messenger came to say that heaven is nothing compared to what transcends it. Mudgala then abandoned his gleaning and "attained the eternal supreme perfection that is marked by nirvāṇa" (247.41d, 43cd). Vyāsa closes with the promise that Yudhiṣṭhira will regain his kingdom. Then, saying, "May the fever of your mind go,"[81] he "returned to his hermitage again for tapas."[82]

20. *Supports Saṃjaya's praise of Kṛṣṇa.* On to the *Udyogaparvan*,[83] Vyāsa arrives when Saṃjaya, taken aside by Dhṛtarāṣṭra and questioned as to who will win the war, tells him he will not answer unless "your father"—that is, Vyāsa!—comes. Saṃjaya will then answer by telling "Vāsudeva's and Arjuna's thought entire"[84]—echoing the phrase that describes the *Mahābhārata* as "Vyāsa's thought entire." As if on cue, "having known the thought of his son and Saṃjaya,"[85] Vyāsa arrives *(abhyupetya)* and invites Saṃjaya to tell everything he knows about Vāsudeva and Arjuna (5.65.8-9). Saṃjaya exalts both, but especially Kṛṣṇa, in a passage cited earlier in this chapter,[86] as "the great yogin Hari [who] undertakes to perform acts like a powerless peasant"; and when Dhṛtarāṣṭra asks Saṃjaya how he knows so much about bhakti (67.4), Saṃjaya answers, "from scripture" (*śāstrād*; 5). Vyāsa then endorses Saṃjaya's words to Dhṛtarāṣṭra, and Duryodhana defies Kṛṣṇa (67.11-68). The sequence concludes Saṃjaya's mission to the Pāṇḍavas and preludes Kṛṣṇa's mission to the Kauravas. As Mangels observes, Saṃjaya "adapts to a hierarchy" here; but she does not notice that this

[81] 3.247.46d: *vyetu te mānasojvaraḥ*.

[82] 3.247.47cd: *jagāma tapase dhīmān punar evāśramam prati*. On the gleaning vow, see chap. 1 at nn. 75-78.

[83] Vyāsa makes no appearance in the *Virāṭaparvan*. Of course the Pāṇḍavas are in hiding and even he must not be able to find them, as it were.

[84] 5.65.7d: *kṛtsnaṃ mataṃ vāsudevārjunābhyām*.

[85] 5.65.8ab: *tatas tan matam ājñāya saṃjayasyātmajasya ca*.

[86] 5.66.14; see above at n. 26.

hierarchy builds from the echo of Vyāsa's "thought entire" to a bold implication that Saṃjaya presents Dhṛtarāṣṭra's (and thus our) opportunity to understand that this "thought entire" is one and the same for the author and the deity.[87]

21. *Gives Saṃjaya the divine eye.* Toward the beginning of the *Bhīṣmaparvan*, with war imminent, Bhīṣma tells Dhṛtarāṣṭra that time has run out for his sons and the other kings: "If you wish during the battle to see it, king, alas, let me give you the eye. Behold this war."[88] Dhṛtarāṣṭra says that seeing the death of kinsmen does not please him. He would rather hear about it with nothing left out (*aśeṣena*; 6.2.7c). So Vyāsa, lord of boons *(varāṇām īśvaro)*, gives a boon to Saṃjaya:

> Saṃjaya will tell this battle to you, king. Nothing in the battle will be out of his sight. Endowed with the divine eye *(cakṣuṣā . . . divyena)*, O king, Saṃjaya will narrate the war and be all-knowing. Manifest or secret,[89] by night or day, even what is thought by the mind *(manasā cintitam api)*, Saṃjaya will know it all. Weapons will not cut him. Fatigue will not trouble him. Gavalgaṇa's son will escape from this battle alive. And I will spread the fame of these Kurus and all the Pāṇḍavas, Bhārata bull. Do not grieve. (6.2.9–13)

Vyāsa then describes the terrifying omens that face the Kauravas,[90] meditates a bit (4.1d), and discourses on time, telling Dhṛtarāṣṭra he should restrain his friends and kinsmen even though Duryodhana is "time *(kāla)* born in the form of your son."[91] Dhṛtarāṣṭra replies:

> I beseech you. You are of immeasurable power *(atulaprabhāvam)*. You show the way *(gatir darśayitā)* and are firm. They are not even under my control,[92] O Maharṣi. You can enable me not to commit

[87]1994, 142–43. Rather, Mangels speculates here about archaic *triṣṭubh* verses, and generally views bhakti passages as overlay (see chap. 1, nn. 17 and 19; chap. 2, nn. 10 and 11). For a passage with similar bhakti "effects," see 3.187.48–55: Mārkaṇḍeya's disclosure that the child god whom he has just described as appearing and vanishing during the dissolution of the universe is none other than Kṛṣṇa Vārṣṇeya who sits beside the Pāṇḍavas listening.

[88]6.2.5d–6: *mā sma śoke manaḥ kṛthāḥ// yadi tvicchasi saṃgrāme draṣṭum enaṃ viśāṃpate/ cakṣur dadāni te hanta yuddham etan niśāmaya.*

[89]6.2.12a: *prakāśaṃ vā rahasyaṃ vā*; see Mangels 1994, 120 and 108, on Saṃjaya's "secretive" use of first person narration in the war books, which she suggests may result from his "exposed position as narrator."

[90]2.16–3.43; of some note iconographically, "The images of the deities *(devatāpratimāḥ)* even tremble and laugh, and they vomit blood from their mouths and sweat and fall down" (6.2.26). Note also the birthing of varied "monsters" (*vibhīṣanān*; 3.2b).

[91]6.4.2–5. Duryodhana is the incarnation of Kali, demon of the Kali yuga.

[92]6.4.12c: *na cāpi te vaśagāḥ*, refering to his sons.

> sin here. Surely you are dharma, the purifier, fame, glory, bearing, and memory, and you are the revered grandfather of the Kurus and Pāṇḍavas.[93]

When the old blind king says his sons are not under his own control, he is allowed the glimmer of a thought that Vyāsa could do something about it: that they are not under his control but under Vyāsa's. But Vyāsa quickly turns such thoughts aside by asking what Dhṛtarāṣṭra *is* thinking: "What turns in your mind? Share as you wish. I am the cutter of your doubt" (4.14). Dhṛtarāṣṭra wants to know the good omens that portend victory in battle, not the bad ones just described. Vyāsa then expounds on these (15-35), and "having so spoken to the insightful Dhṛtarāṣṭra, he went" (*yayau*; 5.1).

Meditating briefly himself, Dhṛtarāṣṭra asks Saṃjaya about the earth over which her rulers contend. Saṃjaya imparts a long cosmology lesson,[94] and then recalls and rather amplifies Vyāsa's boon just as he is about to begin his war report:

> Hear of horses, elephants, and heroes of unlimited energy seen with my own eyes,[95] and seen by the strength of yoga *(yogabalena)*; and, earth protector, may you not set your mind on grief. Past, present, and future are ordained, lord of men. Having saluted your father, the insightful son of Parāśara by whose grace *(prasadāt)* I obtained my unexcelled divine knowledge, and sight beyond the senses, O king, as also hearing from afar, and discerning others' minds, and the past and future, and awareness of portentious happenings,[96] and always the ability to move in space, and unaffectedness by weapons in battles, by

[93]6.4.12–13, ending: *tvaṃ hi dharmaḥ pavitraṃ ca yaśaḥ kīrtir dhṛtiḥ smṛtiḥ/ kurūṇāṃ pāṇḍavānāṃ ca mānyaś cāsi pitāmahaḥ.*

[94]6.5–13; for Mangels 1994, 89, an outrageous break in the narrative build-up to the war.

[95]Had the *Mahābhārata* begun here, this much might have interested some of those who wish it were more like the *Iliad.* Cf. Mangels 1994, 70–71, contrasting the use of such "Hear me" *(śṛṇu . . . me)* passages in the *Mbh* with Homer's use of apostrophe (addresses to a character), and Richardson 1990, 182: "With the apostrophe to a character, the narrator [Homer] . . . crosses into the world of the story. . . . With the invocations to the Muses, the narrator reminds us that he in turn depends on higher powers for every glimpse into the realm of the story he narrates."

[96]6.16.9a: *vyutthitopattivijñānam*, following van Buitenen 1981, 47. Cf. Ganguli [1884–96] 1970, vol. 5, 38: "knowledge also of the origin of all persons transgressing the ordinances" (derived, he says, from Nīlakaṇtha); Belvalkar 1947b, 766: "[discerning] any abnormal occurrence"; Mangels 1994, 128–29 and n. 303: "discerning widely dispersed occurrences" *("die Erkenntnis von weit auseinanderliegenden Vorgängen* [?]*")*, noting that it is problematic. Perhaps "discerning the arising of swerving from duty" (see MW, 1040 on this *Mbh* meaning of *vyutthita*).

the gift of the boon of the high-souled one, hear from me in detail this varied, most wondrous, hair-raising, great war of the Bhāratas as it happened. (6.16.5–10)

Saṃjaya has the "divine eye" until he sees Duryodhana's death and ascent to heaven, whereupon he loses it amid his grief—as Belvalkar says, "as soon as [its] purpose is served" (1947, 321). Presumably he should also keep his invulnerability, mentioned along with the "divine eye" in both passages, until that point as well.

Yet as we have seen (n. 26 above), Saṃjaya has "anticipations" of the "divine eye" before he gets it from Vyāsa. He has sampled it momentarily when Kṛṣṇa makes him one of five beneficiaries whom he allows to see his theophany in the Kuru court.[97] He previews at least one of its powers when he discloses, with Vyāsa's blessing, the "thought entire" of Vāsudeva and Arjuna (§ C.20 above). And he also enters a trance to envision the strength of the Pāṇḍava forces to answer another of Dhṛtarāṣṭra's fearful questions about the odds against his sons.[98] Mangels divides these passages according to her textual stratigraphy. The first two result from an overlay that subsumes Saṃjaya's older, self-sufficient bardic powers under the later narrative omniscience of the purāṇic bardic tradition exemplified by Vyāsa and Vaiśampāyana, which, when it is a question of such "important themes as *dharma*, *Kṛṣṇa*, *Gītā*, etc.," pushes the "little Sūta Saṃjaya" into the background (1994, 143–44) and subordinates him through the "divine eye" itself, which he originally does without. The third passage is then illustrative of this prior Saṃjaya's "'ontological basis' in the fictional space of the main action, which allows him to air his own meaning, so long as it deals with *fabula*" (ibid.). To sustain this division, however, Mangels is led to "speculate" on a thoroughgoing "correction" of the war books (144), and to argue that for Saṃjaya, the "divine eye" is a "literary sediment of practical yoga technique" (130), "a Buddhist pendant" (137, n. 324), and a belated addition to make his narration credible (117, 125, 131). This is a rather severe reduction of such a supple device, whose uses may remind us of Homer: "Physically, the narrator has the ability to move at will and instantaneously to any location. The two manifestations of this power pertinent to the Homeric poems are the abrupt change of scene and the perspective on the scene from on high. More impressive is his knowledge: he knows what none of the mortal characters can know, especially about the activity of the gods; he can see into the characters'

[97] 5.129.13; see Mangels 1994, 137.

[98] 5.49.9–14: he heaves long sighs, faints, falls, and loses consciousness before replying. See Mangels 1994, 143.

minds; and he knows beforehand what is going to happen" (Richardson 1990, 109).[99] Of Saṃjaya's [and Vyāsa's] powers, Homer truly lacks only invulnerability in battle, which, distanced in time and stature (174–78) from the events he narrates, he does not require, since he can access his battle scenes through the Muses and apostrophe (see n. 95). In the *Mahābhārata*, the "divine eye" not only thematizes Vyāsa's authorship in relation to several characters beside Saṃjaya, but is perfectly capable of threading an alternance and interplay between "devotional" and other modes of vision.

Meanwhile, according to Belvalkar, Saṃjaya is "correctly conceived as . . . a 'special war-correspondent' . . . able to secure all the advantages that an expert army of camera-men, radios, specially chartered aeroplanes and television would give to his twentieth-century prototypes" (1947a, 315). But Belvalkar feels obliged to trim Saṃjaya to this modern image: like Mangels, he is "forced to make an appeal to Higher Criticism" (323) to allow Saṃjaya to report to Dhṛtarāṣṭra every night rather than with the flash-forwards at the beginning of each war book, in which Saṃjaya rushes back from the battlefield to announce to Dhṛtarāṣṭra the death of the Kaurava general of that book, and for the rest of the book then narrates the days of battle that conclude with that general's killing.[100] This rationalization of a literary experiment undercuts one of the epic's daring examples of what Morson calls "backshadowing" or "foreshadowing after the fact": a technique of treating the past "as if it had inevitably to lead to the present we know and as if signs of our present should have been visible to our predecessors."[101] Such a "he should have known better" motif is striking here because Dhṛtarāṣṭra is precisely the blind king who should have known better, who will hear over and over from Vyāsa and Saṃjaya why he "should not grieve" for what could never have been otherwise, and the antidote to which is *kālavāda*, Vyāsa's "doctrine of time."[102]

Belvalkar observes that Saṃjaya's powers are further extended, in the course of the narration—or composition—of the war books, to "minor miracles without end that Saṃjaya is able to perform as a consequence of Vyāsa's boon" (1947a, 317): for example, witnessing Arjuna's dream in which he and Kṛṣṇa visit Śiva to insure the next day's use of the Pāśupata

[99]See Richardson's fuller discussion of Homer's "special abilities," including his omniscience that extends to the "plan of Zeus" (1990, 109–39).

[100]Cf. R. M. Smith 1953, 283; Mehendale 1995b, 3; Reich 1998, 107.

[101]1994, 13 and 234, continuing: "in effect, the present, as the future of the past, was already immanent in the past" in "a more or less straight line."

[102]See further Hiltebeitel and Kloetzli forthcoming.

weapon.[103] Most important, Vyāsa's boon gives us the *Bhagavad Gītā*. Just after Arjuna finally tells Kṛṣṇa that "by your grace *(tvat prasadāt)* my doubts and confusion are dispelled," Saṃjaya concludes this text by telling Dhṛtarāṣṭra that he "heard by Vyāsa's grace *(prasādāt)* this supreme secret yoga from Kṛṣṇa the lord of yoga speaking it himself in person."[104] As noted earlier, this is the epitome of the doubling of the grace of the author and the deity.

22. *Stops Yudhiṣṭhira from fighting Karṇa.* When Yudhiṣṭhira is driven to grief over killings—most notably Ghaṭotkaca's—which he thinks do not match their provocation, he takes out after Karṇa, whom he blames for these deaths. Kṛṣṇa sees this, tells Arjuna it cannot be, and the two set out behind Yudhiṣṭhira from a distance (7.158.51–52). Seeing Yudhiṣṭhira endangered, Vyāsa approaches *(abhigamya)* him and tells him to appreciate the good fortune by which Arjuna remains alive to kill Karṇa: in five days Yudhiṣṭhira will rule the earth; for now he should continue to "reflect on dharma, noncruelty *(ānṛśaṃsya)*, tapas, gifting, patience, and truth. Where dharma is, there is victory." So saying, Vyāsa "vanished" *(antar adhīyata*; 53–62). Vyāsa thus drops into the very thick of battle to see to it that Yudhiṣṭhira does not step out of character.

23. *Describes Nara and Nārāyaṇa to Aśvatthāman.* Running from the battlefield after his father Droṇa's death, Aśvatthāman suddenly "sees" Vyāsa "standing" *(sthitam)* before him (7.172.43–44). Vyāsa explains why Aśvatthāman's weapons are ineffective against Arjuna and Kṛṣṇa. The pair are the eternal yogis, Ṛṣis, and ancient gods Nara and Nārāyaṇa, born in age after age. Kṛṣṇa knows past, present, and future, the near and the far; Śiva and Kṛṣṇa worship each other. Vyāsa also knows Aśvatthāman's previous lives in which he pleased Śiva and was his bhakta. Accepting all this, Aśvatthāman bowed to Śiva and acknowledged *(mene)* Kṛṣṇa (7.172.45–91).

24. *Describes Śiva to Arjuna.* Wondering about the fiery being he has seen preceding him in battle and killing foes, Arjuna questions Vyāsa who "arrives by chance" *(yadṛcchayāgatam*; 7.173.3). Vyāsa reveals that this being is Śiva, whose hymn he recites. Then "he went as he came."[105]

25. *Saves Saṃjaya in battle.* After Śakuni's death, Duryodhana, standing alone, sees no remaining allies and determines to enter a lake: one whose name, the Dvaipāyana Lake *(hrada)*, surely suggests a pun—depths, transparencies . . . —linking the author and his recourse to fictions. As we learn from Saṃjaya, three of Duryodhana's allies still live—Aśvatthāman, Kṛpa, and Kṛtavarman (9.28.16–34). Now as Saṃjaya

[103] *Mbh* 7.57; Belvalkar 1947a, 317 and passim; and Mangels 1994, 124.
[104] *BhG* 18.73 and 75 = *Mbh* 6.40.73 and 75.
[105] 7.173.10–107, ending *jagāma . . . yathāgatam*.

describes a Pāṇḍava rush against the leaderless Kauravas and mentions the three Kaurava survivors whom he alone sees, he catches us off guard[106] by telling what Dhṛṣṭadyumna had to say about Saṃjaya's very own capture—as if his own plight were a mere coincidence, or that to describe it would demean his tale:

> Then having seen me, Dhṛṣṭadyumna said to Sātyaki, smiling, "Why is this one seized? There's no point in his living!" *(kim anena gṛhītena nānenārtho 'sti jīvatā)*. Hearing Dhṛṣṭadyumna's word, Śini's grandson, the great chariot fighter [Sātyaki], lifted his sharp sword and prepared to kill me. Having arrived *(āgamya)*,[107] Kṛṣṇa Dvaipāyana of great wisdom said to him, "Let Saṃjaya be released alive. In no way is he to be slain" *(mucyatām saṃjayo jīvan na hantavyaḥ kathaṃcana)*. Having heard Dvaipāyana's word, Śini's grandson folded his hands. Then, releasing me, he said, "May it be well, Saṃjaya. Go ahead." So permitted by him, taking off my armor, weaponless, wet with blood, I left at evening toward the city. (9.28.35–39)

On his way, Saṃjaya sees Duryodhana alone, weeping, disoriented. "For a while I could say nothing, overwhelmed with sorrow. Then I told him all about my capture and release alive in battle through the grace of Dvaipāyana" (*dvaipāyanaprasādāc ca jīvato mokṣam āhave*; 42cd–43). Although neither the smiling Dhṛṣṭadyumna nor the distraught Duryodhana is meant to understand what is at stake in these exchanges, we may understand the irony.

Mangels (1994, 123) argues that Saṃjaya's rescue here contradicts Vyāsa's boon to him of invulnerability, and notes that the rescue verses are not confirmed by the shorter Śāradā and Kaśmīrī manuscripts usually (but not here) favored by the Critical Edition (see below, n. 128). True, but I take the scene as narratively suspenseful: Vyāsa keeps his boon from being contradicted precisely by intervening, just as he does to save that other indispensable character, Yudhiṣṭhira—which Mangels does not notice.[108] Saṃjaya will continue to live so that he can narrate, down to the bitter end, only by the author's grace. Vyāsa portrays the blind old king as so passionate to hear about the struggles of his son that he barely allows his narrator to skip a beat to mention his own story, the main

[106]We may also suspect that he would catch Dhṛtarāṣṭra off guard here.

[107]Ganguli [1884–96] 1970, Vol. 7, *Salya Parva*, 35, adds "just at that juncture." Cf. Mehendale 1995b, 4: "he was saved by the timely intervention of Vyāsa."

[108]Cf. Athavale 1946, 138–40, fancying that, rather than appearing to save his "war correspondent," Vyāsa must have given him "something like a passport."

thrust of which is to indicate that Saṃjaya can answer Dhṛtarāṣṭra's yearnings thanks only to the author.

Saṃjaya thus quickly returns to what he has to tell the father about the son: how Duryodhana rallies. Gathering his wits, Duryodhana had asked Saṃjaya about his allies, and heard, "Only three chariot fighters remain on your side, king. So at the time of setting out Kṛṣṇa Dvaipāyana told me" (*iti prasthānakāle māṃ kṛṣṇadvaipāyano 'bravīt*; 46). Note that we—that is, the blind old king who listens for us and limits what we can know by the questions he does and doesn't ask—cannot pin down what Saṃjaya means by "the time of setting out." Did Vyāsa tell Saṃjaya about the three Kuru survivors just before this while seeing to his release? Perhaps, but Saṃjaya had just before this indicated that he already knew about the three survivors. Is it then Vyāsa's prewar gift of the divine eye that would allow Saṃjaya to say "Kṛṣṇadvaipāyana told me"? Or is the uncertainty a hint that Vyāsa "informs" his narrator in varied ways? Note also that Saṃjaya tells Duryodhana only the *number* of the three survivors, not their names, which becomes crucial in what follows.

Saṃjaya continues: "Sighing long and looking at me repeatedly, touching my shoulder, your son said, 'Other than you I see none alive here in battle, Saṃjaya, I see no second here. And the Pāṇḍavas have their followers. Saṃjaya, tell the lord king whose eyes are his wisdom, "Your son Duryodhana has entered a lake"'" (47–49). It is only after Duryodhana enters the lake that the three survivors "came to that region" (*taṃ deśaṃ samupeyuṣaḥ*; 53d), appearing to Saṃjaya in person. Glad for another survivor, they ask him whether Duryodhana still lives, and he updates them about his submergence in the Dvaipāyana Lake. "Having seen that broad lake, Aśvatthāman wailed in grief, 'Alas, the lord of men does not know we are alive. Surely, if he reached us we could fight with the foes'" (59). It is now clear that, along with the availability of a Dvaipāyana lake, it is Saṃjaya's selective words that keep Duryodhana and his three allies from prematurely reuniting. Vyāsa—or, should we say, Saṃjaya—has other tales to tell that require the continued separation of their ways. They are not to meet until the three find Duryodhana with his thigh broken after his duel with Bhīma, and are motivated to carry out the night massacre of the Pāṇḍava camp.

For now, the three can only weep until they see the Pāṇḍavas coming. Kṛpa then takes Saṃjaya on his chariot to the Kaurava camp, whence everyone flees to the city.[109] Everyone, that is, but Saṃjaya. Although he had headed for the city at the beginning of this passage, Vyāsa still

[109]Including the camp-following Kaurava women, who "tore their heads with their nails and hands and disheveled their hair (*luluvuś ca tadā keśān*), shrieking everywhere, crying out, 'Alas,' and beating their breasts" (66–67b).

requires him to report not only the rest of the *Śalyaparvan* but the *Sauptikaparvan* up to the death of Duryodhana.

26. *Appears between the weapons.* After the night massacre of the Pāṇḍavas' sleeping allies and children, Aśvatthāman parts company with the other two Kaurava survivors and goes to Vyāsa's hermitage on a bank of the Ganges (10.13.12c). Seeking to satisfy Draupadī's call for Aśvatthāman's death and the gem on his forehead, the Pāṇḍavas find him there sitting among many Ṛṣis. Aśvatthāman releases his doomsday weapon and Arjuna, at Kṛṣṇa's bidding, counteracts it with his own. Vyāsa and Nārada then save the worlds by intervening.

> When the two lofted weapons were burning the worlds with their energy *(tejas)*, the two great Ṛṣis then appeared *(darśayāmāsatus)* together there—Nārada and the dharma-souled grandfather of the Bhāratas—to appease *(śamayitum)* the two heroes. . . . The two Munis, wishing all beings' welfare, knowing every dharma, of supreme tejas, stood in the middle *(madhye sthitau)* of the two blazing weapons. Unassailable *(anādhṛṣyau)*, splendrous, having approached that interval *(tadantaram . . . upagamya)* to appease the weapons' tejas, desiring the worlds' welfare, the two best of Ṛṣis, ablaze there like fire, were unassailable *(anādhṛṣyau)* among the living, esteemed by gods and demons. (10.14.11–15)

While the "omniscient author" and the "eternal Brahmacarin" position themselves in the "interval"—a nuclear free zone, a nick of time, an empty authorial space—between the two weapons that could detonate the worlds, the author vouchsafes their unassailability not only by the weapons themselves, but "among the living"—by which he must, of course, mean his characters. At first the two speak in one voice: "Formerly, there were great warriors past who knew diverse weapons, but they never released this weapon on men" (16). Then Arjuna, whose extraordinary brahmacarya enables him to do so, withdraws his weapon, but warns the Ṛṣis that unless they "lay hold *(saṃhartum)* of the worlds' welfare and our own," the unscrupuled[110] Aśvatthāman will "consume us all without remainder" (15.1–10).

"Seeing the two Ṛṣis standing before him," Aśvatthāman tells Vyāsa, who from now on leaves Nārada speechless, that his fear *(bhaya)* and wrath *(roṣa)* make him incapable of recalling his weapon. The mantra he uttered to impel it with such base motives—*apāṇḍavāya*, which could

[110] "Ill-acting" or "sinful" *(pāpakarman)* is the word used here (15.3) and repeatedly (16.1, 16.9) to describe Aśvatthāman in this episode. He is also "low-minded" *(dīnamanas*; 15.12) and a "sinful wretch" *(kāpuruṣam pāpam*, 16.9).

mean "for the destruction of the Pāṇḍava,"[111] but which, he says, "was contrived for finishing off the Pāṇḍavas' descent"—must still take effect (11–18). Vyāsa, after praising Arjuna, then asks,

> Why are you desirous of his and his brothers' and kin's death? A kingdom where the Brahmaśiras (Head of Brahmā) weapon strikes another high weapon gets no rain for twelve years. For that reason the strong-armed powerful Pāṇḍava doesn't even strike this weapon of yours, desiring the welfare of creatures. The Pāṇḍavas, you, and the kingdom are always to be protected by us. Therefore, withdraw this divine weapon, great armed one. Let yourself be wrathless. Let the Pārthas be free from ill. Surely the royal Pāṇḍava sage[112] doesn't desire to conquer by adharma. Give them the jewel that stands on your head. Taking that, the Pāṇḍavas will grant your life. (22c–27)

Presumably Vyāsa speaks for himself and Nārada as the protective "us" here, but later, when he endorses Kṛṣṇa's curse of Aśvatthāman,[113] the "us" might extend to Kṛṣṇa.

Vyāsa thus sets the terms of appeasement while introducing a new twist, which puts new ideas into his characters' heads: Draupadī had asked not for Aśvatthāman's head-jewel but his life. To this, Aśvatthāman now describes his jewel's incomparable value and its talismanic potencies: "I can no wise part with it. But whatever the lord *(bhagavān)* tells me is to be done by me immediately *(anantaram)*. This is the jewel. This am I. The blade of grass will fall into the wombs of the Pāṇḍāva women. It has not been raised in vain" (10.15.30c–31). Vyāsa replies, "Do so, but not any other act on your mind. Having released it into the wombs of the Pāṇḍava women, cease!" (32). Aśvatthāman speaks in a rush here, as if he were cutting off Vyāsa, whose command he cannot deny. Whatever Vyāsa says, Aśvatthāman must do it "immediately," that is, "without an interval," again using the term *antaram* as a time-space that only the author controls:[114] there being "no interval" between the thoughts of author and character. Vyāsa allows Aśvatthāman to interrupt him to get

[111] I.e., Bhīma, who was the Pāṇḍava to first endanger him here.

[112] Yudhiṣṭhira, who is a rājarṣi or "royal Ṛṣi."

[113] He says to Aśvatthāman after Kṛṣṇa has spoken, "Since having disregarded us you have done this cruel act" (10.16.16).

[114] As we shall see in chap. 3, the term is used technically for intervals in a sacrifice, as for example those during which the *Mbh* is doubly narrated and "framed." It is also used for the four intervals of Buddhist cosmology.

his words in edgewise, but he is at the same time shaping those words and prompting and limiting the thoughts behind them.[115]

Vaiśampāyana then concludes the adhyāya: "Then the intensely sick *(bhṛśāturaḥ)* Aśvatthāman, having heard Dvaipāyana's word, released that high weapon into the wombs" (10.15.33). Again, the author's word affects Kaurava women internally in their wombs (as in § C.2 above). It now remains only for the "delighting" *(hṛṣyamāṇa)* Kṛṣṇa to tell how he will make all this turn out well by reviving Arjuna's stillborn grandson Parikṣit; for Kṛṣṇa to curse Aśvatthāman to three thousand years of solitude (16.1–15); and for Vyāsa to endorse this (16–17). When Aśvatthāman accepts his exile with the words, "May the speech of this Puruṣottama be true, O Bhagavan," we are again reminded of the interplay between the "two Bhagavāns" (18), Kṛṣṇa and Vyāsa, who are also two Kṛṣṇas (Hiltebeitel 1984, 1985a). Finally, Draupadī will accept Aśvatthāman's jewel (33).

27. *Tells Dhṛtarāṣṭra about the lifting of the Earth's burden.* Inconsolable after the war, Dhṛtarāṣṭra tells Saṃjaya he should have listened to Vyāsa and Nārada, among others (11.1.13). Vidura then tries to console Dhṛtarāṣṭra, but when the old king falls senseless to the ground, Vyāsa is present, without prelude, among those who sprinkle him with cool water (11.8.2–3). Bereft of his hundred sons, Dhṛtarāṣṭra tells Vyāsa, his own father, he will now end his own life (7–11), but Vyāsa dissuades him. He says Duryodhana was the root cause of the destruction, that all was fated. And he authenticates this by recalling his own presence at the unveiling of the cosmic drama: at a counsel in the Hall of Indra, he "visibly heard" *(mayā pratyakṣataḥ śrutam)* the goddess Earth call for the lifting of her burden by the slaughter of warriors at Kurukṣetra (19–26). Of some interest is Vyāsa's arrival among the celestial gods and Ṛṣis: "Formerly, overcoming fatigue, I went quickly *(tvaritas)* to the Hall of Indra . . ." (20ab). Perhaps he started from not so far away. Once Dhṛtarāṣṭra has agreed to stay alive and try to bear his grief, Vyāsa "vanished then and there" (*tatraivāntar adhīyata*; 48).

28. *Intervenes among the mourners*. Dhṛtarāṣṭra, having set off for the battlefield and shared grief with the Pāṇḍavas, permits them to approach Gāndhārī. But Gāndhāri wants to curse Yudhiṣṭhira for her sons' deaths.

> Seeing her sinful intention against the Pāṇḍavas, Satyavatī's son, the Ṛṣi, fully cognized it ahead of time *(prāgeva samabudhyata)*.

[115]B. Sullivan is minimally correct that Aśvatthāman "was allowed by Vyāsa to kill the Pāṇḍavas' offspring" (1990, 47), but I think misses too much by his emphasis on Vyāsa's mediation and failed reconciliation (62–63). Cf. Mehta 1990, 106: Vyāsa "again turns up in the company of Nārada, to explain and to find a solution to the difficult problem."

> Touching clean and fragrant Gaṅgā water, that supreme Ṛṣi reached that region with the speed of mind *(taṃ deśam upasaṃpede paramarṣir manojavaḥ)*. Seeing with the divine eye and a humble mind,[116] he fully cognized *(samabudhyata)* there the heart of every living being.[117] Kindly spoken, of great penance, he spoke to his daughter-in-law in time *(kāle)*, rejecting the time of cursing, praising the time of peace *(śāpakālam avākṣipya śamakālam udīrayan)*. (11.13.3–6)

Vyāsa can thus read his characters' thoughts before they have them, know the hearts of all the beings *there* (again, first and foremost, the hearts of his characters), and with the "speed of mind" intervene "in time" between their thoughts and actions. It is perhaps not insignificant that he touches Gaṅgā water as he mentally takes flight.[118]

Vyāsa more or less convinces Gāndhārī, of course. She soon expends what's left of her anger with a glance below her blindfold that only blackens Yudhiṣṭhira's fingernails (11.15.6–7). Then she views the battlefield and its personal horrors from a distance with the "divine eye" *(divyena cakṣuṣā)* and "power of divine knowledge" *(divyajñānabala)* that Vyāsa has given her (16.1–3). Dhṛtarāṣṭra is then "given leave" or "authorized" *(abhyanujñāta)* by Vyāsa, who doesn't seem to have gone anywhere since speaking to Gāndhārī, to go with the Pāṇḍāvas, Kṛṣṇa, and the Kaurava women to Kurukṣetra to "see" the battlefield directly (16.9).

Shortly after Gāndhārī uses the "divine eye" to view the battlefield, we learn that Yudhiṣṭhira also can avail it. Dhṛtarāṣṭra feels certain that Yudhiṣṭhira is omniscient,[119] and asks him the number of slain warriors and the worlds to which they have gone. Having answered, Yudhiṣṭhira explains how he was able to do so: he gained the power of recollection *(anusmṛti)* from the Ṛṣi Lomaśa while on pilgrimage in the forest, and before that, "I acquired the divine eye *(divyaṃ cakṣur)* through the yoga of knowledge" *(jñānayogena*; 11.26.19–20). Neither of these two faculties[120] is the "knowledge *(vidyā)* called *pratismṛti*" (3.37.27), another visionary power, more Vedic in its overtones, that Yudhiṣṭhira

[116]*Manasānuddhatena*: or perhaps he has "an unopposed mind." See MW, 33 s.v. *ánuddhata*.

[117]*Sarvaprāṇabhṛtāṃ bhāvam* (11.13.5c), literally "the heart, mind, or experience of all those bearing life or breath." I will sometimes render *bhāvam* as "heart" to best catch this range.

[118]Gaṅgā's waters embody the mingling of time and eternity; see Hiltebeitel in press-d.

[119]11.26.11: "To my mind you are surely all-knowing *(sarvajño)*," he says.

[120]Mangels 1994, 137, observes that Yudhiṣṭhira's words mark a distinction: the *anusmṛti* accounts for the number of the fallen, whereas the "divine eye" accounts for where the fallen have gone—a trait of the "divine eye" *(dibba-cakkhu)* also in Buddhist sources (132).

received from Vyāsa at the beginning of the exile, and further passed on to Arjuna (see above, § C.15). By now Vyāsa has given the "divine eye" to Drupada, Saṃjaya, and Gāndhārī, and has also offered it to Dhṛtarāṣṭra. It is instructive that in contrast to the *pratismṛti* and the *anusmṛti*, Yudhiṣṭhira has won the "divine eye" on his own by yoga. He seems to be the only hero of the main story to have done so.[121]

29. *Contributes to the beginning of Yudhiṣṭhira's postwar education.* Once Yudhīṣṭhira has seen to the cremation of the hundreds of thousands of slain kings (11.26.38), he heads from Kurukṣetra to the Gaṅgā, putting Dhṛtarāṣṭra before him and bringing the weeping Kaurava women along.[122] Having reached the river and performed water rites for the deceased, culminating with Karṇa's, whom Kuntī now reveals was Yudhiṣṭhira's older brother (11.27), the gathering remains beside the Gaṅgā as the *Strī Parvan* ends. As the *Śānti Parvan* begins, the Pāṇḍavas determine to spend the month of purification *(śaucam māsam)* there, whereupon a host of Brahman Ṛṣis "arrived" *(abhijagmur)*, headed by Vyāsa, who does not seem to have made the mourners' trek from Kurukṣetra. The others mentioned are Nārada, Devala, Devasthāna, and Kaṇva "and their disciples" (12.1.1–4), but we do not know whether this includes Vyāsa's disciples, or where any of them have come from. When hundreds of thousands of Brahmans (8) sit down to console Yudhiṣṭhira, Nārada—as so often, the mouthpiece of the author's bitter ironies—asks the leading question: "Now that by your great heroism and Mādhava's [Kṛṣṇa's] grace this whole earth is won by dharma, Yudhiṣṭhira" (10), aren't you happy?[123]

Yudhiṣṭhira is, of course, not happy, and Nārada's question is the opening for the postwar phase of his education. Inclined to renounce his hard-won kingdom, Dharmarāja must first hear arguments to the contrary from Nārada, Devasthāna,[124] Draupadī, and his brothers before Vyāsa reinforces their united message (12.23–28). Vyāsa begins by stressing that the householder stage is foremost among the four lifestages (12.23.2–6), that wielding the staff of chastisement *(daṇḍadhāraṇam)* is the principal Kṣatriya and kingly duty (23.10–24.30), and that the king has sacrificial obligations. Then, in response to Yudhiṣṭhira's grief at his loss of kinsmen and failure to find peace *(śānti)* among the weeping women who

[121]The blind Dhṛtarāṣṭra also "foresees" with his "eye of wisdom" (*prajñā-cakṣus*; 1.1.101; see Mangels 1994, 141), but it is more commonly his ironic epithet; as his questions to Vyāsa, Saṃjaya, and Yudhiṣṭhira suggest, it is a far more limited faculty than the *divya-cakṣus*, and probably innate to him rather than won (although Bhīṣma tells Yudhiṣṭhira one seeking liberation may acquire it [12.265.19]).

[122]Droṇa's disciples precede them with Kṛpī before them after Droṇa's cremation (23.42).

[123]Paraphrased.

[124]Who addresses Yudhiṣṭhira at 12.20–21.

have lost their husbands and children (26.2–3), Vyāsa—"best of those who know yoga, knowing dharma, and fully conversant with Veda"—tells the "wise" king how the wise know how time always recycles thirst, suffering, and happiness (5–31).[125] He then reiterates his points about kingly duties (32–36). But Yudhiṣṭhira still agonizes over the deaths he caused and prepares to sit in the vow of *prāya* ("going forth") until he dies (27.1–25). Vyāsa briefly "dispelled his grief" (*śokam apānudat*; 28.1) by telling an "old story" about King Janaka (2–4). But Vyāsa says nothing about the grieving women, although he does respond to Yudhiṣṭhira's grief over his kinsmen:

> Thousands of mothers and fathers, hundreds of wives and sons, are experienced in (the worlds of) saṃsāra. Whose are they? Whose are we? No one else can be anyone's own, nor can one become anyone else's own.[126] This is just a meeting on the path with hosts of friends, kin, and wives. Where am I? Where shall I go? Who am I? How am I here? Whom do I grieve for and why? So saying, the mind may be stabilized when companionship with those dear is transitory and saṃsāra goes round like a wheel. (28.38–40)

Closing this session with, "The earth is won by kṣātradharma (military duty). Enjoy it, son of Kuntī. Do not resist me" (*mā viṣādīḥ*; 28.58), Vyāsa yields to Kṛṣṇa, "who was not to be transgressed *(anatikramanīya)* by Dharmarāja." Indeed, "known from youth, Govinda was dearer to him [to Yudhiṣṭhira] than Arjuna" (29.5). Kṛṣṇa tells the king his version of the "Sixteen Kings Story," and Nārada follows with the story of Gold-spitter.[127] But seeing Yudhiṣṭhira still speechless with grief, Vyāsa, who by most accounts has told him these two stories before, in the *Droṇaparvan*,[128] resumes. He discourages Yudhiṣṭhira from "complete renuncia-

[125]The passage has a Buddhist flavor.

[126]*Naivāsya kaścid bhavitā nāyaṃ bhavati kasyacit/ pathi saṃgatamevedaṃ dārabandhu-suhṛdgaṇaiḥ*; 12.28.39. On similar questions, see chap. 7.

[127]A boy who could spit gold, only to be killed like the goose that laid the golden egg; he could be resurrected, unlike Abhimanyu, because he left the world without having fulfilled all his virtues (see Hiltebeitel [1976] 1990, 347–48).

[128]To Yudhiṣṭhira, with variations, to console him after the death of Abhimanyu. The present "doubling" by Kṛṣṇa, again to console Yudhiṣṭhira, follows an author/deity convention that should no longer surprise us, or beg for the text-critical scalpel. Rejecting Vyāsa's tellings on the questionable grounds that one of two Śāradā manuscripts and a few Kāśmīrī ones that basically copy it (Reich 1998, 112) "are really secondary elaborations of the same legends in the Śāntiparvan" (De 1958, xvi), which is hardly likely, the CE accepts the deity's retelling but not the prior telling by the author. It thus also dispenses with Vyāsa's concentration of these two stories with a third: his important prefatory story—*not* "doubled" by Kṛṣṇa, but left till later in the *Śāntiparvan* to be told by Bhīṣma (12.248–50)—of the

tion of self" (*ātmaparityāga*; 32.22), i.e., suicide, for the now-familiar reasons. But Yudhiṣṭhira continues to hold himself solely responsible for so many deaths (33.1–6) and to worry about the cries and reproaches of the Kaurava women, who, he says, should they die in their present plight, would go to the realm of Yama leaving him[129] accountable for the murder of women, for which one goes head-first to hell (7–11)!

Now Vyāsa shows his hand slightly, "considering keenly (or cleverly) with his intellect"[130] what to do next. It is as if he acknowledges that Yudhiṣṭhira's grief is tough to crack and that a character *can* "resist" an author. He reassures Yudhiṣṭhira about what he has already said: time does indeed account for everything; Yudhiṣṭhira need not continue this "delusory mental ensnarement"[131] that is his grief. But if it pleases him, he should perform an expiatory horse sacrifice following the example of Indra after the gods' war with the armed Śālāvṛka Brāhmans (34.17–34). As part of Vyāsa's design for this rite, which will be partly followed in the *Āśvamedhika Parvan*, Yudhiṣṭhira and his companions should go to the various realms of the kings slain at Kurukṣetra and consecrate their brothers, sons, or grandsons; and "of those who have no sons, consecrate, the daughters. The class of women *(strīvargaḥ)* surely has desires and wishes. So grief will disappear. Having so consoled every kingdom, sacrifice with the horse sacrifice as did the victorious Indra of old. O Bull among Kṣatriyas, those Kṣatriyas are not to be mourned" (34.33–35b). Vyāsa seems to be plotting a diversion. The notion of consecrating some women among the heirs of the slain kings can have nothing to do with the Kaurava women who torment Yudhiṣṭhira, since their destiny remains in Hāstinapura where Yudhiṣṭhira has succeeded their husbands himself. Is Vyāsa distracting Yudhiṣṭhira? Is he deferring the matter in question to the *Putradarśana Parvan* in the fifteenth book, where he will finally relieve Yudhiṣṭhira of the Kaurava widows? It is as if he speaks of the other women to take Yudhiṣṭhira's mind off the question he has yet to resolve about the ones most persistently at hand.

Vyāsa goes on to speak at length about sins, expiations, food, and gifts (12.35–37) until Yudhiṣṭhira rather abruptly says he wishes to hear about

origin of the goddess Death (Mṛtyu) whose tears, shed at the thought of killing creatures, ultimately become their diseases (*Mbh* 7, App. I, No. 8, lines 118–225). Cf. chap. 1 at nn. 38–40; Vaidya [1905] 1966, 28–29; Sukthankar 1936, 39–42; Belvalkar 1961, 649–50; Hiltebeitel [1976] 1990, 346–49 and 1978, 783–85; Reich 1998, 49, 110–55.

[129]He uses a royal "we" here, but could also be including his wife and brothers.

[130]12.34.1cd: *samīkṣya nipuṇam buddhyā*; note that MW's first meaning for *nipuṇam* is "in a clever or delicate manner" (550).

[131]12.34.12ab: *vyalīkam . . . cittavaitaṃsikam*. But it could be worse, following MW, 1028: "very false or untruthful, lying, hypocritical." *Vaitaṃsika* denotes a net for catching a bird, here Yudhiṣṭhira's "mind" *(citta)*.

the duties of kings *(rājadharmān)* and of conduct appropriate for times of distress *(āpatsu)*. Although it has been somewhat slow going, Yudhiṣṭhira has found joy in Vyāsa's discourse on expiations. Now he asks how to reconcile the conduct of dharma with ruling a kingdom, a subject on which he remains confused, although he thinks about it constantly (38.1–4). Vyāsa then casts his eyes *(samabhiprekṣya)* at the ancient all-knowing Nārada, and says, "Ask Bhīṣma."[132] And so it goes. This knowing glance would seem to register not only that Yudhiṣṭhira has suddenly turned receptive, but that this turn now sets the agenda for the next two sections of the *Śānti Parvan*.[133] Nārada now attests to all the ancient and celestial sources Bhīṣma knows and can cite (cf. Mangels 1994, 61–62; Hiltebeitel in press-d). He has seen the gods, gratified the Devarṣis led by Bṛhaspati, learned variously from the Asuras' preceptor Uśanas, from such other Ṛṣis as Vasiṣṭha, Cyavana, Sanatkumāra, Mārkaṇḍeya, and Rāma Jāmadagnya, and from Indra (38.7–13). The epic does not tell us when Bhīṣma visited Rāma Jāmadagnya's ascetic grove or Mārkaṇḍeya's hermitage, but it is probably safe to assume that he had most of these encounters before he returned to earth to meet his father: that is, at some time in his youth, which he spent wherever he went at birth when he was carried away, presumably upriver, by his mother, the celestial Gaṅgā.[134] But now Yudhiṣṭhira has one more pang of grief: How, he asks Vyāsa, can he confront Bhīṣma whose fall he helped to instigate? Now Kṛṣṇa intervenes, telling Yudhiṣṭhira to cease his "excessive obstinacy in grief" *(atinirbandhaṃ śoke)*. He should do what "lord *(bhagavān)* Vyāsa" says (21) and heed his command (*niyoga*; 24). Yudhiṣṭhira then heads to Hāstinapura for his coronation. There he begins his just rule protecting the women who lost their husbands and sons in battle, as well as the poor, blind, and helpless, displaying thereby the quality of "noncruelty" *(ānṛśaṃsya)* that is indeed one of the difficult and important teachings the author is trying to get across to the king (42.10–11; see chapter 5).

30. *Present for most of Bhīṣma's battlefield oration*. Leaving no trace of his intermediate movements, Vyāsa is next present among the Ṛṣis who surround Bhīṣma at Kurukṣetra just before and after Yudhiṣṭhira and

[132]12.38.5–6. See Mangels 1994, 99, on this passage among others where Vyāsa "authorizes" other narrators.

[133]The *Rājadharma* and *Āpaddharma* subparvans, which are to be followed by the *Mokṣadharma*.

[134]Bhīṣma did not visit Rāma Jāmadagnya's hermitage when he fought him over Ambā; they met at Kurukṣetra (5.177–78), and in any case did not pause over stories. See Hiltebeitel in press-d on the celestial implications. Note that Vasiṣṭha is Vyāsa's great grandfather. Kṛṣṇa will also confirm that Bhīṣma was Vasiṣṭha's disciple (12.46.10).

company arrive there, and on through some of the *Anuśāsana Parvan.*[135] Notably, he is there when Kṛṣṇa gives Bhīṣma the "divine eye" *(cakṣur divyam)* or "eye of knowledge" *(jñānacakṣus)* with which to see all things "truly like a fish in clear water."[136] Before Vyāsa's presence at Bhīṣma's side is mentioned, Kṛṣṇa has already told Yudhiṣṭhira that Bhīṣma already knows past, present, and future (12.46.19), and once we know that Vyāsa is there, Kṛṣṇa adds that he has bestowed on Bhīṣma from afar the "divine knowledge of seeing the triple-time" *(traikālyadarśanaṃ jñānaṃ divyam)* by means of their mutual meditation on each other (47.65). Moreover, Vyāsa is there to hear from Kṛṣṇa that whatever Bhīṣma says "will stand on earth as if it were a declaration of the Veda" *(vedapravāda)*, and that it will have "validity" (*pramāṇa*; 54.29–30). It could not be clearer that Veda Vyāsa and Kṛṣṇa have their act together.[137]

During Bhīṣma's long oration, Vyāsa should thus ostensibly remain in attendance to hear Bhīṣma repeat Vyāsa's teachings to his son Śuka (12.224–47; Bedekar 1966, ccxiii–ccxv) and narrate their father-son story (310–20), as well as to hear himself cited at several other points.[138] In this company, Vyāsa also recalls that he had recited Śiva's thousand and eight names on Mount Meru to obtain a son (i.e., Śuka), and is the first of the Ṛṣis surrounding Bhīṣma to recommend to Yudhiṣṭhira that he too chant this hymn (13.18.1–3). Among the Ṛṣis who concur is also Vyāsa's father Parāśara, who attests that the hymn secured him Vyāsa as well (27–32): granting Parāśara's wish, Śiva predicted that "in the creation of Manu Sāvarṇa," Vyāsa would be one of the Seven Ṛṣis, the arranger of the Veda *(vedānām . . . vyastā)*, maker of the Kuru lineage *(kuruvaṃśa-kara)*, author of a history *(itihāsasya kartā)* for the welfare of the universe *(jagato hitaḥ)*, and dear to Indra (30–31). Bhīṣma last quotes Vyāsa when Yudhiṣṭhira asks him to define Brahmanicide, which, Bhīṣma recalls, Vyāsa took to imply practically anything that disturbs Brahmans' livelihood in the Vedas, their reputation and mental peace, or cows'

[135]Vyāsa is mentioned as present both before (12.47.5) and after (50.10, 58.25, 59.3) the Pāṇḍavas and Kṛṣṇa "descend upon Kurukṣetra" (*avatīrya kurukṣetram*; 48.1–3), and is next mentioned as present in the *Anuśāsana* (13.14.4; see further below).

[136]52.20–22; see Mangels 1994, 99–100, 126, 148.

[137]As mentioned in n. 19 above, Mangels remarks that the epic poets betray a sense of the limits of fiction: in not permitting Saṃjaya and Bhīṣma to obtain the "divine eye" on their own through yoga, they show that they are not ready to take the risk of leaving these two "narrated figures" who also narrate to be answerable to the "odium of fiction" (1994, 148).

[138]12.200.3: cited as an authoritative source on Viṣṇu-Kṛṣṇa, along with Nārada, Asita Devala, Vālmīki (!), and Mārkaṇḍeya; 247.1; 327–38 (*Nārāyaṇīya* citings); 13.325 (quoted on Brahmanicide, as mentioned below; 13.118–20 (story of the worm, discussed in chap. 5); 13.121–23 (conversation with Maitreya); 13.146.23 (composed the *Śatarudrīya*).

access to water (13.25.5–12). Shortly thereafter, following Bhīṣma's response to Yudhiṣṭhira's question about tīrthas (13.26), Vaiśampāyana describes Vyāsa's departure among the Ṛṣis who had gathered to see Bhīṣma on his bed of arrows (13.27.3, 9). Naming forty-five such Ṛṣis who have come from all times and places, including Dhruva (the Pole Star), Agastya (Canopus), various other celestial Ṛṣis, Nārada, and Mārkaṇḍeya (27.4–8), Vaiśampāyana describes their farewell to the dying patriarch:

> Honored on comfortable seats, those great Ṛṣis told stories related to Bhīṣma that were very sweet and delighted the senses. Having heard the stories of those pure-souled Ṛṣis, Bhīṣma, filled with the highest satisfaction, thought himself in heaven *(mene divistham ātmānaṃ tuṣṭyā paramayā yutaḥ)*. Then, taking leave of Bhīṣma and the Pāṇḍavas, the great Ṛṣis all vanished in the very sight of all who were looking *(antardhānaṃ gatāḥ sarve sarveṣām eva paśyatām)*. The Pāṇḍavas all praised and bowed repeatedly to those high-fortuned Ṛṣis even after they had vanished *(antardhānagatān api)*. With cheerful minds those best of the Kurus all waited upon Gāṅgeya [Bhīṣma], like those who are skilled in mantras wait upon the rising sun. Seeing all the directions illuminated by the radiance of those Ṛṣis' tapas, they all became highly amazed. (10–15)

Bhiṣma will lie on his bed of arrows until the sun rises on the winter solstice, at the end of the half year that is equated with a night. With the disappearance of the Ṛṣis around him, nothing could be clearer than that he has been among the stars, whose disappearance lingers in all directions like an anticipatory dawn.

31. *Back for Bhīṣma's end and Yudhiṣṭhira's return to Hāstinapura.* Again with no trace of his intermediate movements, Vyāsa is suddenly present among the Ṛṣis for Bhīṣma's final fifty days on his bed of arrows (13.152–54) and for the launching of Yudhiṣṭhira's reign (14.1–14). The reappearance is foreshadowed by Bhīṣma's last response to Yudhiṣṭhira, whose final questions to Bhīṣma are, "What is good for a man here? Doing what does he grow happy? By what may he be free from sin? Or what is destructive of sin?" Bhīṣma responds, "Surely the list of deities together with the list of Ṛṣis *(ayaṃ daivatavaṃśo vai ṛṣivaṃśasamanvitaḥ)*, recited at the two twilights *(dvisaṃdhyam paṭhitaḥ)*, O son, is the supreme remover of sin" (13.151.1–2).[139] Bhīṣma tells the names of the

[139]Cf. 14.15.7ab: Once Yudhiṣṭhira takes up the reins and Arjuna and Kṛṣṇa can enjoy the victory, they would "recite the vaṃśas of the gods and Ṛṣis" *(ṛṣīṇāṃ devatānāṃ ca vaṃśāṃs tāv āhatus tadā)*.

gods and Ṛṣis that are to be recited at dawn and dusk, and Vyāsa is mentioned not once but twice. First, along with Nārada and Parvata (8), he is counted among the gods (*devatān*; 29–30). Then, along with forty-six other Ṛṣis who are numbered in groups by the celestial quarter they occupy, he is mentioned among the Ṛṣis of the northern quarter (36).[140] I believe the poets leave it for us to understand that when Vyāsa and the other Ṛṣis surround Bhīṣma for the final three adhyāyas that follow, it is because he has just invoked their names at a twilight.

Vyāsa reenters the scene along with, or through, a prolonged silence:

> When Bhīṣma became silent then, (it was) like a picture drawn on a woven cloth. And as if meditating awhile *(muhūrtam iva ca dhyātvā)*, Vyāsa said to Bhīṣma lying there, "O king, the Kuru king Yudhiṣṭhira has regained his nature *(prakṛtim āpannaḥ)*. . . . He bows to you, tiger among kings, together with the intelligent Kṛṣṇa. You can give him leave to go back to the city." Thus addressed by lord Vyāsa, the river's son gave leave to Yudhiṣṭhira. . . . (152.1–4)

In this beautiful moment, the poet portrays himself in midscene, meditating on the canvas of his own creation, before he allows himself to reemerge within the narrative to tell Bhīṣma that this phase of Yudhiṣṭhira's education is over. Bhīṣma then tells Yudhiṣṭhira he should return to Hāstinapura and then come back to Kurukṣetra when the sun begins to rise toward the north. When Yudhiṣṭhira does this fifty days later, Vyāsa is still there, at the head of the Ṛṣis who surround Bhīṣma (153.13–17).

Amid his final words, Bhīṣma will then remind Dhṛtarāṣṭra that he "heard from Vyāsa the mystery of the deities" (*śrutaṃ devarahasyaṃ te kṛṣṇadvaipāyanād api*; 153.32) and recall that he himself learned from Vyāsa and Nārada that Arjuna and Kṛṣṇa are Nara and Nārāyaṇa (43). Vyāsa is the first mentioned of the Ṛṣis present who see the miraculous healing of Bhīṣma's arrow-ridden body as he leaves it for heaven (154.3–4). Once Bhīṣma is cremated beside the Gaṅgā, Vyāsa follows the Pāṇḍavas to Hāstinapura with the Bhārata women *(bharatastrībhir)*, among others, behind him (16). As the *Anuśāsana Parvan* ends, he and Kṛṣṇa then console Gaṅgā for her son's death (33).

When, however, at the beginning of the *Āśvamedhika Parvan*, Yudhiṣṭhira loses his "nature" once again and falls back into grief—now over Bhīṣma's passing—Vyāsa is still there. Kṛṣṇa has some harsh words about the relapse: You have just heard from Bhīṣma, Vyāsa, and others

[140]Lomaharṣaṇa and Ugraśravas (151.39) are curiously both mentioned here among the "Brahmans" (*viprān*; 151.30).

about rājadharma; don't take the "course of the stupid" *(mūḍhānāṃ vṛttim)*; slain warriors go to heaven . . . (14.2.5–8). When Yudhiṣṭhira presses Kṛṣṇa for leave to seek peace in the forest, and asks how he can be free "from this cruelty" *(asmāt krūrād)* and purify his mind (12–13), Vyāsa "addressed him as he was speaking so" (*tam evaṃ vādinaṃ vyāsas tataḥ provāca*; 14). Vyāsa thus interrupts Yudhiṣṭhira, showing his renewed exasperation with this most resistant of his characters. But he also doesn't let Kṛṣṇa answer. It will thus not be Kṛṣṇa who keeps Yudhiṣṭhira from going to the forest but the author himself. Indeed, when the author thus supervenes for the god, we might wonder whether the god might have said something else. Vyāsa seems to have given up on the possibility that Yudhiṣṭhira might "purify his mind":

> Your mind is not perfected, child. Again you are stupefied by childishness. Do we drone on and on into empty space?[141] You know about the duties of Kṣatriyas who live by warfare. . . . You have heard the entire mokṣadharma. . . . Unfaithful, dull-witted, you are constantly losing your memory.[142] (14.2.15–18)

Indeed, the author has more cruelties in store for Yudhiṣṭhira that the god might have had the means to resolve. Rather, steering Yudhiṣṭhira toward a ritual solution to his problems instead of a devotional or yogic one, Vyāsa tells Yudhiṣṭhira that he is not fully using his wits:[143] he has heard about all the expiatory rites at his disposal. Vyāsa would thus seem to remind Yudhiṣṭhira that the horse sacrifice was recommended for just this occasion. But Vyāsa doesn't stop there.

On the precedent that the gods gained ascendancy by sacrifices, Vyāsa says, "Offer the Rājasūya and Aśvamedha, and the Sarvamedha, O Bhārata, and the Naramedha, O lord of men" (*naramedhaṃ ca nṛpate*; 14.3.8). Then he immediately retracts to recommend the horse sacrifice only, as it was performed by Rāma Dāśarathi and Yudhiṣṭhira's ancestor Bharata (9–10). Thus, as Bruce Sullivan nicely puts it, "only the Horse Sacrifice engaged the attention of Yudhiṣṭhira" (1990, 32). But Vyāsa clearly does his prompting by upping the ante. From the conventional epic royal sacrifices—the Rājasūya and Aśvamedha—as a pair in the dual case, he mentions the Sarvamedha in which "the sacrificer should give in

[141]Literally, "into all space": *akṛtā te matis tāta punar bālyena muhyase/ kim ākāśe vayaṃ sarve pralapāma muhurmuhuḥ* (14.2.15).

[142]14.2.18: *aśraddadhāno durmedhā luptasmṛtir asi dhruvam.*

[143]14.3.1ab: *yudhiṣṭhira tava prajñā na samyag iti me matiḥ.* Karṇa says the very same words to Duryodhana, which van Buitenen translates, "Duryodhana, I do not think you entirely have your wits about you" (1973, 381; 1.194.1ab).

dakṣiṇās all he has conquered, and having resumed the fires in himself, . . . betake himself to the forest" and "not return any more" (Heesterman 1985, 41), and the human sacrifice or Naramedha, which Vyāsa punctuates by addressing Yudhiṣṭhira as "lord of men *(nṛ)*." I have long liked Thomas Hopkins's argument that Kṛṣṇa "is intentionally rude and simplistic" in his preliminary arguments to Arjuna in the *Bhagavad Gītā* when he tells him the half-truths that support the claim that it doesn't matter if you kill someone—which, as we have seen, Kṛṣṇa has exasperatedly just repeated to Yudhiṣṭhira.[144] Vyāsa seems to recognize that Yudhiṣṭhira will not find this argument persuasive, and brings him around to the same point by another means. In effect, by a process of elimination he leads the stubbornly confused Yudhiṣṭhira back to the Aśvamedha that he, Vyāsa, has already seeded in his mind. Yudhiṣṭhira has already performed a Rājasūya, which has brought trouble enough (see § C.12 above). His other options now are a Sarvamedha that would supply the very thing he wants—total renunciation of his kingdom and retreat to the forest—but is what the author and the god won't allow him; or, just what he doesn't want, he can offer a human victim—"lord of men, offer a human sacrifice!"—as he has already done in millions in the sacrifice of battle.

Yudhiṣṭhira now weighs in: "No doubt the horse sacrifice purifies even the Earth" (14.3.11)—if not, perhaps, the mind? But he has no wealth to perform it. "Having meditated awhile" (*muhūrtam anusaṃcintya*; 19c), Vyāsa tells him where to find the riches left behind from a sacrifice on Mount Himavat by the emperor Marutta,[145] whose story he tells. More specifically, the sacrifice was performed on "the big golden base (or foothill)" *(kāñcanaḥ sumahān pādas)*[146] that one reaches by approaching Mount Meru from the north side of Himavat (*himavatparśve uttare*; 4.25): a mountain named Muñjavat "on the back of Mount Himavat" *(girer himavatḥ pṛṣṭhe)* where Śiva performs tapas in the company of Umā and their hosts (8.1–3). No ordinary mountain, Muñjavat glows like gold on all sides with the same radiance as the morning sun, and cannot be seen by the living with their "natural fleshy eyes" (*prākṛtair māṃsalocanaiḥ*; 7–10).[147] Yudhiṣṭhira is delighted to hear about this

[144]T. Hopkins 1971, 90. As Sutton 2000, 92, observes, Yudhiṣṭhira "is dissatisfied with Nārada's explanation" of Duryodhana's winning a place in heaven by his death in battle (18.1.14)—one of Kṛṣṇa's supporting arguments (*BhG* 2.32) on this point to Arjuna.

[145]14.4.23: a cakravartin, whose grandfather Kāraṃdhama is also an emperor (saṃrāj; 18).

[146]Cf. 7.55: *haime himavataḥ pāde*, as cited in Sörensen [1904] 1963, 471.

[147]Muñjavat, "having sedge grass." In the Vedic Agnicayana, the Soma merchant brings Soma from Mount Mūjavat (Staal 1983, 347), which seems to have found this new spelling, location, and luminosity in the *Mbh*. Thanks to T. P. Mahadevan for the reference. On the other mountains and features mentioned, see chaps. 7, § D and 8.

unexpected resource, and, after Kṛṣṇa offers some further spiritual guidance of the very sort that Vyāsa seems to have so recently preempted,[148] the king is described as "conciliated *(anunīta)* by the lord *(bhagavatā)* of wide fame himself [that is, by Kṛṣṇa], by Dvaipāyana Kṛṣṇa," and by numerous others including various Ṛṣis, the other Pāṇḍavas, and Draupadī. Moreover, he has "left behind that suffering born of grief, and also his mental anguish" (14.2–4). He now wants to undertake the sacrifice, and tells Vyāsa, "Protected[149] by you, grandfather, we shall go to Himavat. Surely one hears the region is a great wonder" (9). All the Maharṣis then give their assent. And with Vyāsa presumably among them, those Ṛṣis "became invisible then and there to all who were looking" *(paśyatām eva sarveṣāṃ tatraivādarśanaṃ yayuḥ*; 12cd).

32. *Reconfirms and safeguards Parikṣit's miraculous birth.* After Kṛṣṇa, who is with his parents in Dvārakā, narrates the death of their grandson Abhimanyu, Vaiśampāyana describes the obsequies performed for Abhimanyu there and suddenly switches scenes to Hāstinapura where similar grieving continues for the same youthful hero:

> So also the Pāṇḍava heroes in the city named after the elephant found no peace without Abhimanyu. For a great many days, O lord of kings, the daughter of Virāṭa [Uttarā, Abhimanyu's wife] did not eat, afflicted with grief for her husband. There was great distress that the embryo in her womb was completely dissolved *(saṃpralīyata)*. Then Vyāsa came, having known with his divine eye.[150] Having come, the visionary one *(dhīmān)* said to large-eyed Pṛthā and to Uttarā, "O greatly illustrious one, let this grief be completely abandoned. Your son will be born, O illustrious one, famous lady, by the power of Vāsudeva and also by my utterance.[151] After the Pāṇḍavas, he will protect the earth." (14.61.7–10)

Turning to Arjuna, in view of Yudhiṣṭhira, Vyāsa then adds:

[148]Kṛṣṇa tells Yudhiṣṭhira, as he did Arjuna in the *Gītā*, that he is his own worst enemy (14.11.5) and must now fight the war alone that has arisen with his self (11–12). He sings a *Kāma Gītā* (13.11–16) about the indestructibility of desire, which takes the guise of whatever a person seeks to defeat it with. He says Yudhiṣṭhira's desire now takes the form of offering sacrifice, which Kṛṣṇa now also enjoins him to perform (18–19).

[149]Or perhaps "hidden," "preserved" by you: *tvayā guptā* (14.14a).

[150]14.61.9ab: *ājagāma tato vyāso jñātvā divyenacakṣuṣā*. See above, nn. 26, 59, 71, 78.

[151]14.61.10cd: *prabhāvād vāsudevasya mama vyāharaṇād api*. *Vyāharaṇa* could be taken as creative word, evoking the cognate term *vyāhṛti*, "the mystical utterance of the names of the seven worlds, . . . the first three of which, called 'the great Vyāhṛtis,' are pronounced after *oṃ* by every Brāhman after saying his daily prayers" (MW 1039).

> Your grandson will be great-armed and high-minded, and he will protect the earth to the limit of the seas. Therefore, best of Kurus, conquer grief, O foe-mower. You have nothing to doubt. It will be true.[152] What was formerly spoken by the Vṛṣṇi hero Kṛṣṇa, O joy of the Kurus, will be so. Let there be no doubt.[153] Gone to the imperishable self-conquered worlds of the gods, he is not to be mourned by you, child, nor by the other Kurus. (12–15)

These words from his "grandfather" (16a) Vyāsa cheer Arjuna, who stops grieving. Then Vaiśampāyana tells Janamajeya that *his* father, Parikṣit, "increased in the womb like the moon at the time of the bright fortnight" (17), and concludes:

> Then Vyāsa roused the king, Dharma's son, concerning the Aśvamedha. Then he vanished.[154] So the intelligent Dharmarāja, having heard the word of Vyāsa, set his mind on going to get the wealth. (18–19)

In this compact passage, three things are brilliantly sustained: the seven generations of genealogical continuity from Arjuna's "grandfather" Vyāsa to Arjuna's "grandson" Parikṣit and *his* son Janamejaya, Vaiśampāyana's audience; the enigma of transmission from Vyāsa to Vaiśampāyana who can turn us (and Janamejaya) without blinking from Vyāsa as speaker within the text to Vyāsa as a presence behind the telling—indeed, in attendance at Janamejaya's snake sacrifice to hear his own story told;[155] and the interchangeableness of Vyāsa and Kṛṣṇa, author and god. The passage has been overlooked—perhaps because it looks redundant, perhaps because it gets forgotten—by many, including myself, when they recount the miraculous revival of the lunar dynasty through Kṛṣṇa's revival of the stillborn Parikṣit, son of the moon-splendored Abhimanyu.[156] Vyāsa intervenes, just before this revival happens, to soothe and reassure, but also to unsettle: How can one doubt the god's word when it is vouched for by the author's? I believe the question is artfully left open.

[152] 14.61.13cd: *vicāryam atra na hi te satyam etad* [corrected] *bhaviṣyati.*

[153] 14.61.14cd: *puroktaṃ tat tathā bhāvi mā te 'trāstu vicāraṇā.*

[154] 14.61.18: *tataḥ saṃcodayāmāsa vyāso dharmātmajaṃ nṛpam/ aśvamedham prati tadā tataḥ so 'ntarhito 'bhavat.*

[155] See § C.40 below and chaps. 1, § B and 3, § C.

[156] See § C.26 above for Kṛṣṇa's promise and *Mbh* 14.65–69.11, especially 68.18–24 for its fulfillment. See Hiltebeitel [1976] 1990, 337–38 (Abhimanyu's birth from the lunar splendor that is dynastically revived through Parikṣit's birth) and 349–50 (the revival scene); cf. 1991a, 431. Naturally, this passage about Vyāsa is omitted in abridgments.

33. *Assists the Pāṇḍavas in obtaining Marutta's gold.* With no traces of his intermediate comings or goings, Vyāsa is present in Śiva's mountains for Yudhiṣṭhira to have him lead the Pāṇḍavas to Marutta's wealth there (14.64.8), and to give Yudhiṣṭhira permission to return to Hāstinapura with the treasure (19). Perhaps he was among the numerous unnamed Brahmans who made the trip with the Pāṇḍavas (14.62–63), but nothing indicates it, and much more—as we keep seeing—suggests that the region of Meru to the north or back of Mount Himavat is a place one can find Vyāsa very much at home. The episode is told as if Vyāsa's "protection" through these "wondrous" mountains goes by without hitch or need of further elaboration.[157]

34. *Manages Yudhiṣṭhira's horse sacrifice.* A month after Parikṣit has been revived by Kṛṣṇa at Hāstinapura, the Pāṇḍavas return there from their successful quest for Marutta's wealth (14.69.12); and, "after several days" (*katipayāhasya*, 70.10a), Vyāsa arrives—with nothing more said about it. Yudhiṣṭhira tells him he wants to start the Aśvamedha, and Vyāsa gives permission, seconded by Kṛṣṇa (70.10–25). Yudhiṣṭhira then asks Vyāsa to determine the right time for his consecration *(dīkṣā)*, and Vyāsa promises that with Paila (one of his four disciples) and Yājñavalkya, he will perform every rite at the proper time (71.1–3). Vyāsa soon says the horse should be released, and when Yudhiṣṭhira asks who should guard it, Vyāsa answers Arjuna, and lauds his prowess (11–20). Yudhiṣṭhira appoints Arjuna and others to the tasks Vyāsa indicates (20–26). The sacrificial horse is then released "by that *brahman*-speaker Vyāsa himself of unlimited energy."[158]

About a year later, three days after Arjuna returns with the horse, Vyāsa comes to Yudhiṣṭhira and tells him to begin the remaining ceremonies, which, he says, will purify his sins when he takes the final bath *(avabhṛtha)* if he has distributed three times the ordinary amount of gold to the Brahmans (90.11–16). While the rites are underway, "Vyāsa's disciples were always in that sacrificial enclosure" (*sadas*; 37ab)—presumably not only Paila, but Sumantu, Jaimini, and Vaiśampāyana, the narrator. Once the horse is sacrificed and Yudhiṣṭhira and his brothers smell the sin-cleansing smoke rising from the burning of its omentum *(vapā)*, Vyāsa and his disciples exalt the king (91.4–6). Yudhiṣṭhira then follows the Aśvamedha precedent *(smṛte)* of giving away the earth to Brahmans. He offers it to Vyāsa along with ten billion gold pendants to the sadasyas; and when Vyāsa returns the earth to him as a "ransom" *(niṣkraya)* for more gold, Yudhiṣṭhira says he will enter the forest (12), and adds:

[157]See closure of § C.31 above.

[158]14.72.3: *hayas . . . svayaṃ sa brahmavādinā utsṛṣṭaḥ . . . vyāsenāmitatejasā.*

> "O best of Munis, I do not wish to take what is the Brahmans' own. This has always been on my mind and my brothers', O sinless ones." When he was saying this, those brothers and Draupadī also said, "It is so." It was thrilling.[159] Then, O Bhārata, a voice in the sky said "Bravo! Bravo!"[160] Sounds of praise were heard from the crowds of Brahmans. Thus addressed, the Muni Dvaipāyana, saluting this *(idaṃ sampūjayan)* in the middle of the Brahmans, again said to Yudhiṣṭhira, "Given by you to me, I give her back to you. Let gold be given to these Brahmans. The earth is yours." Then Vāsudeva said to Yudhiṣṭhira Dharmarāja, "As the holy one Vyāsa says, so you should do." (91.13–18)

Vyāsa speaks literally for the Brahmans to negotiate their extraordinary sacrificial stipends.[161] But there is perhaps some coyness when it comes to what he salutes. No one could be surprised that Yudhiṣṭhira has always yearned for the forest and doesn't want what belongs to Brahmans. Perhaps what is "thrilling" is the Pāṇḍavas and Draupadī's concurrence that it was always on their mind too. But this is ambiguous, since they could be simply confirming what has been on Yudhiṣṭhira's mind while keeping mum about what has long been on their own: their determination to keep him from dragging them into the forest once again. Vyāsa salutes not only the words of Yudhiṣṭhira, his brothers, and Draupadi, but the celestial mechanics of cosmic approbation—that is, the most obvious of his authorly tricks—and the praise of the Brahmans for whom he serves as spokesman. On the other hand, perhaps by now the other Pāṇḍavas and Draupadī *have* developed a longing for the forest.

Though it goes unmentioned, Vyāsa is presumably still there at the rites' completion when a gold-headed, gold-sided mongoose comes out of his hole to disparage the Aśvamedha. It is not equal, says the mongoose, to the measure of powdered barley given as a "pure gift"[162] to Dharma, disguised as a mysterious hungry guest, by an uñcavṛtti Brahman and his wife, son, and daughter-in-law, who dwell in a hut at Kurukṣetra and practice the pigeon-like vow of gleaning. As we have seen, Vyāsa has told Yudhiṣṭhira about this vow before (see § C.19 above), where the grain gleaned is rice *(vrīhi)* rather than barley. With this story, the first in a series that closes the *Āśvamedhika Parvan*, Yudhiṣṭhira learns,

[159]Or "hair-raising" (*romaharṣana*; 14.91.14d).

[160]14.91.15b: *sādhu sādhviti.*

[161]After the Brahmans take the wealth they want and leave some for the other castes and Mlecchas (14.91.25), Vyāsa gives Kuntī the considerable gold that has come to him (27).

[162]14.93.57a: *śuddhena tava dānena.*

though it is not the parvan's last word on the subject,[163] that his sin-cleansing Aśvamedha is inferior to a form of rigorous tapas, just as earlier he was told, without ever quite accepting it, that it would be a poor second to the grief-conquering wisdom that there is neither the slayer nor the slain.

35. *Sanctions Dhṛtarāṣṭra's retirement to the forest.* With no fanfare, Vyāsa came (*abhyetya*; 15.7.19) and went (*gate*; 8.19) to tell Yudhiṣṭhira to accommodate Dhṛtarāṣṭra's repeated requests for permission to go to the forest, which Dhṛtarāṣṭra then does. Dhṛtarāṣṭra is joined by Gāndhārī, Kuntī, Vidura, and Saṃjaya, and departs to the loud wailing of the Pāṇḍava and Kaurava women (15.5.18–23).

36. *Among those who help the elders in the forest.* Having gone to the bank of the Gaṅgā, Dhṛtarāṣṭra and company make their way from there to Kurukṣetra (15.25.1–8), as if this were but a short distance.[164] There they go to the hermitage of Śatayūpa, a former king of the Kekayas who has retired to the forest after conferring the kingdom on his son (9–10). This king, whose name means "Having a hundred sacrificial stakes," now presents an opposite figure to Dhṛtarāṣṭra: having left one son legitimately on the throne whereas Dhṛtarāṣṭra has left none, his name recalls Dhṛtarāṣṭra's hundred sons slain in the sacrifice of battle. Dhṛtarāṣṭra goes "together with him" to Vyāsa's hermitage *(vyāsāśramam)*, where Dhṛtarāṣṭra receives dīkṣa (presumably from Vyāsa); and the two kings then return to Śatayūpa's hermitage where, at Vyāsa's assent *(vyāsasyānumate)*, Śatayūpa instructs Dhṛtarāṣṭra in the full rule of forest life (*sarvaṃ vidhim . . . āraṇyakam*; 11–13). Dhṛtarāṣṭra now undertakes a life of severe tapas, and Gāndhārī and his other companions follow his example.

Vyāsa is barely present for this visit, and this is the first mention of his hermitage at Kurukṣetra.

37. *Joins the storytellers around Dhṛtarāṣṭra.* When Dhṛtarāṣṭra sets himself and his elderly companions to asceticism, the Munis Nārada, Parvata, and Devala "came" *(abhyayuḥ)* to see them, and so do Vyāsa,

[163]See Reich 1998, 319–21: The last story of the parvan (14.96) undercuts the mongoose's words by revealing that he was formerly Anger personified, and was cursed to revile Yudhiṣṭhira in this fashion. Cf. chap. 1 at nn. 76–78: the uñcavṛtti vow seems to have some special importance for the poets, but not without their having some ambivalence.

[164]It is roughly a hundred miles northwest, and would require crossing the Yamunā. Belvalkar (1947a, 328–29) notes that "utter nonsense" arises if one literalizes Saṃjaya's travels between Kurukṣetra and Hāstinapura; and to allow Saṃjaya to travel twice a night between the two, he finds support from 7.61.5–10 to shorten the distance. Here, Dhṛtarāṣṭra says that "today" *(adya)* he does not, as on other days, *hear* sounds of joy from the Kaurava camp as it prepares to fight for Jayadratha's life. But surely Dhṛtarāṣṭra is just wrapped up in the story.

his disciples, other mindful perfected ones *(siddhāścanye manīṣiṇah)*, and the old royal Ṛṣi Śatayūpa (15.26.1–2). "There, O child, those supreme Ṛṣis fashioned righteous stories, delighting Dhṛtarāṣṭra. . . . But in a certain interval in a story, the divine Ṛṣi Nārada, seeing everything that pertains to the senses, told *this* story."[165] He tells of Śatayūpa's grandfather and other kings who went to heaven by their forest tapas (6–14), and then says, "By Dvaipāyana's grace you too (have?) this forest of penances. Having reached what is hard to reach, you will go to the highest perfection."[166] One hardly knows whether Vyāsa's grace has given Dhṛtarāṣṭra the forest, the penances, or the promise of perfection.

Nārada promises heavenly rewards for Dhṛtarāṣṭra, Gāndhārī, and Kuntī, saying, "We discern this, O king, by the divine eye."[167] Granting that Nārada knows "the truth and end of every matter with the divine eye" (27.4ab), Śatayūpa says Nārada has "increased the Kuru king's faith" (*śraddhā kururājasya vardhitā*; 27.2). But he wants to know the time left and the specific heavenly worlds that await his royal friend. Nārada replies: "Having gone by chance *(yadṛcchayā)* to the abode of Śakra" (27.8ab), Nārada was told the "story of Dhṛtarāṣṭra" as a "divine secret" *(devaguhyam)* by Indra. Dhṛtarāṣṭra has three years left and will go to the abode of Kubera (9–14).[168] Once Nārada has finished this pleasing tale among others, "Having seated themselves around Dhṛtarāṣṭra with stories, the insightful ones scattered as they wished, resorting to the way of the perfected."[169]

Again Vyāsa is a more or less silent presence. Here he comes and goes with Nārada among the storytellers and the stories.

38. *Promises a wonder and asks a leading question.*[170] Worried about Kuntī (15.29.11), Yudhiṣṭhira and his brothers lead a vast party—which includes Draupadī and the Kaurava widows—to visit the elders. Having "descended *(avātarat)* into Kurukṣetra, and gradually crossed *(krameṇottīrya)* the Yamunā," they see the elders' ashram on a bank of the Yamunā (15.31.2, 6). The ashram is "frequented by Siddhas and Caraṇas, crowded by those desirous of seeing [Dhṛtarāṣṭra] like the firmament with hosts of stars" (31.20).

[165]15.26.4–5: *tatra dharmyāḥ kathās tāta cakrus te paramarṣayaḥ/ . . . kathāntare tu kasmiṃścid devarṣir nāradas tadā/ kathām imām akathayat sarvapratyakṣadarśivān.*

[166]15.26.15: *dvaipāyanaprasādāc ca tvam apīdaṃ tapovanam/ rājann avāpya duṣprāpām siddhim agryāṃ gamiṣyasi.*

[167]15.26.19cd: *vayam etat prapaśyāmo nṛpate divyacakṣuṣā.* The "we" should take in Vyāsa.

[168]It seems Nārada must have gone to Indraloka rather recently.

[169]15.27.16: *evaṃ kathābhir anvāsya dhṛtarāṣṭraṃ manīṣiṇaḥ/ viprajagmur yathākāmamaṃ te siddhagatim āsthitāḥ.*

[170]The next two sequences condense Hiltebeitel 1999a, 476–81, but with some changes and additions, especially concerning the hanging question and the closing paragraph.

After Vidura dies (15.33.24–27), the rest pass an "auspicious night furnished with constellations" (34.1). At morning, "the great Ṛṣis who dwell at Kurukṣetra came with Śatayūpa" to join Dhṛtarāṣṭra and the Pāṇḍavas, and so too "the lord Vyāsa, worshipped by the hosts of divine Ṛṣis, showed up *(darśayāmāsa)*, surrounded by his disciples" (34.21–22). Bidding everyone to be seated after he has seated himself (25–26), Vyāsa explains Vidura's passing and then tells Dhṛtarāṣṭra he will show, as the fruit of his tapas, a wonder unprecedented even among the great Ṛṣis. What does Dhṛtarāṣṭra wish to see, touch, or hear? he asks (35.24–25). The question is left hanging as an adhyāya ends.

39. *Shows the survivors their slain loved ones.* Although nothing says that Vyāsa left, much less went very far, he "came there" *(tatrāgamad)* again after a month that the Pāṇḍavas spent with their elders. Other Ṛṣis led by Nārada, Parvata, and Devala soon join them (15.36.7–9) to hear Vyāsa's "most virtuous heavenly stories" (14). But soon, having gotten no answer to his month-old pending question, Vyāsa says he knows what is in the old king's heart *(hṛdi)*, as also the hearts of Gāndhārī, Kuntī, Draupadī, and Subhadrā (36.16–18): their grief for their sons. Dhṛtarāṣṭra admits he mourns his sons and wonders where they have gone (30). Gāndhārī too laments them along with their hundred widows, who surround her with mourning (37.12). Kuntī also grieves for Karṇa (38). Waiting no longer for anyone to tell him what they'd like to see, touch, or hear, Vyāsa reveals the resolve that was already in *his* heart *(hṛdaye)* before they spoke (39.3): he will show them their sons and other loved ones slain in battle. Disclosing the celestial and demonic origins of both the dead and living heroes, he tells the gathering to proceed to the Gaṅgā (18), to do which the elders must now cross the Yamunā and travel at least forty miles.[171]

Once at the Gaṅgā, the "ocean of folk" (15.39.21) awaits nightfall (23). Their evening rites finished, all sit down (40.1–3). "Then the great Muni Vyāsa of great energy, having plunged into the Bhāgīrathī's meritorious water, summoned all the lokas—the slain warriors of the Pāṇḍavas and Kauravas collectively, including kings from other lands. Then, O Janamejaya, a tumultuous sound arose within the water from the armies of the Kurus and Pāṇḍavas, just as it was before" (4–6). As the dead rise from the Gaṅgā with celestial bodies and apparel, Vyāsa, gratified with Dhṛtarāṣṭra, gives him celestial sight to see them, while the blindfolded Gāndhārī sees them with the power of her celestial knowledge (17–18):

> It was as highly intoxicating as a festival, agitating the thrilled women and men. He saw the army approaching like a picture gone onto a

[171]Assuming they start from the closest point between the two rivers within reach from Kurukṣetra. Cf. n. 164 above.

> woven cloth. Dhṛtarāṣṭra, seeing them all with his divine eye, rejoiced, best of Bhāratas, by the grace of the Muni *(prasādāt . . . muneḥ)*. (20–21)

The living and dead delight all night as if they were in heaven (41.8). And then in a moment or twinkle (*kṣaṇena*) Vyāsa dismisses *(visarjayāmāsa)* the dead to reenter the auspicious triple-pathed river and return to the (starry) worlds from which they came (12–13).

Having fulfilled this purpose of "*his* heart," Vyāsa now turns to a purpose he hasn't admitted. Standing in the water, he says:

> "All those Kṣatriya women whose lords are slain, those foremost women who desire the worlds won by their husbands, unwearied, let them quickly *(kṣipram)* plunge into the Jāhnavī's (Gaṅgā's) water." Hearing his words, having faith *(śraddadhānā)*, taking leave of their father-in-law [Dhṛtarāṣṭra], the beautiful women entered the Jāhnavī's water. Released from human bodies, these chaste women all joined their husbands, O king. Women of good conduct, women of the family, they all in course, having entered the water, were released, and obtained residence in their husbands' worlds. (41.17e–21)

As a "giver of boons" *(varada)*, Vyāsa, we are told, gave everyone there what they desired "at that time" (24). But of course he has brought them to that time. Through this episode, the Pāṇḍavas dispose of grief for their elders. The elders dispose of grief for their sons. But the Kaurava widows' grief for their husbands is a surplus that is disposed of by Vyāsa. As we have seen, he hints repeatedly that the Kaurava widows are a burden to Yudhiṣṭhira and delinquent in becoming satīs. Satī is evoked by analogy here, but the *Mahābhārata* knows it.[172]

Coming at the end of the *Putradarśana Parvan*, the "Book of Seeing the Sons," the removal of the widows to heaven is both that episode's culmination and a major moment in the series of stories that finishes the epic with the deaths of the war's survivors. Preceded by the deaths of Bhīṣma and Vidura; soon followed by those of Dhṛtarāṣṭra, Gāndhārī, and Kuntī, which are in turn followed by those of Kṛṣṇa, some of his wives,[173] and the rest of the Yādavas, including Balarāma; and with final closure on the heavenly ascent of Draupadī and the Pāṇḍavas, the "salvation" of the Kaurava widows is the only case where the author

[172]See Dhand 2000, 122, on "an extraordinary reversal"; Sutton 2000, 87, 144, 264–65, 430; Hiltebeitel 1999a, 480 and n. 10, on this scene and oral epic ones; and below at n. 188.

[173]Four of whom become satīs (16.8.7).

eliminates the survivors himself. As with Vyāsa's siring of Dhṛtarāṣṭra and Pāṇḍu, it is a good question whether he does it "without cruelty." One gets used to his promptings, but this "quickly" is a bit much.[174] Although Vyāsa begins his marvel by prompting those who wish to see their sons, he extends his final prompt only to those who wish to rejoin their husbands. No one enters the water to rejoin her sons. Indeed, it is clear from the repeated references to the Kaurava widows, both before and after Vyāsa enters the scene,[175] that they have been at the center of authorial interest through the whole episode. "Seeing the Sons" is how Vyāsa finally makes the Kaurava widows invisible.

40. *Goodbyes to Parikṣit and Dhṛtarāṣṭra.* We have noticed that the phrase "by Vyāsa's grace" has brought with it five wonders: Saṃjaya's boon, the *Gītā*, Saṃjaya's rescue from death in battle, Dhṛtarāṣṭra's forest of penances, and the *Putradarśana.*[176] Other such references do not go beyond these wonders,[177] and none occur beyond the current episode and its sequel, where most of the references cluster. Needless to say, the phrase "by the grace of" is used *more* often only for Kṛṣṇa.[178]

The sequel is twofold. First, there is a sudden dip to the epic's outer frame to hear Sauti—that is, the bard Ugraśravas—narrate events that occur within the inner frame when Janamejaya responds to Vaiśampāyana's account of Vyāsa's marvel.[179] Then, resuming with the inner frame, Vaiśampāyana tells how Vyāsa comes back one last time to see Dhṛtarāṣṭra.

Although our thread in this chapter is Vyāsa's movements through the "main story" as told in the inner frame, his final scenes with the elders are best traced through this dip to the outer frame, since it extends the theme of Vyāsa's grace through both frames, and thus through all six generations of the author's descent. Once Janamejaya has heard the *Putradarśana* story, he is thrilled and asks how the "coming again" or

[174]For a different opinion, see Belvalkar 1959, xlii: "The problem of the future of these poor and helpless ladies had hence to be faced and settled"; xliv: "Fortunately, with Vyāsa's special favour, most of these were united with their dead relatives."

[175]See above, § C.28–30, 35, and n. 172. Cf. § C.2 and 7 on his wider handling of Kaurava widows.

[176]See § C.21, 25, 37, and 39 above, all with ablatives of *prasāda*.

[177]See 1.2.215 (refering to the *Putradarśana*); 6.5.8 (Saṃjaya invited to begin using his boon); 7.165.57 (Saṃjaya uses the boon to see the heavenly ascent of Droṇa).

[178]Using Tokunaga's machine-readable text, I note nineteen instances just by the combination of *prasādāt* with one of Kṛṣṇa's names or a pronoun: 2.30.18; 42.47; 5.78.9; 6.40.56, 58, 62, and 73 (cited § C.21 above); 46.20; 7.123.27; 124 6, 9, 12 and 13; 9.62.15; 12.1.10 (cited § C.29 above); 54.17 and 23; and 55.21. The instrumental *prasādena* is not comparable.

[179]Belvalkar 1959, 155, sees the passage as interpolated, but has only his own logic to support this.

"reappearance" *(punarāgamanaṃ prati)* of his "grandfathers" was possible. Vaiśampāyana explains how karmic recall can apply not only to bodies but features (15.42.1–4), and reaffirms that Dhṛtarāṣṭra "obtained the sight of his sons in their own form by the grace of the Ṛṣi *(ṛṣiprasādāt)*"; indeed, whereas Vidura "reached perfection through the power of tapas," Dhṛtarāṣṭra did so from "having met (or sat down with) the tapas-possessing Vyāsa!"[180] This provokes Janamejaya to say,

> If the boon-giving Vyāsa *(varado vyāso)* may also show me my father in his form, clothes, and age, I will have faith in all you say *(śraddadhyāṃ sarvam eva te)*. It would please me. I would be fulfilled and resolute. By the grace of the son of the Ṛṣi[181] let my wish succeed. (15.43.4–5)

It is a matter of grace and faith, miracle and resolve, just as it is when Vyāsa gives the Kaurava widows their chance to "quickly" enter the waters of paradise.

Sauti now chimes in: "When the king had so spoken, the majestic and insightful Vyāsa showed grace *(prasādam akarod)* and brought forth Parikṣit" (15.43.6). Janamejaya sees not only his father and his ministers, but other figures (8–11) whom we come to know from Sauti's outer frame narratives that open the *Mahābhārata*. Most intriguingly, Sauti reports a conversation between Janamejaya and the Ṛṣi Āstīka, of whom we will say more in chapter 3. Here Āstīka says the snake sacrifice in which Janamejaya has "heard a marvelous tale"[182] is now over, and that "the snakes led by their ashes have gone the way of your father" (13)—that is, of Parikṣit. The tale Janamejaya has heard is, of course, the *Mahābhārata*, which is fine as long as we remain in the outer frame from which Āstīka is speaking. But Āstīka is also supposed to bring about the end of Janamejaya's sacrifice as the closure to the inner frame, in which Janamejaya cannot have heard the whole *Mahābhārata* by now if he is listening to Āstīka at this point in the story. The frame shift thus produces a temporal incongruity, which it now leaves open as Janamejaya asks Vaiśampāyana to return to "what is distinctive about the story" *(kathā-viśeṣam)* of the elders' residence in the forest (18).[183] As elsewhere, different chronicities flow almost unnoticed through a "rough join."

[180]43.1–3, ending: *samāsādya vyāsaṃ cāpi tapasvinam.*

[181]Vyāsa is the son of the Ṛṣi Parāśara.

[182]15.43.13ab: *śrutaṃ vicitram ākhyānam.* One could take *ākhyānam* as "telling," "narrative," etc.

[183]Alternately, the rest of this episode and what follows would have to be told *after* the snake sacrifice is over, which would be inconsonant with what else we know.

In reporting this exchange, Sauti provides a transition for the narrative to return to Vaiśampāyana, who can begin the next adhyāya back in the forest. Here, once Dhṛtarāṣṭra returns to his hermitage and "the supreme Ṛṣis" (with Vyāsa evidently not among them) depart "as they wished at Dhṛtarāṣṭra's leave," the Pāṇḍavas still linger in attendance of their elders (15.44.1–4). Finally Vyāsa, with the most minimal attention to his movements, "went" *(gatam)* to Dhṛtarāṣṭra to convince him to tell the Pāṇḍavas it is time to return home and rule their kingdom (5–12).

41. *Visited by Arjuna.* Thirty-six years after Kurukṣetra, the Yādavas, cursed for insulting the three Ṛṣis Viśvāmitra, Kaṇva, and Nārada, slaughter themselves at Prabhāsa, near Dvārakā (16.2–4).[184] Balarāma (more accurately, Baladeva, Kṛṣṇa's elder brother) enters the ocean and Kṛṣṇa ascends to heaven.[185] After the slaughter but before his world-departure, Kṛṣṇa, back in Dvārakā, sends for Arjuna to protect the Yādava women, soon to be menaced by robbers (*dasyu*; 5.3–4). Arjuna arrives to see the city bereft and hear the wails of Kṛṣṇa's sixteen thousand wives (6.4–6). Kṛṣṇa's agonized father Vasudeva wonders how his son, the lord of the universe *(jagataḥ prabhuḥ)* who slew Kaṃsa, Keśi, Śiśupāla, and others, could have overlooked *(abhyupekṣitavān)* the slaughter of his own kinsmen (7.9–11). Then he tells Arjuna Kṛṣṇa's parting prophetic words: At the proper time Arjuna will attend to[186] the Yādava women and children, and to Vasudeva's own funeral rites; and when Arjuna leaves Dvārakā, the ocean will deluge the city (7.16–17).

Arjuna says he cannot look at the earth without Kṛṣṇa, and that his brothers and Draupadī feel the same. He also knows it's time for them all to move on.[187] But first he will bring the Vṛṣṇi women, children, and aged to Indraprastha (8.2–5). In the Yādava court, he tells the Brahmans and others to be ready to depart in seven days (8–12). Spending the last night in Kṛṣṇa's residence, he is overcome with grief

[184]B. Sullivan thinks the Buddhist *Jātaka* story, where it is Vyāsa rather than Viśvāmitra, Kaṇva, and Nārada, is the older account, and that the *Mbh* is oral up to the first few centuries A.D. (1990, 103–6). The *Jātaka* has Vyāsa killed, but not the *Arthaśāstra.* Possibly the *Arthaśāstra* picks up part of the *Jātaka* version. I suspect the Buddhist variant is designed to "kill the author" (cf. Hiltebeitel [1976] 1990, 64–65), whereas Sullivan thinks the *Mbh* has evolved the story toward keeping the author alive. But that is quite a stretch. Cf. Sullivan 1990, 107–8: the Buddha was Dīpāyana in his former life.

[185]16.5.12–25. Balarāma is discussed in chaps. 3, § D and 4, § B. Bigger 1998, 9, makes the important point that the later name Balarāma is not used in the *Mbh*, but I will continue to use it since it is more familiar than Baladeva.

[186]*Pratipatsyati*, which could also mean "will consider" or "convey," or, as Ganguli translates, "do what is best for" ([1884–96] 1970, vol. 12, *Mausala Parva*, 265).

[187]*Saṃkramaṇa*, for which Ganguli translates "depart" ([1884–96] 1970, vol. 12, *Mausala Parva*, 266), and which can mean "passage into another world, decease, death" (MW). The prefix *sam-* suggests that the action will be done "together."

(14). But before he can set out, Vasudeva dies and goes to heaven. Arjuna sees to his cremation and the satīs of four of his wives (24–25); then he performs obsequies for all the slain Yādavas, including Balarāma and Kṛṣṇa's cremations (15–31). Finally a vast exodus of refugees sets out under his command, including all the widows: Kṛṣṇa's sixteen thousand, and the Bhojas, Andhakas, and Vṛṣṇis' "many thousands of millions and ten millions" (*ca sahasrāṇi prayutānyarbudāni ca*; 38ab). Dvārakā is flooded (40–41). When the march reaches the Punjab (*pañcanadam*), "sinful," "covetous" Ābhīra robbers see easy prey (43–48). Arjuna smiles at their audacity, but when he can barely draw his bow and cannot invoke his celestial weapons, he is shamed (49–54). While women are being carried off, he can only pummel the Mleccha marauders with the curved ends of his bow (55–61). Considering fate (*daivam*) to have prevailed, he turns away, and with the remainder (*śeṣam*) of the women and wealth, "descends to Kurukṣetra" (*kurukṣetram avātarat*; 62–65). From there he sets up residences where sons of the slain Vṛṣṇi and Bhoja leaders can resettle with some of the women, while other women retire to the forest or—in the case of five of Kṛṣṇa's wives—become satīs at Indraprastha (65–72).[188] That is where Arjuna has last been when, with nothing further to trace his movements, this awful adhyāya ends as follows: "Having done this as was suited to the occasion, Arjuna, covered with tears, O king, saw Kṛṣṇa Dvaipāyana seated in a hermitage."[189]

The next adhyāya, the last of the *Mausalaparvan*, then begins: "Entering the truth-speaker's hermitage, O king, Arjuna saw the Muni, Satyavatī's son, seated in a lonely place" (*āsīnam ekānte*; 16.9.1). According to Mehta, whose powerful reading of this passage will now engage us, in "one of the most touching scenes of the epic, we see Dvaipāyana for the last time, after all is over and the great sacrifice has claimed its last offerings, sitting alone, for once, in his own *āśrama*" (1990, 110). All the more remarkable, then, that when at last, and for his last intervention, we find Vyāsa "alone, for once" in such a place, it could not be anywhere more indefinite. We are, to be sure, in something called Vyāsa's hermitage, but it could be that Vyāsa is in a "lonely place" in a hermitage that is "his" only in the sense that he is there now. The

[188] I cannot agree with Dhand (2000, 233) that "the number of *satīs* is negligible" in the *Mbh*, and that "the characters who become *satīs* are inconsequential." See Hiltebeitel 1999b, 89 on the consequences of satī etiquette for low status wives such as Mādrī and Jambavatī and a "favorite" like Rukmiṇī.

[189] 16.8.74cd: *kṛṣṇadvaipāyanaṃ rājan dadarśāsīnam āśrame*. Ganguli [1884–96] 1970, vol. 12, *Mausala Parva*, 269, has "Arjuna . . . then entered the retreat of Vyasa," as it is in the first verse of the next adhyāya. But it is something more vague than that.

impression is given that he is somewhere in north central India, in fact, not far from Delhi.[190] But for all he tells us, the author could have brought Arjuna to the back of Mount Meru.

> Having approached the dharma-knower of high vows, he stood near *(upatasthe)*. Having told his name to him, "I am Arjuna,"[191] he then saluted him. "Welcome to you," said the Muni, Satyavatī's son. "Be seated," spoke the great Muni of tranquil self. Having seen him sad of mind *(apratītamanasam)*, sighing again and again, despondent of mind *(nirviṇṇamanasam)*, Vyāsa said this to Pārtha. "Are you not born of a hero? Are you damaged?[192] Has a Brahman been killed by you? Or are you defeated in battle? You look as if you've lost *Śrī*.[193] I do not recognize you *(na tvā pratyabhijānāmi)*. What is this, bull of the Bhāratas? If it is to be heard by me, Pārtha, you can tell it quickly." (16.9.2–6)

All this is said as if Vyāsa doesn't know what he is about to hear. For the moment, we must forget that when Arjuna comes before him "sad of mind, despondent of mind,"[194] Vyāsa knows his characters' thoughts. Moreover, Vyāsa affects not to recognize the change in his own most "perfected" character.

As Mehta recognizes, Arjuna now tells the story "to his creator, the author himself!" (1990, 110). Instead of making the hero hear his own story, like Rāma, Vyāsa makes himself momentarily his hero's audience.[195] Arjuna tells all that has happened, beginning with the death and departure to heaven of "he who has the form of a cloud."[196] Kṛṣṇa's parting leaves Arjuna helpless and despairing:

> Like the drying of the ocean, like the moving of a mountain, like the falling of the sky, and also like the cooling of fire, I consider

[190]The part of Old Delhi around the Purana Khilla, supposedly the fort of the Pāṇḍavas, is usually identified with Indraprastha.

[191]Arjuna "presents himself with the simple words: 'I am Arjuna'" (Mehta 1990, 110).

[192]16.9.5ab: *avīrajo 'bhighātas te*. The Vulgate and some other northern and southern texts have a different reading and preceding line (16.51*), both probably interpolated, where Vyāsa begins by asking about Arjuna's ritual purity, including, according to Nīlakaṇṭha, whether he had sexual contact with a menstruating woman (Kinjawadekar 1929–33, VI, *Mausalaparva*, 11; Ganguli [1884–96] 1970, vol. 12, *Mausala Parva*, 270).

[193]*Śrī* has many pertinent connotations here: prosperity, radiance, the favor of Viṣṇu's wife.

[194]*Manas*, also "heart," as in Arjuna's "heartbreak" (*mano me dīryate*; 16.9.15c) just below.

[195]Behind this, he is also listening to Vaiśampāyana tell this exchange to Janamejaya.

[196]16.9.7a. Further along, deepening this devotional and iconic vein, Arjuna describes Kṛṣṇa as "that Puruṣa of immeasurable self, the bearer of the conch, discus, and mace, four-armed, yellow-clad, dark, with long lotus eyes" (19).

> incredible *(aśraddheyam ahaṃ manye)* the death of the wielder of the Śārṅga bow. Made to be without Kṛṣṇa,[197] I do not want to stay here in the world. And there's another more painful thing here, O storehouse of penances, by which my heart breaks from repeatedly thinking about it. Hear it. While I was looking, thousands of Vṛṣṇi wives, O Brahman, pursued by Ābhīras, went, carried away by those who dwell in the land of the five rivers. (16.9.14–16)

Kṛṣṇa's departure is "incredible," "unbelievable," and, as such, a test of faith. Completely despondent *(parinirviṇṇa)*, disoriented,[198] Arjuna asks Vyāsa to instruct him (22–24). Making now his last speech within the inner frame of the *Mahābhārata*'s "main story," Vyāsa has two messages.

First, deepening the epic's theodicy, he explains that the destruction comes from the Ṛṣis' curse; yet more important,

> It was overlooked *(upekṣitam)* by Kṛṣṇa even though he was able to negate it. Indeed, to do otherwise he might check *(prasahed anyathā kartum)* the whole triple world of the stationary and moving. What then the curse of the insightful ones? He who went in front of your chariot holding the cakra and mace out of affection for you is the ancient Ṛṣi, the four-armed Vāsudeva. Having achieved the removal of the broad earth's load, O broad-eyed one, bringing release to the whole universe, he is gone himself to the highest station. (26c–29)

We are reminded that Vasudeva, using similar language, wondered how his son, "the lord of the universe," could have "overlooked" the slaughter of his own kinsmen (7.11). But even from the moment of the Ṛṣis' curse, and with language that anticipates both Vasudeva's agony and Vyāsa's closure, "the lord of the universe *(jagataḥ prabhuḥ)* did not wish to achieve the termination otherwise" (*kṛtāntam anyathā naicchat kartum*; 2.14cd).

Mehta's reading deserves appreciation here:

> Then, for the first time, this Kṛṣṇa speaks about that other Kṛṣṇa: 'He, the Lord of the three worlds, could have prevented the disaster, but chose not to. . . .' Now that the story of the inter-play between the two, of this two-in-one, has been told, the author too relinquishes his authorial function as a servant of the Goddess of Speech and reverts

[197] 16.9.14d: *kṛṣṇavinākṛtaḥ*. One might ask, by whom would he have been so "made"?

[198] "Hearing that Viṣṇu is gone, even the four directions confuse me" (*śrutvaiva hi gataṃ viṣṇuṃ mamāpi mumuhur diśaḥ*; 16.9.23cd).

> to his proper status as a Muni, one who meditates in silence. By virtue of his creative imagination . . . he gave shape to his narrative and to his characters, with only Kṛṣṇa as the reality transcending his authorial grasp, not at his disposal. (1990, 110)

Mehta is right to feel that this is the first time Vyāsa speaks "about that other Kṛṣṇa" in a certain way. Perhaps we could say it is with finality and interpretation. But it is hardly the first time he speaks about him. As we have seen, one of his incessant reiterations, indeed, interventions, is to keep reminding characters and readers that Arjuna and Kṛṣṇa are Nara and Nārāyaṇa. What Vyāsa says here for the first time *himself* (Gāndhārī and Uttaṅka say it elsewhere)[199] is that, had Kṛṣṇa chosen, he could have prevented disaster. But as usual, he leaves a loophole. He says Kṛṣṇa could have prevented the destruction of the Vṛṣṇis,[200] but unlike Gāndhārī and Uttaṅka, he does not say whether or not Kṛṣṇa could have prevented the destruction of the Kurus. Nor is it enough to say that Kṛṣṇa transcends the author's grasp and is not at his disposal. Yes, as a necessary grounding of the text in a transcendent reality; as a "reality effect"; as a conventional bhakti statement that destiny lies in divine hands; as an authorly disavowal of ultimate accountability, and a way of letting him say his story is an act of god, and thus absolutely true. Vyāsa cannot say "I made it all up!"[201] But also, no. Kṛṣṇa *is* at Vyāsa's disposal. As with so many other characters from Bhīṣma on, the author has just disposed of him. Moreover, although the passage marks a parting of the ways for author and god, it is not ultimate. In the *Nārāyaṇīya*, when Vaiśampāyana explains Vyāsa's relationship to Nārāyaṇa, he says, "Know that Kṛṣṇa Dvaipāyana Vyāsa is Nārāyaṇa the lord, for who other than the lord could be the author of the *Mahābhārata*" (*mahābhāratakṛd bhavet*; 12.334.9)?

Second, Vyāsa once again moves the story along. He tells Arjuna that, now that he and his brothers have done the gods' great work (16.9.30–31ab),

> The time is come for going. To my mind that is surely best. Strength, intellect, energy, and foresight, O Bhārata, arise when times of well-being come to nought in reversal. All this has its root in time, the seed of the universe, Dhanaṃjaya. Time alone takes everything away again

[199]Gāndhārī (11.25.36–42), charging (thrice) that Kṛṣṇa "overlooked" *(upekṣita)* the Kurus whose destruction he could have prevented; similarly Uttaṅka (14.52.20–22).
[200]As Kṛṣṇa says in confirmation of Gāndhārī's curse, "the destroyer of the circle of Vṛṣṇis is none other than myself" (*saṃhartā vṛṣṇicakrasya nānyo mad vidyate*; 11.25.44ab).
[201]See above, nn. 19 and 137, on the limits of *Mbh* fiction.

> also by chance *(yadṛcchayā)*. . . . It is time for you to go the foremost way, O Bhārata. I think that is surely supremely best for you, Bhārata bull. (16.9.31c–33, 36)

This "word of the unlimitedly splendored Vyāsa" (37ab) is a reminder to Arjuna of something that we know that he already knew when he arrived in Dvārakā:[202] it is time for the Pāṇḍavas' great departure. The *Mausalaparvan* closes with Arjuna's return to Hāstanipurā to relay all this to Yudhiṣṭhira.

Here too, however, it is not quite enough to say Vyāsa is henceforth silent. Through two more books of the *Mahābhārata*, Vaiśampāyana and Ugraśravas continue to recount his "entire thought."[203] What he has told Arjuna is really directed at Yudhiṣṭhira, who will be the focus of the last two books. As Buddhadeva Bose perceives, Arjuna, who has heard little of what actually happened at Prabhāsa, can tell Yudhiṣṭhira no more than the minimum. But Yudhiṣṭhira reads the whole. Suddenly decisive, it is his story from now to the end (Bose 1986, 171–74). Of the two parts of Vyāsa's last speech, the first brings closure to Arjuna's role as Kṛṣṇa's great bhakta. The second is the author's last indirect message to Yudhiṣṭhira, whom he now entrusts to take over the rest of the story with the final tests of his lifelong education.

Tracking Vyāsa in this fashion, especially along with Yudhiṣṭhira and Arjuna and in relation to Kṛṣṇa, one familiarizes oneself with recurrent emplotted patterns and themes. A clear epic-long pattern is that while the deity and author work together, the god deals primarily with Arjuna and the author with Yudhiṣṭhira.[204] Even in this last scene where Vyāsa addresses Arjuna (something rare, in fact), his real message is to Yudhiṣṭhira. Into these patterns are woven themes: vedic and epic intertextualities; tensions between author and characters; unsettling and antiphonal portrayals of character, including that of the "real hero" and "real king," or if one insists, the two "real heroes"; overlap between author and deity; rhythms of concealment and disclosure. These themes are carried along by compositional conventions that are built into the text: mirror effects, enigmas, including enigma verses; questions, including ones left unanswered;[205] an author convention, or function, if you will;

[202]See above at n. 187.

[203]He also speaks "outside the text" in the *Bhārata Sāvitrī* (see chap. 8, beginning).

[204]Cf. Sutton 2000, 318, on Yudhiṣṭhira's "repeated insistence on placing moral ethics above those of *svadharma*"—in particular Kṣatriya svadharma, as preached by Kṛṣṇa to Arjuna in they *Gītā* (296), and as exemplified in Duryodhana (305-8; cf. Gitomer 1992). Sutton notes "a sympathy on the part of the authors for the goodness of Yudhiṣṭhira" (320), which, we might add, is communicated through "the author."

[205]See especially chap. 7.

the divine eye by which the author, like the deity, can know everything—above all the thoughts of his characters, and which only the author and deity ever impart to others;[206] the author's intervention in his characters' thoughts; his "quick" disposals of characters, especially Kaurava widows; his "grace," which converges with the deity's, doubled especially in giving us the *Bhagavad Gītā*; tropes of instruction via dialogue and narrative; messages especially to a king about grief and cruelty by an author who has griefs and cruelties of his own—among them, the spaces and moments he creates for this king and others to ponder the cruel and wondrous ways of God; perspectival inversions of time and space; signifiers of reversible time like the wink, blink, or moment (the *nimeṣa*) and the interval *(antaram)*; double structures of recursivity and deferral, contingency and determinism, finality and unfinalizability. As we are drawn into the mechanics of the text, slow dramas like these, dramas of the text itself, can be a reader's delight.

[206]Nārada also has the divine eye (§ C.37), as does Śuka (12.315.28; see chap. 8), and the Ṛṣi Kaṇva knows with his what Śakuntalā has been up to (1.67.24d; Mangels 1994, 135). None of these seem to impart it to others. And Yudhiṣṭhira wins his on his own (§ C.28).

3 Conventions of the Naimiṣa Forest

Vyāsa's comings and goings from his "hermitage somewhere" have started us thinking about the *Mahābhārata*'s outermost frame. We have also begun to understand some things about the inner frame, having located Janamejaya's snake sacrifice at the historically and geographically incongruous site of Takṣaśilā,[1] and noticed how Vaiśampāyana's recitation there knits together seven lunar dynasty generations from the author as progenitor to his distant descendant and "first audience," King Janamejaya himself. Between these two frames, however, is what I call the outer frame, which has the possibility of telling us more than we yet know about the other two. Let us establish a few working definitions. The first frame, which I call the outermost, can also be called the authorial frame, in that it allows the author to move in and out of the spatio-temporal constraints and possibilities of his text. The second, the inner frame, can also be called the historical or genealogical frame. It is a linear frame (the main story of a dynasty through seven generations) in which the author is present not only to sire the second generation, but to hear his story told to Janamejaya five generations later. The third, the outer (and now also "middle") frame, can also be called the cosmological frame, as it will be the task of this chapter and the next to show. It is this "middle frame," set in the Naimiṣa Forest, that is most *pivotal* to the chronotope through which the *Mahābhārata*'s fuses its "spatial and temporal indicators."[2]

It is well known that the *Mahābhārata* is recited at the Naimiṣa Forest, and that many purāṇas likewise make this spot both the gathering place

[1]See chap. 1 at n. 47. At least that is where the poets locate it when they close the inner frame, having Janamejaya return from there to Hāstinapura when the rite is stopped (18.5.29). In the *Ādiparvan*, however, nothing is said of this location, and it looks there like the rite would have occurred somewhere near Hāstinapura (see 1.3.177; 1.47.9–10).
[2]Bakhtin 1981, 101, as quoted in chap. 2, above n. 20.

for storytelling and the frame story for the occasion of doing so. We will now consider the gathering place and the frame story as two interrelated *Mahābhārata* "conventions." Indeed, Thapar anticipates our usage, observing that the setting of purāṇa recitation at the uncertainly located Naimiṣa Forest "may be just a convention."[3]

A. Narrative Conventions and Symposia

The frame story has been noticed at its possible inception in the Brāhmaṇas by Witzel (1986, 1987c), in its great unfolding in the *Mahābhārata* by Minkowski (1989), as a feature of the epic's literary composition by Sukthankar (1936, 72), or its written redaction by Mangels,[4] Oberlies,[5] and Reich.[6] Both Witzel and Minkowski suggest that this device may have its origins in India, which I regard as highly unlikely,[7] though it is certainly the case that Indian epic and postepic usages of it influenced other usages in the world's literatures.[8] In any

[3]Thapar 1991, 10 and n. 36. For a preliminary statement on these matters, see Hiltebeitel 1998a. For purāṇic unfoldings, see Pargiter [1922] 1997, 305: in *Vāyu Purāṇa* 2.14–23, Purūravas "coveted the golden sacrificial floor of the rishis of Naimiṣa forest and was killed by them"; Hiltebeitel 1999a, 90 n. 7, 220, 265–66, 281, 285–93.

[4]Mangels 1994, 42–44, diagrams the frames as a "box-structure" *(Schachtelstruktur)*, and draws on Bailey's (1986, 4) differentiation of horizontal-sytagmatic and vertical-paradagmatic axes for purāṇic frames to distinguish a purāṇic style from the *Mbh*'s. As "a dialogic structure upon which the entire narrative can be hung" (Bailey 1987–88, 31; Mangels, 85), the purāṇic horizontal axis supplies an "architechtonic framework for the *surface* of the text" (Bailey 1986, 4 [my italics]; Mangels, 85) to accommodate loosely if not arbitrarily connected vertical-paradigmatic elements; but in the *Mbh* such a paradigmatic element, while not lacking, applies only to narrative and didactic digressions (86–88, 92). Yet Mangels sees the epic's frame structure affected by late purāṇic "corrections" (144).

[5]Oberlies makes the frame stories superficial—something I do not see in Mangels (whom he ignores) or Minkowski, and in any case disagree with myself. For Oberlies, the outer frame or "first dialogue level" is part of a re-"surfacing" of the text, one that, with its setting at a sattra sacrifice, reorients it toward Vedic ritual and provides a Brahmanized "roundcoating" *(Unmantelung)* of the epic by the same late author of the *Nārāyaṇīya* who "ritualizes" elsewhere in the name of Nārada. Seeing the outer frame as a "horizontal" arrangement linked with a "vertical" one whose ground principle is "emboxing" *(Einschachtelung)*, he suggests that framing in its entirety would not have been a feature of the "'old' narrative" (1998, 128, 138, 140–41). Cf. chap. 1, n. 14; chap. 2 n. 41; n. 4 above on Bailey and Mangels; and Grünendahl 1997, 240.

[6]Reich shows that Minkowski's notion of the frame structure as "the source of the epic's growth" (Minkowski 1989, 406) can be "misleading" (Reich 1998, 61), and distinguishes usefully between the frames and other devices for expansion (1998, 56–75).

[7]Plato uses frame stories in the *Timaeus*; see Derrida 1998, and below, chap. 8 § B.

[8]See Witzel 1986, 205–11; 1987c for Vedic precedents, especially in *JB*, of "ring composition" (1987c, 411), emboxing stories within stories, and even double frames (404), and Minkowski, suggesting (1989, 412–13) that as a literary device, the frame convention may have been passed on into other Indian texts (cf. R. M. Smith 1953, 282–83) and on

case, as both observe,[9] it is likely that uses of the frame convention in the Sanskrit epics relate to the special attention given in India to the structured embeddedness of Brahmanic ritual,[10] one feature of which is that the *intervals* of certain rites—notably the year-long Aśvamedha[11]—were a time designated for the telling of stories. Rituals that embox other rituals around a central rite could thus also enframe stories that enframe other stories. And this could be done in reverse, as narratives could enframe rituals. As Witzel shows, this is one way to think about how a story about rituals in the Brāhmaṇas also emboxes other stories (1987c, 413–14). More complexly, the *Mahābhārata* makes the technique "self-referential" and turns it into one of literary composition: "An epic frame story is more than embedded: it is the story about the telling of another story" (Minkowski 1989, 402).

For Minkowski, there are only two frames in the *Mahābhārata*: our inner and outer ones. Not conceiving of an outermost authorial frame, he considers our outer frame to be the "highest, most inclusive frame" (1989, 407). But he exerts his greatest ingenuity on the inner frame of Janamejaya's snake sacrifice, and the persuasive hypothesis, already noted, that as a sacrifice of a type called *sattra*—a "sitting" or seated "session"—it supplies not only the intervals in which Vaiśampāyana recites, but a ritual source and model for the literary framing device that the epic poets deploy.

But what about the outer frame of the Naimiṣa Forest, where Śaunaka and the sages are again performing a sattra? Is it no more than an allusion to an old site of Vedic sattra sacrifices (see Minkowski 1989, 416 and n. 72)? As Minkowski vividly puts it, the *Mahābhārata* plays "what may appear to be a dangerous game" by having two frames, and thus posing the "threat of an infinite regression."[12] For if, as he says, a frame story "is a story about the telling of another story" (1989, 402), and if the story about Ugraśravas recitation at the Naimiṣa Forest "answers the simple question: who is telling the story of Vaiśampāyana?" (406), the question of infinite regression—that is, who tells the story of Ugraśravas?—is left unresolved and open. As Minkowski sees it, although "the presence of Ugraśravas is felt throughout the epic" in every scene describing exchanges between Vaiśampāyana and Janamejaya (405), the

into world literature. In such a vein, the folklorist Theodor Benfey (1801–91) could imagine India as the "home of story-telling and of tale-types" (Claus and Korom 1991, 56–57).

[9]Minkowski 1989, 413–20; 1991, 385–91; cf. Witzel 1987c, 410, 413.

[10]See also Staal [1990] 1996, 85–114.

[11]Karmarkar 1952; Hazra 1955; Dumont 1927, 44–49. It is during intervals in his Aśvamedha that Rāma hears the *Rām* from his twin sons Kuśa and Lava; see chap. 8.

[12]1989, 404, 406; cf. Mehta 1990, 101–2; Shulman 1991a, 12.

poets stop short of asking who recounts exchanges between Ugraśravas and Śaunaka.[13] Rather, "The infinite regression is the image of the transmission of the story through history" (421). But why the image of transmission through history? I believe a better preliminary image would be a message in a bottle.

Minkowski underestimates the outer frame, considering it "brief and insubstantial" and "much less carefully elaborated and much less organically connected with the Bhārata story" than the Janamejaya frame (1989, 407, 405). Yet he formulates a philosophical conclusion that is of some interest: "But it is also true that in an ideological system that includes an absolute transcendent reality, nothing can regress indefinitely. It must always end up striking bottom. It appears to me that the attribution of the story to Vyāsa, and setting the story in the Naimiṣa forest, serve the purpose of fixing the text at a level beyond which, as the texts say, one can go no further" (420). But here again, I think the image is misleading. The Naimiṣa Forest does not fix the text at a level beyond which one can go no further. It supplies a location that is not fixed at all but rather bottomless and open.[14] Moreover, Minkowski leaves us in the dark as to what he sees as the connection between this alleged "fixing" and "the attribution of the story to Vyāsa."

But let us not get ahead of ourselves. Realizing that the site of this potentially infinite regression is the Naimiṣa Forest, let us ask where the *Mahābhārata*'s likely innovation of this literary convention brings us. Though few have given it much thought, Naimiṣa is a forest with a give-away name: "lasting for a moment, a twinkling" (from *nimeṣa*, *nimiṣa*, a moment or wink). Biardeau has caught a sense of it: "The name of this place, a proper one for sacrificial activity, derives from *nimeṣa*, the

[13]Much of the interaction between Ugraśravas and Śaunaka occurs in the epic's opening *parvans* through the *Āstīkaparvan* as segue to the Janamejaya frame, and in the *Nārāyaṇīya* (Oberlies 1998, 138). But the poets sometimes remind us that Śaunaka is listening, as when Ugraśravas tells Śaunaka how Vyāsa fulfills Janamejaya's request to show him his deceased father Parikṣit (see chap. 2, § B.40). Śaunaka is mentioned with one last vocative at the epic's end (18.5.44) in a verse that a southern Grantha manuscript precedes with an outer frame-closing exit story: Śaunaka and all the "Naimiśeya Maharṣis" are mentally thrilled (*prahṛṣṭamanasa 'bhavan*). They honor the sūta, who circumambulates the "maṇḍala of Munis," blessing cows and Brahmans. The sages pronounce the work "well" or "accurately said" (*saṃyaguktam*), honor the seer-singer-poet (*vipram*; apparently Ugraśravas; perhaps Vyāsa), and each, delighted, goes to his own home (18, App. 1, No. 2, lines 11–22; cf. Minkowski 1989, 405, n. 16).

[14]Minkowski does not explain why or how the story's setting at Naimiṣa Forest fixes the text at a transcendent level. Cf. Oberlies 1998, 140, for whom the outer frame's "fixing" of the text is but a late literary closure. Here the text-critical method claims the opposite of what the outer frame actually does: rather than fix an outer form, it opens the possibility of an endless drop, a game even more dangerous than the one envisioned by Minkowski.

'blink of an eye,' and has the primary meaning of 'momentary,' 'transitory'" (1999, 1750; my translation). But this primary meaning would seem to apply less to sacrificial activity as such than to what goes on in the *intervals* of sacrifices: the telling of stories. Let us also consider Giorgio Bonazzoli's terms: if, as he suggests, the Naimiṣa Forest is not so much a place as a process through which more ancient purāṇa is "absorbed into a new stream" for the Kali yuga,[15] then the name Naimiṣa might suggest that the stream connects past, present, and future in the twinkling of the eye. The *Mahābhārata*'s Naimiṣa Forest might be thought of as the "Momentous Forest," or even the "Forest of Literary Imagination,"[16] the forest where bards like the "hair-raising" Lomaharṣaṇa and his "frightful-to-hear" son Ugraśravas[17] can enchant Brahman Ṛṣis: a "momentous" forest where stories, to put it simply, transcend time and defy ordinary conceptions of space.

The dizzying outer frame thus points beyond itself. When Minkowski argues that with the deepening of the frames, we move from Janamejaya's interest in "the content of the main story" to the sages' interest in "the ontological status of the epic" (404), this can only be a pointer. As already suggested, the concern of the Naimiṣeya Ṛṣis is more cosmological than ontological. It is the outermost authorial frame that defines the epic's ontology around the status of the "entire thought" of the author. Minkowski tosses in "the attribution of the story to Vyāsa" without examining it, implying that it is no more than a corollary to the outer frame's Naimiṣa Forest setting. But it is something more.

We shall, of course, never really know whether the *Mahābhārata* poets established a naimiṣa convention in this precise semantic sense. The terms *nimeṣa* and *nimiṣa* (wink/blink/moment) are, however, used widely in the text with metaphorical and theological power,[18] and there is a philosoph-

[15]1981, 49, 52–61; his historicization of this evolution as an "enthusiastic movement" of missionary Ṛṣis spreading out from Naimiṣa and Kurukṣetra to give shape to the *Mbh* and purāṇas at the beginning of the Kali yuga (58–59) is, however, pure whimsy.

[16]Rajan observes the temporal fluidity of the tales told at Naimiṣa (1995, xxii) and the "array of literary devices" used by Vyāsa and his disciples there "with superb artistry: flashbacks, prophesies, the curse, recollection (remembrance or smaraṇa) and recognition. These devices serve to effect a fusion of time, to bring time past and time future into the present moment" (xxxiii). But Rajan does not perceive the connection between the devices and the name of the location.

[17]These are meanings of their names.

[18]E.g., 5.195.8–11: with a glance at Kṛṣṇa, Arjuna says that, joined with him on their one chariot, he could destroy the three worlds, three times, and all beings "in the blink of an eye" *(nimeṣād)*; 3.36.1–6: Yudhiṣṭhira, says Bhīma, while the Pāṇḍavas wait idly in the forest, is a mortal bound by time who has made a compact *(saṃdhi)* with time/death that brings their lives closer to death with every blink; 15.33.23–27: Vidura's unblinking death as he dissolves into Yudhiṣṭhira; 14.45.1 (the moment as the "foundation" or "diameter"

ical context in which to look further into the text's ontology.[19] But for now, it is perhaps best to share Sukthankar's impression that the poets are winking at us,[20] and turn to another sense in which the *Mahābhārata* establishes a Naimiṣa convention: the sense of convention as "convocation," as with the convention of bard and sages at Naimiṣa Forest that rounds off the epic's telling. To keep the distinction clear and not wear out the pun, I will henceforth call the first type the convention of the receding frame,[21] and the second the symposium. It is worth noting that this second sense (if not also the first) was appreciated in medieval Tamil. Amid the series of floods that are followed by the founding of the Tamil Caṅkams (Saṅgams, Tamil Literary Academies) of Madurai, we learn that after one such deluge, at the redrawing of the city's boundaries by the serpent Ādiśeṣa, "the Vedas, newly emerged from the *praṇava* [the syllable Oṃ] after a universal destruction, are expounded to the sages of the Naimiṣa Forest in Maturai"![22] Naimiṣa conventions and symposia thus move the Vedic revelation not only through both time and geographical space, but through texts in different languages.

B. The *Mahābhārata*'s First Two Beginnings

Aside from brief and allusive references,[23] the Naimiṣa Forest is described seven times in the *Mahābhārata* as the site of significant ritual

[*viṣkambha*] of the wheel of time [1–12 for the full allegory]); 7.51.17 and 15.4.18–21 (unblinkingly "staring death in the face"). Other instances will be cited.

[19]I would look to what the *Mbh* does with yoga—a vast topic (to begin with see Hopkins 1901; Bedekar 1966; Larson and Bhattacharya 1987, 115–23; Schreiner 1999)—in relation to Buddhism and the Yoga system, which inventory the moment *(kṣaṇa)*. The *Yogabhāṣya* says the whole universe undergoes change in a single moment (*kṣaṇa*: "look" or "glance"). As in Sāṃkhya, where change occurs within the internal modification of matter, the "three times"—past, present, future—have no reality of their own (Balslev 1983, 48–53). *Yogabhāṣya* 3.52 thus rejects the notion that time as such is a real entity (Halbfass 1992, 216 and n. 66). Moments have objective reality, but a time-continuum is a mental construction *(buddhi-nirmāṇa)* (Balslev 1993, 173). The adept seeks to become aware of all the constituents of the perception of the moment in order to inventory the contents of consciousness and isolate the soul. The *Mbh*, however, fuses yoga with bhakti, making its author and deity masters of yoga who unify Time, save souls, and can envision their "entire thought" as a divine plan in which they can intervene. Note *Mbh* 14.48.3: the nimeṣa as the interval for the yogin's self-realization. See Hiltebeitel and Kloetzli forthcoming.

[20]Sukthankar actually has Kṛṣṇa winking, not the poets—and at "European savants"; and it is not exactly a wink but his "inscrutable mask" as "the Unknowable pulling faces at them, and enjoying their antics" (1957, 25). Let us for once leave such differences aside. . . .

[21]See O'Flaherty 1984, 197–205; cf. 1988, 147–53; White 1991, 74 and 246, n. 9.

[22]Shulman 1980, 69 and 370, n. 95. On flood myths linked with eras and changing precessional orientations, cf. W. Sullivan 1996, 9–45, 128–31, 204–5, 351–54.

[23]The most important of which is reference to Naimiṣa in the story of the Brahman who learns the merits of gleaning from the snake king Padmanābha (chap. 1, § C), which, as we shall see in chap. 4, probably alludes to another sattra there.

gatherings or symposia. The fifth, which may be momentarily set aside, finds King Yayāti, the Kaurava ancestor, bounced from heaven for a moment of sinful pride. Permitted to choose to fall "among the good *(pateyaṃ satsu)*," he makes his way to Naimiṣa Forest by descending the Gaṅgā-like river of smoke that he has seen rising from the Vājapeya sacrifice of his four grandsons (5.119.8–14). Dumézil takes the "good" to be Yayāti's grandsons themselves (1973, 31), but they would probably also include the Naimiṣas or Naimiṣeyas (people? Brahmans? Ṛṣis? of Naimiṣa Forest), who are among the "good" *(santo)* and "distinguished" *(viśiṣṭāḥ)* in a passage that contrasts them with "impure" Madrakas (8.30.61-62). That the "good" of Naimiṣa would be forest-dwelling Brahmans is consonant with the other passages, as well as with the epic's shorter references to this place. This is the only passage that shows Naimiṣa Forest to be the venue of a royal sacrifice by Kṣatriyas; in the others, the rites—always sattra sacrifices—are by Brahmans, or in one case by gods.[24] I will consider these six passages in their textual order, the first two in this section, the others in section D, hoping to show that they are illumined by the questions we are asking.

The first two, which open the *Mahābhārata*, are very different descriptions of the same event: coming from Janamejaya's snake sacrifice, Ugraśravas arrives at Naimiṣa Forest to recite the *Mahābhārata* to Śaunaka and the sages.[25] It is the intriguing problem of the double introduction of the *Mahābhārata*, which is compounded by the complex question of the so-called Bhṛguization of the text, since Śaunaka, a Bhṛgu or Bhārgava Brahman, shows himself, but only the second time, to be especially interested that Ugraśravas begin his narration with a cycle of Bhārgava tales. It is Sukthankar's tour de force on "The Bhṛgus and the Bhārata" (1936) that poses these two sets of issues—the double introduction and the question of Bhṛguization—as inseparable and indispensable to his consideration of the formation of the *Mahābhārata*.[26] In discussing the second passage, we must consider Sukthankar's important thesis. But first things first.

[24]One of the seven passages mentions another sattra as precedent for a sattra that follows a prior one at Naimiṣa (9.40.26–27); it takes place not at Naimiṣa itself but at a tīrtha where the river Sarasvatī appears as she does at Naimiṣa; see § D below.

[25]As observed in chap. 1 at n. 50, Yardi allows this trip five hundred years between Vaiśampāyana's primary "text" (ca. 950 B.C.) and the Sauti-Ugraśravas' "text" (ca. 450 B.C.); Vaidya allows over two thousand five hundred years.

[26]The double introduction is a textual problem, and not to be confused with the bard's statement in his first beginning that there are three places in the *Ādiparvan* from which Brahmans *(viprāḥ)* "learn" *(adhīyate)* the *Bhārata* (1.1.50)—a statement often twisted to say that the three would be optional bardic beginnings (e.g., van Buitenen 1973, 1) or stages in composition (Jani 1990, 73–75; Bhattacharji 1992–93, 469).

1. Version one of Ugraśravas' arrival (1.1.1–26), which truly begins the epic, opens with a motherlode of coded gestures and textually recurrent formulae:[27] "Lomaharṣaṇa's son Ugraśravas, a sūta (bard) and paurāṇika, approached the strict-vowed Brahman Ṛṣis seated in Naimiṣa Forest at the twelve-year sattra of Śaunaka, the leader of the group *(kulapater)*" (1.1.1–2b). Whatever *kulapati* means, I take it that Śaunaka is the "leader of the group" of Brahman sages at Naimiṣa Forest, and thus begin with this minimal translation. At the bard's arrival, "the Naimiṣa Forest-dwelling ascetics gathered round there to hear wonderful stories *(citrāḥ śrotum kathās)*" (3). It is thus established from the start that the Naimiṣa ascetics *(tapasvinaḥ)* are Brahman Ṛṣis *(brahmarṣīn)*, to whom Ugraśravas must make a proper bow *(vinayāvanato bhūtvā)* and fold his palms *(kṛtāñjali)* before they invite him to sit down—which he does only after they have reseated themselves first (4–6). Now when hosts seat themselves first, they are not treating their guest with much respect. Thapar puts the problem before us archly in discussing the "ambivalence" one senses in purāṇic texts as to whether purāṇic composition "should be ascribed to *brāhmaṇ* authorship or to the bards and chroniclers": Lomaharṣaṇa, who is said to have taught the purāṇa tradition to six Brahman disciples and his son Ugraśravas, was "of course not a *brāhmaṇ*"; his son Ugraśravas, "being a bard, recited it for a living" (1984, 136). The *Mahābhārata* passages under discussion are an earlier expression of this ambivalence and a source of its purāṇic unfoldings. But in this epic-opening passage, despite the room it leaves for tension between hosts and guest, Brahmans and bard, they are on the most cordial terms.[28]

Ugraśravas now relates that he comes from Janamajaya's snake sacrifice, where he has heard the various auspicious stories "told" *(kathitāḥ)* by Vaiśampāyana that had been (first) "proclaimed" *(proktāḥ)* by Kṛṣṇa Dvaipāyana (Vyāsa) (1.1.9). As Minkowski shows, in cases like this where the *Mahābhārata* uses forms of the verbs *kath* or *kathay* and *pra* + *vac* together, "they appear to convey different notions of spokesmanship": whereas *kathay* is "nearly a *Mahābhārata* neologism," meaning "narrate" or "tell," *pra* + *vac/proktaḥ*, with its Vedic over-

[27]On oral and written formula, see discussion of Grintser above, chap. 1, above n. 88. Cf. Mehta 1973, 547: "The interesting feature of the beginning of the epic is the two identical introductions in the form of formula-like prose headings in adhy. 1 and adhy. 4." Actually, the first sixteen syllables in each opening are identical, after which identical phrases are differently positioned. The poets thus deploy formulas not only in epic verse but prose.

[28]Nonetheless, to get the sense of deference which Brahmans might expect from a sūta, one should read how Ganguli *over*translates the "humility" with which Ugraśravas bows and "humbly" takes his seat ([1884–96] 1970, 1:1). I thank R. Venkataraman for opening my eyes to the dynamics of these Brahman-bard interactions.

tones, has "the sense of an original utterance" (1989, 402, 411-12). Having heard these stories "of varied import, inherent to the *Mahābhārata*" *(vicitrārthā mahābhāratasaṃśritāḥ)*,[29] Ugraśravas has since wandered over many tīrthas and sanctuaries, including Samantapañcaka (= Kurukṣetra) where the *Mahābhārata* war was fought, wishing to see the Naimiṣa sages whom he considers to be *brahman* itself (10-12).[30] Seeing that the sages have completed various ritual acts of their *sattra* and are now seated at ease (13)—Minkowski is probably right to suggest that Ugraśravas here "has not disrupted the rite, but rather has arrived at an interval within it" (1989, 404)—he asks the sages what they want to hear, and they ask for the "ancient lore proclaimed *(proktam purāṇam)* by the supreme Ṛṣi *(paramarṣi)* Dvaipāyana, which was revered (or "approved": *abhipūjitam*) by the gods and Brahman Ṛṣis when they heard it" (15).

Here we come to a turning point. As the Naimiṣa sages state their request, it is clear that their appetite is not only for the "wonderful" stories "of varied import, inherent to the *Mahābhārata*" that Ugraśravas has offered them:

> We wish to hear that wonderworker Vyāsa's collection *(saṃhitā)* of the *Bhārata*, the history *(itihāsa)*, that most excellent communication *(ākhyānavariṣṭha)*, diversified in quarter-lines and sections *(vicitrapadaparvan)*, with subtle meanings combined with logic *(sūkṣmārthanyāyayukta)* and adorned with Vedic meanings *(vedārthair bhūṣita)*, which the Ṛṣi Vaiśampāyana properly recited with delight at the sattra of Janamejaya by Dvaipāyana's command—holy, connected with the meanings of books *(granthārthasaṃyuta)*, furnished with refinement *(saṃskāropagata)*, sacred, supported by various Śāstras *(nānāśāstropabṛṃhita)*, equalled by the four Vedas, productive of virtue, and dispelling of the fear of sin. (1.1.16-19)

Let us appreciate how accurately this opening salvo describes the *Mahābhārata*: in particular the audience's intertextual (including especially Vedic textual) interests.[31] Granted that it was proclaimed by Vyāsa and narrated by Vaiśampāyana, what the Ṛṣis want to hear is

[29]On *saṃśrita* in both epics' usage as "inherent to, peculiar to," see MW, 1118. Van Buitenen's "that form part of *The Mahābhārata*" (1973, 20) is misleading. Cf. Shulman 1991a, 10: "relating to the *Mahābhārata*."

[30]Following Minkowski 1989, 404; Ganguli ([1884-96] 1970, 1:1), Dutt (1895-1905, 1:1), and van Buitenen (1973, 20), also plausibly, take *brahmabhūtā hi me matāḥ* as referring to the sages being considered as Brahmā.

[31]Cf. Fitzgerald 1980, 7-8, 14; 1991, 163-64.

something that has clearly passed through the hands of such Brahmans as themselves and taken its place among "books." Indeed, Ugraśravas soon confirms that the *Mahābhārata* weighs more on a scale than the four Vedas (1.1.208), which suggests a written book. It is the Brahman Ṛṣis of Naimiṣa Forest, not the bard, who are in charge of this composition. The "bard" and all the others who figure in the epic's three frames are fictions of the text: fictions, let me propose, of real Brahman authors who must have enjoyed creating them in some complex image of themselves.[32] Of course it is nothing new to argue that the double introduction reflects Brahman redaction.[33] But without establishing that we can talk about *all Mahābhārata* characters as fictional ones in a work of fiction, we resign ourselves to a hopeless and nonsensical deadlock.[34] The poets have provided us not only with a fictional author, but *two* "unreliable narrators"[35] as its oral performers.

Ugraśravas now begins. Or more accurately, he makes his first beginning. His actual storytelling opens with a cosmogony that builds to "a somewhat austere vision" of the wheel of life, and a resume of the *Mahābhārata* that culminates in the insight that time "cooks all creatures."[36] But before the storytelling he lauds the highest gods with "some *mangala* stanzas" (Sukthankar 1936, 59) and announces, "I will proclaim the thought entire of the infinitely splendid Vyāsa *(pravakṣyāmi matam kṛtsnaṃ vyāsasyāmitatejasaḥ)*. Some poets *(kavayaḥ)* have told it before, others tell it now, and others too will tell this history *(itihāsa)* on earth. It is indeed a great knowledge established in the three worlds that is held (or "possessed": *dhāryate*) by the twiceborn in its particulars and totalities *(vistaraiś ca samāsaiḥ)*" (23–25).

Since sūtas are not twiceborn *(dvija)*, the bard has made it explicit that the *Mahābhārata* belongs to the Brahmans, and no matter who the "poets" are who will continue to tell it on earth, they will henceforth have to get it ultimately from them. Yet what Ugraśravas recites—"Vyāsa's thought entire"—is something rather fine. We soon learn that Vaiśampāyana had earlier impressed Janamejeya twice, in the

[32]See chap. 1 at n. 79.

[33]See Sukthankar 1936, 68–70; Mehta 1973; and Fitzgerald 1991, 163–65, who notes that Śaunaka and his co-sattrins are "cleverly" made to appear ignorant of military matters, which, as will become clear, can hardly be the case. Cf. Shende 1943, 68, 73, 80–81; Goldman 1977, 140, on the *Mbh* as a Brahman vehicle for "control of the past." Cf. Biardeau and Péterfalvi 1985, 26–32.

[34]I make this point via Gellrich 1985, 26. On fiction, cf. chap. 2, § A.

[35]See Booth 1983, 158–59, 271–74, 295–96. Of course, in being able to tell the author's thought entire, they become his omniscient narrators, as do Saṃjaya, Bhīṣma, and various Ṛṣis; see chap. 2, § C.

[36]Cf. Shulman 1991a, 11 on this passage, *Mbh* 1.1.27–190. Cf. chap. 2, n. 25.

company of Vyāsa himself, with the very same words: "I will proclaim the thought entire of the infinitely splendid Vyāsa" (1.55.2 and 1.56.12). But we have only Ugraśravas' report of this (from the outer frame) to rely on. "Vyāsa's thought entire" can never be handed over entirely. As something prior and superabundant to the text—it includes not only all purāṇa but the entire Veda, and may be considered as this epic's term for its own primary process.[37] With it, we may have one more hint that as the place where Vyāsa's "whole thought" is now so fully at play and so universally promulgated, the Naimiṣa Forest is a poetic convention for the conditions in which the epic's real poets, Brahmans, attune themselves to this interplay between the "whole thought" of Vyāsa, which the bard relays to them, and the words that the Brahman Ṛṣis supposedly hear, which real Brahman poets would have transmuted into writing.

2. Version two of Ugraśravas' arrival (1.4.1–5.6) opens, as several have noted, with virtually the same prose lines as version one.[38] But things quickly take a different turn: one that, as far as I know, has drawn no comment. Ugraśravas folds his palms as before. But now, rather than showing deference with a bow and a courteous pause to let his hosts resume their seats before sitting down himself, he asks (more briefly) what the sages want to hear, and is greeted with a deferral which seems rather haughty:

> Very well, son of Lomaharṣaṇa. We will ask you and you will tell us. Let your story repertoire be eagerly heard.[39] But meanwhile the lord Śaunaka is seated in the fire hall. He is one who knows the divine stories told about the gods and Asuras. He knows the stories of men, snakes, and Gandharvas completely *(sarvaśas)*. And at this sacrifice *(makhe)*, O Sauti, the learned one—twiceborn, skilful, firm in his vows, wise, and a guru in Śāstra and Āraṇyaka—is the lord of the

[37]On my use of this term, see Hiltebeitel in press-a and below chap. 7, § D. For now, as Śaunaka will later put it, the *Mbh* story *(kathā)* is "sprung from the great Rsi's oceanic mind *(manaḥsāgarasaṃbhūtāṃ maharṣeḥ)*" (1.53.34). Cf. Shulman 1991b, 10, who takes Vyāsa's "thought entire" as suggesting "the fluidity and open-ended quality of this text." Minkowski misses these senses in the translating *matam kṛtsnam* as "entire composition."

[38]Thus 1.1.1 (translated above) is similar to 1.4.1. See the ever-interesting Vaidya [1905] 1966, 11–12, who traces this recognition to Nīlakaṇṭha: "The commentator has seen the absurdity of these two beginnings . . . and gives the usual explanation based on the supposition of two Sutas belonging to different Kalpas." See Kinjawadekar 1929–33, 1:54. Cf. Sukthankar 1930, 182–86; 1933, lxxxvii; 1936, 59–60, 68–70, tracing recognition of Bhārgava handling to Holtzmann 1893, 2:12; Mehta 1973, 547 (discussed in n. 27 above); Yardi 1986, 7–8.

[39]1.4.3: *paramaṃ lomaharṣaṇe prakṣyāmas tvāṃ vakṣyasi ca naḥ śuśrūṣatāṃ kathāyogam.* Apparently taking *paramam* as "later," van Buitenen (1973, 55) begins, "Later we shall ask you, son of Lomaharṣaṇa . . ."—which seems to get the right sense.

group *(kulapati)*. A truth-speaker, devoted to calm, an ascetic of strict vows, he is esteemed by us all. Meanwhile he must be waited for. When this guru is seated on the most honorable seat, then you will say what the best of the twiceborn asks. (1.4.3–7)

Ugraśravas can hardly feel much esteemed at hearing that Śaunaka already knows "completely" all such stories as Ugraśravas might tell him. Rather than gathering round him to hear wonderful stories, these Naimiṣa-dwellers put such interests well behind the pompous timetable of their guru's sacrifice and the loftiness of his seat. Again, it is not clear at what point in the ritual Ugraśravas arrives. It could be that the wait here is for Śaunaka to finish the entire sacrifice: "having finished the entire ritual (or all his duty) in the proper sequence" *(kāryaṃ kṛtvā sarvaṃ yathākramam)* (1.4.9). Sukthankar takes it that Śaunaka has "duly performed his round of daily duties" (1936, 60), and I will follow that traditional interpretation.[40]

Well portrayed as "reciting for a living," Ugraśravas says, "So be it. When the great-souled guru is seated, questioned by him, I will tell meritorious stories on varied topics" (1.4.8). At last Śaunaka finishes his rites and approaches "the place of sacrifice where the perfected Brahman Ṛṣis, going in advance of the sūta's son *(sūtaputrapurahsarāḥ)*, were seated, firm in their vows. Then the leader of the sattrins *(gṛhapati)*, Śaunaka, seated among the seated priests and attendees, spoke" (10–11). Translators have given Ugraśravas a seat before the Ṛṣis here,[41] but it is clear that *purahsarāḥ* in the plural modifies the Ṛṣis who are seated before Ugraśravas. It is *not* clear whether Ugraśravas is left standing or given a seat. I assume the former, and that at some point perhaps a simple hand gesture, unrecorded in the text, invites him to relax.[42] It is clear, however, that Śaunaka—a *gṛhapati* now as well as a *kulapati*—waits to sit on his most honorable seat, which the seated priests and attendees (*sadasyas*: literally, "those seated" in the sacrificial enclosure) have kept waiting for him, before he says a word to Ugraśravas. Let us note that we have precise Vedic designations for three different types of "seated" actors at this sattra: a *gṛhapati*, literally "master of the house," primus inter pares among the sattrins (cf. Falk 1986, 34–35; White 1991, 96); the other sattrins as priests (*ṛtvij*s); and

[40]Cf. 18, App. 2, line 17: a southern interpolation also has the Naimiśeya Ṛṣis listen to the bard "in the interval(s) of the sacrificial rites *(yajñakarmāntare)*."

[41]Ganguli [1884–96] 1970, 49; Dutt 1895–1905, 29; van Buitenen 1973, 56.

[42]There are, however, bards who sing while standing: e.g., those who perform in the *burrakatha* style in Andhra Pradesh, and the Pāratiyārs (*Mbh*-reciter) and assistants at the Kūvākkam Kūttāṇṭavar festival in Tamilnadu (Hiltebeitel 1999a, 417, n. 13; 438).

the sadasyas. These terms come alive in the telling. In particular, it will become clear from the title *gṛhapati* that it has been correct to translate Śaunaka's other title *kulapati* as "leader of the group."[43]

What Śaunaka has to say now only intensifies the hauteur expressed by his group and the superfluity of the bard. "Your father, my boy *(tāta)*, formerly learned the complete purāṇa *(purāṇam akhilam)*. Have you too learned it all, son of Lomaharṣaṇa? In the purāṇa are divine stories and the original genealogies *(ādivaṃśāḥ)* of the wise. These were told before, and heard by us formerly from your father. First therein I wish to hear the Bhārgava genealogy. Tell that story. We are ready to hear you" (1.5.1–3). Instead of winding up on the high note of the "whole thought of Vyāsa," the second overture directs attention to Śaunaka's Bhārgava vaṃśa, and begins with the descent of Bhṛgu rather than the origin of the universe. Ugraśravas assures Śaunaka that he has completely learned what his father learned, which was completely learned and narrated by such great-souled Brahmins as Vaiśampāyana, and urges Śaunaka to listen to the honored Bhārgava genealogy—which Ugraśravas now lauds with divine encomiums while letting us know for the first time that it is of course Śaunaka's own genealogy—such as it is found in the purāṇa (4–6).

Again, but in shorter shrift, it is affirmed that the bard is a conduit between texts that originate with Brahmans (Vyāsa and Vaiśampāyana) and the new intertextual situation (Śāstra and Āraṇyaka) that Brahmans (represented by Śaunaka and his group) control.[44] Reduced to a convenient fiction, the bard is there to tell the Ṛṣis stories that they—wise Brahmans—already know, here, via Lomaharṣaṇa. But now we may recall that in the first opening, the sages tell Ugraśravas they wish to hear the "ancient lore proclaimed by the supreme Ṛṣi Dvaipāyana, that was revered (or 'approved') by the gods and Brahman Ṛṣis when they heard it" (15). When was this! Either way, certain sages already know the lore that the Naimiṣa Forest sages are about to hear. In the first opening, unnamed Brahmarṣis know it along with the gods; in the second, the Naimiṣeya Ṛṣis know it through the bard's father. One cannot say whether we have two different prior Ṛṣi audiences here, or one. What one can say is that, whereas Janamejaya has something to learn from his listening to Vaiśampāyana, the Naimiṣeya Ṛṣis greet the bard with a certain sense of *déjà écouté*.

[43]Van Buitenen (1973, 19 and 56) translates both *kulapati* and *gṛhapati* as "family chieftain," a fudge in both cases. Ganguli ([1884–96] 1970, 1:1, 49) and Dutt (1895–1905, 1:1, 29) treat "Kulapati" as a name and leave *gṛhapati* untranslated.

[44]I take Āraṇyaka (the "Forest Treatise") here not just as the body of Vedic texts by that name, but as a collective name reflecting the high profile given the Vānaprastha ("Forest-dwelling") mode of life in both epics; see Biardeau in Biardeau and Malamoud 1976, 34–35, 70 (the *Mbh* attributes knowledge of Āraṇyaka rather than Upaniṣad to its Ṛṣis; the Vānaprastha is possibly an epic invention); and Biardeau and Péterfalvi 1985, 32.

C. Reconsidering Bhṛguization

We thus come back to Sukthankar's theory of Bhṛguization.[45] Drawing on his groundwork as chief editor of the *Mahābhārata*'s Critical Edition, he writes on "a subject which, having engaged my attention for a number of years, has acquired considerable fascination for me": the "veritable thesaurus of Bhārgava legends" dispersed throughout much of the *Mahābhārata* (1936, 3). Having traced such material through the epic's eighteen books, he saves the second opening (as noted) for his summation. It "totally ignores the first," he says, in order to introduce a "nest of Bhārgava legends" that "the Sūta obediently proceeds to relate" immediately upon Śaunaka's prompting. The result is the eight chapters (5–12) that form the *Paulomaparvan*, which are "*entirely* consecrated to an account of the wonderful deeds of some of the Bhārgavas, an account which is not even remotely connected in actual fact with the incidents or characters of our epic. It is a digression pure and simple . . ." (1936, 60; author's italics).[46]

"Digression," however, is Sukthankar's misleading translation of *upākhyāna* (1936, 14; cf. 17), a term used for tales told to the epic's heroes, including such famous ones as the stories of Yayāti, Nala, and Rāma; it means no more than "subtale" or "episode," the latter being Sukthankar's alternate translation (65, 70). He asks "how precisely this Bhārgava element, which we find concentrated mostly in the *upākhyānas*, came into the cycle of the Bhārata legends." His answer, admittedly "a matter of speculation," is to run through the supposed cumulative "recensions" of the text. Ruling out those he attributes (uncritically) to Vyāsa and Vaiśampāyana, he finds the "case . . . different with the next recorded recitation of the Mahābhārata" by Ugraśravas at the Naimiṣa Forest, "the sylvan retreat of the Bhṛgus" (70).[47] Whatever he means by "recorded," he now comes to his crucial question:

> Is the Sūta then responsible for the conversion of the Bhārata into the Mahābhārata? Now I do not doubt that some of the Sūtas probably were gifted versifiers, able to compose *ex tempore* short bardic poems and to improvise lays to suit them to varying tastes and requirements of the audience. But if we consider these Sūtas capable of composing

[45]For an earlier version of this section, see Hiltebeitel 1999c, 158 ff.

[46]For a different view of the *Paulomaparvan*, see M. M. Mehta 1973, 549.

[47]It is a frequent fancy that Vyāsa, Vaiśampāyana, and Ugraśravas produced or provide cover-names for sequential *Mbh* recensions: see Vaidya [1905] 1966, 31–36, 49; 1907, 20–21, 29–44, 69, 98–99, 180–81, 200–21, 261–64; Yardi 1986, passim; Gokak 1990, 1; and Fitzgerald forthcoming-b, 48, trying to relate the Vaiśampāyana and Ugraśravas frames to two of "four, or more, distinct poetic or redactorial efforts." Cf. above, chap. 1, n. 100.

> on the spur of the moment such masses of narrative episodes and didactic discourses as we find in our Mahābhārata, we shall be crediting these minstrels with an accomplishment far beyond their natural capacity. (71)

"Spur of the moment" and "natural capacity" are rhetorical flourishes. With the former, which strangely (and no doubt unintentionally) echoes the etymology of Naimiṣa Forest as the Momentous Forest, Sukthankar ignores Ugraśravas' assertion that he has brought the "whole thought of Vyāsa" with him from Janamejaya's snake sacrifice: no spur of the moment matter, at least in any ordinary sense. With the latter, he does not anticipate the effects of the Parry-Lord thesis on oral epic formulaic verse, which has convinced some scholars that oral poets have the natural capacity to do just about anything, except write.[48]

Yet Sukthankar is probably right, even for today, that no one is "so credulous nowadays as to imagine the Sūta as the author" of such "extensive innovations" as would have given the text its present dimensions. For that, he says, we must turn to Bhārgava Brahmans: "The entire story that the Sūta had heard the epic at its first recitation by Vaiśampāyana and reproduced it *verbatim* at Śaunaka's bidding, having committed it to hearing, is so obviously unnatural and improbable that it seems clearly more appropriate to regard it merely as a poetic fiction, a 'frame-story,' the most popular of Indian devices of literary composition" (1936, 72). Ugraśravas is "kept on" as an "image" of the bards "who used to recite the poem in the Heroic Age" (73). Once having completed their "first important diaskeusis," the Bhārgavas then undertook "further additions . . . in the centuries that immediately followed," keeping the text "for some time" as their "exclusive property." These Bhārgava "anchorites, full of age-old wisdom and wonderful masters of the art of myth-weaving, took from the Sūtas the Bhārata and gave back to the world the Mahābhārata, the same book yet different" (75).

Sukthankar is caught between two irreconcilable worlds: his world of Indian literature, in which he rightly recognizes the literary artistry of the frame story convention, and his world of Germanic higher and lower textual criticism (see Morgenroth 1978–79), in which literary artistry (that is, as much of it as is conceded) is at best a screen the scholar must penetrate to excavate historical truths behind pieces of the text that can be all too conveniently separated to meet the demands of the argument.[49]

[48]See chap. 1, n. 74, and note Sukthankar's remark, gratuitous to his theory, that the sūta's version must have been "recorded" (it sounds like he imagines some kind of fieldwork).

[49]See chap. 1. Again, Alter 1981 is most pertinent here; see especially "The Techniques of Repetition" (89–113), "Characterization and the Art of Reticence" (114–30), and

As we have observed,[50] Sukthankar's posthumously published last work (1957) shows him critical of the "European savants" (25) whose methods he had adopted. More than this, as Robert P. Goldman has pointed out,[51] Sukthankar says nothing in this last work about his Bhārgava hypothesis. Without renouncing it, he had in any case finally determined to say something about the *Mahābhārata* as having some literary, religious, and conceptual unity after all. Quoting at the very beginning of these 1942 lectures on the text's "meaning" the verdict of Oldenberg that the *Mahābhārata* is a "monstrous chaos,"[52] he saves for the very end the comment that "it would be a pardonable hyperbole to say that" the *Mahābhārata* is more a cosmos than a chaos (1957, 1 and 124).

Yet Sukthankar's Bhārgava argument has supplied a powerful instrument of *Mahābhārata* interpretation, and, for some—including at least the "early" Goldman, Minkowski (1991), Bigger (1998, 105–7), and J. Brockington (1998, 155–57)—a persuasive myth about *Mahābhārata* mythmaking.[53] I do not suggest that *Mahābhārata* scholarship will get beyond such mythmaking in the matter of the text's origins and authorship, so I consider both the tool and the myth to be major achievements. I attend to them closely because Sukthankar has identified a set of real problems, and because some of his solutions are close to my own. In most of my disagreements, I concur with criticisms made by others. N. J. Shende points out that references to Āṅgirasa Brahmans (including Bṛhaspati, his incarnation Droṇa, and Droṇa's son Aśvatthāman) are more numerous in the *Mahābhārata* than Bhārgava references (1943, 69–70), while for Sullivan, Sukthankar "overstates the impact on the epic of material about Bhārgavas, material which constitutes about five per cent of the text" (1990, 19). Mehta argues that

"Composite Artistry" (113–54). See further Alter 1992 on "the marginalization of the Bible's literary characteristics" by "academic biblical studies" (26), and the chapter "Allusion and Literary Expression" (107–30); Sutton 2000, xiv–xv.

[50]See chap. 1 above n. 57, and n. 20 above.

[51]At the Pondicherry conference on the "Sources of History," January 1997.

[52]See chap. 1, nn. 1 and 2.

[53]See Goldman 1977, 81–147 on "Bhārgava mythmakers." Other would-be follow-ups get lost in fantasies that Bhṛgu was a Dravidian or "Indid" (Karmarkar 1938–39; Weller 1936–37), or that the Bhārgavas were among a riot of vested interest groups that fed interpolations into the *Mbh* in its final stages (Katz 1989, 11), or were partners with Materialists in "telling it like it is" (Alles 1994, 71). Belvalkar 1966, ccii attributes the epic's "dominant Bhakti colouring" to the Bhārgavas. Bhattacharji's capacious sense (see chap. 1, n. 13) of "the Bhārgava section" or "Bhārgava interpolation" finds it offers for the "first time a theology and scripture for a sectarian religion, centering mainly around two gods, Śiva and Kṛṣṇa" (1992–93, 471), and the first seeds of superstitious, foreign, and royally repressive notions that "later evolved into Hinduism" (482). Cf. Shende 1943; Katz 1989, 11; Mukherjee 1994, 11–13.

the first and second openings, with the story material each ties into, must be by the same archetypal "redactorial agency" (1973, 549). And Minkowski makes three telling critiques: there is no evidence for "the existence of a distinct Bhārgava movement"; "it lacks sensibility to maintain" that there is no connection between "the Bhṛgu myth cycle and the Bhārata story," since there are countless parallelisms between them;[54] and the theory suggests a kind of manipulation and conspiracy in the takeover of the text, and presumes a passivity of the "collective audience" faced with that ideological takeover, that are not adequately supported (1991, 399–400).[55]

Although I agree (Hiltebeitel 1993, 19) with Minkowski's critique of conspiracy and takeover theories, I do not share his "no doubt" that the Bhārgava cycle's "origins were separate from the Bhārata story," or his notion that we should "reconsider the process that brought the Bhṛgu material into the Mahābhārata" (1991, 400). In fact, the scholarly convention that Sukthankar, Minkowski, and many others promote of some meaningful contrast between *Bhārata* (thought to have been limited to a main narrative) and *Mahābhārata* (derivative, massive, and comprising narrative and interpolations) has little support from the text, where the two terms are with all but one exception used interchangeably (see 1.1.16–19 and 50), and *Bhārata* never used with implications of priority. Far too much has been made of the verse that says Vyāsa composed a twenty-four thousand verse *Bhāratasaṃhitā* without *upākhyānas*, which the wise call *Bhārata* (1.1.61). It does not, contrary to many scholars' assumptions (most tendentiously Hopkins 1898a) and van Buitenen's translation (1973, 22), say he did this "First"—as if it were done before a *mahā-Bhārata*. Since the passage describes Vyāsa's afterthoughts, it is more plausible to think of this as a digest. A hundred-thousand verse *Bhārata* is also mentioned (12.331.2). Yardi (1986, vi) and Reich (1998, 6), for instance, have tried to connect the twenty-four thousand verse *Bhārata* with the one recited by Vaiśampāyana, but this contradicts Vaiśampāyana's statement that he recites Vyāsa's "thought entire" (1.55.2).

We thus cannot assume that the Bhārgava material in bulk is originally separate from the epic. In fact, one of Sukthankar's insights is that some of it is older than the epic and some is not. Here it seems better to suspect that some Bhārgava material is *created* with the *Mahābhārata* and related within it to older Vedic Bhārgava material that is *recalled* within

[54]Sullivan 1990, 19, also makes this point. Sukthankar denies connections so many times (1936, 4, 10, 13, 14, 17, 30, 33-35, 60, 62, 65, 67, 69, 70) that one has the impression he "protests too much."

[55]For further criticism, see Reich 1998, 154, and Fitzgerald 1999, 2000, and forthcoming-b.

it. In particular, Sukthankar convincingly shows that what is most strikingly new to the *Mahābhārata* in the repertoire of Bhārgava stories is the figure of Bhārgava Rāma, and the relentless reiteration of stories and formulaic verses about him and his annihilation of the Kṣatriyas: a demonstration that Goldman richly develops. Bhārgava Rāma is of course Paraśurāma, "Rāma with the Axe," although in the *Mahābhārata* he does not yet have this latter name or avatar status.[56] Yet although Sukthankar recognizes Bhārgava Rāma as an epic novelty, he still argues that because he belongs to a distinct Bhārgava cycle and comes from an earlier yuga, he is to be distinguished from the "epic characters" he encounters.[57] But Bhārgava Rāma *is* an "epic character" no less than the Pāṇḍavas and Kauravas, and the multiple persons identified with the processes of the text's authorship, transmission, and reception, including the Ṛṣis of the Naimiṣa Forest. Indeed, let us observe that it is never stated that the other Naimiṣeya Ṛṣis are Bhārgavas, although it is the scholarly consensus that they are. As we shall see, there are rather good reasons to suspect that the Naimiṣa Forest Ṛṣis come from all gotras.[58]

In any case, to support his distinction about "epic characters," Sukthankar operates with a limiting notion of symbol and myth. That Bhārgava Rāma survives a yuga to become the guru of Bhīṣma, Droṇa, and Karṇa "is only symbolical, but the basis of the symbolism is significant": he is the suitable guru because he is formulaically "the best of all weapon-bearers" *(sarvaśastrabhṛtām varaḥ)*; "Once the symbol is accepted, it is treated as real, and the myth is worked out in great detail" (1936, 13). To put it simply, Sukthankar's symbol works diachronically (*from* symbol *to* myth) but not synchronically, where it would *connect* Bhārgava Rāma with other "epic characters" not only when they actually meet, but amid the parallelisms mentioned by Minkowski, which enrich the text. These are strange shortcomings, since Sukthankar saw countless connections elsewhere.

[56]See Sukthankar 1936, 24, 48, on a passage where avatar identity is perhaps incipient. As Sutton 2000, 156–57, observes, although the term *avatāra* is never used in the *Mbh*, the "concept is central to the narrative" (cf. 172). Moreover, the concept is frequently subject to allusion by usages of the verb *ava-tṛ*. Cf. Biardeau 1999, 1621, n. 2. I do not agree with Hacker 1960 or Fitzgerald forthcoming-b, 30, that there is one original meaning behind it.

[57]Sukthankar 1936, 13. On Bhārgava Rāma's yuga-spanning appearances in the *Mbh*, see also 17–18, 21, 25, 35–37, 63, 65; Goldman 1977, 132; and especially Thomas 1996, focusing additionally on the correlation between his unusual temporal profile and his appearances in both epics as an indicator of early developments of avatāra mythology.

[58]Vasiṣṭha dwells there, for one (*Mbh* 1, App. 1, No. 36, lines 42–43). For Pargiter [1922] 1997, 65, the "wildest instances [of "chronological confusion"] are the lists of rishis who assembled at the twelve-year sacrifice at Naimiṣa forest" (in *Padma Purāṇa* 6.219.1–12).

With these remarks in mind, let me suggest a new tack. Rather than looking for what Sukthankar calls an "ulterior motive" (1936, 67), I suggest we look for an interior motive. More specifically, rather than thinking of Śaunaka and the Brahman sages of the Naimiṣa Forest as signs of a final Bhārgava redaction and ongoing takeover to allow for further interpolations, I propose that we look at Śaunaka (the only Naimiṣa sattrin explicitly a Bhārgava) and other Bhārgavas mentioned in the epic simply as characters in the *Mahābhārata*. No doubt the composition reached some kind of completion that is reflected in the epic-opening Naimiṣa Forest stories, and no doubt it was done by Brahmans for whom this scene and its stories were symbolic. But there is nothing to suggest that the composing Brahmans were Bhārgavas. Indeed, it is far more likely that they were not, or not just; or in any case, it is unlikely that the group was limited to a Bhārgava movement or cabal. Our question then is: What do the Bhārgavas symbolize in the *Mahābhārata* to Brahmans in general? Once we ask this question, we find that Sukthankar and especially Goldman have paved much of the way. With his notion of "metamyth," Goldman in particular calls attention to the dialogue between Cyavana and King Kuśika (the *Cyavanakuśikasaṃvāda*; 13.52–56), a passage in which Cyavana figures as "the only Bhṛgu who is himself a purveyor of Bhṛguid mythology, . . . [who] becomes at once a model and an inspiration for the whole cycle and the mythic personification of the mythmakers themselves" (1977, 104–11, 136–37)—Brahman mythmakers, that is, who tell stories about all kinds of Brahmans, Bhārgavas included, who sometimes tell stories themselves.

As has been obvious to both Sukthankar and Goldman, Bhārgavas are portrayed in an unfavorable light. Says Sukthankar, in their cycle of "conflicts the Bhārgavas are represented in our epic as irascible sages, domineering, arrogant, unbending and revengeful. To our epic bards they are at the same time omniscient and omnipotent Supermen, who had become so chiefly by their rigid austerities and the magical or spiritual powers acquired by them" (1936, 64). Some of this could describe our friend Śaunaka in the epic's second opening, although he is never among the Bhārgava characters under Sukthankar's review.[59] Goldman goes further:

> The central concerns of the Bhṛgus appear from the mythology to have included death, violence, sorcery, confusion and violation of class roles *(varṇāśramadharma)*, intermarriage with other varṇas *(varṇasaṃ-*

[59]Cf. Shende 1943, 81: when Śaunaka asks Ugraśravas to begin with his own Bhārgava genealogy, "This is quite appropriate if we bear in mind the egotistical tendencies of the Bhṛgus. . . ."

> *kara)*, and open hostility to the gods themselves. In addition, several of the Bhārgava sages are shown in the epic to have engaged with impunity in such activities as theft, drinking liquor, and killing a woman, acts that are condemned unequivocally in the law texts as especially improper for brahmans. One of the greatest of the Bhṛgus is everywhere said to have served as the priest and chaplain of the *asuras*, the demon enemies of heaven and of order *(dharma)*. (1977, 5)

These are not expressions of modern squeamishness, but perfectly accurate descriptions of important details and shadings of the Bhārgavas in the text. Convinced, however, that this mythology *of* the Bhārgavas is mythology *by* the Bhārgavas, neither Sukthankar nor Goldman ever asks why Bhārgavas would have portrayed themselves so unfavorably. Given all the other criticisms of the Bhṛguization theory, the answers one might expect—their portrayal expresses the Bhārgavas' power over the text, perhaps in combination with an omnipotence fantasy, or the determination to convince others of their omnipotence—are, I think, hardly plausible.

I cannot review here the many Bhārgava details and shadings that back up the quoted profiles, but some patterns arise that suggest an answer to what Bhārgavas symbolize in the epic. One such pattern becomes clear from an insight of Goldman's: such themes "unequivocally mark the Bhṛgus as a group set apart from their fellow brahmans" (1977, 4). They are repeatedly portrayed as "degraded Brahmans" (81–82, 85, 97, 141–42), military Brahmans (99), violent Brahmans, caste-mixing Brahmans, nearly all of whose males marry Kṣatriyā women (98), and who—as Sukthankar notes (1936, 63)—provide for one of their daughters "the only *pratiloma* [hypergamic or "against the grain"] marriage on record in Brahmanical literature"—the marriage of the Bhārgava Śukra's daughter Devayānī "down" to the Kṣatriya king Yayāti. As I see it, Bhārgavas are portrayed as vehicles for defining, and if necessary correcting, the status relations *of Brahmans*. Goldman shows that they vie constantly with princes and gods (1977, 93–128), but they never vie, as far as I can see, with other Brahmans (even Śukra, opposite number as chaplain of the Asuras to Bṛhaspati, the Āṅgirasa Brahman chaplain of the gods, accommodates Bṛhaspati's son Kaca in taking him on as his disciple and ultimately transmitting the mantra of regeneration to him).[60] I suggest that this is because Bhārgavas represent those other Brahmans: they speak and act for them in certain ways. And these ways are not far to seek. As has been repeatedly perceived, they are champions of the

[60]Beyond Sukthankar and Goldman's discussions of Śukra's myths, see Dumézil 1971, 133–238; Defourny 1978, 57–105.

cause of Brahmans (Sukthankar 1936, 66). Linked with the Āṅgirasas as Brahmans of the *Atharva Veda*, they are the *Mahābhārata*'s experts in black magic, curses, *dhanurveda* (the Veda of the bow), and mantra-sped divine missiles.[61]

On this matter, it is instructive to consider ways in which the *Mahābhārata* differs from the *Rāmāyaṇa*. Whereas the *Rāmāyaṇa* portrays Bhārgavas only minimally,[62] the *Mahābhārata* makes the Bhārgavas a kind of last resort of the Brahmanical world order, with Kṛṣṇa descending from Bhṛgu in his maternal line and revealing that among his "supernal manifestations" *(vibhūtis)* he is Bhṛgu himself among Ṛṣis.[63] Rāma learns his divine weapons from Viśvāmitra, who, albeit a Kṣatriya-turned-Brahman, is one of the august group of Seven Ṛṣis, ancestors of the most exalted Vedic Brahman clans. Most of these Seven—the main exception is the Bhārgava Jamadagni—parade through the *Rāmāyaṇa* to guide Rāma through his life.[64] Presumably Jamadagni does *not* make such an appearance because he is deceased well before Rāma's career. Thus when Bhārgava Rāma avenges Jamadagni's death at the hands of the sons of Kārtavīrya Arjuna, it is attributed to earlier times, ordinarily a previous interval between the Kṛta and Tretā yugas (Thomas 1996). Yet Jamadagni's absence is compensated for by Bhārgava Rāma's singular appearance. When Rāma Dāśarathi meets him, he has exterminated the Kṣatriyas "long ago" (*Rām.* 1.73.20; 74.24–26), and, as something he never quite completes, it looks as if he has come prepared to kill Rāma, a regenerate Kṣatriya prince. Appearing just after Rāma and Sītā's wedding, he withdraws only after he has learned from seeing Rāma's prowess with the bow that Rāma is no *mere* Kṣatriya but Viṣṇu (75.3–17).[65] In receding as no more than a kind of temporarily menace, he thus leaves other regulative Vedic Ṛṣis to supervise the martial as well as the moral education of a prince who is also an avatar. In contrast, *Mahābhārata* heroes learn their divine weapons primarily

[61]Sukthankar 1936, 66–67; Shende 1943, 71–78; Goldman 1977, 99–101, 107, 147; Biardeau 1981, 85. In this light, it will not suffice to say that for the Brahmanic redactors, "les Bhargavas étaient des brahmanes par excellence" (Bigger 1999a, 4).

[62]On Bhārgavas in the *Rām*, see Sukthankar 1936, 69; Goldman 1976a; 1977, 150, n. 13.

[63]See Defourny 1978, 67–68, on the Bhṛgu-to-Kṛṣṇa descent, which passes through Yayāti via Śukra's daughter Devayānī. On *vibhūtis*, see *BhG* 10.25.

[64]See Hiltebeitel 1979b: Viśvāmitra, Vasiṣṭha, and Bharadvāja instruct Rāma directly; Atri indirectly through the story of his wife Ahalyā, and Jamadagni and Kaśyapa more indirectly, through descendants. See also Hiltebeitel 1977a, 347, on *pravara Ṛṣis*, the seven, and Agastya, linked with the south (to which he further directs Rāma) and, as with all the rest, with the stars. On Viśvāmitra's exceptional status in this group, see White 1991, 78–79.

[65]On Rāma Jāmadagnya's incomplete job in both epics of effacing the Kṣatriyas and their lineages, see Hiltebeitel in press-c, and 1999a, 458–62.

from Bhārgavas and Āṅgirasas, and their moral and military educations are split. The former is given by varied forest Ṛṣis headed by Vyāsa, but including such a Ṛṣi as Pulastya, ancestor of Brahmarākṣasas (see Koskikallio 1999, 359); by Kṛṣṇa, God and avatar; by Bhīṣma, whose lengthy postwar oration has Vyāsa's prodding and Kṛṣṇa's inspiration (see chap. 2, § C.29 and 30); and by their mixed-caste and in any case non-Brahman uncle Vidura. And their martial instruction is left primarily to "flawed" Bhārgava and Āṅgirasa Brahmans: Bhārgava Rāma and the Āṅgirasa Droṇa. The dharma has so declined that these are the primary Brahmans left to help restore it, with the avatar secretly one with the primal Bhārgava ancestor. Such a restoration can come only at a price, since Bhārgava correctives are inherently violent.

We see the cycles of violence begin to unfold with Bhārgava involvements even in the epic's first beginning. Ugraśravas' main narrative in this segment, the *Pauṣyaparvan* (1.3), culminates when Uttaṅka, a Bhārgava, seeks revenge against the snake Takṣaka for stealing a pair of earrings he has taken some trouble to get. Uttaṅka goes to Janamejaya to tell him for the first time that Takṣaka had killed Janamejaya's father Parikṣit, and thereby provokes the latter to undertake his snake sacrifice as a double retaliation (although Uttaṅka doesn't mention his own reasons; 1.3.136–195).[66] Then with the second beginning, the cycles truly start to unravel when Śaunaka demands to hear the Bhārgava genealogy. What Ugraśravas tells of this in the *Paulomaparvan* (1.4–12) concerns only one of the clan's less violent branches: the one that leads to Śaunaka.[67] But the culminating story about Śaunaka's forefather[68] Ruru further overdetermines the vendetta against snakes. Having learned that the only way to bring his snake-bitten fiancée back to life is to give her half the lifetime still ahead of him, Ruru does this, but then goes around clubbing snakes to death until he learns from a lizard, whom he is ready to kill as a snake, that he is acting more like a Kṣatriya, and in particular like Janamejaya, than a Brahman. When Ruru asks to hear about Janamejaya's sacrifice, the lizard—who is of course a Ṛṣi under a curse that has now been relieved by the sight of Ruru—tells him he will hear the story from a Brahman. The lizard-Ṛṣi disappears, and Ruru has to go hear the story from his father Pramati (1.8–12).

[66]When a later *Āstīkaparvan* passage presents a rather different account of how Janamejaya first hears that Takṣaka killed his father, Janamejaya finally decides on a revenge that will be for both Uttaṅka's pleasure and his own (46.41). On the relation of these accounts, see Mehta 1973, 548–49. On the snake sacrifice amid *Mbh* cycles of vengeance, see Malamoud 1989, 195–205, especially 197.

[67]On the three main branches of Bhṛgu's descent, see Sukthankar 1936, 4.

[68]*Pūrvapitāmaha* (1.5.8): forefather or "ancestor" (Ganguli [1884–96] 1970, 1:50). Van Buitenen's "grandfather" (1973, 56) is unlikely. The short genealogy at 1.5.6–8 (Bhṛgu > Cyavana > Pramati > Ruru > Śunaka) gives Śaunaka no father to close the descent line.

While Pramati's non-"authoritative" Bhārgava account of Janamejeya's sacrifice is thereby quickly lost to us, Ugraśravas continues to build up to his own telling by transitioning to the "large" (1.13.4) *Āstīkaparvan*, which his father Lomaharṣaṇa taught him after hearing Vyāsa himself recite it at the Naimiṣa Forest, making Lomaharṣaṇa in fact a sixth "disciple of Vyāsa *(śiṣyo vyāsasya)*" (6–7), though not necessarily the sixth in time. The *Āstīkaparvan* is thus "authorized" by Vyāsa, but it comes from a different time and place than the inner frame of the *Mahābhārata*, which Ugraśravas has now already told us comes from Vyāsa via Vaiśampāyana as it was narrated at Janamejaya's sacrifice. But what was Vyāsa doing in the Naimiṣa Forest? All we can say for now is that this location seems once again available to resolve a literary leap, this time required by the fact that the events of *Āstīka* build up to the sacrifice where Vaiśampāyana will recite what is now obviously his less complete version of Vyāsa's "thought entire" than Ugraśravas's version.

In the *Āstīkaparvan*, the cycle of vendettas now roles into it such interspecies feuds as those between Snakes and Birds, Gods and Demons (at the Churning of the Ocean), and Rāhu (the eclipse demon) and the Sun and Moon. The snakes now consult as to how they might avoid their "compete extinction" (*sarvavināśam*; 33.6) in Janamejaya's sacrifice, which their mother Kadrū pronounced on them when they did not do her immediate bidding in her rivalry with her sister Vinatā, mother of birds.[69] The snakes' solution requires them to nurture a snake mother with the same name as her future husband, Jaratkāru, so that a son Āstīka can be born to become the snakes' savior. And so it becomes clear that all these vendettas underlie and enfold the rivalry between the Pāṇḍavas and Kauravas, which Śaunaka will at last ask to hear at the beginning of the next parvan, the "Book of the Descent of the First Generations."

That the *Pauloma* and *Āstīka* parvans are a narrative continuum is made clear by Śaunaka himself as he reaches this point: "You have told me the entire great story beginning from the genealogy of the Bhṛgus, my boy *(bhṛguvaṃśāt prabhṛtyeva tvayā me kathitaṃ mahat/ ākhyānam akhilaṃ tāta)*. I am pleased with you, Sauti. I ask you further to tell me the story composed by Vyāsa and recited at the snake sacrifice . . ." (1.53.27–29). At last Ugraśravas can report how Vaiśampāyana responds to Janamejaya's question about the "breach" *(bheda)* that led to the "great war" between "all my grandfathers" (1.55.19–20), and get to the "real" *Mahābhārata*. But now, as Ugraśravas narrates not only Vaiśampāyana's lesser version of Vyāsa's "thought entire," but Janamejaya's deliberations in the course of a snake sacrifice that is to be the ultimate fulfillment of

[69]On the textual complications of Kadrū's curse, see Mehta 1972.

so many feuds against snakes, it becomes clear that there is an overhanging question. As one cycle of violence builds upon and reverts back to another, as different species feed off each other in the cauldron of time, is there no appeasement? It forces the question of the *Eumenides*: have the Furies no end? And of course the answer is always yes, although the resolutions always leave ambiguous remainders.

In the case of Janamejaya's sacrifice, the drama hinges on whether Takṣaka, "Fashioner,"[70] will be sucked into the flames like so many other snakes. The gruesome sattra is, at least implicitly, a rite of black magic *(abhicāra)* designed to kill an enemy. The priests are all dressed in black while the seated attendees *(sadasyas)*, a group that includes Vyāsa seated with his disciples and son—presumably Śuka, though that will have to be explained[71]—and several sages well-known from the Upaniṣads, seem to be clothed ordinarily. We now see how this distinction becomes important. The Hotṛ, in charge it seems of invoking the snakes into the fire and the leading priest mentioned, is one Caṇḍabhārgava, "Terrible Bhārgava," and when Āstīka arrives seeking to ask Janamejaya for the boon that the sacrifice be stopped, the grim Caṇḍabhārgava makes Janamejaya wait until he is certain Takṣaka is doomed. But once Janamejaya offers the boon, there is just an "interval" *(antaram)*, a nick of time, for Āstīka to make his request, and Takṣaka is left hanging in mid-air until his fate is determined by the sadasyas, who adjudicate that Āstīka's boon should be granted and are among those who joyously applaud the rite's termination (1.51–53). The "moment of decision" thus belongs to this "elusive"[72] group that includes Vyāsa, the "author," and his disciples and son, the disseminators of his composition.[73] "Terrible Bhārgava," whom neither Sukthankar nor

[70]See Biardeau 1978, 140, n. 1, opposing Takṣaka in this "fecund" and "creative" aspect to Śeṣa-Ananta, who denotes "formlessness, chaos."

[71]*Sadasyaścābhavadvyāsaḥ putraśiṣyasahāyavān* (1.48.7ab). Van Buitenen has, "was a sadasya in the midst of his sons (sic!) and pupils" (1973, 114), which fails to reckon that of his four sons, three—Dhṛtarāṣṭra, Pāṇḍu, and Vidura, long deceased—can hardly be there, and that the other, Śuka, on whom see chap. 8, is one, along with Vaiśampāyana and three other Brahmans, of his five pupils. Ganguli has correctly, "Vyasa with his son and disciples" ([1884–96] 1970, 1:119).

[72]See Heesterman 1985, 222, n. 24 on the "equally elusive *sadasya* (apparently a representative of the guests)"; 1963, 34: a sole sadasya in later ritual supervises like the Brahman, and seems to be the survivor of a group of sadasyas who are still mentioned in older texts as dakṣiṇā recipients. Ugraśravas should also be a sadasya.

[73]The *antaram* as "nick of time" is also a narrative "moment" (*nimiṣa, nimeṣa*) or "instant" (*kṣaṇa*), these terms having a certain overlap. Cf. chap. 2, n. 114, and Derrida 1995, 54, 65, 68, 71–72, 77–79, 95–96, on the "instant of decision" and its "madness" in that most-discussed interrupted sacrifice—of Isaac. On one point of comparison here, Vyāsa sits in the place of God.

Goldman mentions, is thus pitted against the author and the disseminators of the text.

But all this is without even mentioning the more violent Aurva branch of the clan, which plays out its own multigenerational feud with the Kṣatriyas. This branch passes from Aurva (who blinds all the Kṣatriyas at the sight of his lustrous birth, and threatens to destroy the universe) to Ṛcīka (who masters the *dhanurveda* for the destruction of Kṣatriyas) to Jamadagni (who orders the beheading of his own Kṣatriyā wife) to Rāma Jāmadagnya (who exterminates the Kṣatriyas twenty-one times over and remains after that to haunt the heroes of both epics). Other branches of Bhārgavas would seem to continue, but this line stops with the exterminator.[74] As far as the larger epic is concerned, the Bhārgava genealogy centers on this Aurva branch, which has no continuation after Bhārgava Rāma's "retirement."[75]

Although Fitzgerald justly cautions that Rāma Jāmadagnya's epic portrayals would draw from several strands (forthcoming-b), Goldman is still right to stress Sukthankar's insight that, as the epic's new Bhārgava, with no Vedic debut (1936, 2, 16, 64–66), this Rāma is a "deliberate creation of the epic bards" (Goldman 1977, 136): a non-Vedic cathecting figure for their whole "pastiche" of Bhārgava myths that otherwise have numerous Vedic elements. Goldman further argues that many Bhārgava motifs (again, often partially Vedic) are not unique to Bhārgavas, but are shared with (and Goldman thinks traceable to) mythologies of other Brahman gotras (78, 86, 103, 135, 144, 159, n. 4). Although virtually all the unfavorable features of the Bhārgavas—caste mixture, degraded Brahmans, Brahmans as kings, black magic, curses, feuds, extreme and uncontrolled violence—find analogs in the Bhārata story, it is clearly their culmination in Bhārgava Rāma that forms their contact point with it.

Of all the generic Bhārgava features, three stand out for the ways they relate Bhārgava Rāma to the central story. First, Bhārgava Rāma suggests an intolerable model. Having exterminated the Kṣatriyas, he has become de facto a Brahman king, as Sukthankar (1936, 40–42) and Goldman

[74]The continuity of the other main Bhārgava branches is intriguing. It may be presumed in the case of Śaunaka, who is a householder. The line of Śukra passes through his daughter Devayānī's marriage with Yayāti (see above at n. 60) into the Kṣatriya lines of their sons Yadu (in which, as noted, one finds Kṛṣṇa) and Turvasu. This is a maternal descent, but as one appreciates in the case of Āstīka, whose birth is arranged to save the snakes of his maternal line, this is not insignificant. The feud of the Aurva line of Bhārgavas is with Haihaya Kṣatriyas of the Yādava line, and is thus not only a feud between Brahmans and Kṣatriyas, but between paternal and maternal descendants of Bhṛgu. Also, as Defourny (1978, 68) observes, from a purāṇic perspective, Bhṛgu is the ancestor of two avatāras: Kṛṣṇa and Paraśurāma.

[75]For variants, see Goldman 1977, 99–101, 135–40, 143; Fitzgerald forthcoming-b.

(1977, 104, 108) both show. Second, suggesting narrative links, is the tradition of Bhārgava service to demons. While in former ages Bhṛgus serve as priests of Asuras and of the quasi-demonic thousand-armed Arjuna Kartavīrya, in the *Mahābhārata* Bhīṣma, Droṇa, and Karṇa—the Kauravas' three most formidable champions—are all disciples of Bhārgava Rāma in the arts of war. The Kauravas they serve are also incarnate demons. Bhārgava Rāma's role as guru of those who serve the demons[76] thus seems to provide the chief reason for his reactivation from prior yugas. Third, a symbolic convergence, is the theme of annihilation itself, which is so important for its parallels in the rivalry of the Kurus: whether it is total or not, and whether and how cycles of destruction can come to an end.[77]

Ugraśravas in fact launches this third theme in the *Mahābhārata*'s first beginning when he tells Śaunaka about Bhārgava Rāma's deeds while reporting on his own stopover—on the way from Janamejaya's snake sacrifice to Naimiṣa Forest—at Samantapañcaka, "the country where the war was fought between the Kurus and Pāṇḍavas and all the kings of the earth" (1.1.11):

> In the juncture between the Tretā and Dvāpara yugas, Rāma the best of weapon-bearers, impelled by outrage, repeatedly slew the royal Kṣatra (class). Having annihilated the entire Kṣatra by his own energy, that one of fiery lustre made five lakes of (their) blood at Samantapañcaka. (Standing) in those lakes of bloody water, insensate with wrath, he satisfied his fathers with sprinkling rites of blood.[78] So we have heard. Then his Fathers led by Ṛcīka, having approached, restrained that bull among Brahmans, saying, "Forbear" *(kṣama)*. Then he stopped. (1.2.3–6)

The Vulgate adds eight lines (1.71*) for his "pleased" Fathers to grant Bhārgava Rāma the boon he requests of freeing him from the sin of annihilating the Kṣatra while "overcome by anger *(roṣābhibhūta)*." Perhaps one of the functions of Śaunaka's character in the text is to not

[76]On Śukra and the demons, see Goldman 1977, 114, 120, 124–27; on Bhārgavas as priests of Kārtavīrya, 96; on Bhārgava Rāma as guru of the three Kaurava marshals, see Sukthankar 1936, 13, 17–18, 21, 25, 35–37, 63, 65; Goldman 1977, 132. Note that Śukra's opposite number Bṛhaspati, like Droṇa in whom he becomes incarnate, is an Āṅgirasa, it being the job of chaplains of both groups to master Atharvanic magical powers. Fitzgerald finds this "unpersuasive," perhaps because he regards Bhārgava Rāma's instruction of Bhīṣma, Droṇa, and Karṇa as three different "themes" (2000, 5; forthcoming-b, 40).

[77]See Sukthankar 1936, 8, 12 19, 40–41, 65; Goldman 1970.

[78]*Saṃtarpayāmāsa rudhireṇa*; the reference is to *tarpaṇa* rites for the ancestors, normally done with water.

mind hearing this gory story about one of his clansmen over and over again, often in even gorier terms.

Yet before Śaunaka hears it (or at least hears this version from Ugraśravas) in the Naimiṣa Forest, the initial audience for many other stories of Bhārgava Rāma is Janamejaya, a king who hears it, mixed in with the story of his own ancestors' feuds, while carrying out his own ghastly vendetta against snakes. If, as Biardeau has put it, the *Mahābhārata* "author's concern was primarily focused on the svadharma of Kshatriyas as opposed to that of Brahmans" (1981, 76), and if, as James Fitzgerald has argued, the usage of *śānti* in the *Śāntiparvan* carries the implication of the "pacification" of Yudhiṣṭhira after the violence of the *Mahābhārata* war,[79] the main target of this message is Janamejaya, the last king to hear it not only as it as it is told to him, but in several of its tellings, as it had earlier passed through the ears Yudhiṣṭhira and Janamejaya's other royal ancestors. The svadharma of kings must include not only the means to violence, but the means to its appeasement. When a "pleased chorus of cheers" greets the attendees' (including the "author's") decision that Janamejaya's snake sacrifice should end, Janamejaya too becomes "pleased" and gives the priests and attendees great riches (1.53.9–11). Janamejaya "gets" the author's "message" and, in so doing, terminates the grim and destructive project of his Bhārgava priest. One of the chief objects of the *Mahābhārata* is thus to instruct kings and other Kṣatriyas in how to curb endless cycles of violence, particularly as such cycles effect and implicate Brahmans.

So it is that the Bhārgava cycle intertwines with all these vendettas, and is inseparable from the literary "work" of the non-Bhārgava author. It can hardly be kept apart as a separate strand of authorship or a layer of textual history.

D. Further Sattras at Naimiṣa Forest

There are four more occasions in the *Mahābhārata* where one hears explicitly about sattras at Naimiṣa Forest.[80] These sattras precede the lives of the main heroes rather than follow them, yet it is not the Pāṇḍavas or Kauravas who hear about them,[81] but secondary figures: Draupadī's father Drupada and Kṛṣṇa's brother Balarāma, who will emerge, despite his obscurity in the epic, as a central figure in our

[79]See Fitzgerald 1980, 137–51; 1991, 166 on *śānti* as "pacification" and "neutralization" of Yudhiṣṭhira's grief through Bhīṣma's *Śāntiparvan* instruction.
[80]The remainder of this section slightly modifies Hiltebeitel 1998a, 164–70.
[81]The Pāṇḍavas go to Naimiṣa Forest in their forest wanderings (3.93.1-2), but there is no Ṛṣi there to tell a story (as there is in so many other forests), much less tell stories about Naimiṣa Forest.

discussion. What is most revealing about these narratives is that they show the epic poets not only making new conventions about Naimiṣa Forest sattras, but being familiar with older Vedic ones. These passages are saturated with Vedic allusions to Naimiṣa Forest as a place of Vedic sattras. Indeed, let me admit a methodological choice. Rather than looking at Vedic sacrifices as prior forms or schemas by which the epic poets "ritualize," "transpose" or indeed *allegorize* an older story into another register,[82] I argue that they make knowing *allusion* to Veda, its rituals included, within the primary texture of their composition.[83]

Of the four occasions, the first is the most familiar, coming after Drupada hears that all five Pāṇḍavas have decided to marry his daughter. Yudhiṣṭhira tries to reassure him, but can only say that even though he doesn't know why, the polyandrous marriage must be subtly dharmic because he says so, since "my voice does not speak untruth" (1.187.29; 188.13). Drupada, not much convinced, says he needs time to think. Vyāsa "by chance arrived,"[84] and after asking what others have to say, he takes Drupada aside to "authorize" Yudhiṣṭhira's certainty by telling the episode of the Former Indras.[85]

"Formerly," he begins, "gods sat at a sattra at Naimiṣa Forest": perhaps all the gods, perhaps a group. I adopt the second reading: as yet, as far as I know, untried. Consecrated *(dīkṣitaḥ)* to perform the office of "suffocator priest" or *śamitṛ*, Yama, who is the only deity specifically identified as a sattrin, stops killing "creatures" *(prajā)*, who thus increase, no longer subject to death brought on by time (189.1–2). A group of gods—again, it is not indicated whether they are among the sattrins, but they include Indra, Kubera, Varuṇa, the Sādhyas, Rudras, Vasus, and Aśvins, but not, let us note, the Maruts—grow anxious about the proliferation of humans (*mānuṣyāḥ*, not just "creatures") and appeal to Brahmā: "Mortals have become immortals. There isn't any distinction. Agitated by nondistinction, we come for the sake of distinction."[86] These gods base their appeal on the need for clear categories, with immortality the distinction they wish to regain for themselves. The concern for clear categories is also that of the wise lizard in the story of Ruru: a topic for chapter 5.

[82]This has been the premise of Oberlies 1998, and before him of Gehrts 1975 and van Buitenen 1975, 3–30, as it was for Dumézil 1968 with his notion of the transposition from myth to epic. See chap. 1, n. 99.

[83]On allegory and allusion as interpretative strategies, see Quint 1993, 15.

[84]1.187.32d; see chap. 2, § C.12, at n. 58.

[85]See Hiltebeitel [1976] 1990, 169–91, and Scheuer 1982, 105–16, for earlier looks at this myth.

[86]1.189.6: *martyā hy amartyāḥ saṃvṛttā na viśeṣo 'sti kaścana/ aviśeṣād udvijanto viśeṣārtham ihāgatāḥ.*

Brahmā says that while Yama is occupied with the sattra, humans will not die; but when he has finished giving his undivided concentration to completing it *(tasminnekāgre kṛtasarvakārye)*, his "body will be strengthened joined with your power; that body will surely be their end at the time of death, having power over men."[87] The matter is curious. If Yama is a *śamitṛ*, he should presumably be killing creatures in the ritual itself. Either he ceases killing creatures in the world at large while temporarily limiting his specialty, causing death, to this sacrificial role, or his function as śamitṛ is not to perform sacrificial killings in the sattra itself but to be invigorated by the sattra so as to be able kill creatures outside it in the world. It seems to be the latter. In any case, once Brahmā has reassured them, "the gods sat where the gods were sacrificing" *(devā yatra devā yajante/ samāsīnās . . .)*—suggesting a distinction between gods who are sacrificing and being invigorated and others who are seated, like sadasyas, and help to invigorate. Indra, who seems to be among the latter group, now sees golden lotuses floating down the Gaṅgā. He traces them upriver to the tears of the goddess Śrī, who weeps over the fall of four former Indras at the river's source. Drupada now hears that the Pāṇḍavas and Draupadī are the five Indras and Śrī, ordained by Śiva to become mortals and marry. Embroiled in time itself, they are subject to the same laws of karma as the very humans that the gods wanted to reestablish their distinction from; only by karma that will be "unbearable" *(aviṣahya)* and lethal to many others will they be able to regain Indraloka by their "own karma" *(svakarmaṇā)* (25–26). We begin to see that the two phases of the story tie together: Yama will not be alone in bringing death to the human world. The conclusion of the gods' sattra will take place in the slaughter of Kurukṣetra.

The last three passages are a cluster, all found in the account of Balarāma's forty-two day pilgrimage to thirty-six tīrthas, mostly along the Sarasvatī River,[88] on which he departs in a rage when Kṛṣṇa rejects his prewar proposal to aid the Kauravas as well as the Pāṇḍavas (9.34.10–12). The pilgrimage ends when he comes to Kurukṣetra just in time to see the final mace-duel between his disciples Duryodhana and

[87]1.189.8: *vaivasvatasyāpi tanur vibhūtā/ vīryeṇa yuṣmākam uta prayuktā// saiṣām anto bhavitā hyantakāle/ tanur hi vīryaṃ bhavitā nareṣu* (189.8). The CE shows numerous variations, the Vulgate, for instance, simplifying the last line to "there will be no power among men" *(na tatra vīryaṃ bhavitā nareṣu)*, thus omitting the second reference to Yama's "body, person, self" *(tanus)*. But the prior reference is without exception.

[88]I modify Dandekar's list of thirty-five (1961, liii); it is sometimes not possible to distinguish which āśramas to locate *at* tīrthas and which ones to identify *as* tīrthas.

Bhīma. Until very recently,[89] Balarāma's pilgrimage has received no more than passing scholarly interest, when suddenly, over no more than a few years, three scholars independently understood the same thing: that Balarāma's pilgrimage replicates a certain Vedic ritual journey up the Sarasvatī river.[90] A Draupadī cult analogy suggests a preliminary parallel. As Balarāma zeroes in on Kurukṣetra, he does something similar to what Aravāṉ does at the Draupadī cult *paṭukaḷam* (ritual battlefield). As each in effect "circles" the battlefield, he is a representative of Ananta-Śeṣa, the "Endless"-"Remainder" snake, who encircles the world and time, and, by implication, all ritually constructed sites—Kurukṣetra being the exemplary Vedic and epic ritual terrain as sacrificial altar of the gods *(devayajana)*.[91] In the *Mahābhārata* Balarāma is Seṣa incarnate, whereas in the Draupadī cult Aravāṉ is Śeṣa's daughter's son. Each is present to represent the "endless" principle of what "remains" at the end of the eighteen-day war.[92] Instructively, the Draupadī cult retains the principle while applying it to a different person.

But the epic obviously reworks something older. Most immediately, the pilgrimage allows the poets to relate the two sanctities of Kurukṣetra

[89]See Biardeau CR 90 (1981–82), 145–47, attempting to link the plough-bearing Balarāma and Kurukṣetra in terms of a ploughing of the "earth of acts" *(karmabhūmi)*. Cf. Biardeau CR 89 (1980–81), 245, 249; Kaveeshwar 1972, 7–8, 24–26; Feller 2000, 87: "to create suspense at a decisive point" and "a pretext to narrate many legends."

[90]See Oberlies 1995, 1998, who probably deserves credit for the first recognition; Bigger 1998, 1999a. I wrote in 1996 before seeing the other pieces. I leave what appears here and in chap. 4, § B largely as I wrote it, although I benefit from both authors and thank Bigger for some helpful comments (E-mail, September 1999) that have led to improvements.

[91]Balarāma seems to "buttonhook" Kurukṣetra, passing through it and out from its "gate" (*dvārāt . . . niṣkramya*; 9.51.25), and then doubling back to it for the final mace-duel. On Aravāṉ's definition of the boundaries of the Draupadī cult ritual battlefield *(paṭukaḷam)*, equivalent to Kurukṣetra as a Kālī temple, and his connection with Ādiśeṣa as serpent-encloser of this terrain, see Hiltebeitel 1991a, 309–12.

[92]On Balarāma's parallellism with Śeṣa within the *Mbh*, see Feller 1999, 813–14: like Balarāma, Śeṣa withdraws from a cousin-rivalry, that between the snake and bird offspring of Kadrū and Vinatā. Feller disagrees here with Bigger's argument (1998, 161) that Balarāma and Śeṣa bear only a late connection. Balarāma incarnates Śeṣa at *Mbh* 1.61.91, with unfoldings at 1.189.30–31 (formed of a white hair of Viṣṇu, evoking the link between snakes and hair at 1.18–20) and 16.5.11–16 (upon Balarāma's dying, Śeṣa parts as a white snake from his mouth, resumes his thousand-headed form, and returns to join the other great *Āstīkaparvan* snakes in the ocean). Here he closes out the "end" of the Yādavas at Dvārakā just as he does with the Kurus at Kurukṣetra. Cf. 18.5.15 and 23*. The emphasis on the serpent-matriline (with *Mbh* antecedents; see Hiltebeitel 1995a, 448) recalls the story of Āstīka. On Aravāṉ in the Draupadī cult, see Hiltebeitel 1988, 316–32, especially 323, 329–32 on Ādiśeṣa; 1991a, 283–319, especially 309–12 on Ādiśeṣa. On Aravāṉ's own related Tamil cult as Kūttāṇṭavar, see idem, 1995a; 1998a; 1999a, 414–38 (also on Aravāṉ's multiform Barbarīka, known in Andhra and much of north India); and 1999d—all of which develop "end-of-the-war" themes. Cf. above, at n. 22, on Ādiśeṣa at Madurai.

and Sarasvatī, to which our three passages add a third: Naimiṣa Forest. The first two stories, launched when Balarāma learns that Vinaśana tīrtha is named for the place where the Sarasvatī disappeared "because of her hatred of Śūdras and Ābhīras,"[93] are based on Sarasvatī's inherent responsiveness to Brahmans, which comes from her being not only preeminent among Vedic rivers and the purifier of the heartland of early Vedic culture, but in classical times the goddess of Brahmanic learning, arts, and speech.[94]

In the first passage, Balarāma is drawn to a place called Naimiṣeya Kuñja (Bower, Bend), where the westward-flowing river wondrously turned back to flow eastward "for the sake of beholding the great-souled Naimiṣeya Ṛṣis."[95] This occurred in the aftermath of a "great big twelve-year sattra" that the "Naimiṣeya ascetics" undertook "formerly in the Kṛta Yuga." When the vast gathering of Ṛṣis was finished with this sattra in Naimiṣeya (the name for the place in this passage), they came in droves along the tīrthas on the southern bank of the Sarasvatī, up to Samantapañcaka (Kurukṣetra). One is struck by their mass migration from Naimiṣa at the end of their sattra. On their way, they beautified the river but crowded its tīrthas so much that those along the southern bank looked like cities *(nagarāyante)*, and at Kurukṣetra, finding no space left, the Ṛṣis were reduced to measuring the ground for their Agnihotras and other rites with their sacred threads (39–49). Seeing that "crush *(sāṃghātam)* of despairing Ṛṣis riven by anxiety," Sarasvatī out of compassion took a turn at the spot where Balarāma now finds himself; there she made watered bowers *(kuñjān)* for the Ṛṣis, and then resumed her westerly flow so that the Ṛṣis' visit there would not be in vain (50–53).[96]

[93]9.36.1–2; but at 3.130.4, it is out of her hatred for Niṣādas! Bharadwaj 1986, 21–43 reviews debates on the whereabouts of Vinaśana, which is clearly no longer to be located (and certainly not in Bharadwaj's Indus Valley speculations). Ābhīras—who become Ahirs in Hindi—are the caravan raiders who shame Arjuna in the episode recounted in chap. 2, § C.41 below n. 188.

[94]See 9.41.29–31 in this sequence and the fascinating 12.303.6–12, where Sarasvatī possesses or enters *(pra-viś)* Yajñavalkya's body with a burning heat, revealing the Veda, its appendix, and the "whole Śatapatha" (i.e., the *Śatapatha Brāhmaṇa*), which Yajñavalkya is told, "you will compose" *(praṇeṣyasi*: which could also mean anything from "promulgate" to Ganguli's "edit" [1884–96] 1970, 10, 458). This passage is suggestive as to how the epic poets imagine the composition of a "fifth Veda."

[95]9.36.35–36; Naimiṣeya Kuñja is now "apparently . . . Prācī-Sarasvatī," the name "given to the river where it turns eastward near Pṛthūdaka or Pehoa in district Kurukṣetra" (Bharadwaj 1986, 131; cf. *VāmP* 23.43). *Kuñja* must derive from *kuñc*, "to bend, curve, be crooked," implying the river's many bends (I thank Michael Witzel for this observation: personal communication, December 1996).

[96]Clearly 9.40.19 speaks of "watery bowers (or curves)" *(apāṃ kuñje sarasvatyās)*, which Roy and Dutt translate as "watery receptacles." The abbreviated version of this episode in

Sarasvatī thus appears to the Ṛṣis not at Naimiṣa itself, but while they are out of station. Vaiśampāyana then recalls to Janamejaya a bower at Naimiṣa that is apparently one he has mentioned to him earlier (at 3.81.92; cf. Dandekar 1961, 491), saying, "Thus, O king, there is a watery bower (singular) in Naimiṣeya, it is recalled. At Kurukṣetra, best of Kurus, perform *(kuruṣva)* great sacrifices" (54). And Balarāma, before continuing on toward Kurukṣetra himself, then marvels at the watery bowers (plural) "there" at the site he is visiting (55).[97]

Balarāma makes his next visit to the Sapta Sārasvata Tīrtha, the tīrtha of the Seven Sarasvatīs, where the river goddess mingled together seven forms in which she had appeared elsewhere (37.27–28).[98] The seven appearances, each under a different name, show that Sarasvatī comes wherever she is "invoked by the powerful *(āhūtā balavadbhir)*" (37.2). One of the seven spots was Naimiṣa itself: "Having assembled, the Munis sat together at Naimiṣa. There were wonderful stories about Veda *(citrā kathā hy āsan vedam prati)*, O king. Having assembled, those Munis who were knowledgeable about various modes of recitation recalled Sarasvatī. Thus meditated on by those sattra-sacrificing Ṛṣis, the highly blessed and meritorious Sarasvatī came there to assist the great-souled Munis assembled there. Among the sattra-sacrificing Munis in Naimiṣa, she is (called) Kāñcanākṣi, Golden-eyed" (9.37.15–18). Once again Balarāma hears about a place along the Sarasvatī that recalls a connection with the Naimiṣa Forest, but doesn't go to Naimiṣa himself. This time, rather than the Naimiṣeyas traveling up the Sarasvatī, Sarasvatī travels to the Naimiṣeyas, who stay at Naimiṣa for the whole story, and do not leave it. As if at a symposium, they assemble for "wonderful stories" about Veda, as they do in the *Mahābhārata*'s first opening. But this time they seem to generate the stories themselves without any itinerant bard. "Golden-eyed," the special name which these Naimiṣeyas have for Sarasvatī, may remind one of the trail of golden lotuses formed by the

VāmP Saro Māhātmya 21.3–6 renames the tīrtha Yajñopavītika, presumably after the detail of the sacred threads, though it doesn't mention it. The account begins, "The Naimiṣeya Ṛṣis assembled at Kurukṣetra for bathing in the Sarasvatī, but did not obtain access to it *(praveśaṃ te na lebhire)*." Seeing the region full of Brahmans, she made bowers *(kṛtvā kuñjāni)* for them.

[97]Which is thus not to be confused with Naimiṣa, although translators have done so, further placing Naimiṣa at Kurukṣetra (Ganguli [1884–96] 1970, *Salya Parvan*, p. 115; Dutt 1895–1905, *Shalya Parva*, p. 74).

[98]Bharadwaj 1986, 131, is disingenuous in calling these "seven tributaries." In four of the seven cases, Sarasvatī appeared as the river Suprabhā to Brahmā and the Ṛṣis at Lake Pushkar in Rajasthan (37.11–14), to King Gaya as the River Viśālā at Gaya in Bihar (19–20); to Audālaka as the Manohradā River in northern Kosala or Śrāvastī in Oudh (21–23; Dandekar 1961, 492); and to Dakṣa at Hardwar on the Gaṅgā (26)!

tears of the goddess Śrī, which float by Naimiṣa Forest on the Gaṅgā during the sattra of the gods. Yet Sapta Sārasvata, where Sarasvatī makes present the Golden-eyed form in which she appeared at Naimiṣa Forest, is not on the Gaṅgā but the Sarasvatī.

One begins to appreciate that Naimiṣa Forest could manifest itself anywhere that the Sarasvatī—that is to say, Vedic knowledge—could. We have seen a Naimiṣa Forest crop up in Madurai. When Yama and the gods sit at their sattra at Naimiṣa, Indra is near enough to the Gaṅgā to see a golden lotus float by. We also noticed in chapter 1 that a Brahman visits Naimiṣa Forest to learn from the snake king Padmanābha that his "highest dharma" would be to take up the vow of gleaning. Here Naimiṣa Forest is on a bank of the Gomatī River (12.343.2c), which is the main river to run east of the Gaṅgā and west of the Sarayū, more or less parallel to each. The *Rāmāyaṇa* also (7.82.13; 83.2–4) puts Naimiṣa Forest on the Gomatī. Rāma selects that site for his Aśvamedha, telling Lakṣmaṇa, "Let a very grand sacrificial enclosure be ordered near the Gomatī in Naimiṣa Forest, O great-armed one, it has surely the highest sanctity."[99] There he arrives with his army to admire the enclosure Lakṣmaṇa has built (83.2–4), and there too come all the kings, great Ṛṣis, Rakṣasas, and monkeys who attend the rite's first year (4–16); and, after that year, it is further the site of the dramatic appearances of Rāma's sons Kuśa and Lava, his wife Sītā and the poet Vālmīki, and the god Brahmā.[100] In brief, it is where Kuśa and Lava tell their father his own story, some of which is still yet to happen. This indicates that Vālmīki—or, if one prefers, the "late" *Uttarakāṇḍa*—has adopted the narrative convention of linking Naimiṣa Forest with collapsible stories in frames. Yet as V. V. Mirashi shows (1968, 28–35), even the Gomatī identification has been split. Some relate the *Rāmāyaṇa* associations to the usual location of Naimiṣāraṇya (Naimiṣa Forest) at Nimsar, which is on the Gomatī.[101] Others look to the tradition that Rāma's Aśvamedha was performed near Vālmīki's hermitage, not much easier to locate,[102] for which Mirashi divines a spot closer to Ayodhya. According to the *Bhaviṣya Purāṇa*, however, Naimiṣa Forest is found at the "purifying lotus forest served by the Muni Vālmīki, the foremost iron bolt consisting of brahman on the bank of the Gaṅgā" (*BhvP* 3.3.28.3).

[99] *Rām* 7.82.13: *yajñavāṭaś ca sumahān gomatyā naimiṣevane/ ājñāpyatām mahābāho tadd hi puṇyam anuttamam.*

[100] 7.84–88 and 7, App. 13. I will discuss these episodes further in chap. 8.

[101] Near Misrikh, in Sitapur District, Uttar Pradesh; see Ragam 1963, 261–64; Mirashi 1968, 29; Bharadwaj 1986, 129–30.

[102] Kuśa and Lava tell Rāma that Vālmīki has "arrived" (*saṃprāpto*; 85.19d) for Rāma's sacrifice, suggesting some indeterminate distance. The *Bālakaṇḍa* places Vālmīki's hermitage on the Tamasā River, a tributary to the Gaṅgā (1.2.3; Goldman 1984, 280). See Kibe 1946, juggling river names and sizes to find it "close to the Tamasā" (431).

It is best to be aware that the *Mahābhārata* poets show no great mastery of north Indian geography (see Biardeau 1991, 83, n. 12), and that in this they are probably like purāṇic authors, who delight in fudging geography while fusing old references. Yet even with such variation, there is no reason to think that the original Naimiṣa Forest had no location at all. With the allusions now noted to Vedic linkages of Naimiṣa Forest with Kurukṣetra and the Sarasvatī, not to mention older Vedic traditions themselves that do the same, one might gravitate toward the position of P. V. Kane (1930-62, 4: 738) and O. P. Bharadwaj (1986, 130-34) that (in Bharadwaj's terms) the earliest references are to a Naimiṣa Forest that "was only a part of Kurukṣetra," or of Witzel that it was somewhere in (Eastern?) Kuru-Pañcala country" (1987b, 191). For Bharadwaj, such a position allows for numerous later purāṇic references to the two sites to be interchangeable. Bharadwaj "does not rule out the possibility that in course of time the name Naimiṣa or Naimiṣāraṇya moved eastward" (1986, 134), and indeed, it seems we see this process beginning in the hesitancies and relocations within the *Mahābhārata*, and carried further by the *Rāmāyaṇa*'s relocation of Naimiṣa to the Gomatī. But I think all such efforts to pin down Naimiṣa Forest to geography are bound to fail.[103] It is best to say for now that he *Mahābhārata* poets create a proximity for Naimiṣa and the Sarasvatī that is only partially geographic.

This brings us to the last spot where Balarāma learns about Naimiṣāraṇya: the Hermitage of Baka Dālbhya. Once again, although he keeps hearing about Naimiṣa Forest on his Sarasvatī travels, he doesn't actually go there. Here he hears not just Vedic allusions but the retelling of a Vedic story from *Kāṭhaka Saṃhitā (KS)* 10.6. Several scholars have briefly considered the two passages, but only from Vedic studies perspectives.[104] In terms of epic studies, it is worth beginning with Macdonell and Keith's observation, regarding the Dhṛtarāṣṭra in question, that there is "no good reason to deny his identity with the Dhṛtarāṣṭra of

[103]Van Buitenen 1973, x, claims to draw on an earlier edition of Schwartzburg [1978] 1992, and maps "Naimiṣa" as the whole area between the Sarasvatī and Dṛśadvatī Rivers. But Schwartzburg [1978] 1992, 14, on his *Mbh* maps, puts "Naimiṣa" between the upper Gomatī and the Gaṅgā on the map of natural features, and "Naimiṣas" between the Gomati and the Sarayū on the map of regions, peoples, and cities, and gives Naimiṣa no location on his *Rām* map (13)!

[104]Caland 1908, 51-53; Heesterman 1963, 29-30; Falk 1986, 58-60; White 1991, 97; Koskikallio 1999, 305-6, 324-25, whose statment, "Ritual information does not differ much from the original while some details have been added for clarification" (325) underestimates difference and, I think, mistakes refitting and readjustment for "clarification." Caland and Falk translate the *Kāṭhaka* passage.

the Śatapatha Brāhmaṇa, king of Kāśi."[105] That is, the two versions may differ on the home, not to mention the "dynastic" identity, of Dhṛtarāṣṭra, who in the *Mahābhārata* rules not from Kāśī (Banaras) but Hāstinapura, and is the father of the Kauravas. The epic poets seem to make one bold stroke to try to correct this. In the *KS*, the visit to Dhṛtarāṣṭra follows a cattle expedition against the Kurupañcālas, suggesting that Dhṛtarāṣṭra rules elsewhere than among the Kurupañcālas. In the epic, the visit to Dhṛtarāṣṭra follows a cattle expedition against only the Pāñcālas (9.40.3), leaving the Kuru kingdom to be implicitly identified with what the passage calls Dhṛtarāṣṭra's city.

When the *Mahābhārata* speaks of the "city" of Dhṛtarāṣṭra and uneasily folds the passage into the dynastic history of the Kurus, it is being very free with the Vedic precedent of the *Kāṭhaka Saṃhita*, which tells us no more than that Dhṛtarāṣṭra is a rāja with attendant Brahmans who is visited in person without mention of his realm. The *Kāṭhaka* tells us nothing about a Sarasvatī pilgrimage site. The retelling is thus motivated by epic amplification—and not only in these areas, but in details and modifications on the Vedic ritual. Yet as Falk shows, the *Kāṭhaka* version is clearly known to the epic narrator, who faced a familiar but partly unintelligible Vedic text that he attempted to improve where he found it to be corrupt.[106] I summarize the epic's retelling, and mention matters concerning the *Kāṭhaka* mainly in notes:

> Balarāma then went near the āśrama of Baka Dālbhya, crowded with those whose source is Brahman, where Baka Dālbhya burnt severe tapas. There, performing tapas for the sake of cattle, the energized (*pratāpavān*; 9.40.2 and 6) Baka Dālbhya poured out the kingdom of Dhṛtarāṣṭra, son of Vicitravīrya.[107]
>
> Formerly, at the twelve-year sattra of the Naimiṣeyas, when the end

[105][1912] 1967, 1:403; see *ŚB* 13.5.4.21–22, in which, however, Dhṛtarāṣṭra has no patronymic "Vaicitravīrya." Cf. Dandekar 1961, 493, not noticing the patronymic in *KS*.

[106]1986, 59–60: Falk calls the epic "Version" an adaptation or revision (Bearbeitung). Cf. Caland 1908, 51, on "some distortions" *(einigen Abweichungen)* in the *Mbh* version, and above, n. 104.

[107]7.40.1: *juhāva dhārtarṣtrasya rāṣtram*. *KS* 10.6 has "all that belonged to Dhṛtarāṣṭra was poured out," taking *avakarṇam* as a corruption of *avakīrṇam* (Falk 1986, 59, n. 170). The epic poet thus retains the theme of "pouring out the kingdom" in different terms, as if he knows it but does not recognize the terms for it in the *KS*, and repeatedly gives *avakīrṇam* the sense of "crowded, scattered" (ibid.). In *VāmP* 39.24–35 (= *Saro Māhātmya* 18.27–33 [Gupta 1968, 190–91]), Avakīrṇa becomes the name of Baka Dālbhya's tīrtha, collapsed with Pṛthūdaka and Brahmayoni tīrthas (cf. *Mbh* 9.38.22–33; 46.20–21) also along Balarāma's Sarasvatī route (see Kane 1930–62, 4:736).

of the All-Conquering rite (Viśvajit)[108] was completed, the Ṛṣis went to the Pāñcālas. There the wise ones asked the king for twenty-one strong and healthy young bulls as dakṣiṇās.[109] But Baka Vṛddha (Baka the Old, as he is called just this once)[110] then told all the Ṛṣis, "Divide the cattle (among yourselves).[111] Having relinquished these cattle, I will solicit the best of kings."[112] The best of Brahmans[113] then went to the abode (or palace: *bhavanam*) of Dhṛtarāṣṭra.[114] Having come into the presence of the lord of the people, Dālbhya begged cattle. Irritated *(ruṣita)*, Dhṛtarāṣṭra, seeing that some cows were by chance dead, said, "Quickly take these cows if you wish,

[108]No Viśvajit is mentioned in *KS* 10.6, but the rite is enfolded into numerous sattras (Caland [1931] 1982, 595, 606-7, 609, 614-15, 622-23, 638)—yet not at the end, although as a nightlong rite, it could begin or end a sattra (ibid., 585). The Viśvajit and Abhijit sacrificer (who should perform the two sequentially or simultaneously) gives away his all (excepting ground and people) in dakṣiṇās by dispersing a thousand cows in each rite. He then retires with his wife to the forest in a kind of renewed dīkṣā for twelve days in three-day parts: staying under a fig tree living on fruits and roots; staying among Niṣādas; staying among alien people, either Vaiśyas or rivals; staying with their own relatives, after which the pair can return to their previous state, reestablished in *śrī*. The rites originally established the supremacy of Indra; ibid. 430-38, 451-52; cf. Heesterman 1963, 14, 19-20; 1985, 40-41, noting in them a possible source for "the vicissitudes of the Pāṇḍavas and Rāma"; Koskikallio 1999, 325 and n. 8). Janamejaya hears that one of his and the Pāṇḍavas' ancestors, a prior Janamejaya son of Pūru, offered a Viśvajit before entering the forest (*Mbh* 1.90.11).

[109]*Vatsatarān*, "more than a calf," of which they obtain twenty-seven (cf. Koskikallio 1999, 325). Ganguli ([1884-96] 1970, 123) thinks dakṣiṇās are "to be given away . . . (in the sacrifice they have completed)." Dakṣiṇās are not given to or received among the participants in a sattra, but they may be passed on to others.

[110]*Vṛddho* is uncertain in the CE, with the variants *dālbhyo*, *dālbho*, and *vipro*. But Baka Dālbhya's old age is a rich post-Vedic theme, on which see Koskikallio (1999, passim).

[111]*Vibhajadhvam paśūn iti* (9.40.5); similarly *KS*: "You divide these yourselves *(yūyam evaitān vibhajadhvam)*."

[112]There is no echo of the reason in *KS*, where Vaka Dālbhya says, "He will make me houses" *(sa mahyaṃ gṛhān kariṣyati)*. One wonders whether obtaining "houses" reflects on his role as *gṛhapati*, "lord of the house(-s?)."

[113]Baka Dālbhya is apparently a Brahman "ritualist from the Naimiṣa Forest" (Koskikallio 1999, 305) in this *KS* passage, and in other Vedic passages a Sāma Vedic singer "with connections to *sattra* groups among the Kurupañcālas" (307). He serves, for instance in *PB* 25, under the alter ego Glāva Maitreya as the Prastotṛ (a Sāma Veda assistant) at a "snake sattra" whose serpent sattrins include "Dhṛtarāṣṭra, the son of Īravat" as the Brahman, Janamejeya as one of two Adhvaryus, etc. As Caland observes, "in this *sarpasattra*, this sattra performed by the serpents, we have to see the prototype of the *sarpasattra* (the *sattra*, where the *sarpas* are sacrificed) of Janamejaya in the Mahābhārata" ([1931] 1982, 641, n. 1). Keśin Dālbhya, another well-known Dālbhya in such texts, is, however, usually a Kṣatriya, and "sometimes he is explicitly introduced as a king" (Koskikallio 1999, 307).

[114]As remarked, *KS* provides no such residence, and has Vaka Dālbhya go to him only in person.

unworthy Brahman *(brahmabandhu)*."[115] Having heard such words, the dharma-knowing Ṛṣi considered, "Alas, cruel indeed is the speech *(aho bata nṛśaṃsaṃ vai vākyam)* I am addressed in the assembly *(saṃsadi)*." Having reflected, enraged, the best of the twiceborn set his mind to the destruction of King Dhṛtarāṣṭra. Having cut up the dead meats, he poured out the kingdom of the lord of men. Having lit a fire on the crowded *(avakīrṇe)* tīrtha of the Sarasvatī, observing high mental discipline *(niyamam param āsthitaḥ)*, Baka Dālbhya poured out Dhṛtarāṣṭra's kingdom by those very meats.[116] When that very harsh sattra was begun according to prescription, Dhṛtarāṣṭra's kingdom wasted away. Like an endless forest cut with an axe, it was struck down and even scattered insensate *(avakīrṇam acetanam)*.[117] Seeing it so, Dhṛtarāṣṭra became distressed, as did his Brahmans; but their efforts to free the kingdom were vain. Then he asked his fortunetellers *(vaipraśnikān)*, who said, "Offended by you about the cattle, the Muni Baka pours out your kingdom with the meats. When this kingdom is offered by him, the wasting is great. His ascetic rite leads away what is yours. Placate him at the watery bower of the Sarasvatī."[118]

Dhṛtarāṣṭra then went to the Sarasvatī. Falling with his head to the ground, joining palms, he said, "I placate you, lord. Forbear my

[115]Falk (1986, 59, n. 165) takes it that the prior line is also addressed to Baka Dālbhya, but does not explain how he could be called *nṛpasattama*, best of kings, in this line and a Brahman elsewhere. "Best of kings" makes more sense as a vocative addressed by Vaiśampāyana to Janamejaya. Cf. *KS*: "He (Dhṛtarāṣṭra) did not trouble about him. He incited him, 'These cows, you Brahmabandhu,' he said, 'Paśupati killed the cows. Take them far away and cook them.'" The cattle are thus killed by Rudra Paśupati rather than "by chance" *(yadṛchayā*; *Mbh* 9.40.8). In both texts, Baka Dālbhya is insulted as a *brahmabandhu*, a "nominal Brahman." Cf. *Mbh* 8.39.33: Yudhiṣṭhira calls Aśvatthaman a *brahmabandhu* to decry his falsification of Brahmanhood by fighting.
[116]Cf. n. 107 on Avakīrṇa as a purāṇic name for this tīrtha. The distillation in *VāmP Saro Māhātmya* 18.28–30 is revealing: "The Naimiṣeya Ṛṣis formerly went for the sake of dakṣiṇās. Baka Dālbhya thereupon begged Dhṛtarāṣṭra. There a lie about cattle *(paśvanṛtam)* was uttered by him (Dhṛtarāṣṭra) for the sake of censure *(nindārtham)*. Then, with great wrath, having cut flesh at the great Pṛthūdaka tīrtha called Avakīrṇa, he [Baka Dālbhya] then poured out the kingdom of the king of men Dhṛtarāṣṭra." No sattra, cattle raid, or dead cattle are mentioned; and Dhṛtarāṣṭra's insult is reduced to "a lie about cattle." Baka Dālbhya appears to offer his own flesh (as Gupta 1968, 190, translates) rather than the dead cattle's. The Ṛṣis have just "gone" for dakṣiṇās (inappropriate at a sattra). The new lesson of the thoroughly Brahmanized passage is: Never show contempt to Brahmans (18.34). Cf. Koskikallio 1999, 326, emphasizing this, and also Baka Dālbhya's connection with tīrthas.
[117]In *KS*, the rite consists of black rice kernels offered on potsherds to Agni Rudravat. *KS* also has no forest metaphor.
[118]In *KS*, there is no counterrite by Dhṛtarāṣṭra and his Brahmans, whom the epic poets seem to feel obliged to introduce even when they are useless. It is, however, again fortunetellers *(vipraśnikāḥ)* who say, "These Brahmans practice black magic *(abhicarati)* against you. Seek their protection."

offense. I am wretched, covetous, and struck with stupidity. You are the way, and you are my lord, able to make placation."[119] Seeing him bewailing and struck with grief, Baka Dālbhya felt pity *(kṛpā jajñe)* for him; placated, he dismissed his anger and released the kingdom. Then he offered a counter-offering *(punarāhuti)* for the release of the kingdom.[120] Then, having released the kingdom, having taken hold of many cattle, self-gratified, he went again to Naimiṣa Forest. The virtuous-souled Dhṛtarāṣtra, whose great mind was now sound, returned to his city possessed of great success. (9.39.32–40.25)

The *Mahābhārata*'s version has four identifiable locations: Naimiṣa Forest, which is definitely where the Naimiṣeya Baka Dālbhya returns at the story's end, and which is probably where the first sattra performed by the Naimiṣeyas takes place at its beginning; Pāñcāla country, where the "wise" Naimiṣeya sattrins go after the sattra to rustle up some cattle; the city of Dhṛtarāṣṭra, visited independently for more cattle (rather than houses, as in the *Kāṭhaka*) by Baka Dālbhya; and the pilgrimage site on the Sarasvatī where Baka Dālbhya performs a second vengeful sattra to pour out Dhṛtarāṣṭra's kingdom. If Baka Dālbhya has followed Dhṛtarāṣṭra's insulting cooking instructions to the letter—"Take them far away and cook them" (which does present a problem of transportation)—this last site should be "far away" from Dhṛtarāṣṭra's city.

The *Kāṭhaka saṃhitā* calls this second rite abhicāra (black magic) without calling it a sattra, and mentions no location for it. It is hardly done with "high mental discipline," one of the limbs of yoga (one that perhaps ironically includes *ahiṃsā*). But most important, what the *Mahābhārata* poets adapt, and at times maladapt, to their epic purposes is the Vedic story of a cattle-raiding expedition by Vrātyas—a distinctive type of Vedic sodality about which a fair amount has been written, but for the most part as if it were a live topic only for Vedic times.[121] The

[119]The *KS* has no such prefiguration of Canossa. In *VāmP Saro Māhātmya* 18.32–33, Dhṛtarāṣṭra, having had no prior consultation with fortunetellers, goes with his purohita and placates Baka by giving him all his jewels.

[120]I follow Koskikallio 1999, 324, on this "counteroffering." In *KS*, Dhṛtarāṣṭra "gave much" to Vaka Dālbhya and the Brahmans, who remove the affliction with an offering of white rice kernels on eight potsherds to Agni Surabhimat. No locations are mentioned. The epic passage adds that Bṛhaspati performed the prototype for Baka Dālbhya's rite by pouring out an oblation with meats for the nonexistence *(abhāva)* of the Asuras and the existence *(bhāva)* of the gods, after which the Asuras wasted away and were shattered by the gods, who appeared like conquerors in sacrificing (40.26–28).

[121]Steps in epic and other post-Vedic directions have been taken by Reich 1998 and

Kathaka leaves the place and length of the initial sattra vague: "The Naimiṣiyas once held a sattra. Having arisen (from it and set out), they acquired young bulls among the Kurupañcālas" *(naimiṣiyā vai satram āsata ta utthāya sampaviṃśatiṃ kurupancāleṣu vatsatarān avanvata).* Presumably they leave the Naimiṣa Forest, but one never knows. "Rising" at the end of a sattra with the verb *ud-sthā* connotes setting out on such an expedition (Falk 1986, 34). *Vatsatarān*, strong and healthy young bulls, literally, "more than a calf," are dakṣiṇās only in the epic. In the *Kathaka*, dakṣiṇās would be inappropriate, since sattrins do not receive dakṣiṇās. One learns of the value of young bulls in "mobile sattras" *(yātsattras)*, where they may be used to increase the herd from a hundred to the heavenly number of a thousand (*PB* 25.10.19), or they may serve as food for the performers (Caland [1931] 1982, 637). Vrātya rites invigorate the sattrins, just as Yama must be invigorated to bring about death on earth and restore distinction to the gods.

Yama and the gods perform their sattra at a Naimiṣa Forest on the banks of the Gaṅgā; the Naimiṣeya Baka Dālbhya performs his second sattra at a bower on the Sarasvatī. It begins to appear that just as Naimiṣa Forest moves about in the epics, so do the Naimiṣeyas bring the Naimiṣa Forest's sattra conventions to new locations. What is striking is that the poets retain not only Vedic rites and stories about Naimiṣa Forest, but make new conventions about this "momentous" place the setting and outer frame of their whole story.

Koskikallio 1999. Reich sees Vrātya themes in the epic as "echoes of Vedic motifs" (260): generally in "archaic agonistic elements" (269, 272) and especially in the *Virāṭaparvan* (268, 340, 371), for which she posits a background in "popular cults" (341). But her examples stress the "residual" (268), lack specificity (see further 229–30, 369), and in one case err: the "fantastic genocidal rite" of Janamejaya's snake sacrifice "takes place in the Naimiṣa forest, the center of the *vrātya* cult according to the earlier texts" (269). Reich conflates the sattra-sites of the two frame stories. The snake sacrifice occurs at Takṣaśilā (see n. 1 above). Koskikallio, concerned with Baka Dālbhya and figures with related names from the Vedas on, treats Vrātya rites and practices only in Vedic texts, and for later ones makes connections only in stories that "faintly mirror" them or in features that they might "explain" (374; cf. 360, 368, 373). But as we shall continue to see in chap. 4, the *Mbh* makes deliberate *allusions* to Vrātya rites and practices that are something more than mirrors and echoes. See n. 83 above.

4 Moving along with the Naimiṣeya Ṛṣis

There is no end to the maze one could trace between the Veda and the *Mahābhārata*,[1] or more particularly between Vedic precedent and epic sattras,[2] so there should be no need to explain why one must still take up the threads. Keeping matters to essentials, we must bear two questions in mind: what are the features of Vedic sattras that the *Mahābhārata* evokes, and how does it rework them into its narratives? But our main purpose in this chapter will be to continue to explore the Vedic precedents for the epic's two types of Naimiṣa conventions: the collapsible narrative and the symposium.

As we saw in chapter 3, of the seven narratives in the *Mahābhārata* that explicitly describe gatherings at Naimiṣa Forest, six are sattra narratives: two, doubled as the epic's introduction, tell of the sattra of Śaunaka and the other Ṛṣis assembled with him; one is a sattra of Yama

[1]See chaps. 1, n. 70; 3, nn. 104–21. For Biardeau, much unfolds from her premise that the *Mbh* presents a bhakti rereading of the Vedic revelation that itself encompasses a yogic one; on "the manner, at once both very free and very savant, in which the epic utilizes Vedic texts," see CR 91 (1982–83), 168 (my translation), 168–73, and CR 85 (1976–77), 167: "Avouons que dans cette épaise forêt, on n'a souvent pas d'autre méthode d'exploration que celle des *trials and errors*." Cf. Biardeau 1997a, 85, 87; Gopal 1969, 399, on Vedic echoes in the story of the four Śārṅgaka birds rescued from the burning of the Khāṇḍava forest: "It is quite likely that the author of the *Mbh*. skillfully blended together the ideas and phrases contained in different texts to show off his scholarship"; Fitzgerald 1980, 17–20; 1991, 156–65; Hiltebeitel 1984; Jatavallabhula 1999; Feller 2000; Gombach 2000, 94–113; and Inden 2000, 50, 89, for pertinent Barthesian refections on Veda, purāṇa, and epic.

[2]See Minkowski regarding sattras: "it appears that there is more Vedic precedent for the *Mahābhārata*'s frame story than for the epic itself" (1989, 415). Yet I must demur: the frame stories link with other conventions and allusions (see chaps. 1, n. 70; 3, nn. 82–83) to make the *whole appear Vedic*. See also Oberlies 1995, 178, n. 10; 192 on Minkowski's contribution, noting (187–91) that the larger consideration of Veda and epic he precipitates takes impetus from studies of the epic's treatment of specific brāhmaṇic rituals, notably the Rājasūya. But Oberlies 1998 takes such "ritualization" to be superficial (see chaps. 1, nn. 14 and 99; 2, nn. 41 and 65; 3, n. 5).

and other gods that Vyāsa recites to disclose the divine origins of the Pāṇḍavas, Draupadī, and Balarāma; and the other three are recounted during Balarāma's pilgrimage up the Sarasvatī River. If we review these, along with the sattra that is Janamejaya's Snake Sacrifice, some recurrent themes are apparent. In their connections with extreme violence, Yama's sattra and Baka Dālbhya's second sattra beside the Sarasvatī are like Janamejaya's sattra—and for that matter, like the Bhṛgu mythology that comes into focus through the epic's outer frame at the Bhārgava Śaunaka's sattra. Baka Dālbhya's first sattra is also violent, in that it concludes with a cattle raid of the Pāñcālas (in the Veda, the Kurupañcālas). This unleashing of the sattrins, which occurs in the third Naimiṣa narrative that Balarāma hears, also bears comparison with the postsattra spillover of Ṛṣis to Kurukṣetra that follows the first Naimiṣa narrative he hears. This cluster, and the frame story of Balarāma's pilgrimage to Kurukṣetra, will take us back to the Vedic Naimiṣa Forest as a possible source for the convention of the collapsible narrative.

Once we are there, we can then ask what kind of Vedic symposia occur at Naimiṣa Forest, and consider the precedent they set for the two epic sattras at which Ṛṣis gather at Naimiṣa to hear "wonderful stories about Veda": one, the second Naimiṣa narrative Balarāma hears; the other, Śaunaka's sattra, which provides the epic's outer frame. Let us simply register the impression that the phrase "wonderful stories about Veda" has a certain interchangeability with "the *Mahābhārata*."

A. The Vrātyas: Vedic Precedent and Epic Usages

Behind all these sattras we must now consider the Vrātyas. Heesterman, who has worked longest on the subject, remarks: "As is now generally recognized, both the *dīkṣita* and the sattrin[3] derive from the *vrātya*, the aggressive warrior moving about in sworn bands" (1993, 178) on so-called Vrātya expeditions, which could be undertaken by *rājaputras*, princes or "king's sons" (ibid., 183), as well as by the "sons of the Kuru Brahmans" (1963, 6, 17).[4] Heesterman's claim of consensus is possible thanks mainly to Falk, who amplifies Heesterman's groundbreaking 1963 essay, "Vrātya and Sacrifice."[5] Witzel summarizes

[3]One "consecrated" to perform a sacrifice *(dīkṣita)*, and one engaged in performing a sattra (*sattrin*).

[4]One need not follow Heesterman's theoretical reconstruction of a preclassical Vedic sacrifice to work with his account of "derivations" from the preclassical Vrātyas and the "reformation" of sattras.

[5]See Heesterman 1993, 278, n. 18, on Falk 1986, 17–30, as adding "further details and comparative materials." Falk also adds new insights, as does Koskikallio 1999.

the advances that can now be appreciated: "The Vrātyas are poor, mostly younger Brahmins and Kṣatriyas who in search of a 'start capital' form a dark, ominous sodality which demands ransom from the local, well-settled *gṛhasthas* and even from the kings" (1989, 235–36). The classical systematization of śrauta ritual, which rejected such crossover between Kṣatriyas and Brahmans, separated the sattra "session" from the Vrātyastoma. It regularized the sattra into a rite requiring seventeen Brahman sacrificers, and reformed the Vrātyastoma into a single-day soma sacrifice *(ekāha)*. Earlier the Vrātyastoma was performed for the beginning and end of Vrātya expeditions.[6]

Frequently, as in the *Kāṭhaka Saṃhitā* version of the Baka Dālbhya story, one must read behind descriptions of sattras to see the older Vratya pattern, since the term *vrātya* is not mentioned (Falk 1986, 60). But as Falk shows, two stories of Budha Saumya or Budha Saumāyana, after whom one of the primal ancestors of the lunar dynasty seems to be named,[7] describe a leader of sattras performed by Vrātyas themselves. In one, he is the *sthapati* (interchangeable with *gṛhapati*,[8] one of Śaunaka's two titles) of a group called the Daivā Vrātyas, who are typically associated with the plundering Maruts.[9] In the other, he is the sthapati of a Vrātya band that performs a sixty-one-day sattra of a type associated with the sixty-one-day cold period *(śiśira)* of winter.[10] In the latter account (*PB* 24.28.2–9), the old is kept with the new, and "the concepts of Vrātya, sattrin, and dīkṣita are inseparably interrelated" (1986, 57).

[6]Heesterman 1963, 14–15; Falk 1986, 31. See Heesterman 1963, 3, 32–33; 1993, 178–79; Falk 1986, 40–41 on the anomalous character of the Vrātyastoma in the śrauta classification system.

[7]Budha is the son of Soma (the Moon, a.k.a. Candra), first in descent from Soma in the lunar dynasty's origins; see Hiltebeitel 1977a, 330. Although not called Saumya or Saumāyana ("son of Soma" [Caland (1931) 1982, 621]; "descendant of Soma" [Macdonell and Keith (1912) 1967, 2:69]), the epic poets are likely to have played upon such Vedic names, as they do upon Dhṛtarāṣṭra Vaicitravīrya's (see chap. 3, § D), in constructing the line of lunar descent: Brahmā-Atri-Soma-Budha-Purūravas-Āyus-Nahuṣa-Yayāti, etc. (7.119.4–5).

[8]See Heesterman 1963, 3, and n. 8; Falk 1986, 18; 31, n. 70. *Gṛhapati* is used for both Vrātyas and sattrins; *sthapati* likewise in the present passage.

[9]*Baudhāyana Śrauta Sūtra* 18.26, translated and discussed in Falk 1986, 55–57. On the *daivā vrātyāḥ* being like Maruts and their leader like Indra, see Heesterman 1963, 4–5, 17–18, 32–33; White 1991, 95–96 and 256, n. 47. I thank Michael Witzel (personal communication, December 1996) for also pointing out that the Snakes who become Ādityas in *PB* 25.15, and who elsewhere rival the Āṅgirases, are like the Daivā Vrātyāḥ: "having left aside their old hide, [they] creep further, for they had vanquished death. The Ādityas are the serpents"; see chap. 3, n. 113 on this passage. As in other sections of *PB* 25, the sattra stories recall Vrātya practice.

[10]See Falk 1986, 28, 31, 34, 40; White 1991, 96–99.

For its bearing on *Mahābhārata* sattras, we must consider certain features of this text, which I summarize:[11]

> The Vrātyas, adherents of "the God" (apparently Rudra), held a sattra with Budha as their sthapati. They consecrated themselves (or the sacrificial place, *devayajana*), without asking King Varuṇa. Varuṇa cursed them, precluding them from a share in the sacrifice and from knowing the path leading to the gods. Now, at that time there was neither juice in the herbs nor butter in the milk nor fat in the flesh nor hair on the skin nor leaves on the trees, but since the Vrātyas performed this sixty-one-day rite, they obtained these potencies and were full of lustre, full of sap. With regard to this, three verses *(ślokas)* are handed down, telling that:
>
> > Budha Saumāyana, raising the earth for his dīkṣā, brought fat into the milk and over the protruding bones of the cattle, delighted his whole band, and received their strength in his flesh.
>
> Those who settle down on the devayajana to undertake the sixty-one-day sattra should ask Varuṇa's agreement. Those who do so thrive in all ways.

As Falk observes, the three śloka verses recall an older situation than the surrounding prose. In the ślokas, Budha Saumāyana's dīkṣā temporarily relieves his band's hunger and restores fat to cattle that are threatened with perishing. A Vrātya expedition for cattle of the type led by Baka Dālbyha could then follow. In the prose, the restoration of sap and strength to nature is permanent, and Budha's dīkṣā is only the origin of a sattra for Brahmans, and not a model for repetition of a rite that could end with a Vrātya expedition (1986, 58). As to Budha's dīkṣā itself, we have here a clear instance of the leader's role as dīkṣita in undertaking the dīkṣā vows for his Vrātya band and/or co-sattrins (Heesterman 1963, 32; 1993, 182). Such an undertaking brings impurity and "evil" *(pāpman)* upon him, yet he is also invigorated by the group's participation.[12] The Vrātyastoma is classed as a Soma sacrifice, and the "central evil" is "the killing of Soma or of the sacrificial substance in general, whether animal or cereal" (22). But secret Vrātya sattras in the forest seem to have emphasized cow sacrifice with overtones of human sacrifice, identification

[11]From Caland [1931] 1982, 620–22, and Falk 1986, 57–58. Cf. Heesterman 1963, 11, 16–17.

[12]1963, 8–9, 12–13, 24. Cf. Witzel 1984, 215–16; such a power, ritually generated, can also invigorate the sun and the "ascension" of the Milky Way.

with dogs, and the self-sacrifice and rebirth of the gṛhapati-sthapati himself.[13]

We can quickly see that much of this resonates with the Baka Dālbhya story, which is awkwardly refitted from Veda to epic. His presumed role as single dīkṣita and sattra-leader in giving away all the cattle to his co-sattrins recalls the older Vrātya practice of the leader dispersing his collected goods as dakṣiṇās (which the reformed sattra no longer includes, having no dakṣiṇās, since all seventeen priests circulate goods only to each other).[14] His second sattra is performed with offerings of dead cattle. With Baka Dālbhya in mind, certain things also become clear about the gods' sattra at Naimiṣa Forest on the Gaṅgā, where Yama is explicitly the dīkṣita, and thus presumably the gṛhapati as well.

As suggested in chapter 3, the gods who "sit" at the sattra of the dīkṣita Yama are distinguished from other gods who are clearly "more immortal" than they, yet see even that immortality imperiled. This latter group, which is able to leave the sattra to appeal to Brahmā, cannot be sattrins themselves, who would have to remain "seated" to perform their conjoint priestly functions with Yama. I have suggested they are sadasyas, who would presumably have more leeway in coming and going, and noted that their number does not include the Maruts. The non-mention of the Maruts in this group hardly serves to place them in the other. But the image of the Vedic Maruts as Vrātyas, and as prototypes for "human Vrātyas,"[15] fits elegantly into the slot left for Yama's unspecified divine co-sattrins. Says Heesterman, "The relevant opposition seems not to be divine vrātyas as against human vrātyas—indeed the texts never speak about *mānuṣā vrātyāḥ* [human Vrātyas]—but of *devāḥ* [Gods] as against *daivyā vrātyāḥ* [divine Vrātyas]. When the gods go to heaven the *daivyā vrātyāḥ* stay behind and rejoin them later on. They belong to the gods but at the same time are opposed to them. They are said to have offended Rudra (Īśāna) or Vāyu or Varuṇa" (1963, 17). Indeed, "human Vrātyas" are really those who self-designate themselves as *daivyā vrātyāḥ* (ibid.), those who seek divine immortality like the Maruts and Yama (a god, after all, who begins as the first mortal). Koskikallio marks the distinction by calling them "earthly vrātyas" (1999, 311).

As Brahmā says to Indra and the other Gods who have come to him, Yama must be invigorated by these others: his "body will be strengthened

[13]See especially White 1991, 96, 99, 101; cf. Heesterman 1963, 14, 25; 1993, 175; Falk 1986, 38–42, 60–65; Koskikallio 1999, 306, 315.

[14]Heesterman 1963, 13; 1993, 36–37, 178; Falk 1986, 33, 40: the gṛhapati gives himself as dakṣiṇā.

[15]See *Baudhāyana Śrauta Sūtra* 18.26 as discussed in Heesterman 1963, 16–17; Falk 1986, 55.

joined with your power *(vīrya)*." In terms of what is lost and regained through the conduct of the Vrātya dīkṣita, this same quality of energy or strength *(vīrya)* can be called *indriya vīrya*, "Indra force" (Heesterman 1963, 8–9, 12, 22). The narrative connection in this story between Yama and Indra begins with the concern that Yama as dīkṣita obtain this "Indra force." The Vrātya leader is supposed to be Indra-like, while the group is like the Maruts when he unites them (ibid., 7).

I have suggested that the sattra Yama leads at Naimiṣa Forest seems to invert features of a human sattra. If so, the inversions conform to what we know about Vrātya sattras. Instead of offering a cow for the invigoration of cows which may then be captured and increased, paving the way for humans to reach heaven, Yama avoids sacrificing "creatures" so that humans can be killed, leaving immortality (rather than the older Vedic heaven) as the preserve of gods. Instead of killing (i.e., sacrificing) for the invigoration of all creatures, and even of the cosmos through the invigoration of the sun in the sixty-one day winter sattra,[16] the gods (or at least certain gods including Yama), thinking only of their own welfare, take time out from killing so that divine life can be invigorated beyond the sattra by the killing of humans—the very thing that will restore the gods' distinction.

Moreover, this killing will take place by a virtual divine raid into the human world led by five Indras, "consecrated" as dīkṣitas for this mission by Śiva's curse that they be reborn in human wombs (which are prefigured for the four former Indras by their gestation in a Himalayan cave). Like the Vedic Maruts as *daivyā vrātyāḥ*, the former Indras are in this lowered state because they have offended Rudra-Śiva, as has the current Indra. Their raid ultimately takes them, through the humans they incarnate, to Kurukṣetra, sacrificial altar of the gods, where, like Vrātyas who attain heaven through the Vrātyastoma (Heesterman 1963, 6), they can regain heaven only through Vrātya-like cruel deeds.[17] Indeed, the Pāṇḍavas, who undergo further symbolic dīkṣās to make them dīkṣitas for the sacrifice of battle,[18] are precisely five former Indras with the chief

[16]See Witzel 1984, 215–16; Falk 1986, 28, 31–34, 40–41; White 1991, 96, 98–99.

[17]Heesterman 1963, 6, 11: The Vrātya on campaign assails "those who are not to be assailed," especially Brahmans and Veda scholars, and commits "cruel, unappeased deeds" (*krūra, aśānta*; *JB* 2,223). Cf. Witzel 1984, 221. Recall that the Pāṇḍavas will regain Indraloka only after performing "unbearable" lethal karma (see chap. 3, after n. 87).

[18]See Biardeau 1976, 207–8; 1978, 149–57, 187–88, and n. 3; CR 82 (1973–4), 94; Biardeau and Malamoud 1976, 133. Biardeau regards the generalized dīkṣā theme as "doubled" in the person of Arjuna, whose wrestling match with Śiva, when the latter is disguised as a hunter (*kirāta*), involves a transformation of Arjuna's "offered" body into a divine one, permitting him to ascend to heaven and attain divine weapons to be used in the "sacrifice of battle" (1976, 227, 241, 245; 1978, 149–59). Oberlies 1995, 179 also observes

among them, Yudhiṣṭhira, none other than the son and incarnation of Yama-Dharma himself: that is, of the dīkṣita of the gods' sattra at Naimiṣa Forest, through whom this whole divine raiding operation is launched.

It seems that the full story of Yama's sattra describes a dīkṣā in two stages. First Yama is dīkṣita; then the five Indras undergo a kind of dīkṣā as well. Only for Yudhiṣṭhira is it doubled. Yama as dīkṣita becomes "Indra-like" in the convergence that gives birth, through this story, to Yudhiṣṭhira, who is both a former Indra and the son and "portion" *(aṃśa)* of Dharma-Yama. The other four Pāṇḍavas are also both former Indras and "portions" of different gods (Bhīma of Vāyu, Arjuna of Indra, the twins of the Aśvins), but none of those gods has been a former *dīkṣita* at a Naimiṣa Forest sattra.

The story Vyāsa tells Drupada to explain why Yudhiṣṭhira is unknowingly right that Draupadī can marry five men thus draws not only on the convention of Naimiṣa Forest sattras, but on deeper resonances of those sattras with Vrātyas and death.[19] In doing so, Vyāsa reveals some dark and hidden things, but at the same time seems to conceal the Vedic connections with Vrātyas.[20] He reveals that the marriage is dharmic, and that it has beginnings that have to do with death. But he never fully reveals that Dharma is actually Yama, or that Dharmarāja Yudhiṣṭhira's identity as the son of Yama-Dharma "consecrates" him for a sacrifice of battle that will accomplish the same ends as the sixty-one-day Vrātya rite of Budha Saumāyana: a renovation of the earth.[21] Dharma's identity

that the Pāṇḍavas are heavily armed "kriegerliche Pilger [warrior pilgrims], Dīkṣitas" when they set forth on their *Āraṇyakaparvan* pilgrimage. Cf. Hiltebeitel 1980b, 149–50, 168–74 and for a *Mbh-Rām* comparison on this matter, 1985b, 47–51.

[19]Cf. Heesterman 1963, 20, on the use by Death (Mṛtyu) of Vrātya "weapons" (lute-playing, dancing, frivolity) in losing his sacrificial rivalry with the calculating Prajāpati; and 1993, 176, on death and the sattrin.

[20]The *Mbh*'s "dark" extractions from the hidden corners of Veda are similar to those of Dante and Chaucer from the Bible, as discussed by Gellrich 1985, 126–33, 157, 165, 173, n. 20, 201. Both Gellrich (123, n. 80) and Handelman (1982, 29–30) acknowledge Auerbach's treatment of the Bible as "fraught with 'background'" (1968, 15): an apt phrase too for what the *Mbh* knows and reencrypts as Veda. See chap. 2, n. 28, and at n. 18. Cf. also Derrida 1995, 10, n. 5: "Literature concerning the secret is almost always organized around scenes and intrigues that deal with figures of death." The *Rām* touches on its Vedic "background" more "lightly"; see Biardeau 1997a, 87.

[21]Bhaṭṭa Nārāyaṇa's *Veṇīsaṃhāra*, which makes explicit things about Draupadī's hair that the epic treats implicitly (Hiltebeitel 1981), does the same for Yudhiṣṭhira's unique dīkṣita status: says Bhīma to Draupadī, in "the sacrifice of war *(raṇayajña)*, . . . [the younger Pāṇḍavas] are the officiating priests; Lord Hari is the director of rites; the king [Yudhiṣṭhira] is the one consecrated *(dīkṣitaḥ)* for this sacrifice of war; [our] wife is the one whose vow is maintained" (Hiltebeitel 1981, 193; *Veṇīsaṃhāra* 1.25). Cf. the *Śrī Tiraupatātēvi Māṉmiyam*'s version of the former Indras' myth, where Yudhiṣṭhira is both

with Yama is, however, borne out in numerous resonances, not least of which is Yudhiṣṭhira's thirteenth-year disguise as a carrion-eating "heron" *(kaṅka)*[22] and his prior encounter with the death-dealing Dharma, who is himself disguised as a carrion-eating crane *(baka)* by a lakeside in the forest-book episode of the Yakṣa's questions.[23] Indeed, the name of Baka Dālbhya also resonates in the epic with this Crane disguise of Yama-Dharma.[24] It is perhaps appropriate that "Mr. Crane Dālbhya" should "pour out" the kingdom of Dhṛtarāṣṭra at a watery bower on the Sarasvatī,[25] just as the crane-disguised Yama-Dharma nearly ends the lives of the Pāṇḍavas by a lakeside before asking Yudhiṣṭhira the Yakṣa's questions that enable their recovery. But there is also an analogy between Yudhiṣṭhira and Baka Dālbhya: each oversees a sacrifice that nearly "pours out" the kingdom of Dhṛtarāṣṭra: one at Kurukṣetra, the other at a spot along Balarāma's pilgrimage route to Kurukṣetra that takes him past so many Sarasvatī tīrthas. As we have seen, Balarāma, although he never goes there, hears about Naimiṣa Forest at three of these tīrthas. Moreover, we have also noted another link between these four Naimiṣa narratives.

The same Balarāma who hears three Naimiṣa stories on his pilgrimage has also been born, along with the Pāṇḍavas and Draupadī, as a result of

a former Indra and a portion of Yama rather than Dharma (Hiltebeitel 1991a, 485). Yudhiṣṭhira's "compact" with "time the winged finisher" (*saṃdhiṃ kṛtvaiva kālena antakena patatriṇā*; 3.36.1) is also a compact with death.

[22]In disguise, Yudhiṣṭhira also identifies himself as a gambling "Brahman of the Vaiyāghrapādya [Tiger paw] line" (*vaiyāghrapadyaḥ punar asmi brāhmaṇaḥ*; 4.6.10.b), giving himself for Vedic precedent a name of Aupoditi Gaupālāyana Vaiyāghrapadya, the sthāpati of a band of "earthly Vrātyas" who seek the heaven attained by their *daiva vrātya* counterparts (*Baudhāyana Śrauta Sūtra* 18.26; see Koskikallio 1999, 311). Note also that Vrātyas are "poison-swallowers" (Koskikallio 1999, 318), a trait partially matched by Bhīma's resistance to snake poison (1.119.39–41). On the "heron," cf. Fitzgerald 1998, for whom the carrion-eating of the *kaṅka* contradicts heron behavior. Fitzgerald thinks that although *kaṅka* probably does cover herons, the carrion-eating "giant stork *Leptopilos dubious*, a grotesquely ugly bird that presides over the carrion-littered battlefield, . . . supplies an even more compelling emblem" of *Mbh*'s 'Dharma King' (1998, 258).

[23]On Dharma understood as Yama in the *Mbh*, see Belvalkar 1959, xxix; Karve 1974, 67; Biardeau 1976, 171–72; 1978, 94–106; Hiltebeitel 1988, 431–32; 1991a, 50–52, 128, n. 13, 485; Scheuer 1982, 120–22; and Kantawala 1995, 103–4, 109 (in the Aṇīmāṇḍavya episode, which establishes this identity "from the start" [see chap. 5, § B]). There is little to recommend Dumézil's view of Dharma as a "rejuvenated" Vedic Mitra (1968, 172), or Gonda's that Dharma is an independent deity in an epic that "scarcely knows Dharma as Yama" (1971, 125).

[24]As does the cannibal demon Baka whom Bhīma slays to protect a Brahman village (Hiltebeitel 1988, 174).

[25]Dālbhya is probably from *darbha*, the pointy grass used in sacrifices whose sharpness can make it a weapon (Hiltebeitel 1991a, 394). Cf. Koskikallio 1999, 314, 316; Sarma 1968, 240, on Keśin Dārbhya or Dālbhya, disrespectfully called "*darbha.*"

Yama's sattra at Naimiṣa Forest. More precisely, after Śiva has ordained the births of the Pāṇḍavas and Draupadī in the human world, the gods then go to Viṣṇu, who confirms all of Śiva's arrangements and then, plucking a white and black hair from his head, ordains the births of Balarāma and Kṛṣṇa (1.189.31). Balarāma and Kṛṣṇa thus complete the core of divine births at the heart of the epic's divine plan,[26] which as we have seen is also a divine raiding operation. Unlike the Pāṇḍavas and Draupadī who are ordained by Śiva to lives of unbearable and lethal karma, Balarāma and Kṛṣṇa are ordained by Viṣṇu to in a certain manner direct and contain their violence—especially at Kurukṣetra, where both Balarāma and Kṛṣṇa are noncombatants. Indeed, it is Balarāma's pilgrimage that keeps him out of the fighting.

Further, not only are the four Naimiṣa narratives saturated with Vedic allusions; so are the stories of several of the other Sarasvatī tīrthas Balarāma visits.[27] But most important, as was anticipated in chapter 3, Balarāma's Sarasvatī pilgrimage as a whole recreates, and refits to epic ends, a precise Vedic ritual precedent called a *yātsattra* or "moving session,"[28] a type of journey that provides a "clear case" of the "traces of vrātya ritual in the śrauta sacrifice" (Heesterman 1963, 34).

[26]See chap. 1 at nn. 19 and 42; chap. 2, § C.27; and chap. 3, n. 92; Hiltebeitel 1999a, 241–54. Cf. Sullivan B. 1990, 66–73, on "Brahmā's plan," which is ultimately Nārāyaṇa's—unless one prefers to call it the author's. Cf. Inden 2000, 62, on the "divine plan" of the *VDhP* as an imperial world wish; Richardson 1990, 187–96, and Redfield 1994 on the "plan of Zeus" in the *Iliad.*

[27]See the curing of Soma at Prabhāsa (9.34.36–76; cf. 42.38–42 and 49.65–50.2 on Soma), the coolness of the herbs *(oṣadhi)* at Udapāna (34.80–81), the birth of the Maruts at Sapta Sārasvat (37.30–32; cf. 46.22–28 on the Maruts), Vasiṣṭha and Viśvāmitra's rivalry for Sarasvatī's favor at Vasiṣṭhāpavāha (41.1–39), the concealment of Agni in the śamī at Agnitīrtha (46.12–20), and especially the miraculous salvation of the Veda and Vedic recitation through a twelve-year drought by the boy-Muni Sārasvata at Sārasvatamunitīrtha (50.2–50)—not to mention the details on Kurukṣetra, Plakṣaprasravaṇa, Kārapacana, and Yamunā mentioned below. Dandekar's eye for further Vedic detail also enriches his notes on this passage in the CE (1961, 489–97).

[28]See chap. 3, n. 90, on Oberlies and Bigger's studies. For what follows, I do not share these authors' view that the *Mbh*'s pilgrimage lists and narratives are interpolations that can be broken down into originally separate components ("plains" pilgrimages and mountain ascents coming from separate textual units [Oberlies 1995]; circular pilgrimage routes that are later than up-river ones [Bigger 1999a, 7–8]); that they correlate with textual strata and are evidence for theories of textual growth or the evolution of pilgrimage; that Balarāma's is not only the oldest pilgrimage insertion, but divisible into further separately interpolated components (Bigger 1998, 73–74; 1999a, 3); that the Pāṇḍavas' pilgrimage comes next from a Bhārgava layer (see chap. 3, § B above) because some Bhārgava stories are told during it; that the lack of Bhārgava stories during Balarāma's pilgrimage might mean that Bhārgava redactors left it alone because the Pāṇḍavas' pilgrimage served their purposes better; or that Arjuna's tīrthayātrā enters last and probably from a Pāñcarātra layer because it mentions Nara and Nārāyaṇa (1999a, 3–5). The method is catch-as-catch-can and speculative.

B. Moving Sessions along the Sarasvatī

Yātsattrins, like Vrātyas, "go along 'killing and cursing,' this being an expression of force *(ghnanta ākrośanto yanti, etad vai balasya rūpam)*."[29] Their journeys are "moving sessions," marching eastward along the Sarasvatī (or its tributary the Dṛṣadvatī) and ending at the Yamunā. Crossing rivers with their sacrificial fires, they move the *gārhapatya* (domestic) fire eastward each day by the distance of the throw of a *śamyā*—"a wooden pin used, inter alia as a marker when measuring out the place of sacrifice." So as to continually relocate the *mahāvedi*, the eastward-extending trapezoidal "great altar" used for animal and soma sacrifices, wheels are provided for carts to portage the larger ritual components and drag a special *yūpa* (sacrificial post) whose mortar-shaped base makes it easier to pull. They take with them a hundred cows and a bull "with the aim of having them multiply to the mythic number of a thousand" (Heesterman 1993, 128–29; 1963, 35–36). A thousand cows represent the height and reaching of heaven,[30] and for yātsattrins heaven's attainment. Similarly, the Maruts are said to have performed Sarasvatī yātsattras when attempting to attain heaven.[31] For the yātsattra along the Dṛṣadvatī, the yātsattrin's "final bath in the river Yamunā" suggests "ritual suicide" in the statement, "There he disappears from among men."[32]

That Balarāma's pilgrimage is a yātsattra refitted to epic ends can be supported both by his route and by details of his expedition. He sets out not alone but "together with all the Yādavas" (9.34.12)—all, that is, but Sātyaki and Kṛtavarman, who, as the passage mentions (9.34.13), side with the Kauravas and Pāṇḍavas respectively at Kurukṣetra, and of course Kṛṣṇa.[33] The Yādavas are Kṣatriya warriors and a branch of the lunar dynasty that descends from Yayāti's oldest son Yadu, and parallels the branch (which includes the Kurus) that descends from Yayāti's youngest son Pūru. Their accompaniment of Balarāma signifies that Kṛṣṇa keeps "all the Yādavas" out of the fighting. Yet the epic Yādavas already have

[29]Heesterman 1963, 34–35, citing *JB* 2.298; see Caland 1919, 201; cf. also Witzel's translation, 1984, 221.

[30]"'The world of heaven is as far removed from this (earthly) world' they say, 'as a thousand cows standing the one above the other.' Therefore, they say, 'He who sacrifices with a sacrifice at which a thousand dakṣiṇās are given, reaches these worlds'" (*PB* 16.8.6; Caland [1931] 1982, 440); the gaining of all by the offering of a thousand cows is also compared to the winning *kṛta* throw in dice (*JB* 16.9.4). See further Witzel 1984, 221.

[31]Heesterman 1963, 34–35, citing *JB* 2.297–99; Caland 1919, 201.

[32]*PB* 25.23.4; Heesterman 1993, 175 and n. 64; Witzel 1984, 220, 224, 255, n. 77.

[33]According to Sörensen [1904] 1963, 761, Yādava is "commonly synonymous with Vṛshṇi," a term that frequently describes Sātyaki and Kṛtavarman.

associations with herding that both anticipate later identifications of Yādavas as herders,[34] and, on this pilgrimage, evoke earlier Vedic patterns of "transhuming treks of warrior bands carrying their fire and belongings with them" (Heesterman 1985, 104). We see this best when Vaiśampāyana whets Janamejaya's appetite to hear more about Sarasvatī tīrthas with a summary of the Yādavas' departure and the trek. Balarāma ordered, "Bring all the provisions and paraphernalia *(saṃbhārān . . . upakaraṇāni ca)* for a tīrthayātra: the sacrificial fires in Dvārakā, and also sacrificers *(ānayadhvaṃ dvārakāyā agnīn vai yājakāṃs tathā)*. Bring gold, silver, cows, robes, horses, elephants, chariots, and also ass and camel vehicles. Quickly bring everything necessary for a tīrthayātra. Moving quickly, go against the stream of the Sarasvatī *(pratisrotaḥ sarasvatyās)*. Bring Ṛtvijs and hundreds of Brahmans" (34.15–17). The haste reminds us that the journey will all occur "during the calamity (*vaiśase*) of the Kurus" (34.18). Among the provisions and paraphernalia he orders,[35] Balarāma, like a good yātsattrin, remembers to bring the sacrificial fires in Dvāraka, and clarifies that he will be accompanied by a plurality of journeying "sacrificers" (*yājakas*: presumably those who are then called "Ṛtvijs and friends [*suhṛd*]" in distinction from "other Brahmans" [19a]).[36] Among the mobile units that combine features of a caravan with those of an epic army (chariots, elephants, horses), there is also no forgetting the cows. The wealth of all kinds that is brought along to be given out along the way takes above all the form of "thousands of milk cows, their horns cased in gold and covered with beautiful cloths" (30). The recipients are the weak and weary, children and the elderly (20), and Brahmans and Kṣatriyas (24); but it is especially and most persistently, of course, Brahmans who are to receive this wealth as dakṣiṇās (21–26, 29–31). In a yātsattra, dakṣiṇās would only be a by-product, since the performing "sacrificer-priests" would not receive them but give them to others. The epic makes dakṣiṇās focal, turning the yātsattra into a pilgrimage with dakṣiṇās for the Brahmans who write them into the text, making sure the cows go to them. As to the trek itself, along a route furnished not only with trees and creepers but shops and markets (28), "The path shone, O king, bringing pleasure to all, like heaven then, O hero, for the men who were going there."[37]

Balarāma's intention is to go "against the stream of the Sarasvatī," which is further specified as "approaching the Sarasvatī against the

[34]Biardeau 1978, 204–37; Hiltebeitel 1988, 185–86, 220.

[35]*Upakaraṇāni* could include sacrificial implements.

[36]The priests in a sattra are also yajamānas, "sacrificers"; see Witzel 1984, 220.

[37]*Sa panthāḥ prababhau rājan sarvasyaiva sukhāvahaḥ/ svargopamas tadā vīra narāṇāṃ tatra gacchatām* (34.27).

stream [beginning] from the ocean *(sarasvatīṃ pratisrotaḥ samudrād abhijagmivān)*" (34.18). The concept of following a river upstream is a commonplace: we have, for instance, seen Indra leave the Naimiṣa Forest to follow the Gaṅgā to its source, and can mention the Buddhist "stream-winner" as the best-known parallel. But the approach "from the ocean" signals one of the ways the epic poets redefine the Vedic yātsattra into a classical pilgrimage. Whereas the Vedic yātsattra would begin at the fourth tīrtha along the epic route, the epic extends the beginning westward to start "from the ocean" near where the Yādavas live. In the epic's (and purāṇas') expanded pilgrimage geography, Sarasvatī, which already in Vedic texts is said to have gone underground at the fourth tīrtha,[38] is allowed to empty into the sea at Prabhāsa after reemerging from underground at Camasodbheda (the second tīrtha on the Yādavas' route) after reaching there below Udapāna (the third, which shows the river's presence under it by the coolness of its herbs).[39] The Yādavas thus begin their pilgrimage near Dvārakā at the oceanside tīrtha of Prabhāsa: the very place that they will go to from Dvārakā on their final tīrthayātra (16.4.6–9) to end their days in a drunken brawl, with Balarāma leaving the world by emitting from his mouth the white world-supporting snake Śeṣa, who returns to the ocean.[40] The westward extension of the beginning of the yātsattra to the ocean thus bespeaks widening horizons and new bhakti connections, but it does not change the yātsattra's underlying cosmological scheme, as we shall see.

From the fourth tīrtha on, each of the four sites indicated in *Pañcaviṃśa Brāhmaṇa* 25.10, the Brāhmaṇa literature's fullest account of the Sarasvatī yātsattra,[41] is either mentioned, or finds ready equivalents in Balarāma's tīrthayātra:

1. The Vedic yātsattrins undertake their dīkṣā "on the southern bank" of the Sarasvatī at Vinaśana "where the (river) Sarasvatī is lost

[38]See below; Kane 1930-62, 4:555–59, argues that the Sarasvatī was dry before the *Aitareya Brāhmaṇa*. I will not comment on the current debates about a "Sarasvatī Civilisation" that would have preceded this disappearance of the river in question other than to say that it is unknown to the epic poets.

[39]9.34.78–80; see Dandekar 1961, 490, on Camasodbheda.

[40]16.5.12–13. See chap. 2, § C.41 for the surrounding events. The pilgrimage from Prabhāsa recalls that Arjuna stopped there to marry Subhadrā on *his* so-called pilgrimage (1.210.2–8), and that the Pāṇḍavas also passed through on their forest tīrthayātrā (3.118.15; see Oberlies 1995, 182). It now marks the beginning of the movements of the Yādavas that will end there with their destruction.

[41]See Caland [1931] 1982, 634-37, trans.; Witzel 1984, 231, partial trans. Cf. *ŚŚS* 13.29 (Caland 1953, 368–70), mostly reiterating.

(in the sands of the desert)."[42] Vinaśana is where we have seen Balarāma learn that the Sarasvatī went underground because of her hatred of Śūdras and Ābhīras (9.36.1–2).

2. Proceeding upstream on the southern bank, yātsattrins reach a section where "they move along the eastern part (of the stream), for at this (part) one single (other stream) flows into (it): the Dṛṣadvatī."[43] The "eastern part" is probably still on the southern bank of one of the river's bends. Here the match between the yātsattra and the Yādava tīrthayātra is least clear, but presumably it is with the segment that runs from what Dandekar calls the "Eastern *tīrthas*" to Naimiṣeya Kuñja or Prācī-Sarasvatī, where the river is said to turn east (9.36.32–36; i.e., the eleventh and twelfth tīrthas on the route).[44] In approaching these, the Yādavas are on the Sarasvatī's southern bank (36.28) for at least the stretch between Śaṅkha Tīrtha and Dvaitavana (the eighth and ninth tīrthas).[45]

3. From here the yātsattrins go to Plakṣa Prāsravaṇa, which is "a distance of forty days on horseback from the spot where the Sarasvatī is lost" (i.e., Vinaśana). From here heaven can be reached: in *Pañcaviṃśa Brāhmaṇa* 25.10.16, at the distance of another forty days on horseback; in *Jaiminīya Brāhmaṇa* 2.297, Plakṣa Prāsravaṇa is itself "the end of the word" *(vāco 'ntas)*—that is, the end or source of the Sarasvatī as Vedic speech and the place beyond description: heaven (*svargo loka*) itself (Caland 1919, 200–1; Witzel 1984, 221 and 249, n. 51). Plakṣa Prāsravaṇa, "probably representing the middle of the world," is where yātsattras may end, which they should do through one of three "accomplishments":[46] "when the cows they have taken with them have increased tenfold, or, conversely, when they [the

[42]Caland [1931] 1982, 634, translating *PB* 25.10.1; *JB* 2.297 provides the detail of the southern bank *(dakṣiṇe tīre)*; see Caland 1919, 200–201.

[43]Caland [1931] 1982, 636, translating *PB* 25.10.13–14.

[44]The epic makes no mention of crossing the Dṛṣadvatī, which is thought to have entered the Sarasvatī from the south (Kane 1930–62, 4:682). In *PB* 25.10.15, they offer boiled rice to Agni as Apāṃnapāt; in *Āpastambha Śrauta Sūtra* 23.12–13, they offer an *iṣṭi* here to Agni Kāma (Kane, 4:558), but in *PB* 25.10.22, this is done at Plakṣa Prāsravaṇa. The *Mbh* does not echo such details. However, at Aruṇā tīrtha (number 19; 42.1–38), Balarāma and company bathe at what is either "a particular form of the river Sarasvatī, formerly blood-red from the curse of Viśvāmitra; or a tributary of the Sarasvatī flowing between that river and the Dṛśadvatī" (Dandekar 1961, 494); and at Aujasa tīrtha (number 21) they worship Āpāṃpati Varuṇa (45.92, 46.4, 9). In this stretch would be Saptasārasvata (number 13) and the Hermitage of Baka Dālbhya (number 16).

[45]At Pṛthūdaka (the fifteenth), they are on the northern bank (38.29). The Dṛṣadvatī yātsattra takes place entirely on its southern bank (*PB* 25.13.2 and 4); this is not said of the Sarasvatī yātsattra.

[46]See Witzel 1984, 221, 251, n. 65, on these "accomplishments."

yātsattrins] have lost all their property, or, finally, when their leader [*gṛhapati*] dies."[47] Thus the gṛhapati Sthūra died and was seen going directly to heaven,[48] and one Namin Sāpya, King of Videha, went directly to heaven it seems from Plakṣa Prāsravaṇa itself (*PB* 25.10.17). Correspondingly, Balarāma's epic pilgrimage lasts forty-two days. One hears of his passing the night only three or four times, so it is uncertain how many of the forty-two were passed between Vinaśana and Plakṣa Prasravaṇa.[49] But of the nights mentioned, only one, at Camasodbheda,[50] comes before reaching Vinaśana (itself one of the more indefinable places [chapter 3, n. 93]), leaving it possible that the forty-two-day pilgrimage is meant to encompass the forty days prescribed for a yātsattra from Vinaśana to Plakṣa Prasravaṇa.[51] Balarāma hears some stories near Plakṣa Prasravaṇa, as we shall see, so perhaps the epic poets do not think of it as the "end of speech."

In any case, as Balarāma approaches Plakṣa Prasravaṇa, the thirty-fourth tīrtha on his itinerary, he does so "having gone out from the doorway of Samantapañcaka *(samantapañcakadvārāt . . . niṣkramya)*" (9.51.25ab), which I take to mean that he already has passed *through* Samantapañcaka-Kurukṣetra, and now pauses before going beyond it to ask the Ṛṣis about Kurukṣetra's merits.[52] Kurukṣetra, he learns, is the "eternal high altar *(uttaravedi)* of Prajāpati" where the gods performed sattras (52.1–2, 20); there too, the Kaurava ancestor Kuru performed such austere "tillage" *(-kṛṣ)* that Indra granted him, as "fruit of the field" *(kṣetrasya . . . phalam)*, that ascetics who died there and those slain there in battle would directly reap heavenly worlds.[53] As Bigger observes, this is a matter that correlates with Duryodhana's determination, two adhyāyas later, to transfer the place of his final mace duel to Kurukṣetra for the

[47]Quoting Heesterman 1985, 84, summarizing *PB* 25.10.18–21. See above at n. 30.
[48]See *JB* 2.299; Heesterman 1985, 84; Caland 1919, 201–2.
[49]Not Prāsravaṇa, as in the Vedic passages.
[50]9.34.79; Camasodbheda is "usually mentioned in association with Prabhāsa" (Dandekar 1961, 490), and thus perhaps not requiring of an extra day at the latter.
[51]The other nights mentioned after Vinaśana are at Sapta Sārasvat (38.2), Aujasa (45.94), and arguably at Kārapacava (308* after 53.12), on which there is the question raised by Kaveeshwar as to whether it can rightly be deemed an interpolation, Kaveeshwar arguing that it describes a night between Śalya's death and the final mace duel (1972, 24–26).
[52]Cf. Witzel 1984, 221 and 249, n. 51: Approaching Plakṣa Prāsravaṇa, yātsattrins "go toward the east, across the whole of Kurukṣetra *(te prāñco yanti samayā kurukṣetram)*. This territory *(kṣetram)* is the sacrificial ground *(devayajanam)* of the gods. They cross by the sacrificial ground of the gods *(devānām eva tad devayajanena yanti)*" (*JB* 2.297 [number 156]). Translation of Witzel n.d., slightly modified in last sentence.
[53]9.51.25; 52.6, 13–14 (Indra adds the reward for even animals who die here in battle).

same reason.[54] Balarāma now gives away "portions *(dāyān),*" presumably to the Ṛṣis. "Having seen Kurukṣetra," he now approaches a "very large heavenly āśrama" *(āśramaṃ sumahad divyam)* thick with trees of many kinds, including plakṣas and banyans *(plakṣanyagrodhasaṃkulam)* (53.1–2). Note, however, that while it has plakṣa trees, it has no special plakṣa tree. Having seen this āśrama, he asks the Ṛṣis whose it is, and learns that it is where Viṣṇu duly performed his eternal yajñas, and where, through yoga, an exceptional brahmacāriṇī obtained the highest heaven and the supreme yoga, as well as the fruit of a horse sacrifice (4–8).[55] The poets' refitting of yātsattra to pilgrimage thus centers the latter on yoga, bhakti, and more generalized notions of sacrifice.

Balarāma now salutes the Ṛṣis with a respectful adieu, and begins his approach to the next āśrama: "On the side of Himavat, having made his entire entourage leave him, he ascended the mountain *(pārśve himavato cyutaḥ/ skandhāvārāṇi sarvāṇi nivartyārūruhe 'calam)*" (53.9).[56] He is highly amazed *(vismayaṃ paramaṃ gataḥ)* at seeing "the meritorious tīrtha of Plakṣa Prasravaṇa, the source of the Sarasvatī" (10),[57] and we too might be surprised by the geography, since one does not usually think of Himavat as rising from Kurukṣetra. Yet Witzel, who locates Plakṣa Prāsravaṇa in the Siwaliks (1984, 271, fig. 2), urges that we think of this source of the Sarasvatī as being "in the foothills of the Panjab Himalayas" (1995b, 8), and that may be within range of what is meant. Let us note that whereas plakṣa trees are mentioned at the previous tīrtha, none is mentioned at Plakṣa Prasravaṇa. It is possible that the poets, unfamiliar with local features, have split such details between the two sites.

[54]9.54.3–7. See Bigger 1998, 74–75; 1999a, 6. Again (see n. 28 above), I see this as evidence of first-order textual adjustment rather than belated maladjustment via interpolation. The same holds for the dialogue-shift to Balarāma as primary audience for the stories about pilgrimage sites once he gets to Kurukṣetra (9.51.25). I see this as a deepening of the narrative's purpose rather than evidence of another layer of interpolation (Bigger 1998, 74).

[55]This tīrtha is evidently more powerful, or else more liberalized by the new ideology of yoga, than Vṛddhakanyā Tīrtha, the Tīrtha of the Old Maid (number 30), where Balarāma hears of an old maid who learned that being a brahmacāriṇī was not enough to reach heaven, and had to marry first (9.50.51–51.24).

[56]I have accepted Andreas Bigger's translation of *skandhāvārāṇi sarvāṇi nivartya* (E-mail correspondence, September 6, 1999; cf. 1998, 52). Many northern texts have instead *saṃdhyākāryāṇi sarvāṇi nirvartya* (e.g., Vulgate 9.54.10), "having accomplished all his evening rites"—which might lend support to Kaveeshwar's thesis of an intervening night (see n. 51 above).

[57]*Prabhavaṃ ca sarasvatyāḥ*, with, however, numerous variants, including most frequently *prabhāvam* ("excellence") for *prabhavam* ("source"). One wonders whether Dandekar as CE editor favors the Vedic precedent familiar to him. In any case, "source" is one of the readings. On this source's possible locations, see Bharadwaj 1986, 8–19.

4. Back to the yātsattrins: "At Kārapacava, they descend for the lustral bath into the Yamunā" (*PB* 25.10.23). This refers to the final bath or *avabhṛtha*. According to Witzel, this *avabhṛtha*, as its name indicates, leads the yatsattrin yajamāna, who has become a semidivine person, "down" *(ava-)* from the celestial world to the earth, where he once again becomes a normal man who hopes to live a hundred years (1984, 250–51, n. 61)—that is, the yātsattrin who has not achieved "accomplishment" number 3 and gone straight to heaven.

Balarāma meanwhile goes to Kārapacana (9.53.11), his thirty-fifth tīrtha, which is obviously the same as Kārapacava.[58] Here he gives away gifts, bathes in the cool water, and possibly spends the night (see n. 51). He then goes, evidently nearby, to the ashram of Mitra and Varuṇa (12), his thirty-sixth and last tīrtha, also on the Yamunā. Bathing there too, he obtains supreme satisfaction *(parāṃ tuṣṭim)*, and then sits with Ṛṣis and Siddhas listening to "splendid stories *(kathāḥ śubhāḥ)*" until the divine minstrel Nārada arrives (53.14–15). "Provoker of strife and always fond of strife *(prakartā kalahānāṃ ca nityaṃ ca kalahapriyaḥ)*" (18), Nārada brings Balarāma up to date on the "excessive destruction of the Kurus," and says that if Balarāma is curious, he should go see the terrible duel between his two disciples, Bhīma and Duryodhana (20–31). Balarāma then "dismissed *(visarjayāmāsa)* all the Brahmans together with those who had accompanied him, and ordered his followers, 'Go to Dvārakā'" (32). Here the yātsattra as pilgrimage may be supplemented by a *vaisarjana* such as one finds concluding the Aśvamedha, "which is interpreted by the Kāṭhaka as a dissolution of a war band after the battle has been won" (Heesterman 1993, 178).

We would expect Balarāma to move on from the bank of the Yamunā near Kārapacana. But we immediately find him back at Plakṣa Prasravaṇa, and may be surprised once again at how quickly he must move to keep this symbolic geographical terrain together: "Descending from that best of mountains, from auspicious Plakṣa Prasravaṇa *(avatīryācalaśreṣṭāt plakṣasravaṇācchubhāt)*" (53.33), he sings the glories of Sarasvatī, and then hops a chariot (36) to Kurukṣetra to see his disciples' last fight.

Plakṣa Prasravaṇa thus retains an aura for the epic poets as the true end of the Sarasvatī pilgrimage, and as a kind of cosmic concentration point for movement between earthly and heavenly worlds. True, the poets

[58]Kārapacana has nine similar variants showing considerable guesswork (Dandekar 1961, 387; cf. 497), but none of them Kārapacava.

have refitted none of the Vedic rites or persona mentioned in connection with Plakṣa Prāsravaṇa except the bathing, and have left mention of plakṣa trees to the previous tīrtha. But they know the yātsattra or Sarasvatī sattra in surprising detail. Balarāma is not the only epic hero to have gone this way. When Dhaumya advises the Pāṇḍavas on pilgrimage routes they should take, he mentions Plakṣāvataraṇa as "the holiest tīrtha, where the twiceborn, having sacrificed with [sacrifices that pertain to] the Sarasvatī *(sārasvatair iṣṭvā)*, go after the avabhṛtha bath"; further, he says one finds there a holy spot named Agniśiras[59] where a certain Sahadeva (Sahadeva Sṛñjayaputra according to Nīlakaṇṭha)[60] "sacrificed [after measuring the terrain] with the throw of a yoke peg" (*sahadevo 'yajad yatra śamyākṣepeṇa*; 3.88.3–4). Then, when the Pāṇḍavas reach the area on the very route that Balarāma's pilgrimage will overlap, at the "doorway *(dvāra)* of Kurukṣetra" the Ṛṣi Lomaśa, now their guide and traveling companion, directs Yudhiṣṭhira's attention to a spot that (presumably) lies before him, and tells him to touch water *(upa-spṛś)* there, since it affords vision of all worlds: "There Yayāti performed sacrifices, pleasing Indra. . . . This tīrtha of the Yāmuna is called Plakṣāvataraṇa. Those of insight call it the doorway of the back of the firmament *(nākapṛṣṭhasya dvāram)*.[61] There the foremost of Ṛṣis, sacrificing with the sacrifices that pertain to the Sarasvati, having mortars for their yūpas, went for the avabhṛtha."[62] Having touched water there, Yudhiṣṭhira is able to see through the worlds to Arjuna, who is in Indra's heaven (3.129.12–20). Like Sahadeva Sṛñjayaputra with his yoke peg, these Ṛṣis with mortars for yūpas[63] performing Sārasvata yajñas are clearly yātsattrins[64] on their way to Plakṣa Prāsravaṇa, now also called

[59]On Balarāma's pilgrimage, Agnitīrtha is mentioned (46.12–20) as twenty-first among the thirty-six tīrtha's he passes, but on the Sarasvatī, not the Yamunā. Agniśiras is not mentioned on his route, and Sörensen [1904] 1963, 24, has no other reference for it.

[60]An ancient king of the Pāñcālas; see Kinjawadekar 1929–33, 2:252 (Nīlakaṇṭha knows nothing about yātsattras or Sārasvatī sattras); Sörensen [1904] 1963, 606. Ganguli ([1884–96] 1970, 2:208), no doubt having consulted Nīlakaṇṭha, helpfully inserts "king" for Sahadeva; van Buitenen omits verse 4 about the *śamyā*-throwing (1975, 402). Clearly it is not the listening Sahadeva Pāṇḍava, who has yet to make this trek.

[61]As translated in another context by Witzel 1984, 219: *"dos du firmament."*

[62]3.129.11–14; *atra sārasvatair yajñair ījānāḥ paramarṣayaḥ/ yūpolūkhalinas tāta gacchantyavabhṛthāsrjat* (14). Cf. Oberlies 1995, 185: *sārasvata yajña* would be the epic's gloss here for the older Vedic *sārasvata sattra*. Thus the "sacrifices" mentioned above in brackets for the passage at 3.88.3c are implied by *sārasvataiḥ*.

[63]Van Buitenen (1975, 468) translates *yūpolūkhalinas* as "carrying poles and mortars," while Ganguli ([1884–96] 1970, 3:277) comes I think closer with "making use of the sacrificial stake for their pestle."

[64]Not those performing sacrifices "with *sārasvata* brahmins," as van Buitenen, following Nīlakaṇṭha, suggests (1975, 827).

Plakṣāvataraṇa, the "Descent of the Plakṣa tree" that is also the doorway to the back of the firmament. The forest-wandering Pāṇḍavas thus hear epic renditions of yātsattra and Vrātya lore about both kings and Ṛṣis, and the four who wander here below first follow a route that Arjuna has himself taken, and then ascend along the Sarasvatī to glimpse him in heaven at the destination where yātsattrins could likewise see through the heavenly vault.[65] All this, let us note, is part of Yudhiṣṭhira's Vedic education; Arjuna, meanwhile, is learning the mastery of divine weapons through his encounters with Indra and Śiva.

Witzel's discussion of Vedic passages on Plakṣa Prāsravaṇa and the Sarasvatī pilgrimage makes it clear what the epic's refitting must be about. Sarasvatī yātsattras, says Witzel, are among developments having to do with the "rise to a new mythology of the region" of Kurukṣetra in the formation of the Kuru state in the early post-Ṛg Vedic period: "the river Sarasvatī itself is the personification on earth of the Milky Way in the Vedic texts; this falls down on Earth at Plakṣa Prāsravaṇa, the world tree at the center of heaven and earth, and then continues to flow through the land of the Kuru people,—which is identified with the whole earth. The area was conceived as the 'center of the world.'"[66] The Plakṣa tree in question is also upside-down, making it clear that the alternate epic name Plakṣāvataraṇa, "descent of the Plakṣa tree," is describing just such a tree.[67] Monier-Williams gives two identifications of plakṣa: one, "the wave-leafed fig tree, Ficus Infectoria (a large and beautiful tree with small white fruit"; the other, "the holy fig tree, Ficus Religiosa" (MW, 714)—that is, the *aśvattha* or pipal. In Vedic texts, the former is often meant, and one wonders whether its small white fruit could have been visualized as stars. In the epic's descriptions, it is impossible to say which tree is meant. In Vedic passages on the Sarasvatī yātsattra, the mythological associations of the plakṣa at Plakṣa Prāsravaṇa may have shifted from the wave leaf fig to the *aśvattha*. The upside-down world

[65]Cf. Oberlies 1995, 181–86, on the patterned links between the Pāṇḍavas' pilgrimage and Arjuna's movements, first in his earthly pilgrimage in Book 1 as the mock celibate who must atone for breaking in on Yudhiṣṭhira's privacy with Draupadī (1.207–12; see Hiltebeitel 1988, 215–23), and second in his heavenly ascent in Book 3 to obtain divine weapons, and on the convergence of these overlapping narratives leading to the brothers' and Draupadī's reunion with Arjuna through their vision of him in heaven from Plakṣa Prāsravaṇa.

[66]Witzel (1995a, 11) traces the idea to *ṚV* 3.53.11, where the Bhārata king Sudās, settling on the Sarasvatī, identifies it as *vara ā pṛthivyāḥ* "the best place on earth."

[67]Ganguli ([1884–96] 1970, 3:277), translating "descent of the banyan tree," is right about everything but the tree. Van Buitenen (1978, 169), translating "the descent upon the *plakṣa* [wavy fig tree]," may be right about the tree but wrong that one descends "upon" it, and in inferring that Yayāti must have been the one to do so when he was bounced from heaven. He descended on the Naimiṣa Forest (see chap. 3 after n. 23)! Yayāti's descent there among the "good" and his sacrifice at Plakṣāvataraṇa are different events.

tree held by Varuṇa in *ṚV* 1.24.7 is unspecified,[68] but, once detached from Varuṇa, it comes to be identified as an upside-down aśvattha in *Kaṭha Upaniṣad* 6.1 and *Bhagavad Gītā* 15.1-3. As originally Varuṇa's tree, it probably also had associations with the circulation of soma and the waters, and may thus also be identical with, or had another of its destinies to become, the "Soma-yielding aśvattha" *(aśvattha somasavana)* of *Chāndogya Upaniṣad* 8.5.3.[69] In any case, as Witzel translates, Plakṣa Prāsravaṇa is "the Plakṣa tree of 'forth streaming,'" the upside-down tree from which the Sarasvatī itself flows from heaven about the time of the winter solstice.[70]

More than this, Witzel considers the Sarasvatī, by name "the possessor of many ponds," to be the Ṛg Vedic term for the Milky Way (1984, 217), and one that yields in subsequent Vedic texts to a new term for the Milky Way: "*svargá- loká-*, which means literally 'the luminous world,' 'luminous space.'"[71] One wonders whether the *Mahābhārata*'s emphasis on "bowers" *(kuñja)* does not suit this image of "ponds." *Svargaloka* and *svarga* are thus not exactly "heaven," as usually translated; indeed, the heaven of the gods is higher than the Milky Way and, unlike *svargaloka*, it does not move.[72] Epic references to *svargaloka* and *svarga* often retain such allusions to stars of the night sky. Luminous bodies are obtained in svarga loka by good deeds (3.247.7, 12–13) and by visiting various tīrthas, with details often recalling the Sarasvatī yātsattra. Where Sarasvatī enters the ocean, one obtains the fruit of giving a thousand cows; after three nights there one shines like the moon (3.80.79–80); one goes from Aujasa on Balarāma's route through the "tīrtha of the Kurus" and the "doorway of heaven" *(svargadvāram)* to the worlds of Nārāyaṇa, Śiva, and Umā (81.143–51); Sarasvatī flows from a plakṣa tree *(plakṣādevī srutā . . . sarasvatī)*, but also has water that rises from an anthill; and six *śamyā* peg throws from an anthill (perhaps not the same one) is a hard-to-find *(sudurlabham)* tīrtha where one obtains the fruit of giving a thousand cows and an Aśvamedha (82.5–9).[73] Meanwhile, as

[68]Though a "riddle-hymn" (*ṚV* 1.64.22) identifies the cosmic tree, which could also be the one held upside-down by Varuṇa, as the *aśvattha* (Kuiper 1983, 76–77; cf. 145–46).

[69]Kuiper 1983, 76–77, 143–46; cf. Witzel 1984; 1995a, 25, n. 99, also citing *Taittirīya Āraṇyaka* 1.11.5. Note that Balarāma reaches Plakṣa Prasravaṇa after he goes to the Viṣṇu's tīrtha with plakṣa trees where a maiden practices yoga, possibly reiterating the connection between the upside-down tree, Viṣṇu, and Yoga that one finds in the *KU* and *BhG*.

[70]Witzel 1995a, 11, 25-26, nn. 99, 101, 103; 1984, 221–25; 1995b, 8. See also Kloetzli's suggestive observations about the leaf and mountain shapes of the star-pointers on the upper disc (the *rete*, "web" or "net") of the astrolabe (1985, 124, 145).

[71]Witzel 1984, 215, as translated in Witzel n.d., 2. Cf. 216, 221–22, and nn. 20, 27, 70.

[72]Witzel 1984, 219–20, 230, and nn. 38, 43 (the gods have even closed their heaven), 55.

[73]For yātsattra lore learned by the Pāṇḍavas, cf. 3.81.62; 82.23–25; 58–67 (esp. 62–63); 83.15–16.

the pilgrimaging Pāṇḍavas wait for Arjuna to return from heaven, they look toward Mount Meru and hear about the sun's unwearied movement through the northern and southern regions, turning at "winter," on the "uncrowded" and "indescribable path" around Meru, pulling all creatures including the stars (the Seven Ṛṣis headed by Vasiṣṭha among them), while above Meru is the ever-luminous abode of Nārāyaṇa where the same stars cease to shine (160.12–37). Similarly, above the lunar and solar worlds and the worlds of Varuṇa and Indra, on "the back of the firmament *(nākasya pṛṣṭhe),*" are four worlds: the Prājāpatya lokas, source of all worlds; the world of cows; *svargagati*, again a "luminous way," which is the world of the Self-born Brahman; and, the highest, a world of certain Vedic rituals (13.105.40–54).

Now as already noted, Balarāma's pilgrimage route follows a "path" that "shone, O king, bringing pleasure to all, like heaven [*svarga*/the Milky Way] for the men who were going there."[74] In going "against the current" and "rising toward the east and north along the length of the Sarasvatī—the terrestrial reflection of the Milky Way—one rises also along the Milky Way, a new portion of which becomes visible in the east and northeast each morning" (Witzel 1984, 223 [n.d., 7]). As *Jaiminīya Brāhmaṇa* 2.297 puts it, "The counter-current is, so to speak, the shining world" *(pratīpam iva vai svargo lokaḥ)*: "i.e., the movement of the Milky Way, in the morning, from December to June."[75]

As to the "doorway at the back of the firmament," which the Pāṇḍavas hear about as something to be seen at Plakṣāvataraṇa, and through which they see Arjuna in Indra's heaven, it is not mentioned when Balarāma gets to the same place under its yātsattra name of Plakṣa Prā[a]sravaṇa. But this is not surprising when we learn that this "doorway" is an island or dark spot near the bifurcation of the Milky Way, at the eagle constellation, which, at Kurukṣetra, would not become visible in the east until it can be seen in mornings, just before dawn, around the winter solstice (Witzel 1984, 223, 233, and figures). Balarāma's pilgrimage cannot be fully a yātsattra because he arrives at Plakṣa Prasravaṇa too early; the winter solstice is still being awaited about fifty days hence by Bhīṣma.

Further, where the Milky Way divides just beyond this island, it forms two branches: the Sarasvatī flows to earth as a continuation of its western branch, the Yamunā as a continuation of its eastern branch.[76] One

[74] 9.34.27, as cited n. 36 above.

[75] Witzel n.d., 5; 1984, 221, 233, 249, n. 51. The shaman-priests' upstream pilgrimage of the Vilcamayu River (River of the Sun; W. Sullivan 1996, 36, 66, 99, 351–54) is one of the remarkable parallels between Indian and Inca star-related myth and ritual complexes.

[76] Witzel 1984, 222–24, 255, n. 77; by the Yamunā one returns to earth lest one disappear, go crazy, or enter the land of the Fathers.

wonders whether the Yamunā branch has any "islands" that might correspond to the birth place of Vyāsa, "the island-born Dark one" (Kṛṣṇa Dvaipāyana), who was born on an island in the Yamunā. Be that as it well may, this "doorway" or "island"[77] also appears in mornings at the summer solstice, in June and July, in the west, after which it disappears beyond the west, not to reappear until it comes up in the east around the winter solstice. It is thus significant that the spot where yātsattrins and Balarāma reach the earthly source of the Sarasvatī is near a span of the Yamunā.

Finally, during the time that one follows the Sarasvatī upstream, the "doorway" must thus be "'up above' the earth, . . . moving toward the east" where it will reappear. This movement "is advanced" by a ritual called Gavāmayana ("march of the cows"). Culminating in colorful ceremonies performed at the time of the two solstices—the Viṣūvat day ["peak day"] in summer and the Mahāvrata in winter—the Gavāmayana invigorates the sun,[78] just as a yātsattra may invigorate the Maruts or a band of Vrātyas.

This linkage of Plakṣa Prāsravaṇa with the heavenly Sarasvatī as Milky Way is one that could be expected to have undergone shifts in its refitting from Veda to epic, since the *Mahābhārata* has shifted the Milky Way from the heavenly Sarasvatī to the heavenly Gaṅgā.[79] But the *Mahābhārata* relates the two rivers. For instance, its brief account of Bhagīratha bringing down the heavenly Gaṅgā (6.7.26–28; 41–47) mentions that after Gaṅgā flows from Brahmaloka, she divides sevenfold, with the Sarasvatī as one her seven branches (6.7.44–45), and that she descends from the top of Mount Meru "bearing milk" (*kṣīradhārā*; 26).[80] Despite vast changes in cosmology from Veda to epic, the

[77]On this terminology, see Witzel 1984, 226, 251, n. 64.

[78]Witzel 1984, 215–16, 222–23, 233, and nn. 22, 72, 77 on these rituals and the power generated by them.

[79]See Wilson [1840] 1972, 188, n. 29: "The situation of the source of the Ganges of heaven identifies it with the milky way"; Zimmer 1962, 113; Kramrisch 1975, 242; Witzel 1984, 217 and n. 31; Kloetzli 1985, 138–39, 146–47; de Santillana and von Dechend 1977, 260. See *Mbh* 3.82.23: Hardwar as the "gate of the Gaṅgā *(gaṅgādvāra)* is doubtless equal to the doorway of heaven *(svargadvāra).*" On the heavenly Gaṅgā *(ākāśagaṅgā)*, see Bhīṣma's upbringing "by her there" (chap. 2, at n. 134), the "viewing of the sons" (chap. 2, § C.39), and Yudhiṣthira's bath in it (18.3.26; chap. 7, § D). Cf. 12.315.46; 239.42; Vulgate 3.142.11 (= CE 3, App. 16, line 22). On Gaṅgā coming from the sky *(gaganāt)*, cf. 13.27.70–71; 134.17.

[80]The *Rām* version (1.42) is more extensive. Cf. Witzel 1984, 225, on the Plakṣa at the confluence of the Ganges and Yamunā, where the Sarasvatī in classical cosmology joins from underground; and the *Mokṣadharma* dialogue in which Bhṛgu tells Bharadvāja that in a former day of Brahmā, the Ṛsis ascertain the origin of the world after standing a hundred divine years meditating in silence, whereupon "the celestial Sarasvatī came to them out of

Mahābhārata thus seems to retain the basic cosmological pattern underlying the Vedic Sasasvatī "pilgrimage," transforming it around the figures of Balarāma, incarnation of Śeṣa, and Bhīṣma, the son of Gaṅgā, who will be the one to await the winter solstice.

In the Vedic pattern,[81] when the sun and Agni enter the netherworld at evening, they enter the "womb" or "seat of the Ṛta," which is also the western ocean of Varuṇa. There, Varuṇa and Mitra "hold both earth and heaven." Says Kuiper, the "fact that in later times the same function is attributed to the Serpent Śeṣa is particularly interesting because in the *Atharva Veda* Varuṇa has authority over the serpent world. Like Śeṣa, Varuṇa must have been conceived as supporting heaven and earth 'from below' by means of the cosmic axis. . . . While in later times this axis was identified with Mount Meru," the *Ṛg Veda* speaks of a primordial hill, and of a cosmic tree that arose from that hill whose roots Varuṇa holds aloft (1983, 68). The *Mahābhārata*, of course, still regards Varuṇa as lord of waters and of the west, including the western ocean. Indeed, as Kuiper observes, it hardly looks coincidental that Dvārakā, "City of Gates or Doors," from which Balarāma and the Yādavas go to Prabhāsa, "is situated on the western-most part of India on the shore of the 'western ocean' (like Pylos in Greece!). It may be suggested that the town was originally considered the sacred gate to Varuṇa's world," which itself has a thousand doors (68, 73). It would also seem that Dvārakā is where the "doorway of the back of the firmament," which in Vedic cosmology opens to Varuṇa's world, and in the epic's cosmology to other higher worlds, would be last seen before it disappears to the west. The epic has probably relocated the point at which this "doorway" disappears: from Vinaśana, where the Sarasvatī goes mysteriously underground, to Prabhāsa near Dvārakā, where it goes into the western ocean itself. Balarāma thus begins his upstream pilgrimage from the very site at which he will return his innermost "portion" to the ocean at the end of his epic mission, when Śeṣa emerges from his mouth and slips back into the ocean to resume upholding the regenerated earth. It is possible that the flooding of Dvārakā near the end of the epic (17.1.43) completes the epic's portrayal of the end of a yuga,[82] and further, that it evokes a

ethereal space" *(divyā sarasvatī tatra sambabhūva nabhastalāt)* with the sweet sounds of dharma (12.176.8; Fitzgerald 1980, 369; cf. Sutton 2000, 405).

[81] I condense here mainly from Kuiper (1983, 66–89, 130–58) and Witzel (1984, 1995b), both drawing from a variety of Vedic texts.

[82] Kṛṣṇa's death, coincident with Dvārakā's flooding, generally defines the Kaliyuga's beginning in the purāṇas, but not in the *Mbh*, which usually associates the yugas' turning with the *Mbh* war: generally, as a war that took place "when the interval between (the) Kali and Dvāpara (ages) arrived" (1.2.9); and specifically, with the Kali yuga arriving (says Kṛṣṇa) at the death of Duryodhana (9.59.21)—perhaps Kali is released following

precessional "sinking" of a sign of the zodiac below the equatorial plane (great ocean).[83]

As to the Plakṣa tree at the other end of the Sarasvatī, it is in Vedic terms linked with the east, with the dawn, and with the return of Agni and the sun, which have had to pass through the "stone house" of Varuṇa in the depths of the cosmic mountain, from which Agni was born before becoming the navel of the radiant firmament. The sun's nightly journey from the western to the eastern horizon is expressed in terms of an ascent, and a passage not only through Varuṇa's abode but Yama's, which is within Varuṇa's realm, and is the dwelling-place of the dead. Cows are also penned up in the stone of the netherworld, and, with their release, are identified with the dawns (Kuiper 1983, 68–74, 82–83). In the Gavāmayana ritual, which invigorates the sun's rising each day from a different point on the horizon and against the background of different stars, Uṣas, goddess of dawn, is a cow, *gau*, whose appearance each day corresponds to the three hundred and sixty-five cows whose march constitutes the ritual (Witzel 1984, 253–54, n. 72).

These Vedic images of the sun's movement from night to dawn require a perspectival shift. As Kuiper shows, at night, Varuṇa's netherworld "extends over the earth as the night-sky. The cosmic waters are at that time a celestial ocean" (74), with its river of stars.[84] The netherworld at night "was thought of as hanging over the earth *in an inverted position*" (76 [Kuiper's italics], cf. 145–46). Seen from this perspective, Varuṇa's stone house—which the *Mahābhārata* still evokes as the "back

Duryodhana's incarnation of him while alive, as Kali, once disembodied from Nala, enters the tree that produces the dice whose throws define the yuga-names (3.70.34). For an alternate reading of Duryodhana's role, see Biardeau 1976, 153–54; 1997a, 111. The coming of the Kali yuga is also associated with Kṛṣṇa's incarnation (6.26.7–8 [= *BhG.* 4.7–8]; 6.62.39; 12.326.82) and Vyāsa's (12.337.42–44), and with numerous usages of such terms as *kali*, "discord," *yugānta*, "end of a yuga," and *kāla*, "time" in prophesies and tropes to convey that the *Mbh* war was an age-ending turning point in "history" (e.g., 2.45.50; 3.148.37; 3.187.5–7; 5.47.59; 5.72.18; 6.4.2–5 [see chap. 2, n. 91], 6.11.14). Yet as Koskikallio 1994, 264, points out, according to the *Yuga Purāṇa*, the change of yugas comes with the death of Draupadī! Gonzales-Reimann 1998 attempts to atomize the epic's yuga references, but without success.

[83]See chap. 1 at nn. 41–42; chap. 3, n. 22.

[84]Witzel (1984) is convincing that stars in the celestial river(s) (the Milky Way variously considered as the Sarasvatī, as dividing into the Sarasvatī and Yamunā [220], as *svargaloka*, and as the Rasā [226 and 258, n. 92]), must be differentiated from other stars and star-groups, which are also of major mythological and soteriological importance (228–29, 260–61, n. 105), and that the night sky as ocean *(samudra)* is both the underworld as seen at night and at the edges of the world at sunrise and sunset (226; 240, n. 12; 259, n. 102). Sattras are crossings of the ocean (251, n. 64, citing *ŚB* 12.2.1.1); the hundred thousand-versed *Bhārata* is an ocean churned by Vyāsa (12.331.2).

of the firmament"[85]—is seen upside-down as the "spotted rock" studded with stars that each night revolves around the pole star and the horizon.[86] One must especially appreciate the mythic cask or casket "crammed with goods" that Varuṇa can tip so that it flows earthward (149; cf. 139), which Witzel seems to have finally identified from Atharva Vedic and early Upaniṣadic references as the "bowl" or "cup" *(camasá)* of the Big Dipper (or Seven Ṛṣis). Each night, or through the year when observed at the same time each night, the bowl tips upside-down as it turns like a waterwheel (1996). The *Mahābhārata* seems to know of this bowl when it adds to the starry path of the yātsattra, before Vinaśana, a stop at Camasodbheda near the start of Balarāma's pilgrimage (see above at n. 39). One of the few tīrthas where Balarāma explicitly stays the night, Camasodbheda is, by name, the place where the "bowl" *(camasa)* either "bursts forth" (like a spring or fountain) or, only slightly more prosaically, "becomes visible" *(udbheda)*.

Similarly, the ashram of Mitra and Varuṇa at the very end of Balarāma's pilgrimage (9.53.12), where Nārada arrives to find Balarāma between Kārapacana and his "descent" from Plakṣa Prasravaṇa to the Yamunā, probably recalls the idea that the yātsattra along the Sarasvatī follows the northeastward "march *(ayana)* of Mitra and Varuṇa," representing day and night (*PB* 25.10; Witzel 1984, 231, 263, n. 117). Not only does Balarāma obtain "supreme satisfaction" here; so did Indra, Agni, and Aryaman obtain *prākprītim* (9.53.13), which can be translated as "former joy" or "eastward joy." If, as now seems likely, Kaveeshwar is right that the night spent at Kārapacana is not an interpolation (see n. 51), the epic poets are, it seems, precise that at the beginning and end of his journey, at spots near celestial observatories at the beginning and end of the former yātsattra route, Balarāma stays overnight.

C. Setting the Universe in Motion

The *Mahābhārata*'s use of these conventions can now be appreciated from several angles. The timing of Balarāma's pilgrimage is intriguing. When he reaches Plakṣa Prasravaṇa and Kurukṣetra and turns back to Dvārakā the same day after seeing Bhīma's foul-play in slaying

[85]*Mbh* references to the *nākapṛṣṭha* are rich in cosmological allusions; see especially 2.11.12: the hall of Brahmā (the world of brahman) is "self-luminous *(svayaṃprabhā)*, beyond the moon, sun, and fire, established on the back of the firmament"; 2.31.25: the assembly of kings and Brahmans at Yudhiṣṭhira's Rājasūya "shone like the back of the firmament with its immortals." On reaching various tīrthas, and especially those on mountains, one rejoices "on the back of the firmament" (3.80.45; 83.19; 83.87; 86.20; 87.15). Cf. n. 61 above; 1.3.14; 1.214.29.

[86]Witzel 1984, 228–29, 260, nn. 103–4, referring especially to *AV* 10.5.20.

Duryodhana (9.59.26), there remain, as we have noted, fifty days before the winter solstice. The war's survivors keep returning to Kurukṣetra for those fifty days until the dakṣiṇāyana is over—that is, until the winter solstice—to hear Bhīṣma and indulge his vow to remain alive for the fifty-eight days it will take him, on his bed of arrows, to coordinate his heavenly ascent with the sun's turn northward (6.114.49).[87] The *Mahābhārata* war and the entire "pacification" *(Śāntiparvan)* and "further instruction" *(Anuśāsanaparvan)* of its survivors thus occur during the dakṣiṇāyaṇa, the time of the sun's descent through the half year that is equivalent to a night. If one recalls the dawn imagery, the consoling of Gaṅgā, and Bhīṣma's celestial source-citations[88] as he lies on his bed of arrows, it is perhaps not surprising that he knows such celestial Ṛṣis as are mentioned there. The period he spent growing up with his mother Gaṅgā was spent with the Heavenly Gaṅgā, not the earthly one (see n. 79), and it would be to the former that he returns at the turn of the solstices. Balarāma's incomplete Sarasvatī yātsattra is thus in effect completed by Bhīṣma's coordinations with the celestial Gaṅgā.

The netherworld as an upside-down mountain and womb-like enclosure also resonates with the cave in the Himalayan mountain where Śiva confines the four Indras and directs the fifth, who become the five Pāṇḍavas. Yama's twelve-year sattra at Naimiṣa Forest ends when these five are reborn to undertake harsh deeds on earth. One begins to suspect that Yama's sattra at Naimiṣa Forest not only inverts human and divine orders, but also takes place in some kind of night, and that the world Yama-Dharma is born into as Yudhiṣṭhira extends that night toward the dawn of a new yuga.

Now if Heesterman is right that stationary Vrātya sattras, including the sixty-one- and ten-day sattras performed in the cold period of winter for the invigoration of cattle and the sun, are the base upon which the mobile Sarasvatī and Dṛṣadvatī yātsattras developed (1963, 34–35), one may suspect that Plakṣa Prāsravaṇa, as the site where such mobile sattras would end, would have some equivalent in the place where seated sattras ended. Seated sattras, of course, ended where they began, and numerous locations are mentioned. But one, as we know, emerged—probably around the same time as the mythology of Plakṣa Prāsravaṇa[89]—to become exemplary, and that is the Naimiṣa Forest.

[87]Bhīṣma fifty-eight days on his bed of arrows begin with eight days of fighting left.
[88]See chap. 2, § C.29–31. Similarly, the story about gleaning that ends the *Śāntiparvan* has passed to Bhīṣma via Cyavana, Janaka, Nārada, Indra, and the Vasus (340.4; 353.2–5).
[89]See Witzel 1995a, n. 103: Plakṣa Prāsravaṇa's "pilgrimage" mythology "is unmatched by any other area in the Vedic texts; places like Prayāga and Kāśi or even the Naimiṣa Forest (though mentioned already in KS 10.6 [as cited above]) attain this kind of fame only well after the Vedic period." Minkowski (1989, 416, n. 72) cites three other Vedic references to sattras at Naimiṣa, or by the Naimiṣeyas, but not in connection with "pilgrimage."

In fact, the *Mahābhārata* seems to know at least one more sattra at Naimiṣa Forest, but without mention of the term *sattra* in describing the event. In the story exalting gleaning that ends the *Śāntiparvan* (see chap. 1, § C), the Brahman who will decide to glean learns where he will get an answer to his questions from the snake Padmanābha in the following terms: "Where, according to the laws of an earlier creation,[90] the wheel of the dharma was set in motion, there, in Naimiṣa (Forest) on the bank of the Gomatī, is a city named after the Nagas. When all the thirty-three gods were there, there was a sacrifice . . . where Māndhātṛ the best of kings overstepped Indra."[91] Māndhātṛ's sacrifice *(iṣṭam)* could be something other than a sattra, but the setting in motion of the dharmacakra to create the universe is associated with Naimiṣa Forest in the purāṇas. At Nimsar-Naimiṣāraṇya[92] is a spot called "Tīrtha of the Wheel" (Cakratīrtha), unmentioned in the *Mahābhārata* but heralded, it would seem, in this passage.[93] According to the *Brahmāṇḍa Purāṇa*, the Naimiṣīya Ṛṣis, born in Naimiṣa, ask Brahmā how to reach a "land of merit" *(deśam puṇyam)*, and he tells them to follow a radiant divine wheel to the place where its felly is broken. Then, as the gods perform a thousand-year divine sattra with Brahmā as master of the penance-house *(tapogṛhapati)*, Mṛtyu (Death) as *śamitṛ*, and so on, the Ṛṣis follow the dharmacakra's whirling course till it breaks the earth's plane at Naimiṣa Forest on the Gomatī, which is apparently—at least in these passages—where the celestial and earthly Naimiṣa Forests intersect.[94]

Vedic precedent is again instructive. A persistent strain in three of the epic's sattras at Naimiṣa Forest is that they are of the twelve-year variety: Śaunaka's, which we never hear the end of (1.1.1; 1.4.1) even when we have finished the *Mahābhārata* (see chapter 7, § D), by which time we

[90]See Belvalkar 1954, 2233: "*pūrvābhisargeṇa*, 'according to the laws or requirements of an earlier Creation.'"

[91]12.343.2–3: *yatra pūrvābhisargeṇa dharmacakraṃ pravartitam/ naimiṣe gomatītīre tatra nāgāhvayaṃ puram// samagrais tridaśais tatra iṣṭam āsīd dvijarṣabha/ yatrendrātikramaṃ cakre māndhātā rājasattamaḥ.*

[92]On which see chap. 3, n. 101.

[93]The story's names now seem rather transparent. The Brahman is named Dharmāraṇya, "Forest of Dharma"; at the very end he goes off for his gleaning to another forest (12.353.9). The snake-king Padmanābha, "Lotus-Navel," has a cosmogonic name of Viṣṇu, which perhaps evokes the latter's relationship with Śeṣa. Nāgāhvayaṃ puram, the City named after the Snakes, is synonymous with Hāstinapura (8.1.17), the contested Kaurava capitol, in which case it means City named after the Elephant. Nāgāhvaya is equivalent to Nāgasāhvaya, Hāstinapura's more frequent name (seventeen usages to one, according to the Tokunaga machine-readable text). Cf. Sörensen [1904] 1963, 494.

[94]See Hiltebeitel 1999a, 291–93. The path seems to be evoked at another point when Yayāti descends the Gaṅgā-like river of smoke that takes him from heaven to join the "good" at Naimiṣa Forest; see chap. 3, § B.

should have realized that no one can finish the *Mahābhārata*; Baka Dālbhya's (9.40.3), which seems to end with the cattle raid that follows the Viśvajit sacrifice; and that of the Naimiṣeya Ṛṣis (9.36.39), which explicitly ends with their crowding of the Sarasvatī's southern banks. *Pañcaviṃśa Brāhmaṇa* 25.6 says twelve-year sattras were originally performed by Prajāpati and have the following characteristics:

> By means of this (sattra), Prajāpati came into the state of setting in motion the whole (universe). They who perform this (sattra) come into the (state of) setting in motion the whole (universe).
>
> [This sattra has four three-year segments, each defined by chanting hymns of different numbers of verses.]
>
> By means of this (sattra), the inhabitants of Naimiśa [Naimiśīyas] throve in all possible ways. They who undertake it thrive in all possible ways.
>
> They broke off this sattra [after the ninth year]. They said: "He who among our progeny will thrive he shall finish this sattra." Therefore, the Brāhmins perform this sattra, wishing to finish it.[95]

Not only do the Naimiṣeya Ṛṣis thrive in performing this sattra; in following the twelve-year model of Prajāpati—which presumably marks a celestial cycle like that of the zodiac—they set in motion the whole universe.[96] They also thrive even though they leave their sattra incomplete. In the epic, the only Brahmans still wishing to finish a twelve-year sattra would be Śaunaka and his co-sattrins, who are not only Brahman Ṛṣis but Naimiṣeya Ṛṣis. We never hear what their session is for, so there is no reason to reject Vedic precedent. Since it is all we know of their sattra, hearing the *Mahābhārata* from a bard would thus be their chief means to "thrive" through their twelve years, and as such, it can also be considered a means of "setting in motion the whole (universe)." On the one hand, they achieve this by hearing the "thought entire" of Veda-Vyāsa, beginning with a cosmogony (1.1.23, 27–38). On the other, if one regards Śaunaka and his co-sattrins as names, like Vyāsa, for those engaged in facets of the actual authoring of the

[95]*PB* 25.6.2–5 as translated in Caland [1931] 1982, 631–32 [bracketed portions summarized]. Cf. Minkowski 1989, 416, also noting the Vedic texts on this twelve-year sattra, the three epic twelve-year sattras, and other incomplete sattras. Caland notes the spelling "Naimiśa" throughout both the *JB* and the *PB*. It is also found in the southern recension of *Mbh*.

[96]It is perhaps significant for the connection between the Naimiṣeya Ṛṣis and the sun's ascent to the dawn that not only Prajāpati "sets in motion the universe" by a sattra, but so does Savitṛ, the sun as "Impeller," through one of seven forty-nine-day sattras (*PB* 24.15,3; Caland [1931] 1982, 618).

Mahābhārata, as I am inclined to do, it would appear that the *Mahābhārata* is designed to set in motion the entire history of the universe down to and just past the *Mahābhārata* war, to the "dawn" *(saṃdhyā)* of "our times," the Kali yuga (see n. 82).

With this suspicion we come as far as we can toward considering the origins of Naimiṣa Forest conventions. White is probably right that as the site for early sattras such as Baka Dālbhya's,[97] Naimiṣa Forest begins its etymological history as "the 'twinkling' forest" (1991, 97), the place where the stars would shine especially during darkening winter nights. Yet although it becomes increasingly clear that precise knowledge of star groups can be important in understanding Vedic and epic cosmologies, myths, and rituals, and although more such precision is surely to be attained, I do not think that this "twinkling forest" is any more a precise constellation than it is a precise geographical location. Rather, I believe it is the entire ever-changing visible night sky, which gods, Brahmans, Ṛṣis (Brahman and Royal), warriors who die in battle,[98] Fathers, and also Nāgas fill to all its reaches.[99] There the heavenly Sarasvatī can still appear, retaining her Ṛg Vedic associations with the Milky Way, to symposia of Naimiṣeya Ṛṣis virtually anywhere they happen to gather. As Witzel observes, the ascent of the Sarasvatī as Milky Way correlates with the "path of the gods" *(devayāna)*, and its descent with the "path of the Fathers" *(pitṛyāna)*, but other stars range "above" it such as the Seven Ṛṣis, and "below" it such as Agastya and others associated with the "south" and the world of Yama.[100] Indeed Yama's sattra at Naimiṣa Forest makes him a kind of Naimiṣeya god. A "bizarre interpolation" (Sukthankar 1933, ci) found in a few northern and southern texts also lets us know that the "Ṛṣis who dwell in Naimiṣa Forest" (*Mbh.* 1, App. 1, No. 36, line 43) include Vasiṣṭha, one of the stars of the Big Dipper, and tells that he and his wife Arundhatī, a dim star beside his, come to the Yamunā to solemnize the marriage of Parāśara and Satyavatī, the parents

[97]Baka Dālbhya, along with Śunaka and Aṇīmāṇḍavya (see chap. 5, § B), is among the many timeless Ṛṣis who greet Yudhiṣṭhira upon first entering his *sabhā* (2.4.8–10); at a holy spot on Lake Dvaitavana, he also urges Yudhiṣṭhira to obtain a purohita and let such Brahmans accompany him in the forest (3.27.5–25). See Koskikallio 1999, 326–29, on these and other passages, one outside the CE, that affirm his watery habitats and old age.

[98]Recall *BhG* 2.32: "Provided as if by chance, the open doorway of heaven *(yadṛcchayā co 'papannam/ svargadvāram apāvṛtam)*. Happy warriors, Pārtha, obtain such a war."

[99]See 12.262.22–23 (they obtain the "infinity" that is "Vedic": *ānantyam . . . vaidikam*); 12.201 (Fitzgerald 1980, 262, 288); and 13.103.36–37 (they remain so long as the twinkles of their eyes; see Hiltebeitel 1977a, 347–50 for this and other examples).

[100]See Witzel 1984, 218–19, 223, 245–46, n. 38 on Yama's world; on Agastya, see Hiltebeitel 1977a, 339–50; Kloetzli 1985, 140–43.

of Vyāsa.[101] Again, one is left to wonder whether this is the earthly Yamunā or the heavenly one.

But most informative is what the exiled Yudhiṣṭhira and his brothers (minus Arjuna) learn about Naimiṣa Forest amid the rush of information they absorb—just after hearing the story of Nala—about pilgrimages that can take them to svarga loka and the door at the back of the firmament:[102] Naimiṣa is "frequented by Siddhas; there Brahmā always resides surrounded by hosts of gods";[103] by dwelling there a month, bathing, and observing restraint and a meager diet, one "obtains the fruit of a Gavāmayana sacrifice *(gavāmayasya*[104] *yajñasya phalam)* and purifies his lineage for seven generations"; one who dies there while fasting "would rejoice, established in the heavenly world *(sa modet svargalokastha)*" (3.82.53-57). The fruit of the Gavāmayana, which was to invigorate cows and the sun at the solstices, is now equivalent to the fruit of a yātsattra: residence in the "shining world" of the Naimiṣa Forest.

Naimiṣa Forest would thus provide many places—both in the night sky itself, and under it, "down to earth"—for Ṛṣis to gather for symposia and to "frame stories."[105] The ten-day sattra, whose ten days were embedded in the twelve nights of the Vrātyas' twelve-days sattra ("actually ten nights of sacrifice, framed by two days" of sattra; White 1991, 105), is especially interesting in this regard for the consideration it has received as a prototype for the medieval "ten-day" Dasarā festival of Hindu kings. Several have argued for the intermediacy of the royal Vedic rites of the Rājasūya and Aśvamedha, where the king becomes the dīkṣita and replaces the *gṛhapati*, and for which one finds plausible continuities at the folk level.[106] Dasarā marks the end of the rainy season rather than the winter solstice, but as Falk argues, this can be

[101]Couples are supposed to gaze at this faithful pair during marriages to assure fidelity.

[102]3.80-83; one would like to know the connection between this information and the Ṛṣi who gives it: Pulastya, ancestor of Rākṣasas.

[103]*Tatra nityam nivasati brahmā devaganair vṛtah*; 3.82.53cd. Recall that Ugraśravas comes to Naimiṣa Forest wishing to see the Naimiṣa sages whom he considers to be *brahman* itself (chap. 3 at n. 30).

[104]Used only two other times in the epic (13.109.44; 110.24) and equivalent to Gavāmayana, which the epic does not use; the CE clears away some misunderstandings (3.82.56 notes).

[105]This can only be proposed metaphorically for Vedic texts, there being, I believe, no Vedic passages connecting Naimiṣa or Naimiṣeyas with the late Brāhmaṇic *(JB)* composition of the earliest frame story narratives (see Witzel 1986, 1987c). On hosts of stars as celestials compared to epic assemblages, see 2.31.25 (cited n. 85 above) and 15.31.20.

[106]Falk 1986, 41; White 1991, 104-5; both discussing Sontheimer 1981 and 1984 on folk Dasarās involving ritual and mythical dogs (cf. Hiltebeitel 1988, 123-24, 365; 1991a, 369-70, 390-93); Heesterman 1963, 13, 36; 1993, 178, 183-84 on the intermediacy of the Vedic royal rites.

plausibly accounted for by changing experiences of geography, climate, and the seasons (1986, 43–44). Vrātya sattras and Dāsaras both end with the invitation to raid one's neighbors (that is, in the parlance of Dasarā, with the opening of the season for military campaigns). Two *Mahābhārata* interpolations say the epic is to be studied or recited during the four months of the rainy season.[107] So too with *Ālhā* (Hiltebeitel 1999a, 310).

No less interesting, with the end of the rainy season, the stars reappear in the sky. People can stay out all night and listen to stories (or, if the stories are told in the day, it is still the nightly half of the year). We know from Minkowski that sattras provided "intervals" for storytelling (1989, 402, 413–20), and that in its *pāriplava*—"whatever rushes on or is repeated again and again"—the Aśvamedha provided for a revolving ten-day cycle of legends *(ākhyānas)* during the whole year of the horse's wandering. The *pariplava* consisted of ten topics, similar to those by which one might classify the *ākhyānas* of the epics and especially the *purāṇapañcalakṣaṇa* or "five characteristics of the Purāṇas." The topics rotated so that each would be covered thirty-six times during the year (Hazra 1955; cf. Karmarkar 1952). It is presumably during such *pāriplava* intervals in his Aśvamedha that Rāma hears his own story told to him by his sons at the Naimiṣa Forest.

Yet the Vedic precedent of the "twinkling forest" is most intriguing when we recall the story Balarāma hears at the tīrtha of the Naimiṣeya Bowers. When the Naimiṣeya Ṛṣis break up their "great big twelve-year sattra" in the Kṛta Yuga, they come in such droves along the southern bank of the Sarasvatī that by the time they reach Kurukṣetra, the tīrthas along this bank look like cities, and at Kurukṣetra there is so little space that they cannot properly perform their Agnihotras. The Agnihotra, like the Gavāmayana, invigorates the sun, but daily (Witzel 1984, 215–16). The constrained Ṛṣis, however, are reduced to measuring their ritual terrains with their sacred threads (perhaps an echo of the measurement of the journey by throwing a wooden *śamyā* peg, but also a foreshadowing of the crush of warriors at Kurukṣetra).

Since the Naimiṣeya Ṛṣis start their journey at the Sarasvatī's western end, far from any of the Naimiṣa Forest's "known locations," we may now suspect that they do not begin this sattra in any earthly location at all, but, as it were, from one of the points where the Sarasvatī has gone underground—Vinaśana or Prabhāsa—in the western ocean of the night

[107] 1,494* lines 1–2 (apud 1.56.494) and, according to Hopkins [1901] 1969, 364, at 18.6.21 ff., which would be in a glorification of the *Mbh* recitation omitted from the CE (I do not find the reference in Kinjawadekar 1929–33, 6).

sky.[108] Their movement up the southern bank of the Sarasvatī is then an ascending movement through a night. And although they are Ṛṣis, their overcrowding and despair recalls something of the violence and hunger of the yātsattrin, whose "killing and cursing," it would now appear, involves a movement through the same netherworld. This outburst of Ṛṣis is also like the gods' raid into the world of humans after Yama's Naimiṣa Forest sattra, and like the encompassment of the battle of Kurukṣetra into the end of a cosmic night that is measured from Balarāma's pilgrimage (a circling of the battlefield by the underworld-serpent Śeṣa's "portion") to Bhīṣma's ascent to heaven. When the Sarasvatī miraculously turns east to create bowers for the Naimiṣeyas, she is making their eastward countercurrent journey with them. The city-like crowds of Ṛṣis along her heavenly night-course suggest a population like the stars of the Milky Way gathered for a dawn.

D. The *Mahābhārata* Symposium

So far we have considered the Naimiṣeyas (including the "Naimiṣeya gods" with Yama) primarily when they are on the move, once they have broken up their sattras and gone on their under- or other-worldly raids. But what do Naimiṣeyas do when they are just sitting at their sattras before breaking camp? As two such sessions have made clear, they listen to wonderful stories about Veda. One such occasion is the sattra Balarāma hears about at the Sapta Sārasvata tīrtha, and the other is the sattra of Śaunaka at which we—along with Śaunaka and his co-sattrins and sadasyas—hear the *Mahābhārata*. In the first case, as was noted, the Naimiṣeya Ṛṣis hear wonderful stories about Veda among themselves, whereas in the second, they listen to them recited by a bard, even though Śaunaka is supposed to know them all already. Either way, as has been the argument of this and the preceding chapter, the Naimiṣa Forest and its sages provide "conventional" images through which the epic poets describe something about their own art and manner of composition.

If this is so, among many implications, for me, it means that the rubric "encyclopedic" is inadequate to describe such a project and misleading as analogy.[109] I do not see anything to recommend the freefall hypothesis that goes with this attribution, but even if it were true,

[108]Not surprisingly, Vinaśana is one of the places near which medieval geography (the *Kṛtyakalpataru* of Lakṣmīdhara) located Naimiṣa Forest, as does Bharadwaj 1986, 211 (citing the passage). Bharadwaj tries to adjudicate between two attempts to locate Plakṣa Prasravaṇa: the source of the Sarasvatī (which he favors), or where the Sarasvatī reappears after vanishing at Vinaśana (1986, 8–9). Ironically, not understanding that this is cosmography rather than geography, he fails to realize that both are right.

[109]See chap. 1 at n. 56 on usages of the term.

the analogy would be poor. If some encyclopedias undergo "continuous revision" for a time, they are all launched over relatively short periods, written with totalizing plans and designs, are mostly multi-authored, are in principle selective in their educational or propagandistic purpose, and don't drape themselves around long stories.[110] Were the premise altered to fit such a description, the analogy would begin to be useful, but only if one started with the encyclopedic novel.[111]

Yet most important, insofar as those who use the analogy often relate it to what the *Mahābhārata* says about itself, the analogy is philosophically "off." The epic's famous claim—"Whatever is here *(yadihāsti)* may be found elsewhere; what is not here *(yannehāsti)* does not exist anywhere" (1.56.33; 18.5.38)—is not an encyclopedic slogan, as many have made it out to be,[112] but an *āstika* ("Vedic," "those who say 'it is'") proclamation or affirmation that the epic is about what "is" and "is not." In this regard it is like a verse from the *Kaṭha Upaniṣad*, which it may recall: "Whatever is here, that (is) there. Whatever is there, that, too, is here (*yad eveha tad amutra, yad amutra tad amviha*; 2.1.10)"—this in a "yogic Upaniṣad," frequently echoed in the *Mahābhārata*, that ends with the affirmation of Viṣṇu as the Puruṣa who can be apprehended only by saying "it is," or "he is" *(astīti)*. In its own yogic-devotional terms, the *Mahābhārata*—to steal a phrase—engages in an ontological debate about "being and what there is."[113] The story of Āstīka, who preserves the remnant of the snakes at Janamejaya's snake sacrifice and is so named "because his father had left saying '*asti*'" "It

[110]See Collison 1966. Cf. Patton 1996, xv, xxv, 25, 29, 32–35, using the same analogy for the *BD*, emphasizing that the encyclopedia is one of the West's "'eclectic' forms of knowledge" whose analogic usefulness lies in its claim "to an all-encompassing, total reorganization of knowledge," a totalization that is intertextual and inherently selective, and a selectivity that follows from an interpretative relation to "canon." One might suspect that whereas the *BD* seeks to close off the canon around a totalizing Mīmāṃsaka vision of the sufficiency of ritual, the *Mbh* keeps the canon open as a "fifth Veda" oriented around bhakti. On the last point, Dahlmann is an exception, using the analogy to speak of the *Mbh* as having an "encyclopädische" genesis in its didactic teachings, to which the central story is secondary (1899, 173; see Fitzgerald 1980, 38).

[111]I thank Walter Koenig for suggesting this line of thought.

[112]E.g., van Nooten 1971, 2–3; Bailey 1983, 109; Goldman 1984, 77; Pollock 1986, 41; Shulman 1991a, 8; cf. Sukthankar 1936, 68, 72; Mehta 1971, 68; and Fitzgerald 1980, 34–38, 46.

[113]Halbfass 1992; cf. Patton 1996, 34: "As the final verse [of the *Bṛhaddevatā*] states, the one who knows the *ṛṣi*, the meter, and the deity of a Ṛg Vedic *sūkta* 'enters into *brahman*, the immortal, the unending, the final source of that which is and that which is not, big and little, the Lord of all and the highest light' (8.140)." See above, n. 110 on the "encyclopedic" comparability of these two texts.

is,"[114] can also be read as such an affirmation—one embedded in Āstīka's very name and applauded, as we have seen, by the author, who sits among the sadasyas who approve the termination of the snake sacrifice's spiraling violence and cruelty (see chap. 3 at n. 77). The epic's treatment of "heresy" (*nāstikyam*, *nāstikas*, "those who say it/he isn't") is consistent with this thrust. When Draupadī says creatures are like wooden dolls *(dārumayī yoṣā)* in the hands of a capricious creator (3.31.22ff.), Yudhiṣṭhira replies, "Resolving that 'all is,' abandon heretical opinion *(vyavasya sarvamastīti nāstikyaṃ bhāvam utsrja)*. Do not revile the lord of beings . . ." (3.32.38–39; cf. 1–5). That Kṣatriyas who flee from battle are like Nāstikas fleeing from the Veda (7.76.4) is surely a loaded simile. Great merits come from teaching the *Mahābhārata (Kārṣṇa Veda)* to those who do not say 'It is not' (*anāstikān*; 1.56.17). The "wise" (e.g., Mārkaṇḍeya [3.181.20; 188.22; 198.66], Vidura [5.36.16; 35.40; 39.48, 59], Bhīṣma and others [frequently in books 12 and 13]) often inveigh against *nāstikyam* (Hopkins [1901] 1969, 86-90). Meanwhile, the epic maintains a virtual silence regarding the *real* Nāstika opposition of Buddhists, Jains, Ājīvakas, and Materialists; if it were "encyclopedic" in any ordinary sense such as the analogy implies, these movements would have suitable entries.[115]

Yet if the "encyclopedia" analogy overlooks the epic's design, its principal fault is that it tells an accompanying story that detracts from the text it describes. Scholars who have made up stories about higher criticism, strata, development, interpolations, orality, encyclopedias, and literary monstrosity have convinced themselves and general readers—but, to judge from the lack of agreement, not each other—that they were producing cumulative results. On the contrary, scholars who explore the intricacies of the epic's design—and this does not exclude some of the "excavators"—have shown some progress. There is much to be worked out in terms of the design, manner of composition, and the spirit behind

[114]Mehta 1972, 7; *Mbh* 1.43.38: Āstīka's father Jaratkāru says this "It is" with reference to his wife Jaratkāru being pregnant with Āstīka—"He of Whom One Says It Is"—as he abandons her. See below, § E.

[115]Sutton 2000, 51, notes a reference to Ājīvakas at 12.86.21. The Rākṣasa Cārvāka seems by name to hold place for the Materialists: a "friend of Duryodhana" around since the Kṛta yuga, he tells Yudhiṣṭhira he should be cursed for those who died in battle, and is slain when Yudhiṣṭhira's court Brahmans utter the syllable *"hum"* (12.39.22–47). The Jain concept of colors of the soul seems to lie behind 12.270. And, as was observed in chap. 1, § C, Buddhism is most often treated by negative allusion (see also Sutton 2000, 9, on 12.211 as "a polemical attack on Buddhist doctrines"; and Ganguli [1884–96] 1970, 9:124–25 and notes). Cf. Reich 1998, 37, 252, 256–57, 283–84, 328–29, 337, 372–75, on indirect reference to the heresies, especially Buddhism, as in part a form of "ideological containment" (257). On similar silences in the "encyclopedic" *VDhP*, see Inden 2000, 33, 39, 54, 64, 90.

the work. But we are coming to appreciate that the motivations are extraordinarily subtle in combining bold instructive teachings with a delight in concealment; that the composers are not averse to rough joins, repetitions and reiterations, multiple and deepening causalities, overdeterminations, and intriguing contradictions;[116] that the design infuses whatever is foundational in the text down to places where some have least expected it, including the manner in which the births of the Pāṇḍavas, Draupadī, Balarāma, and Kṛṣṇa tie in not only with Yama's sattra, the former Indras, and the conventions of the Naimiṣa Forest, but with other narratives as well;[117] and that when the author himself tells this myth, it is more a revelation, an opening into further enigmas, than a piece of fluff.[118] Scholars attentive to the epic's intricacies have also made up stories about its composition, several around the notion of a written archetype. If these cannot be said to have reached cumulative results, they can at least be said to be cumulatively more instructive, and in any case, I think, better stories. We have noted some of these in

[116]See Hiltebeitel 1993, 9; Reich 1998, 216, 293–94; Bigger 1998, 16: "Breaks *(Brüche)* therefore should not be hidden *(übertüncht)* but should be brought to the fore, since they are part of this synchronic text"; Fitzgerald 1980, 168, on the problem in the *Mokṣadharma* "of explaining why a redactor would introduce [a] discourse with a question that does not fit it well," and 171, conjecturing "it may have been considered part of the value of the text"; also 195; Feller 2000, 17, 135–36, on traces of piecing together multiple narratives. Cf. Witzel 1987c on inconsistencies, clever joins, tense shifts, transitions between old and new, colloquial shifts, and other signs of "'repair' work" composition in the precedent-setting frame story-telling of *JB*. See also Richardson 1990, 168, on "seams and joins" in Homer, and Gellrich 1985, 179–90, on Chaucer's highlighting of "joints and seams" in his references to Dante.

[117]It can now be studied further for its conjunction other epic references to the overpopulated earth (de Jong 1985); Lady Death's (Mṛtyu's) refusal to cause death until it results from her transformed tears (see chap. 2, n. 128); and the sequence of Indra's travels (12.220–21), first to the mountain cave (220.11) where he meets the Asura Bali, learns that Bali is one of thousands of former Indras (39–41), waxes eloquent about "time cooking" (90–94, 102), and then, when he bathes at dawn in the Gaṅgā's "source at the gate of the pole star" *(dhruvadvārabhavāṃ gaṅgām)*, sees Śrī rising like a second sun, her ornaments shining like stars (10–14; cf. Hiltebeitel [1976] 1990, 160–61). Cf. 12.169.9: "The world is assaulted by death" *(mṛtyunābhyahato loko*; Fitzgerald 1980, 348).

[118]See above at n. 26. Reviewing the CE of the *Ādiparvan*, Winternitz reluctantly retreats to viewing the myth as "childish and contradictory" (1933–34, 174), after having certified it thirty-five years earlier in a lengthy attack on Dahlmann 1895 as a "late addition" (1897, 754) of three originally separate components (746) that is "nothing but a collection of fragments of stories patched together by a very unskilled hand" (735). Cf. van Buitenen's reassertion that it is an example of "silly" and "inept mythification" (1973, xix–xx); and Bigger's view that its story of incarnations is "*im MBh nicht wieder angesprochen*" (1998, 100; cf. 159: "it stands isolated in the MBh") and is later than the list of incarnations in 1.61 (29–30, 57, 72)—a Śaivite interpolation with a Viṣṇuite insertion (107, cf. 161, 163).

chapters 1 and 3.[119] In closing this chapter, I would like to cite one more, and move along with my own.

With her stance against the Critical Edition and her view that the epic is originally oral,[120] Biardeau cannot be expected to contemplate an archetype. But after rejecting the "received opinion of a slow collective and disordered elaboration," and insisting that "the refinement of construction and invention that imbue the *Mahābhārata* can only be the work of a genius, and I see nothing to gain by pluralizing him," she admits to two lines of thought: "If it were necessary, I would imagine a father, a son, and a maternal uncle of the father or son working together, and, in a corner out of the way, just beyond voice range, a woman, wife of the father, mother of the son, and sister of the uncle. This schema is drawn from the *Mahābhārata* itself, but it situates the composition of the poem in south India rather than north . . . but that is another story. For my part, I prefer to suppose the creation of a sole Brahman of genius."[121] Like Sukthankar, Biardeau's first line imagines a relation of embeddedness between composers and the text. What is new here is the south Indian woman.

E. What Fits

My story continues with the theme that Śaunaka and his co-sattrins and sadasyas, along with Ugraśravas (who may or may not get to sit down at the Naimiṣa Forest sattra), and Vyāsa and his disciples (who *do* sit down at Janamejaya's sattra), and of course the term sattra itself, may be names for processes and even roles of people that went into the making of the *Mahābhārata*—an ironic narrative device by which the epic poets embedded reflexive images in their poem. In making the Naimiṣa Forest the intermediary setting between the outermost frame of the author and

[119]See chap. 1, § C at nn. 91–98 and 120, and chap. 3, § C, on Sukthankar's story about Bhṛguization. Dahlmann and Vaidya (see Proudfoot 1987, 212, n. 71) could be considered here too. Cf. also van Buitenen 1973, xvi: "The grand framework was a *design*."

[120]On orality, see Biardeau 1968, 116–17, 123; 1997a, 87, and Proudfoot's criticism (1987, 212, n. 69). However, cf. 1997a, 118–19, on the adoption by Brahmans of "the narrative and poetic form" in the epics and purāṇas as an "apparently literary event" that served to make "a brahmanial literature . . . accessible to practically everybody." On the CE, see Biardeau 1968, 1970a, 1970b.

[121]Biardeau and Péterfalvi 1985, 27 [my translation]. Biardeau hints further at a Buddhist presence in the political background during a long period, and the need to posit socio-religious conditions among Brahmans for the text's rapid dissemination, again, possibly beginning from the peninsula (30; cf. 1999, xxxiii). More recently, she also includes royal patronage in her story, making her single author "a Brahman living in dependence of a royal court," and suggesting that the epic's first diffusion occurred inside royal courts, and then spread "very fast to Viṣṇu temples" (1997a, 87–88).

the inner frame of the narration to Janamejaya, they transformed the outer frame from the "Twinkling Forest" of the Vedic heavens into the "Momentous Forest" (no less twinkling, but now more winking) of the Literary Imagination," where any frame can recede and collapse.[122] These devices clearly tie in with the epic's emphasis on the relentlessness of time, and also find theological expression in the *Gītā*'s revelation that the deity is himself the totality of time, creating and collapsing worlds: a formulation that is in all likelihood an answer to the time-emptying and deconstructive Buddhist teachings of radical momentariness (see chapter 3, n. 19).

Now one thing about sattras that the epic never tells us in describing them, and that none of the authors cited so far ever mentions either, is that in a sattra, where "all the priests jointly count as Sacrificers, . . . [a]s they are all yajamānas, they all need wives" (Jamison 1996, 31). Indeed, wives are known to have made considerable noise at one of the sattras most pertinent to our argument: the Gavāmayana sattra, which, as its name—the "Course" or "Progress of the Cows"—suggests, holds reminiscences of the mobile yātsattra and the cattle expeditions of the Vrātyas (see n. 78). One end of the Gavāmayana sattra is celebrated on the winter solstice with a carnal ceremony called the Mahāvrata. Here, the ritual requirement of multiple wives "ensures quite a band—and that is in fact what the wives form." While lewd exchanges and ritual copulation "are going on, the wives play musical instruments: lutes and flutes of assorted types."[123] As Jamison says, "What a New Year's Eve!" (98).

I suggest that with all their knowing allusions to Vrātya and yātsattra themes in their sattra narratives, the epic poets cannot have forgotten the women they omit to mention at the Naimiṣa Forest sattra of gṛhapati Śaunaka, the "master of the house." Like Biardeau, I see the women as perhaps beyond earshot, but definitely heard. The epic's status as fifth Veda is enough to explain why they would be out of earshot from the "Vedic" recitation. That van Buitenen could sense that the story of "Nala and Damayantī" is written "from a woman's point of view" (1975, 184) is one of many hints that the poets have listened to their mothers, wives,

[122]Compare the eagle in the dream by which Chaucer frames his *House of Fame*, which takes Chaucer toward the Milky Way, through planets, constellations, and "sterres" (937–1017), preceding this by "learned discourses" on the origin of sound (753–852)! The House of Fame, not unlike Naimiṣa Forest, is situated "Ryght even in myddes of the weye between hevene, erthe, and see" (714–15; 846): a "cosmic center" (see Gellrich 1985, 185–94).

[123]1996, 98 and 283, n. 224, for citations. The ceremony is akin to the ritual copulation of the chief wife with the strangled horse in the Aśvamedha; on Mahāvrata as a Vrātya rite and the Aśvamedha, see ibid., 96–98, 145–46; Hiltebeitel 1991a, 381–87.

sisters, and daughters, and probably sometimes listened well.[124] The women who cannot not be there are, I submit, one of the ironic presences at this dark and subtle sattra, and their real human counterparts, the epic poets' wives, are probably one of the reasons that so many of the epic's women, and in particular Draupadī, come to life. Indeed, one might even imagine that the impoverished and golden-tear-weeping Śrī whom Indra finds at the source of the Gaṅgā is not only the goddess whom Draupadī incarnates, but another image of the wives: impoverished like their sattrin husbands should be too, yet also images of prosperity, at the periphery of a sattra.[125]

Śaunaka and company's sattra thus conveys the image of a group. Though I prefer the term "committee" (see chapter 1, n. 79), it could also be described as a syndicate (M. M. Mehta 1971, 101), or a symposium. Indeed, it would be just as useful to compare the *Mahābhārata* with Plato's *Symposium*, where the subject is love, and where Socrates finds his inspiration from a woman, Diotima, as with the *Iliad*, where the subject is anger. We can benefit from both analogies, without giving one priority. Like the Tamil Caṅkams for Caṅkam literature, like the Buddhist Saṅgha for the "Dharma and Vinaya," like the putative translators of the Septuagint for the Torah,[126] the epic would seem to supply its own story, or better stories, of the group behind its transmission and composition.

Yet not surprisingly, the Mahāyāna yields the closest parallel in its of the telling of the *Lotus Sūtra*.[127] Śākyamuni preaches the *Lotus of the True Dharma (saddharma)* on the Vulture Peak. More exactly, he preaches the *Puṇḍarīka of the True Dharma*, evoking a type of lotus, the *puṇḍarīka*, that also lies behind the name of an eleven-day Soma sacrifice called *Pauṇḍarīka*, which secures "supremacy" for Prajāpati or any "most exalted Lord" after an all-night Viśvajit and the bestowal of a

[124]I agree with van Buitenen that it is "profitless to speculate" on whether "Nala" (or other passages that could provoke similar thoughts) "was written by a woman" (1973, 184). But note the unconsidered concession that it "was written."

[125]Curious here is the story of the gleaner whose emaciated wife wears cast-off peacock feathers. Summoned to be his partner in sacrifice *(yajñapatnī)*, she complies, but unwillingly, fearing her husband's curse (12.264.6–7; see chap. 1, n. 78). But he is a gleaner, and apparently not a sattrin.

[126]The *Letter of Aristeas* tells that during the reign of Ptolemy II Philadelphus in Egypt, the Hebrew Pentateuch was identically translated into Greek by seventy-one translators in seventy-one separate rooms, all within a year and a day.

[127]See Lopez 1993 on this "locus classicus for the legitimation of the Mahāyāna" (363) through "fiction," and its place among "sūtras . . . purporting to be the word of the historical Buddha (or sanctioned by him)" that "were, in fact, literary compositions, written in such a way as to preserve the conventions of recorded discourse" (360).

"myriad of cows" as dakṣiṇās[128]—in the epic, it obtains for one the world of the Sun *(sūryaloka)*.[129] As Śākyamuni sermonizes, the Stūpa of the "extinct" Buddha Prabhūtaratna rises five hundred yojanas[130] above him, issuing a voice that congratulates him for recycling the *Puṇḍarīka* teaching. But now, as happens thanks to Prabhūtaratna's vow whenever the *Puṇḍarīka* teaching is promulgated by a Lord Buddha, Buddhas of the Buddha-fields of the ten directions converge "in the sky above" as "an assembled congregation" to hear the *Puṇḍarīka*, each not only with "his own troops of Bodhisattvas," but backgrounded so that "in each direction of space" there are "many hundred thousand myriads of koṭis of Buddha-fields, similar to the sands of the river Ganges." After this, the four classes of Śākyamuni's earthly congregation are also equally uplifted to be exhorted to preach the *Puṇḍarīka*, and Mañjuśrī elevates to the same heights the Nāga-bodhisattvas whom he has brought to enlightenment by preaching the *Puṇḍarīka* under the sea (Kern [1884] 1963, 227–50). I thank Michael Witzel for his suggestion that the elevated Nāgas can be compared to the snakes of *Pañcaviṃśa Brāhmaṇa* 25.15, who "vanquish death" and become the Ādityas by their sattra.[131] Let us also recall that the snake Padmanābha inhabits the Naimiṣa Forest. This story frames Śākyamuni's preaching of the *Puṇḍarīka* not on the boundaries of the text, but at its very heart, allowing him to fill out the text with parables that expand from this center, and use "fictional" means to bring beings to the truth that there is but a single vehicle that elevates this host (Lopez 1993, 363–71, 377–78), so that whenever the *Puṇḍarīka* is promulgated, the congregation of enlightened beings assembles like the sands of the celestial Gaṅgā, the stars of the Milky Way.[132] The *Lotus* and some other early Mahāyāna sūtras—probably from "the first centuries of the Christian era" (Lamotte 1988, 574–75)—would seem to have an answering relation to the *Mahābhārata*, though little has been done to figure it out.[133]

[128]*PB* 22.18 (Caland [1931] 1982, 584–85). A certain "son of Puṇḍarīka" is said to have thrived by performing this rite (22.18.7), and presumably given it his name. It is an *ahīna* (a rite of more than one and less than thirteen days) rather than a sattra, but the distinction is not absolute (see *PB* 22.3.3).

[129]3.82.99; I thank Randy Kloetzli for recalling the Pauṇḍarīka sacrifice from a talk by Frits Staal. Note that the golden lotuses Indra traces from Yama's sattra to the weeping Śrī are *puṇḍarīkas* (1.189.9), and Kṛṣṇa is Puṇḍarīkākṣa, "Lotus-eyed."

[130]500 x 9 miles (Monier-Williams's best estimate of a yojana) = 4,500 miles.

[131]Witzel, personal communication, December 1996; see above, n. 9.

[132]On the "sands of the Ganges" as stars in Buddhist cosmology, and their relation to the cosmology of "innumerables" such as the numbers just mentioned in the *Lotus*, see Kloetzli 1983, 52, 93, 114, 119–227. A *koṭi* is ten million.

[133]See Lévi 1918–19; Pisani 1939, 175–76 for preliminary insights. Cf. Walters 2000, 110 relating the Sanskrit epics to earlier Buddhist texts.

As Lopez observes, one purpose of such Mahāyāna sūtras is to "wrest . . . authority" away from multiple "Hīnayāna" texts and arhats, "and restore it solely to the absent Buddha" (361). In the *Mahābhārata*, however, authority remains in a multisigniferous Veda. Rather than claiming it in a "Buddha's word" *(buddhavacana)*, it relocates it in something more displaced: a "fifth Veda" that is its author's "entire thought," never spoken by him but only transmitted by others. Nor does the audience have to be elevated to the heavens. Like the author, the Naimiṣeya Ṛṣis are already there, but also here. Together with this author, always present in his characters thoughts, his disciples, and a bard, they make their story while they live it. Their group has some time, but not so much time (the sattra lasts twelve years), for certain people to work intensely together under the direction of a "master of the house," for some to sit and listen to the composition as it proceeds in intervals, for others to come and go, and for all the men and women to listen to each other. Somewhere in back of all this the author spent three years on this work[134]—perhaps, as Vaidya saw it, doing such "splendid plot-laying" as to rival Shakespeare.[135] No doubt the bard represents oral tradition—in particular, narrative skill[136] and, as we shall see, perhaps even a gift for improvisation. But the rest are all Brahmans, and it is their project. The inner core, the sattrins or committee, would no doubt have had a philosopher and a dharmaśāstra connoisseur among them,[137] and perhaps a retired Brahman general (a *senāpati*), while the master of the house kept them all to a common purpose.[138] The design with its parvans ("joins, knots") and subparvans suggests that different units would have been "joined" together, leaving awkward fits and provocative contradictions among the endless riches to ponder. This, I suggest, would have been one of the more enjoyable parts of the work under the guidance of this inspired and usually appreciative "leader of the group."

About this Śaunaka, there are further hints. One concerns his connec-

[134]1.56.32: "For three years the Muni Kṛṣṇa Dvaipāyana always got up making this superb *Mahābhārata* story" *(tribhir varṣaiḥ sadotthāyī kṛṣṇadvaipāyano muniḥ/ mahābhāratam ākhyānaṃ kṛtavān idam uttamam)*.

[135]1905 [1966], 49. See chap. 1 at n. 62.

[136]Śaunaka knows all the stories, but it never said he knows how to tell them.

[137]Yardi's statistical results define five styles, which, if they mean anything, might indicate authorly orientations: in Draupadī and other women (1986, vii, 18, 27–28), Kṛṣṇa (ix, 44, 78–81, 97–98), and Bhārgavas (ix), with no style distinctive for didactic passages alone (x).

[138]Cf. Inden on the "composite authorship" of the *VDhP*: "To summarize: the 'author' of the text was a complex agent, one consisting of Pāñcarātra adepts, palace priest, king of kings, and counsellor, as well as the chronologer himself, each of whom participated in the process of composition from a different perspective and brought to bear a different expertise or commitment" (2000, 41)—including entries on the science of weaponry and warfare (39, 58, 60, 80; see chap. 1, n. 120 on Inden's short time-frame for this virtual committee).

tion with the subterranean Vrātya themes we have traced to Naimiṣa Forest sattras. Until now I have left largely aside the insights of Falk, Koskikallio, and especially White connecting Vrātyas and their descendants with dogs.[139] But there can be no doubt that although Śaunaka's name belongs to numerous sages of the Śunaka *gotra*, which derives from his ancestor Śunaka, the son of Ruru,[140] it means "doggish," or "of canine descent," being related to *śunaka*, "dog," and to the basic word for dog, *śvan* (akin to Germanic *Hund*, hound). As a parallel, a Naimiṣa Forest sattra is "held by the Śunakas, 'Whelps'" in the *Chāgaleya Upaniṣad*.[141] There seems to be nothing canine about any of our Naimiṣa Forest sattras, but at another epic sattra the dogs steal the show.[142]

The story opens the *Pauṣyaparvan*, in which Ugraśravas supplies the main narrative content of his first opening of the *Mahābhārata*.[143] Once, while Janamejaya and his three brothers sat for a long sattra at Kurukṣetra, a son of the celestial bitch *(devaśunī)* Saramā approached and was beaten by the brothers. When the pup ran howling to Saramā, she assumed it had been beaten for some offense. But assured of its innocence, she went to the sattra and pronounced that an "unseen fear" *(adṛṣṭam . . . bhayam)* would come upon Janamejaya (1.3.1–10). Mehta thinks this story may point to "an old version of the Janamejaya-sacrifice before it was connected with the Mahābhārata or composed in its present form as found in our Āstīkaparvan" (1973, 549). But the snake sattra takes place at Takṣasilā rather than Kurukṣetra (see chapter 3, n. 121), and this sattra involves no snakes. In context, the story seems to plant the fear that will result in Janamejaya's hearing about his father Parikṣit's death, from which the snake sacrifice follows. What is intriguing about it has been noted by Vaidya ([1905] 1966, 221–22) and Mehta (1973, 549): unusually for the *Mahābhārata*, the story is broken off. We learn no more about the haunting fear or the dogs. Yet given all the Vrātya allusions that run through other sattras, and the fact that it is Janamejaya who must perform his snake sacrifice with this lingering fear still in mind, one wonders.

[139]See Falk 1986, 20–21, 28, 40; White 1991, 96–100, 104–5; and above, n. 13.

[140]See chap. 3, n. 68 for this genealogy. See also Chakravarty 1969, 169 and passim.

[141]*Naimiṣe 'mī śunakāh sattram āsata*—"In Naimiṣa Forest those dogs sat (for) a sattra." See Falk 1986, 40, n. 107 (whom I translate here); White 1991, 97.

[142]See White 1991, 97, who, however, confuses things, calling Śaunaka Śunaka, locating the sattra in Naimiṣa Forest rather than Kurukṣetra (cf. chap. 3, n. 121), placing Janamejeya at Naimiṣa in the presence of this "Śunaka" (he never meets Śaunaka), identifying the sattra as a snake sacrifice, claiming that the sacrifice in question was never ended (which it explicitly is; 1.3.10), and identifying it with the outer frame of the epic.

[143]See Feller 2000, 168, n. 2, and above, chap. 1, n. 70, on her discussion of other Vedic echoes in the *Pauṣyaparvan*.

Yudhiṣṭhira, a portion of Yama-Dharma consecrated to carry out the battle of Kurukṣetra like a Vrātya raider from the world of the gods, punctuates his career by a series of meditations on dogs. As peace negotiations reach their end before the war, he tells his last ambassador, Kṛṣṇa, "With the prevention of conciliation it becomes terrible, like a trifle among dogs, as marked by the wise: tail-wagging, a bark, a bark back, backing off, baring the teeth, howling, and then the fight begins. The one who is stronger, having won, eats the meat, Kṛṣṇa. So it is too among humans; there is no distinction at all *(evam eva manuṣyeṣu viśeṣo nāsti kaścana)*" (5.70.70–72; cf. Sutton 1997, 336). Having just won the war, he is appalled by its devastation: "We are not dogs, but we are like dogs greedy for a piece of meat. And now our meat has disappeared, and those who would eat the meat have vanished too" (12.7.10; Fitzgerald trans., 1980, 128). Just after this, Arjuna rebukes him for thinking of becoming a beggar: "Abandoning blazing prosperity, you cast your eyes around like a dog" (12.18.12). There is more on this theme to be noted in chapter 7, until finally, like a yātsattrin ascending from Plakṣa Prāsravaṇa, Yudhiṣṭhira goes bodily to heaven after rejecting Indra's counsel that "there is no cruelty" (*nṛśaṃsam*; 17.3.8 and 10) in casting off the unnamed dog that has made his heavenly ascent with him. Having thought the dog was simply "devoted" *(bhakta)*, he finds that it is his father.

Is the one dog story at the beginning of the epic left off to be picked up by the other at the end?[144] Would Janamejaya's hearing it at the end have anything to do with his having abandoned the snake sacrifice at the beginning? Does the lesson about noncruelty to a dog tell Janamejaya how to relieve his "unseen fear" by ending his cruelty to the snakes? Are these further Vrātya ironies of poets who depict their leader as some kind of sly or shaggy dog, and who save a dog for the end to reveal the unity of Yudhiṣṭhira not only with Dharma but with Yama? Is one to be reminded that Yama's messengers are two dogs, sons of Saramā, the celestial bitch who in the *Ṛg Veda* crosses the cosmic night and its Milky Way to retrieve cows for Indra from the cave of the Paṇi demons?[145] Such obscure elements are not meant to be fitted together like a puzzle, but neither do they so easily come apart.

Secondly, there is little reason not to identify the Naimiṣeya Śaunaka with the Ṛṣi Śaunaka who appears three times at transitional moments or

[144]Cf. Witzel 1986, 206–7 on the framing device already used in the *JB* of leaving themes, once introduced, "while another motif is taken up, and only then, or still later, the original theme is reverted to again."

[145]Kramrisch 1975, 240–43; Witzel 1984, 225–27, nn. 32, 50, 92; cf. Macdonell [1898] 1974, 173.

"joins" in the *Āraṇyakaparvan*. The forest-rover Śaunaka's first appearance (3.2.14–79) makes him interesting as Yudhiṣṭhira's first instructor upon entering the forest: "Delighting in the higher self, he [Śaunaka] is skilled in Sāṃkhya and Yoga" (3.2.14). Let us follow scholarly convention and take such epic references to Sāṃkhya-Yoga as being to a "proto-Sāṃkhya."[146] Śaunaka tells Yudhiṣṭhira he already has an "eight-limbed awareness *(aṣṭāṅgam buddhim)* that destroys all that is not beneficial, and is informed by Vedic revelation *(śruti)* and tradition *(smṛti)*" (17). Yudhiṣṭhira learns from him about the endlessness and beginninglessness of "thirst" *(tṛṣṇā)* that is rooted in affection *(sneha)* (33–36); that the fool driven by his penis and stomach (62) comes only to be "bewildered by sports and food, does not know the self when sunk in the great mouth of bewilderment, falls into saṃsāra and womb after womb, and is moved round like a wheel by ignorance *(avidyā)*, karma, and thirst" (66–67). Yudhiṣṭhira's eight-limbed awareness is his basis for his learning that there is an "eightfold path" *(mārgo 'yaṃ dharmasyāṣṭavidhaḥ*; *aṣṭāṅgenaiva mārgeṇa)*, for which Śaunaka gives two explanations. For "the good" *(sat)* who follow the Vedic precept, "Do the rite and renounce it *(kuru karma tyajeti ca)*," it allows them to complete the itineraries of both the "path of the fathers" and the "path of the gods." Four practices (offering oblations, Vedic recitation, gifts, and tapas) are for traveling the former, and four (truth, forbearance, restraint, and nongreed) are for ascending the latter (70–73). But for those of purified soul *(viśuddhātmā)* who wish to conquer saṃsāra, the eightfold path achieves liberation by (1) right *(samyañc, samyak)* binding of intention *(saṃkalpasambandha)*, (2) right subjugation of the senses *(indriyanigraha)*, (3) right distinction of vows *(vrataviśeṣa)*, (4) right service to one's guru *(gurusevana)*; (5) right discipline about eating *(āhārayoga)*, (6) right approach to recitation, i.e., of the Vedas *(adhyayanāgama)*, (7) right abandonment of rites *(karmopasaṃnyāsa)*, and (8) right stopping of thought *(cittanirodhana)* (74–75). All this brings "success in yoga" (*yogasiddhim*, 77). Considering the echoes of Buddhist language here, it would seem that Śaunaka's instructions for the forest life combine a preemption and subversion of Buddhist teachings about forest enlightenment and the eightfold path with a strongly Vedic interpetation (or anticipation?) of an eight-limbed Yoga.

Śaunaka next appears among the great Ṛṣis who applaud when Baka Dālbhya tells Yudhiṣṭhira he should surround himself with Brahmans and

[146]See Larson and Bhattacharya 1987, 3–15, 110–17, with other citations, all, however, looking only to acknowledged philosophical passages (*BhG*, *Mokṣadharma*, etc.). Note that Vyāsa is described a "knowing Sāṃkhya and Yoga" at the end (18.5.33), and that it is highlighted in his and others' teachings to his son Śuka (see chap. 8).

appoint one as his chaplain (3.27.23). And third, he appears just after Nārada finishes narrating to Yudhiṣṭhira what Pulastya once told the pilgrimaging Bhīṣma (80.10–25) as his recommended route for visiting tīrthas that open the doorway to heaven (see chapter 2, n. 39). As Pulastya vanishes and just before Nārada turns the Pāṇḍavas over to Lomaśa to guide them to some of the tīrthas Pulastya has recommended, Nārada mentions sixteen Ṛṣis who await the Pāṇḍavas, ready to accompany them, including Śaunaka (here, with a son), Vyāsa, Mārkaṇḍeya, and Vālmīki (83.102–4). It is curious that Pulastya, the ancestor of Rākṣasas, including Brahmarākṣasas,[147] is among those who make numerous allusions to Vrātya practices in his guide to tīrthas (3.80–83.95). Indeed, Koskikallio (1999, 334) notes that Pulastya's narration includes the story of "Darbhin," probably Baka Dālbhya, who creates the Avatīrṇa tīrtha along the Sarasvatī and collects the four oceans there (3.81.131–36). Nārada tells Yudhiṣṭhira that the tīrthas they will now approach are "filled with hosts of Rākṣasas, and no one can go there but you" (83.100). Pulastya seems to have recommended that the Pāṇḍavas free up a route that has been overrun by his descendants.

Now if the two (or more?) Śaunakas are one, it would only mean that Śaunaka would have to live about as long as Vyāsa (a small feat, considering the longevity of their companion Vālmīki here, not to mention "old" Baka Dālbhya and Mārkaṇḍeya), and hear about himself at these points from Ugraśravas' account of what he heard from Vaiśampāyana, without it being mentioned that he is doing so. This might explain how Śaunaka had already heard all the stories Ugraśravas tells him. Or the relation between this forest-roving Śaunaka and the forest-sattrin Śaunaka could be one of the epic's planted uncertainties. In any case, the name cannot be an accident: it connects him not only with the ideological containment of Buddhism (see n. 115) and with Vrātya rites and characters, but with a whole school of Vedic exegesis.[148]

[147]Hiltebeitel 1988, 179; Koskikallio 1999, 359.

[148]Patton 1996 writes: "it is quite clear . . . that Śaunaka and those attached to his school were concerned with the correct boundaries and applications of the Ṛg Vedic canon—in its meter, its *anuvāka* divisions, its authorship, its deities, and its ritual and everyday uses" (16); "The point of view of this school is not only that the Vedas are eternal . . . , but also that Vedic language, particularly in the form of *mantra*, can be infinitely applied to any number of situations" (xix); not only commenting on canon but tending to compete with it, it "extends beyond the domestic and public sacrificial realms and into the everyday life of the Brahman" (454–55). This school composed the "encyclopedic" *BD* (see nn. 110 and 113 above), and in the *Ṛg Vidhāna*, it stressed more than any other "the capacity 'to bring the deity to mind' in the midst of the sacrifice" (188–89). Considering that the Ṛṣis of the Naimiṣa Forest are probably not all Bhārgavas (see chap. 3 at n. 58), it might be more fruitful to think of a "Śaunaka school" contributing to the *Mbh* than a Bhārgava "clan."

This brings us to our last matter, which concerns the sense one gets that our first (if not only) Śaunaka appreciates improvisation and delights with his co-sattrins in making (if not also appearing in) the "joins" in their work. It concerns the two Jaratkārus, male and female: the bizarre parents of the "ontologically" all-important Āstīka, he of whom the father Jaratkāru says "it/he is" with reference to his being the embryo in the mother Jaratkāru's womb, who will be born to save the snakes.[149]

Before making this fateful pronouncement, the male Jaratkāru had aged in his asceticism while neglecting to produce offspring, and when his Fathers revealed the terrible straits this was putting them in, he agreed to rescue them by marrying and bearing a son; but only on the condition that the maiden have his unusual name. The only female Jaratkāru to be found, sister of the great snake Vāsuki, had been raised by the snakes as an ascetic snake-virgin to meet this anticipated name-requirement, since her snake-kin knew that the pair's son would be their savior at Janamejaya's sattra (1.13, 34–36.7, 41–44, 49). Now, when Ugraśravas has built the story to the point where the snakes prepare to introduce their sister to the desperately searching male Jaratkāru as his only conceivable match, Śaunaka asks Ugraśravas to tell him the etymology *(niruktam)* of "Jaratkāru" (36.2). The scene already looks amusing, since the Brahman thus requests the bard to show *his* adroitness at *nirukta*, "etymology," one of the six *vedāṅgas* or "limbs of the Veda," about which a bard might be expected to know much less than a Brahman sattrin. The bard replies:

> "*Jarā*, they say, means 'destruction' and *kāru* implies 'horrible.' His body was horrible, and the wise one gradually caused its destruction by severe tapas, so it is said. Likewise, O Brahman, the sister of Vāsuki is called 'Jaratkāru.'"
>
> Having heard this, the virtuous-souled Śaunaka burst into laughter, and he saluted Ugraśravas, saying, "It fits!"[150]

Like the names of the bards Lomaharṣaṇa ("Horripilating"), the father, and Ugraśravas ("Terrible to Hear"), the son, and like so much else in the *Mahābhārata*, Jaratkāru signifies something frightful: a "Horrible (body of) Destruction."[151]

[149]See chap. 3, § B on the parents and on Āstīka, and above, n. 114.

[150]1.36.3–5: *jareti kṣayam āhur vai dāruṇaṃ kārusaṃjñitam/ śarīraṃ kāru tasyāsīt tatsa dhīmāñśanaiḥ śanaiḥ// kṣapayāmāsa tīvreṇa tapasetyata ucyate/ jaratkārur iti brahman vāsuker bhaginī tathā// evamuktas tu dharmātmā śaunakaḥ prāhasat tadā/ ugraśravasam āmantrya upapannamiti bruvan.*

[151]Van Buitenen (1973, 97) prefers "monstrous" for *dāruṇam*; Ganguli ([1884–96] 1970, 1:98) has "huge."

Clearly "It fits!" or "That fits!" is a good translation of *upapannamiti*,[152] which occurs just this once in the entire *Mahābhārata*.[153] The commentator Nīlakaṇṭha would even allow us to translate, "It joins!" (*upapannaṃ yuktam*: Kinjawadekar 1929–33, 1:88). But what an odd fit it is, as Nīlakaṇṭha shows by imagining further stories to make it fit: most notably that the female snake-Jaratkāru also withered her body away as a young unmarried lady (ibid). Ugraśravas, with his "likewise" *(tathā)*, never quite tells us that the name "fits" her for the same reason as her husband, even though Nīlakaṇṭha tries to fit the bard's words to that expectation. Most of all, the etymology is incongruous. One has to look hard for other females with Sanskrit names that end in short "u."[154] *Jarat* from *jarā*, "old age," is passably explained as *kṣayam*, "destruction."[155] But Ugraśravas's other gloss doesn't seem to fit the Sanskrit language. It looks like the bard might be speaking wittily from a vernacular with common -u endings. Or perhaps he conceals an obscure pun on Vedic *kārú*, a kind of bardic eulogist or "proclaimer" sometimes said to "praise *(jarate)* with hymns" (*ṚV* 7.68.9) or to "wander about praising *(járan)*" (see Gonda 1969, 479–80). But *kāru* has no Sanskrit meaning that can be glossed by *dāruṇam*, "horrible, monstrous, harsh, etc." As Monier-Williams, citing this passage, puts it in dictionary shorthand: "(only etymological) horrible" (MW, 275). In other words, Ugraśravas has made it up it for the occasion! Moreover, as van Buitenen says, one has the right to wonder "how this etymology can inspire merriment" (1973, 444). Yet it is clearly the etymology that makes Śaunaka laugh, and not, as Nīlakaṇṭha further invents, the marriage of two people whose deformity and old age are equal.[156] Merriment indeed!

Now as Minkowski has indicated, the epic poets play a "dangerous game" with their double frame, which invites thoughts of infinite regression. They usually make it appear that they suppress such an implication by reporting the exchanges between Ugraśravas, Śaunaka, and

[152]It was van Buitenen's "That fits!" (1973, 97) that caught my eye. Cf. Mangels 1994, 72: "Gelungen!" ("Success!"). Mangels thinks that Śaunaka is testing his bard (71–72).

[153]At least, judging by the Tokunaga machine-readable text of the *Mbh* based on the CE.

[154]See Whitney [1889] 1960, 123: feminine -u endings are found, but "a special feminine-stem is often made by lengthening the *u* to *ū*," as in Kadrū or Sarayū. Women's names popular today like Bhanu and Madhu do not seem to be used in classical Sanskrit.

[155]The element *jarā* figures in destructive contexts in the hunter Jarā who kills Kṛṣṇa and in the Rākṣasī Jarā who "puts together" the two halves of the Magadhan despot Jarāsandha.

[156]Kinjawadekar 1929–33, 1:88. Cf. Tschannerl 1992, 112, who may be right that whereas the male Jaratkāru's name suggests that his body becomes old and frail through his strict mortification, the young woman Jaratkāru's name suggests that her body would have grown old more quickly because she lacked sexual activity.

the other Naimiṣa Forest sattrins rather matter-of-factly, as if to prompt such a question would be gauche. But here they force the question. Śaunaka and Ugraśravas leap out of the outer frame. Who hears Śaunaka's burst of laughter? The author? The reader? Who takes such delight in how things fit? Here we glimpse the *Mahābhārata* poets tipping their hand as framers who are both beyond and within the outer frame. What a strange, dark sense of humor, and what a daring sense of fit it is that they reveal. These authors, ghost-writing in collaboration with the fictional Vyāsa under the cover of the Naimiṣeya Ṛṣis, set in motion the hearing of a new understanding of life as it begins from what is.

5 Don't Be Cruel

In a plainly Marxist study, Walter Ruben finds that "fighting against despots in old Indian literature" "plays a fairly big role" (1968, 11). Sampling the epics, purāṇas, and some other texts, he lists thirty-one literary despots beginning with Duryodhana, Rāvaṇa, Kaṃsa, Jarāsandha, and Arjuna Kārtavīrya (all from the epics), and ends with the observation that only one, "Sarvārthasiddhi, the last Nanda, was an historical king" (114). The other thirty are "mythological" (111). He concludes that there was "no revolutionary class in ancient India," and that, while Brahman literatures (including the epics) encouraged kings to be nondespotic and Buddhist Jātakas even envisioned mass resistance, the people "suffering under despotism" were "consoled with religious stories" (116–17). Turning to history, he runs through the record of patricides and other assassinations that distinguish early imperial Magadha, and suggests the implications of this history for Indian mythology.

> According to Buddhist tradition Bimbisāra of Magadha was killed by his son Ajātaśatru and the four following kings were also patricides; then the people supplanted this dynasty of murderous despots by electing the minister Siśunāga as king. The last Saiśunāga was killed by the first Nanda, allegedly a barber and paramour of the queen. The last Nanda [mentioned above] was killed by the Brahmin Kauṭalya. The last Maurya was killed by the Brahmin Puṣyamitra, founder of the Suṅga-dynasty. The last Suṅga, Devabhūmī, was killed by Vasudeva, who founded the Brahmanical Kāṇva-dynasty. Then followed centuries of war and political trouble caused by foreign invaders from the North-west. . . . Thus, in the course of five hundred years between 500 B.C. and 30 B.C., people in Northern India became accustomed to the idea that it was the right and even the duty of this or that man to assassinate a king. . . . These five hundred years were basic for the evolution of Indian civilization, for the growth of epic and Buddhist literature and for the development of Vaiṣṇava and Śaiva mythology and morals. (114)

As we have seen, others too have looked to this period to understand the polito-religious background of the composition of the Sanskrit epics. But Ruben's insights are important for singling out despotism—and patricide as one of its recurrent features—as an underlying moral problematic to which both Sanskrit epics respond.

More than this, Ruben's comments focus us on the imperial character of this grim history. Fitzgerald, alert to this issue, identifies the "period after the rise of the Mauryan empire" as the background in which "the mind of the creator of the [*Mbh*] text" would have provided "an early Brahmanic Vaiṣṇava ideological grounding for an empire—whether as an unfulfilled fantasy, an imaginative projection intended to inspire such action, or a retrospective justification for something already accomplished or attempted" (1983, 625). Perhaps a better formulation would be an imagined history as charter for a better future. I do not think a justification for something already accomplished, that "the Śuṅgas, the Guptas, or some ambitious or merely fanciful petty king sometime in between" (ibid.), need have had anything to do with sponsoring the *Mahābhārata*: as indicated in chapters 3 and 4, I think the sattra-performing Brahmans of the epic's outer frame are more likely to provide a key to its composition than Janamejaya, the king of the inner frame, who is probably no more than a great king from the past idealized as a royal audience. But even if the Mauryans, and Aśoka in particular, stand out in this imperial history, it is its relentlessness as a whole that seems to impinge on the epic poets.[1]

To begin with, they trace Magadha's imperial history back to the figure of Jarāsandha, king of Magadha in the time of the Pāṇḍavas. Bimbisāra and Ajātaśatru both supposedly descend from Jarāsandha (*Viṣṇu Purāṇa* 4.23). Jarāsandha alone stands in the way of Yudhiṣṭhira's intention to claim imperial status *(saṃrājya)* through a Rājasūya ritual. As Kṛṣṇa tells Yudhiṣṭhira, Jarāsandha's rival imperial intentions are evidenced by his plan to exterminate the Kṣatriyas. In thanks to Śiva, who helped Jarāsandha defeat the kings in battle, he now intends to sacrifice a hundred kings from the hundred and one lines, that is, all those of lunar and solar descent with the one exempt line his own (2.13.4–8). Having already imprisoned eighty-six of the hundred kings in Girivraja, a "mountain corral," in an "enclosure for men *(puruṣavraja)*" (64),[2] he needs only the remainder before he begins this cruelty (*krūram*;

[1]I follow Biardeau here (in Biardeau and Péterfalvi 1985, 30), cited also in chap. 4, n. 121. On other views, see chap. 1, § C.

[2]There are perhaps echoes here of the mountain cave (see 2.13.62), "former Indra," and cattle-release themes noted in chap. 4. A *vraja* is a corral for cattle, and Jarāsandha treats the kings like *paśu*, "cattle," to be offered to Śiva-Paśupati, "Lord of cattle." On this theme and its relation to Kṛṣṇa, raised in Vraja, see Hiltebeitel 1989, 94–95.

14.20). Thus, says Kṛṣṇa, he must be killed. Jarāsandha seems to be given a number of crypto-Buddhist traits,[3] apparently folded into his identification as a pre-Buddhist worshiper of Śiva.

But the epic poets, like purāṇic poets who carry the epic histories forward, also seem to reflect upon recurrent patterns that emerge within the period of early Buddhist history itself. As Ruben's glance shows, the patricides are Buddhist, most of the assassins are Brahmans, and "true Kṣatriyas" are nowhere to be found. Although Buddhists and Jains treat some of the Magadha dynasties as Kṣatriya, purāṇic genealogies consider them non-Kṣatriya and mostly low (Nandas as Śūdra; Mauryas implied as such; Śuṅgas as Brahman).[4] "Of the Nandas it is specifically said that they will exterminate all the *kṣatriyas—kṣatra vināśa kṛt*" (Thapar 1991, 22); Mahāpadma Nanda in particular is called *sarvakṣatrāntaka*, "finisher of all the Kṣatriyas": "Like another Paraśuráma, he will be the annihilator of the Kshatriya race; for after him the kings of the earth will be Śūdras."[5] These prophesies describe a period in which the Kṣatriya has to be reinvented.[6]

Despite Buddhism's appeal to nonviolence *(ahiṃsā)*, early Buddhist rulers were murderous despots[7] and, from the purāṇic perspective, not Kṣatriyas anyway. The murder of such rulers by Brahmans is no solution, since it is a vicious cycle uncongenial to Brahmans, and, from the standpoint of epic and purāṇic history, there are no Kṣatriyas left to replace the despots anyway. No doubt there were families of Kṣatriya extraction in the period of the epics' composition, but they are not recognized as such by the purāṇas, or prefigured by the epics. From what these texts tell us, they are of no political or historical interest. Rather, the epics tell how Kṣatriyas were long before this exterminated twice over: first, before the *Rāmāyaṇa*, by Bhārgava Rāma,[8] and second,

[3]See Hiltebeitel 1989, 98–99 (written in 1979): his daughters Asti and Prāpti, whom he marries to Kaṃsa, have names for concepts of Sarvāstivāda Buddhism; his name evokes the wheel of time "put together by old age" (the Buddhist *bhāvacakra* is joined at the point where "old age and death" are linked with "ignorance"); the *caitya* peak outside his city.

[4]Thapar 1978, 358; 1984, 141–42; 1992, 152–53 (the Mauryas with links to the Buddha are Sūryavaṃśin-Ikṣvākus in Buddhist genealogies). Aśoka thinks he is a Sūryavaṃśa Kṣatriya in the *Aśokāvadāna* (Strong 1983, 205, 272, 281).

[5]Wilson [1840] 1972, 374; cf. Sircar 1969a, 150.

[6]Cf. Hiltebeitel 1999a, 455–56; in press-b; in press-c.

[7]Even in Buddhist accounts. This problematic is brilliantly taken up by Obeyesekere, not only for early Indian history but in its continuation in Sri Lanka, as a "psychic structure of the long run" (1990, 71–214, esp. 147–60, 182–89 on Bimbisāra and Aśoka). Cf. Strong 1983, 40–56, 209–33 (Aśoka kills his elder brother to obtain the throne), 275–76, 283–85 (the *Aśokāvadāna*'s Jekyll-Hyde portrayal of Dharmāśoka and Caṇḍāśoka ["Righteous" and "Fierce Aśoka"], who remains "fierce" in appalling ways even after his conversion).

[8]The *Rām* also knows this myth (1.73.20; 74.24), but does not, like the *Mbh*, problematize

having barely avoided extermination by Jarāsandha, at Kurukṣetra[9]—each time with some mysterious remainder that is left for the Brahman theorists of these texts to define.

Fitzgerald also suggests that the epic poets reflect upon this period's history: "the type of political integration and subordination required to produce a harmoniously disciplined society and imperial state certainly must not have come easy to the imagination of the old political elites of Aryan society, which were fractious and agonistic (Heesterman)" (1983, 625). To be sure, it would not have come easy. But I do not think these "old political elites" were in any position to effect a "transformation" toward such a society by composing the *Mahābhārata* as a "forceful argument" for the "great social cost involved," or that the epic symbolisms of patricide and annihilation are a "metaphor" for the "required annihilation" of an "old order" that "involves the awful sacrifice of something cherished, fundamental to, and formative of oneself" (1983, 625–26). The "old Kṣatriya order" which the *Mahābhārata* envisions, and, as Fitzgerald says, often seems to loathe (1983, 624), probably had its only real historical foothold in the early post Ṛg Vedic period. As the early Upaniṣadic saying—"Where in the world are the Pārikṣitas?"[10]—indicates, it is long gone by then: well before the time of the epic's composition. In advocating the replacement of this old order, the *Mahābhārata* replaces and indeed rethinks an order defined by Vedic texts that no longer describe a current political situation. If the epic recommends a "transformation," it is, as Fitzgerald of course recognizes, an inner one; but it is not a political one over which current Kṣatriyas—"legitimately" recognized as such in the epic or purāṇic sense—are in any way envisioned as contributors.

The epic and purāṇic interpretation of the political history summarized by Ruben raises important questions for the epic's treatment of spiraling violence. In chapters 3 and 4 we met this concern in connection with Bhārgavas, Janamejaya's snake sacrifice, and Vrātya expeditions. Let us now ask what kind of "old order" it is that the epic envisions as ending

the question of how the Kṣatriyas revived, in particular by the time of Rāma Dāśarathi. See Goldman 1984, 80, n. 48: that the *Rām* "nowhere recounts his proper legend" suggests "a *Rāmāyaṇa* application of a figure drawn from the *Mahābhārata*"—but not, I would add, an "interpolation."

[9]Cf. Fitzgerald (1980, 128, n. 3) on the "similarity of the phrase" Yudhiṣṭhira uses at the end of the war for the extinction of his clan's descent to that used for Rāma Jāmadagnya's extinction of the Kṣatriyas: *jñātīn niṣpuruṣān kṛtvā*, "making our kin to have no men" (12.7.3), and *pṛthivīm kṛtvā niḥkṣatriyām* and variants, "making the Earth to have no Kṣatriyas." Yudhiṣṭhira tells Kṛṣṇa that a peace won by the total eradication of an enemy is "crueler (*nṛśaṃsataram*) than the heart-eating disease of heroism" (5.70.55–56).

[10]*BĀUp* 3.3; see Olivelle 1998, 81 and 482; Macdonell and Keith [1912] 1967, 493–94.

with the *Mahābhārata* war, and what kind of dharma it recommends as arising out of that old order for life in our times, the Kali yuga.

A. The Passing of the "Old Order"

The *Mahābhārata* certainly does describe an old order in the throes of its passing, and symbolizes it in vivid ways. In the boastful Jarāsandha, Kṛṣṇa's first choice for elimination and ready for any kind of fight, van Buitenen sees "Quite the old baron!" (1975, 18). Duryodhana's final words glorify the "kṣatriya ethos" that has followed him to its doom.[11] Fitzgerald sees Bhīṣma on his bed of arrows as "the dying exemplar of the old Kṣatriya order" (1980, 364). As a fallen "emblem of the *kṣatriya* dharma," he is a "constant reminder" to Yudhiṣṭhira "of the fratricidal and patricidal war" just finished (142); for a "new age," he also promulgates "a new statement of all the facets of *dharma* [that] has its ultimate source in Kṛṣṇa" (364).[12] Or as Biardeau has observed, the "old Kṣatriya order" is self-consciously personified in the person of Vṛddhakṣatra, "Old Kṣatra." Engaged in tapas near Kurukṣetra, he has vowed that if anyone causes his son Jayadratha's head to touch the ground, the slayer's head will burst to pieces. Kṛṣṇa, knowing this, directs Arjuna to relay Jayadratha's severed head with his arrows into Vṛddhakṣatra's lap, and when "Old Kṣatra" inadvertently lets it fall to the ground, it is his head that explodes (7.121.17–33). More than being just aged, he seems to signify the old Kṣatriya order that Kṛṣṇa, like Bhārgava Rāma, is bound to remove from the earth (Biardeau 1978, 169; Hiltebeitel 1988, 404–5, 416). In one case, a dying paragon of the old order finds words through Kṛṣṇa for the "pacification" *(śānti)* that brings the great cycle of violence to some resolution. In the other, Kṛṣṇa sees to it that another exemplar of the old order simply self-destructs from the absurdity of his retaliatory vow.[13]

But as Biardeau also sees, the epic represents the old order most insistently, weaving Vedic precedents and names into its narrative through a complex of intertwining stories, in its Pañcāla cycle: its stories of the

[11]Cf. Gitomer 1992, 229, and chap. 1, n. 25.

[12]See chap. 2, § C.30. Kṛṣṇa has placed his *buddhi* ("intellect") in Bhīṣma (12.54.27–30), communed with him, and eased his pain, all for this purpose (Fitzgerald 1980, 139–44). This is an important point: the whole "instruction" in the *Śānti* and *Anuśāsana* parvans, which often (but not always) seems like anything but bhakti teaching, is inspired, according to the epic poets, by the same divine "intellect" that utters the *BhG.*

[13]See Witzel 1987a on the agonistic character of Vedic (mainly Upaniṣadic) dialogues, which can result in a "shattered head" by asking ultimate questions that go "beyond the limits of one's knowledge" (372). There is no dialogue with "Old Kṣatra," but perhaps that is just the point.

people of Draupadī.[14] Indeed, the Pañcāla cycle is so deeply embedded in the *Mahābhārata*'s central narrative that some have convinced themselves that it formed the epic's original nucleus (see chapter 1, n. 10), that the nucleus was a Kuru-Pañcāla cycle without the "parvenu" Pāṇḍavas, who, along with Kṛṣṇa, have so often been targets for the scalpels of "higher critics." Once we recognize the Pañcāla cycle as part of the epic's archetype and primary design, however, we find again a cycle of spiraling violence that would be unending[15] were it not for the conniving of Kṛṣṇa and the intercession of Vyāsa, "the author." In outline:[16]

1. Droṇa, a Brahman, and the Pāñcāla king Drupada, a Kṣatriya, are childhood friends.
2. Grown up, Droṇa, now a father of Aśvatthāman and poor, seeks wealth from his former friend, but Drupada says insultingly that friendship is not possible between people of different status.
3. Having since chosen a career of weapons obtained from Bhārgava Rāma, Droṇa trains the Kaurava and Pāṇḍava princes in weapons, and for his guru's fee asks that they conquer Pañcāla. Victorious, Droṇa gives his "friend" Drupada back the southern half of his own kingdom and keeps the northern half for himself.
4. Knowing his sons to be no match for Droṇa, Drupada hires two priests to ritually produce a son for him who will kill Droṇa. When this son, Dhṛṣṭadyumna, is born from the ritual fire, Draupadī is born unasked for from the earthen sacrificial altar *(vedi)*.
5. Draupadī marries the Pāṇḍavas, consolidating Kuru-Pañcāla relations between Drupada and the Pāṇḍavas (who are as much Kurus, descendants of Kuru, as are the Kauravas). This does not heal the enmity between Drupada and Droṇa, who sides with the Kauravas.
6. Drupada along with three of his grandsons is slain by Droṇa on

[14]On Vedic names connected with the Pañcālas and their story cycle, see Biardeau 1976, 242, n. 2: while Droṇa is named for the Vedic soma vessel, Drupada is named for a synonym of the *yūpa*, the sacrificial post. Cf. CR 87 (1978–79), 153–55; 1985, 14; and Biardeau and Péterfalvi 1985, 117, on these and other names (one need not accept them all to accept the principle) in the Pāñcāla line, which "evokes the ensemble of the socio-cosmic order that comes unhinged"; cf. 1986, 146–47.

[15]As Reich 1998, 353, observes, "the agonistic sacrifical paradigm lacks a mechanism for stopping the cycle of violence."

[16]I do not encumber this outline with many citations, since the episodes are well enough known. For discussion and documentation, see Biardeau 1976, 241–54; 1978, 120–26; 1993, 234–37; CR 87 (1978–79), 151–60; Biardeau and Péterfalvi 1985, 116–17, 126–27, 154–56; 1986, 147–48, 272–73, 283–95; Hiltebeitel [1976] 1990, 250–54, 312–35; 1988, 192–95, 419–35 esp. 427; Scheuer 1982, 293–339.

the morning of the fifteenth day of battle at Kurukṣetra; Dhṛṣṭadyumna vows to kill Droṇa that same day (7.161.28–37).

7. Later that day, Droṇa kills many more Pañcālas, including twenty thousand at once with his doomsday weapon *(brahmāstra)*, until Agni and the great Ṛṣis appear in the sky to dissuade him from such unrighteous fighting (7.164.87–92). Dhṛṣṭadyumna beheads Droṇa after Droṇa has dropped his weapons and sat down in *prāya* (fasting unto death); he then hurls Droṇa's "great head" into the van of the now headless Kaurava army (7.165).

8. Aśvatthāman kills Dhṛṣṭadyumna, all Draupadī's other brothers, other Pañcālas, and Draupadī's and the Pāṇḍavas' five sons in a night raid while they are sleeping in a camp that Kṛṣṇa has knowingly talked the Pāṇḍavas into abandoning so as to protect the Pāṇḍavas, but not the Pañcālas.

9. Draupadī demands revenge: Aśvatthāman's death and the forehead-jewel he was born with (10.11.20); she vows she will sit in prāya until she gets it.

10. Out of love for Draupadī (Biardeau, in Biardeau and Péterfalvi 1986, 295), Bhīma and Nakula go after Aśvatthāman. But when Kṛṣṇa warns that Aśvatthāman will hold the doomsday weapon against them and could destroy the world, Kṛṣṇa drives Arjuna and Yudhiṣṭhira (10.13.5–6, 16) to confront Aśvatthāman (Draupadī seems to be left with Sahadeva). Seeing the three Pāṇḍavas assaulting him, Aśvatthāman releases his doomsday weapon, and Arjuna retaliates in kind. Vyāsa and Nārada appear, seemingly in midair, between the weapons to prevent them from detonating. Urged by Vyāsa to withdraw their weapons, Arjuna can do so by his yogic power, but Aśvatthāman's wrath allows no such restraint. Vyāsa convinces him to give the Pāṇḍavas his forehead-gem, but he still directs the weapon into the wombs of the Pāṇḍava women—Draupadī included—to make them barren. The "author" then tells Aśvatthāman he must never use the weapon again (see chapter 2, § C.26).

11. Kṛṣṇa promises the Pāṇḍavas he will revive the child in the womb of Uttarā, wife of the slain Abhimanyu. The stillborn child Parikṣit, revived, will thus be the remnant of the Kuru line. Bhīma then convinces Draupadī to abandon her vow and accept Aśvatthāman's head-gem without his death.

Clearly, it has been pointless to try to reclaim an original kernel by cutting the Pāṇḍavas and Kṛṣṇa, not to mention the intervening "author," from this cycle. But one can now see that the epic poets do describe a vicious cycle of violence at the heart of the story by representing the Pañcālas as *the* central element of the old Kṣatriya order. They recall the early post-Ṛg Vedic order of what Witzel calls India's first state, the Kuru realm in which Kuru-Pañcāla, with Kurukṣetra as its ritual center, formed one of the two major groups among some sixteen kingdoms:[17] "Both tribes, the Kurus and the Pañcālas, form a 'people,' of two large 'tribes' with separate chieftains whose families, however, intermarry. In other respects as well, the two tribes form a ritual union within a large chiefdom; it is based on competition between two moieties: for example, they exchange their roving bands of vrātyas. . . ."[18] Again, this is not a society that immediately precedes that of the epic poets, and which the poets might actively "transform";[19] rather, it is one they recall to life—often by deliberate techniques of archaization—only through their knowledge of Veda.[20]

Moreover, the epic poets portray the Kuru-Pañcāla relationship much as Witzel reconstructs its Vedic past. The Kurus and Pañcālas raid one-another's territory. As among Vrātyas, there is overlap between Kṣatriyas and Brahmans. Drupada and Droṇa begin their friendship as youngsters without noticing their Kṣatriya-Brahman difference. Droṇa accompanies the Kuru raiding party of young Pāṇḍava and Kaurava princes.[21] The young Pāṇḍavas appear at Draupadī's svayaṃvara in the guise of Brahmans. And when the two "moieties" intermarry, the father of the bride allows his daughter to take five husbands when he hears not only that the five princes he thought were Brahmans are actually incarnations of five Indras, but part of a plan to restore death to the human world that follows from a sattra of the gods in the Naimiṣa Forest. If Drupada exemplifies the Pañcālas' position at the heart of the "old Kṣatriya order," it is perhaps understandable that he is the one to hear this secret story, and that he "alone" should find it appealing.

What is striking, however, is that while Kṛṣṇa guarantees the continuity of the Kuru line, he sees to it—along with Droṇa and

[17]1995a, 3—the other being Kosala-Videha, about which *Rām* and Buddhist stories develop.

[18]1995a, 4; cf. 1987b, 182–205; 1989, 111, 243 [maps], 235–36, 247–51.

[19]Witzel argues that between the Kuru realm and the emergence of Magadha, royal centers intervened at Pañcāla and Videha (1989a, 236, 241).

[20]Cf. Biardeau 1985, 13, n. 9, warning not to presume consecutive historicity between Brāhmaṇa passages and epic ones linking Kurus and Pañcālas. Cf. Reich 1998 on "deliberate archaisms" (125) in the *Mbh* around "archaic 'agonistic' elements" (269; cf. 230, 259–69), including Vrātya "echoes" and "residues" (on which, however, see chap. 3, n. 121). On metrical and linguistic archaization, see chap. 1, n. 70, and van Buitenen 1966, a classic study of archaism in the *BhgP*.

[21]1.128.3. His son Aśvatthāman joins the princes' training, but does not join the raid. A fuller account in southern and some northern manuscripts (1, App. 1, No. 78) has Arjuna bring a halt to the raid because "the best of kings Drupada is a relative of the Kuru heroes" (line 116)—this, before the Pāṇḍavas' marriage to Draupadī, although it can be explained through the lunar vaṃśa.

Aśvatthāman—that the Pañcālas are exterminated. If, as seems evident, the old Kṣatriya order is represented by the agonistic dyad of the Kuru-Pañcālas, the new order that emerges from it into a unified and miraculously continuing Kuru state is achieved by the eradication of its former Pañcāla component. For like the Bhārgava line of the Aurvas that goes no further than Bhārgava Rāma, the Pañcālas, as far as the epic is concerned, end with Draupadī, who loses not only her father and all her brothers and other kinsmen, but her sons and her capacity to reproduce (cf. Katz 1991, 135). As Yudhiṣṭhira says definitively to Gāndhārī when he is about to leave his elders to end their lives in the forest: "This whole earth is now empty. It is not pleasing to me, auspicious lady. Our kinsmen are diminished,[22] our strength not what it formerly was. The Pañcālas are utterly destroyed with a girl their only remainder.[23] I see no family-founder anywhere for them, auspicious lady. They were all reduced to ash by Droṇa alone in battle, and those that remained were slain by Droṇa's son at night" (15.44.31–33). The Kuru line continues not through this "girl" Draupadī (how courtly of Yudhiṣṭhira to refer to the middle-aged heroine, who is present to hear him,[24] as a girl or maiden [*kanyā*]!), but through her co-wife Subhadrā (sister of Kṛṣṇa) and the Matsya princess Uttarā: Subhadrā's daughter-in-law, wife of the slain Abhimanyu, mother of Parikṣit, grandmother of Janamejaya.[25]

If we ask, as we did with the Bhārgavas, what this Pañcāla component represents, we have thus the beginnings of a useful answer—one that owes much to the work of Heesterman—in this elimination from the lunar dynasty of the principle of agonistic rivalry that lies at the heart of what

[22]*Parikṣīṇa*, implying that Parikṣit will be their lone survivor. Note the contrast with those "utterly destroyed" (*kṣīṇāḥ*) in the next line, cited in the next note.

[23]*Pāñcālāḥ subhṛśaṃ kṣīṇāḥ kanyāmātrāvaśeṣitāḥ* (32): Northern mss. have the equally interesting *kathā* for *kanyā*: the Pāñcālas "remain only as a story." Cf. 5.47.93: Arjuna says elderly astrologers predict the "great destruction of the Kurus and Sṛñjayas [Pañcālas], and victory for the Pāṇḍavas" (cited chap. 1 after n. 42). Cf. also Hiltebeitel 1988, 210: at Draupadī's Svayaṃvara, Kāmpilyā, the Pañcāla capitol, is just this once called the "the City of the Śiśumāra," i.e., "of the child-killer," often translated "crocodile": "With the roar of the surging ocean, all the citizens approached Śiśumārapuram, and the kings assembled there" (1.176.15). As suggested, this odd note for a marriage may be a foreshadowing of the fate of Draupadī's children, Pāñcāla relatives, and the entire Kṣatra.

[24]Among the party that leaves the capital to see the elders, she gets to see Vyāsa raise the slain warriors, including her sons and brothers, from the Gaṅgā (15.36.13; 37.7; 38.2; 39.14; 41.4). It is sixteen years after Kurukṣetra. See Hiltebeitel 1999a, 477–82.

[25]Note also that the Pāñcālas' destiny is largely parallelled by that of the Matsyas (15.44.34), whose king Virāṭa is killed simultaneously with Drupada, and who are fully effaced with the Pāñcālas during the night raid. After this, as Biardeau observes, "All that subsists of the two kingdoms Pañcāla and Matsya is the two princesses Draupadī and Uttarā" (Biardeau and Péterfalvi 1986, 273). Cf. Hiltebeitel 1985b.

the epic poets recall from the Vedic ritual and mythological system.[26] But for us, a more pressing question now emerges. What does this tell us about Draupadī, who, with the death of all her kinsmen, becomes the sole Pāñcāla survivor. Does she remain to represent that agonistic principle throughout her life? Or is she too "transformed"? Indeed, does the *Mahābhārata* offer her, too, an education? These are questions we can return to in subsequent chapters.[27] For now, we may frame them by noting that while she begins her life emerging from this agonistic principle's cornerstone, the sacrifice, saddled with some of its darkest implications, she at least, under the most trying circumstances, brings the Pañcāla cycle of revenge to an end by dropping her demand for the death of Aśvatthāman.

Draupadī's "dark" associations are, of course, evident from birth and throughout her life by her name Kṛṣṇā, "the Black (or Dark) Lady," through which she complements Kṛṣṇa, Vyāsa, and others who spin out the poem's darker workings (Hiltebeitel [1976] 1990, 60–78; 1985b). Indeed, even before she is born, the luminous but weeping Śrī whom she incarnates in the myth of the former Indras has come to be "of impoverished share" (*mandabhāgya*; 1.189.13), the very term by which Yudhiṣṭhira describes Draupadī when he is about to tell her of the loss of her sons and brothers (10.10.26). But it is especially Draupadī's birth that demonstrates the epic poets' determination to identify her with a nefarious darkness that arises from the agonistic dimensions of her identity as a Pāñcālī, a daughter of Pañcāla. The rite by which Drupada seeks retaliation against Droṇa, which will involve him in returning to fight the Kaurava half of the Kurus at Kurukṣetra, is by implication a rite of *abhicāra*—"black magic." Like Janamejaya's snake sacrifice, it is designed to fulfill a desire to kill an enemy. Indeed, as Biardeau observes, not only is the rite of a type frowned on by the Brahmanical conscience for its intention of violence; "the present example is particularly thorny since it is a question of killing a Brahman, an abominable crime in itself."[28]

The poets are indirect in telling us anything about the rite, and the term *abhicāra* is not used. Of the actual rite, all we learn is that Drupada

[26]Clearly they do not know what Witzel extracts from the Vedic texts, that the Pañcālas survived the Kuru kingdom (see n. 19).

[27]See also Hiltebeitel 1999a, 508–11, where they are raised of both the classical epic heroine (I suggest that "Draupadī and Yudhiṣṭhira are each other's mutual education" [509], but that is a bit premature), and of the subsequent Draupadīs of India's regional oral martial epics. For a somewhat analogous study, see Suzuki 1989.

[28]Biardeau and Péterfalvi 1985, 155; Biardeau 1993, 134–37; cf. CR 87 (1978–79), 153; 1989, 129. *Manu* 11.33 says that Brahmans may employ it "without hesitation" to kill their enemies (Türstig 1985, 93–95). Drupada's case is the reverse.

goes to considerable trouble to find priests willing to perform it; that it begins when he pronounces his aim of obtaining a son to kill Droṇa; and that "at the end of the offering *(havanasyānte)*" his queen is summoned but told the rite is efficacious no matter what she does.[29] Immediately, the fire-hued Dhṛṣṭadyumna, incarnation of Agni, rises armed from the sacrificial fire and rides forth on a chariot; as the thrilled Pāñcālas roar approval, an "invisible great being *(mahadbhūtam adṛśyam)* in the sky" announces, "This fear-dispelling prince *(rājaputra)*,[30] making the Pañcālas' fame, is born for the death of Droṇa to dispel the grievance of the king."[31] That should obviously be it: at "the end of the offering" the rite's purpose has been fulfilled. But immediately, entirely gratuitously (cf. Biardeau 1997a, 97), and, in a double sense, beyond the stated end (purpose, completion) of the rite, Dṛṣṭadyumna has a twin sister:[32]

> And also a Pāñcālī girl *(kumārī)* arose from the middle of the sacrificial altar *(vedi)*, well-apportioned[33] with limbs one ought to see, a waist like a vedi,[34] a delight to the mind. Dark *(śyāmā)*, her eyes like lotus petals, hair dark-bluish *(nīla)* and curling, having taken human form clearly possessing the hue of an immortal,[35] her fragrance, like that of the blue lotus, wafted for a league. She bore a supreme form that was without its like on earth. And just as that full-hipped one was born, a disembodied voice said: "Best among all women, Kṛṣṇā will lead the Kṣatra to destruction. The fair-waisted one will in time accomplish the work of the gods. Because of her, a great fear will arise for the Kṣatriyas." Having heard all this, the Pāñcālas roared like a pride of lions, and the Earth did not tolerate [*sehe*: bear, endure, suffer] them filled with joy. (155.41–46)

[29]See van Buitenen 1973, 313 and 462, n. to verses 1.155.30-35 on the exchange with the queen. It seems that she must necessarily be summoned at the wife's typically peripheral position in the Vedic sacrifice, but can also be told that it is immaterial whether she cohabits with the king or not.

[30]That Dhṛṣṭadyumna is a fire-born "Rājaputra" has not gone unnoticed by some who would give Agnikula Rajputs an epic pedigree; see Hiltebeitel 1999a, 473, 475. It would be interesting to study how the epic contextualizes the terms *Rājaputra* and *Rājaputrī*.

[31]1.155.33-40. Note that *śoka*, "burning grief," covers both the revenge-seeking "grievance" (1.155.2, 40) of Drupada and the "griefs" without motives of vengeance of Dhṛtarāṣṭra and Yudhiṣṭhira, which supply a narrative thread from Books 6 through 13.

[32]"Thus the twin children of Drupada were born in that great sacrifice" (*tathā tanmithunaṃ jajñe drupadasya mahāmakhe*; 155.50).

[33]*Subhāga*: opposite, for now, of *mandabhāgya*?

[34]The vedi, a kind of woman's torso, tapers at the middle, between its "shoulders" and "hips"; see Hiltebeitel 1991a, 119 (map), 132.

[35]*Sākṣādamaravarṇinī* (155.42): van Buitenen 1973, 318, leaves us here with "a lovely Goddess." That her dark color is that of the immortals is surely provocative.

There could be no clearer statement that the Pāñcālas, roaring in exhilaration at the news of their own (or at least their own Kṣatriya class's) imminent destruction, represent the "old Kṣatriya order" caught up in a death embrace that has snapped the tolerance of the Earth.[36] Further, as the two announcements of the heavenly voice indicate, Draupadī's birth is the outcome of the fact that the purpose of the gods exceeds the purpose of the rite. Born from the middle of the earthen altar, she is the dark means by which the gods' work—the Earth's renovation through the destruction of the Kṣatra—is to be achieved.

Beyond the description of the ritual itself, the poets surround its performance with further allusions to abhicāra. The slight disreputableness of the two Ṛṣi brothers who serve as priests is evident from the manner in which the younger, Upayāja, first refuses for a year to perform such a lethal rite; then, "with a sweet voice," recommends his elder, Yāja, because he is unscrupulous in observing rules of purity; and finally breaks his own scruples when his elder pressures him to join him in performing the death-dealing rite for payment (155.1–30). One should appreciate that abhicāra rites are well-known and readily referred to in the epics,[37] and that the *Mahābhārata* in particular ascribes the births of the Pāṇḍavas to abhicāra (Türstig 1985, 87). The boon that Kuntī obtains from the irascible sage Durvāsas to allow her to call down gods to impregnate her is "a canon of mantras joined together by abhicāra *(abhicārasaṃyuktam . . . varam/ mantragrāmam)*" (1.113.34). And although all five Pāṇḍavas are born by this black magic mantra, its sorcery is doubled by abhicāra rites in the case of the firstborn, Yudhiṣṭhira. When the impotent Pāṇḍu, having just learned of his wife Kuntī's boon, decides to put it quickly to the test, he tells Kuntī to first "Call Dharma. . . . Solicit Dharma with abhicāra rites of service" *(upacārābhicārābhyāṃ dharmam ārādhayasva)* (39, 42). Pāṇḍu does not seem bothered that these are rites designed to kill an enemy. His stated purposes in choosing Dharma first are to assure that the world will consider his sons "lawful" or "legitimate," and that his oldest son will be one to "uphold the law" (40–41). But the poets have told us more than Pāṇḍu or Kuntī can know: that Dharma is also Yama, with deep destructive designs.

Once we recall that abhicāra rites make use of pointed yūpas called *śūla*, "stake" (Hiltebeitel 1991a, 138–44), it is further notable that Draupadī is described by allusion to the śūla and other piercing instruments. Immediately upon hearing the story of her miraculous birth,

[36] Cf. Biardeau 1993, 137: ". . . les kṣatriya seront détruits, Pañcāla inclus."

[37] See Türstig 1985, 100, n. 1, citing *Mbh* 1.104.6 and 13.33.7; Hiltebeitel 1991a, 140 and n. 27, on Indrajit's abhicāra in *Rām*.

"the sons of Kuntī were as if pierced by spears *(śalyaviddhā ivābhavat)*, and those great chariot warriors all became mentally unstable *(asvasthamanaso)*" (1.156.1). This is more than the convention of spear-like eyes, which Tamil poets assign to Draupadī, since the Pāṇḍavas have yet to see her. And when she exits from the *Mahābhārata* reenthroned in heaven with her solar radiance, Indra tells Yudhiṣṭhira that she had been Śrī herself, "fashioned by the holder of the trident *(nirmitā śūlapāṇinā)* for the sake of your pleasure *(rati)*" (18.4.10).

This is more than just a reminder that it was Śiva who ordained her birth in the story of the former Indras and its companion piece, the story of the overanxious maiden who asks Śiva for a husband, but, when she says it five times, is ordained five instead. We can now understand something of the relationship of the two stories of the preconditions of Draupadī's birth. Just after the Pāṇḍavas are "spear-pierced" upon hearing of her birth and have decided—at Kuntī's advice—to head rather derangedly toward Pañcāla (1.156), Vyāsa arrives to give them purpose. As we have seen, he tells them the overanxious maiden story to inspire them to want to marry Draupadī jointly (1.157). It is thus not surprising that Yudhiṣṭhira has some idea that his words must be true when he tells Drupada that it will be appropriate for Draupadī to marry them all (see chapter 2, § C.10 and 12). But he knows only this story, and for reasons we can only guess,[38] refrains from telling it to Drupada. Vyāsa then takes Drupada aside to tell him the deeper story of the former Indras and show him the Pāṇḍavas and Draupadī in their celestial bodies (1.189.35–41). And then he repeats the overanxious maiden story presumably to let Drupada know that the marriage flows not only from a divine plan, but from Draupadī's own karma (41–48). Upon hearing both stories, Drupada says, "Do it" (49).

But it is something else Vyāsa tells Drupada that alerts us to another abhicāra feature of the rite that brings forth Draupadī's birth. So far, we have learned from the event's description that it occurs after the "end of the offering." But Vyāsa, in his deeper story, tells Drupada something more, and this just after revealing that Kṛṣṇa and Balarāma were born from Viṣṇu's black and white hairs (they are still in the background at this point, having attended Draupadī's svayaṃvara). Finally revealing that the Pāṇḍavas are former Indras from the mountain cave, and that Draupadī, Lakṣmī incarnate, is appointed to be their wife, Vyāsa asks, "How else could a woman be born at the end of the ritual from the

[38]Perhaps, like Winternitz and van Buitenen, he thinks it might sound a little "silly" (see chap. 4, n. 118). Indeed, Winternitz has some fun with Yudhiṣṭhira's seeming memory lapse (1897, 736–37).

surface of the earth than by the power of divine fate?"[39] Draupadī is born "at the end of the ritual" *(karmaṇo 'nte)*.

Similar things happen elsewhere in the epic. Duryodhana, humiliated when his attack of the "helpless" Pāṇḍavas in the forest turns into his own humiliation, vows to fast unto death (3.238.19; *prāya* again). His closest companions cannot dissuade him. The netherworld *(pātāla)* demons, knowing that his death would (as van Buitenen nicely puts it) "wreck their party" (1973, 691; *te svapakṣakṣayam*; 2.239.19), set their Brahmans to performing Upaniṣadic rites with mantras from the *Atharva Veda*. Again, the details of the rite are minimal: milk is offered into the fire, and "at the completion of the rite *(karmasiddhau)*" a gape-mouthed Kṛtyā (a female personification of black magic) rises up to receive her command to bring Duryodhana to the netherworld, which, "in the twinkling of an eye" *(nimeṣād)*, she does (3.239.18–24). Duryodhana now hears that he has many divine and demonic forces still working for him, and is returned by the Kṛtyā with his confidence restored. One expects this Kṛtyā to rise "from the fire," as van Buitenen has her do (1973, 691), and as many have taken Draupadī to have done. Indeed, commentarial literature defines one meaning of *kṛtyā* as "a woman caused through abhicāra-spells to rise from a fire for killing an enemy."[40] But the epic says no such thing.

On the other hand, when Indra's wife Śacī implores Bṛhaspati to find Indra (who is hiding in a lotus stalk) so that she can avoid the sexual demands of Indra's foe Nahuṣa, Bṛhaspati offers something unmentioned into the fire, and Agni appears in "a marvelous woman's form" (*strīveṣam adbhutam*; 5.15.27). This female form of Agni then searches everywhere but the waters and reports back in another "twinkle" (*nimeṣāntaramātreṇa*; 28) that Indra remains to be found, whereupon (s)he (Agni) is then lauded so that (s)he can enter the waters, recover Indra, and pave the way for his return once Nahuṣa is ousted from heaven (16.1–9).

These are both abhicāra-type rites, linked with the intention to kill enemies. Both mirror aspects of the scene of Draupadī's birth. The first

[39] 1.189.34: *katham hi strī karmaṇo 'nte mahītalāt/ samuttiṣṭhed anyato daivayogāt*. "Yoke of divine fate" is tempting; *daiva* here is clearly divinely appointed and coordinated "fate," involving what is ordained by Brahmā, Śiva, and Viṣṇu on top of the intentions of Yama. Van Buitenen's "by God's intercession" (1973, 373) is at this point a monotheistic oversimplification.

[40] Türstig 1985, 75, part of an excellent discussion of *kṛtyā* and Kṛtyās, including Ṛg and Atharva Vedic background, in relation to abhicāra and other forms of sorcery (75–81, 89). Pertinently, "expelling a *kṛtyā* belongs to 'pacification' *(śānti)*"; as a one of the six ritual activities *(ṣaṭkarmāṇi)* of abhicāra, śānti's "main purpose . . . is to counteract the other varieties of *abhicāra*" and their "cruel karma" (108–9).

mirrors it through the birth of a female embodiment of black magic "at the end of the rite." Like the dark Draupadī, "*kṛtyā* is said in the ṚV and AV to be blue and red *(nīlalohitā)*"; as a goddess, Kṛtyā is later "called 'Ugrakālī', the fierce Kālī, a form of Durgā" (Türstig 1985, 89, 76). A Jain tradition views Draupadī herself as a Kṛtyā (Karve 1974, 82). A "*kṛtyā* is clearly and always a female entity, deliberately produced for a malevolent purpose" (81), and whoever deploys her, especially against a Brahman, suffers pollution, and must undergo rites of expiation (93–94). We never hear of Drupada's expiation, so we may wonder whether his own death must follow. But most important, his malevolent purpose is fully met by the birth of Dhṛṣṭadyumna. Droṇa's death is entirely *his* business, not Draupadī's. From the standpoint of Drupada's malevolent intent, Draupadī's birth is superfluous. We could almost say that her birth has nothing to do with malevolent purpose. But we know that it results not from Drupada's purpose but the purpose of the gods. Whether the gods are malevolent is a difficult question.

The second episode of the birth of Agni holds a mirror to the births of both Draupadī and her brother, who is Agni's incarnation. Agni is born in female form directly from fire itself. We seem to be being told that a "black magic woman" is felt by the epic poets to be too impure to emerge *directly* from the sacred fire.[41] She must emerge after "the completion of the rite" as a kind of surcharge or leftover. Or if a female form should so rise up, it can only be that of Agni *him*self. Worshipers of Draupadī obviously do not feel the same way.

If we may recall Draupadī cult folklore for a moment, these scenes are revisited not only in terms of the goddess's birth from fire, but in a chain of associations from the implicit to the explicit in the matter of impalement. The two Ṛṣi brothers hired in the Sanskrit epic to generate a son to kill Droṇa, and who produce Draupadī by accident, reappear in Draupadī's Tamil folklore to bring her forth a second time, without her brother, as the Supreme Śakti. This time she is born from the sacrificial fire itself bearing the pointed and other ritual weapons that, in a variant, she otherwise obtains from Pōttu Rāja, the personification of the pointed sacrificial stake. Here too it is an abhicāra-type ritual, performed by a king, a Pāṇḍava descendant, to kill an enemy. But now Draupadī kills the enemy herself, severing his hundred heads, and needing the assistance of Pōttu Rāja only to keep the last head from touching the ground. The demon, a grandson of Bakācuraṉ (Baka, "Crane"), is sometimes also known as the demon of the Gingee Fort (Hiltebeitel 1988, 81–84, 368–93). This makes the demon the Draupadī cult's regional multiform

[41]The kṛtyā's blue and red color may be identified with the blood of defloration; see discussion of *ṚV* 10.85.28 in O'Flaherty 1981, 273, n. 27, and Türstig 1985, 76.

of Mahiṣāsura, the Buffalo Demon, who on the grand scale gets impaled by the goddess Durgā.

B. Vidura's Birth and the Limits of Impalement

As we have seen in the last chapter (§ A), the Dharma whom Yudhiṣṭhira incarnates is implicitly Yama—an association that is explicit in Draupadī cult folklore.[42] Such a Dharmarāja Yudhiṣṭhira accepts the violent self-sacrifice of Arjuna's son Aravāṉ as a preliminary offering to Kālī, goddess of the battlefield, even though he would prefer to offer a buffalo or some other animal (Hiltebeitel 1988, 321–22). In certain villages that name Draupadī temples after Dharma (or Dharmarāja), there is a tendency to find him, as the chief deity in the sanctum, faced from just outside the entrance by a pointed yūpa-like post representing his "disciple" Pōttu Rāja (1991a, 101–16). Dharma-worship involving impalement-laden rituals as a form of self-sacrifice is also found in the Dharma Gājans of Bengal, where the rituals have heroic exemplars in the regional folk epic of Lausen, and in which Dharma (or Dharmarāja) has a lordship over death that would again point to an identification with Yama.[43]

If the *Mahābhārata* makes such connections with death only allusively and indirectly with Yudhiṣṭhira, it gives them grounding in the person of his double, the epic's other and "lower" incarnation of Dharma: his uncle Vidura, Vyāsa's son with a Śūdra woman.[44] Let us revisit the scene (see chapter 2 § C.2–4). When, at his mother's request, the appallingly unkempt and smelly "author" has intervened to restore continuity to the Kaurava line by performing the rite of levirate with the widows of the deceased king Vicitravīrya, he first sires two defective sons, the blind Dhṛtarāṣṭra with Ambikā, who has closed her eyes in fright, and the pale Pāṇḍu with her sister Ambālikā, who has only blanched. When Ambikā is then called upon to endure a second impregnation by Vyāsa, it is too much. Taking her jewels, she decks one of her servants *(dasī)* with them. This woman, beautiful as an Apsaras and, as we soon learn, a Śūdrā, spends a glorious night with Vyāsa, and in the morning he gratefully promises her not only that her days of servant life are over, but that she

[42]See Hiltebeitel 1991a, 50–51; 128, n. 13; 485.

[43]See Hiltebeitel 1991a, 182–207, 302–8, 373–76. Cf. also Kakar 1991, 59, 64–66, 86 on Yama known as Dharmarāja and Pretarāja in Rājasthan, before whom exorcistic rites are performed that include mortifications.

[44]When Vidura dies, he fixes Yudhiṣṭhira with a steadfast unblinking *(animiṣo)* gaze and, with his yoga-power *(yogabala)*, as if alight with spiritual energy *(tejasā prajvalanniva)*, enters *(viveśa)* Yudhiṣṭhira's body limb by limb, breaths by breaths, senses by senses (15.33.24–27).

will bear a son versed in dharma. Vaiśampāyana then deepens the story by telling that Vidura is an incarnation of Dharma himself, born because the god was cursed to take birth in the womb of a Śūdrā by the sage Māṇḍavya.

This prior fatality is then the prompt for a singularly uncomfortable story—one that until recently was rarely discussed in epic scholarship,[45] but has suddenly gained interest.[46]

> Māṇḍavya, a great Brahman ascetic and yogin, performs tapas under a tree with his arms raised and keeping a vow of silence. A band of fleeing thieves (Dasyus) hides their loot, and then themselves, in his ashram. Pursuing royal guards ask which way they went, but Māṇḍavya holds his posture and says nothing. Searching the ashram and finding the thieves and loot, the guards suspect him and bring him and the thieves to the king, who sentences them all, and Māṇḍavya in particular to be "strung on a stake" *(śūle protas)*. Remaining impaled for a long time, without food but keeping himself alive, Māṇḍavya calls on the Ṛṣis, who, distressed at his condition, come in the form of *śakuna* birds and ask him, committed as both he and they are to the doctrine that the fault must be his, what sin *(kiṃ pāpam)* he has committed to effect such torture. The king, overhearing, claims that whatever injury he has caused was done out of delusion and ignorance, and, seeking to appease Māṇḍavya, lowers him from the top of the stake. But when the king is unable to pull the stake out, he cuts it off at the base *(mūle)*. And so Māṇḍavya goes about with the stake inside him, winning hard-won worlds by his tapas. People call him 'Māṇḍavya-of-the-Stake' [Aṇīmāṇḍavya]. At last he goes to Dharma's abode *(sadana)*, where, finding Dharma seated, he calls attention to the power of his tapas and demands to know at once what "ill-performed karma" he had unknowingly done that brings him such retribution. "You had stuck blades of grass in the tails of flying insects," explains Dharma, referring to some boyhood mischief.[47] Indignant, Aṇīmāṇḍavya curses Dharma to be reborn in the womb of a Śūdrā *(śūdrayoni)*, and establishes that henceforth there shall be a

[45]See Kantawala 1995, reviewing especially N. B. Utgikar, "The story of Aṇī Māṇḍavya in Sanskrit and Buddhistic Sources," *Proceedings of the Transactions of the Second Oriental Conference, January 28–February 1, 1922*, Calcutta, pp. 227ff., which I have not been able to obtain.

[46]See especially Goldman 1985, 418–25, on anxieties behind the story's acceptance of karma theory; Kantawala 1995 on variants and other recent studies.

[47]See Goldman 1985, 418, n. 14: In the CE, one knows only "by inference, through the character of Māṇḍavya's exclusion of childhood actions from the realm of effective *karma*," that he was a child; the southern recension clarifies that he was so (1, 1000*).

"limit *(maryādā)* on the fruition of dharma": that sins committed before the age of fourteen shall not be counted an offense.[48]

One should appreciate the "gallows humor," as the "śūla-stationed" Ṛṣi with his "soul of dharma" *(śūlasthaḥ . . . dharmātmā)* wins worlds of tapas "mostly out of the reach of others" (13, 21; van Buitenen 1973, 238).

As Kantawala says, Dharma, seated (comfortably, unlike Aṇīmāṇḍavya) on his throne and meting out "justice," is here "a functional name given to Yama."[49] As we saw in chapter 4, § A, Yama is the hidden identity of Dharma that is also "partially" incarnate in Yudhiṣṭhira. Whereas Vidura is Dharma reborn directly through Aṇīmāṇḍavya's curse, Yudhiṣṭhira is the son of Dharma and the primary means by which the Naimiṣa sattrin Yama restores death to humans at Kurukṣetra to restore the immortal distinction of gods. As we have also seen, Yudhiṣṭhira's birth incarnates Dharma through the invocation of enemy-destroying black magic. The Dharma that Vidura incarnates, however, goes further, evoking Yama through the even more severe and "lower" principle of impalement, although again at several removes. Dharma or Yama does not impale, nor is he impaled himself. The story achieves what Obeyesekere calls "symbolic remove" (1990, 253–54 and passim) while at the same time acknowledging what can't be removed from it. As Goldman says, Māṇḍavya "does not transgress directly against Dharma. Nor does the god curse him. The sage's crime is not so much against Dharma as against dharma; and so the god has dispassionately assigned fitting retribution: He who sticks things up the rectum of a creature shall, in the course of time and in rigid keeping with a Hammurabian principle of justice, have things stuck up his."[50] Now that Yama-Dharma is to become Vidura and sire Yudhiṣṭhira, he is a Dharma whose depersonalization becomes, somewhat paradoxically, also more humane.

While Yama's sattra and its aftermath restore the distinction between gods and humans, it also provides opportunity for the poets to underscore what is left for humans to distinguish themselves. In the present story,

[48]*Mbh* 1.101; quotes from van Buitenen 1973, 237–38. Kantawala translates the sin as sticking needles into the tails of moths (1995, 102), and notes a *Padma Purāṇa* variant of impaling grasshoppers *(śalabha)* on a little stake (*śūlikā*; 107–8).

[49]1995, 104–5; cf. Goldman 1985, 420: "Yama or, as he is often called, Dharma." Cf. Malamoud 1989, 201–2.

[50]Again, one knows that it is anal impalement in Māṇḍavya's case only by the inference that the punishment fits the crime. On anal impalement as more widely implicit, and sometimes explicit, in the ritual use of sacrificial stakes for the abhicāra treatment of enemies, symbolic or otherwise, see Hiltebeitel 1991a, 163–64, 226.

Dharma's harshness is softened by the mitigations pronounced by the sage. The result is a Dharma or Yama more appropriate to human frailties, one given to compassion, indeed, one whom the sage curses not by Dharma-Yama's own harsh prior principle of lex talionis (Kantawala 1995, 107), which would result in another impalement in the series, another stake for a stake, but by the new principle of *maryādā*—"limit," "propriety"—which submits Dharma or Yama to function as the impersonal principle of dharma in response to such specifically human traits as childhood sexuality and violence, amnesia (Aṇīmāṇḍavya forgets that he tortured the insects), latency, and adult accountability.[51] It is clearly more "humane" to be born in the womb of a Śūdra than impaled, although there is no evidence that the text views either as any more or less human.

C. Talking with Animals

As an epic that frames itself by an obvious parallelism between its heroes and snakes, and by less obvious affinities between its poets, heroes, and dogs, the *Mahābhārata* anticipates a prominent aspect of much of the fable literature that seems to have adopted its device of the receding frame: it has lots of talking animals.[52] Clearly, talking animals make their way rather easily into frame stories because, just as frame

[51]See Goldman 1985, 418–25, on childhood memories, amnesia, and conflict (violent and sexual) with gods, fathers, mothers, and gurus. Yama-Dharma is a "father" here only at several removes, but conflict with the father over childhood sexuality and violence is direct, explicit, and similar in the *Śiva Purāṇa*'s Sandhyā story, where the fixing of limits on accountability for feeling and arousing sexual desire at the time of birth results in Sandhyā's satī. Like Māṇḍavya, Sandhyā gets to set a "limit" *(maryādā)* on feelings of sexual arousal in childhood, and accountability for them, after she has had such feelings for her father Brahmā and her brothers. To accommodate her last wish before she becomes a satī, Śiva rules that children will no longer have such feelings; during life's four phases—infancy, childhood, youth, and aging—only in the third will embodied beings become desirous, or in some cases (Śiva equivocates) at the end of the second! (Hiltebeitel 1999b, 73–75).

[52]See Minkowski 1989, 412–13, on some pertinent fable literatures; Lévi-Strauss's 1963, 89: animals are "good to think"; Lakoff and Turner on the "folk theory of forms" in which the "generic level metaphor" of the "great chain" of beings (inanimate objects-plants-animals-humans . . .) is pitched toward "distinctions" at the "highest level properties" of each class and species for metaphoric reference in proverbs, stories, etc. (1989, 80–83, 166–73, 193–213); Gellrich 1985, 34: "every creature is a book" (Alanus de Insulis); 114: Augustine on "constructing similitudes" on "the nature of animals, stones, or plants." Cf. Malamoud 1989, 8, 150, 209, on man's distinction from animals as the only creature who both is sacrificed and sacrifices, has the four goals of life, and can conceive of abstention from violence to other creatures; B. K. Smith 1994, 241–86, on early Indian animal taxonomies, especially 241–42 on reflexivity and man's highest place (241–42); Thite 1972; Doniger 1993b, especially 52–54, on interrupted love and the language of animals theme, brilliantly linked with the inspiration for poetry (on which see chap. 8).

stories have a "self-referential character" (Minkowski 1989, 402), so, at least in the *Mahābhārata*, does the relationship between poets, heroes, and animals.[53] We have met one of the most interesting such talking animals, nearly the first—he comes after the dogs and snakes of the *Pauṣyaparvan*—whom the poets put on the epic stage: the lizard, mistaken for a snake, who arrests the murderous club of the Bhārgava Ruru, ancestor of Śaunaka, and tells this blindly furious Brahman that he is acting too much like a Kṣatriya (see chapter 3 below n. 68). It is not that the lizard speaks for the snakes, who are perfectly capable of speaking for themselves. Rather, he speaks primarily for himself, secondly for the snakes, with whom lizards share a likeness but different joys and sorrows (1.10.3–4), and more generally for all animals who may find themselves so unexpectedly beset by the murderous excesses of human beings.

As may be evident already, this brief, playful passage offers a serio-comic glance at the problem of category-formation in relation to the laws of karma and the lessons of the evidence of perception. In his former life, when the speaking lizard *(ḍuṇḍubha)* was a human child *(bālya)*, he made a straw snake *(tārṇam . . . uragam)* that frightened an irascible sage. The sage cursed the boy: Having scared me with a "powerless snake" *(sarpa)*, you will become a "powerless *bhujaṃga*" (11.1–4). Van Buitenen sensibly translates *bhujaṃga* as "reptile" (1973, 62), and, noting that his translation of "lizard" for *ḍuṇḍubha* "is merely approximate," finds "a kind of legless lizard" as a meaning that meets his expectation that this lizard would look, at least to a crazed sage, like a snake (62, 442). But *bhujaṃga* itself just means "snake," not "reptile." Somehow the sage's curse has bent the karmic mechanism and the Sanskrit language a little out of shape.[54] But then it was the cursing sage's twisted perception itself, his perceptual error of mistaking a "kind of rope" for a snake, that caught the boy up in the philosophically loaded trap that turned him into this strange "kind of snake."

One begins to see that the lessons of many of the epic's animal stories relate the adjustment of perception to themes of cruelty and violence, especially in its excesses. To deal first with more familiar stories, the lizard, like Aṇīmāṇḍavya, suffers disproportionally for something he shouldn't have done "with animals" as a boy in his previous life. But

[53]It is similar in the *Rām* with its tender-hearted vulture, multitalented monkeys (especially Hanumān with his perfect spoken Sanskrit), and wise old bear. *Mbh* characters rarely talk with animals, but hear many more stories *about* talking animals. For some discussion, see Patil 1983, 176–91.

[54]In more recent parlance, the poets have allowed a break between the bond of the signifier and the signified.

unlike the human sage Aṇīmāṇḍavya, the lizard remembers![55] Even when the animals don't speak to these issues themselves, they are often spoken for. Dharma shows up in the guise of a silent dog for Yudhiṣṭhira's penultimate test before entering heaven, which the hero passes by rejecting Indra's argument that there would be "no cruelty" in leaving the dog on the high frozen wastes (see chapter 7, § D). Again, Dharma as a crane poses the lakeside questions that offer Yudhiṣṭhira his only chance to revive his suddenly slain brothers (3.297.11–19). Analogously, Baka ("Crane") Dālbhya starts to "pour out" the kingdom of Dhṛtarāṣṭra with the meat of dead cows when he hears Dhṛtarāṣṭra's "cruel speech in the assembly" (see chapter 3, § D). And Yudhiṣṭhira dons the guise of a "fish-eating crane-Brahman" in Matsya, the "kingdom of the fishes."[56]

There is a thread through these stories that has to do with classification, and the need to keep categories distinct. If one vows to kill snakes, one shouldn't kill lizards by mistake. This problem overlaps with the wider problems of maintaining distinctions between castes, and between gods and humans. As Yudhiṣṭhira puts it, war reduces everyone to acting like dogs. It is when the dharma of caste breaks down that the "law of the fishes" takes over. Caste mixture and confusion are the great dread of the *Bhagavad Gītā*, and of countless other epic passages. At the root of the Pañcāla cycle of violence is the confusion of caste (and other categories) between Droṇa and Drupada. And, from the standpoint of the story of the former Indras, it is the loss of distinction between gods and humans—and, we can now add, demons—that lies at the root of the whole *Mahābhārata* war. There is also the important question of whose violence it is that exceeds the appropriate limits. The end of the story of the former Indras leaves a clear distinction between human violence, for which Dhṛṣṭadyumna is born, and divine violence, for which Draupadī is born. But at Kurukṣetra all such distinctions collapse, in part because demons, who push all limits by their inherently violent nature, have become human kings to challenge the gods; in part because gods have taken on human portions; but also, in part, because of Kṛṣṇa and Vyāsa.

Once one looks into the epic's wider reaches, these patterns continue to unfold. When Yudhiṣṭhira asks about the sorrow of Kṣatriyas who give

[55]Animal memory can be elephantine; cf. 3.191: King Indradyumna goes from Mārkaṇḍeya to an owl to a crane to a tortoise before he can find anyone who remembers him—which he must, to regain heaven.

[56]See Hiltebeitel 1988, 202–4: Yudhiṣṭhira's disguise, the Matsya kingdom, and the "law of the fishes" (*matsya nyāya*: "the big fish eat the little fish") connote a king or kingdom out of control; 210: Drupada's southern Pañcāla capital as Śiśumārapura is another kind of "kingdom of the fishes" (and another point of parallel between Matsyas and Pāñcālas) to be devoured by the *Mbh* war (see above, n. 22). See also Biardeau 1997b.

up life in battle, and about this seeming waste of human birth, Bhīṣma tells him the story of a conversation between Vyāsa and some kind of biting worm.[57] "Knowledgeable about the course of every creature and understanding the language of animals,"[58] Vyāsa asks a worm he sees hastily crossing a busy road why he doesn't prefer to die, being just a worm. The worm explains how each creature finds its own life dear, and says he became a worm because in his last life as a wealthy Śūdra he was "unfavorable to Brahmans *(abrahmaṇya)*, cruel *(nṛśaṃsa)*, stingy, a usurer," envious, and vile in countless other acts "fraught with the quality of cruelty" (*nṛśaṃsaguṇabhūyiṣṭam*; 13.118.18, 25). Yet he honored his mother; and he once honored a Brahman: that kept his memory for this next life. Vyāsa then reveals he can rescue the worm by the sight of his person, and assures him he can become a Brahman, or any other status he prefers. But just then a chariot comes along, cuts the worm to pieces, and turns it into—a Kṣatriya! In gratitude, the new being exults at the difficulties he has overcome to reach this birth: he had been a hedgehog, iguana, boar, deer, bird, dog-cooker (Caṇḍāla or Outcaste), Vaiśya, Śūdra, and worm; now, "having obtained wormhood, I have become a Rājaputra! *(yadahaṃ kīṭatāṃ prāpya saṃprāpto rājaputratām)*" (119.11). He is only a Kṣatriya, Vyāsa reveals, because he has yet to destroy the sins of cruelty he committed as a Śūdra. But Vyāsa holds out the higher hope: "Here, from the status of a Rājaputra, you will obtain Brahmanhood, having offered up your own breaths for the sake of cows or Brahmans, or on the battlefield" (21); then he will enjoy in heaven the imperishable happiness of one who has become Brahman: thus one may rise from the lowest animal to the highest human and divine ranks (22–26). So, concludes Bhīṣma, just as the worm obtained the "highest eternal Brahman," Yudhiṣṭhira should not grieve over slain Kṣatriyas (120.13–14). This is one of our Brahman poets' most trenchant expressions of their attitude toward Kṣatriyas,[59] and one of their clearest

[57]That the *kīṭa* bites or bores is evident from its appearance in Karṇa's story: Indra sends a kīṭa which Karṇa allows to bury into his thigh while Bhārgava Rāma sleeps with his head on Karṇa's lap (8.29.5). Only a Kṣatriya could endure such pain, says Rāma, seeing through the disguise that Karṇa hoped would allow him access to Rāma's knowledge of weapons—again, a nexus of cruelties and deceptions between a "worm," a Kṣatriya, and a Brahman. Kīṭas can also be other biters: a "scorpion" or "a kind of insect."

[58]13.118.8ab: *gatijñaḥ sarvabhūtānām rutajñaśca śarīriṇām*; *rutajña* means "understanding the cries" of animals, but "language" is implied, since what is understood is always "translated" into human speech. Cf. 12.137.6.

[59]A similar message comes from the mongoose who steps forth from a hole at Yudhiṣṭhira's Aśvamedha to announce that this sacrifice (and by implication, the battle of Kurukṣetra) had less merit than a Brahman practicing the vow of gleaning *(uñcha)* at Kurukṣetra (14.92). The emaciated wife of the Brahman in this story, who gives away her portion of the gleaning, suggests another image of the woman of the impoverished share *(mandabhāgya)*. See chap. 1, § C and nn. 77 and 78; chap. 2, § C.19 and 34.

indications of the correlation between the law of karma and a great chain of beings.[60]

Interspecies violence thus repeats itself, with man at the center, and each animal and human species speaking ultimately for itself alone, though all in a distinctly human voice. Foreshadowing the destruction at Kurukṣetra, the burning of the Khāṇḍava Forest finds Arjuna and Kṛṣṇa working as "Man" (Nara) and "God" (Nārāyaṇa) in tandem—"the two Kṛṣṇas on one chariot" for the first time—to feed Agni by destroying nearly all the forest's animal population. Four fledgling Śārṅgaka birds, among the six creatures to survive, are really sons of a Ṛṣi who deemed birth as a bird a quick way to satisfy an ancestral demand for sons. The fledglings are saved because their bird-father lauded Agni and received the boon that Fire would spare them (1.220.22–32). When Agni licks at the fledglings' nest, they too, Ṛṣis themselves, laud him in the hope of being spared (223:6–19). But offered a boon, and learning that they need not waste it on a redundant request for their own lives, the opportunistic little darlings ask Agni to kill the cats that always bother them "together with their relatives *(sabāndhavān)*," which Agni quickly does (24–25).[61]

More whole species are nearly exterminated: Rākṣasas by a vengeful sattra (1.172); speaking frogs by a vengeful massacre (3.190.1–42). Violence erupts when distinctions are not observed. A boa nearly strangles Bhīma before telling Yudhiṣṭhira what he recalls from his previous life: that he was the Pāṇḍavas' great ancestor Nahuṣa, cursed to his present state for having misruled heaven. A human king of heaven in place of Indra who demanded Indra's divine wife, Nahuṣa had treated the great Brahman Ṛṣis like lowly slaves.[62] But perceptions are misleading, and distinctions all too easily missed. A shy Ṛṣi and his wife can change into deer to avoid humans and (it seems) enhance their sexlife. When Pāṇḍu shoots such a pair on a forest hunt, his "cruelty" *(nṛśaṃsa)*, says

[60]See Lakoff and Turner 1989, especially 212–13: "Many political revolutions have been fought to rid society of some part of the extended Great Chain. . . . For whatever reason, [it] is widespread and has strong natural appeal. This is frightening." Cf. Lovejoy [1936] 1960, 184, 251–54, on the critiques of Voltaire and Samuel Johnson of eighteenth century "great chain" ideas, and 326–29, on the ultimately "unbelievable" and "instructive negative outcome" of the "sweeping" hypotheses of rationality, plenitude, continuity, and gradation underlying this "experiment in thought." Cf. Handelman 1982, 102, contrasting Patristic "verticality" with the "horizontal" readings of Rabbinic hermeneutics. In India, the great chain is reinforced by the law of karma and theory of reincarnation; Inden 1985.

[61]See Gopal 1969; Biardeau CR 79 (1971–72), 140–41; chap. 4, n. 1; and Hiltebeitel 1976, 219; 1984. On the cat's cruelty from the perspective of the mouse, and its competition with a Caṇḍāla hunter for the birds in trees, see the cat-mouse dialogue *(mārjāramūṣakasaṃvāda)* at 12.136.18–193.

[62]See 3.174.18–178 on the boa story, and Hiltebeitel 1977a on epic versions of his misrule in heaven.

the dying buck in a human voice, is not that he shot them (the Ṛṣi accepts having taken the risk of turning into deer), but that he lacked the "noncruelty" *(ānṛśaṃsya)* to wait until they were finished making love; thus Pāṇḍu will die when overcome by love.[63]

Most interesting, however, is the story of the Muni and the dog whose heart (or disposition) had gone human.[64] The Muni, the lone human in a great forest, secures a peaceable kingdom by such qualities as tranquility, Vedic recitation, and purity of soul. All the wild carnivorous animals[65] come and go, asking him agreeable questions and behaving like his humble and solicitous disciples. But one village animal *(grāmyas . . . paśus)*—the dog whose heart has gone human—weak and emaciated from living peacefully off fruits and roots like the Muni himself, becomes attached to the Muni out of affection *(snehabaddho)* and remains permanently at his side, ever the attached devotee *(bhakto 'nuraktaḥ satatam)*. One day the dog spots a cruel *(krūra)* leopard preparing to eat him and tells the Muni, "This leopard, an enemy of dogs, desires to kill me. By your grace, relieve my fear."[66] To allay this fear, the Muni turns the dog into a leopard, and as such he is able to roam the forest fearlessly. But the problem only escalates. The Muni turns the leopard into a tiger (who starts eating meat) to protect him from a tiger; the tiger into an elephant to protect him from an elephant; the elephant into a lion to protect him from a lion; and the lion into a fierce eight-legged śarabha to protect him from a śarabha "prone to the killing of all creatures."[67] For a while the śarabha "born in the womb of a dog" lives happily beside the Muni, but then, having eaten or scared away all the food of the forest, he wishes to eat the Muni. The sage, knowing its intentions, turns it back into a dog and expels it from his hermitage. As the dog leaves,

[63]1.109.5–31, with verses citing 23, 25, and 26 on "cruelty" and 18–19 on the "noncruelty" that should have been observed. The dying deer-Ṛṣi six times mentions one or the other term or a cognate.

[64]*Manuṣyavad gato bhāvaḥ* (12.117.10); cf. Ganguli ([1884–96] 1970, 8:268): "with a heart like that of a human being." The passage calls him a Muni twelve times, a Ṛṣi eleven. I prefer "Muni" because a kind of carnivorous and liquor-drinking forest sage called Muṉi or Muṉicuvaraṉ appears, usually with dogs, in the remote Tamil countryside. Quite possibly such Muṉis are relatives of this anonymous epic sage. See Masilamani-Meyer in-press, 70–73 ("Muṉi and others") and plates.

[65]Lions, tigers, śarabhas (see below), maddened elephants, leapords, rhinosceri, bears, and others who are *kṣatajāśanāḥ*, "eating from wounds" (12.117.6–7).

[66]The Vulgate and numerous northern manuscripts add here that the Muni "understood the cries of all creatures" *(rutajñaḥ sarvasattvānām)* and that the dog had cause for fear (12.270* *apud* 12.117.14).

[67]*Sarvaprāṇivihiṃsakaḥ*; 12.117.33. The śarabha is a mythical beast, the fiercest of animals; in some purāṇic myths and temple iconography (e.g., at Dharasuram) it is a form Śiva takes to counter Viṣṇu's fierce Man-lion (Narasiṃha) form.

it has become extremely wretched, depressed *(paraṃ dainyam upāgamat)* (12.117–118.1).

Step by step it is a question of the perception of class or species identity, as is made clear when the dog-turned-elephant becomes a lion and does not consider the wild lion dangerous "because of their connection to the same class of creatures": that is, their common lion *jāti*.[68] But in each case it is a question of escalating species-misperception. Between animals, the wild animals misrecognize the transformed dog, and the dog misrecognizes himself. But the dog begins his troubles by misrecognizing himself as a "kind of human." His final wretchedness is to remain just a dog. Yet it is ultimately not the human heart or disposition of the dog that is under question, but that of the Muni whom the wild animals questioned so submissively at the beginning of the story. The Muni's response to the dog's expression of human-enough fears, and, not only that, to the dog's devotion *(bhakti)* and request for refuge *(śaraṇam)*, is to turn him into a series of increasingly wilder and fiercer animals, and ultimately to cast him off wretched and depressed, a dog once again. Of course the Muni is "putting the dog in his place." But why should he need to do this? It appears that he is a very cruel Muni. The dog's affection for the Muni is never reciprocated. Rather, the "refuge" the Muni offers his "devotee" is a power trip of his own devising that ends by callously reestablishing the distinction between the superior human and the low and mistakenly humanized "village animal." As the story begins, the human heart's disposition to cruelty is exemplified in a dog; by the time it ends, it is exemplified in the Muni.

It is, of course, with Bhīṣma speaking here from his bed of arrows, Yudhiṣṭhira who is the chief listener to this tale. And so he is with many of the other animal tales just cited: either he or Janamejaya, and in either case, "the king." When Yudhiṣṭhira asks Bhīṣma how a king should rule during the waning of a yuga, Bhīṣma says, "He should move with the sight of a vulture, the crouch of a crane, the striving of a dog, the valor of a lion, free from apprehension, with the suspicion of a crow, and the motion of a swerving snake *(bhujaṃga!)*."[69]

While Bhīṣma tells Yudhiṣṭhira many stories about animals, the story of the Muni and the dog is of particular interest because Yudhiṣṭhira, as

[68]*Tulyajātisamanvayāt*; 12.117.30. Cf. 12.271* apud 117.16: the wild leopard, "seeing him agreeably like himself *(ātmanaḥ sadṛśaṃ śubham)*, immediately found his nonincompatibility *(aviruddhas)* with him."

[69]12.138.62: *gṛdhradṛṣṭir bakālīnaḥ śvaceṣṭaḥ siṃhavikramaḥ/ anudvignaḥ kākaśaṅkī bhujaṃgacaritaṃ caret*; and just earlier, he should conceal his limbs like the tortoise, think toward ends like the crane, be bold like the lion, seize like the wolf, and rush forth like the rabbit (12.138.24–25)!

we have already seen, is quite preoccupied with dogs. Before and after the war he has claimed to see "no distinction" between dogs and humans.[70] Yet at the end of the epic, his treatment of the dog who is his *bhakta* is just the opposite of the Muni he has heard about from Bhīṣma. Unlike the Muni who seems to find his "human" affinity with the dog intrusive, Yudhiṣṭhira and the dog maintain a hidden affinity and identity (as Yudhiṣṭhira finally learns), since one is a form and the other the son of Dharma.[71] But most important, Yudhiṣṭhira refuses to abandon the dog. These differences between the Muni and Yudhiṣṭhira are differences in the human heart. Yudhiṣṭhira has developed a quality that the Muni seems to lack: the quality of noncruelty, *ānṛśaṃsya*.

D. Noncruelty and Nonviolence

Since chapter 2 I have flagged epic passages that highlight two terms and the cluster of ideas and themes associated with them: *ānṛśaṃsya*, which I have translated as "noncruelty" (with corollaries translated by "cruelty" or "cruel"), and *ahiṃsā*, "nonviolence." These are major concepts. As Mukund Lath observes in a very suggestive article, the *Mahābhārata* proclaims each as the "highest dharma."[72] Lath introduces *ānṛśaṃsya* as "a new word" (1990, 113): "outside the *Mahābhārata*, whether in the literature preceding the *Mahābhārata* or following it, the word hardly has the significance it has in the epic" (115). This is a promising point, since it suggests an intention of the poets. Lath interprets the relation in the epic between *ānṛśaṃsya* and the more widely attested *ahiṃsā* as one between this-worldly and other-worldly pursuits. He concludes,

> *Ahiṃsā* . . . is an ideal which is central to what is called the *nivṛttimārga*, the *mārga* of *saṃnyāsa* [the way of renunciation]. But the *Mahābhārata* is, if anything, a great text of the *pravṛttimārga* [the way of turning toward the world]. It argues for the *pravṛttimārga*,

[70] A similar point is made from a different angle by Viśvāmitra, who decides that "dog and deer are the same" when it comes to eating a dog's haunch to save his life during a famine (12.139.71).

[71] This "identity" rests on the epic's standard endorsement of the proverbial identity of father and son, and the example set by the identity between Vidura and Yudhiṣṭhira as the reborn "form" and son of Dharma respectively. When Vidura dies and is dissolved into Yudhiṣṭhira, we are told, "Surely whoever Dharma is, he is Vidura; whoever Vidura is, he is the Pāṇḍava" (15.35.21; cf. 16–22). See also n. 44 above.

[72] Lath 1990, 114: *paro dharmaḥ* for ānṛśaṃsya; *paramo dharmaḥ* for ahiṃsā. Cf. Halbfass 1988, 554, n. 95, noting the double strain. The difference between *paro/param* and *paramo/paramam* seems to be purely metric.

> though it is very much attracted by *nivṛttimārga* and *ahiṃsā*. But total *ahiṃsā* cannot be practiced, because the human condition is such that some *hiṃsā* has to be there for the practice of both the *gṛhasthadharma* [householder's dharma] and the *rājadharma* [king's dharma]. Therefore, what the *Mahābhārata* preaches is not *ahiṃsā* but *ānṛśaṃsya*. This latter is one of the most outstanding moral concepts of the epic. *Ānṛśaṃsya* is *ahiṃsā* adapted to the *pravṛttimārga*. (118–19; my brackets)

These are rich insights, and one must look forward to Lath's promised further study. Yet so far, at least, I think he overlooks something in the relation between ahiṃsā and ānṛśaṃsya: a tension pulling away from ahiṃsā, even occasionally a critique of it, that is more consequential than the implied translation of other-worldly into this-worldly values, which goes on in other texts, especially *Manu*.

To be sure, ahiṃsā, literally "not having the desire to kill," is a function of post-Vedic interpretations of Vedic sacrifice through such familiar arguments as "to kill in sacrifice is not to kill"; one should act (and thus sacrifice) "without the desire for the fruits" of one's actions; the animal consents to its sacrifice; the victim goes to heaven (Biardeau 1976, 53–54; 1993, 125–34); the real self is unslain. But I believe Lath is right that the epic treats ahiṃsā as a nivṛtti value, and, more than this, that the term holds ambiguous associations that derive from its promulgation by the rival nivṛtti systems of Jainism and Buddhism. As a virtue, ahiṃsā bears the ascetic imprint of the *desire* not to kill or harm creatures, which, in its ascetic framework, is a desire to overcome the desire for life. While the *Bhagavad Gītā* includes it in several lists of advocated virtues (10.5; 13.7; 16.2; 17.14), its purpose is to revitalize an ideal Kṣatriya who will fight to reestablish an *ārya* dharma convinced by such arguments, and particularly the second (action without the desire for fruits), fourth (death in battle as a ticket to heaven; 2.32), and fifth (the real self is unslain; 2.17–26). These are precisely non-Buddhist and non-Jain arguments: that ahiṃsā can be adjusted not only to the practice of sacrifice, but to the sacrifice of battle. As we saw in chapter 2 (§ C.31 and n. 144), Kṛṣṇa also tries these arguments out on Yudhiṣṭhira before his Aśvamedha, but with less effect, since Yudhiṣṭhira has already taken his main cues from Vyāsa, who has a little more attachment to life than the deity. Kṛṣṇa's main purpose with such arguments is to convince a warrior before the war rather than to console the king after it.

Lath mentions the impracticability of "total ahiṃsā" in the lives of householders and kings, and puts his finger on what is, I believe, the real nerve center in the epic poets' unease over ahiṃsā: its absolutism. The epic anticipates what Halbfass calls the "major 'philosophical' achievement" of the ritual exegesis of the Pūrvamīmāṃsā: "its method of shielding the Vedic dharma from the claims of philosophical, i.e., argumentative and universalizing thought, its demonstration that it cannot be rationalized or universalized within the framework of argumentative and epistemologically oriented thought, and its uncompromising linkage of dharma to the sources of the sacred tradition and the identity of the Aryan" (1988, 325; cf. 329–30). This "eternal" Vedic ārya dharma treats ahiṃsā not as an absolute ascetic guideline for the monastic life; rather, as Bhīṣma tells Yudhiṣṭhira: "The proclamation of dharma is done for the sake of the power of beings. What is connected with ahiṃsā would be dharma, that is certain. Dharma is (derived) from upholding, they say. By dharma beings are upheld apart *(dharmeṇa vidhṛtāḥ prajāḥ)*. What is connected with upholding would be dharma, that is certain."[73] As Halbfass renders the key phrases, ahiṃsā is "a form of *dhāraṇa*, 'upholding'" by which "creatures are kept apart, i.e., upheld in their respective identities by dharma"—an "upholding which is incumbent on qualified men; but it is also the condition under which such upholding is possible. It protects its protectors" (318). This well describes how the lizard might appeal to ahiṃsā as the "highest dharma" in reminding Ruru that he is not a snake: in upholding a dharma that holds creatures apart, he advocates his own protection by a principle whose value lies in its particularities rather than in any universality, since he is admittedly less concerned about snakes than he is about himself.

The "good" *(sat)*, the "respectable" *(sādhu)*, and the "cultured," "learned," or "strict" *(śiṣṭa)* who uphold this āryadharma were, of course, not invented by Kumārila.[74] All these terms are elegantly set forth in one epic passage by the "dharmic hunter" *(dharmavyādha)*, a figure whose story (3.197–206) recapitulates with some irony themes from many of the epic's other animal and hunt stories, while also presenting the only voice other than Bhīṣmā's to say that both ahiṃsā (3.198.69) and ānṛśamsya (203.41) are the "highest dharma." It begins when a Brahman ascetic glares to death a female crane *(balāka)* that just defecated on his head. Chagrined at his excessive anger, he seeks advice from the dharmic hunter who lives in the exemplary kingdom of Janaka. Although the hunter keeps a meatmarket, he is a vegetarian, and leaves

[73]12.110.10–11: *prabhāvārthāya bhūtānāṃ dharmapravacanaṃ kṛtam/ yat syād ahiṃsāsaṃyuktaṃ sa dharma iti niścayaḥ// dhāraṇād dharma ityāhur dharmeṇa vidhṛtāḥ prajāḥ/ yat syād dhāraṇasaṃyuktaṃ sa dharma iti niścayaḥ*. The CE adopts the "more difficult reading" here; see its verse notes. Cf. Biardeau 1993, 131, on passages that virtually equate dharma and daṇḍa, the royal "staff of punishment."

[74]See chap. 1 at nn. 112–13, and chap. 3, § B on the "good" and "distinguished" (or "very strict": *viśiṣṭāḥ*) Naimiṣeyas. Cf. Halbfass 1988, 327–29 on Kumārila's depiction of such legitimizers of the Vedic dharma, and his insistence that the Buddha did not teach dharma.

others to do the hunting. He finally confirms what the Brahman comes to suspect: he was a Brahman in his previous life. Once he had accompanied a king, his friend, on a hunt that had strayed too near an ashram, and had shot a Ṛṣi by mistake, thinking him a deer, who then cursed him to become a Śūdra hunter; but out of ānṛśaṃsya (206.3) he allowed him to keep his memory.

Hearing the "dharmic hunter's" story in the forest, the Paṇḍavas and Draupadī learn about the ways of the "unrespectable" (*asādhu*; 3.198.43) and the "conduct of the strict" (*śiṣṭācāram*; 56–94) that defines the "supreme path of the good *(satām mārgamanuttamam)*" (92, cf. 89; 200.42). We have also met the Naimiṣeyas among "the good" who occupy the old Vedic homeland (see chapter 3, § B). The "strict," says the hunter, "shun cruel *(krūra)* heretics *(nāstikān)*, fixed on sinful thoughts, whose limits of propriety are broken *(bhinnamaryādān)*" (198.66). As to *ahiṃsā*, the dharmic hunter relativizes it in relation to a justification of sacrifice: "Surely what was said by those astonished men of old was, 'Ahiṃsā!' *(ahiṃseti yaduktaṃ hi puruṣair vismitaiḥ purā)*. Who in this world does not harm living beings? Having given it much consideration, no one in the world does ahiṃsā *(iha vai nāsti kaścid ahiṃsakaḥ)*. Even ascetics (Yatis) devoted to ahiṃsā surely do himsā, although by their effort it may be lessened" (199.28–29).[75]

In Kumārila the Mīmāṃsa argument against Buddhism is explicit (Halbfass 1988, 329–30); in the *Mahābhārata* (and probably *Rāmāyaṇa*) a similar argument is woven into stories and dharmic instructions through a wink and a nod.[76] It is not hard to see the link between a resistance to absolutizing ahiṃsā and the perception that heretics are "cruel," since so many early Buddhist emperors who would have supported both Buddhist and Jaina monks who taught ahiṃsā as an absolute could have been perceived as murderous and low non-Kṣatriya despots. In the case of Aśoka, even Buddhists considered him cruel. Strong observes the discrepancy between the "fierce"- versus-"dharmic" Aśoka of the legends and the Aśoka known through his inscriptions, who announces his abandonment of violent means in the name a Buddhist dharma after what he admits was a vast destruction of the Kalingas. This latter "nonviolent" and "converted" Aśoka is a favored construct of modern writers. But his

[75]Arjuna agrees, telling Yudhiṣthira ahiṃsā is not only impossible but delusory, in his first postwar rebuke of the latter's renunciatory bent (12.15.20–28; see Biardeau 1993, 132).
[76]Cf. the "stubborn particularism" and resistance to universalizations of Rabbinic *midrash* (Handelman 1982, 12, 75; Neusner 1965, 23). Like the *Mbh* as "fifth Veda," midrash as oral Torah carries forward written Torah as law and story; but the *Mbh* is not "map without territory" (Neusner 1979). See Alles's fine treatment of Aśoka and the Mauryas, noting their emphasis on didactic rather than narrative discourse (1994, 65–66, 71–72).

Brāhmī inscriptions were deciphered only in 1837, and were illegible for over a millennium before that to Indian readers (1983, 3–18). One would hardly expect surviving Kalingas to have appreciated the imperial about-face of the self-promotional inscriptions without remembering a very real fierce Aśoka behind them. Aśoka writes: Whereas the "ceremony of Dharma" *(dharmamaṅgala)* produces effect in this world and the next, ceremonies performed on the occasions of "sicknesses, marriages of sons and daughters, children's births, and departures on journeys," and especially the "many diverse, trivial, and meaningless ceremonies" performed by women, bear "little fruit" in this world and none in the next (Nikam and McKeon 1966, 46–47). Aśoka also "banned religious assemblies *(samājās)* except for those that propagate his *dhamma*" (Rock Edicts 1.3–5, 9.7–9; Alles 1994, 172, n. 52). Assuming an Aśoka recallable to epic authors, the "strict" would not have seen much difference between the legendary Aśoka and the Aśoka of the inscriptions, not to mention other "cruel" despots with whom he ruled in train.

It is thus not just a question of the impracticability of "total ahiṃsā" in the dharma of householders and kings, but the fact that heretical absolutizing despots who murdered their fathers and brothers favored such a notion. The Sanskrit epics are written in counterpoint. The *Rāmāyaṇa*, concerned to establish a rule of primogeniture, has Rāma dissuade Lakṣmaṇa from overthrowing their father Daśaratha (2.18.8; 20) and killing their brother Bharata (90.18–20) to eliminate Rāma's hurdles to the throne. The *Mahābhārata* describes Yudhiṣṭhira's "despair" at having "occasioned the killing of his fathers, brothers, sons, affinal kin, and allies" (1.2.196), even though the "patricides" in question are his grandfather (Bhīṣma), guru (Droṇa), elder brother (Karṇa), and maternal uncle (Śalya): the four Kaurava marshals at Kurukṣetra.[77]

Indeed, the question of fratricide is also faced openly in the convoluted scene on the seventeenth day of battle when Yudhiṣṭhira, upset that Arjuna should delay in slaying Karṇa (whom they have yet to know is their eldest brother), tells Arjuna to give his bow to someone else, and Arjuna, who had vowed to kill anyone who ever spoke that insult, prepares to kill Yudhiṣṭhira. Kṛṣṇa, to calm Arjuna and find a way out of this impasse, tells him his vow is childish (*bāla*; 8.49.23), rebukes him as one who has not learned to serve the elderly (14), says that not killing is always considered preferable to killing, and asks, "How, best of men, like just another uncultivated man *(prākṛto 'nyaḥ pumān iva)*, could you wish to kill your elder brother, a king who knows dharma?" (21). To make the point that keeping to the truth of one's vow does not always

[77]The translation (1980, 73) and the point (109, 115; 1983, 624) are Fitzgerald's. Cf. Goldman 1978 on such "father figures" (329).

conform to dharma, he then tells the story of an inverse case: a very cruel *(sudāruṇa)* act of killing by a hunter named Balāka, another "Mr. Crane," who shot a blind beast he had never seen before, yet was nonetheless carried off to heaven because the beast had vowed to kill all creatures (31–40).[78]

That the epic resists the universalization of ahiṃsā, however, is nowhere clearer than from a glance at the uncertain status it accords it among the "highest dharmas." As we have seen, ahiṃsā and ānṛśaṃsya are both the "highest dharma." Yudhiṣṭhira, who has every right to be confused on this issue by the end of the war, makes the "highest dharma" of the king his first and most enduring question to Bhīṣma (12.56.2; 161.48; 353.8). Of the fifty-four instances I have found in the *Mahābhārata*, the tally for the different excellences said to be the "highest dharma" is ānṛśaṃsya, 8;[79] truth, 5;[80] ahiṃsā, 4;[81] what is in the Veda, 2 (3.198.78; 13.129.5); offspring, 2;[82] following your guru, 2 (2.61.80; 3.183.15); speaking what is applicable to dharma when one knows it, 2;[83] Viṣṇu-Nārāyaṇa, 2 (12.271.26; 335.76); seven different excellences for kings (*1*, kingship itself;[84] *2*, restraining the wicked, cherishing the good, and not retreating from battle [12.14.16]; *3*, administration of justice [*daṇḍanīti*; 12.70.31]; *4*, protection of subjects [12.72.26–27]; *5*, accepting the consequences of victory and defeat [12.107.27]; *6*, restraint and Vedic recitation [13.128.49]; and *7*, retirement to the forest for royal sages [15.8.12]); three for Brahmans (*1*, keeping vows; *2*, mendicancy; and *3*, sacrifice plus ahiṃsā);[85] two for Kṣatriyas (*1*, doing one's "own dharma" [3.149.25]; and *2*, death in battle [9.13.12]); one for the householder: honoring guests even by offering one's wife (13.2.69); one for women: fidelity to the husband (presumably, given the typical priorities, even when offered to his guest [12.347.10]); one for sons: their father's command [12.358.10]; and eleven more single entries: celibacy (1.159.13), inheritance law (3.183.5), wealth (5.70.23), the householder stage (12.23.2), various philosophical insights (12.210.1), aspects of yoga (12.242.1–4),

[78]Bhīṣma also alludes to this story (12.110.7). See Hiltebeitel 1984, 24, on the further outcome that Kṛṣṇa advises: Arjuna's "killing himself" by self-praise.

[79]3.67.15; 203.41 (the dharmic hunter); 297.55 and 71 (counted as one); 5.32.11; 12.220.109; 316.12; 13.47.2; 159.6.

[80]1.69.24; 3.198.69; 12.156.24; 319.11; 13.74.31.

[81]1.11.12 and 14 (the lizard, counted as one); 3.198.69 (the dharmic hunter); 13.116.1; 117.37–41.

[82]1.97.13; 3.277.15, each in paradoxical circumstances.

[83]2.61.80 (Vidura says this about Draupadī's question, on which see chap. 7); 3.183.15.

[84]3.49.13; 12.56.2; 12.161.48 (Yudhiṣṭhira's question of Bhīṣma).

[85]All in one passage: 13.128.35, 36, 41.

friendship to all creatures and inoffensiveness (12.254.6), nirvāṇa (12.330.16), gleaning (12.353.8),[86] giving (13.129.10), and breath (14.93.33). This counts only usages with *para* and *parama* (see n. 72 above); *uttara*, used more rarely for "highest" in this sense, gives only further variety. According to the serpent princess Ulūpī, when she desires Arjuna, his "highest dharma" is the injunction to save her life by making love to her (1.206.30). For Bhīma about to burn Yudhiṣṭhira's arms, it is to remember not to overreach one's older brother.[87] For kings of old, it was ahiṃsā (13.116.72). And so on.

The highest dharma seems to be knowing the highest dharma for whatever particular situation one is in, and recognizing that situation within an ontology that admits virtually endless variation and deferral in matters of formulating and approaching "the highest."[88] Those who "know the highest dharma" also make a short and interesting list: Yama (3.42.16), Vyāsa (13.80.11),[89] Vyāsa's son Śuka (12.319.23 etc.), Brahmans who sire Kṣatriyas after the latter are exterminated by Rāma Jāmadagnya (1.98.33), and King Śibi while cutting his flesh to save a dove from a hawk (3.131.16), an act said elsewhere to typify ānṛśaṃsya (1.88.19). Āstīka (1.43.38), Nārada (12.30.40), and Bhīṣma (12.47.9) are also among a few who have the "soul of the highest dharma" *(parama-dharmātmā)*, as does Pāṇḍu when at last he dies out of love in the arms of his second wife Mādrī (1.116.12; see above at n. 64). It is suggestive that a search for similar usages in the *Rāmāyaṇa* yields much less. The exiled Sītā—and let us note how revealing it is that she is Vālmīki's primary figure to voice this value—tells Hanumān to remind Rāma that he once told her ānṛśaṃsya was the highest dharma (5.36.34); Kaikeyī, for her own devious reasons, finds it in truth (2.12.3); and Vasiṣṭha (1.72.12), Rāma (32.29; 3.5.6), and, according to Rāma, Bharata (2.103.25), "know the highest dharma," which in Bharata's case could well be ānṛśaṃsya, since Rāma trusts him with the kingdom because he has this quality (2.41.6). The *Rāmāyaṇa* does not present a Dharmarāja so beset with ambiguities. Yudhiṣṭhira is never said to know the highest

[86] See chap. 1 at n. 75: the *Śāntiparvan* and its *Mokṣadharmaparvan* end on this note.

[87] 2.61.8; see chap. 7 on this passage and as a delicate topic.

[88] The same is true of the movement in the *BhG* from uncertainties about what is "better" (*śreyas*; 2.6–5.1) to statements of what is "highest" *(param, paramam*; 5.16–8.28) to deepening revelations of the "most hidden" *(guhyatamam)* and "highest" *(param)* "royal mystery" (*rājaguhyam*; 9.1-2, 10.1, 11.1, 14.1-2, 15.20, 18.53-68, and 75). Cf. Handelman 1982, 14, 56, contrasting Rabbinic "what if" statements with Greco-Christian "what is" ones. The *Mbh* is concerned with both: with "what is" (*sat, āstikya*, etc.; see chap. 4 at n. 114), but also with the "if" *(yadi)* and especially the "as if" *(iva)*, one of its more disarming narrative conventions.

[89] See B. Sullivan 1990, 56, for related expressions.

dharma or to recognize it so easily in a brother.[90] If Rāma would seem to incarnate it, Yudhiṣṭhira must learn it.

E. Tempered Cruelties

If the *Mahābhārata* tells us different things about the highest dharma, it is ānṛśaṃsya that has the most occurrences. This quality is especially promulgated to Yudhiṣṭhira. When we realize by the epic's end that he departs this world through his noncruelty toward a dog, we see that it has been a long and painful lesson. Although Yudhiṣṭhira has some prior ideas of his own on the subject, as we shall see in chapter 7, we first find him *hearing* about ānṛśaṃsya through edifying encounters in the forest: listening to the story of Nala and Damayantī (as we shall see in chapter 6); to the boa who is his ancestor Nahuṣa (3.177.18); to the story of the dharmic hunter (as already noted); and in answering the riddling questions of Dharma ("really" Yama) after Dharma has turned from a crane into a Yakṣa. Here the triply disguised Yama, who as we have just seen "knows the highest dharma," asks Yudhiṣṭhira what it is, and Yudhiṣṭhira answers ānṛśaṃsya (3.297.54–55). When the Yakṣa gives him the boon of being able to select one brother to be revived, Yudhiṣṭhira exemplifies this quality by selecting Nakula so that each of his mothers should have one living son (71); and the Yakṣa, now identifying himself as Dharma, says he is pleased with this ānṛśaṃsya and grants further boons.[91] By this time Dharma confirms something Yudhiṣṭhira has had at least twelve years to think about.

During the year spent incognito and as he prepares for battle, Yudhiṣṭhira begins to advocate ānṛśaṃsya himself (4.32.47; 5.30.38) and exemplify it to the Kauravas (4.27.26; 5.32.11; 34.83; 52.10). But just before the *Bhagavad Gītā*, in a moment that clearly anticipates it, he has doubts. He looks out over the battlefield and asks Arjuna how so few can conquer so many, and Arjuna answers that victory comes not so much by strength "as by truth and ānṛśaṃsya, as also by dharma and perseverance" (6.21.10). Then in battle, there is the exemplary scene noted in chapter 2 in which Kṛṣṇa has engineered the death of Bhīma's half-Rākṣasa son Ghaṭotkaca by inducing Karṇa to use up the weapon that he was intending for Arjuna. Yudhiṣṭhira is driven to such grief that he

[90]None of Yudhiṣṭhira's brothers have ānṛśaṃsya, although Arjuna recognizes the quality in Droṇa (4.53.6) and Yudhiṣṭhira (4.65.20; 6.21.10), and Bhīma once taunts Arjuna with inclining toward it (7.168.8) in battle. Arjuna's deeds, however, are not nṛśaṃsa (3.142.15, 25; 254.13; 4.61.21), at least before the war.

[91]3.298.10; see Lath 1990, 114–15. It is perhaps indicative of his ānṛśaṃsya that he saves Nakula for a mother, Mādrī, who is (among the) dead! Cf. Shulman 1996, 157–58, 163, for a rather different reading.

sets off to challenge Karṇa, but Vyāsa intervenes, emerging to tell Yudhiṣṭhira to count his blessings and bide his time: for now, he says, "Reflect on dharma, ānṛśaṃsya, tapas, giving, patience, and truth. Where dharma is, there is victory."[92]

After the war, there is time for reassessment. In the only case I find where Yudhiṣṭhira admits his own cruelty, riven by grief, he tells Gāndhārī, "I am the cruel slayer of your sons *(putrahantā nṛśaṃso 'haṃ tava)*, the cause of this destruction of the earth," and urges her to curse him (11.15.3). Bhīma and Arjuna rebuke him for making noncruelty, along with other benevolent qualities, an excuse to abandon the kingship he has just won (12.10.3; 18.37). Soon, having heeded the advice to undergo his coronation, Yudhiṣṭhira begins his just rule displaying ānṛśaṃsya by protecting the war widows and mothers who have lost their sons, as well as the poor, blind, and helpless.[93] Bhīṣma then gives him many further illustrations of ānṛśaṃsya's value, some of which we will note, and saves for his parting words, as he prepares to ascend to heaven, a recommendation of Yudhiṣṭhira to Dhṛtarāṣṭra for his devotion to ānṛśaṃsya and to elders (13.155.34), and a final admonition to Yudhiṣṭhira to always live with self-controlled, righteous, and ascetic Brahmans devoted to ānṛśaṃsya (48). Yudhiṣṭhira continues to exhibit this quality while attending Dhṛtarāṣṭra (15.2.3), and finally, again, with the dog. And then the last twist: when Dharma puts Yudhiṣṭhira through his final "third test," the upside-down experience of heaven and hell that we will consider more closely in chapter 7, Yudhiṣṭhira "censures" Dharma for what is in effect his cruelty.

The quality of noncruelty thus carries Yudhiṣṭhira a long way. At the end, when he censures his father Dharma, he also, of course, censures dharma, the principle. But the god is definitely there to answer, as he is, where it is clear that the same god is Yama when he is censured *(upa-ā-labh)* by Aṇīmāṇḍavya (1.101.22). We might even propose that the Dharma who puts Yudhiṣṭhira to these excruciating tests of ānṛśaṃsya, and who is alone among the gods to endorse this quality, has come to embody it as a result of Aṇīmāṇḍavya's curse, which softens and "humanizes" the Yama who administers the karmic mechanism of reincarnation. Aṇīmāṇḍavya curses Yama, as Dharma incarnate, to take "form" as the truly uncruel Vidura. But Dharma's three tests are hardly uncruel. And for Yudhiṣṭhira, who absorbs it, ānṛśaṃsya is a cruel and paradoxical standard not only at these three trials but at many other points, such as Vyāsa's counsel to "just think about it" after the death of Ghaṭotkaca, or Kuntī's lady-Kṣatriya message, via Kṛṣṇa, to Yudhiṣṭhira

[92] 7.158.53–62, esp. 61; see chap. 2, § C.22.

[93] 12.42.10–11; see chap. 2, § C.29.

before the war: "You will do an extreme cruelty" *(sunṛśaṃsam kariṣyasi)* if you do not fight (5.133.5). Indeed, we might even wonder whether, in censuring Dharma and dharma, Yudhiṣṭhira is censuring not only his father but this uncompromising quality that has compromised his life.

In any case, ānṛśaṃsya is no more an absolute than ahiṃsā. It is a "highest dharma" only in its bearing on particular circumstances, and although these circumstances are of supreme importance in the *Mahābhārata*, it is not, as Lath suggests, "the supreme *dharma* from the highest point of view."[94] That formulation is too absolute and vague. If the epic's Brahman poets regard any dharma as supreme from their highest point of view, it would be their slippery concept of "truth," in which ānṛśaṃsya (12.316.12) and ahiṃsā (3.198.69; 12.156.24) are both rooted, and which they relativize—one might even say narrativize or fictionalize—at every turn. Ānṛśaṃsya is a "highest dharma" as a teaching for the king, and must be looked at in its narrative contexts.

"The Āryas call forebearance, truth, ānṛśaṃsya, and uprightness *(ārjavam)* the best" (12.288.12), says Prajāpati, in the form of the wandering gander *(haṃsa)* who represents the soul, to the ancient and exalted Sādhya gods in a story Bhīṣma tells Yudhiṣṭhira. Cruelty *(nṛśaṃsya)*, on the other hand, is *anārya*, as is exemplified by the words and actions of the Kauravas to Draupadī at the dice match (2.60.30; 5.126.12), or, as Aśvatthāman charges, by Yudhiṣṭhira's hypocritically carrying the "banner of virtue" yet uttering the "exceedingly cruel *(sunṛśaṃsya)* and *anārya*" untruth that enables the killing of Droṇa.[95] Jayadratha, son of "Old Kṣatra," was both "*anārya* and cruel *(nṛśaṃsa)*" according to his widow Duḥśalā (14.77.38); and other characters commit cruelties, such as Purocana (who tries to burn the Pāṇḍavas in the lacquer house; 1.36.3), Śiśupāla (2.42.6–7, 11), Kīcaka (4.29.5), and Kaikeyī (3.261.32), that are *nṛśaṃsa* with no need to add *anārya*.[96] Ānṛśaṃsya is a "trickle-down" virtue that flows from a king who first (as Bhīṣma instructs) should surround himself with "self-controlled, righteous, and ascetic Brahmans" devoted to the quality (cf. 12.80.4). The boa Nahuṣa tells his descendant Yudhiṣṭhira that when "authority *(pramāṇa)*, truth, and the brahman" extend to all four classes, both ānṛśaṃśya and ahiṃsā can be found in any of them,[97] as is indeed exemplified by the "dharmic

[94]1990, 115. Kumar's reflections (1995, 241) on the "universal principles" of the Dharmarāja lead one in a similar misdirection.

[95]7.166.19. Cf. 12.1.28: Yudhiṣṭhira recalls Duryodhana's similar charge against him.

[96]Kaikeyī, like Jayadratha, Śalya, and Śakuni and the latter's sister Gāndhārī, are from that "northwest frontier," which both epics typify as a zone of mixed *ārya* and *anārya* practices.

[97]3.117.18; cf. 12.285.23–24, where the two, with ānṛśaṇsya first, head the list of "eternal dharmas" *(dharmāḥ sādhāraṇāḥ)* listed by Vyāsa's father Parāśara.

hunter," the Śūdra who instructs the irascible Brahman in the righteous kingdom of Janaka.

Ānṛśaṃsya does, however, seem to have its limits. The exemplary King Yayāti, son of Nahuṣa, "satisfied the gods with sacrifices, the Fathers with śrāddhas, the wretched *(dīnān)* with desired favors, Brahmans with desires, guests with food and drink, the people with protection, Śūdras with ānṛśaṃsya, and Dasyus with suppression *(saṃnigraheṇa)*" (1.80.2–4). Dasyus in the *Mahābhārata* are often brigands,[98] but carry their Vedic connotation of subdued or conquerable outsiders into an overlap with forest peoples (3.31.15), Abhīra Mlecchas of the Panjab (16.8.44–61), and warlike mountaineers who are not Kṣatriyas (2.24.15; 25.17). They are also interchangeable with the "cruel *(krūra)*, fierce Mlecchas who eat anything" and terrorize Brahmans at the end of a yuga (3.188.52–61; cf. 16.8.61). They are particularly known for breaking the limits *(maryādā)* of dharma (12.79.18; 131.10), but there is also a Robin Hood "good Dasyu" who teaches his band of brigands the maryādā they should observe: above all, don't slay women and, naturally, when plundering, exempt Brahmans.[99] The Kaurava and Matsya kings are said to practice Dasyu dharma when they allow cruelties to Draupadī.[100]

What is most interesting about ānṛśaṃsya, however, is not that it is retractable and dispensed from above, but that it is also expandable. Unlike ahiṃsā, which, beyond the life of the recluse, is seen in the epic as susceptible to a calculus of perceptions and distinctions that can be hypocritical for a king who cannot fully practice it, ānṛśaṃsya is a matter of the human heart that can expand and contract as character and circumstances allow. Whereas ahiṃsā proclaims a value that must either be applicable to all beings or to a calculus that posits such an equivalence while denying its administration, ānṛśaṃsya begins from a feeling of the "absence of injuring *men*" *(nṛ)*, including, as we are already beginning to see, women, as if that were a good and realistic starting point for a species trying to imagine a way out of its own cycles of violence. Thus as Lath shows, "the word has more than a negative connotation; it signifies good-will, a fellow feeling, a deep sense of the other"; it "occurs often with . . . *anukrośa*, to cry with another, to feel another's pain" (1990, 115), which is perhaps best translated as commiseration. By the combination of these two qualities, Yudhiṣṭhira upholds dharma out

[98]As in the stories of Aṇīmāṇḍavya and of the Ābhīra marauders who make off with Kṛṣṇa's widows from the defenseless Arjuna (see chap. 2, § C.41).

[99]12.133; cf. Jha 1995, 242, who somehow sees this code as a contribution to the "nation."

[100]3.11.17; 4.15.24. Cf. Thapar 1984, 132, 154; Halbfass 1988, 175–80, 507, n. 5, 508, n. 9. Mleccha equals Dasyu in the *BhvP*: see Hiltebeitel 1999a, 272–73.

of respect for Dhṛtarāṣṭra before the war (5.34.83); when Indra sees the Asura Bali resolutely accepting defeat, he exclaims, "Ānṛśaṃsya is the highest dharma. Thus I commiserate with you *(anukrośas tathā tvayi)*."[101] We shall note other examples. As such, ānṛśaṃsya can contract from a fellow-feeling for "men" into one for the ārya inclusive of Śūdras (itself already an important expansion). Or, as Yudhiṣṭhira's expressions of ānṛśaṃsya and his hearing others tell him stories about it, and occasions to display it, show, it can expand to a fellow-feeling for a former foe, for a half-Rākṣasa like Ghaṭotkaca, for the lowly and destitute;[102] for slave girls, dependent hunchbacks, and cripples (5.30.38); for not only the living but the dead;[103] for a dog; or even for a tree, as one last animal story is meant to show.

Yudhiṣṭhira asks Bhīṣma about the qualities of noncruelty, dharma, and devout folk *(bhaktajana)* (13.5.1). Bhīṣma responds: A fowler of Kāśī went hunting antelopes. We can now say that the hunt, and particularly what van Buitenen calls the "motif of the 'mishap of the deer hunt'" (1973, 447), is another convention by which the epic poets make the stories turn. In this one, the fowler's poisoned arrow hits a mighty forest tree by mistake. The tree withers, but a parrot in it doesn't leave his nest because of his "devotion to the lord of the forest" (*tasya bhaktyā vanaspateḥ*; 6); it withers with the tree. Amazed at the parrot's extraordinary resolution and knowledge of the sameness of happiness and suffering, Indra asks, "How can this bird experience *ānṛśaṃsya*, which is impossible for animals?" (9). He goes disguised as a Brahman, and asks why the parrot doesn't leave the tree for one with fruits and leaves. The parrot says with a sigh that it has been born, has grown up, obtained his good character, and received protection in this tree; it will remain out of devotion to ānṛśaṃsya, and because anukrośa is the great dharma and perennial happiness of the respectable (*sadhūnām*; 22–23). Delighted, Indra offers the parrot a boon, and the parrot, "ever devoted to noncruelty," requests the revival of the tree. While ahiṃsā tightens the great chain of beings, ānṛśaṃsya softens it with a cry for a *human* creature-feeling across the great divides.

Yet ānṛśaṃsya extends not only to the hearts of gods, demons, humans, animals, and trees; in a passage glorifying Kṛṣṇa as the supreme being *(puruṣottama)* and explaining his divine names, Saṃjaya closes with the statement that it also extends to Kṛṣṇa, who will come to the Kuru court "for the sake of ānṛśaṃsya" (5.68.14; cf. 69.4). Let us note that

[101]12.220.109; *hyanukrośaśca me tvayi* (12.227.111d) in the Vulgate, making it clearer that it is Indra's *anukrośa* for Bali.

[102]See 12.42.12 and the epigram repeated at 1.82.8; 2.59.6; 12.288.8; 13.107.56.

[103]See the case of Mādrī, above, n. 91.

Kṛṣṇa says nothing about ānṛśaṃsya himself; these are words by which Saṃjaya speaks (as always) for the author, here in defining Kṛṣṇa's mission.

When Saṃjaya says this to Dhṛtarāṣṭra, it is for once beyond the hearing of Yudhiṣṭhira, who might have had a question. Indeed, Yudhiṣṭhira also does not hear Saṃjaya add in the same breath that Kṛṣṇa's mission is to terrify Dasyus (5.68.6), or draw the terrifying implication of what Saṃjaya has told the Kauravas just before this: that Arjuna conceives his joint mission with Kṛṣṇa as that of killing Dasyus, among whom he includes the Kauravas (47.59–76). In any case, Kṛṣṇa does not speak for ānṛśaṃsya. This quality comes not from God but from the author: either directly from him, or from his divine, sagely, bardic, and animal surrogates and fictions. This author, however, gives his readers an opening to question whether he practices what he preaches when he has his mother admonish him to sire the heroes' fathers "with noncruelty" and "out of commiseration *(anukrośa)* for beings."[104]

Could we say the same of Saṃjaya's statement about Kṛṣṇa: that it opens a question? Could we say that Dharmarāja, left out of earshot, is not only here but elsewhere the king whose education requires that he must withstand not only the cruelties of his father Dharma-Yama, but those of the deity and the author? We know Kṛṣṇa does not undertake the final negotiations before the war to bring peace or to practice ahiṃsā, as Yudhiṣṭhira thinks and wishes. How then is Kṛṣṇa "noncruel"? It is the big question, the question of theodicy. It is beyond Yudhiṣṭhira's earshot but not ours, and others in the epic have raised it. More than a matter of Yudhiṣṭhira's censuring of Dharma, it is easy to see how for many of Vyāsa's characters who grow on our sympathies—for Duryodhana, Gāndhārī, Uttaṅka, Balarāma, even Śiśupāla,[105] and, on some strong occasions, Draupadī[106]—the *Mahābhārata* is an argument with God.

[104] 1.99.33; see chap. 2, § C.2 and n. 49.

[105] These characters make famous speeches or protests holding Kṛṣṇa accountable for the epic's disasters. See Matilal's important discussion "in defense" (1991). On Uttaṅka and Gāndhārī, see chap. 2, § C.41 at n. 199. On Duryodhana, see Gitomer 1992 and chap. 1 at n. 25; on Balarāma, see his distaste for what Saṃjaya calls Kṛṣṇa's "semblance of dharma" *(dharmacchalam)* in defense of Bhīma's treacherous felling of Duryodhana (9.59.17–25). On Śiśupāla, see 2.34–42.29; Dumézil 1971, 59–132.

[106] 5.80: her argument that Kṛṣṇa's embassy should seek war, not peace, especially verse 24: "While the Pāṇḍavas were looking and you were alive, Keśava," she was molested at the dice match; 3.31: her "heretical" puppet speech. See further chap. 7, § B.

6 Listening to *Nala* and Damayantī

To overstate the premise of this chapter, the story of Nala and Damayantī has a double *Mahābhārata* purpose. First, its primary audience, the Pāṇḍavas and Draupadī, listens to it in the company of a lot of forest Brahmans. More precisely, four of the five Pāṇḍavas are present with Draupadī, while the fifth, Arjuna, has set off for the Himalayas to seek weapons from Śiva. As with other frames, it matters in the epic who listens to what, and how textual units are adjoined and juxtaposed. Second, it poses to its live audience, those who read "Nala" within the larger epic and listen in, such reflections and enigmas as are posed—not only retrospectively but prospectively—to this primary audience by their hearing of this story within the story. Shulman indicates that a Tamil chapbook retelling, the *Nalaccakkiravarttikatai* or "Story of Emperor Nala," "boldly and simply declares itself as the *sāra*, the 'essence' or 'pith,' of the *Mahābhārata*" (1994, 2). I believe this would not be an idle boast were it made for *Nala* (the name to be used henceforth for the title) in the Sanskrit epic. If the *Mahābhārata*'s frames within frames can be thought of as emboxing some surprises, *Nala* is surely one of them. We proceed from outer frames to an inner miniature that frames nothing more than its own reflections.[1]

[1]Cf. Handelman 1982, 25, 53, 74–80, 88, on inference by juxtaposition, *smuchin*, in Rabbinic hermeneutics, and Reich 1998, 293–94, and passim. The principle applies to "invention" in what I have called "background myths" in the *Mbh* (Hiltebeitel 1976, 210–23; [1976] 1990, 312–13; 1984, 15 and n. 42), and to "paradeigma" or "inset tales" as "mirror stories" in Homer (Andersen [1987] 1999, 479–81): "the hearer establishes . . . the *secondary or key function* of the paradigm. The paradigm now becomes a *sign* of the main story and a comment on its own context and so on the actual situation and even on the *Iliad* as a whole" (476; cf. Willcock 1964, 142). The inset tale "brings time to a complete standstill and locks our attention unremittingly on the celebration of the present moment" (Austin [1966] 1999, 414). *Nala* is for the *Mbh* a kind of "mise en abyme" (Bal 1978).

A. Characters in Search of Each Other

The story is told early during the Pāṇḍavas' twelve years in the forest. There Draupadi has been complaining of how she was violated in the dice match, and has been trying to goad Yudhiṣṭhira to seek what he argues is premature revenge. They both miss Arjuna. So Yudhiṣṭhira is miserable, and asks the forest sage Bṛhadāśva, "Who is more miserable than I?" At the end, after reciting *Nala*, Bṛhadaśva sums up his answer: "Nala's suffering *(duhkha)* was such as this. He was all alone. But you are surrounded by your brothers and Draupadī, and attended by lordly Brahmans. What (is your) complaint *(kā paridevanā)*?" (78.6–9). He then gives Yudhiṣṭhira the "heart of the dice" that saved Nala in the story, and provides Yudhiṣṭhira—until now hopeless at gambling—with a talent by which to disguise himself.

We must thus begin with the inventory already in hand (mainly from two articles by Biardeau [1984, 1985]) of the interreferential correspondences, what Biardeau calls the "mirror effects" (1985, 17), between *Nala* and the larger epic. Biardeau has brought out the main reciprocities, and Shulman, speaking of "a hypothetical relation of parallelism or, more profoundly, of encapsulation" (1994, 2), has found a good term for the relation of the part to the whole. *Nala* is perhaps the exemplary subtale in this regard, "encapsulating" the epic narratively as the *Gītā* does theologically.

Methodologically, however, both Biardeau's and Shulman's approaches leave us with the sense of an important point still left unsaid. Mirror effects and encapsulation are interpretative strategies that confront *Nala* and the *Mahābhārata* as two texts, but stop short of envisioning them as one. For Biardeau, the problem is one of treating "two such disproportionate texts" (1985, 3) by attending to their symbolic oppositions and inversions (16–17). For Shulman, *Nala* is twisted to fit a *Mahābhārata* setting. In classifying *Nala* with its happy ending as a fairy tale or Märchen,[2] he sees the ending as one with an ironic sting in its epic context, since the analogy between Nala, who regains his kingdom peacefully, and Yudhiṣṭhira, who does so disastrously, is, he says, "falsely constituted" (1994, 6). This is untenable. Would it be truly constituted if it were a perfect fit? Incongruity is, once again, what makes a fit interesting. Moreover, it is not just a matter of oppositions,

[2]1994, 5–6. Similarly, Biardeau says its optimistic ending gives it the flavor of a "conte" (1985, 4); cf. van Buitenen 1975, 183–85; J. D. Smith 1992, 13: "essentially light reading. . . . in sharp contrast to the grimness of the epic narrative which surrounds it," yet, as he shows, with no easy parallels among folktales (15–19). I suggest it is romance (or romantic epic) within epic (or martial epic); see Quint 1993, 182, on "attempt[s] to lend romance variety to the epic narrative by interweaving episodes of love."

inversions, and fits, but of interpenetrating stories. If the *Mahābhārata* Critical Edition does not allow us to pass *Nala* off as an interpolation or to derive a prior folktale behind it, then the challenges posed by a one-text approach are unavoidable. I hope to show that they are also fruitful.[3]

Both Biardeau and Shulman angle at such an approach: Biardeau around the issue of *Mahābhārata* "substories" *(sous-récits)*;[4] Shulman around the theme of loss and recovery of self. Toward the end of her *Nala* essay, Biardeau says that one of its results is to verify "the necessity . . . postulated of not separating the study of a well-individualized substory" like *Nala* "from the ensemble of the epic that includes it."[5] The mirror effects are more, she says, than "a universe already delimited by an ensemble of organizing values" that would doom the poetic imagination to divert its well-inculculated audience with indeterminate repetitions, and leave the modern interpreter with something akin to Adela Quested's cave of echoes—a reduction to repetition without meaning.

> The gearing down (démultiplication) of the principal intrigue into well-constructed "substories," or, again, secondary stories destined to "explain" an abnormal situation, also responds to other demands. *The narration wants to be cryptic*: this deployment of planes of signification imbricated within one another is one of the story's charms, but this charm supposes that at one moment or another such a plan suddenly becomes clear, by favor of a term repeated with insistence, or of a situation that is perfectly incongruous, or of a detail set in relief, which forces the opening toward a new meaning. The "substory" is one of the privileged means that the authors gave themselves to make their audience blink. (1985, 32 [my italics])

Indeed, blinking is a trait of the Naimiṣa Forest, whose Ṛṣis comprise another audience for *Nala*. And of course it is a motif in the tale itself,

[3]See n. 1. Cf. Ramanujan 1991, 424: *Nala* illustrates nested repetition in the *Mbh*. Opposed, see Sukthankar 1939, 294: "the episode is a palpable 'interpolation,' impeding annoyingly the march of the epic story, and is forced upon the reader of the Epic in the most barefaced manner"; J. D. Smith 1992, 15: "not appropriate to treat *Nala* as heavily symbolic, and as existing chiefly to reinforce the outer epic which frames it." Smith makes an admittedly useless search for a common tale type, and then a formalist attempt to "concentrate on *Nala* itself" and its "structure," whose "essence" he defines around Nala's "various gifts" (16, 21): the loss of some and their recovery by the display of others. He does not solve his final problem—Nala's heroic "passivity"—without noting that Yudhiṣṭhira is listening (28–29).

[4]Recall the discussion of Sukthankar's views of such *upakhyānas* in chap. 2, § B.

[5]Biardeau has also taken up this epic-and-subtale problem in studies of "Śakuntalā" (1979) and in recent work on the *Rāmopākhyāna* (personal communication); cf. her studies of Reṇukā, Arjuna Kārtavīrya, and Rāma Jāmadagnya (1969; 1970a; 1976, 188–203).

for the final sign by which Damayantī can distinguish the human Nala from her other suitors, four gods, is that he is "revealed by a blink" (*nimeṣeṇa ca sūcitaḥ*; 3.54.24d). As in that famous scene, the image offers a kind of litmus test for other audiences. Do the Pāṇḍavas also blink? Do readers? How often?

As to Shulman, the intratextual game is one of riddles about man and text: "questions and answers" that explore the limits of language as it traces a "hero's perception of his disastrous inner development." His approach has been groundbreaking. Yet the narrative connections between *Nala* and the *Mahābhārata* are "surface similarities," "epiphenomena" that express "a much more deeply rooted affinity in meaning and internal debate" (Shulman 1994, 2). Depths and surfaces aside,[6] it is again like the question "who blinks." That is, it is not only a question of what readers hear in these echoes, but of what the primary audience might hear. Do we read the *Mahābhārata* by listening in or by tuning out?

There is one other important point that I think both Biardeau and Shulman undervalue. For all their attention to mirrors and echoes, one never quite understands from either that *Nala* is perhaps classical India's greatest love story.[7] A 1993 Madison, Wisconsin, panel on "Nala and Damayantī" showed that it remains at heart a love story in its vernacular folk tellings as well.[8] Biardeau is quick to find Damayantī's pining insufferable (1984, 259–61), and to allegorize the hero's and heroine's associations into philosophical abstractions. Shulman is more attentive on this score, but with his focus a bit narrowly on Nala.

In following the conventions of the intertextual game, I will concentrate mainly on three characters—Nala, Damayantī, and Nala's charioteer Vārṣṇeya. Nala is a homonym for Nara, which means "Man." This connects Nala with Arjuna, who was a sage called Nara in a previous life, and who is himself recursively identified with Nala by the disguise he takes in the *Virāṭaparvan* as a eunuch under the name Bṛhannalā, "the great Nalā," which, with its feminine ending, means "the Great Man, as Woman."[9] Damayantī evokes these connections herself

[6]As I see it, to distinguish them in this text is false privileging. See chap. 1, n. 14.

[7]Cf. Sukthankar 1939, 294, "without doubt one of the most beautiful love stories in the world"; van Buitenen 1975, 183–84: one of the earliest examples of the theme of love in separation. Of course there are contenders: the *Mbh* stories of Śakuntalā and Savitrī; Kālīdāsa's *Meghadūta*. Whatever one's favorite, no other *Mbh* or *Rām* story raises profound questions about love at such a pivotal juncture for India's epic heroes (except, perhaps, Rāma's hearing his own story from his sons before and after his abandonment of Sītā).

[8]I thank Velcheru Narayana Rao for bringing out this point, one that has since been made beautifully by Doniger (1999, 149–54, 157–63) in her comparison of the semiotics of reunion in *Nala* and the homecoming of Odysseus to Penelope in the *Odyssey*.

[9]Shulman follows Biardeau (1985, 3) on the Nala-*nara*-Nara equation (1994, 18 and n. 28),

when, with mixed joy and bitterness upon sensing Nala's return, she says, "Nala has been like a eunuch to me" (71.14). The "dark" *(śyāma)* and Śrī-like Damayantī is an image of Draupadī, who is the dark incarnation of Śrī.[10] Indeed, Draupadī can recognize herself not only physically in this heroine, but emotionally: for instance, when she hears Damayantī wondering whether it is her "impoverished share" or "ill fortune" *(mandabhāgya)* that makes her suffer.[11] And Vārṣṇeya, Nala's charioteer, is a homonym and mirror figure of Vārṣṇeya Kṛṣṇa, and thus, as Biardeau puts it, a "fugitive" figure of the avatāra (Biardeau 1985, 5–6, 8–9, 16–17, 31–32). Shulman ignores this last connection, while Biardeau rather surprisingly minimizes it.[12]

But Nala is also a king like Yudhiṣṭhira, and Arjuna is absent at *Nala*'s telling. The tale is primarily for the ears of Draupadī and Yudhiṣṭhira, and recalls—to us as it must to them—the dice match and Draupadī's outpourings of anger that build up to Yudhiṣṭhira's "complaint" and *Nala*'s telling. Nala does *not* bet Damayantī when he is crazed by the dice (cf. Biardeau 1984, 253, 266). This enables Damayantī to "take refuge" (57.16) in Vārṣṇeya as the rescuer of Nala's horses and chariots and their children. Nala does, however, wager her once he has obtained whatever self-knowledge has come to him with the "heart of the dice." Unlike Yudhiṣṭhira, he *wins* the final bet. This is all a powerful message for Yudhiṣṭhira, since it is he who wagered Draupadī as his final stake, and then could not, or would not, answer the famous question she posed as to whether he could have dharmically wagered her after he had bet and lost himself. Once Draupadī asks this question—which is not only about the "self" of King Dharma (Yudhiṣṭhira) but, as we shall see, about the "subtle" self or essence of dharma, which it is the function of the avatar to preserve—it hovers over the entire *Mahābhārata*, *Nala* included, since no one ever resolves it. Yudhiṣṭhira, as I will argue in chapter 7, is still trying to figure it out when he curses Dharma at the very end for

from which the rest readily flows. Cf. J. D. Smith 1992, 14–15, favoring a phallic sense of *Bṛhannalā* here ("she of the big prick"), of which more could be said (see Hiltebeitel 1980b, 155–56). But Smith invokes this meaning only to inveigh, rather contradictorily, against "'symbolic' interpretation" (see n. 3 above), with the effect of denying ambiguity.

[10]On Damayantī as *śyāma*, see Biardeau 1984, 264; 1985, 8, 32; as Śrī-like, 1984, 256, 259. Cf. Shulman 1994, 18. Damayantī is Śrī-like in hidden ways that require others' recognition (50.12 ["long-eyed like Śrī"] = 62.290*, line 4; 65.9).

[11]On this term, relating Śrī and Draupadī, see chaps. 2, § C and 4, § B. Cf. 5.8.35: Śalya reminds Yudhiṣṭhira that Draupadī's misfortune *(aśubham)* was like Damayantī's.

[12]As "effaced" (1985, 8) or "reduced" (16). This underestimation seems likely to have resulted from singling out the avataric dimensions of Nala (1984, 270; 1985, 24) and especially Damayantī (1985, 6–8, 6, 31–32) in the absence of a full dharmic and cosmic crisis that would require a real avatar of Viṣṇu. Doniger also ignores Vārṣṇeya (1999, 140–54).

confronting him with his last awful test: that of being ready to abandon his wife and brothers in hell, much as he had abandoned them to his demonic cousins by wagering them. So if Yudhiṣṭhira and Draupadī have a love story, it must take a long time to work out. *Nala* can only give them pause, hope, and, as Bṛhadaśva says, fewer complaints.

B. Nala's Possession

If love and dharma pose such long-term questions during the exile, questions of possession and "dispossession" are closer to hand. This point of intersection in *Nala* deserves a closer look.[13] I will discuss Nala's possession: his possession by Kali, "Discord," the demon of this age, the Kali Yuga, a "portion" of whom is also incarnated in the demonic Duryodhana, as it relates to this background.[14] More specifically, when Draupadī asks the question whether Yudhiṣṭhira had bet himself before betting her, it is the question of whether he possessed a self when he did so—or, if not, whether by implication he was possessed by something else. During the dice match Yudhiṣṭhira does not have the precise excuse of being possessed. But—much as in Draupadī cult dramas[15]—the scene of the dice match, which precedes her question, finds both Duryodhana (2.55.5; 60.1, 5) and Yudhiṣṭhira (58.18) drunk or crazed, *matta*. And during the whole time that the authorities in the gambling hall argue over Draupadī's question, from the moment it is asked of Yudhiṣṭhira, "he did not stir, as though he had lost consciousness, and made no reply . . . whether good or ill" (2.60.9). So if he is not possessed, he is *dispossessed* of wealth, loved ones, and language, and stripped of all that has up to now identified him. *Nala* seems to confront Yudhiṣṭhira with the fact that he does *not* have the excuse of demonic possession to explain his wager of his loved ones. Yet Yudhiṣṭhira must see himself in Nala, who also, as we shall see, falls silent during his dice play, "his senses gone."

[13]Biardeau puts "possession" in quotes, as if it were metaphoric (1984, 25, 262; 1985, 5–6, 8, 18); Shulman makes it rather abstract, linked with traversal of "identity boundaries" in an "axis of innerness" distinct from an an "axis of otherness" linking Nala and Damayantī (1994, 20–24). Note that Damayantī's big question to Nala when he emerges from possession is, "Who are you"—the "all-pervasive question addressed to [possessing] spirits" in Tamilnadu (Nabokov 2000, 7; see 78–85, 96, 105–8, 119, 132–33, 147–48, 172).

[14]Duryodhana is a "portion" of Kali (*kaleraṃśa*; 1.61.80a; 11.8.27c). Cf. 15.39.10: Vyāsa tells Gāndhārī that she should know him as Kali, Śakuni as Dvāpara, and the other Kauravas from Duḥśāsana on as incarnate Rākṣasas. See also chap. 4, n. 82. On demonic possession in the *Mbh* involving forms of the verb *ā-viś*, see 3.92.10–11 (Daityas and Dānavas possessed by Kali); 3.240.13 (Duryodhana's allies possessed by Dānavas); Hiltebeitel 1995b, 450, and below; F. Smith 1994.

[15]These portray the Pāṇḍavas and Kauravas during the dice match as "madmen" (*piccarkaḷ*); see Hiltebeitel 1988, 267–68, 273, 276, 443–48.

Nala has a rich stock of Indian possession tropes: possession as ownership, dicing, running wildly, the swing *(dolā)*, the flying horse. But the starting point is love, of whom Nala is, or "possesses," the very image *(mūrti)*: "Nala, tiger among men, with a form matchless on earth, was as if Love himself was possessing an image with form *(kandarpa iva rūpeṇa mūrtimān abhavat svayam)*" (50.14). When the gods see him approaching Damayantī's svayaṃvara, he looks "like Manmatha himself incarnate with the perfection of his beauty" *(sākṣādiva sthitaṃ mūrtyā manmathaṃ rūpasaṃpadā)* (51.26). Kandarpa and Manmatha are names for Kāma, the Indian Cupid. So Nala is love personified, enformed: all this, we now know, before Damayantī even sees him.

Then there is the intervention by one of the epic's most memorable talking animals, the gold-bedecked gander *(haṃsa)*. Unable to bear the desire in his heart, Nala retreats to the woods, and sees the haṃsa decked in gold, who says, "Within Damayantī's hearing I shall so speak of you that she will never think of any man *(puruṣam)* but you" (50.20).[16] Each of our principals is, in a sense, possessed by the haṃsa, but Damayantī only by the haṃsa, whereas Nala is also possessed by Kali, Dvāpara, the dice, and some *śakuna* birds. How does a haṃsa possess? We get some sense of this from the *Rāmāyaṇa*, when Rāma embraces his estranged brother Bharata after the latter comes to try to bring him from the forest: "Rāma drew his brother, who was dark *(śyāma)*, of eyes large as lotus petals, to him, and spoke with the voice of an amorous/intoxicated haṃsa" (*mattahaṃsasvara*; 2.104.15). If we accord the haṃsa its proverbial meaning of the bird that represents the higher flights of Brahmā as the highest transmigrating soul,[17] perhaps it "possesses" with the breathing sound of self-recognition—*so 'ham, so 'ham*, "I am this, I am this"—which, these epic scenes seem to suggest, is found through love of another. I am, of course, arguing that *Nala* is a text alive to both philosophers and lovers: Yudhiṣṭhira and Draupadī included.

Having heard the haṃsa's words, Damayantī is "no longer herself *(nasvasthā)* on account of Nala" (51.1)—dejected, sighing, "looking like a woman crazed" (*babhūvonmatta-darśanā*; 3). So taking her signs of madness as readiness for marriage, her father decides to hold her svayaṃvara: the "self-choice" ceremony that will allow her to choose her husband. When she first sees Nala, she still acts strangely. The words of the gander "consume me *(māṃ dahati)*. . . . If you reject me, I'll seek

[16]Damayantī later calls on this truth even while it is still unknown to her: accosted by a lecherous hunter who rescues her from a python, she calls upon the truth that she has never thought of anyone but Nala, and the hunter instantly self-combusts (60.34–38).

[17]See *Mbh* 12.288.12, cited in chap. 4 § D. Cf. Zimmer 1962, 47–50; Biardeau 1984, 251; 1985, 4, linking the haṃsa with Brahman and with other Brahman intercessors in *Nala*.

mercy from poison, Agni, water, or rope" (53.3–4). Note that the vocabulary of loss of self that introduces Damayantī is not, as with Nala, couched in the semantics of the ātman, but in a repetition of terms built on the prefixed possessive *sva*: "self" as what is, ultimately provisionally, "[one's] own" used as a pronominal adjective, as in *a-svasthām*, *na-svasthām*, "not self-standing," "not self-abiding" (51.1, 4, 5). Basically, in such usages Damayantī is "not herself" in the sense of not being in charge of herself, not possessing her (better) self, out of character as she wants to know herself. But she is entirely in character—in what Paul Ricoeur calls her *idem* self, the self of character as continuum (1992, 2–3, 113–26)—for her primary audience and readers.

Throughout *Nala*, there are only three places where Damayantī gets to "think of herself," or is "thought of," with reference to her reflexive self, her ātman—in Ricoeur's terms, her *ipse* self, a self held up to itself through constancy or promise (ibid., 265–71, 318). In each instance, this self of Damayantī's is defined in relation to her husband or her marital family. First, when she is being squeezed by a python, she even then "mourns Nala more than herself" (*ātmānam*; 60.21). Second, she tells the ascetics she meets after Nala has left her that if she doesn't find Nala soon, "I will yoke *myself* to a better world by abandoning my body" (61.84). Finally, Nala calls on her to remember that "women of family save themselves by themselves *(ātmānamātmanā)* and surely conquer heaven" (68.8). In echoing two famous verses from *Bhagavad Gītā* (3.43; 6.5), Nala's words leave no doubt that Damayantī has a self to save herself with: she is a *pativratā*, a woman whose "vow to her husband" defines a self through promise that always holds itself before her. In Doniger's terms, we are left with the gendered asymmetry of "his identity and her fidelity, the two qualities that are implicitly equated and essentialized: where he must prove who he is, she must prove that she is his."[18] These relatively few usages show that Damayantī's fidelity leaves her unendangered by such "loss of self" as Nala's, whose *ātman* is in danger of being possessed by, and submerged in, a demonic other.

Nala, meanwhile, must await news of Damayantī's svayaṃvara. When he receives it, he sets off, "his self undepressed *(adīnātmā)*, avowed to Damayantī" (3.51.25). The negative in "undepressed" warns of things to come. We may also take it as a signal that the term ātman as "self" is important, despite a century of efforts to undertranslate it by anything but its-"self."[19] From this "undepressed self," let us follow Nala through

[18]1999, 167; cf. 153, 163; again, Doniger is comparing Nala and Damayantī's reunion with that of Odysseus and Penelope.

[19]See the debate between Goldman 1976b, 470, and van Buitenen 1976, 472. *Ātman* can refer primarily to the "mind" or "body" in the Upaniṣads and epics, and is often easily

those points in the story where his ātman is specifically brought into question, taking our cue from Shulman, who suggests that to follow Nala's "axis of innerness (what goes on inside him)" involves tracking him through "an evolving series of partially overlapping self-images" in a text that articulates not only "the obvious and difficult question of whether two can ever be one, . . . but also the even more troubling and rooted problem of whether *one* can ever be one" (1994, 18).

Kali and Dvāpara arrive late for Damayantī's svayaṃvara (55.1–4). What does it mean that the demons who personify the two most deteriorating yugas, and the two lowest and losing dice throws, arrive late? Among other things, probably that events occur under the role of the dice, and are to take place under the sign of the "twilight"-time that is the interval between Dvāpara, "deuce," and Kali, "discord." This is, of course, the time of the primary audience and the story they inhabit. Moreover, the parting gods, who have given Nala important gifts and sanctioned his wedding, are presented as the four Lokapālas, regents of the four directions. Actually, only three of the conventional Lokapālas come: Indra, Varuṇa, and Yama. Agni replaces Kubera, with important repercussions (Biardeau 1984, 249, 251, 261; 1985, 2–3, 27). The gods of space thus yield to the powers of time, for a time. Yet when Kali says he wants to choose Damayantī and Indra laughs and says he has come too late, it is, to use an epic mode of speech, "as if" Kali's yuga has missed its turn, and, with Nala and Damayantī's marriage, a Kṛta ("Perfect") yuga can begin. Enraged, Kali announces that if Damayantī has chosen a man among the gods, she deserves to be punished (55.6). Kali is thus introduced by his desire and anger. The gods say they let her choose Nala themselves, and go to heaven. But Kali says to Dvāpara: "I cannot control my anger. I shall enter *(vatsyāmi)* him and unseat him from his kingdom, and he shall not have the pleasure of Bhīma's daughter. You must enter *(samāviśya)* the dice and give me assistance" (12–13).

This is one of the points where it has been misleading to view *Nala* and the *Mahābhārata* separately. According to Biardeau, in underplaying the larger epic's themes of dharmic and cosmic crisis, *Nala* leaves the figure of Kali adrift to "float a little" as a rather disembodied presence, while Dvāpara merely "seconds" him feebly and episodically. Although Kali still evokes the Kali Yuga and the worst dice throw, the crisis in *Nala* is not so great as to make him a demon (1984, 270; 1985, 4, 9). But it is not so easy to dismiss the demonic in a matter of possession.

translated as "soul." But for *Nala*, at least, one gains by tracing its primary sense of "self." Among the gains is an appreciation that what holds for "*Nala* as *Mbh*" holds also for *Mbh*: most clearly in the *Gītā*. *Ātman* may mean several things, but, from the Upaniṣads on, its meaning of "self" is probably always "in question."

Biardeau has cleverly detected that Ṛtuparṇa, who plays a vital role in *Nala* as king of Ayodhyā, is the story's only figure with an explicit Asuric trace. With his patronym Bhāṅgāsuri, "son of the Asura Bhaṅga," Ṛtuparṇa, who wants to marry Damayantī at her "second svayaṃvara," has an "Asuric ascendance." Although *Nala* never calls Kali or Puṣkara demons, their desire to marry Damayantī "suffices to place them in the Asura camp" (1984, 266–67). Given these insights, it is surprising that Biardeau relies only on the "explicit" for a contrast on this very point: in *Nala*, "only one person is marked as an Asura, Ṛtuparṇa: there to communicate the secret of dice to Nala, not to oppose him. In the epic, on the contrary, Kali and Dvāpara are Asuras, in close rapport with each other as maternal uncle and nephew" (1985, 4)—that is, incarnate in Śakuni and Duryodhana. Biardeau finds a "weakening" of the Asuric theme in *Nala*, which leaves Kali not only disembodied but with no "independent place in the society: he 'possesses' Nala, that is his only 'status'" (ibid.). But this accounts only for human society. Indra and other gods see Kali and Dvāpara coming to Damayantī's wedding. Kali will also communicate with Puṣkara. We know Kali immediately by his anger, and Dvāpara by his ability to "enter" (or "possess": *sam-ā-viś*) the dice at Kali's behest. In *Nala*, one yuga demon possesses the dice and the other possesses the king. Kali's status as possessor of Nala is hardly negligible if we consider that it is the connivance of Kali incarnate in Duryodhana with Dvāpara incarnate in Śakuni that raises the stakes to a madness bordering on possession in the central epic dice match. *Nala* does not extract itself from the *Mahābhārata* to "weaken" Dvāpara and Kali's demonic status, or let us forget that Śakuni and Duryodhana incarnate these same yuga demons.[20] Indeed, the parallel allows readers to realize that if Yudhiṣṭhira sees himself in Nala possessed by Kali, he was also like Duryodhana in being "possessed" by the dice at the main epic dice match.

Having made his covenant with Dvāpara, then, Kali waits twelve years, evoking in miniature the twelve thousand years of a Kali yuga (including twilights), and the twelve-year exile of the Pāṇḍavas and their twelve-month period incognito, during each of which Duryodhana—Kali incarnate—plots their destruction. Finally, Kali sees "his interval" *(antaram)* when Nala forgets to purify his feet after urinating before his "twilight" rites. Kali now "possesses" Nala *(āviśat, samāviśya)*. Then he approaches Puṣkara and tells him to challenge Nala to dice, promising that with his help Puṣkara will win. As the game unfolds, Damayantī looks on. "Being possessed by Kali in the game *(āviṣṭāḥ kalinā*

[20]Of the four yugas, only the last two have yuga demons. They would seem to draw time toward negativity in forms that center on deceit (as with Śakuni) and "discord" (the meaning of *kali*). Cf. Hiltebeitel 1999a, 253–83, on Kali's collusions with Kṛṣṇa in the *Ālhā*.

dyūte)"—Kali's possession takes effect in the dicing—Nala loses gold, wagons, clothes, etc. "Crazed by the thrill of the dice *(akṣamadasaṃmattam)*," he is beyond help from friends, who try to restrain him while he is "witlessly gambling" *(divyamānam acetasam)*. Townspeople and ministers come, but cannot stop the "sick" *(āturam)* king. His charioteer—one soon learns that this is Vārṣṇeya—tells Damayantī to remind him of his royal responsibilities. Grief-stricken, she tells him he should go see the citizens and ministers at the gate, who are "occupied with devotion to the king *(rāja bhakti puraskṛtaḥ)*."[21] Nala, possessed by Kali *(āviṣṭaḥ kalinā)*, says nothing. The wellwishers say, "He is lost," and dejectedly go home. It goes on many months, and Nala keeps losing (56).

Seeing Nala's wits gone *(gatacetasam)* in the game, as one maddened, but unmaddened herself *(unmattavad anunmattā)*, possessed of fear and grief *(bhayaśokamāviṣṭā)*,[22] Damayantī calls on her nurse Bṛhatsenā to bring Nala's councilors. But now, seeing Nala unwelcoming of the people, and that the dice remain hostile to him, she turns again to Bṛhatsenā and says, "Go once more and bring Vārṣṇeya the charioteer here on Nala's orders *(nalaśāsanāt)*." Damayantī speaks gently to Vārṣṇeya, "knowing time and place, and that the time had come" *(deśakālajñā prāptakālam*; 57.10–11).[23] Her knowledge of time must include at some unknowing level that Dvāpara and Kali are at play in the dice match. It is time to respond. She calls on Vārṣṇeya, and asks his aid now that the dice are in Puṣkara's power. Since Nala does not heed my word, she says, "I have come to you for refuge, charioteer, please do as I ask" (*śaranaṃ tvām prapannāsmi sārathe kuru madvacaḥ*; 15ef). She tells him to take Nala's horses, chariot, and their twins to her parents in Vidarbha. "You may stay there, or go elsewhere" (18). Echoing the epithet Kṛṣṇa Pārthasārathi for Kṛṣṇa as charioteer *(sārathi)* of Arjuna (Biardeau 1985, 6), *Vārṣṇeyo Nalasārathiḥ* (57.19b) does as she bids, and goes to Vidarbha, where he leaves the twins, chariot, and horses with Damayantī's parents. Then he goes on to enter the services of the aforementioned Ṛtuparṇa of Ayodhyā, as *his* charioteer (22–23).

Let us pause for a moment to take stock of what our primary audience is hearing. Damayantī knows time and place. So Damayantī intercedes

[21] Is it significant that Vārṣṇeya prompts this rāja-bhakti?

[22] *Ā-viś*, "to enter, to possess," also describes Damayantī as she calls Nala to his final self-recognition: seeing him at last, "she was possessed by a bitter anguish" (*tīvraśokasamāviṣṭā*; 74.7).

[23] This stress on Damayantī's "knowledge," not to mention what she does with it, undercuts Biardeau's insistence that she typifies a heroine's representation of unconscious matter, blind ignorance, and illusion (1984, 259–64, 268; 1985, 6–8, 13–16, 19, 29). I leave this subject for chap. 7, § C to focus the discussion there on Draupadī.

after Nala has been possessed and all but lost himself, but before he loses his most personal treasures. Draupadī, not long ago, has interceded after Yudhiṣṭhira lost his treasures, and asked whether, in wagering himself before he wagered her, his losing himself nullified his wager of her. In both cases, the heroines save the heroes and themselves, but both also "take refuge" in Vārṣṇeya: in one case, Vārṣṇeya Kṛṣṇa, soon to be charioteer of Arjuna, who comes to rescue Draupadī and the Pāṇḍavas by preventing Draupadī's disrobing; in the other, Vārṣṇeya Nalasārathi, "charioteer of Nala," who rescues Damayantī and Nala by saving their children, and probably the horses and chariot that will eventually allow Nala to regain his kingdom. If our primary audience catches some of this, it provokes them to consider a momentous difference. Unlike Yudhiṣṭhira, Nala bets neither himself nor, at this point, his wife. "After Vārṣṇeya's departure," says *Nala*, "Nala kept gambling; and Puṣkara took the kingdom and whatever wealth Nala had left." Puṣkara laughs and says, "Let the game go on, what do you have left to stake? Only Damayantī remains to you *(śiṣṭā te damayantyekā)*, I have taken everything else. Well, stake Damayantī." Hearing this, Nala's "heart was riven with rage and he made no reply." "Gripped by fury, he glanced at Puṣkara and threw down all the jewels on his body" (58.1–5). What if Yudhiṣṭhira had done the same . . . ?

The game over, Nala and Damayantī go forth from the city, each wearing a single garment. They camp for three nights living only on water, the people unable to treat them hospitably because of Puṣkara's malicious interdiction. Starving, Nala sees some "śakuna birds with feathers that seemed made of gold." Hoping to eat them, he casts his single robe over them, but the birds grip it, take it into the sky, and cry out, "We are the dice, fool, and we came to take your robe too, for it did not please us to see that you still went clothed." "Seeing the dice gone and himself left naked *(ātmānaṃ ca vivāsasam)*," Nala says to Damayantī, "they through whose fury I was unseated from my kingdom"—that is, the dice—"have become śakuna birds and flown off with my robe. I have become highly unstable, suffering, my mind gone" *(vaiṣamyam paramam prāpto duḥkhito gatacetanaḥ)* (58.6–19).[24]

This is the second key point describing Nala's ātman: it is naked, unclothed—*vivāsasam*. The deepest resonance for readers is with *Bhagavad Gītā* 2.22: the self puts on garments from life to life; unclothed, it is either between earthly identities or liberated. But the *Gītā* comes later in the epic. Our primary audience has a better chance to be reminded of the dice match. The dice in the form of golden-seeming

[24]Nala becomes both *gatacetasa* and *gatacetana*, with perhaps not much to distinguish them; I translate them respectively as "his wits gone" and "his mind gone."

śakunas, that is, birds of ill omen playing dice, recall Śakuni, who is named after the same bird and who, like the dice, is an incarnation of Dvāpara, who plays dice against Yudhiṣṭhira. In both cases, it is Dvāpara and Kali incarnate who strip the kings—Yudhiṣṭhira and Nala—to their naked selves.[25] Nala thus sees himself/his self naked, and even recognizes his increasing derangement; but he never has to lose his self as wager. His loss of self occurs in an area that Yudhiṣṭhira, Bhīma, and Draupadī must ponder: the area of emotively expressed love described in Nala's rage at his brother's challenge to wager Damayantī. Nala's physical expression of outrage is reminiscent not of Yudhiṣṭhira at the dice match but Bhīma, who reacts to the staking of Draupadī by wishing to burn Yudhiṣṭhira's arms for letting Draupadī be treated worse than a whore (2.61.1–6).

Nala now encourages Damayantī to take a path to Vidarbha, where her parents live, or elsewhere (3.58.19–22). But Damayantī refuses to go without him, to leave him: "My heart trembles," she says, "and my limbs all weaken when I reflect over and over on your intention *(saṃkalpam)*. . . . How could I desert you in the unpeopled forest, when you have lost your wealth, and are unclothed, hungry, and tired? . . . Physicians know of no medicines in all sorrows that equal a wife—this is *truth* I tell you" (25–27). Nala agrees and reassures her: "Why do you fear, I'd abandon myself *(ātmānam)* before abandoning you, innocent wife" (29). As Shulman notes, Nala has already begun to register (at 58.19) a series of *viṣama/vaiṣamya* states (cf. 59.2; 68.3,4): "not-same, uneven" states—that is, painful dislocations (1994, 14–15). Damayantī asks why, if he doesn't want to leave her here, he points out the way to Vidarbha? "I know, king, that you should not desert me, but with your wits deranged *(cetasā tvapapakṛṣṭena)* you might" (58.31). If you want me to go to Vidarbha, she says, let us go together; my father, the king, will honor you. Nala says he could go there recognized as a king, but not *viṣamasthaḥ*, on such "uneven standing" (59.1–2).[26]

So, "covered by half her garment," "the two covered between them with one robe" *(tāv ekavastrasaṃvītāu)*, they wander about wearied, hungry, till they come to a "sabhā" or "hall" (59.4–5). This *sabhā* in an "empty forest" (*vane śūnye*; 25), which van Buitenen tries to imagine as a "lodge" (1975, 333), perhaps for wayfarers, is rather, as Biardeau perceives (1985, 19), a daring incongruity in the poets' play of correspondences with the Kaurava dice match, since it is in the Kaurava sabhā that Yudhiṣṭhira has abandoned Draupadī, as Nala is about to do

[25]Cf. Biardeau 1984, 258; 1985, 18–19 on these correspondences.
[26]Peile 1881, 98: "standing on difficult ground."

to Damayantī. The couple sits there on the ground—Nala "naked, dirty, hairless,[27] covered with dust" (59.6)—and Damayantī falls asleep.

But Nala cannot sleep, "for his *cittātmā* was churned up by grief" *(śokonmathitacittātmā)*. This anguished churning of this "mental self," or perhaps "self-understanding," is vividly described. He broods, saying maybe she'd be better off without him and find her way back to her family. He thinks it over, back and forth, and decides it would be better *for her* should he leave her. He cuts the saree in two with a sword he finds in a corner of the hall. He leaves her sleeping and runs away, his "mind gone *(gatacetanaḥ)*" but "his heart still bound" *(nibaddha-hṛdayaḥ)*. He goes back to the hall, looks at her, and weeps. He sees his own madness in her—"clothed here in a cut-up skirt, she of happy laughter and beautiful hips, as though she were crazed"[28]—as though *she* were crazed. And he asks how she will be when she wakes up in the terrible forest. "He went and went, but came back to the hall every time, drawn forth by Kali, drawn back by his love *(sauhṛdena)*"—"drawn" *(ākarṣa)*, another term linked with black magic and possession portraying Kali as a kind of mesmerist,[29] compelling Nala by a power of fascination, "drawing" Nala "toward" him, pulling apart two selves that in Nala's heart are one: "The suffering man's heart was torn in two *(dvidheva hṛdayaṃ tasya duḥkhitasyābhavat tadā)*"; "like a swing *(dolā)*" it kept going back and forth. Then, "drawn forth by Kali, bewildered, Nala ran forth *(prādravat)*," deserting his sleeping wife. "Lost of self *(nāṣṭātmā)*, touched *(spṛṣṭa)* by Kali, not recognizing this or that, grieved, the king went, abandoning his wife in the empty forest" (59.23–25).

So Nala is on his own. But not quite. As Shulman has put it, Nala is "not even aware, yet, of the alien presence that has taken over part of his inner existence" (1994, 14). This is Kali's most intense possession. Nala's ātman has been naked but not lost, it appears, so long as he has Damayantī with him, and the garment, even the half-garment-the half of *her* garment—that has bound what remains of their twoness into one. But now that ampler self of his is lost, destroyed *(naṣṭātmā)*, as Kali pulls and draws him away (both *ā-kṛṣ* and *apa-kṛṣ*) by his actual "touch."

Now for Damayantī, I limit discussion to the states that describe hers as a madness mirroring Nala's, but without such "loss of self." She wakes up, runs about in all directions; crazed (*unmattā*; 60.18), she cries, "Ah I am lost and dead" (*hā hatāsmi vinaṣṭāsmi*; 60.3), and—in

[27] *Vikaca*: has Nala had to shave his head? Alternately, some manuscripts have *vikaṭa*, "without a mat" (see, e.g., Kinjawadekar 1929–33, 3:101, for 3.62.6a).

[28] 3.59.20: *iyaṃ vastrāvakartena saṃvītā cāruhāsinī unmatteva varārohā.*

[29] See Türstig 1985, 104, on *ākarṣaṇa*, "attracting persons," as a form of *vaśya*, "subjugating, bringing others under control."

anticipation of the final scenes of Nala's self-recovery—calls, "Show yourself, lord" (*darśayātmānam īśvara*; 7). "Burning with grief," she worries about him, and curses Kali, not knowing him but by his effects: "Whatever creature it is by whose curse the suffering Nala finds more suffering, that creature shall reap even greater grief than his" (15–16). When she comes upon a caravan, she looks "like a mad woman afflicted with grief, covered in half a garment, thin, pale, dirty, her hair overlain with dust" (61.110). After the caravan is destroyed, she travels on with some Brahmans and enters a city of the king of Cedi (roughly, Bundelkhand) in a half-skirt, "pale, wan, loose-haired *(muktakeśī)*, unwashed, walking like a crazed woman" (*unmattāmiva*; 62.19)—as Draupadī was "loose-haired" when she was dragged into the dicing hall (2.70.9; 71.18, 20). The king's mother questions Damayantī, who says she is a *sairandhrī* "hairdresser" (26)—now anticipating Draupadī's future disguise,[30] whose husband, though of countless qualities, has lost his wits *(gatacetasam)* to gambling (29-31). The king's mother assigns Damayantī to her daughter Sunandā (43).

Meanwhile, when Nala deserts Damayantī, he comes upon a big forest fire, hears the loud cry of a creature calling him, enters the center of the fire using a power bestowed on him by Agni, and sees a Snake-King lying in coils, trembling, looking at Nala with folded hands. This talking snake, Karkoṭaka, cannot move from this place, having been cursed by an innocent Brahman Ṛṣi whom he had captured. Nala tells Karkoṭaka not to fear, and the snake becomes light—the size of a thumb, so that Nala can pick him up (3.63.1–8). As Biardeau remarks, "the account borrows from the Upaniṣads the image of the 'measure of the thumb' that is applied to the immortal and luminous being present in the heart of each individual" (1984, 262; cf. Feller 2000, 161). In evoking the indestructible soul, this thumb-sized snake is like the gander: complementary bird and snake images of the soul,[31] each working mysteriously, as it were from opposite ends, to unite Nala and Damayantī. From its cosmic grandeur as the haṃsa that brings two selves together, the self is reduced to its minimum in the single heart, all but lost from the love of is partner.

Karkoṭaka, thumb-size in Nala's hand, now tells him to walk on, count his steps, and expect a favor. The snake, who must be devious to impart this favor, bites Nala on the tenth step, responding to the word "ten" *(daśa)* as if it meant "bite" *(daśa)*, and Nala's form instantly changes.

[30]As Biardeau observes, Damayantī's *sairandhrī* disguise is less motivated than Draupadī's, suggesting it is again the "mirror effects" that count (1984, 256–57, 261, 267; 1985, 31).
[31]On bird-snake oppositions in the *Mbh*, see chap. 3, n. 92; Biardeau CR 89 (1980–81), 236–37; O'Flaherty 1986, 17–23, 37–38; Hiltebeitel 1995a, 448–51.

Astonished, he now sees the snake in his prior shape, and sees "himself deformed *(ātmānaṃ vikṛtam)*," and, as we later learn, dwarfish.[32] Karkoṭaka says he has changed Nala so that people will not know him, and that the one who has caused all Nala's troubles "will henceforth dwell in you and hurt from my poison." Karkoṭaka's bite thus neutralizes Kali's poison. Karkoṭaka then tells Nala to go disguised as a charioteer named Bāhuka to King Ṛtuparṇa of Ayodhyā, who will teach Nala what he needs to know: "When you become a knower of dice, you will be united with fortune and rejoin your wife." He gives Nala a pair of celestial clothes to use whenever he wants back his appearance, and vanishes (63.12–24). Although Kali now "dwells" *(ni-vas)* in Nala, he no longer "possesses" *(ā-viś)* him. Nala is no longer maddened, feeling the pain caused by Kali; but he is now deformed, and for a duration that he can himself determine. Nala has yet to recover himself fully, but Kali is under constraint.

After ten days, Nala goes to Ṛtuparṇa and introduces himself as Bāhuka, an incomparable charioteer and cook. Ṛtuparṇa employs him, and by now also has Vārṣṇeya and a Brahman named Jīvala working for him. Nala settles down in Ayodhyā with these two, and in the evening recites a verse: the first of the riddles by which his hiddenness eventually becomes known. For this first riddle, all we need note is that it is Jīvala, not Vārṣṇeya, who asks what woman Nala always grieves for. Presumably Vārṣṇeya, were he to ask, would have to figure things out too soon, since he has not only been Damayantī's confidante, but her "refuge." Nala answers Jīvala: "Some nitwit, a fool, got separated from his woman, and now, of foolish self,[33] runs around in misery day and night, remembering his grief over her, singing one couplet" (64.1–14). Regarding this "foolish" ātman, Nala has once again become self-referential.

Once Damayantī is found and goes home to her parents, she convinces her father to send out a Brahman messenger to look for Nala. From here, riddles get carried back and forth between the two, first enabling Damayantī to find Nala, and finally enabling Nala to regain himself. Part of the first such riddle revolves around something Nala would remember, since Damayantī quotes him on an important point: "Renowned, wise, high born, and with the capacity to compassionately cry out *(sānukrośaḥ)*, you have turned uncompassionate *(niranukrośaḥ)*; I fear my portion would perish. Great archer, have pity *(dayām)* on me, bull among men. Noncruelty *(ānṛśaṃsya)* is the highest dharma, so indeed I heard from

[32]68.6: deformed *(virūpa)* and dwarfish or short *(hrasva)*.

[33]*Mandātmā*: or, "of impoverished self," on a contrastive analogy with *mandabhāgya* for heroines? See n. 11 above.

you!" (67.14–15). The point, as we have seen, is also important to Yudhiṣṭhira, though we have still not yet seen how important. Let us appreciate again the link observed by Lath between *anukrośa* and *ānṛśaṃsya*, and, within *Nala*, a suggestive symmetry in *Nala*'s only two usages of the related term *nṛśaṃsa*, one before and one after Damayantī's message. Damayantī and Nala each use the same phrase, "Alas, what cruelty!" *(nṛśaṃsam bata)*, to cry out to the absent partner: Damayantī when she thinks Nala, who has really left her, must be hiding in the bushes (60.9); Nala when he thinks Damayantī is seriously planning the infidelity of a second marriage (69.5).[34] *Nala* centers the question of noncruelty around the little cruelties of intimacy and, once again, around the gendered opposition of male identity and female fidelity (see n. 18).

Just as Damayantī's first coded message is meant not only for Nala's ears but Yudhiṣṭhira's, so Nala's first coded reply is meant not only for Damayantī's. He concludes: Knowing her husband's trials and afflictions, "consumed with anxieties, a dark woman could not anger *(ādhibhir dahyamānasya śyāmā na kroddhum arhati)*. . . . Having seen her husband without *śrī*, an unseated king, a dark woman could not anger *(bhrastarājyaṃ śriyā hīnaṃ syāmā na kroddhum arhati)*" (68.10–11). Nala's words to Damayantī are the storyteller Bṛhadaśva's words to Draupadī.

Damayantī directs her next message to Ṛtuparṇa, inviting this Ayodhyā king of demonic descent to join the suitors coming to her second svayaṃvara. The announced svayaṃvara is a lover's lie. She plans no such thing, and has worked out the whole plan with her mother while keeping her father in the dark as to her real intentions (68.13–20). Damayantī has just had her mother's help also in getting her father to send out the first messengers (67.1–6). And the mother of the Cedi king who sheltered her in her sairandhrī disguise turned out to be her maternal aunt (66.11–14). Van Buitenen is surely right that Damayantī's prominence as a daughter—she is the favored older sister of three brothers (50.9)—and access to sympathetic maternal kin shows that the story engages a "woman's point of view" (1975, 183–84). How poignant, moreover, from the position of the first woman listener, Draupadī, who is born the byproduct of a ritual meant only to produce a son,[35] whose

[34]The phrase (even reversing the terms) is used only four other times in *Mbh*, one of them familiar: by Baka Dālbhya, describing Dhṛtarāṣṭra's cruel speech offering him dead cows (9.40.9; see chap. 3, § D). Cf. 3.119.12 (Balarāma to Kṛṣṇa after Dhṛtarāṣṭra and his sons' treacheries at the dice match); 3.261.32 (Bharata, decrying his mother Kaikeyī's perfidy); and 7.118.4 (Bhuriśravas, when his arm has been cut off by Arjuna from an unseen position). Only Damayantī and Nala address the phrase to a spouse.

[35]Cf. Biardeau 1984, 250, and above, chap. 5, § A.

mother is peripheralized and unnamed, and who has no access to female relatives anywhere, so far as the epic informs us—especially during her forest trials surrounded entirely by men.

Damayantī says if Ṛtuparṇa wants to make it, he must travel the hundred yojanas in a day, hoping this will induce him to order his charioteer Bāhuka, whom she now suspects to be Nala, to take the reins. When Nala hears of it, and when he thinks of Damayantī "cruelly" contemplating remarriage, he reflects, vascillates, blames her and himself, not knowing, swings again emotionally but is not swayed. Knowing she wouldn't remarry, especially since she has the children, he gives Ṛtuparṇa his word to get him there in a day and readies the horses.

Then something superfluous happens: "Then that best of men, illustrious king Nala, O king, eased the spirited, powerful horses, controlling them with his reins, and lifting the charioteer Vārṣṇeya *(sūtamāropya vārṣṇeyam)*, set out with great speed" (69.19–20). There is no reason for Vārṣṇeya to be on this chariot unless it be to remind us of Kṛṣṇa. Vārṣṇeya's presence there is framed not only by this beginning, but by the following ending, when Damayantī, having heard the telling sound of Nala's horses entering Vidarbha, "almost unconsciously" *(naṣṭasaṃjñeva)* mounts the palace stairs, and sees Ṛtuparṇa together with Vārṣṇeya and Bāhuka still on the chariot: "Then Vārṣṇeya and Bāhuka, descending the superb chariot, unyoked the horses and secured the chariot" (71.18). The superfluity is again striking: Why two charioteers for a job that can only be done by one? Though the usage of the verb *ava-tṛ*, as in *avatāra*, is conventional for getting down from a chariot, the singling out of Vārṣṇeya by the phrase *avatīrya vārṣṇeyo* suggests an accentuation of Vārṣṇeya's role as a double of Kṛṣṇa, who "descends" as avatar and drives Arjuna's chariot.[36] The sound of the horses, which draws Damayantī "almost unconsciously" to the palace stairs, reminds us that the last time she saw Vārṣṇeya was when she acted out of her "knowledge of time and place" to send him off as her "refuge" with the children, horses, and chariot. Damayantī is being reawakened to something that would seem to have made her blink.

Lest we get ahead of ourselves, however, let us appreciate that the journey has been as momentous as the arrival, since it is on this journey, in the company of the superfluously mounting and descending Vārṣṇeya, that Nala is finally fully dispossessed of Kali. The speed of the horses

[36]It is as if the poets want to give only this barest hint, having Bāhuka's descent share the verb with Vārṣṇeya in this verse, and having Bāhuka and Ṛtuparṇa likewise "descend" alone from chariots just before (70.20) and after (71.19) this. See chap. 3, n. 56, on avatar and allusion, and recall 9.53.33 (cited in chap. 4, § B, p. 145), where Balarāma approaches Kurukṣetra, "descending *(avatīryā)* from . . . Plakṣa Prasravaṇa."

bewilders and astounds Ṛtuparṇa, but has a different effect on Vārṣṇeya: when he "heard the roar of the chariot and saw the driver's control of the horses, he wondered" (69.23); and, having thought it through, he is convinced, in suitably convoluted but revealing terms, that Bāhuka must be Nala: "Men of great ātman," he says, "roam the earth in disguise when they have been yoked by fated decree and scripture-spoken disfigurements."[37] It is thus Vārṣṇeya's function to be the first, after Damayantī, to recognize Nala, and the very first to do so in his company, while on the way to Damayantī's second svayaṃvara—just as it is one of Kṛṣṇa's functions, his first in the *Mahābhārata*, to be the first to recognize Arjuna at Draupadī's svayaṃvara.[38] Vārṣṇeya recognizes Bāhuka-Nala as *mahātman*, a "great self," evoking for readers Kṛṣṇa and Arjuna on the chariot in the *Gītā*, and also Arjuna's disguise as "the great Nalā."

Meanwhile, both Vārṣṇeya and Ṛtuparṇa enjoy the ride until Ṛtuparṇa realizes that his shoulder cloth has fallen. Ṛtuparṇa tells Nala to stop so that Vārṣṇeya can retrieve it. Nala says it is four or five miles—a yojana—back. Ṛtuparṇa then sees a certain tree, a *bibhītaka*, whose nuts are used in the ancient Indian dice game, and tells Nala to observe his extraordinary skill in counting its nuts and leaves. Nala wants to check Ṛtuparṇa's count, and says, "Go on, with Vārṣṇeya as charioteer *(yāhi vārṣṇeyasārathiḥ)*." Is Nala still possessed? He suddenly seems to have forgotten Damayantī! Is this Kali's last stirring inside him? Ṛtuparṇa insists: "It's on account of you I have hopes of reaching Vidarbha. I take refuge in you" (70.17c)—the same words Damayantī had earlier for Vārṣṇeya.[39] Bāhuka persists in counting, and the king finally agrees to wait. Astonished, Nala gets the same exact count, and wants to know the king's counting "magic" *(vidyā)*. Ṛtuparṇa answers: "Know that I know the heart of the dice" *(akṣahṛdayam)*. Bāhuka offers to exchange his

[37]3.69.29: *pracchannā hi mahātmānaś caranti pṛthivīm imām/ daivena vidhinā yuktāḥ śāstroktaiśca virūpaṇaiḥ.*

[38]Hiltebeitel [1976] 1990, 83. Cf. Biardeau 1984, 266–69; 1985, 17, 31, on the interreferentiality of the multiple dice games (including Yudhiṣṭhira's dicing in Matsya) in *Nala* and the *Mbh*. Note also that Śiva's curse of Śrī and the former Indras follows the interruption of his dice game with Pārvatī (1.189.9–17).

[39]In a third instance found only in Northern texts (3.330*), when Nala now wants to curse Kali, Kali also "takes refuge" *(śaraṇaṃ tvām prapanno 'smi)* in him—using the same words as Damayantī when she takes refuge in Vārṣṇeya and as Ṛtuparṇa when he takes refuge in Nala (Biardeau 1984, 265). Biardeau shows that such cumulative bhakti phrases and motifs in *Nala* resonate within the *Mbh* (1984, 249, 252; 1985, 25–26); moreover, Nala gives pardon to Kali and fearlessness to Karkoṭaka "as if he were the supreme deity of bhakti" (1985, 262). Thus both Vārṣṇeya and Nala bestow "refuge"; as Pollock demonstrates, not only do avatars liberate, but kings (1991, 50–51, 71–74; cf. Biardeau 1984, 257, 261–62, 272). Indeed, in Kali's case, the "fugitive figure of the avatāra" is present with Nala.

knowledge of the "heart of horsemanship" for Ṛtuparṇa's "heart of the dice." Ṛtuparṇa eagerly agrees, and gives Bahuka what he wants right then (69.33–70.26).

As soon as Nala learns the heart of the dice, Kali exits from his body, along with the vomit of Karkoṭaka's bitter poison and the burning fire of Damayantī's curse of whoever possessed Nala, i.e., Kali. Emaciated by Kali, Nala "had for a long time been *anātmavān*"—"one without a self," "not self-possessed" (70.27–28). Meanwhile Kali, "himself freed *(vimuktātmā)* from that poison, resumed his own form" (70.29). Here at last the two selves—possessor and possessed—are disengaged. Kali now enters the bibhītaka tree, which, like the dicing nuts that come from it, will henceforth be "inauspicious due to its association with Kali." Nala, his fever gone "now that Kali had disappeared, . . . sped the flying horses on with a joyful inner self *(prahṛṣṭenāntarātmanā)*"—even though he was still "disunited from his own body" (70.27–39).

Once Nala arrives in Vidarbha's capital, and Damayantī senses that it is he, she sends her maid Keśinī to test Bāhuka with part of the first message he had responded to earlier. But before she poses Damayantī's riddle, Keśinī poses a puzzle of her own, which is an important piece of the textual puzzle. Keśinī, whose name means "the hair-lady" or perhaps "the Coiffured," is a double for Damayantī, who, as Draupadī will be, has been disguised as a hairdresser-maid or *sairandhrī* herself. Only Keśinī can ask the question and retain the mystery, since Damayantī already knows the *overt* answer herself. Keśinī asks: "This third (man) in your party, where does he come from and whose is he? And whose are you, and how is it that this work fell on you?" (73.10). She clearly recognizes Vārṣṇeya as a charioteer, but does not know him personally (as Damayantī does), and is thus puzzled not only as to why Nala drove, but why two charioteers! Once Nala replies that Vārṣṇeya was Nala's charioteer, and that he himself is Ṛtuparṇa's, Keśinī asks further, "Does Vārṣṇeya know where King Nala has gone? Has he said anything in your presence?"

Here at last Nala replies definitely—he begins to tell his own story—about his ātman: Vārṣṇeya, he says, "left the two children of that Nala of inauspicious karma here, and then went off as he wished. He does not know Nala. And no other man *(puruṣa)* knows Nala, good woman. The king moves hidden in this world, his form lost *(naṣṭarūpo)*. The self *(ātmā)*[40] surely knows Nala and she who is nearest him. For there are no signs *(liṅgāni)* that betray Nala."[41]

[40]In the nominative. That is, the sentence's subject is Nala's self.

[41]72.14–16; there is a suggestive juxtaposition here in the usages of the terms *puruṣa*, which only Nala knows, perhaps suggesting a Sāṃkhya isolation of puruṣa, and ātman, which

Here we have some crucial phrasing. First, *Nala*, in its play here and elsewhere on "signs," provides Doniger with another rich point of comparison with the reunion story of Odysseus and Penelope (1999, 135–72). Damayantī and Penelope are not figures through whom something feminine is signified (land, prosperity, the prize or cause of war, etc.) but semiotically talented women who give, exchange, and read signs. That is, they are women who sense, know, and test their men by being signifiers themselves. Here again we should not forget that Draupadī and Yudhiṣṭhira are listening. Second, Nala shows in his answer that he now sees himself, to date, through three pairs of eyes: Vārṣṇeya's, his own, and Damayantī's.

In saying that Vārṣṇeya does not know him, Nala says something untrue, but still true to his knowledge. Vārṣṇeya does know him, and is, I have argued, the hidden avataric presence and double who has recognized the "hidden king." Indeed, as the one *puruṣa* who knows Nala unbenownst to Nala, Vārṣṇeya looks like a *puruṣa* not just in the sense of "man" (as just translated) but in that of the "soul" as "witness" *(sakṣin)*—the witnessing double so nearly concealed by his seeming superfluity in the text.

Second, Nala now recognizes the autonomy of his own self: that his self is not Nala who knows himself, but the self that knows Nala *(ātmaiva hi nalaṃ vetti)*. It is in this vein that he will finally be able to make his troubling disclaimer to the weeping Damayantī at his moment of anagnorisis to her: "That my kingdom was lost I myself was not its doer; that was done by Kali, timid one, as also that I abandoned you" (74.16). Nala's disclaimer—*nāhaṃ tatkṛtavān svayam*: as van Buitenen and Shulman put it, "it was not my own fault"[42]—is consonant with the wisdom of the dharmic hunter of Mithilā: "Having committed a sin, a man should think, 'Not I!'"[43] These disavowals are troubling, perhaps because they are meant to be: like Arjuna's hearing from Kṛṣṇa that the self is neither slayer nor slain in the *Bhagavad Gītā*. They work for Arjuna, who isn't listening here; but not for Yudhiṣṭhira, who is.[44]

Third, regarding Damayantī, Nala combines his own reflexive self-knowledge with her ability to recognize it: "The self surely knows Nala

knows itself. Cf. the promise of the golden gander, image of the ātman, that Damayantī "will never think of any man *(puruṣam)* but you" (50.20).

[42]See Shulman's fine discussion (1994, 8–11, 26–27), and van Buitenen 1975, 359.

[43]3.198.51ab: *pāpaṃ kṛtvā hi manyeta nāham asmīti puruṣaḥ*; cf. chap. 5, § D on the dharmic hunter; also 13.1: a talking snake bites a boy, but it is neither his fault, nor that of Death (Mṛtyu) or Time (Kāla), but the boy's own karma. On commitment to karma—not only a child's, but that of a child in a previous life—as the bottom-line explanation for suffering, see the Aṇīmāṇḍavya story (chap. 5, § B).

[44]See chap. 2, § C.31, and nn. 144 and 204.

(ātmaiva hi nalaṃ vetti) and she who is continuous with it" *(yā cāsya tadanantarā)"—tadanantarā*: "she who is next to it," "she who has no interior apart from it."[45] As Peile remarks, almost wistfully, "This next to self (ātman) is apparently buddhi" (1881, 213).[46] This might sound like she is nothing without him, but the story, like the philosophical implications, suggests just the opposite. In any event, the self that knows Nala and the self that Damayantī knows is one self which knows itself as one-another, yet one in which the two selves are also not quite altogether different or the same. Reuniting what has been riven, recalling the two selves made one by the gander, Nala now recognizes that there is "no interior," "nothing between," the self that knows Nala and the Damayantī who knows that self. Yet here, as distinct from what he says of Vārṣṇeya, Nala knows that he is known. Thus he also couches a truth in an untruth. Unbeknownst to him another male knows him. But of *she* who knows him—that is, more precisely, who knows the self that knows him—he can say there are no signs that betray Nala *except* those that can be known by her.

C. Further Prismatics

So, who knows Nala? And what might *Nala*'s primary audience know about themselves from hearing it? Philosophically, the point seems to be that, if only the self knows Nala, each self must know *Nala* in itself, himself, or herself.[47] Textually, the game of signs, echoes, and mirrors is really a game through which the poets give us *Nala* to allow themselves, and (other) readers after them, to imagine the Pāṇḍavas and Draupadī as they might reflect upon themselves.

One carryover soon follows for Draupadī when she is reminded of an enigmatic figure named Indrasenā Nāḍāyanī. Still on pilgrimage with her husbands minus Arjuna, Draupadī hears of various model wives who served their husbands in the forest, including Damayantī and "Indrasenā Nāḍāyanī, always submissive *(vaśyā nityam)* to Mudgala" (3.113.23–24). Then in the *Virāṭaparvan*, Bhīma reminds her a bit more pointedly of this second woman (among others) while urging her to endure Kīcaka's affronts and serve the Pāṇḍavas more quietly in the hardships of their concealment: "And Indrasenā Nāḍāyanī, if you have heard of her beauty, formerly served her ancient thousand-year-old husband" (4.20.8). There

[45]Cf. Peile 1881, 213: "'and that in him which is next to it,' i.e., to self. . . . 'that which has no between.'" But he takes *anantara* without a feminine ending.

[46]*Antara* can also mean "other" (see Peile 1881, 87), which would give "she who is not other than it."

[47]See Ricoeur 1992, 150: "But what is selfhood, once it has lost the support of sameness?" Cf. 146–63 on narratives of self-loss and "the unity of a life."

is something cryptic in this reminder, which comes soon after Arjuna has disguised himself as Bṛhannaḍā.

Keeping ourselves to the Critical Edition, we know that Nala and Damayantī's daughter is named Indrasenā (3.229* *apud* 54.37; 57.21; 73.24). Given the same fluctuation of consonants that engenders the alternates Nala/Naḍa/Nara and Bṛhannalā/Bṛhannaḍā, the name Indrasenā Nāḍāyanī could, with similar riddling, be a patronymic for "Indrasenā daughter of Nala." But such a connection seems at most to be allusive,[48] leaving open interpretive possibilities that seem to have been developed only in the *Mahābhārata*'s southern recension and Tamil variations, where Draupadī's prior lives are fused in the person of Nāḷāyaṉi, wife of Mudgala,[49] who, however, appears to have nothing do with Nala and Damayantī's daughter.

We do not, however, have to go such epic fringes to probe the impact of *Nala* on its primary audience. The clincher is something so far unnoticed that emerges from setting *Nala* face to face with the *Virāṭaparvan*. I still hold that this parvan may show each of the Pāṇḍavas to be a mini-Śiva as complement to Draupadī, incarnation of the goddess.[50] More clearly, however, each of them is a refraction of Nala as complement to Draupadī, mirror image of Damayantī.

One hardly needs to reiterate the many ways that the poets draw us into obvious identifications of Nala and Damayantī with Yudhiṣṭhira, Arjuna, and Draupadī. Several have been highlighted in passing, and Biardeau has worked out many more, defining one of her main problems

[48]One anonymous commentator on the reference in the *Virātparvan* identifies Nāḍāyanī the wife of Mudgala as the daughter of Nala; see Scheuer 1982, 102–4.

[49]In the southern recension (Scheuer 1982, 99–127), *Villipāratam* (1.5.73–88; Subramanian 1967, 47), and the Draupadī cult's "Glorification of Draupadī" (Hiltebeitel 1991a, 484–85), the "secret" of Draupadī's polyandry turns on her prior life as Nāḷāyaṉi, which fuses the stories (separate in the CE; see chap. 2, § C.10 and 12) of the "overanxious maiden" and the "ill-fortuned" goddess who marries the five Indras: Nāḷāyanī's service to the decrepit Maudgalya/Mudgala is rewarded by his pleasing her so amply—in five distinct forms—that when he wants to pursue renunciation, she wants her joys prolonged. Provoked, he curses her rebirth as a princess in the line of Drupada, and to have five sweet-looking *(madhurākāra-)* husbands to satisfy her (77–80)—a decree that Śiva soon mitigates, saying her mates will be like Indras, she will retain her virginity for each one, and she should stand in the Gaṅgā, where Indra will find her tracking upstream the golden lotuses that come from her tears (CE 1, App. 1, no. 100; Scheuer 1982, 100–2). As Scheuer (99, n. 37) and Sukthankar (1933, lxvii) note, the northern commentator Nīlakaṇṭha knew the story, proving that he used Southern manuscripts. The southern strain of Draupadī's unbounded libido is amplified in the Tamil "sixth man" theme that has her desire one more husband (Hiltebeitel 1988, 288–89). Nāḍāyanī-Nāḷāyaṉi probably also resonates with Nārāyaṇī: the goddess in such forms as Yogamāyā, Lalitā, Durgā, and Śrī-Lakṣmī (see Scheuer 1982, 103–4).

[50]As argued in Hiltebeitel 1980b; cf. Goldman 1995, 90–97.

for *Nala* around them.[51] Her question is whether Nala is more like Yudhiṣṭhira the dicer, the nonmartial king with an "aptitude for pardon," or like the "dark" Arjuna, the "perfect king," for whom his wife mourns in his absence (1985, 3, 5–6, 17).

Biardeau, however, curtails her comparisons of the Pāṇḍavas with these two brothers, since she ignores the twins here and finds Bhīma more like Damayantī. Biardeau finds this latter rapport in violent contexts where Damayantī must act on her own in ways that may recall Bhīma's exuberances, which usually occur in the service of Draupadī. Draupadī usually has this strongman to call on as her "right arm," but Damayantī must sometimes act like Bhīma for herself.[52] But Bhīma is also like Nala. We have noted this at one crucial point in the dice match, where Bhīma alone draws comparison with Nala for holding the line at the wager of one's wife. This is not surprising, since it is Bhīma whose love for Draupadī is most open and passionate among the brothers. Nala's love for Damayantī is certainly one of the things that keeps him from betting her, overriding even the effects of Kali and Dvāpara—unlike Yudhiṣṭhira, whose passion for dice overrides, at least at this point, his hardly negligible passion for his wife.[53]

Moreover, the affinities between Nala and the five Pāṇḍavas are mainly ones that have to do precisely with Nala's emergence from his hidden nature. In the case of Yudhiṣṭhira, such affinities are explicit in his obtaining Nala's mastery of dice. The "heart of the dice" allows Nala to win back his kingdom, this time, self-assured, with Damayantī as stake (77.5–20); transmitted to Yudhiṣṭhira, it will enable him to pass his year incognito triumphantly. For Arjuna disguised as the eunuch Bṛhannalā, we have noted the allusions in Damayantī's plaintive words, upon sensing Nala's return, that "Nala has been like a eunuch to me" (71.14). There is also the play on Arjuna and Kṛṣṇa with Vārṣṇeya as Nala's charioteer.

But the other three Pāṇḍavas come clear as fragments of Nala when Damayantī sends Keśinī to confirm her suspicions that Bāhuka is Nala: that is, in the very context of Damayantī and Nala's exchange of signs.[54] On Keśinī's first visit, it is in the midst of Nala's answering her about Vārṣṇeya that Bāhuka tells Keśinī how he obtained work from Ṛtuparṇa.

[51]See Biardeau 1984, 259–67; 1985, 8, 13, 15, 26–28, 33 (the heroines and the suffering Earth); 1984, 263–67; 1985, 8–9, 32 (their darkness and evocations of the smoky fire); 1985, 3 (Indra and Yama as Pāṇḍava fathers and Lokapāla suitors of Damayantī).

[52]Thus Damayantī and Bhīma share a capacity to curse, episodes with a python, and episodes involving fragrant lakes that result in destruction and betray their "ignorance" (1985, 19–29, 27–30).

[53]Evident in what he says before he wagers her; see chap. 7, § C.

[54]Biardeau 1984, 270, finds that the following recognition sequence is "banal and conforms to dramatic canons that appear to us longish."

He gained it as one skilled in horses and excellent at cooking (72.12). These are the skills that will define the disguises of Nakula and Bhīma. This is not enough for Damayantī, who sends Keśinī a second time: now, not to ask anything but to watch Bāhuka while withholding fire and water from him even if he asks for them. Keśinī reports that she has seen Bāhuka prepare food for Ṛtuparṇa in a tub that fills with water merely at his glance, and light fire spontaneously and handle it without being burnt (73.1–14). Affinities with water and fire are precise traits that distinguish Nakula and Sahadeva, respectively, and Sahadeva has a mastery over fire.[55] All that remains for Damayantī to confirm that Bāhuka is Nala is to taste the meat he has cooked (73.22) and hear his show of tenderness as he embraces their children (25–28).

These correspondences, "saved for the end," thus mark a rapport between the disclosure of Nala's identity to Damayantī and the disguises that will conceal the identities of the Pāṇḍavas and Draupadī in Virāṭa's court. Listening, if Draupadī and the four Pāṇḍavas do not blink, it would have to be because they are yet to know what their disguises will be. But readers should blink. Yet the matches do not go full-circle. All the Pāṇḍavas and Draupadī share decisive traits with Nala and Damayantī. But one of them is an exception when it comes to choosing a disguise. Yudhiṣṭhira, Bhīma, Arjuna, Nakula, and Draupadī will pick disguises that recall Nala and Damayantī, but Sahadeva becomes a keeper of cows. Moreover, some of these defining traits can be traced backward as well as forward. Mastery over water, fire, and cooking were the gifts given by Varuṇa, Agni, and Yama respectively to Nala at Damayantī's svayaṃvara (3.54.28-32). We thus see one of the reasons why Agni was necessary among the Lokapālas. But Yama gives two gifts to Nala: the "essence" or "taste of food" *(annarasam)*, which comes to serve Bhīma, and "utter firmness in dharma" (*dharme ca paramāṃ sthitam*; 3.54.31), which belongs to Yudhiṣṭhira. These swerves and connections may reconverge again if we wonder whether Yudhiṣṭhira in his "Heron" disguise in the Kingdom of the Fishes will not also retain something from the dark side of Yama's "taste for food." Such feints and dodges keep the question before us of what the Pāṇḍavas and Draupadī "take in" from hearing *Nala*. It is, again, "as if" they have each heard something that is not only revealing about the love that keeps them together during hard times, but something useful about their hidden selves.

[55]Wikander 1957, 73 (Nakula sent to fetch water [3.196.6]; Sahadeva to fetch fire [2.61.6]), 89–95 (Sahadeva's contest with king Nīla, who also, under Agni's protection, has mastery of fire [2.28.11–37]). On Nala's powers over nature and "mastery of *māyā*" in this episode (which recalls Duryodhana discomfiture in the Pāṇḍavas' sabhā), see Biardeau 1985, 8.

7 Draupadī's Question

If hearing *Nala* lifts its listeners' spirits, it would be not only because it holds up mirrors, but because it raises questions. Or, more exactly, it mirrors certain questions and keeps them alive. At the Pāṇḍava-Kaurava dice match, having bet all his wealth and brothers, Yudhiṣṭhira is prodded into losing himself and then Draupadī. The wager lost, Duryodhana orders that Draupadī be brought to Dhṛtarāṣṭra's house as the slave *(dāsī)* of her new masters.[1] Draupadī asks the messenger a question, refuses to come with him, and challenges him to ask it in the dicing hall, which he does. Draupadī's question is a *praśna*, and as Shulman observes, "The Epic is fond of such *praśnas*: this is the term Draupadī uses when she tries to save herself and her husbands at the dice-game. . . . There, as elsewhere in the text, the *praśna* points to a baffling, ultimately insoluble crystallization of conflict articulated along opposing lines of interpretation" (1996, 153). Draupadī's question unsettles the authorities, brings forth higher authority where it is silenced or absent, and opens the question of authority to multiple voices, including her own and the poets'.[2] The sabhā is the epic's ultimate setting for constructing, deconstructing, and rethinking authority.[3]

We have already made some observations about this question and the

[1]59.1; 60.4, following Mehendale 1985, 182, who clarifies that the second verse explains the first: when Duryodhana orders the "usher" to "bring Draupadī," it is to Dhṛtarāṣṭra's house, not the sabhā.

[2]Cf. Suzuki 1989 on the "metamorphoses" of epic heroines beginning with Helen, and "woman as a figure that questions" (3). Given Homer's poetic voice and vision (40, 54–55), Helen in particular interrogates the authority of the epic's heroic code (28, 33) that scapegoats women in the name of men's heroic struggles.

[3]See Lincoln 1994, 12: had he discussed India, the *Mbh* "court" scene would have to have been the obvious counterpart to his choices from Greece, Rome, and Germanic sources, especially for his interest in "authorized speech and significant silence" (9–12, 25–27, 51–53, 55–56, 75), stripping (25), and questions raised about women (90–102). See also Higonnet 1994 on the "erasure of women from the history of war literature" (160); Hess 2001 on the continuing praśna literature built on questions about, or of, the *Rām*.

scene that provokes it: that it has to do not only with the self of King Dharma (Yudhiṣṭhira), but the "subtle" self or essence of dharma, and that the scene provokes two expressions about what is the "highest dharma." To Bhīma, about to burn Yudhiṣṭhira's arms, Arjuna says the highest dharma is to remember not to overstep one's eldest brother (*bhrātaraṃ dhārmikaṃ jyeṣṭhaṃ nātikramitum arhati*; 2.61.8cd)—a somewhat troubling point, since he says this to his own older (if not eldest) brother Bhīma.[4] And for Vidura, it is speaking what is applicable to dharma when one knows it (61.80). As Biardeau puts it, for Vidura, leaving Draupadī's question unanswered puts the dharma itself at stake.[5] I have also suggested that the question hovers over the entire *Mahābhārata*: that no one ever resolves it, and that Yudhiṣṭhira will still be trying to figure it out at the very end. With this has gone the suggestion that it also has something to do with love as it is tested in Draupadī's marriage to Yudhiṣṭhira as one of her five husbands.

Draupadī is not the first to raise one aspect of her question. This is first voiced by Vidura, who incarnates Dharma, but whose authority is undercut by his having a low caste mother: the wager of Draupadī may be invalid, he says, since "I think she was staked when the king was no longer his own master *(anīśa)*" (59.4). Vidura's words are part of a warning of disaster, but he says them to Duryodhana, who ignores them, having already ordered that Draupadī be led away and enslaved in the house of his father. It is the question's insolubility and the impasses it opens that provoke the two violent scenes of Draupadī's hair-pulling and disrobing. Let us follow the question as it unfolds through these events.[6]

A. Hair Pulling

It is Draupadī who raises the actual question, which emerges as her fourth in a series. When Duryodhana's "usher," whose approach to

[4]A point missed by Söhnen-Thieme 1999, 150.

[5]1985, 10, with reference to 2.61.52: "dharma is harmed *(pīḍyate)*" if it is unanswered.

[6]I have elsewhere discussed these and related matters in Hiltebeitel 1980a; 1980–1981; 1981; 1985b; 1988, 228–38, 263–81; 1991b; and 2000b. Only this study and the latter have benefited from Mehendale 1985 and 1990: thoughtful and helpful pieces, especially the former, by which I have been able to sharpen what follows, despite disagreeing with their main arguments. Mehendale is correct that I have "a different view of the role of the epic author," whose business, he says "is to narrate the event as it happened in the past" (1990, 287). This realism finds its explanation in an article attempting to turn the tables on van Buitenen's fruitful argument (1972; 1975, 3–30) that the epic's Rājasūya-plus-dice-match is modeled on the Vedic Rājasūya: "The epic war, on archaeological evidence, is supposed to have been fought C. 1200 B.C., i.e. at a time much anterior to the formalization of the Rājasūya as represented in the ritual texts. . . . Thus one may attempt to explain the game of dice becoming part of the Vedic ritual on the basis of incidents similar to the one found in the epic, and not vice versa" (1992, 68). *What* archeological evidence?

Queen Draupadī is compared by Vaiśampāyana to a dog's (60.3), tells Draupadī she is to come with him as a slave, she asks three questions in a burst: "How do you speak so, an usher? What Rājaputra would wager his wife? The king was befooled and crazed by the dicing.[7] Was there nothing else for him to stake?" (5). In these questions, she sounds angry, incredulous, and then sarcastic. But when the usher has explained the betting sequence, with Yudhiṣṭhira having bet himself before he bet her (6), she uses her wits: "Go to the game. Having gone, ask in the sabhā, what did you lose first, yourself or me *(kiṃ nu pūrvam parājaiṣīr ātmānam māṃ nu)*? Having learned that, then come to take me" (7). Draupadī formulates her question in a way that opens up two things that might work in her favor. She definitely wants the question raised "in the sabhā," where she can expect it to be treated "in court" as a case of "law," dharma. And, whether cleverly or inadvertently—and if we grant that she is clever to address the court, she is probably being clever here too—in asking Yudhiṣṭhira a question whose answer she has already obtained, she makes it clear at least to readers that her question is about more than it says. Listening in, we may ask whether Yudhiṣṭhira too can read behind her words, even though he will only hear those she has imparted to the usher. Draupadī seems to give him a precious riddle. For although one is forced to translate, "What did you lose first, *your*self or me?" what she also says, literally, is, "What did you lose first, self or me?" Several scholars have followed up the legal side of Draupadī's question,[8] but few have recognized its obvious philosophical import as a question about the nature of the self,[9] and none have discussed it.[10]

[7]She is quoting what the usher has just told her (60.4). See also chap. 6, p. 213.
[8]See Mehendale 1985, 183, on slave status and whether Yudhiṣṭhira could rightfully bet Draupadī after he had bet himself; Kulkarni 1989 and Shah 1995, 30–31, on the husband's authority over the wife; Vassilkov 1989–90, 388, 393–94, noting that only "lawful (dharmic) wives" would be forbidden to enter the sabhā; Devi [1981] 1988 (fictionalized) and Agarwal 1995 on rape and revenge; M. C. Smith on vexed "subtle dharma questions" and themes of alliance (1992, 60, 118). Söhnen-Thieme 1999, picking up on Smith's argument that Vedic triṣṭubh verses provide the epic's oldest stratum (see chap. 1, n. 70), sees it "a somewhat futile question" when Draupadī, in a "short passage" in ślokas, sends the messenger to ask Yudhiṣṭhira whom he bet first, since "the Prātikāmin had just told her" (143). Based on triṣṭubhs, the question is "not so much whether Yudhiṣṭhira had lost himself before staking her or not, for this was made known to her already . . . , but whether Yudhiṣṭhira's staking her was in agreement with the law (dharma) and thus valid" (147). This reduction to law of Draupadī's question yields a "'genuine triṣṭubh version'" (148) that is truncated and purely hypothetical (see chap. 1, n. 70); indeed, the contrast noted between dialogues and discussions in triṣṭubh and narration in śloka (150) seems to suggest a complementarity (cf. van Buitenen 1973, xxxix). Söhnen-Thieme also rejects the return dice match.
[9]Although I will not pursue the comparison, Yudhiṣṭhira is put into the position of raising for himself and the others in the court, including incarnate demons, the Pascalian/Faustian question of what it means to have "wagered one's soul" (see Hiltebeitel 1987).
[10]Shulman, as indicated (after n. 1 above), is suggestive, but does not explore the point. In

Returning to the court, the usher doesn't change Draupadī's question in any essentials, but quotes her on a further question before he repeats the one we have heard: "'As the owner of whom did you lose us' *(kasyeśo naḥ parājaiṣīr)*? So queries Draupadī. 'What did you lose first, (your-) self or me' *(kiṃ nu pūrvam parājaiṣīr ātmānam atha vāpi mām)*?" Here, "Yudhiṣṭhira did not stir, as if he had lost consciousness *(niścesto gatasattva ivābhavat)*, and made no reply . . . whether good or ill."[11] The questions snowball even as their meanings double: "As owner of whom?" or, "As master, or lord *(īśa)*, of what?" One may ask, did Draupadī really ask this new question? In effect, the "usher" joins Draupadī's question with Vidura's observation that Yudhiṣṭhira was "not his own master or lord" *(anīśa)* when he bet her. "As if" Yudhiṣṭhira had lost consciousness. Had he? If so, for how long? If not, of what do Draupadī's words make him conscious? One has much to ponder already.

Duryodhana has some reason to be surprised at Draupadī's response, for as Mehendale points out, when he had first ordered her taken to the Kaurava quarters, he "and probably everyone in the Assembly" assumed "that Draupadī had lost her status as a free woman. But now, for the first time, he realizes that Draupadī does not agree to this position. . . . He tacitly admits that her question is justified" (1985, 183). Seeing also the potential to catch Yudhiṣṭhira in a lie, he says, "Let Kṛṣṇā Pāñcālī come here and ask the question herself. All the people here shall hear what is her word and his" (60.10).[12] The usher goes back to Draupadī. Finding her in what van Buitenen calls "the king's lodgings" *(rājabhavanam)*, he tells her apologetically that she is summoned. Draupadī reflects: "So now the All-Disposer disposes, touching both who are touched, the wise and the fool. He said, 'In this world dharma is alone supreme.' Protecting, he will dispose peace."[13] We are not told who the "he" is whom she quotes: the All-Disposer? Viṣṇu-Kṛṣṇa? Dharma? Yudhiṣṭhira? No one says such precise words in the epic, either earlier or later. The name

calling Draupadī's question "the ultimate riddle" (1975, 30), van Buitenen is also suggestive. Meanwhile, Lipner 1994, 197–212, 218–20, 229, 231, 286 unpacks the story around the axis of "freedom and determinism," but lumps Dhṛtarāṣṭra's helpless fatalism with Yudhiṣṭhira's enigmatic and implicitly correct reading of fate *(daiva, vidhi)*, which is something not just at odds with "choice," but "at play" and "divinely disposed." Contrast Lipner 1994, 199–201 and 229, with Biardeau's decisive discussion (1976, 143–44).

[11] 60.8–9: Good or ill, or straight or crooked, right or wrong *(vacanaṃ sādhvasādhu vā)*.

[12] Ganguli's translation catches an important sense here: "Let everyone hear in this assembly the words that pass between her and Yudhishthira" ([1884–96] 1970, 2:189). Duryodhana wants play them off against each other. But they won't fall for it.

[13] 2.60.13: *evaṃ nūnaṃ vyadadhāt saṃvidhātā/ sparśāvubhau spṛśato dhīrabālau// dharmaṃ tvekaṃ paramaṃ prāha loke/ sa naḥ śamaṃ dhāsyati gopyamānaḥ*. Lipner 1994, 204, takes this line as evidence of Draupadī's "touching faith" that Dharma brings peace when "obeyed" (for *gopyamānaḥ*, as modifying Dharma).

sounds fitting for Viṣṇu or Kṛṣṇa, while the words sound more like Yudhiṣṭhira, and as if she is quoting him, as Damayantī does Nala. In any case, at this point the Critical Edition text itself becomes contestable. As Edgerton, the *Sabhāparvan* editor, sees it, Draupadī seems to come to the sabhā twice: first, with a "trusted messenger" *(saṃmataṃ dūtam)* sent for her by Yudhiṣṭhira (14); then, with Duḥśāsana.[14] This second arrival would occur when the usher balks at approaching Draupadī a third time after a northern "interpolation" has returned him a second time to the sabhā (531* line 6 *apud* 2.60.13). But these movements are uncertain. What is clear is that she is accosted by Duḥśāsana in what van Buitenen calls a "dwelling" (*veśman*; 19), and that she then runs from this place toward the women around Dhṛtarāṣṭra. There Duḥśāsana grabs her by the hair (21–22).

It is tempting to adopt Edgerton's view that, "Clearly we have here parts of two entirely different versions of the story," and his inclination to drop the two verses concerning Yudhiṣṭhira's messenger, which involve a change of meter, as an interpolation. He is certainly right that "attempts to smooth over the inconsistencies" are indeed interpolations.[15] And he is also right about the ludicrous effect produced by some northern manuscripts to put the second of these verses, the famous description of Draupadī's arrival in the sabhā before Dhṛtarāṣṭra, into Yudhiṣṭhira's mouth as a command: "In a single garment, a waistcloth below,[16] weeping, having her period, having come to the sabhā, she came[17] before her father-in-law" (2.60.15), is turned into Yudhiṣṭhira's order, "Come[18] before your father-in-law in a single garment, a waistcloth below, weeping, having your period!" Not only is this preposterous marital cruelty out of character; it makes Yudhiṣṭhira speak when we

[14]Cf. Mehendale 1995a, finding this to be but one of five "contradictions" at the dice game, and evidence that "at one time there were current different versions of the game." But he tortures the text to produce the others.

[15]Edgerton 1944, xxxi–xxxii: *531 (as already noted, giving the usher a second return to the sabhā); *532 (clarifying that Draupadī has arrived in the sabhā in front of Dhṛtarāṣṭra, with the implication that when Duḥśāsana goes for her, she is no longer at "the king's lodgings"); *533 (giving her a "residence" [*bhavanam*] where Yudhiṣṭhira's trusted messenger can find her).

[16]*Adhonīvī*: having a low waistcloth/petticoat? or: with her waistcloth below [her navel] (Ganguli)? or: "her waist-cloth dropped" (Edgerton). If she is *ekavastrā*, it would seem that either the *nīvī* is the *ekavastra* ("single garment") itself, or is so low it doesn't count.

[17]*Abhavat*, literally "was" or "became," although of course better translated as "stood" or "came."

[18]*Bhava*: literally "be" or "become," although likewise better translated as "come" or "stand." See the sample from different northern scripts in the notes to 2.60.15. The Vulgate has *bhavet*, "she should be . . ." (Ganguli [1884–96] 1970, 2,140), as if changing Yudhiṣṭhira's words from an imperative to an optative would soften them.

have been told he is mindless and silent. Indeed, such a command would answer Draupadī's question prematurely: having bet himself, Yudhiṣṭhira would exemplify by this command that he still retains his husbandly rights over Draupadī. No such cruelty or authorly stupidity need be imagined, except that someone did *change* the text by imagining it. Clearly someone who didn't like something about Draupadī's question wanted to settle it in favor of an extreme male arrogance.

It is indeed surprising that the epic poets lend to this confusion by using such imprecise terms *(bhavana, veśman)* to describe the places of Draupadī's movements near or within the sabhā. But I think the Critical Edition gives us a readable text that is better for what it has removed, and not necessarily a conflation of "two entirely different versions of the story." As it stands, while the usher is still with Draupadī, Yudhiṣṭhira sends his trusted messenger, but we don't know the message. Left to do this silently, as if by a signal, Yudhiṣṭhira could still be thought of as appearing witless. Draupadī comes to the sabhā in front of Dhṛtarāṣṭra. Duryodhana then, "gleeful" at what he sees in the faces of the assembly, tells the usher, who could quite naturally have come back to the sabhā with Draupadī (and the "trusted messenger") unmentioned, says, "Bring her right here, usher. Let the Kurus speak to her visibly."[19] Terrified by Draupadī's anger, which he has already glimpsed, the usher, "abandoning his pride," asks what he should say to Kṛṣṇā. Duryodhana, rash and thinking the usher to be afraid of Bhīma, which he is not, tells Duḥśāsana, who *should* be afraid of Bhīma, he has nothing to fear from "our powerless rivals," and orders, "Fetch and bring Yājñasenī yourself." "Then the Rājaputra [Duḥśāsana] rose up, having heard his brother, eyes red with wrath," and entered that "veśman of the great chariot warriors" (60.16–19). This appears to be an area off to the side of the sabhā to which the Pāṇḍavas would have repaired after the dicing, and where Draupadī seems to have gone, and not evidence of a second story in which Draupadī is still in "the king's lodging." I would be just as happy to drop the two verses about Yudhiṣṭhira's trusted messenger and the first description of Draupadī's bloodstained appearance in the sabhā, since the former is awkward by any reckoning and the latter reiterated endlessly. But it seems better not to ignore them,[20] and to consider them among the "more difficult readings."

[19]Dissatisfied by the imprecision of the usher's movements and the reasons for Duryodhana's glee, Mehendale invents a conversation between Draupadī and the usher and the latter's prior return to account for them: Duryodhana is gleeful because no one no one would answer Draupadī's question (1985, 184).

[20]Rather than add a "little insertion," as above (see n. 19), Mehendale now decides to "neglect" these two verses as "extremely inconsistent with the narration" (1985, 184 n. 1).

In any case, Duḥśāsana now drags Draupadī's hair, and doesn't stop to ask or answer questions. "Come, come, Pāñcālī, you are won, Kṛṣṇā. . . . Enjoy the Kurus *(kurūn bhajasva)*" (60.20). She runs toward the Kaurava women's quarters, but Duḥśāsana rushes after her; "He seized by the long black flowing hair the wife of the Indras among men," and led her to the sabhā. While she was being dragged, "she spoke softly, 'I'm having my period now! I have one garment, fool! You cannot lead me to the sabhā, you non-Ārya!' But forcefully holding her down by her black *(kṛṣṇa)* hair, he said to Kṛṣṇā, 'Cry out for help *(trāṇāya vikrośa)* to Kṛṣṇa and Jiṣṇu, to Hari and Nara. I will lead you for sure. *Be* in your period, Yājñasenī, in a single garment or with no garment. You are won at dice and made a slave. With slaves one delights as one wishes'" (60.22–27). Duryodhana has summoned Draupadī to let her raise her question, which includes the question of her slavery, but Duḥśasana simply calls her "slave" *(dasī)* "time and again."[21] She answers, "You whose conduct is non-Ārya, of cruel acts, don't unclothe me, don't drag me" (30). It is the cruel and non-Ārya Duḥśāsana who orders Draupadī, "Be in your period," not Yudhiṣṭhira.[22]

Duḥśāsana's taunts are also a prelude to what follows: the disrobing and Draupadī's "cry for help" to Kṛṣṇa, or, more exactly to Kṛṣṇa, also known as Hari, and to Arjuna, also known as Jiṣṇu and Nara. *Trāṇa* stands here for more than just "help": Draupadī's *trāṇāya vikrośa* will be her "cry for salvation."

B. Disrobing Draupadī, Redressing the Text

Draupadī now gets to ask her question in the gambling hall, furious at her mistreatment, dragged and tossed about by Duḥśāsana, hair disheveled, menstrual blood spotting her single garment, taunted as a dāsī. During all this she challenges the men in the court "who have studied the śāstras" to consider her question, which she frames in a surprising statement about dharma and Yudhiṣṭhira that we may read, I suggest, as her assertion of faith that things have not gone totally awry: "The king, son of Dharma, is firm in dharma; dharma is subtle, to be understood by the adroit (*dharme sthito dharmasutaśca rājā/ dharmaśca sūkṣmo nipuṇopalabhyaḥ*; 60.31ab)." Her husbands are "inflamed" by her "sidelong glances" (*kaṭākṣa*; 35cd), which hurt them more than the loss of

[21]Quoting Mehendale (1985, 185), for whom her slavery is the whole question. Not also the repeated uses here of the name Yājñasenī, basically "She whose army is connected with the sacrifice," cf. Hiltebeitel 1988, 194, 338, 392.

[22]2.60.27: *rajasvalā vā bhava yājñaseni*; cf. n. 17 above, where it is the same imperative verb put into Yudhiṣṭhira's mouth.

kingdom or riches. But we find that although the subtlety of dharma is admitted right and left, none of the śāstra-knowing men are adroit enough to answer her question, which they bandy about from every angle.

Bhīṣma responds first, as he should since he is the senior śāstric authority on such matters: "Because of the subtlety of dharma, dear, I am unable to solve your question the proper way *(na dharmasaukṣmyāt subhage vivaktum/ śaknomi te praśnam imaṃ yathāvat)*" (60.40ab). He equivocates twice, first over the issue of the wife as property and then over more legalistic subtleties that border on the ethical and the philosophical: "One having no property cannot bet another's, but considering that a wife is under a husband's authority *(asvo hyaśaktaḥ paṇitum parasvam/ striyaśca bhartur vaśatāṃ samīkṣya)* . . ." (40cd). The property issue is itself philosophically coded; one could translate, "One with no 'his' cannot bet another's 'his.'" But while Bhīṣma seems to know this, he contents himself with the inconclusivities of dharma as "law": "Yudhiṣṭhira could abandon the whole abundant earth before he would abandon truth. And 'I am won' was said by the Pāṇḍava. Therefore I cannot decide this. Śakuni is second to no man at gambling. The son of Kuntī was free to choose with him. The great-souled one does not consider him deceitful. Therefore I cannot speak to your question."[23] Bhīṣma sticks to the surface of *what has been said*, which, as a good "lawyer," is all that is admissible as evidence in the sabhā as court. Yet we know that silences refute and extend this admitted evidence: we know that Yudhiṣṭhira knows at least that Śakuni cheats, although he may not know how he does so or whether he does in any particular instance;[24] and we know that there can be more to truth than what is said, and that what is said is precisely where dharma is subtle, where there is more to dharma than meets the eye, more than language can express. There is thus something unpleasant here.[25] Bhīṣma's equivocality amounts to an

[23]2.60.41–42: *tyajeta sarvām pṛthivīṃ samṛddhām/ yudhiṣṭhiraḥ satyamatho na jahyāt// uktaṃ jito 'smīti ca pāṇḍavena/ tasmānna śaknomi vivektum etat// dyūte 'dvitīyaḥ śakunirnareṣu/ kuntīsutas tena nisṛṣṭakāmaḥ// na manyate tāṃ nikṛtim mahātmā/ tasmānna te praśnam imam bravīmi.*

[24]Shulman 1992. Indeed, at the start of the game, Yudhiṣṭhira says, "Sakuni, don't defeat us by crooked means and cruelly *(amārgeṇa nṛśaṃsavat)*" (2.53.3).

[25]Cf. Biardeau 1985, 20: Bhīṣma remains obstinately mute, "recusing himself" not only before Draupadī but Ambā; Karve 1974, 14: "in the court where he sat as the eldest he did not lift a finger to halt the indignity to a woman"; the most callous and indifferent of all *Mbh* men toward women, Bhīṣma exhibited "an almost inhuman treatment" toward them (11–14, 25); Mehendale 1985, 194: "his attitude . . . was unbecoming of him; and since Draupadī was not only insulted with abuses, she was also a victim of molestation, his attitude must be judged unpardonable . . . ; improper . . . ; he should have told Duḥśāsana he was in the Assembly of civilized Kṣatriyas and not in the den of hooligans." Even Thakur 1992, 141–47, gives his hero no excuses here.

equivocation, a refusal to honor this "more," as Draupadī herself suggests, refuting his points term for term, but rather too interpretatively,[26] and insisting on an answer to her question (45): words that come with tears.

These are greeted with insults from Duḥśāsana and an outbreak of dissensions on both sides. Among the Pāṇḍavas, in a scene we have noted, Bhīma now denounces Yudhiṣṭhira for treating Draupadī worse than an ordinary gambler treats a whore: although he is "the master *(īśa)* of all we possess" (61.4), he has "gone too far" in staking Draupadī: "I shall burn off your arms! Sahadeva! Bring fire!" To which Arjuna replies that while Yudhiṣṭhira has kept to the Kṣatriya's dharma of meeting a challenge, Bhīma "oversteps" his "highest dharma" of not overstepping his eldest brother.[27]

As the hair pulling turns into the second violation of the disrobing, the responses to Draupadī's question become polarized. In the epic's only expression of pro and con views, Karṇa joins in a carefully constructed debate with Vikarṇa, an otherwise obscure[28] youngest brother of Duryodhana, whose name, in this context, suggests a contrived opposition: Vikarṇa as "good demon" and Karṇa as the Sun god's son gone demonically awry.[29] Vikarṇa takes what seems to be a compassionate view, although as Shah points out, this "defence does not turn out to be a defence at all but a mere debate on technicalities. His arguments do not in any way contradict the general belief that the wife is her husband's property" (1995, 31). Says Vikarṇa, the throw is null for three reasons: (1) Draupadī was staked after Yudhiṣṭhira bet himself; (2) it was only due to the prodding of Śakuni that Yudhiṣṭhira bet her; and (3) the "faultless" *(aninditā)* Draupadī is "common to all the Pāṇḍavas" (*sādhāraṇī ca sarveṣām pāṇḍavānām*; 61.23–24). Karṇa, outraged at such assertions by a mere youth, offers a close rebuttal:[30] (1) it is irrelevant

[26]Or "pathetically" (Lipner 1994, 206). Yudhiṣṭhira was an innocent who did not wake up until he'd lost all, and thus cannot be said to have had any choice, she says (60.43–44)—as if she could perhaps still hope that it was a vast right-wing conspiracy.

[27]2.61.5–9; see above, n. 4, and on Bhīma's outrage, chap. 6, after nn. 25 and 52.

[28]Though "considered to be one of the four important *(pradhāna)* Kauravas" (Mehendale 1985, 194, n. 1, citing 1.90.62), this is his sole moment, one for which the Tamil Draupadī cult elevates his profile (Hiltebeitel 1988, 235–36, 272–77).

[29]Mehendale 1990 and Dhavalikar 1992–93, 525, n. 8, take me to task for my appeal to "nature mythology" in Hiltebeitel 1980a. I accept Mehendale's criticism of my attempt to extend the color symbolism of Draupadī's garments to an evocation of the colors of the three guṇas (288), but the Draupadī-Karṇa/Earth-Sun correlations are simply part of the poets' stock of tropes. Mehendale's argument combines a realism about the epic's past (287; cf. n. 6 above) with a determination to require metaphor to meet the tighter requirements of allegory (286).

[30]Mehendale 1985, 185–86, contra Hiltebeitel 1980a, 98, on this breakdown and my phrase

when she was wagered: Yudhiṣṭhira could bet her because Draupadī is "included within his total property" (*abhyantarā ca sarvasve draupadī*; 32); (2) Śakuni may have prodded Yudhiṣṭhira, but he did it audibly and her wager was allowed by all the Pāṇḍavas (*kīrtitā draupadī vācā anujñātā ca pāṇḍavaiḥ*; 33); and (3), the twist on which everything turns, being "common to all the Pāṇḍavas," Draupadī cannot be "faultless" at all: "Or if you think it was through adharma that she was led into the sabhā in a single garment, hear my final word. One husband per wife is ordained by the gods, O scion of Kuru; but she, whose submission is to many, is for certain a whore."[31] A whore is common to all and protected by none—a reminder that Bhīma cannot protect Draupadī even though he denounces Yudhiṣṭhira for treating her worse than a whore.

More than this, recalling Duḥśāsana's taunt—"*Be* in your period, Yājñasenī, in a single garment or with no garment"—Karṇa continues: given that she is a whore, "leading her into the sabhā is not strange, to my mind, whether she is wearing a single garment or even naked. . . . This Vikarṇa is a very childish speaker of wisdom. Duḥśāsana! Strip the clothes of the Pāṇḍavas and Draupadī (*pāṇḍavānāṃ ca vāsāṃsi draupadyāś cāpyupāhara*)."[32]

"point for point rebuttal" (softened here), sees Vikarṇa making two points: (1) Yudhiṣṭhira lost Draupadī by his gambling addiction, one of the four addictions that lead one to abandon dharma; (2) Śakuni prompted him, with varied repercussions that include my point one. That Mehendale combines my first and second points is trivial, but his neglect of the third suggests that he finds Karṇa's response to it distasteful (cf. 1985, 179, n. 3, on "incidents one would be ashamed to repeat" that he opines to be "unauthentic," and below, n. 32). I omit his first point because it makes no argument that Draupadī has not been lost, and because Karṇa ignores it. Indeed, it would be an untenable argument for Yudhiṣṭhira and the Pāṇḍavas, from whom Duryodhana, most crucially, has invited concurrence. In finding it "difficult to agree" that Karṇa offers a close rebuttal, Mehendale thinks Karṇa's whole reply, dismissed as "not important," "must belong to some other version . . . in which Yudhiṣṭhira loses [everything] . . . not piecemeal, but in a single game in which he staked" all at once (186; cf. 1995a, 35, n. 3). For a four-point breakdown, including Vikarṇa's addiction argument, cf. Mehendale 1995a, 34; Söhnen-Thieme 1999, 150.

[31] 61.34–35: *manyase vā sabhām etām ānītām ekavāsasam/ adharmeṇeti tatrāpi śṛṇu me vākyam uttaram// eko bhartā striyā devair vihitaḥ kurunandana/ iyaṃ tvanekavaśagā bandhakīti viniścitā*. Cf. Shah 1995, 90 and 1.114.65: Kuntī, rejecting Pāṇḍu's request, after Arjuna's birth, that she take on further divine mates to provide him more sons, scolds him for not recalling the "law" that a fourth union (implying levirate) makes a woman "loose" and a fifth makes her a "whore" (*bandhakī*)—or for Lipner, a "slut" (1994, 206).

[32] 61.36–38. Mehendale 1990, 290, n. 2, says my translation "strip" for *upāhara* (it is also Tadpatrikar's [1929, 327], van Buitenen's [1975, 146], Spivak's [1988, 196], and Lipner's [1994, 206–7, 212]) "goes beyond the text," preferring "remove" (1990, 287). He (like Dhavalikar 1992–93, 322) wants to maintain that the "clothes" (*vāsaṃsi*) here are the Pāṇḍavas *and* Draupadī's "upper garments" (*uttarīyas*). Draupadī's uttarīya *is* mentioned earlier (60.47b), but clearly it is not all she was wearing; and here, while the Pāṇḍavas do shed their uttarīyas (61.39c), Duḥśāsana seizes Draupadī's undefined "garment"—perhaps

Once again, the textual contestation is especially rich. How was Draupadī protected by inexhaustible sarees? The Critical Edition makes it an unexplained wonder, and Edgerton, as the *Sabhāparvan*'s editor, thinks "cosmic justice" is "apparently implied" (1944, xxix). Or was it the story Duḥśāsana's words anticipate, and which everybody knows, including, as we shall see, Draupadī and Kṛṣṇa *later* in the Critical Edition, that Draupadī prayed to Kṛṣṇa? Let us look at the apparatus.[33] Based on the Critical Edition's own criteria, Edgerton's judgment that "the evidence of the manuscripts is entirely conclusive" (1944, xxviii) is warranted, and it seems that the passage is an interpolation. Yet a reexamination of northern and southern variants provides a case where the editorial protocols may yield a nugget, though not necessarily the one that Edgerton imagined. Indeed, they may require us to reopen the question.

Edgerton's comments focus mainly on matters of style and continuity, but he also cannot avoid some of the theological implications of the presumed alterations:

> No prayer by Draupadī; no explanation of the miraculous replacement of one garment by another; no mention of Kṛṣṇa or any superhuman agency. It is apparently implied (though not stated) that cosmic justice automatically, or "magically" if you like, prevented the chaste Draupadī from being stripped in public. It is perhaps not strange that later redactors felt it necessary to embroider the story. Yet to me, at least, the original form, in its brevity, simplicity, and rapid movement, appeals very forcefully. (ibid., xxix)

Within the context of the passage itself, the Critical Edition's accumulated evidence leaves no grounds to refute these conclusions. The reconstituted text has continuity without Kṛṣṇa's intervention, and the tendency of later redactors (both northern and southern) to embroider the story is evident. Southern and northern variants of Draupadī's plea differ significantly, and both recensions provide what Edgerton calls "prime" and "excellent"

even differentially—"by force" (*balāt*; 40b). Considering that Draupadī's bloodstained "single garment" is repeatedly called a *vastra* (60.15a), *vāsa* (60.25c), *vāsasa* (61.34b), and *ambara* (60.27c and 61.36c), but never an *uttarīya* or for that matter an *adhonīvī* (see above, n. 16), and that Karṇa has inflamed Duḥśāsana by saying that as a "whore" she might as well be naked, Mehendale and Dhavalikar's argument must be viewed as an inept attempt to claim a purer past than the text allows: "strip" is a good translation.

[33]In revising this section on textual transformations from Hiltebeitel 1980a, 98–101, I make changes in three directions: renewed caution about the CE as the reconstruction of an original; wariness of generalizations about the textual process based on single passages; and insistence that we not lose sight that the CE bears the stamp of modern editorial interests.

manuscripts that entirely omit it.[34] Rarely does the epic offer a better passage in which to examine a process of textual layering.

One must, however, still be cautions. The reconstituted text is a twentieth-century reconstruction, and not proof of an "original." One must thus admit that, with no known original, Edgerton's choice could merely typify the eagerness of the Critical Edition's editors to excise bhakti by stripping the text. The manuscript evidence of variants could be no more than a collection of embellishments upon something that is indeed fully acknowledged elsewhere in the Critical Edition. At their base, Kṛṣṇa's intervention could be implied all along, but be told with different images and words of invocation that reflect the story's popularity. *Mahābhārata* poets often imply more than they tell, as when Draupadī's hair is called a "path" that the Pāṇḍavas followed to victory (12.16.25)—without it ever being clear what Draupadī did with her hair (Hiltebeitel 1981, 200–1). Moreover, just as the whole disrobing scene is omitted at some Draupadī festival drama cycles because of its inauspicious near-exposure of the goddess's impure (menstruating) nakedness (Hiltebeitel 1988, 228–29), it is possible, as analog, that late sectarian copyists might have omitted Kṛṣṇa's part in rescuing Draupadī to rescue *him* from "textual contact" with her impure single garment. What makes certain manuscripts "excellent" in the eyes of the Critical Edition editors is not any proof of their antiquity, but precisely their relative usefulness in shortening the Critical Edition text.

These cautionary remarks take us in opposite directions, but they are not contradictory: at a charged point, a text can be both expanded and contracted. Indeed, the Critical Edition cannot itself solve the problem, since, as has been indicated, it admits two powerful passages that explicitly recall Draupadī's prayer to "Govinda"! One has Kṛṣṇa recall her appeal in a message of warning to the Kauravas:

> This old debt will not glide off from my heart, that Kṛṣṇā cried out, "O Govinda," when I was far away.[35]

And a second has Draupadī keep Kṛṣṇa mindful of this debt herself:

> Five great warrior sons are born to me by five heroes who are lawfully as related to you as Abhimanyu is, O Kṛṣṇa. Yet I, a woman,

[34]Edgerton refers here to the northern Śāradā codex and to two southern manuscripts, one in Grantha script and one in Malayalam (ibid., xi and xxix).

[35]5.58.21: *ṛṇam etat pravṛddham me hṛdayān nāpasarpati/ yad govindeti cukrośa kṛṣṇā māṃ dūravāsinam*. Southern variants are slight: *ṛṇam pravṛddham iva me* for the first pada, *govindeti yadākrośat* for the last. The *Udyogaparvan* editor S. K. De does not take up the issues this passage raises for Edgerton's arguments.

> was seized by the hair when I went to the sabhā while Pāṇḍu's sons were watching and you were living, O Keśava. While the Kauravas, Pañcālas, and Vṛṣṇis were living, I became a slave of sinners, placed in the middle of the sabhā. While the apathetic, motionless Pāṇḍavas looked on, when I said, 'Save me, O Govinda,' you were longed for in my mind *(nirāmarṣeṣvaceṣṭeṣu prekṣamāṇeṣu pāṇḍuṣu/ trāhi mām iti govinda manasā kāṅkṣito 'si me)*. (5.80.23–26)

To retain the argument that the Critical Edition reconstitutes the original disrobing scene, one would have to argue either that the reconstituted *Sabhāparvan* passage has a textual autonomy from the critically reconstructed *Mahābhārata* as a whole, or that the two *Udyogaparvan* references to Kṛṣṇa in the scene reflect a later stratum of the text. Such arguments are possible, and the latter is probably the one that could have been expected of Edgerton, had he read ahead. But there is no compelling evidence that the *Udyogaparvan* recollections are any later than the *Sabhāparvan* episode they surely recall. Indeed, they are very sparse, condensed, and unelaborated. Draupadī and Kṛṣṇa—the two principal "witnesses"—recall virtually the same thing, each in the other's company: each says Draupadī called upon "Govinda" to save her; Kṛṣṇa recalls that Draupadī appealed to him from afar. Although neither mentions Draupadī's clothing, it is certain, at least for the second passage, that the disrobing scene is the setting.[36] If we are to contemplate originals, it is hardly more likely that Kṛṣṇa's intervention was unknown at an early stage of the text than that it was known.

In any case, the rich variations must have a history. The reconstituted text now reads (2.61):

> 40. Then Duḥśāsana, O king, forcibly tore off Draupadī's garment in the middle of the sabhā, and began to undress her.
>
> 41. But whenever one of Draupadī's garments was removed, O king, another garment like it repeatedly appeared.
>
> 42. Then there was a great shout of approval there, a terrible roar from all of the kings, having watched the greatest wonder in the world.[37]

[36]The first could recall Kṛṣṇa coming to Draupadī's aid to fill her cooking pot, discussed below, but this is unlikely since the CE rejects it. Bhattacharya 1995, 188–90, fails to mention these passages in arguing that Draupadī's disrobing is itself an interpolation.

[37]*Tato duḥśāsano rājan draupadyā vasanam balāt/ sabhāmadhye samākṣipya vyapakraṣṭum pracakrame// ākṛṣyamāṇe vasane draupadyās tu viśām pate/ tad rūpam aparaṃ vastram prādurāsīd anekaśaḥ// tato halahalāśabdas tatrāsīd ghoranisvanaḥ/ tadadbhutatamaṃ loke vīkṣya sarvamahīkṣitām.*

It is after verse 40 that most of the variations occur. The main southern variant, to which shorter additions were frequently made, has the distressed Draupadī repeatedly call out "Govinda" and "Kṛṣṇa" *(govindeti samābhāṣya kṛṣṇeti ca punaḥ punaḥ)*, and then recite a one-*śloka* prayer that several versions refer to as a song *(gītā)* taught to her by the sage Vasiṣṭha (547* and 548*, apud 2.61.40). Draupadī's repetition of the name "Govinda" at this point provides a Sanskrit counterpart, and possible source in the southern recension, for her cry "Govinda" at this point in Villiputtūr's Tamil *Makāpāratam*, and in Draupadī cult possession rites (Hiltebeitel 1988, 280–81 and n. 38). The song taught by Vasiṣṭha also includes the name Govinda:

> Holder of the conch, wheel, and mace, whose residence is Dvārakā,
> Govinda, Lotus-Eyed, protect me who has come for refuge.[38]

One sees here a fully articulated and intentionally highlighted bhakti theology, probably colored by Śrī Vaiṣṇava overtones.[39] The fact that the invocation "Govinda" is mentioned in both *Udyogaparvan* passages, however, means it is not restricted to the southern recension.

The chief northern variant (543*), familiar from the Roy and Dutt translations of the *Mahābhārata* from the Vulgate, and commented upon by Nīlakaṇṭha, is actually found "in only a few Devanāgarī manuscripts" (Edgerton 1944, xxix). It is, however, much longer than the main southern variant, and has many more contextual references to other facets of the *Mahābhārata*. Here Draupadī refers to Kṛṣṇa as "Beloved of the Gopī folk" (*gopījanapriya*; 543*, line 2; also 542*, line 1), one of the few allusions to Kṛṣṇa's childhood among the cowherders in the epic. Although we should no longer assume that such allusions are late or interpolated,[40] this one's explicitness in referring to the Gopīs themselves is quite possibly an indication that the passage was worked up by poets familiar with the *Harivaṃśa*, or the work of still later Paurāṇikas or north Indian bhakti sectarians.

The passage also goes to bizarre lengths to achieve a kind of literalism in bringing Kṛṣṇa to Draupadī's aid. At his residence in Dvārakā, "having heard the words of Yājñasenī, Kṛṣṇa was deeply moved. And having abandoned the couch where he slept, the benevolent one came

[38]*Śaṅkhacakragadāpāṇo dvārakānilayācyuta / govinda puṇḍarīkākṣa rakṣa māṃ śaraṇāgatām* (547*; cf. 548 on Vasiṣṭha and his song).

[39]On Śrī Vaiṣṇava "refuge," see Lester 1966, 266–82.

[40]See Katre 1960, 83–85. But let us recall that allusions to Kṛṣṇa's childhood among cowherds are more numerous in the epic than usually perceived (Biardeau 1978, 204–8; Hiltebeitel 1988, 188, 220). Again, the poets seem to imply more than they tell.

there on foot out of compassion."[41] To cover the roughly eight hundred miles from Dvārakā to Hāstinapura "on foot" *(padbhyām)* to rescue Draupadī at a moment's notice is more than would normally be required even of a deity, not to mention a literary convention. In this, the passage is like another that the Critical Edition relegates to an appendix. While the Pāṇḍavas are in exile, the sage Durvāsas visits Hāstinapura, where Duryodhana goes all out to gratify him and finally obtains a boon from him. Visiting the Pāṇḍavas in the forest when they've finished a meal and Draupadī has just lain down to rest, Durvāsas demands food for himself and his thousand disciples. What can Draupadī do but pray to Kṛṣṇa? "With you as protector, O lord of gods, in every distress there is no fear, as formerly when I was set free from Duḥśāsana in the sabhā."[42] Leaving Rukmiṇī's bed, Kṛṣṇa comes immediately, and after some frivolities at Draupadī's expense, takes some "vegetable and rice" (105) left over from the meal and miraculously makes it stuff Durvāsas and his throng's stomachs. Thinking they might anger the Pāṇḍavas by having to refuse the meal, Durvāsas decides to leave, and adds: "I fear still more, O Brahmans, from men who take refuge at the feet of Hari" (line 21). As Sukthankar says,

> With this story disappears one of the very few episodes . . . in which Śrī Kṛṣṇa is represented as hearing from a distance, as it were by clairaudience or divine omniscience, the prayers of his distressed devotees and as either coming instantly to help them in person or providing invisibly the means of their rescue or safety. The other . . . [episode is] the disrobing of Draupadī. . . . They undoubtedly represent a later phase of Kṛṣṇa worship. (1942, xiii n. 1)

All things considered,[43] it seems prudent to agree with Sukthankar that there may be a relative lateness to passages that *elaborate* on Kṛṣṇa's answering from afar, as in the Durvāsas episode and the northern variant of the disrobing scene where he arrives "on foot." But there are still textual grounds to suspect that he can do so mysteriously.

Immediately following the statement that Kṛṣṇa came "on foot" to veil

[41]2.543*, lines 10–11: *yājñasenyā vacaḥ śrutvā kṛṣṇo gahvarito 'bhavat/ tyaktvā śayyāsanam padbhyāṃ kṛpāluḥ kṛpayābhyagāt*. We would seem to have here an allusion to Kṛṣṇa as Viṣṇu-Anantaśāyin, the lord who wakes from sleeping on the serpent-couch to recreate the universe and bestow boons (cf. Hiltebeitel [1976] 1990, 106–7).

[42]*Āraṇyakaparvan*, App. I, No. 25, lines 86-87.

[43]Along with a debasement of the "Śaivite" Durvāsas with his horde of followers, the shift in tone seems to diminish the stature of Draupadī. Kṛṣṇa leaves the bed of Rukmiṇī, whom, rather than Draupadī, another presumably sectarian passage makes the incarnation of Śrī, leaving Draupadī an incarnation of Indra's wife Śacī (Hiltebeitel [1976] 1990, 62, n. 7).

Draupadī with sarees, there is a curious verse (544*). It is found extensively in the northern recension,[44] sometimes after the long rapid-travel passage just cited, but more often directly after verse 40, with the long passage omitted. It shows its anomalous character by being the only verse among all those that recount the scene, whether accepted or rejected by the Critical Edition, that is in the *triṣṭubh* rather than the *śloka* meter.[45] Theologically, however, it is consonant with a śloka verse (553*, *apud* 2.61.41) that is also found widely in the northern recension, and almost uniformly in the same manuscripts as 544*. It would thus appear that verses 544* and 553* together constitute the oldest variant, or perhaps the "original interpolation," in the northern recension. Set into the reconstituted text, the altered passage would read as follows:

> 40. Then Duḥśāsana, O king, forcibly tore off Draupadī's garment in the middle of the sabhā, and began to undress her.
>
> 544* Yājñasenī cried out for salvation *(trāṇāya vikrośati)* to Kṛṣṇa, Viṣṇu, Hari, and Nara. Then Dharma, concealed, the magnanimous, having a multitude of garments, covered her.[46]
>
> 41. Whenever one of Draupadī's garments was removed, O king, another garment like it repeatedly appeared.
>
> 553* Thereupon garments of many colors and whites appeared, O lord, by hundreds, due to the protection of Dharma.[47]

In verse 544* Draupadī does invoke Kṛṣṇa under the first three names mentioned, but the fourth—Nara—usually refers to Arjuna. Here Draupadī is doing almost exactly what Duḥśāsana has said she could do in the nonproblematic Critical Edition verse cited above. In anticipation of her stripping, he taunts, "Cry out for salvation *(trāṇāya vikrośa)* to Kṛṣṇa and Jiṣṇu, to Hari and Nara" (60.26). But the help in verse 544* seems to come not from Kṛṣṇa or Nara, but from Dharma. And in verse 553*, her rescue is even more clearly "due to Dharma's protection" *(dharmasya paripālanāt)* alone, with no mention of any other figure. Indeed, Draupadī has counted on the protection of Dharma from the beginning (see above, n. 13).

[44] As Edgerton observes (1944, xxix), the Śāradā Codex alone omits it, although one Kaśmīrī manuscript has it "written on the *margin*" (Edgerton's italics).

[45] Regarding arguments concerning hypermetric or irregularly metered triṣṭubhs (see chap. 1, n. 70), they would not apply to these regular verses.

[46] *Kṛṣṇaṃ ca viṣṇuṃ ca hariṃ naraṃ ca/ trāṇāya vikrośati yājñasenī// tatastu dharmo 'ntarito mahātmā/ samāvṛṇottāṃ vividhavastrapūgaḥ.*

[47] *Nānārāgavirāgāṇi vasanānyatha vai prabho/ prādurbhavanti śataśo dharmasya paripālanāt.* Mehendale 1990, 288, noting that I rely on Nīlakaṇṭha in translating *virāga* as white (1980a, 107), prefers "having different colours": i.e., that some of the garments were "each one of a different colour" *(nānarāga)* and others multicolored. This is possible.

As noted, Dharma incarnates in Vidura and sires Yudhiṣṭhira: the one, the first to raise an aspect of Draupadī's question and the first to continue pressing for an answer to it immediately after the miracle (61.51c–57); the other, silenced by it and left most to ponder it. To be sure, Dharma, like Nara, could refer to Kṛṣṇa as Viṣṇu, for whom such a name is possible. But in the epic Dharma is more a deity on his own whom we have come to know. Indeed, the "concealed" *(antarhita)* Dharma who rescues Draupadī here is certainly reminiscent of the Dharma who disguises himself as a Yakṣa and a dog to test Yudhiṣṭhira in encounters with death. Yet "Dharma/dharma's protection" would also seem to have an impersonal connotation here. The two verses identifying dharma/Dharma as the source of the miracle were perhaps what Edgerton had in mind when he spoke of "cosmic justice" automatically rescuing the chaste Draupadī. Justice *(dharma)* may be set in motion by a prayer to Kṛṣṇa, but it is available to Draupadī precisely because she is just, virtuous, herself.[48] I think this is apt, yet I think we must also consider the implication that the "concealed dharma" operates here as well through the ignored Vidura and the silent Yudhiṣṭhira.

If these verses are our oldest variant, or "original interpolation" in the northern recension, then it is reasonable to suspect that they could have proved devotionally uninspiring to later northern poets, who could have sought uniformity in the ambiguous references to Kṛṣṇa, Nara, and Dharma by prefacing verse 544* with a long and explicit plea to Kṛṣṇa culminating in the totally unambiguous but ridiculous assertion that he came to Draupadī's rescue "on foot." If one must guess at a chronology, the southern recension's simple devotional "song" is probably later than the verses invoking Dharma and earlier than Kṛṣṇa's fancy footwork and the reference to the Gopīs. As to the verses invoking Dharma, they are *probably* (if they are the original interpolation), but *not necessarily* (if they are the oldest variant), younger than the *Udyogaparvan* recollections of Draupadī's cry to Govinda, which cannot be called interpolations. This leaves us with the question of whether one can profitably argue for a priority between the reconstituted passage that makes no mention of Kṛṣṇa and the critically accepted texts that do, so briefly, under the name "Govinda." I doubt that one can. Lipner links Draupadī's cry to Kṛṣṇa with "popular versions," and says that "in the final analysis" it is dharma that vindicates her (1994, 207 and 344, n. 8). But Kṛṣṇa's intervention

[48]On dharma as having garments with which to "dress one with virtue," sometimes hypocritically, see Hiltebeitel 1980a, 101. Cf. Spivak 1988, 183; Biardeau 1984, 255: when Nala leaves Damayantī in the forest, he "implores the gods to protect her, knowing well that she is 'covered with *dharma—dharmeṇāsi samāvṛtā*'" (3.248* line 2, after 3.59.21), here evoking this "original" dimension of Draupadī's disrobing in an interpolation.

cannot be attributed to "popular versions": the "original interpolation" seems to have been unpopular, and the Critical Edition knows the story elsewhere.[49] Moreover, the Critical Edition has Draupadī call not only on dharma but on the All-Disposer. If the All-Disposer alludes directly or indirectly to Kṛṣṇa, he may be working with dharma all along.

One may ask, what does all this textual variation on Draupadī's cry for salvation have to do with her question? But we need only recall that Karṇa's order to strip her is the outcome of his cruel answer to it. We have already found such connections in *Nala*: the body stripped—to any degree (see n. 32)—is a self laid bare. As Nala is stripped, so is Yudhiṣṭhira. For each, their project becomes that of restoring themselves, their kingdoms, and their marriages. But the women are never stripped. Damayantī retains half a sari, and Draupadī receives endless sarees. For the one a fraction is left by her husband, for the other an infinity is received from . . . what? The textual variations are different commentaries on what saves the heroine who asks about the self of the hero, not only to save herself but to save him, or them. As in *Nala*, it is a question of the self, as ātman, only with the royal hero and not with the heroine. These two heroines have other refuges, one of them being their fidelity, another being riddles. Other than that, what saved Draupadī? Was it God who comes from afar? on foot? even in his absence? Was it the All-Disposer, or Dharma—one of whom, she says earlier, will bring peace? Dharma as law? as justice? as reduced to a question left for those who embody it—the ignored Vidura and the silent Yudhiṣṭhira—still to keep alive? The variants give all the answers but the last, which I think we must nonetheless still keep pending.

Although Vidura says a question raised in the sabhā requires an answer lest dharma be injured (see n. 5), his words are greeted with silence, and Karṇa orders Duḥśasana to take the dasī away to the "houses" (*gṛhān*; 61.81)! But Draupadī stands her ground, saying she will abide by the answer given (62.4–13). Bhīṣma equivocates again (14–21), this time concluding, "I think Yudhiṣṭhira is the authority on this question, whether she is won or not won, so he can give utterance himself *(api svayaṃ vyāhartum arhati)*" (21)—which Duryodhana seems to appreciate. Indirectly daring Yudhiṣṭhira, he taunts Draupadī to get a response from him or, if he will not speak, from another of the Pāṇḍavas: "Let them declare in the midst of the nobles for your sake,

[49]For Lipner, Kṛṣṇa is yet to be divine for the entire the *Sabhā Parvan* (1994, 198), forgetting for a moment that parvan's "bhakti of hatred" story of Kṛṣṇa and Śiśupāla, which he cites later (198; 357, n. 34). Like Mehendale (see n. 30), he posits an "original story" without miracles and with the two dice matches as one (344–45, n. 13). Indeed, he takes the story's bare reference to reincarnation to suggest that it predates the doctrine (231)!

Pāñcālī, that Yudhiṣṭhira is not a master. Let them all make Dharmarāja a liar *(kurvantu sarve cānṛtaṃ dharmarājam)*, Pāñcālī, (and) you will get free from servitude" (25). So cued, Bhīma now says that Yudhiṣṭhira *is* their master (*īśa*; 32–33), which would leave Draupadī a dāsī; but his answer is ignored. Karṇa insults the dāsī some more, and Bhīma flares up. Again Duryodhana taunts Yudhiṣṭhira to answer, now addressing him directly, and shows Draupadī his bared left thigh, goading Bhīma to vow to break it (63.1–16). Again Vidura says the dharma requires an answer, now more urgently than ever, and seems to suggest his own view of the impasse as a kind of mirage: "A stake that one who is not his own master plays would be won as in a dream, I think."[50]

Finally Arjuna seems to pick out of Vidura's gloom the implication that Draupadī is not lost: "The king was formerly our master in the betting *(īśo rājā pūrvam āsīd glahe naḥ)*, Kuntī's son, the great-souled king Dharma. But whose master is he whose self is vanquished *(īśas tvayaṃ kasya parājitātmā)*? Realize this *(taj jānīdhvam)*,[51] all you Kurus" (63.21). Arjuna's words are but another question, one that leaves Draupadī's question hanging. As his question closes the debate on Draupadī's question, it leaves two matters open: not only whether Yudhiṣṭhira has been his own master, but whether indeed his self has been vanquished. Arjuna's opinion, which is of course the opposite of Bhīma's, probably registers what is closest to the dharma's unacceptable truth. But it settles nothing, for at this very moment jackals bark and donkeys bray (23).[52] These terrible omens sound at Arjuna's words.[53] This is probably because he is doing the very thing he had told Bhīma not

[50]2.63.19ab: *svapne yathaitaddhi dhanaṃ jitaṃ syāt/ tad evam manye yasya dīvyatyanīśaḥ*. Cf. van Buitenen 1975, 152: ". . . if the stake is put up by one who does not own it!"

[51]I follow the strongest translation of Mehendale 1985, 188–91, who also gives "take note" for *jānīdhvam*, and argues reasonably against van Buitenen's "decide" (1975, 152) and Ganguli's "judge" ([1884–96] 1970, 2:151). Cf. Biardeau's "Aux Kaurava de le savoir" (1985, 11). But the improvement does not help his argument that Arjuna "settled the issue" (Mehendale 1985, 182). What follows is my disagreement with him on this point.

[52]Mehendale deplores these omens, getting quite carried away: "The Indian tradition has touched a very low point in allowing the stanzas about bad omens to remain where they are for so long. We are unaware of the fact that in doing so we have tarnished the fair image of a person like Śrī Vyāsa" (1985, 193). Despite noting how well they are established in both the text and the Indian tradition (179–81), he wants to find them either "a figment of some interpolator's imagination" (193; cf. 181, 192) or that Dhṛtarāṣṭra, already convinced by Arjuna, ignored them when he decided to give Draupadī her boons (193).

[53]Mehendale does not ask why they do so, requiring his explanations (see n. 52 above) as to why Arjuna's words have been "overlooked" (1985, 190). He rues that "[n]obody has ever sensed that what happened was due to Arjuna's reply" (189), and that Arjuna hit "the bull's eye" (192). But it is Mehendale who misses the point. Lipner, concluding correctly that "[t]he question remains open," cites Bhīma's and the jackals' contributions, but ignores Arjuna's (1994, 209).

to do: he is overstepping his eldest brother, indeed, his two elder brothers, since he is also disagreeing with Bhīma. Whatever the truth of his words, they are an unacceptable truth that cannot be the truth of the story, and are as ominous as the omens that greet them. For were they taken as final, they would be the very thing Duryodhana wants to hear, even at the cost freeing Draupadī: that Yudhiṣṭhira is a liar.

At last these omens prompt Dhṛtarāṣṭra to offer Draupadī the boons that allow her to choose Yudhiṣṭhira's freedom and that of all her husbands, plus their weapons. And Karṇa recognizes that she has been the Pāṇḍavas' salvation *(śānti)* and their boat to shore (64.1–3). As Kṛṣṇa will later confirm, "Kṛṣṇā lifted up[54] the Pāṇḍavas, as also herself, as with a ship from a swell in the ocean" (5.29.35).

C. The Question within the Episode

Let us now look at the implications of Draupadī's question: first, mainly within the episode itself, and then at what lies behind and follows from it at other points in the epic. Even as she is dragged into the sabhā decrying the Kuru's loss of dharma that brings her there, she attests to Yudhiṣṭhira's firmness in dharma and her knowledge that "dharma is subtle" (60.31–33). Yet the dharma is also what subjugates her there in the sarcastic words of Karṇa: "There are three who own no property: a slave, a student, and a woman are nonindependent *(asvatantra)*. You are the wife of a slave, his wealth, dear—without a master, the wealth of a slave, and a slave (yourself)" (63.1). These words resonnate with a famous verse in *The Laws of Manu* (9.3) that describes women as "non-independent" *(asvatantra)*. Draupadī challenges this, speaking about, and perhaps for, women as a class: "These Kurus stand here in the hall, lords of their daughters and daughters-in-law, all considering even my word—answer this question of mine the proper way" (61.45). The men are challenged to consider a question that questions their "ownership" of women.[55] It is by appealing to dharma around a question that brings

[54]On the use of the verb *ujjahāra* here, see Hiltebeitel 1980a, 103, and *Mbh* 12.333.11: "Formerly this earth with her ocean-belt disappeared. Govinda, resorting to boar form, lifted her up." It is Nara and Nārāyaṇa who speak with this avataric vocabulary.

[55]On the contrary, Karve 1974, 87–90, gives an astonishing reading of Draupadī's question as her "greatest mistake": Draupadī "tried to show off her learning"; "by putting on airs in front of the whole assembly, she had put Dharma [Yudhiṣṭhira] into a dilemma and unwittingly insulted him"; "Draupadi was standing there arguing about legal technicalities like a lady pundit when what was happening to her was so hideous that she should only have cried out for decency and pity in the name of the Kshatriya code. Had she done so perhaps things would not have gone so far." Karve compares Draupadī here with Sītā, as does a woman interviewed by Mankekar who, after seeing both heroines portrayed on Indian national television, "felt Draupadi was 'Westernized' because the heroine questioned and challenged her elders on the propriety of their actions" (1993, 552).

both overt and hidden questions to life that she can save herself and the Pāṇḍavas.

Śakuni, Yudhiṣṭhira's deceitful opponent, delivers the probing verse: "There is surely your dear lady *(priyā devī)*, one throw unwon. Stake Kṛṣṇā Pāñcālī. Win yourself back by her *(tayā 'tmānam punarjaya)*" (58.31). "Your dear lady," *priyā devī*. . . . The first meaning of *devī* is of course "goddess," which would be an overtranslation but hardly an overestimation of the lady. More than this, *devī* is the goddess as "she who plays" (Biardeau 1985, 17), and Pāñcālī is a name for Draupadī, used with heightened frequency in this scene (ibid., 11, 13–14), meaning "the puppet." As Yudhiṣṭhira sets to wager her, he speaks from what feels like a reverie:[56] "She is not too short or too tall, not too black or too red—I play you with her *(tayā dīvyāmyahaṃ tvayā)*. . . ." Doll-like, iconic, she is bet and lost, and Yudhiṣṭhira will say nothing until her question frees him. Once in the forest, Draupadī will say we are all puppets, our strings pulled by the Creator—to which Yudhiṣṭhira will reply that she is eloquent with passion, but heretical. As Pāñcālī, Draupadī is thus the doll or puppet who speaks, who even recognizes herself as such; as *devī*, she is the lady who is played who also plays.

But there is more to Yudhiṣṭhira's words as they turn from reverie to silence: ". . . Eyes like the petals of autumn lotuses, a fragrance as of autumn lotuses, a beauty that waits on autumn lotuses—the peer of Śrī in her beauty. Yes, for her noncruelty *(ānṛśaṃsya)*, her perfection of form, the straightness of her character *(śīla)*, does a man desire a woman *(yām icchet puruṣaḥ striyam)*. . . . Her waist shaped like an altar, hair long *(vedimadhyā dīrghakeśī)*, eyes the color of copper, not too much body hair . . . such is the woman, king, such is the slender-waisted Pāñcālī, whom I now throw, the beautiful Draupadī" (58.33–37). It is important that Draupadī is not in the sabhā to hear these words; they are not for her to hear but for Yudhiṣṭhira to remember. We now see that while it is his hearing Damayantī tell Nala, "Ānṛśaṃsya is the highest dharma, so I heard from you" (3.67.15cd; see p. 228 above), that begins Yudhiṣṭhira's long and painful education about ānṛśaṃsya, it is this unforgettable scene—the first to use the term in connection with him, and with he himself, like Nala, the speaker—that grounds "noncruelty" for him, we might say above all, in the big and little cruelties of his marriage.

It is clear that in all this talk about betting oneself, Draupadī's question is a philosophical one about the nature of self, compounded by legal issues of *mastery*, *lord*ship, *proper*ty, *own*ership, and slavery in the

[56]Lipner says that Yudhiṣṭhira "[f]or a moment . . . muses" here (1994, 203); but as we shall see, it is surely more than that.

hierarchical context of marriage, and symbolized around the figure of the ultimate lord, master, and owner, the king, in relation to a subjecthood and objecthood of the queen, his wife. These themes are discernible in the Sanskrit,[57] as are those we have noticed in *Nala* of possession of self verses possession by the madness of dicing, and, one senses, the theme of love and abandonment, of love between six people in one and the same marriage tested to the breaking point especially in Bhīma's and Arjuna's different expressions of near-insubordination. Listen to what Yudhiṣṭhira says when he bets himself just before he wagers Draupadī: "I am left, so beloved of all my brothers. Won, we shall do work for you when the self is itself a deluge" (*upaplave*; 58.27). Slipping into his loving reverie, Yudhiṣṭhira descends into silence once he has lost her. Here we see Draupadī's question from a new angle. Yudhiṣṭhira's loss of self *appears*—it is only described so by others—to be a loss of consciousness, like Nala's. Yet is he unconscious? What is the nature of the "self at stake" in Draupadī's question?

Here we seem to be in an agonistic multidialogical situation that reverberates with Upaniṣadic scenes in which fathers and sons, gurus and disciples, and even men and women churn the oppositional languages of rivalry and status to release the saving knowledge of what is one.[58] Gārgī, whose questions to Yājñavalkya are like arrows; Yājñavalkya to Maitreyī, renouncing the world and saying goodbye forever to his dearer-than-ever "knowledge-discoursing *(brahmavādinī)*" wife: "not for love of the husband is a husband dear, but for love of the ātman . . . ; not for love of the wife. . . ."[59] We should not forget the limits such dialogues impose on the women speakers.[60] But here, where only one of the partners is speaking and the other is silent, the speaker is the woman. Does she speak, at least for now, for both of them, while Yudhiṣṭhira cannot, or will not, speak for himself?

As *Nala* has demonstrated, in the *Mahābhārata*, the language of such questions and answers is compounded by proto-Sāṃkhya-Yoga and bhakti (see chapter 6, § B). Al Collins (1994, 3–4) shows how a sovereign self, male *(puruṣa)*, replicates itself in other selves through a "scale of forms"

[57]The main terms covering these meanings are *īśa* and *anīśa*, which I have cited frequently, translating *iśa* as "master." At two points, Draupadī is also said to be "lordless" *(anāthavat)* or, as van Buitenen translates (1975, 141, 146), "without protectors" (60.24cd, 61.52b).
[58]Cf. Witzel 1987a. One may ask whether Draupadī's question overreaches the limits of her knowledge (371–72). I would argue that it does not; see below on Draupadī and the question of *avidyā*, "ignorance," and her recognition as a "paṇḍit."
[59]See *BAUp* 3.6 and 8, both presenting Gārgī, and 2.4 (esp. stanza 5) and 4.5 (esp. stanza 6), both presenting Maitreyī.
[60]Cf. Falk 1977, 105–7, setting Draupadī and Yudhiṣṭhira's exchanges amid such male-female dialogical situations.

that "presents a problem for male identity formation." Man (and, for that matter, woman), as mind-ego-intellect, is feminine matter, *prakṛti*, living—ultimately unconsciously—"for the sake of puruṣa," of "man" as conscious self or soul. As Collins says, "The problem is not limited to kings" who top this "scale of forms," "but is universal: it is highly dangerous to claim to be a self" (1994, 4). This well describes Yudhiṣṭhira's predicament; no wonder he is silent. Should he claim to be a self who wagered Draupadī first, he simply lies and loses her forever. If he claims to be a self who wagered her after he lost himself, he—or his brothers—might keep her, or maybe just compound their slavery, but he lies about having lost himself.

Indeed, should he claim, like Nala, that in betting and losing his wife, "I myself was not its doer," the self he wagered would be counterfeit, making him a more deceiving gambler even than Śakuni.[61] If *Nala* can lift the Pāṇḍavas and Draupadī's spirits, it cannot retrospectively provide Yudhiṣṭhira with Nala's excuses. No matter how tempted a reader might be to say that Yudhiṣṭhira was "possessed by Kali," who is incarnate in Duryodhana, or even that he was just crazed by the dice (see above, n. 7), Yudhiṣṭhira could not help himself by saying such things, since unlike Nala, he bet his wife.

Buddhists have a story about Aśoka—a king, indeed an "emperor," who topped the scale of forms—that invites reflection here.[62] The "great quinquennial festival" *(pañcavārṣika)* described in Buddhist sources involved, as an extravaganza of imperial *dāna* (gifting), the "custom of divestment and then reacquisition of the royal clothes and jewels" (Strong 1983, 94). In the *Aśokāvadāna*, Aśoka announces he is ready to give away vast wealth to the saṅgha and bathe the bodhi tree.

> This, however, hardly represents the totality of his assets. There follows, therefore, a comic scene in which Aśoka's young son Kunāla indicates with a hand gesture to the crowd that he will double the amount. The crowd laughs and Aśoka is forced to "outbid" his son by tripling his original offer; Kunāla quadruples it. This goes on until finally, Aśoka, retaining only the state treasury, makes a total gift to

[61]See Derrida 1991 and 1992, raising the questions of law, narrative, the aleatory, the gift of time, and of what may be counterfeit in a wager. "The gift must let itself be structured by the aleatory; it must appear chancy," dicey (1992, 122–23, 163). In effect, Draupadī's question is her added throw of the dice, as in a Telugu folk *Mbh* story of her playing the last throw herself (Hiltebeitel 1988, 238).

[62]While the *Mbh* may be considered post-Aśokan (see chap. 1), it is doubtful that the scholarly reconstructions of Aśoka's *history* can provide solid ways to interpret the epic *stories* of Arjuna (Selvanayagam 1992) or Yudhiṣṭhira (Sutton 1997). But the two stories suggest a common milieu, and perhaps a Buddhist reworking of the epic theme.

> the sangha of his whole kingdom, his harem, his ministers, his self, and his son Kunāla. This is the ultimate potlatch, and Kunāla, finding himself part of his father's gift, cannot very well outdo him.
>
> Then, however, having given everything away to the sangha, . . . [Aśoka] buys it all back, . . . and thereby redeems from the sangha his kingship, his wives, his ministers, his son, and his self. (95–96)

The summary is Strong's, who may have been reminded that Marcel Mauss called the *Mahābhārata* dice match "the story of a monstrous potlatch" (see chapter 1, n. 2). But Strong's translation of the episode shows that it is not so comic. It begins, "Now at that time Kunāla's eyes had not yet been put out." Aśoka laughs at the first outbidding, but is "irritated" by the second. When he learns his opponent is Kunāla, it is in perhaps both humors that he makes the encompassing bid that includes "my self, and Kunāla": that is, *both* their selves. He thereby dissolves or nullifies their mock-rivalry by his subsuming wit (264–68). Aśoka loves Kunāla, but is "too attached to his son's eyes," which "resembled a fully blossomed blue lotus." When Kunāla is cruelly blinded by his stepmother, who resents his rejection of her ardor towards him, and fears he might kill her, she lets Kunāla think that it is Aśoka who has ordered the blinding. As a blind minstrel, Kunāla then reconciles with his father, but he cannot save his stepmother from Aśoka's cruel execution, even though saying that he loves her provides the "act of truth" by which he regains his sight (268–85). It is between losing his first and second eyes that Kunāla is enlightened about the impermanence and emptiness of self, making it clear that we have been hearing about Buddhist *non*selves in this contest: fathers and sons, husbands and wives, again hard truths from the dialogical situation.

But what about Draupadī? Biardeau, also insistent that a Sāṃkhya problematic underlies *Mahābhārata* portrayals of heroines, argues that the heroine-goddess represents prakṛti as unconscious matter, blind ignorance given to "obstinacy"; matter that unknowingly yet somehow inerrantly works on behalf of puruṣa (1984, 263) through "blind initiatives"; heroines whose ignorance is unknowing in particular about dharma.[63] Unlike Kunāla, such a dim Draupadī would have no sight to begin with and none to get back. The epic poets do touch on Sāṃkhya themes, but

[63]A key passage is 4.15.34: Yudhiṣṭhira tells Draupadī, when she protests being kicked by Kīcaka, "You are ignorant of time *(akālajñāsi)*, you run about like an actress!" But one cannot generalize on these silencing words. Yudhiṣṭhira may be reminding her she *should* be "acting" like a Sairandhrī, "biding her time" while they keep their disguises; or perhaps of how by contrast she "played for time" in the sabhā. Cf. Biardeau 1997b, 38, 47.

this reading is one-sided.[64] Biardeau says nothing about ignorance when it is a question of a heroine's "knowing time and place,"[65] or exhibiting her ingenuity in posing riddle-questions that prompt a hero's anagnorisis and draw him out of his concealment, riddles about intimacies and pains of love that are a lifeline allowing him *and her* to use their wits, to "play for time," and thus to give time its play. Draupadī certainly knows enough about dharma to question it. It is not just her obstinacy that makes her persist. Her timely "strategy for survival," her "delaying tactics" amidst the craven Kauravas, have "paradoxically . . . involved a concerted effort to freeze time," or better suspend it, by language that undercuts and literally eludes the grasp of patriarchal authority in the "men's court."[66] Yudhiṣṭhira *appears* to be silent: is it that he reads her "signs" and leaves her this chance to play for time?[67]

That is my sense of things, although as we shall see, if it is true, it may work at the dice match without working for all things, since time does eventually run out. Let us touch on a few defining incidents in the relationship of Yudhiṣṭhira and Draupadī over the long haul to see what such an interpretation would entail.

D. Before and After the Question

Once the Pāṇḍavas marry Draupadī, they establish themselves, with Kṛṣṇa and Vyāsa's help, in their new half of the kingdom at Indraprastha (1.199.26–28). Kṛṣṇa then leaves for Dvārakā (50), Vyāsa recedes back into the text, whereupon Nārada "by chance arrived" (*ājagāma yadṛcchayā*; cf. chapter 2, n. 61). He sees the Pāṇḍavas sitting on five thrones with one queen, and once Draupadī has left the room, he tells

[64]Cf. Sutton 2000, 440–41, noting how the renounced mendicant *(bhikṣukī)* Sulabhā makes a Sāṃkhya argument against female inferiority in her teachings to King Janaka (12.308).
[65]Said of Damayantī (3.57.10–11). Cf. chap. 6 at n. 23.
[66]I transpose these quoted phrases from Suzuki's description (1989, 75) of Penelope's "vigilant consciousness of the passage of time," her "strategy for survival in Odysseus' absence, her delaying tactics against the suitors." Note too that "Homer's Helen" repeatedly "poses the question of her responsibility—a question that remains unanswered [not only] in the *Iliad*" (56) but to Penelope in the *Odyssey* (74–75). Cf. above, nn. 2 and 3.
[67]See Shulman 1996, 151: In the epic dice match, with the certainty of losing, "one mostly fights for time." My thoughts on "giving time," the "aleatory," and on dharma as law and justice begin from that quote (from a 1991 draft of Shulman 1996) and Biardeau's discussions of *daiva* and the name Pāñcālī (see above at n. 56), variously enriched by Derrida 1991 and 1992, Grosz 1997, and Caputo 1997a, 160–229. "The gift gives, demands, and takes time. . . . That is one of the reasons this thing of the gift will be linked to the—internal—necessity of a certain narrative [*récit*] or a certain poetics of narrative" (Derrida 1992, 41). See also above, nn. 10 and 61. For a different reading—Yudhiṣṭhira "ostentatiously declines to take any further part in the episode . . . once he knows" Draupadī is menstruating, so as to maintain male purity—see M. Brockington 2000, 4.

them a story to impress them with the need to avoid a breach between them. Two demons, Sunda and Upasunda, were safe in the boon that death could come to them only if they killed each other. Nonetheless, they did so over Tilottamā, whom the celestial architect Viśvakarman had fashioned at the gods' bidding to Śrī-like perfection—from diamonds and all the world's most beautiful things (203.12–17), a truly perfect doll with no prior attachments—to tempt the pair to their own destruction. Having heard this story, which is not that flattering to Draupadī, the Pāṇḍavas make a compact *(samayam)*: "Anyone who would see one of the others while he is sitting together *(sahāsīnam)* with Draupadī must live in the forest for twelve years as a celibate *(brahmacārin)*."[68] We soon learn that "sitting together" is a euphemism and that Nārada, as usual, is prompting as much trouble as he is precaution.

All goes well for a while, but after a "long time" the idyll ends. A Brahman comes crying to Arjuna that thieves have made off with his cows; unless the thieves are apprehended and his cows returned it will be a rebuke to Pāṇḍava rule. Arjuna says, "Don't fear," but faces a dilemma: the Pāṇḍavas' weapons are "where Dharmarāja Yudhiṣṭhira was with Kṛṣṇā." It would be great adharma, thinks Arjuna, for the king were he to overlook this, whereas by protecting the Brahman "it would establish the nonheresy *(anāstikyam)* of all of us in the world." He convinces himself to bravely face death in the forest to avoid this adharma, and in rapid order, "having followed the king in entering *(anupraviśya rājānam)*, taking leave, grabbing his bow, delighted *(saṃhṛṣṭaḥ)*," Arjuna "addressed the Brahman, 'Come quickly'" (205.1–19). Catching these thieves is no problem, but there is one upon his swift return: Arjuna tells Yudhiṣṭhira, "The compact is completely overstepped by my seeing you *(samayaḥ samatikrānto bhavat saṃdarśanān mayā)*. I will go dwell in the forest. That was surely the compact we made" (24). Yudhiṣṭhira, hearing this "disagreeable word unexpectedly *(sahasā vākyam apriyam)*," tries to smooth things over: "What you did, O hero, in following my entry *(anupraveśe)* is not disagreeable *(apriyam)*. I forgive it entirely. It is not a transgression in my heart *(vyalīkaṃ na ca me hṛdi)*. Surely the younger following the entry of the elder *(guror anupraveśo)* is not an offense. The breach of the rule is the eldest's following the entry of the younger *(yavīyaso 'nupraveśo jyeṣṭhasya vidhilopakaḥ)*" (26–27). But Arjuna holds to principle: "'One should not observe dharma through fraud.' So I have

[68]1.204.28. Twelve years according to the CE. Van Buitenen 1973, 446, thinks one year was the "original duration," as does Oberlies 1995, 181. But Arjuna must not only go all around India; for nine months of this "year" he is near Maṇalūra for both the beginning *and end* of Citrāṅgadā's pregnancy with their son Babhrūvāhana (1.209.24).

heard from *you*! I will not waver from truth. By truth I took the weapon." Off he goes to dwell in the forest for twelve years (29–30).

One begins with the obvious question: why did the Pāṇḍavas keep their weapons in the bedroom? But the poets never even ask it, much less answer it. A Draupadī cult analogy is useful again. It is as if the bedroom is like a Draupadī temple, where the Pāṇḍavas *and* Draupadī's weapons are stalled, to be taken out for festival processions, including one reenacting Arjuna's defense of the kingdom of Virāṭa against a cattle raid. But more immediately, the weapons in the bedroom are the Pāṇḍavas' tokens of virility, and Arjuna wants his back.

I have translated the repeated use of *anu-pra-viś-* as "follow in entering," for it certainly carries sexual connotations in the context of the Pāṇḍavas' tenuous marriage protocols.[69] That Yudhiṣṭhira and Draupadī are not just "sitting together"[70] is underscored in the Oriya *Mahābhārata* of Sāralādāsa,[71] in which the complaining Brahman is revealed as Agni:

> Agni came in the guise of an unidentified brahman and insisted on meeting Yudhisthira who was with Draupadi in her harem (bedroom). As a sign for that Yudhisthira left his foot-wears by the side of the door. But Agni, in the form of a dog, lifted those foot-wears. Arjuna, being ignorant of this, went inside the bedroom and saw the coition of his brother and Draupadi. (Misra 1995, 144–45)

It does not take much to realize that if the younger may follow the entry of the eldest but not vice versa, Arjuna *may* find something problematic in Yudhiṣṭhira's having this turn with Draupadī, since these events would transpire after at least one previous cycle of passing Draupadī down by order of seniority, with the result that Yudhiṣṭhira would have "followed in entering" after the turn of *his* youngest brother Sahadeva: indeed, after all four of his younger brothers. Moreover, considering that Yudhiṣṭhira is first called not just the "eldest" but the "guru," Arjuna's "gazing" is a kind of "violation of the teacher's bed" *(gurutalpa)*, one of the worst of sins. Indeed, given that a guru and eldest brother are equivalent to a father, Arjuna sees an approximation of the "primal scene."

Moreover, *anu-pra-viś* also means attack: Yudhiṣṭhira and Draupadī

[69]It is used six times in this episode, including a summation by Ulūpī (1.206.25), and nowhere else in this sense.

[70]Ganguli, however, attempts to keep Draupadī and Yudhiṣṭhira "sitting" throughout the episode ([1884–96] 1970, 1:445–46).

[71]A Śūdra poet from near Cuttack of the fifteenth century, according to Mohanty 1990, 267, and Patnaik 1993, 170; thirteenth century according to Misra 1995, 144. Cf. Boulton 1976, 5: a "ploughman."

are vulnerable when Arjuna "completely oversteps" his compact by "seeing" them.[72] Having by his own admission "completely overstepped" his eldest brother at this first test of their marital concord, it is not hard to see that it foreshadows his warning to Bhīma not to do the same at the dice match,[73] and his finally doing the very same himself.

Of course the poets do not say such things. Yet we know that this scene ends the Pāṇḍavas and Draupadī's idyll, and it seems Arjuna is quite eager to end it. Once the "delighted" Arjuna has invaded the bedroom, stood his ground on the principle of the compact, and left for his twelve years of "celibacy," Draupadī will not again see the man who won her until he has married three other women and brought one of them home: the "auspicious" Subhadrā, sister of Kṛṣṇa, who seems to become his "favorite."[74]

For all six partners, then, it is enough to say that the happy freshness of their honeymoon is over. For Draupadī and Yudhiṣṭhira in particular, it ends with their own intimacy interrupted by the brother who not only won Draupadī, but whom she now comes to start missing in this first of what will be Arjuna's many absences and estrangements.[75] Again, the poets do not have to tell us that Yudhiṣṭhira bends so far to keep Arjuna around, at least in part, to keep Draupadī happy, and that when he claims to find nothing "disagreeable" in his "heart" about Arjuna's interruption and gaze, that his heart would be troubled. They do not have to tell us that if Draupadī begins to find her multiple marriage emotionally less satisfying than it was to this point, she will have no one to blame but Yudhiṣṭhira, who upheld the mother's word that made her polyandry happen.[76] Draupadī will wait until Arjuna has returned with Subhadrā

[72] *Saṃdarśana*, really more than "seeing," is "the act of looking steadfastly, gazing" (MW, 1144): perhaps best, "staring."

[73] It is the same verb: *sam-ati-kram-* here; *ati-kram-* at 2.61.8d. See above at nn. 4 and 27.

[74] See Hiltebeitel 1988, 220, on Subhadrā's auspiciousness and her homecoming, worked out to lessen Draupadī's jealousy; 1988, 215, and 1991a, 378–83, on Subhadrā as "favorite" *(vāvātā)* and Draupadī as "chief queen" *(mahiṣī)* with respect to Arjuna, following Gehrts 1975, 186–87; 1988, 216, and Subramanian 1967, 55, on the Rabelaisian character of Arjuna's "celibacy."

[75] As just noted, his return from this one with Subhadrā is especially bittersweet. Cf. 3.38.19–25: Draupadī's sadness on Arjuna's departure to obtain weapons; 3.142: missing him; 3.144–46: her forest hardships and "colorful frolics" (*krīḍitāni . . . vicitrāṇi*; 145.43) at the prospects of seeing him: 3.161.29: just back from heaven he sleeps beside the twins; 4.23.24 (see Hiltebeitel 1980b, 161): harsh and cryptic words during their estrangement while incognito; 14.89.1–10 (and Dumézil 1969, 164): she won't hear of his having any imperfection on his return from the year of guarding the Aśvamedha horse.

[76] Kuntī says, "Share it [her] all equally" (1.182.1–4), thinking Draupadī is alms (Hiltebeitel 1988, 200). See Mohanty 1990, 279, on Pratibha Ray's Oriya novel *Jajnaseni* depicting

to have her one son with each Pāṇḍava. The five are born a year apart and Arjuna's is named third (1.213.72, 79), so Arjuna must have again taken his turn after his two older brothers. But the account is perfunctory.

So much for what comes before Draupadī's question. The next passage of interest comes early in the forest book in the long exchange between Yudhiṣṭhira and Draupadī that includes what I have called Draupadī's puppet speech. It is the nadir of their relationship, coming between the dice match and Arjuna's departure (at Yudhiṣṭhira's behest) to obtain divine weapons, which itself sinks the remaining Pāṇḍavas in the misery that prompts their hearing of *Nala*. More specifically, it comes between Yudhiṣṭhira's reverie about Draupadī's "noncruelty" with his descent into silence while she raises her question, and their hearing of Damayantī's message-reminder to the estranged Nala that, in Nala's words, "Noncruelty is the highest dharma." The exchange between Yudhiṣṭhira and Draupadī highlights this quality of ānṛśaṃsya. It prompts Yudhiṣṭhira's first expression of how he understands it, and, moreover, how he contextualizes it in relation to intimacy.

Draupadī—introduced here as "dear and beautiful, a scholar *(paṇḍitā)*[77] and a faithful wife *(pativratā)*" (3.28.2)—begins by observing that the cruel *(nṛśaṃsa)* Duryodhana is not unhappy about their suffering (3); Yudhiṣṭhira should act like a Kṣatriya, all of whom have anger, and not like a Brahman (34). Yudhiṣṭhira defends himself:

> Truth is better than falsehood, noncruelty than cruelty *(satyaṃ cānṛtataḥ śreyo nṛśaṃsāc cānṛśaṃsatā)*. Even to kill Suyodhana,[78] how can one like me give reign to anger, which has many faults and is shunned by the respectable *(sādhuvivarjitam)*? . . . An angry man does not see his task correctly, full-hipped one. The angry man considers neither task nor limit *(maryādā)*. . . . If there were no one among men having forbearance like the earth, there would be no peace

Draupadi's final recollections "of her tortuous and suffering life." Nicely written and translated (Ray 1995), it has interesting twists on the marriage, in which Draupadī clearly favors Arjuna, has a rough first night with Yudhiṣṭhira, and wishes she were monogamous (28–83). The present bedroom scene is bowdlerized (she is massaging his feet) but with the other details intact; the surprise is that Draupadī wants to come with Arjuna into the forest as a celibate like Sītā—to which Arjuna cruelly replies that Sītā had only one husband (163–67).

[77]That she is a "scholar" might reflect on the intelligence that lies behind her question that stumps all the experts in the sabhā, some of whom cite paṇḍits in their defense (30.16, 22; 33.56). This is probably the verse Karve has in mind when she says, "In the *Aranyakaparva* Dharma called her a 'lady pundit,' hardly a complimentary epithet in the eyes of the Kshatriyas of the Mahabharata" (1974, 90). See above, n. 55, on Karve.

[78]Yudhiṣṭhira's euphemistic name for Duryodhana, implying that there is something "good" *(su)* about him.

> *(saṃdhi)* among men, for war has its root in anger. If the oppressed were to oppress, if one hit by his guru were to strike back, it would be the destruction of beings and adharma would be broadcast. . . . Were fathers to strike their sons and sons their fathers, husbands to strike their wives and wives their husbands,[79] then in such an angry world there would be no birth, Kṛṣṇā *(evaṃ saṃkupite loke janma kṛṣṇe na vidyate)*; know that the birth of creatures has its root in peace *(saṃdhi)*, lovely one. In such (a world), all creatures would quickly perish, Draupadī. Therefore, wrath is for the destruction of creatures and nonexistence. But since those who possess forbearance like the earth are seen in the world, the birth of beings and existence is carried on. In every distress, beautiful one, a man should be forbearing, for forbearance is declared the existence and birth of beings. . . . Suyodhana is not capable of forbearance and so finds none. I am capable of it and thus forbearance finds me. That is the conduct of the self-possessed *(etad ātmavatāṃ vṛttam)*. This, forbearance and noncruelty, is the eternal dharma, and that I truly do. (3.30.15, 18, 25–26, 28–32, 49–50)

Draupadī won't buy this: "In this world a man obtains prosperity neither by noncruelty and dharma, nor by patience, uprightness, nor tenderness" (31.2). Their suffering, she says, is brought on by Yudhiṣṭhira's putting dharma before the rest of them, betting his brothers and her away with his kingdom. His words make her think they are like puppets being played by a capriciously hurtful divine child (30–39). Yudhiṣṭhira tells her it is heresy *(nāstikyam)* to censure the good heavenward ship of dharma (32.1 and 22), or salvation that comes to the devoted mortal by the grace of the highest deity (40).

I suppose Yudhiṣṭhira is a frustrating husband. But at the heart of his argument, he reveals what he is about, and what he seems to think Draupadī should be about. It was, after all, Draupadī's ānṛśaṃsya that Yudhiṣṭhira recalled just before he wagered her and descended into silence. That was out of her hearing, but it seems that without mentioning his words at that moment, ānṛśaṃsya is the quality, along with "forbearance" *(kṣama)*, that he would like to remind her of now. He tells her it is the maintenance of these two qualities, noncruelty and forbearance, that sustains existence and the birth of beings. Indeed, the *saṃdhi* which these qualities make possible is not just "peace," but "connection," which, in the context here, implies the peace to have sexual connection without cruelty or interruption.

[79]The *han-* verbs here could be translated "kill," but to be consistent with the verse about "striking" a guru and being "struck back," I translate as "strike" or "hit" throughout.

This theme has by now been richly developed. When Yudhiṣṭhira's great-grandmother Satyavatī prepared to tell her son Vyāsa to rescue the Kuru line by siring sons with his half-brother's two widows, she said, "Because beings cry out *(anukrośāc ca bhūtānām)* and for the protection of all, having heard what I say, you must do it with noncruelty *(ānṛśaṃsyena)*" (1.99.33)—as noted (see chapter 2, § C.2), a strange thing to tell an "author" about characters he is about to make love to and father, and we must wonder how well he listened, considering the outcome. We have also seen Pāṇḍu, Yudhiṣṭhira's father, cursed because he lacked the "noncruelty" *(ānṛśaṃsya)* to wait until two Ṛṣis-turned-deer were finished with their pleasure.[80] But most of all, the theme has come into focus because Arjuna has interrupted Yudhiṣṭhira and Draupadī in the bedroom. Did Arjuna show forbearance and noncruelty? Probably not, even though he is portrayed as opposing cruelty (2.61.7; 3.142.15, 25; 254.13; 4.61.21)—without, however, the term *ānṛśaṃsya* in these cases, which so often distinguishes Yudhiṣṭhira. But if Arjuna was hasty and cruel (couldn't he have knocked?), and even eager for some escapades, we understand why Yudhiṣṭhira would never say so, especially to Draupadī, and why he would take such pains to say that what Arjuna did was "not disagreeable."

But there is something more in Yudhiṣṭhira's words. His conduct of forbearance and noncruelty is, he claims, that of "one who is self-possessed" *(ātmavat)*. Is it possible that he is answering Draupadī's question? Has he learned something from the dicing? Is he hinting that he had not really lost himself, but could not say so? That in some sense, his silence meant that he thought he understood her question? He is quite convincingly self-possessed now, and it would not be unreasonable to propose that while he appeared to have "lost consciousness" during the time Draupadī raised the question, he knew enough—perhaps just enough—to "keep to himself" while she played for time.

Draupadī and Yudhiṣṭhira have a few more ups and downs. The bedroom scene is no doubt echoed in the *Karṇaparvan* in one of the many surprising features[81] of the insult-exchange between Yudhiṣṭhira and Arjuna over Arjuna's delay in killing Karṇa while Yudhiṣṭhira nurses his wounds away from the action, but still, of course on the battlefield. Says

[80]See chap. 5 at n. 63. The theme and terms recur in the Mitrasaha story: a Brahman couple enjoy forest sex until Mitrasaha attacks the husband; "While the woman was crying out *(vikrośamāna)*, the king most cruelly *(sunṛśaṃsakṛt)* devoured the husband" (1.173.14); she curses him to become the cannibal Kalmāṣapāda. The bereaved cry of a female *krauñca* bird upon seeing her mate slain in the act of love by a cruel hunter is also Vālmīki's inspiration in composing the *Rām*; see Leslie 1998, and below, chap. 8.

[81]See Hiltebeitel 1984, 24; Reich 1998, 231–45; and above, p. 206.

Arjuna, "Lying on Draupadī's bed *(draupadītalpasaṃstho)* you insult me, and I am to kill great warriors for your sake?" (8.49.83ab; Reich 1998, 235, translating). Once again, Arjuna finds Yudhiṣṭhira in Draupadī's bed; once again, it is a question of Arjuna using his weapons. But this time there are insults. And when the war is over, Draupadī severely upbraids Yudhiṣṭhira once again, now for wanting to abandon the kingdom he has just won, which would turn all their suffering to nought. He is like a eunuch, she says, like a Kṣatriya without a rod *(daṇḍa)* (12.14.12–14); he is like a madman whom his brothers, were they not crazy themselves from following him, should bound with the heretics *(nāstikyaiḥ)*; or he should be treated with drugs (32–34). Yet she speaks these words to him as one who "always took pride, especially in Yudhiṣṭhira, and was ever cherished by the king."[82]

But we hasten to the end.[83] Heading north on their ascent to heaven, self-restrained and rapt in yoga *(yogayuktāḥ)*, the Pāṇḍavas and Draupadī see the great peak Himavat *(himavantam mahāgirim)*. Crossing even beyond it *(apy atikramantas)*, they see an "ocean of sand" *(vālukārṇavam)* and the great mount Meru (17.2.1–2). The ascent combines with cosmological images of the yogic journey, delivered with an appropriate rapidity. To follow Witzel (1984, 228–29), Himavat is often called *giri* or *uttara giri* in Vedic texts, where it may be seen as what remains at dawn on the northern horizon of the "spotted rock," the revolving upside-down subterranean mountain of the night sky studded with stars not contained in the milky way. If the image holds for the epic, the Pāṇḍavas and Draupadī's journey now heads backward from Himavat into the night and forward into a post-Vedic yogic cosmology. Beyond Himavat is an "ocean of sand": a likely image of the stars, which the travelers are said only to *see*, not to cross by walking. And beyond this they *see* (again with no mention of actual footwork) Mount Meru, which is no real mountain but the cosmic mountain by which the totality of the universe is projected as measurable, perceivable, and knowable.[84] While they are holding to their yoga, moving quickly, Draupadī's yoga is ruined and she falls to the ground.[85] Asked by Bhīma why she fell, Yudhiṣṭhira

[82]12.14.4: *abhimānavatī nityaṃ viśeṣeṇa yudhiṣṭhire/ lālitā satataṃ rājñā*. For similar strains and ambiguities in their relationship, see 4.15.30–18.36, especially 18.8 and 35–36: Draupadī's grief for Yudhiṣṭhira's sufferings. Cf. Shah 1995, 72–73.

[83]Cf. chap. 2, § C.41. As noted, from here Vyāsa leaves Yudhiṣṭhira to take over the story.

[84]On Meru as the key to mapping the universe by stereographic projection, see Kloetzli 1985, esp. 135–38. On sand, stars, and images of the wearing away of Meru to dust, see Kloetzli 1983, 114–31. See also chap. 4, after n. 73, on *Mbh* 3.160.12–37, where the Pāṇḍavas look toward Meru and learn about days, nights, the stars, and other celestial movements.

[85]17.2.3: *teṣāṃ tu gacchatāṃ śīghraṃ sarveṣāṃ yogadharmiṇām/ yājñasenī bhraṣṭayogā nipapāta mahītale*.

replies, "Her partiality for Arjuna was especially great *(pakṣapāto mahān asyā viśeṣeṇa dhanaṃjaye)*. That is the fruit she now enjoys" (17.2.6). Yudhiṣṭhira and his brothers (including Arjuna) travel on, leaving her body behind with that thought, which might reopen the whole book on Yudhiṣṭhira, yet will not be his last about her.

His brothers fall, and Yudhiṣṭhira is left with the dog. Indra comes to take him to heaven, but because of his "noncruelty" Yudhiṣṭhira won't leave the dog. The dog turns into Dharma in his own form (17.3.16),[86] who congratulates Yudhiṣṭhira for his "capacity to cry out *(anukrośa)* toward all beings" (17), and tells him that he can now reach his heavenly worlds in his own body, a nonpareil feat (20, 27). The gods provide him a chariot to heaven, where Nārada welcomes him among the royal Ṛṣis. But seeing heaven without his brothers, Yudhiṣṭhira wishes to go where they are. Indra discourages him: "Why do you still draw on human affection *(mānuṣyakaṃ sneham)*? . . . The human heart *(mānuṣo bhāvaḥ)* still touches you, lord of men. This is heaven!" (31–33). Yudhiṣṭhira replies that he wants to be where his brothers are, "where my dear Draupadī is, the best of women, the great dark one *(bṛhatī śyāmā)* rich in spirit, character, and virtue *(buddhisattvaguṇānvitā)*" (36).

This verse, which emphatically ends the *Mahāprasthānikaparvan*, yields this singular compound. It is used only one other time in the epic, where it introduces Āstīka as one whose name means "there is," and who has these same qualities "even as a child."[87] "Rich in spirit, character, and virtue" is van Buitenen's translation for the description of Āstīka (1973, 108), and I have transferred it to Draupadī. But it can hardly be all that is meant, even if one keeps it a copulative compound as "rich in insight, goodness, and virtue." *Guṇa* in the singular is unlikely for "virtue,"[88] but is regularly used in the epic as a proto-Sāṃkhya term. Indeed, *guṇa*, *buddhi*, and *sattva* are all proto-Sāṃkhya terms with Upaniṣadic prehistories and resonances across the *Mahābhārata*. It is tempting to understand this language as describing Draupadī and Āstīka as characters who represent and provoke awareness. One could thus translate it as "having the sattvic quality *(guṇa)* of insight."[89] The

[86]Belvalkar 1959, *Svargārohaṇaparvan* Introduction, xxix, takes "Yamadharma" to have been Indra as well as the dog. Better, I think, the two gods cooperate throughout Yudhiṣṭhira's two last "tests" (see 18.3.2, 30; 3.34).

[87]1.44.19–20. Cf. 3.147.111: in answer to Hanumān's question, "Who is Hanumān?" Bhīma provides a parallel description of Hanumān as *buddhisattvabalānvita*, with *bala*, strength, instead of *guṇa*: perhaps "endowed with power of intellect and goodness," or "endowed with the sattvic power of the buddhi."

[88]I thank James Fitzgerald (personal communication, 1996) for this point: "guṇa is not really the abstract noun 'virtue.'"

[89]Fitzgerald (personal communication, 1996), calling it "one of many depressingly

juxtaposition of "great dark one," feminine, with *buddhi* may hint that Draupadī evokes the dark *pradhāna*, primal matter or prakṛti, which, transformed into buddhi, serves to discipline the five senses and bring about the awakening of puruṣa.[90] There would seem to be something to ponder in Yudhiṣṭhira's final description of the character of his wife.

As the epic's last book, the *Svargārohaṇaparvan*, now opens, Yudhiṣṭhira's resolve hardens. Seeing Duryodhana shining in heaven, he is affronted. He blames Duryodhana for the war and the mistreatment of Draupadī in the sabhā, and doesn't want to be in a heaven with him (18.1.1–10). Nārada, smiling, tells him that here enmities cease; Yudhiṣṭhira should not think of what was done at the dice match, the pain *(parikleśa)* done to Draupadī and the other pains that followed: "This is heaven! There are no enmities here, lord of men" (11–18). But Yudhiṣṭhira still protests, and says he prefers to see the afterworlds of his brothers (including Karṇa), his allies, and Draupadī; "Where they are is my heaven. To my mind this is not heaven" (20–2.12). The gods reply, "If that is where your faith *(śraddhā)* is, son, you may go without delay," and order a celestial messenger, "Show Yudhiṣṭhira's friends *(yudhiṣṭhirasya suhṛdo darśaya)*" (2.13–14). Yudhiṣṭhira's "faith" lies in seeing his *suhṛds*: "those who are dear to his heart."

The messenger takes Yudhiṣṭhira on the foul and slippery path to the edge of hell *(naraka)*. There he hears the piteous cries of his brothers, Dhṛṣṭadyumna, Draupadī, and Draupadī's sons asking him to stay for a time, since he brings them comfort (2.16–33).

> Yudhiṣṭhira then reflected *(vimamṛśe)*, "What now is the effect of destiny *(kasyedānīṃ vikāro 'yam)* by which these have gone to hell? . . . Am I asleep? Am I waking up? I do not seem to understand. Ah,

ambiguous compounds involving these terms," regards both as possible, and tentatively prefers the proto-Sāṃkhya one (for the reason cited in n. 88). But he offers and prefers a third: "to construe *buddhisattva* as a dvandva . . . in apposition to the guṇa(s) with which Draupadī is *anvitā*/endowed": thus "endowed with the virtues of insight and bravery."

[90]On *buddhi* in the epic, I am most tempted here by one of Vyāsa's *Śāntiparvan* teachings to Śuka (12.246.9–15): "Vyāsa compared the human body to a city which was ruled by Queen Intellect; this queen has the mind as her counsellor who harassed the senses which were the citizens" (Belvalkar 1966, ccxiv–xv). Queen Intellect (*svāminī buddhir*; 9b) is also "inviolable" (*durdharṣā*; 12a). The *BhG*, among other things, makes also Kṛṣṇa the embodiment of the buddhi-charioteer of *KU* 3.3–9, and Vyāsa's "buddhi is unlimited" (*vyāsenāmitabuddhinā*; 1.56.21; see Sutton 2000, 27). Kṛṣṇā Draupadī, Kṛṣṇa Vāsudeva, and Kṛṣṇa Dvaipāyana—the three Kṛṣṇas (see Hiltebeitel [1976] 1990, 60–76; 1984; 1985a)—thus all have this "darkly illuminating" sattvic quality. Cf. also Sutton, 171 (on Nārāyaṇa's bestowal of buddhi on Brahmā to create the universe [12.337]); 344–47 (in relation to other faculties); and chap. 4 at n. 146; chap. 6 at n. 46; and chap. 8 for more on Śuka and the buddhi, especially at n. 64.

> this is a mental twist. Or maybe it is the wandering of my mind."[91] So King Yudhiṣṭhira reflected in many directions, overwhelmed by sorrow and grief, his senses agitated by thought *(cintāvyākulitendriyaḥ)*. Then the king, the son of Dharma, intensely gave way to anger, and Yudhiṣṭhira then censured *(garhayāmāsa)* the gods and also Dharma. (42–50)

Yudhiṣṭhira's final contest with his father Dharma holds strong echoes of Naciketas' contests with his father *and* Yama in the *Kaṭha Upaniṣad*, which introduces proto-Sāṃkhya-Yoga language in profusion, especially when Yama gives Naciketas his third boon and describes the ascent to heaven. Yudhiṣṭhira, living out such an ascent, is back to the question that was raised about him in the sabhā: was he conscious or crazed? Now he asks it of himself, compounding it with more proto-Sāṃkhya-Yoga language about the wanderings and "generated products" of thought as he contemplates the vision before him. His "censure" or "accusation" of Dharma (or dharma) comes from these uncertain thoughts, and has no finality, as Indra soon indicates.[92] Yudhiṣṭhira has only glimpsed that he has more to awaken to, and that it is Dharma who keeps putting him through these cruel and intolerable tests.

Despite the foul smell, Yudhiṣṭhira determines to stay where he is, and sends the messenger back to the gods to tell them so. But the gods are soon there and the stench, the underworldly Vaitaraṇī river, and the gloom *(tamas)* disappear with their arrival. Indra comforts Yudhiṣṭhira: He should not make himself angry;[93] he has had to see hell because he killed Droṇa by fraud. For similar reasons the others also experienced hell. Indra invites Yudhiṣṭhira to see them now, freed from sin in their radiant celestial bodies, and to take his supreme place among the greatest of the royal Ṛṣis (18.2.52–3.25). Without Yudhiṣṭhira's having moved an inch, Indra announces what has opened before him: "This is the sacred

[91]18.2.48: *kiṃ nu supto 'smi jāgarmi cetayāno na cetaye/ aho cittavikāro 'yam syād vā me cittavibhramaḥ*. I have translated *cittavikāra* here as "mental twist," leaving it to point to *vikāra* in verse 46: "Whose twist is this?" But this second usage introduces a distinctive proto-Sāṃkhya-Yoga terminology, since *vikāra* refers to the "generated products" of prakṛti, of which classical Sāṃkhya lists sixteen: the mind, five sense capacities, five action capacities, and five gross elements (see Larson and Bhattacharya 1987, 52, 318–19).

[92]Shulman 1996, 160–64 reads this as a "curse" of Dharma/dharma that must include Yudhiṣṭhira himself, and a breakdown of the "battered" linguistically constructed world that Dharma has imparted to him. Granted dharma's fragility as linguistically constructed, I do not see how its breakdown carries if Dharma is doing a test. A separate issue: Yudhiṣṭhira is also not renouncing dharma in the fashion Kṛṣṇa recommends to Arjuna (*BhG* 18.66).

[93]18.3.11: *na ca manyus tvayā kāryaḥ*. As mentioned at nn. 77–79, anger at Dharma or dharma is not the *Mbh*'s answer.

celestial river, O Pārtha, purifier of the triple world, the heavenly Gaṅgā *(ākāśagaṅgā)*, O Indra among kings. Having plunged there, you will go; having bathed there, your human heart will go away *(te bhāvo mānuṣo vigamiṣyati)*. Your grief gone, without troubles, you will be freed of enmity" (3.26–27). This is now twice that Indra speaks of Yudhiṣṭhira's "human heart," first to tell him he is still "touched by it" when he prefers his family's worlds to those of heaven, and now, once he has found his family, to tell him his human heart will "go away." Indra now seems intent on limiting the discussion of what will go away with Yudhiṣṭhira's human heart to the pangs of grief and enmity, since this time he does not mention the ties of affection *(sneha)* that he mentioned before.

But Dharma knows where Yudhiṣṭhira's heart is: "Even as Indra was speaking to that Indra-among-Kauravas Yudhiṣṭhira, Dharma, visibly possessing his own form, addressed his own son. 'Aho, greatly wise king, I am pleased by your devotion to me, your truthful speech, forbearance, and restraint. This is the third test I have made for you, king. Nothing, Pārtha, makes you swerve from your own heart'" (18.3.28–30).[94] Dharma reveals that he was indeed behind the Yakṣa's questions, the dog's devotion, and now this, Dharma's final test, which is of Yudhiṣṭhira's human heart, and by which Yudhiṣṭhira is now "purified" (*viśuddha*; 31–34). Unlike Yudhiṣṭhira's thoughts, his heart cannot swerve. Unlike the Muni who abandons the dog with the human heart, Yudhiṣṭhira does not swerve because he has the virtues Dharma has just mentioned, plus those exemplified in both of the prior tests, and surely also in this one: ānṛśaṃsya and anukrośa. What Yudhiṣṭhira saw, Dharma continues, was an illusion displayed by Indra; hell must be seen by every king. His brothers (including Karṇa) "did not deserve hell for long. And the Rājaputrī Kṛṣṇā did not deserve hell, Yudhiṣṭhira. Come, come, best of Bharatas. See the triple-world-going Gaṅgā" (34–37). These are the last words that pass from this strange father to his son, mixing tenderness with what is almost another cruelty—that is, it seems (and here Dharma contradicts Indra), Draupadī did not deserve hell at all—neither the one Yudhiṣṭhira has just seen her in nor those he put her through. We can assume, I think, that Yudhiṣṭhira has always known this, which is perhaps how Dharma can utter these last words without their being a fourth test. We can also assume that Yudhiṣṭhira does not think Draupadī deserved hell for preferring Arjuna.

Yudhiṣṭhira has not gone anywhere during this conversation, so the celestial Gaṅgā is still before him: "He went together with Dharma and

[94]More literally, "You do not swerve from your own heart (experience, nature), Pārtha, by (any) means"; or ". . . by means (of what comes) from your own heart (etc.)."

all the gods. Having plunged into the sacred purifying divine river sung of by the Ṛṣis, the king abandoned the human body *(tanuṃ tatyāja mānuṣīm)*. Having assumed a celestial appearance *(vapus)*, Dharmarāja Yudhiṣṭhira, immersed in this water, was without enmity, his anguish gone" (18.3.38–40). His body is gone; even his enmity and anguish *(saṃtāpa)*. And his human heart is supposed to go too. But we have just noted how Dharma's last words leave an impression about Draupadī, which it now seems is the last thing Yudhiṣṭhira carries with him.

In heaven, he sees Govinda and his brothers, each in turn in their radiant celestial forms (4.1–6). But when he sees Draupadī, something powerful happens that has been easy to miss. Seeing her garlanded with lotuses, seated in heaven with the splendor of the sun, "suddenly King Yudhiṣṭhira was wishing to question her *(athaināṃ sahasā rājā praṣṭum aicchad yudhiṣṭhiraḥ)*" (8). But Indra, impatient again with lingering affections, cuts him off by telling him about Draupadī's divine origins,[95] and then points out the heavenly abodes of Draupadī's sons, and those of Karṇa, Abhimanyu, Bhīṣma, Droṇa, and many others, who, having abandoned their bodies, won heavens by meritorious words, thoughts, and deeds (9–19).

Quickly, in answer to a question of Janamejaya's that closes the *Mahābhārata*'s inner frame and the "whole story of the Kurus and Pāṇḍavas" (18.5.25), the next and last thing we hear about Yudhiṣṭhira comes amid a long list of the characters who dissolve into divine forms: he "entered Dharma" *(dharmamevāviśat)* along with Vidura (5.19). And we are back in the Naimiṣa Forest (although it isn't mentioned here) to close out the outer frame with Ugraśravas telling Śaunaka how Janamejaya was "pleased" to end his snake sattra after the arrival of Āstīka (26–29). Thirty more verses about Vyāsa, the text, and the merits of its recital finish the epic.

So Yudhiṣṭhira wants to ask Draupadī a question, but he never gets to ask it.[96] This is a tenacious human heart. It goes on questioning into the swirl of its dissolution. I retain the imperfect—*aicchat*, "he was wishing to question her"—because this is the perfect moment for a verb of incompletion. Although Yudhiṣṭhira and Draupadī have their end, the question has no finality, because not only did he not get to ask it or she to answer it, but we will never know what it was. Past, present, and future thus open up with this "imperfect moment." And with all the

[95] It is here we learn that she was "fashioned by the holder of the trident" (18.4.10), as mentioned in chap. 5, p. 187. Cf. Gellrich 1985, 235–36, on narrative ironies of distraction and interruption.

[96] A few mss. have *draṣṭum* or *spraṣṭum* for *praṣṭum*: he wanted "to see" her or "to touch" her rather than "to question" her!

echoes of the sabhā in these two final parvans, and in particular Nārada's insistence that Yudhiṣṭhira should not think of the pain done to Draupadī at the dice match and the other pains that followed, and Dharma's comment that she did not deserve hell, we remain within the rules of this playful text if we suspect two things. First, that a trouble Nārada sees and seems to try to avert is only something that is bound to happen: that our best clue to what Yudhiṣṭhira is thinking about is what Nārada has told him not to think about. And second, that if Dharma knows his son, he knows him to be good at riddles. In any case, whatever Yudhiṣṭhira wants to ask Draupadī, he is reminding us of Draupadī's question.

Writing about the epic dice match as a recharged piece of the Vedic Rājāsūya sacrifice, whose "dead letter" the masterful poets dramatically revive to carry forward the ambiguities of their "point, counterpoint" story, van Buitenen gives us one of his most memorable insights: "the epic is a series of precisely stated problems imprecisely and therefore inconclusively resolved, with every resolution raising a new problem, until the very end, when the question remains: whose is heaven and whose is hell?" (1975, 29). This design is one of deferral.[97] The question Yudhiṣṭhira doesn't get to ask comes even after this, and is the *Mahābhārata*'s very last deferral. Indra distracts Yudhiṣṭhira into the glorious higher worlds of personal dissolution, and Vaiśampāyana and Ugraśravas rapidly tie up the text. Yudhiṣṭhira will never answer Draupadī's question and he will never ask her his own.

[97]On deferred work and deferred speech, see Malamoud 1989, 68. One could see the *Mbh* as "an allegory of reading the Veda" in the sense Gellrich develops for Dante and Chaucer's "allegory of reading" the Bible (and other medieval books): "the allegory of the *Commedia* consists in the structure of temporal distance between the originary *liber* of God, envisioned in the sky at the end of the poem, and the book of written efforts to explain the experience of its meaning" (1985, 165); cf. 188–89: the "continually deferred" "origin" in *House of Fame*; 246: "not completing the narrative" of *Canterbury Tales*. As Gellrich seems to suggest (76–77, 180, 183, 200, 240–47), allegories of reading are also allegories of writing. See also chap. 2, n. 18. For Derrida on this topic, it is perhaps sufficient for now to recall that "difference defers-differs [diffère]" ([1976] 1994, 66).

8 Vyāsa and Śuka: An Allegory of Writing

How does Ugraśravas tie up the text? He repeats to Śaunaka (18.5.44) that "whatever is here is found elsewhere . . . ," tells him that Vyāsa made a "stringing (or binding) together (*saṃdarbham*: i.e., a book)[1] of this *Bhārata*" out of desire for dharma, that Vaiśampāyana sang it to mortals *(martyān)*, Nārada to gods, Asita Devala to the Fathers, and Vyāsa's son Śuka to Yakṣas and Rākṣasas, and that it is "equal to the Veda *(vedasaṃmitam)*" (18.5.38–43). Ugraśravas does not have to tell Śaunaka that the Ṛṣis have heard it from him, and that Ṛṣis have "distinction" as a class beyond mortals. And he does not have to tell us that we have heard it with these Ṛṣis in the Naimiṣa Forest.

Ugraśravas's closing image of "the author" then tells us something further about Vyāsa and Śuka:

> The great Ṛṣi lord Vyāsa, having formerly made this Saṃhitā, caused his son Śuka to recite it *(adhyāpayac chukam)* with four verses:
>
> "Thousands of mothers and fathers, and hundreds of sons and wives, experiencing (worlds of) saṃsāra, go. And others will go. There are a thousand situations of joy and a hundred situations of fear. They affect the ignorant daily, but not the wise. With uplifted arms I cry this aloud, but no one hears me. Artha and kāma are from dharma. For what purpose *(artha)* is it not served? For the sake of neither desire nor fear nor greed should one ever abandon dharma, even for the sake of living. Dharma is eternal, but happiness and suffering are not eternal; the soul *(jīva)* is eternal but its cause is not eternal."
>
> The one who having risen at dawn recites this *Bhārata-Sāvitrī*, having obtained the fruit of the *Bhārata*, goes to the highest Brahman (18.5.46–51).[2]

[1]The term, not used elsewhere in either epic, connotes a wreath or manuscript tied together; "a literary or musical composition" (MW, 491, 1143).

[2]As mentioned in chap. 2, n. 3, Mehta sent me a mimeographed copy of his article with

With just a few more words the epic ends: The *Bhārata* is a mine of precious gems like the ocean and Himavat; it leaves no need for one to be sprinkled with water at Lake Puṣkara (52–54).

Although Ugraśravas recounts this anecdote with its four extra verses, it falls outside the narrations of the inner and outer frames. Their message is clearly for mortals, but its narration must depict a fragment of the outermost frame. Once the education of Yudhiṣṭhira is over, the text thus wraps itself up, taking us quickly through the inner and outer frames to the outermost frame of the author. We know some things about this outermost frame from Vyāsa's comings and goings in the story (see chapter 2). Indeed, he has presences in virtually all the frames. He attends Janamejaya's snake sacrifice as one of the sadasyas. Ugraśravas tells the Naimiṣa Forest sages that what he has heard "told" *(kathitāḥ)* by Vaiśampāyana had been first "proclaimed" *(proktāḥ)* by Vyāsa (1.1.9). The authorial "divine eye" also presences him in two of the epic's interior frames: the war narrative, for which he himself gives the eye to Saṃjaya (6.2.9–13; 16.5–10), and the postwar instruction of Yudhiṣṭhira, for which Kṛṣṇa gives it to Bhīṣma in Vyāsa's presence (12.52.20–22). For Bhīṣma's oration, Vyāsa seems to remain additionally present to hear Bhīṣma tell Yudhiṣṭhira about Vyāsa's teachings to Śuka (12.224–46), which anticipate their father-son story (310–20), the story that tells us the most about the epic's outermost frame.

A. Author and Sons

The story of Śuka has received careful discussion of its epic and purāṇic tellings, with the richest studies being those of Doniger (1993b) and Shulman (1993).[3] Along with such interpretative articles, translations by Ganguli ([1884–96] 1970) and Fitzgerald (1987), the latter kindly made available in a preliminary draft, make one appreciate the value of multiple readings of this highly ambiguous text. So far, however, because the interpreters have not considered the story in relation to the larger epic and have been highly selective in telling it, and because the translations have been largely noninterpretative, there is still need for close reading. I will argue that from the outermost frame, the Śuka story provides a metatext on the poetics of the *Mahābhārata* "at large," and is an important text for the epic's interpretation. More specifically, I regard it

some handwritten marginalia. In one, he incorporates a reference to these verses as bracketed in what follows: "It [the *Mbh*] speaks of a lost time, seeking to integrate it into the present, but aware of the insufficiency of its own 'cry in the wilderness,' [(cf. the *Bhārata Sāvitri* verses)] it also speaks of the future . . ." (1990, 101).

[3]See also Bedekar 1965; Brown 1996.

as an example of the high artistry of the epic poets, one that is especially intriguing for what I will argue is its careful *literary* construction, and for its depiction of the author himself in relation to his larger text, its cosmology, and its characters and audiences. One trace of its careful literary construction is its measured pace through eleven adhyāyas—"lessons," "readings," or "chapters"—whose ten breaks are often worth noting as reminders that the adhyāya divisions of the *Mahābhārata* are suggestive of a written composition.

The first adhyāya (310) opens with Yudhiṣṭhira, now well into his postwar education, asking his nominal grandfather Bhīṣma about some things that we are almost surprised he doesn't yet know. They concern Śuka, the son of Yudhiṣṭhira's real grandfather Vyāsa. Insofar as Vyāsa is the father of Śuka, Dhṛtarāṣtra, Pāṇḍu, and Vidura, Śuka would have to be Yudhiṣṭhira's uncle: his seniormost uncle, one must infer, since there is nothing to contradict the few passages that tell us Śuka's birth preceded those of Vyāsa's other sons.[4] Yudhiṣṭhira asks:

> How did the just-souled Śuka of great tapas, Vyāsa's son, take birth and achieve the highest perfection? Tell me this, grandfather. Upon whom did Vyāsa, that treasure of asceticism, beget Śuka? We do not know his mother *(jananīm)* or that high-souled one's lofty birth. How as just a boy did his mind attain such subtle knowledge as no one else in this world?[5] I wish to hear this in detail *(vistareṇa)*. . . . Tell me, Grandfather, of Śuka's glorious union with the self and consciousness, in the proper order *(yathāvad ānupūrvyeṇa)*. (310.1–5)

Yudhiṣṭhira explicitly asks for a "detailed" and "properly ordered"[6] account, and when Bhīṣma rounds off the tale, he reassures Yudhiṣṭhira that he has indeed told what he has learned from the most impeccable sources: "Thus the birth and course of Śuka, O bull among the Bhāratas, is told by me in detail *(vistareṇa)*, as you have asked me. The Ṛṣi Nārada formerly told it to me, O king, and also the great yogin Vyāsa, line by line amid conversations *(saṃjalpeṣu pade pade)*" (320.40). I follow Doniger (1993b, 49) on *pade pade* here as "line by line," but let us note

[4]Doniger 1993b, 37, nicely sees that the fathers of the Kauravas and Pāṇḍavas "were born only after (and perhaps to compensate for) the loss of his first son, Śuka." Cf. 56: "real sons, to take the place of Śuka." But who is "real" is not such an easy question.

[5]Thanks to Fitzgerald 1987 for clarification on this verse.

[6]Note how *ānupūrvyeṇa* is used here much as in the story of the Former Indras (at 1.187.28), where Yudhiṣṭhira, in insisting that he follows the "proper sequence" of "the ancients" or "the ancestors," refers to the scrambled scene of making "order" out of the "subtle dharma" of Draupadī's polyandry. Possibly *ānupūrvyeṇa* is used dislocatively at such points where one follows time into its inside-out turns.

that it could also be translated "at every step, everywhere, on every occasion" (MW, 583), or even as "word by word" (Fitzgerald 1987, 44)! These prior tellings have an extraordinarily rich vagueness as to their "time and place," as if the story regularly entered Vyāsa's and Nārada's "conversations." Moreover, when Bhīṣma comes to the point of describing how Vyāsa looked when he performed his arduous tapas to beget Śuka, he pulls in a third witness-source: "And by the splendor of his matted locks like the crest of a fire, he [Vyāsa] was seen to be blazing, possessed of immeasurable splendor. Lord Mārkaṇḍeya said this to me. He always told me the deeds of the gods here" (310.23–24).[7] Bhīṣma registers that Vyāsa could not have observed this himself, and Nārada, who comes into the story only later, seems "by chance" to have been elsewhere at the time. The text is thus given its own critical apparatus, with a little extra reassurance on the point that Bhīṣma has a hotline to Mārkaṇḍeya.

Bhīṣma starts his story with another source, a proverb about Vedic learning also found in *Manu*:[8]

> (One is great) not by years, not by gray hairs, not by riches, nor by relatives. The Ṛṣis made the law *(cakrire dharmam)*: "He is great to us who has learning *(anūcāna)*." All this you ask me about has its root in tapas, O Pāṇḍava. . . . I shall now tell you the birth as also the fruit of yoga of Śuka, and the lofty course *(agryāṃ gatim)*[9] that is hard to understand by those of unperfected selves *(akṛtātmabhiḥ)*. (12.310.6–7b, 10)

Hard to understand indeed. Yudhiṣṭhira's "unperfected self" is poised to seek understanding on behalf of all of us.[10] Let us begin by proposing that the story has to do with presenting enigmas of time and space as they relate tapas as "creative fervor" to yoga, both joined with the new potent combination of authorial presencing and literary imagination.

[7]Cf. chap. 2, § B, on other inclusions of Vyāsa among gods. Bhīṣma continues: "Even now those matted locks of the high-souled Kṛṣṇa [Dvaipāyana] shine forth having the color of Agni, O child, ablaze by tapas"—his fiery locks thus haloing his "black" complexion.

[8]As Belvalkar's apparatus notation (1954, 1748) indicates, it is the same as *Mbh* 3.133.12 (van Buitenen 1975, 476) and *Manu* 2.154. Ganguli [1884–96] 1970, 10:495: "They said that he amongst them was great that studied the Vedas." On *anūcāna*, being "adept in the knowledge of the Vedas with their auxiliary parts," see Bedekar 1965, 90–91.

[9]Or "final course" (Fitzgerald 1987).

[10]The phrase is often used, but perhaps most pertinently when Saṃjaya picks up from Vyāsa's invitation to instruct Dhṛtarāṣṭra on what the latter calls "the path where all danger ceases, by which I may reach Hṛṣīkeśa and attain to ultimate peace." Says Saṃjaya, "One of unperfected self can never know Janārdana, whose self is perfected" (5.67.16–17).

Timewise, the passage takes us back to the point hinted at in connection with the Pāṇḍavas' arrival, during their forest wanderings, at the hermitage where Vyāsa mourns Śuka's loss. As suggested in chapter 2, that passage seemed to imply that Śuka must have learned the *Mahābhārata* from Vyāsa before most (if not all) of it occurred. From Yudhiṣṭhira's present questions in the *Śāntiparvan*, we might now wonder whether in the *Āraṇyakaparvan* he had not yet known enough to ask what he now asks about Śuka, or had not yet the inclination. And if we allow that Janamejaya just follows the narration, we would only now begin to wonder why *he* never asks the obvious question about Śuka's premature knowledge of the *Mahābhārata*, which seems to him no more of a contradiction than it does to Yudhiṣṭhira. In any case, the problem returns in certain purāṇas that extend the Śuka story. The *Bhāgavata Purāṇa* makes Śuka its narrator at the dying of Janamejaya's father Parikṣit.[11] And the *Devī Bhāgavata Purāṇa*, while removing Śuka from this role, tells that he ascended to mokṣa before the passing of his grandmother Satyavatī, Vyāsa's mother, whom Vyāsa returns to, depressed after losing Śuka, in time to sire Dhṛtarāṣṭra, Pāṇḍu, and Vidura.[12] Satyavatī is of course long-gone before the demise of her great grandson Parikṣit, and thus, so one would think, her grandson Śuka should also be dissolved by then into the ultimate otherness of mokṣa and unable to recite the *Bhāgavata* at Parikṣit's passing.

Doniger sees the problem, but forces an unsuccessful answer: "Śuka could certainly have told the *Bhāgavata* to Parikṣit *before* his final departure from the earth" (1993b, 57). Such a solution would only screw up time in another direction, leaving us with the impossibility—at least for the *Mahābhārata*—of explaining how Bhīṣma, who dies well before Parikṣit, could tell about Śuka's attainment of mokṣa before it could have then happened itself. Doniger is responding to Ganguli's (not Roy's) view ([1884–96] 1970, 10:530, n. 1), endorsed by Sörensen ([1904] 1963, 219) and quoted with seeming approval by Belvalkar (1966, 2223), that, "It is evident that the Suka who recited the Srimad Bhagavat to Parikshit, the grandson of Arjuna, could not possibly be the Suka who was Vyasa's son." In what must, most curiously, have been a longer version of this note, quoted by Belvalkar and Sörenson, Ganguli continues: "Orthodoxy would be staggered at this; for, the prevailing impression is that it was Vyāsa's son Śuka who recited the Bhāgavata to Parīkṣit." But these

[11]Not surprisingly, the *BhP* offers its answer as Sūta Ugraśravas's reply to a question raised by Śaunaka and the other sages of the Naimiṣa Forest (*BhP* 1.7.9), who are performing a sattra there of the thousand year variety (1.1.4).

[12]Having scrapped the epic's author conventions, the purāṇa fancies that Vyāsa could return to be surprised at *Mbh* stories he has missed (Bhattacharya 1995, 184; Doniger 1993b, 36).

scholars only rationalize what they perceive as linear (Doniger) or historical (the others) contradictions in the text, or force us (in Doniger's case) to imagine further contradictions between the *Mahābhārata* and the *Bhāgavata* were we to accept the attempt at resolution. The tapas of yogic authorship would seem to hold out more daring possibilities.

Śuka tells the *Bhāgavata* to the dying Parikṣit on the bank of the Gaṅgā, showing up "by chance" "with no goal, with no sign to distinguish him, surrounded by women and children, and wearing the garb of a social outcaste" (an *avadhūta*, one who has "shaken off").[13] Contrary to our cut-and-dry expectation that mokṣa should leave no possibilities of return, and contrary even to what we might expect Śuka's story in the *Mahābhārata* to tell us, we must entertain the thought that although it is "hard to understand by those of unperfected selves," there is some narrative play in the comings and goings of the fully liberated.[14] Indeed, Mārkaṇḍeya is the best-known case in point. Likewise, Śuka, as an avadhūta "with no sign to distinguish him," would seem to have returned from the realm of mokṣa.[15] Indeed, the reference to the women surrounding him probably recalls the epic story of his liberation, which we shall examine. If it is a convention in the *Bhāgavata Purāṇa* that Śuka can return from mokṣa "with no sign to distinguish him," there is reason to suspect that it carries this convention forward from the *Mahābhārata*, which does indeed give us what seem to be post-mokṣa appearances of its

[13]Doniger 1993b, 35–36 and 260, n. 13; see further 38 on the "28 Vyāsas" of *DBhP*, and Śuka's transmission of the Mbh to Gandharvas, Yakṣas, and Rākṣasas, cited above. Doniger views Śuka's transmission as "more elitist" than Vyāsa's to his five disciples (38), but it would rather seem it is the least elitist of all.

[14]Brown 1996, 159–60 and 174, argues that in terms of the technical distinction between liberation in a disembodied state *(videhamukti)* and liberation while living *(jīvanmukti)*, the *Mbh*'s version of the Śuka story stands apart from later purāṇic ones in holding to an archaic idea of *videhamukti*: "Here alone does Śuka cast off his physical body in his quest for the Supreme" (160). But this is said only on the basis of the Śuka story itself, without considering Śuka's other *Mbh* appearances or the story's intertextual resonances.

[15]All this seems well understood by Bhaktivedanta, who offers also some thoughtful remarks about parrots and fruits (1972, 57–58); but he seems to forget it when he chides "mundane scholars" for their "diversity of opinion as to the date of compilation" of the *BhP* while claiming it to be "certain . . . that it was compiled before the disappearance of King Parīkṣit and after the departure of Lord Kṛṣṇa" (328). Contrary to what S. Collins says about *nirvāṇa*, that it "gives a full stop (period) in the religious story; . . . [what] Frank Kermode [calls] . . . 'the sense of an ending'" (1992, 233), Śuka's mokṣa is an "open ending." Collins's thought that his "approach could be generalized to other concepts of 'eternal salvation'" (223–24) is likewise not applicable to Śuka. Similarly, Vasiṣṭha, once past his near suicide at the deaths of his hundred sons and having "liberated himself from the peak of Meru" (*sa merukūṭād ātmānam mumoca bhagavān ṛṣiḥ*; 1.166.41ab), can reappear before the Pāṇḍavas in the forest (see chap. 2 at n. 80).

own for Śuka, most notably, as we have seen, at Janamejaya's snake sacrifice.[16]

Yet Śuka's presence at Janamejaya's snake sacrifice cannot solve the riddle of when he learned the *Mahābhārata* from Vyāsa. Śuka cannot tell the *Bhāgavata* to Janamejaya's father Parikṣit from having learned it, or the *Mahābhārata*, at Janamejaya's sacrifice, since Janamejaya performs this sacrifice in revenge for Parikṣit's death! Moreover, on that occasion he would (at least ostensibly) have had to learn the epic (if not the *Bhāgavata*) from Vaiśampāyana rather than Vyāsa. No, Śuka must have learned the *Mahābhārata* along with Vyāsa's four other disciples at some other time and place. Granted, once we open the floodgates of reappearances from mokṣa, it could have been almost any time and place. But if we take the epic on its own terms, Vyāsa's main time with Śuka is the time they spend before Vyāsa mourns him. If that is when Śuka learned the *Mahābhārata* from his father, he must have learned it *before* his *mokṣa*, and at least by the time of the epic's third book, the *Āraṇyakaparvan*, in which we hear of the tīrtha where Vyāsa mourns Śuka's loss. We thus have two main possibilities, the second doubled. Either passages that present temporal contradictions about Śuka are interpolations or oversights, or they are enigmatic by design, leaving open the double possibility that one might return from the otherness of mokṣa, or leave behind traces that might be experienced as one's presence even after one has gone beyond. Yudhiṣṭhira's "heresy" speech to Draupadī in the forest (see chapter 7, § D) suggests that we should favor the second option, with its irresolvable double possibility: "You have seen with your own eyes the Ṛṣi Mārkaṇḍeya of great tapas and immeasurable self going about, long-lived by dharma. Vyāsa, Vasiṣṭha, Maitreya, Nārada, Lomaśa, *Śuka*, and other perfected Ṛṣis are benevolent by dharma alone. With your own eyes you see them, possessed of divine yoga, capable of curse and grace, more venerable than even the gods!" (3.32.10–12). Yudhiṣṭhira does not indicate whether Draupadī has seen the pre-mokṣa Śuka or the post-mokṣa Śuka, but considering what he says of the company Śuka keeps, he can only mean the latter.

These enigmas are indeed mind-boggling, and if the *Mahābhārata* underplays them, it is, I would suggest, to leave the text some play in

[16]1.48.7ab. See chap. 3, n. 71, and § C. Śuka also appears along with various Ṛṣis, his father, and Vyāsa's other four disciples for the opening of Yudhiṣṭhira's sabhā (2.4.9); at 9.48.16–22 (mentioned in verse 19), he has some kind of presence at the Aditya tīrtha on the Sarasvatī, on Balarāma's pilgrimage route, along with various celestials, his father (who, like Asita Devala, attained the highest yoga there), and Kṛṣṇa Mādhusūdana (it is where Viṣṇu slew the Asuras Madhu and Kaiṭabha); and at 12.306.58, he is among various Ṛṣis and gods said to have spoken on the nature of the self.

working its own magic.[17] "Telling the story before it happens" would seem to be a *Mahābhārata* enigma, and not yet what one could call a device or convention. But the *Bhāgavata Purāṇa* treats it as a convention, and so do other purāṇas.[18] More interesting, so does the *Rāmāyaṇa*, which seems to adopt the convention directly from the *Mahābhārata* (see chapter 3 at nn. 99–101). When Rāma has heard his unknown sons Kuśa and Lava, the disciples of Vālmīki whom the latter has trained as bards, sing twenty sargas of the *Rāmāyaṇa* at his Aśvamedha sacrifice, and has recognized them, missed Sītā, summoned her to attest once again to her fidelity, and seen her prefer being taken back into the Earth (*Rām* 7.84–88), there follows a sarga that the Baroda Critical Edition rejects to an Appendix only by making a mockery of its own principles.[19] Rāma threatens to destroy the Earth unless she returns Sītā intact (App. 13, lines 18–20). When Brahmā appears, even as he did after Sītā's fire ordeal, he reminds Rāma once again of his divine origin and invites him to listen with the great Ṛṣis to the rest of his story, which, he makes clear, is yet to happen (lines 21–40). Not only that, once Brahmā has returned to heaven, the great-souled Ṛṣis who reside in Brahmaloka obtain his permission to return to hear the remainder of the *Rāmāyaṇa* and what the future has in store for Rāma, to which Rāma agrees (lines 43–49). Like the Ṛṣis of the Naimiṣa forest who listen to the bard Ugraśravas recite the *Mahābhārata*, the Ṛṣis of Brahmaloka stay with Rāma to listen to Kuśa and Lava recite the *Rāmāyaṇa* to its end—a very paradoxical situation indeed. And where do they do this? Having come from Brahmaloka, the celestial Ṛṣis stay to hear Kuśa and Lava continue their recitation in the Naimiṣa Forest, on the banks of the Gomatī.[20] In the one case, a bard, Ugraśravas, leaves a royal sacrifice, Janamejaya's, to sing the story to the sages at a Naimiṣa Forest that seems to be celestial; in the other the celestial Ṛṣis, two bards, and a king converge at a Naimīṣa Forest that is certainly here on earth. One may note that

[17]It is, in any case, unclear on what basis Shulman states that "only when . . . his sons and grandsons have died, does [Vyāsa] decide to tell the story as he knows it" (1991a, 14).

[18]I take this to be what happens in the *BhP*: Vyāsa told Śuka the story "while Śuka was engaged in withdrawal from the world (*śukam . . . nivṛttiniratam*)" and was "delighting in the self (*ātmārāmaḥ*)" (*BhP* 1.7.8 and 9)—i.e., before the story of Kṛṣṇa could have happened. Cf. Hiltebeitel 1999a, 263–96, on the *Bhaviṣya Purāṇa*.

[19]It appears as *Rām* 7, App. 13. Although the editor U. P. Shah finds it universally attested, he says, "Still however we feel that it is an early interpolation," and "Without this passage of 56 lines, the continuity of narration between sargas 88 and 89 is not hampered and appears in better order" (1975, 29). This editor's feelings also guide him in rejecting 7, App. 7, another passage concerning Kuśa and Lava that requires Śatrughna and his army to keep the secret of the boys' birth from Rāma.

[20]See chap. 3 at n. 99, and also chap. 4, § D, at n. 108.

only the *Uttarakāṇḍa* sets this scene in the vicinity of Naimiṣa Forest. Nothing of this sort is said in the *Bālakāṇḍa*. It is thus precisely the *Uttarakāṇḍa* that adopts and inverts this *Mahābhārata* convention. This could of course mean that it is late. Or perhaps the poet adopted it in midstream, or saved it for the end.

Now as we have seen (chapter 3, § C), Ugraśravas, who of course brings the *Mahābhārata* to the Ṛṣis of the Naimiṣa Forest, supplies us with what we might call a bit of sideshadowing (see chapter 2, § A). Sometime before his recitation there, his father Lomaharṣaṇa had taught him the *Āstīkaparvan* after hearing Vyāsa recite *it too* at the Naimiṣa Forest (1.13.6–7; 14.1–4). The Śuka story may take us back to Naimiṣāraṇya, but for the moment, it begins elsewhere.

B. Coming Here, Going There

Bhīṣma begins his story "in a Karṇikāra forest on the peak of Mount Meru *(meruśṛṅge)*," where "Mahādeva sported, surrounded by his terrible hosts of spirits," in the company of "the daughter of the mountain king [Pārvatī]." There Vyāsa "underwent divine tapas. Having settled himself by yoga, devoted to yoga-dharma, engaged in holding fast [in meditation: *dhārayan*], he did tapas to get a son, O best of Kurus. 'Let my son be endowed with the energy *(vīrya)* of fire, earth, water, wind, and space, O superior one,' he said. Thus by a resolution hard to attain by unperfected selves, engaged in the austerest tapas, he caused Śiva to give a boon" (310.11–15). Vyāsa worships Śiva living upon wind for a hundred years surrounded by such hosts as the heavenly Ṛṣis, world regents, Gandharvas, Apsarases, gods, winds, oceans, and streams. Note that he resolves something difficult for those of "unperfected selves"—a tag that can refer here only to Vyāsa himself, and which was used just a few lines earlier to describe those who will find it difficult to understand this story. Vyāsa's resolve and Yudhiṣṭhira's (and our) effort to understand what he is up to are thus made comparable.

Vyāsa resolves to have a son with the "energy" of the elements, and when Śiva, gratified by Vyāsa's tapas and bhakti, responds, he tells him, "as if with a smile," that he will get just what he asked for. But then Śiva changes the terms: "Your son will be great, as pure *(śuddha)* as fire, wind, earth, water, and space" (26–28). Although no one seems to have noticed it, we must of course suspect that the change from "energy" to "purity" will go on to make all the difference.

As the second adhyāya (311) opens, Vyāsa, churning a firestick[21] to make fire, sees the lustrous celestial Apsaras Ghṛtācī radiating beauty by

[21]*Araṇīm*, singular: 311.1.

her own tejas, and is suddenly befuddled with desire. Seeing him so, she becomes a female parrot *(śukī)* and draws near him. Her parrot form excites him even more, and despite his best efforts to suppress a passion that pervades his every limb, and to work all the harder to start the fire, "his sperm suddenly fell down on the firestick *(araṇyām eva sahasā tasya śukram avāpatat)*. Without mental scruples, the best of the twiceborn churned the firestick *(araṇīm mamantha)* and the Brahmarṣi Śuka was born from it. Of great tapas, Śuka was born when the sperm was churned out *(śukre nirmathyamāne)*. That supreme Ṛṣi and great yogin was born from the womb of a firestick" (311.1–10).

The implication that this scene would have elevated meaning to those of purified souls serves, for those who do not—the author as protagonist, the first listener (Yudhiṣṭhira), and other audiences—to suggest that by its insistent restraints the text designs a kind of cautionary yet enticing screen. As Vyāsa suppresses his desire, so Yudhiṣṭhira sets the model for listeners and readers by suppressing any questions about the "lower" meaning of the enigma he has just heard. But for an enigma, lower meaning is no less than higher meaning, and the screen invites one to look through it at both. What Yudhiṣṭhira has just heard is a crescendo of spiraling complements or doubles: a subject treated by Doniger (1993b), but with a few things still left to notice. These include, first,

> fire : desire,
> Ghṛtācī (whose name means "Sacrificial Ladle full of Clarified Butter")[22] : a female parrot *(śukī)*, and
> the mother (an Apsaras and parrot) : a firestick *(araṇī)*.

Yudhiṣṭhira, who as we know is good at riddles, uses the somewhat impersonal term *jananī*, "genetrix," for "mother," and has left things open to the answer he now receives: that Śuka has no biological mother but rather a series of manipulable female formations detached from any maternal body.[23] Yudhiṣṭhira will soon be able to infer that motherlessness is a distinct advantage for a seeker of mokṣa, for as Nārada will tell Śuka, "an embryo falls into the womb like a calamity"[24] and has no more control over its cooking, digestion, and emergence from a mother's body than does her piss and shit.[25]

[22]See Doniger 1993b, 41, on this along with the single firestick as a feminine symbol.
[23]Patton 1998 treats the increasing tendency in Vedic texts to detach female bodily elements and processes, most notably in relation to the term *garbha* (womb/embryo), from the biological domain to that of manipulable sacrificial ritual and symbolism, as we find here.
[24]318.20: *upadrava ivāviṣṭo yonim garbhaḥ prapadyate.*
[25]"Where food and water are wasted and food digested, even in this belly, why is an embryo

Although *aranī* is a feminine term, it is a convention that the vertical churning stick is male and the "churned" one below it female.[26] The male stick is ordinarily prescribed to be made of aśvattha wood, whereas the female "stick" should be *śamīgarbhāt*, "from the womb of the śamī." Though some texts come to view this as referring to a śamī tree itself, the older meaning is that this stick should be made from an aśvattha tree that has been enclosed by a śamī. Both sticks are thus supposed to be made of aśvattha.[27] Since Śuka is only born from one of them, it is best to suppose that it is the feminine one. Indeed, the text would seem to hold an echo of the Vedic prescription: Śuka is "born from the womb of an araṇī *(araṇīgarbha-saṃbhavaḥ)*"—the feminine araṇī, one assumes. Śuka is thus called Āraṇeya, "Son of the firestick" (12.311.21; 312.41; 314.25).

The narrative then confirms some additional doubles: "As Agni kindled in sacrifice shines when consuming the offering, so the beautiful Śuka took birth as if blazing forth with splendor. Bearing the nonpareil color and form of his father, O Kauravya, he of purified soul then shone blazing like a smokeless fire" (311.10–11). If Śuka has his father's color, it must be dark or black, since one of Śuka's epithets is Kārṣṇi, "son of Kṛṣṇa," after his father's name Kṛṣṇa Dvaipāyana, which is itself explained by Vyāsa's dark complexion. But this might make Śuka's "blazing like a smokeless fire" rather paradoxical, since what makes fires "dark," and more specifically "black-pathed" *(kṛṣṇavartman)*, is the dark smoke from the fat of animal sacrifices. Parrots, however, being green, we may assume a color chart that allows "dark," "green," and "fiery" to be ranged together. Thus the pairs

fire : Śuka
dark : green
dark fire : fiery radiance

Indeed, the "smokeless fire" that Śuka resembles evokes the "purified fire" of vegetal offerings produced by pouring ghee onto the flames from

not digested like food? The passage of embryos, piss, and shit is regulated by its own nature. No one has the power to hold them back or expel them" *(garbhamūtrapurīṣāṇām svabhāvaniyatā gatiḥ/ dhāraṇe vā visarge vā na kartur vidyate vaśaḥ)* (12.318.24–25). I follow Fitzgerald 1987, 36–37 through the digestive tract in this passage. The full passage runs from 318.14–27. On Śuka's motherlessness, cf. Shulman 1993, 119, 121.

[26]Thus Abhimanyu is born like "fire from the churned womb of the śamī" (1.213.61). Both araṇi and araṇī are feminine, but the latter—more singularly Vedic according to Monier-Williams, citing *ṚV* 5.9.3 (MW, 86)—may underscore its femininity at Śuka's birth.

[27]See Biardeau 1989, 51–54; Feller 2000, 88–89. Cf. *BAUp* 6.4.25 on the analogy between sexual intercourse and two "golden fire-drills" *(hiraṇmayī araṇī)*.

the sacrificial ladle identified with his mother's name. Thus the further pairs

animal fat : ghee
sperm : ghee

from which the crescendo builds through further doubles:

sperm *(śukra)* : son
sperm *(śukra)* : parrot *(śuka)*
son (Śuka) : parrot *(śuka)*
churning *(manth)* : churning out *(nir-manth)*
churning the female firestick *(araṇī)* : churning out the sperm *(śukra)*

Note how the pairings circulate through different orders of signification: causality, color association, analogy, allusion, homophony, and opposition, not to mention the varieties of biological, ornithological, sacrificial, and, one begins to suspect, literary symbolism.

But of course both firesticks are involved. Clearly what our strenuously suppressing minds are supposed to half-screen from our unperfected souls is that the author is simultaneously doing at least two kinds of churning: one, a "churning" into the feminine araṇī that is the only firestick mentioned,[28] and the other a "churning out" from a male firestick of which the only one seriously unmentioned (a wooden male araṇī/araṇi would not emit sperm) is obviously the author's penis, brought to life after a hundred years of solitude, of living on wind. Yet I believe that there may be another kind of churning alluded to here—that of churning out text—and that the story of the birth of Śuka may be read as an allegory of writing.[29] If so, tapas or creative fervor as authorship is linked with suffering,[30] sacrifice, even despair, and with something like mental masturbation.[31] Indeed, it so happens that Vyāsa uses this very phrase, "churning out," earlier in the *Mokṣadharma* section of the

[28]See above, nn. 21 and 26.
[29]Here and in the title of this chapter, I take a turn on Gellrich's phrase "allegory of reading," where he treats mainly Dante and Chaucer's *House of Fame*: especially, in the latter, the author's flights on authorship, through even the Milky Way. See Gellrich 1985, 156-57, 176, 219-20, 246-47, 180-201, 245.
[30]Another meaning of tapas.
[31]"Lucubrations of a Derrida!" (again quoting J. L. Mehta 1990, 111; see chap. 2 at n. 2) indeed!—that is, we may be reminded that Derrida attributes a correlation between writing and masturbation to Rousseau ([1976] 1994, 150-55 and 340).

Śāntiparvan in his lengthy instructions to Śuka.[32] Imparting instruction about the higher self *(adhyātmā)*, he tells Śuka:

> The secret *(rahasyam)* of all the Vedas, inaccessible by inference or mere scriptural study,[33] self-confirming *(ātmapratyayikam)*, this instruction *(śāstra)* that I have taught, O son, which is the wealth in every tale *(ākhyānam)* of dharma, in every tale of truth, as well as [in] ten thousand *Ṛk*s [that is, the Veda], having churned out this extracted nectar *(nirmathyāmṛtam uddhṛtam)* as butter from curds and as fire from wood, so also this knowledge of the wise has been well extracted *(samuddhṛtam)* for my son's sake. (12.238.13–15d)

As Sutton recognizes, "Here the word *nirmathya* . . . could be taken as a euphemism for a mode of exegesis," and is "an attempt to represent essentially non-Vedic teachings as the real purpose of the Vedas" (2000, 43, 45). Indeed, set amid many intertextual references, the passage reads like exegesis and echo of the Śuka story itself.

Śuka's birth is greeted with celestial celebrations. First, "The best of rivers, Gaṅgā, approaching in her own form on the back of Meru *(merupṛṣṭhe)*, O king, bathed him with water" (311.11). We note that Vyāsa and son are still on Mount Meru,[34] but now, rather than on its peak, they are at its "back,"[35] upon which the divine Gaṅgā flowing by in her "own form" is by implication the celestial Gaṅgā, the Milky Way. The "back of Meru" would seem to imply something hidden from the "ordinary" vantage point from which one views the cosmic mountain,

[32] 12.224–47; Bedekar 1966, ccxiii–ccxv; see chap. 2 at n. 138.

[33] 12.238.13b: *anaitihyam anāgamam*; cf. Ganguli ([1884–96] 1970, 11:218, and Nīlakaṇṭha on 12.246.13b in Kinjawadekar 1929–33, 5:467.

[34] In the *Nārāyaṇīya* too, Vyāsa teaches the Vedas and the *Mbh* to Śuka and the other four disciples "on Meru, best of mountains, lovely, inhabited by Siddhas and Caraṇas" (327.18).

[35] *Pṛṣṭha*'s primary meaning is "back, hind part." A secondary meaning, "upper side, surface, top, height," allows the translation "peak" (Fitzgerald 1987, 7). But the epic has many precise terms for "peak" or "top" (e.g., *śikhara, śikha, śṛṅga, kūṭa, tuṅga*). At 1.106.8, the diffentiation is clear: Pāṇḍu and his wives roam on "the southern side *(dakṣiṇam pārśvam)* of Himavat . . . and on the backs of mountains *(giripṛṣṭheṣu)*"—suggesting an opposition between southern "sides" and "backs" in the other directions. In the Śuka story too, "back" as the primary meaning simply makes sense, whereas "top" is strained, incomplete, perhaps at best that which one needs to reach in order to *get to* the back, to *see* it. Indeed, not only shall we find that other usages in the *Mbh* resonate with the meaning "back" as something "beyond," but so do several Ṛg Vedic usages, according to Laurie Patton (whom I thank for these references and her comments on their "polysemic" readings): e.g., Agni as *ghṛtapṛṣṭha*, "he whose back is brilliant with ghee"; *ṚV* 6.24.6: "From you, O Indra, they conduct (their procession?) with (their) hymns and rites, like waters from the ridge/back of the mountain *(parvatasya pṛṣṭhād)*"; cf. 5.61.2; 6.73.5 (Patton, personal communication, May 1998).

suggesting that we find Vyāsa and Śuka on "the other side of the mountain." But there is a "ground" or "earth" *(bhūvi)* there for things to fall on from the sky (13), and various divinities drop in with the "requisites which a Brahmacārin . . . requires" (Bedekar 1965, 97).

As soon as Śuka is born, "the Vedas along with their mysteries and abstracts *(vedāḥ sarahasyāh sasaṃgrahāḥ)* presented themselves[36] to [him], as they did to his father." Although Śuka is already "versed in the Vedas, auxiliaries, and commentaries *(vedavedāṅgabhāṣyavit)*," he chooses Bṛhaspati as his preceptor with whom to go and study them further, and then returns home to his father, having also studied "history in entirety and the śāstras *(itihāsaṃ ca kārtsnyena . . . śāstrāṇi)*" (311.22–25)—thus absorbing an extensive curriculum. Back with his father, he adopts celibacy and begins a regime of "fierce tapas," upon which the ādhyāya concludes: "His intellect *(buddhi)*, directed toward mokṣadharma, took no pleasure, O king, in the three lifestages rooted in the householder stage" (27).

The third adhyāya (312) now opens with Śuka's penchant for mokṣa as the tension point of all further developments: "Thus considering mokṣa, Śuka came to his father," whom he regards as "skilled in the observances of mokṣa *(mokṣadharmeṣu kuśalo)*" (1–2). Saying "Study mokṣa, son," Vyāsa directs him to master "the entire Yogaśāstra and Kāpila" (3–4)—that is, Yoga and Sāṃkhya (Kapila being the reputed founder of the Sāṃkhya). When Vyāsa sees that Śuka has finished this course and is "conversant with the knowledge of mokṣa," he then says, "Go to King Janaka, lord of Mithilā. He will tell you the meaning of mokṣa in its totality and particulars" (6). Vyāsa's attitude is intriguing. Showing none of the mixed blessings he keeps for the Bhārata line, his dedication to Śuka is unmixed and total.

Vyāsa's directions for Śuka's journey are said to be "unsurprising *(avismitaḥ)*." Yet they are anything but:[37] "Go by a human path. Don't go by the power of moving through the air *(mānuṣeṇa tvam pathā gacha . . . na prabhāveṇa gantavyam antarikṣacareṇa vai)*" (312.8). Vyāsa tells his "parrot"-son to walk, not fly, but the directions and journey are ambiguous on this very point. Śuka should take a kind of yogic beeline: "Go straight, not by the path of desire for pleasure. Don't pursue distinctions, especially ones involving attachments. Don't exhibit ego *(ahaṃkāra)* before that king who sponsors sacrifices" (9–10b).[38] The

[36]*Upatasthur*, literally, "they approached" him. They make themselves accessible to him with the result that he fully knows them.

[37]Remember, Vyāsa is one of Bhīṣma's sources.

[38]Janaka is Vyāsa's sacrificial patron (312.11; 313.10), and Vyāsa is Janaka's guru (313.2–4)—a relationship and synchronism one does not hear of in the *Rām*, where Janaka is Sītā's father. Indeed, it is a synchronism about which Yudhiṣthira is wise not to ask.

"unsurprising" itinerary alternates flightpaths with landscapes and mixes cosmography with geography. Śuka heads off "on foot, though he was able to traverse the earth with her seas through the sky. Crossing mountains and fording rivers and lakes, as also varied woods filled with many beasts of prey, and the two *varṣas* of Meru and Hari, as also gradually traversing Haimavat varṣa, he came to Bhārata varṣa. Traversing its regions inhabited by Chinese and Huns,[39] he came to *this* region, Āryāvarta, pondering *(vicintayan)*" (12–15).

Śuka thus leaves the forested heavens around his father's hermitage on the "back" of Mount Meru, in the vicinity of Naimiṣa Forest; crossing "down" into Bharatavarṣa, he arrives in Āryāvarta, the Vedic heartland of northern India. Geography aside, he probably takes the same "descending" route that Vyāsa takes when he comes and goes into his story. One senses that the author's charge to his son to do it on foot is meant to cover his own lack of traces, to suggest that his flights of fancy are also grounded. Bhīṣma tells us that Śuka keeps "pondering" the "unsurprising" directions. Not only does Śuka "ponder" as he enters Āryāvarta. Walking "by the command of his father's word, and also pondering its meaning," he traverses "the path like a bird going in the sky. Passing through delightful towns and thriving cities, seeing varied jewels, Śuka did not notice" (312.16–18). We are told he is walking, but his path is like a bird's. His birdy walk across the universe takes "not so long a time" (*acireṇaiva kālena*; 19) to reach the Videhas (plural): both the people and kingdom, and the "bodiless ones,"[40] making the destination as ambiguous as the starting place and the route. The phrase *arthaṃ vicintayan*, "pondering its meaning," is recurrent: Śuka passes by the flourishing gardens of Mithilā and "ponders the(ir) meaning, gratified with the pleasure-ground of self" (24). Reaching the inner palace's chambers, he finds no distraction in fifty ravishing courtesans and reviews the experience before he sleeps by "pondering its meaning" (43).[41] Vyāsa gives his son riddles that we (no doubt with Yudhiṣṭhira) "ponder" with him.

The fourth adhyāya (313) is filled with updated upaniṣadic teachings and set in the upaniṣadic frame of King Janaka's court—Janaka being the Upaniṣadic king who plays host to numerous Brahman sages. His

[39]As discussed in chap. 1, § C. *Varṣa* ordinarily refers to divisions of the earth separated by nine mountain ranges: Kuru, Hiraṇmaya, Ramyaka, Ilāvṛta, Hari, Ketumālā, Bhadrāśva, Kiṃnara, and Bhārata. Śuka thus travels at least from Hari to Bhārata.

[40]The name has this explicit explanation in *DBhP* (Bedekar 1965, 99, 102, 106); cf. Brown 1996, 159–60, 171.

[41]See also 315.12 and 319.12 without the *"artham,"* as at 312.15d. Note also the uses of *anu-cint* (311.23d; 312.1a and 31b; 317.11d, 12b, and 22d; 320.27d).

kingdom's name, Videha, which in the epics often means "bodiless," makes our present dialogue one between Śuka, the innately liberated child, and Janaka, the king who embodies the disembodied condition (see Brown 1996, 159–63, 171–72). After Janaka answers Śuka's openers about mokṣa's meaning, nature, and achievement with an advocacy of its attainment through the four āśramas or lifestages (13–19), Śuka asks his driving question: "When discriminating knowledge and understanding have arisen and are perceptible in the heart, what is the need of living in lifestages and forests? I ask you, lord. Tell it, according to the meaning of the Vedas *(yathā vedārthatattvena)*" (20–21). Janaka's reply seems at first conservatively cautious: "The dharma of four lifestages . . . was practiced by the ancients." (22, 24–25). But he reserves the possibility of shortcutting the four āśramas: "One whose self is purified by past causes through many saṃsāric wombs surely attains mokṣa in the first lifestage" (26). We have no inkling that Śuka might have any previous lives. Indeed, he appears to have sprung forth *de novo*, an advantage in his readiness for mokṣa. Janaka thus concedes that a brahmacārin can attain mokṣa, but he doesn't seem to know that Śiva has made Śuka "pure-souled" from the start, revising the boon that Vyāsa had asked of him. In any case, the adhyāya ends with Janaka encouraging Śuka to realize what is already awakened within him:[42] "Whatever the nature of mokṣa's meaning *(mokṣārthaśca yadātmakaḥ)*, you reside in it, O Brahman. What else do you ask about?" (50–51).

As the fifth adhyāya (314) begins, Śuka leaves Janaka's question about further questions hanging. Emphatically, Śuka has no more questions.[43] Making no reply to his host, Śuka "of perfected self and settled conclusions *(kṛtātmā kṛtaniścayaḥ)*, settling the self by the self, seeing the self by the self, his object accomplished, happy, tranquil, with the qualities of wind, quietly went forth facing north, pointing toward the wintry mountain *(śaiśiraṃ girim)*" (1–2).[44] The wintry mountain is Himavat, to which Nārada now also heads "even at that time" *(etasminneva kāle tu)* (3)—a vague time as usual, and with no more said

[42]Janaka knows this from Śuka's guru (313.41–43)—maybe Bṛhaspati but possibly Vyāsa, who is Janaka's guru; a father is by definition also a guru, and beyond that, Vyāsa will be counted as guru of Śuka among Vyāsa's five disciples (314.37–38). Nīlakaṇṭha is silent.

[43]The last adhyāya's closing quatrain about "mokṣa's meaning" (313.51b) rephrases Śuka's opening question to Janaka, where it is *mokṣārthaśca kimātmakaḥ* (313.13b) instead: from "what?" to "what-ever. . . ." Cf. Ganguli ([1884–96] 1970, 10:505, n. 2), taking *tūṣṇīm*, "quietly," as "without putting further questions to Janaka," in the verse next quoted (314.2b), and noting that Śuka "no longer walked like ordinary men. Without trailing along the solid support of the Earth, he proceeded through the sky."

[44]After this verse, three northern mss. make clear that Śuka heads "quietly north having established himself in yoga" *(prayayau yogamāsthāya tuṣṭo diśam athottarām*; 12.791*).

of Nārada for the moment. Unlike his descending journey, Śuka's return is not pedestrian. "Not alighting *(asajjamānam)* on trees,[45] mountains, or plains, yoked to yoga," he flies "like an arrow" (27). Once at his destination, we find not only that he has gone to Himavat, but that Vyāsa's hermitage has now shifted from Meru to the "back of Himavat" *(himavat pṛṣthe)* (30), which this time is on the latter's eastern side.[46] Śuka spots Vyāsa and his four Brahmin disciples below, and they see him coming like a solar flame-scattering fire in the sky (25–26).

Śuka joins this company, bringing us to an important passage, and one that is possibly quite coy: the *Mahābhārata*'s main narrative of the dissemination of Vyāsa's literary labors. "Teaching his disciples and son, Vyāsa dwelt on the back of Himavat.[47] Then, at some time"—vague as usual: *tataḥ kadācit*—the disciples, having fulfilled their Veda study, requested a favor: "May no sixth disciple of yours attain fame. Be graceful to us about this *(atra prasīda naḥ)*. We are your four disciples and the guru's son is the fifth. The Vedas should abide here. This is our desired boon" (314.33–38). Ostensibly, they ask him to be the sole carriers of his fame as propounders of the four Vedas that he is elsewhere said to have divided. But Vyāsa's answer opens other possibilities. "Knowing the substance and meaning of Veda *(vedārthatattvavit)*" and "considering the meaning of the other world *(paralokārthacintakaḥ)*," he tells them how to disseminate his work: "May you be many. Let this Veda be spread *(vedo vistāryatām ayam)*." Though the disciples are four, they will become many, to spread "*this (ayam)* Veda." Here is the first hint that their charge might be a particular Veda. Vyāsa next describes the qualities they should require from their own disciples, who will further spread "this Veda," and foretells the hardships and rewards of their work, before enjoining: "Let the four varṇas hear, having placed the Brahman in front" (41–45). "This Veda" now seems to have only one possible referent: the *Mahābhārata* as "fifth Veda," through which it will be the four disciples' radical new mission to disseminate "Veda" to all four varṇas, including Śūdras. The four are thrilled that their request is granted, and say, "We wish to go to earth from this peak *(śailād asmān mahīṃ gantum kāṅkṣitaṃ no)* to make the Vedas manyfold *(vedān anekadhā kartum)*" (315.4). Vyāsa then confirms that Himavat is not exactly on earth, saying: "You may go to earth or to the world of the gods, as you like, but you should be careful, for brahman is hidden in manifold fictions" (*apramādaśca vaḥ kāryo brahma hi pracuracchalam*;

[45]Śuka seems very parroty here; cf. Fitzgerald 1987, 17: "paid no heed to trees. . . ."
[46]The side associated with the region of Indra (314.23).
[47]Recall that in the *Nārāyaṇīya*, Vyāsa imparts the Vedas and the *Mbh* to the five on Mount Meru; see above, n. 34.

315.6cd).[48] Indeed, if *brahman* continues to refer to Veda, as it can, and if we recall a point of Foucault's, Vyāsa could be continuing to describe "this Veda"—the *Mahābhārata*—as a Veda whose fictions his disciples should continue to regulate in the author's name.[49] The four disciples then take leave, "descending to earth *(avatīrya mahīm)*," where they lead prosperous lives reciting and offering sacrifice for Brahmans, Rājanyas, and Vaiśyas (8–9). There is no mention of what they recite, or that they yet include Śūdras in their audiences. If we allow for the possibility of consistency, this would be because they are *not yet* reciting this fifth Veda, whose *earthly* dissemination awaits the setting of Janamejaya's snake sacrifice, where Vaiśampāyana will *for the first time* recite the *Mahābhārata* among *mortals*, *humans*. One may thus understand that the "other world" Vyāsa "considers" when he sets his disciples' course is *this* world, the earth. Indeed, if we allow for further consistency, Vyāsa's other three regular disciples must wait for Vaiśampāyana before reciting the *Mahābhārata* on earth themselves, leaving Nārada to recite it to the gods, Asita Devala to the Fathers *(Pitṛs)*, Śuka[50] to the Gandharvas, Rākṣasas, and Yakṣas (1.1.64; 18.5.42)—and Ugraśravas to the immortal Ṛṣis of the Naimiṣa Forest.[51]

"When his disciples had descended *(avatīrṇeṣu śiṣyeṣu)*," Vyāsa remained alone with Śuka and sought solitude in silent meditation. "In time *(kāle)*," Nārada saw him in the hermitage and urged him to resume singing Veda: "Shorn of brahmic sounds, this mountain doesn't shine *(brahmaghoṣair virahitaḥ parvato 'yaṃ na śobhate)*"; as the abode (*ālaya*, as in Himālaya) of the "hosts of gods and Ṛṣis," it is like a village of Veda-lacking Niṣādas that "doesn't gleam *(na bhrājate)*"; as the mountain-abode is itself bedimmed, so "the Ṛṣis, gods, and Gandharvas of great energy *(ojas)* do not gleam *(na bhrājante)* as before, deprived of brahmic sound" (315.10–15). Himavat, suspended between the world of gods and Ṛṣis and the earth to which one may "descend," is thus a vast abode of divine hosts that is brought to full light, along with those hosts, by Vedic singing. There, for now at least, is Vyāsa's hermitage, and there Nārada, the brahmic bard, finds the author in low spirits—we might say depressed—agreeing that things look dim, and asking his visitor for

[48]*Chala*, here "fiction," having the following meanings: "fraud, deceit, sham, guise, pretense, delusion, semblance, fiction, feint, trick" (MW, 405). Cf. ibid., 657 on the compound *pracuracchala* as "hidden in manifold disguises, MBh."

[49]Cf. the beginning of chap. 2, this being my second point taken from Foucault 1979.

[50]Perhaps taking up his father's cue that the disciples may go wherever they like.

[51]See the opening of this chapter. Recall too that the story of the former Indras concerns the restoration of this mortal/immortal "distinction" (see chap. 3, § D).

inspiration:[52] "Make it a command, O poet-sage *(viprarṣe)*, tell me what I should do for you. What should I accomplish, O Brahmarṣi? Tell it. Separated here from my disciples, my mind is not highly thrilled *(viyuktasyeha śiṣyair me nātihṛṣṭam idam manaḥ)*" (18–19). If Vyāsa's four disciples have "descended" to earth and are busying themselves with earthly tasks "for some time" prior to their reunion with him *and Śuka* at Janamejaya's sacrifice, we may infer that Vyāsa is not only missing the four; finished with his literary labors, he is undergoing some kind of postcomposition blues.

Nārada tells Vyāsa to recite the Vedas (plural), and so Vyāsa does, along with Śuka, "filling the worlds with loud precise sound" until "a wind blew excessively, impelled by the gales of the ocean." Vyāsa knows to break off recitation at this particular wind, but Śuka, curious about the interruption, asks where this wind comes from, and "all about the motion of the wind" (315.24–26). One may note that a question about winds would be quite logical from a parrot. In the same vein, Nārada instructs only Vyāsa to sing the Vedas; Śuka only sings along, with a hint that, perched on the threshold of liberation, he is "only parroting."[53] But Śuka still has "curiosity" *(kautūhalam)*: a trait that links him in two immediately preceding verses with both Nārada, whom Vyāsa addresses as "You who know everything, see everything, and are curious everywhere *(sarvajñaḥ sarvadarśī ca sarvatra ca kutūhalī)*" (315.17), and women, whom Nārada then includes in the following aphorism that opens his response: "The Vedas are stained by nontransmission. A Brahman's stain is to be vowless. Outsiders *(vāhīkāḥ)* are the earth's stain; curiosity *(kautūhalam)* is the stain of women" (20).[54]

As if in preparation for this moment, Vyāsa has already included discussion of a vast cosmic wind in his teachings to Śuka earlier in the *Mokṣadharma*: when the dissolution of the five elements proceeds to the point where fire is dissolved into air, a great wind blows in all ten directions; then it, too, dissolves into space, silence, and the absorption of everything into brahman (12.225.6–10). The present recitation-stopping wind is, however, apparently a different one, and, left "utterly amazed"

[52]Note the contrast with the *Rām*: Nārada's inspires Vālmīki to compose the *Rām*, whereas here he shows up after the *Mbh* author's work is finished.

[53]Shulman 1993, 108, 110, and 112, nicely captures the flavor of birdsong throughout the Śuka story. Talking parrots who can "parrot the Vedas" are, Bloomfield shows, a theme in "Hindu fiction" (1914, 350, 353–54); cf. Doniger 1993b, 35.

[54]315.20cd: *malam pṛthivyā vāhīkāḥ strīṇām kautūhalam malam* is close to *malam pṛthivyā bāhlīkāḥ strīṇāṃ madrastriyo malam* (8.30.68cd): "Bāhlīkas (sic) are the earth's stain; Madra women are women's stain"—thus before Śalya drives his chariot, Karṇa insults him and the "dirty" habits of his Madra homeland that is "outside" *(bahis)* the epic's version of the ārya heartland (Hiltebeitel [1976] 1990, 259, 272–78, citing 277).

(paramavismitaḥ) (315.27) by Śuka's question about it, Vyāsa imparts his wisdom about the seven winds:

> You have the divine eye (see chapter 2, n. 206). Your mind of itself is without impurity. Abandoned by tamas and rajas, you are settled down in sattva. As one's own shadow is seen, you see the self by the self *(ādarśe svāmiva chāyām paśyasyātmānamātmanā)*. Having yourself fixed the Vedas into yourself, reflect with insight. The Devayāna is the course *(cara)* of Viṣṇu, the Pitṛyāna that of darkness. Going on these two paths leads to heaven *(divam)* or below. Where winds blow on earth and in midspace there are seven paths *(mārgāḥ)* of the wind. . . . (315.28–31)

Teaching a son who has fused Veda into his self allows Vyāsa to introduce Viṣṇu as the destination of the Devayāna and to integrate the Devayāna into the ascent of yoga.[55] Each wind has higher cosmic and soteriological functions than the preceding, and through them all Vyāsa tells how the cosmic winds circulate through the breaths of "breathing beings."[56] But it is, of course, the seventh wind that has interrupted the Vedic singing, and Vyāsa saves it for last:

> "But this is a great wonder that this foremost mountain suddenly shook when that wind began to blow. This wind is the breathing out[57] of Viṣṇu. When impelled with speed, it suddenly arises, child. Then the universe trembles. Hence brahman-knowers don't recite brahman when it blows over *(ativāyati)*. What is uttered by wind is surely fear of wind. That brahman may be injured *(vāyor vāyubhayaṃ hyuktaṃ brahma tatpīḍitam bhavet)*." Having said such words, Parāśara's son, the lord, having told his son, "Recite," then went to the celestial Gaṅgā *(vyomagaṅgām)*. (54–57)

That destination provides the very last word of the sixth adhyāya.

Vyāsa's hermitage is thus near the celestial Gaṅgā that is in fact associated with the sixth wind called Parivaha; when this wind is "agitated, heavenly waters carry through the sky; it abides, having

[55]In effect, Vyāsa combines the Devayāna teachings of *BAUp* and *ChUp* with the yogic ascent of *KU*.

[56]315.35: "Wind everywhere causes the respective motions of breathing beings *(prāṇinām)*"; 38: the third wind "makes for the incessant rising of the stars, moon (soma), and the rest, which, within bodies, the great Ṛṣis call Udāna. . . ."

[57]Or expiration, or outward sigh.

diffused the propitious water of the celestial Gaṅgā."[58] There on the "back of Himavat," near the celestial Gaṅgā, Vyāsa also resides not so far from the seventh wind, which can rise "impelled from the gales of the ocean" and shake his mountain.[59] We would seem to have caught an allusion to Viṣṇu as Nārāyaṇa breathing out in his yogic sleep on the cosmic ocean; as elsewhere,[60] he would then be the destination of the yogic path that Vyāsa describes. Moreover, the celestial Gaṅgā as Milky Way bares the design that connects the cosmic night, in which Viṣṇu does his sleeping, with the "back of the mountain," which would now seem to be where the sun does not shine if we are on the "northern back," and where the sun does not *yet* shine when we are on the "eastern back." Śuka's birth takes place on a back (maybe the northern back) of Mount Meru, but his ascent to mokṣa will take place from the eastern back of Mount Himavat. From there he will fly toward the rising sun. The author seems to have composed and transmitted "this Veda" while waiting for a dawn.

This setting then carries over to the first quatrain of the seventh adhyāya (316): "In that empty interval *(etasminn antare śūnye)*, Nārada approached Śuka, who was devoted to recitation, to address the desired meanings of the Veda *(vedārthān vaktum īpsitān)*" (316.1). The "interval" or "opening" *(antaram)*[61] is "empty" *(śūnya)* temporally because Vyāsa's recitation has stopped,[62] and "open" spatially because Vyāsa has gone elsewhere, to the celestial Gaṅgā. Fitzgerald can thus translate, "At that time when nothing was happening," and Ganguli, "After Vyāsa had left that spot." The "empty interval" is indeed both a "nothing time" and a "left spot," but also a yogic-textual inner and outer space opened in and for Śuka by the now-absent author's account of the seven winds. It is also a nice opening for Nārada, who takes most of seventh, eighth, and ninth adhyāyas (316.5–318.45) to prepare Śuka for *tyāga*—abandonment, renunciation, flight—by running him through a pithy and absolutely uncompromising eremetical checklist for takeoff,

[58]315.46: *yasmin pāripluve divyā vahantyāpo vihāyasā| puṇyaṃ cākāśagaṅgāyās toyaṃ viṣṭabhya tiṣṭhati* (315.46). So I take this verse, implying, it seems, the diffusion of the celestial Gaṅgā or Milky Way by this wind, which has also to do with the obscuring of the sun and the rising of the moon (47–48).

[59]The Zen feel is appropriately palpable.

[60]As he is under the identity of Aniruddha in the *Nārāyaṇīya* (12.335.12–17, 56–59), which immediately follows the story of Śuka.

[61]On the *antaram* or "interval," see chap. 2, n. 114; chap. 3, nn. 11 and 73.

[62]If Śuka follows his father's command, cited above, he would be reciting alone, which would imply a kind of meaningless redundancy for the reasons mentioned. In any case, it is Vyāsa's breaking off that provides the "interval," and Śuka is not reciting when he converses with Nārada.

from which we have already extracted the gist of its embryology (see above at nn. 24–26). Nārada plays on familiar *Mahābhārata* teachings and conventions: "Noncruelty *(ānṛśaṃsyam)* is the highest dharma, forbearance the highest strength, self-knowledge the highest knowledge. Higher than truth is nothing" (316.12). "There, ever assailed by the woes of death and old age, a creature is cooked in saṃsāra. Are you not awakened as to how?" (26). "Surely life is going by at the measure of a blink *(nimeṣamātram)*. It does not abide. When bodies are impermanent, what does one consider permanent?" (317.22). "This ceaseless succession of dark and bright fortnights wastes away birth and death, not missing a moment *(nimeṣaṃ nāvatiṣṭhate)*" (318.6). But the main message-verse is delivered twice. First it is followed by a brief how-and-why:

> Renounce dharma and adharma, and both truth and lie; renouncing both truth and lie, renounce that by which you renounce. Abandon dharma by absence of desire, adharma by ahiṃsā,[63] both truth and lie by buddhi, buddhi by supreme resolve.[64] Bone-pillared, sinew-strung, mortared with meat and blood, skin-covered, foul-smelling, full of piss and shit, exposed to old age and grief, sick sanctuary of disease, full of passion[65] and impermanent, abandon this abode of beings.[66]

Then, in closure, Nārada repeats the key verse as his countdown's ultimate memorandum.

> Renounce dharma and adharma, and both truth and lie; renouncing both truth and lie, renounce that by which you renounce. This supreme mystery *(paramaṃ guhyam)*[67] is told to you, best of Ṛṣis, by which

[63]Dharma and adharma are renounced along with different kinds of desire, the latter as literally "not having the desire to harm."

[64]Nārada's instructions, and indeed the whole story, make frequent reference to the buddhi functioning in a proto-Sāṃkhya fashion, e.g., just before this passage, "Having renunciation as the wind and buddhi as the boat, one may cross the swift-pathed river *(tyāgavātādhvagāṃ śīghrām buddhināvā nadīṃ taret)*" (12.316.39cd), and after the next quote, Śuka, "possessing the highest buddhi," has still not yet "reached resolve" (318.46: *niścayam* again). See also 311.27 cited above, and 319.21 and 320.2–3 cited below. Buddhi and the boat metaphor both characterize Draupadī; see chap. 7, n. 90 and at n. 54.

[65]Probably the likeliest of several meanings for *rajasvalam*.

[66]316.40–43: *tyaja dharmam adharmaṃ ca ubhe satyānṛte tyaja/ ubhe satyānṛte tyaktvā yena tyajasi taṃ tyaja// tyaja dharmam asaṃkalpād adharmaṃ cāpyahiṃsayā/ ubhe satyānṛte buddhyā buddhim paramaniścayāt// asthisthūnaṃ snāyuyutam māṃsaśoṇitalepanam/ carmāvanaddhaṃ durgandhi pūrnam mūtrapurīṣayoḥ// jarāśokasamāviṣṭaṃ rogāyatanam āturam/ rajasvalam anityaṃ ca bhūtāvāsaṃ samutsṛja.*

[67]The charge to renounce dharma and adharma echoes *BhG* 18.64–66, where the famous

the gods, having renounced the world of mortals, have gone to heaven *(yena devāḥ parityajya martyalokaṃ divaṃ gatāḥ)*. (318.44–45)

"Possessing the highest buddhi,"[68] Śuka reaches his resolve after "reflecting for a moment," or perhaps better, after "considering the hour" *(tato muhūrtaṃ saṃcintya)*, since it will soon be dawn. We hear his brief thought at the turning point: "Great is the pain with sons and wives, great the exertion in transmitting knowledge. What place would be permanent, of little pain and great arising?"[69] Here and for the rest of the story, his and others thoughts are often given without verbs of thinking or address to separate them from the narrative.[70] Thereby Bhīṣma helps us to forget that Vyāsa and his other sources make an extraordinary literary leap—even given the divine eye—into that which is presumably beyond their or indeed anyone's experience: another's liberation. Without telling us or letting anyone ask how Vyāsa or Nārada could know them, Bhīṣma takes us through Śuka's last thoughts as he "reaches resolve" and acts upon it. Now Śuka's thoughts become the heart of the narrative: a narrative of mokṣa that draws Vyāsa and others along behind, but only so far as they can go. Or so, perched with this parrot-boy on the epic's outermost frame, we are left to think.

Śuka's resolve takes form through a long and ostensibly silent soliloquy (318.49–59) which, without verbs of thought or address, leaves open—probably by design—the *possibility* that Vyāsa, who has gone elsewhere, could still be mind-reading from afar; or that Nārada, still present, could somehow be listening: that Śuka's words *could* be spoken to Nārada, and that Nārada *could* thereby have later recounted them to Vyāsa or Bhīṣma, offstage as it were. Two of these verses move Śuka from resolve to conception: "Except by yoga, the supreme way cannot be obtained. Mokṣa's release from bondage is not approached by acts. Therefore, resorting to yoga, having abandoned this home-body *(tyaktvā gṛhakalevaram)*, I will become wind and enter the day-making mass of radiance *(vāyubhūtaḥ pravekṣyāmi tejorāśiṃ divākaram)*" (318.52–53). Setting a course that, already in the Upaniṣads, combines yoga with the

charge to attain Kṛṣṇa as sole refuge by "renouncing all dharmas *(sarvadharmān parityajya)*" forms part of Kṛṣṇa's "highest mystery of all" *(sarvaguhyatamam)*.

[68]12.318.46, as cited in n. 64 above.

[69]12.318.47: *putradārair mahānkleśo vidyāmnāye mahāñśramaḥ/ kiṃ nu syācchāśvataṃ sthānam alpakleśam mahodayam*. I read *mahodayam* in the sunrise context, but it could just mean "great fortune." Note that he mentions no pain "with fathers."

[70]See 318.49–59 and 319.18–19, both discussed below.

"path of the gods" *(devayāna)* through the sun, Śuka "will enter" the sun's "ever-undiminished disc."[71]

Śuka declares himself now ready to "take leave of trees,[72] snakes, mountains, earth, regions, sky, gods, Dānavas, Gandharvas, Piśācas, snakes, and Rākṣasas," and to "enter all beings in the worlds" (318.58–59ab). But before he can do so he must part company with two particular beings: Nārada and his father. With Nārada not a word is wasted, and perhaps none was spoken: "Thereupon, taking leave of the world-famed Ṛṣi Nārada, having obtained his leave, he went toward his father" (60). With Vyāsa it is a little different: "Saluting the great-souled Ṛṣi, the Muni Dvaipāyana, the Muni Śuka, circling Kṛṣṇa to his right, took leave" (61). Vyasa is "pleased" with Śuka's "word" *(vacanam)*, but there is nothing to tell us what it was, or even whether it was spoken. That they communicate as Muni to Muni may suggest that they do so under that term's meaning of "silent sage." Vyāsa, however, then speaks: "Aho aho, son. Stay now so that I may gladden the eye on your account." But "Śuka, having become disinterested, without attachment, his bonds freed, disposing himself only toward mokṣa, set his mind on going. Having completely abandoned his father, the best of twiceborns went."[73] Thus ends the story's ninth adhyāya, according to the Critical Edition. But numerous manuscripts add: "[went] . . . to the broad back of Kailāsa inhabited by crowds of Siddhas."[74] Clearly the un-"improved" text was written by someone who knew how to end a chapter.

The tenth adhyāya (319) then begins: "Having ascended the back of a mountain *(giripṛṣṭhaṃ samāruhya)*,[75] Vyāsa's son, O Bhārata, perched (or settled) in a lone, level, and twigless (or grassless) region *(same deśe vivikte ca niḥśalāka upāviśat)*" (319.1) where "there was no flock of birds, no sound, not even a sight" (*na tatra pakṣisaṃghāto na śabdo nāpi darśanam*; 319.1, 4ab). Śuka can, of course, make such journeys on foot

[71]12.318.55d: *nityamakṣayamaṇḍalaḥ*. Śuka says he will "cast off my body" and "dwell with my inner self detached, invincible in the sun's abode *(sūryasya sadane)*," while bidding the gods and Ṛṣis to see "the energy (or effort) of my yoga" *(paśyantu yogavīryam)* (318.56–57, 59). Entering the solar disc is also the "wonder of wonders" consummated by the gleaner in the story that ends the *Śāntiparvan*; see chap. 1, § C, at n. 75. See also Bedekar 1965, 116 on *Mbh* 5.33.178: "Two penetrate the orb of the sun: the recluse who practises Yoga and the hero who has laid down his life on the battlefield." On pertinent Upaniṣadic precedents and varied follow-ups, see Hiltebeitel 1999a, 273 and 275, n. 38.

[72]Trees coming first for a parrot.

[73]318.63: *nirapekṣaḥ śuko bhūtvā niḥsneho muktabandhanaḥ/ mokṣam evānusaṃcintya gamanāya mano dadhe/ pitaraṃ samparityajya jagāma dvijasattamaḥ.*

[74]12.798*: *kailāsapṛṣṭhaṃ vipulaṃ siddhasaṃghair niṣevitam.*

[75]I use the indefinite article until the mountain becomes clear.

at his father's insistence, but now, as we have just learned, he has stopped listening to his father. Yet we are in the dark as to how he "ascended," and equally in the dark, though only for the moment, as to what mountain it is.[76] It is time for the dawn. Śuka performs various yogic disciplines, and, "facing east when the sun was not long risen," he "laughed forth a laugh, having become aware of the sun *(prajahāsa tato hāsaṃ śukaḥ samprekṣya bhāskaram)*" (2–5). Suddenly he is a great yogin coursing high above the atmosphere on the path of mokṣa. He circles Nārada to take leave once again, this time speaking—that he has found the path and started on it by Nārada's grace. "Then, flying up from the back of Kailāsa, he flew to the sky" *(kailāsapṛṣṭhād utpatya sa papāta divaṃ tadā)* (6–10). We now see what bothered the interpolator at the end of the last adhyāya. Śuka last took leave of Nārada and Vyāsa "on the back of Himavat." The interpolator has tried to keep some economy by making Śuka "ascend" Nārada's current mountain, Kailāsa: textually the nearest one mentioned. But that is only one of three possibilities. Kailāsa and Himavat could be the same mountain: an attractive solution, but one we will soon have to reject. Alternately, Śuka could "ascend" Himavat and fly from there to Kailāsa to find Nārada at his shifted location. Or, as the interpolator seems to suggest, Śuka and Nārada could have both already shifted from Himavat to Kailāsa, leaving Śuka to merely "ascend" the latter. We can only be sure of a few things. Śuka, who was born on the "back of Meru" and instructed on the east-facing "back of Himavat," makes his final departure at sunrise either directly from the east-facing "back of Kailāsa," or, having started from Himavat, made the east-facing "back of Kailāsa" the last fixed point of his final take-off.

Observed now by all beings, Śuka rises with the radiance *(dyuti)* of Garuḍa and the splendor *(prabhā)* of fire, "hastening with the wind of the mind *(manomārutaraṃhasam)*, . . . thus pondering all three worlds *(lokāṃs trīn sarvān so 'tha vicintayan)*" (319.11–13). Prepared by prior instances of the Leitwort *vicintayan*, "pondering,"[77] and by Vyāsa's teaching about winds, one strains to follow. Soon the Apsarases, Gandharvas, Ṛṣis, and Siddhas speak for the astonished "all beings": "Who is this sky-rover *(antarikṣacaraḥ)* who reaches success by tapas? Body below, face upward, he is carried along by the eyes" *(adhaḥkāyordhvavaktraś ca netraiḥ samabhivāhyate)* (16). Continuing to "face east, looking at the sun" *(bhāskaraṃ samutīkṣan sa prāṅmukho)*

[76]That is, setting aside the just-mentioned addition to the end of the previous adhyāya.

[77]See Alter 1981, 92–94, on Martin Buber's coinage of Leitwort for the compositional heightening of intratextual resonances by recurrent use of charged words and their roots: a technique savored in the *Mbh* and evident in the Śuka story with verbs built on the root *cint* (see above, n. 41, and passim).

(17), Śuka is seen to move vertically, as if he were targeting the still rising sun like an Indian Icarus. Wide-eyed Apsarases marvel at his flight (19), and as he passes one Apsaras, Urvaśī, she exclaims, "Aho! What concentration of buddhi. . . . By listening to his father he reached this high nonpareil success. Devoted to his father, of firm tapas, a son well loved by his father, how is he abandoned by that father of undivided attention *(ananyamanasā tena katham pitrā vivarjitaḥ)*!" (21–22). The key closing line has been translated differently, notably by Ganguli, who has Śuka "dismissed by his *in*attentive father."[78] But the point, I believe, is that Urvaśī speaks here for the maternal interests of the Apsarases, among whom Ghṛtācī is Śuka's mother, to scold Vyāsa as Śuka's father. Vyāsa *is* attentive, or at least as attentive as he can allow himself to be. Śuka's flight can hardly escape the attention of the author. One might think it is the son abandoning the father, as has indeed already happened. But at a deeper level it is the father as author abandoning the son, and Urvaśī, as a kind of extended aunt, voices her reproach.

Now we learn that, improbable as it sounds, Śuka listens while in flight. Despite "having completely abandoned his father,"[79] these words from the maternal side move him to a last utterance. "Hearing Urvaśī's word, Śuka, knower of the highest dharma *(paramadharmavit)*, his mind absorbed in her word *(vacane gatamānasaḥ)*,[80] scanned all the regions" (319.23). The author thus allows a final access to his son's last thoughts and turns them, via these maternal words, to the worlds Śuka is leaving. Moreover, Vyāsa reminds us (that is, Yudhiṣṭhira and subsequent audiences) that Śuka knows from Nārada precisely what the "highest dharma" is: noncruelty *(ānṛśaṃsyaṃ paro dharmaḥ)*.[81] Indeed, the point is reinforced. "Then Śuka, knower of the highest dharma, spoke this word, 'If my father should follow me crying "Śuka," then may you all give answer to him combined. Out of affection for me, please carry out this word'" (26–27). This next-to-last adhyāya then ends with nature's response to Śuka's charge: "The directions with their forests and groves, the oceans, rivers, and mountains, answered him from every side" that

[78][1884–96] 1970, 10:527. Cf. Doniger, putting the onus on Śuka: ". . . how has he separated himself from his father who has no one but him in his heart?" (1993b, 48). I follow Monier-Williams (MW, 25) in taking *ananyamanasā* as "of undivided attention," and *vivarjita* not as "dismissed (by Vyāsa)" or "separated himself (from Vyāsa)," which is strained, but "abandoned (by Vyāsa)." So too Bedekar, who paraphrases: "How could his devoted father abandon him?" (1965, 117); and Shulman 1993, 115: "how could his father let him go?" Doniger seems to acknowledge this sense when she notes that Urvaśī is hardly one to cast aspersions on a parent abandoning a child (1993b, 50).

[79]318.63, cited at n. 73.

[80]More literally, "gone into her word."

[81]316.12, cited above after n. 62.

they will do as he commands (28–29). The author thus uses Urvaśī's words to turn Śuka's last thoughts to himself, to Vyāsa. We may ask from time to time whether Vyāsa is cruel to his characters, but he makes his son's abandonment through mokṣa as uncruel to himself, the author-father, as it can be. Yet how cruel or uncruel is it to have had a perfect son and be left with only an echo? Or, as we shall see, a shadow? Śuka's last thoughts leave us to ponder not only whether an author can be cruel to his characters, or whether characters can be cruel to their author, but whether an author can be cruel to himself.

C. Wonders upon Wonders

And so we come to the last adhyāya (320). Its first eleven verses crescendo around three exclamations of the tag phrase, "That was like a wonder *(tad adbhutam ivābhavat)*," spoken for all onlooking beings by Bhīṣma. The first such wonder is that, upon uttering his last word regarding his father, "Śuka rose to perfection *(prātiṣṭhata śukaḥ siddhim)*" by abandoning the fourfold worlds[82] and the three guṇas (1–2). The second is that "in the instant *(kṣaṇe)*" that "he established himself in brahman, that eternal station beyond the guṇas, free of traces,"[83] he "blazed like a smokeless fire"—which now seems to mean "he shined without karmic residue"[84]—while meteors burnt the regions and shook the earth (3–4). So far, the "instant" of mokṣa seems to be a rather straightforward world-transcendence. Śuka thus exits the universe as he entered it: the phrase "blazing like a smokeless fire" also describes his purified self *(bhāvitātman)* as he takes birth from the sperm, firesticks, and intervention of Śiva "on the back of Mount Meru."

As we now come to ponder the third wonder, which concerns that very mountain, it is worth recalling some things we know about the three main mountains of the story. Born in Vyāsa's hermitage on the back of Mount Meru, then present in Vyāsa's hermitage on the back of Mount Himavat for its shaking by the breath of the sleeping Viṣṇu, Śuka's final journey, traced from Mount Kailāsa, now finds him facing Meru and Himavat once again.

[82]I follow Fitzgerald 1987, 42, here for *hitvā lokāṃś caturvidhān* (320.1d), which inspires lots of commentary and could be something less cosmological, like "the four kinds of worldly ways."

[83]320.3: *tasminpade nitye nirguṇe liṅgavarjite/ brahmaṇi pratyatisthatsa.*

[84]Ganguli [1884–96] 1970, 10:524, n. 3, commenting on Śuka's resolve to enter the solar orb, refers to the two soteriological paths of the Upaniṣads as *arcirādi mārgaḥ* and *dhūmādi mārgaḥ:* the first "the path of light or luster, etc." for those who "reach Brahma and have never to return"; the second, "the path of smoke etc." for those who "enjoy felicity for some time and then come back." The "path of smoke"—which, as we have seen, implies "dark smoke" fed by animal fat and semen—is thus synonymous with karmic bondage.

> Trees released branches, and mountains their peaks. And Mount Himavat, struck with sounds, seemed to split.[85] The thousand-rayed sun didn't shine and fire didn't blaze. Lakes, rivers, and even oceans trembled. Vāsava [Indra] rained water that was tasty and very fragrant. A pure breeze blew that bore a divine smell. When the divine nonpareil peak was born of Himavat and Meru conjoined—one yellow-white, the second auspicious and made of beautiful gold—a hundred yojanas crosswise in breadth and in height, O Bhārata, he [Śuka], having resorted to the northern direction, saw it shining.[86] With unhesitating mind, Śuka then rushed forward into the double mountain peak, suddenly rending it. The two were seen, O Mahāraja; that was like a wonder.[87] Then also he suddenly sprang forth from the two peaks of the mountain, and that best of mountains did not obstruct his way.[88] Then the sound of all the heaven-dwellers became great in heaven. From the mountain-dwelling Gandharvas and Ṛṣis, having seen Śuka crossed beyond and the mountain made twain, there was everywhere, O Bhārata, the sound "Sādhu! Sādhu!"[89] (5–13)

In attempting to translate this passage, others have sought to make it geographically, geologically, climatologically, or psychologically comprehensible.[90] But it describes precisely what is out of this world.

[85]320.5cd: *nirghātaśabdaiśca girir himavān dīryatīva ha.*

[86]320.8–9: *sa śṛṅge 'pratime divye himavanmerusambhave/ saṃśliṣṭe śvetapīte dve rukmarūpyamaye śubhe// śatayojanavistāre tiryagūrdhvaṃ ca bhārata/ udīcīṃ diśam āśritya rucire saṃdadarśa ha.* Cf. 12.160.31–32: Where Brahmā and the Brahmarṣis reside "on Himavat's very lovely back, which has stars for its lotuses *(himavataḥ pṛṣṭhe suramye padmatārake)*," it is likewise *śatayojanavistāre*, "a hundred yojanas in extent."

[87]320.10: *so 'viśaṅkena manasā tathaivābhyapatacchukaḥ/ tataḥ parvataśṛṅge dve sahasaiva dvidhākṛte/ adṛśyetām mahārāja tadadbhutam ivābhavat. Sahasā*, "suddenly," could also be taken as "forcibly, vehemently," as also in the next line (11).

[88]320.11: *tataḥ parvataśṛṅgābhyāṃ sahasaiva viniḥsṛtaḥ/ na ca pratijaghānāsya sa gatiṃ parvatottamaḥ. Parvataśṛṅgābhyām* could also be "from the two mountain peaks," as if there were simply two separate mountains, but I translate as "from the two peaks of the mountain" because the second line makes it clear that there is only one "best of mountains" (*parvatottamaḥ*) that does not obstruct him.

[89]320.13: *dṛṣṭvā śukam atikrāntam parvataṃ ca dvidhākṛtam/ sādhu sādhviti tatrāsīnnādaḥ sarvatra bhārata. Sādhu sādhu*: "Bravo! Bravo!" "Straight! Straight!" "A saint! A saint!" "Excellent! Excellent!"

[90]Bedekar 1965, 118: "While Śuka careered flying above the earth, mountain peaks cleft and gave way to him"; Sörensen [1904] 1963, 218: "*Himavat* and *Meru* (the one yellow, made of gold; the other white, made of silver), each 100 yojanas in height and breadth, were in close contact with each other. . . . *Çuka* clashed against them, and they were immediately broken in two"; Fitzgerald 1987, 42: "Śuka saw two incomparable divine peaks that were intertwined, one originating in the Himālaya, the other on Mount Meru. The two shone brilliantly—one, made of silver, was white, the other, made of gold, was yellow—and they

First, Himavat, the mountain that has shaken at the breath of the snoozing Viṣṇu, "seems to split" when Śuka approaches it. Letting this *seeming* barely sink in, Bhīṣma regrounds us with some conventional cosmic side effects; but we may wonder who it is that has begun to see double: the narrator? Śuka? all beings? readers? Then he hits us with what may well be one of Vyāsa's enigma verses. What "seems" to be happening, if we take the language most simply and keep sequence in mind, is that Himavat, which had just "seemed to split," is now seen as a single divine peak become double, an imponderable mass, perhaps spherical or cylindrical, "a hundred yojanas crosswise in breadth and in height," born *(sambhave)* of the yellow-white Himavat and the golden Meru conjoined *(saṃśliṣṭe)*. There is no doubt who sees this: Śuka. Headed north, "he saw it shining." And there is no doubt who now splits the mountain *alone*: "With unhesitating mind, Śuka then rushed forward into the double mountain peak, suddenly rending it." In other words, what first *seemed* to split—perhaps to many—is now split, and seemingly seen, by Śuka alone. To the yogin as he breaks through to liberation, it is one mountain born of Himavat and Meru, shimmering with the distinctive faces of both; one mountain that is *both* Himavat and Meru that he alone now shatters, and which (singular) "did not obstruct his way."[91] All this is possible only through a combination of yogic and literary effects. *Saṃśliṣṭe* here is an instance of its cognate literary term *śleṣa*, "double meaning," as is the verse's other key word, *saṃbhave* ("coming together, meeting; birth, origin"). Both modify one doubled peak *(śṛṅge)* more "naturally" than some kind of connecting ridge where

stretched a hundred *yojanas*"; Doniger 1993b, 48: two peaks very close that he splits in two, though when Vyāsa follows, he sees only one split mountain; 49: "Even though Śuka has shed his physical form, he is able to act upon matter so effectively that he makes the conjoined peak of two mountains into *two separate* peaks, a violent metaphor for his own separation from his father."

[91]See n. 88. Cf. White 1996, 328, for Meru itself as a double mountain when "having the form of two cones, the one inverted and the other upright, joined at their tapered ends." White does not, however, clarify how this doubleness of Meru (for which he cites a purāṇic source [*BhP* 5.16.7; for variations, cf. Mabbett 1983, 66, 71–72; Saxena 1995, 28–29]) would relate to the yogic-alchemical macro-microcosmic body symbolism he discusses, in which the spinal cord is "*meru-daṇḍa*, Meru rod" (White 1996, 328). Within his yogic-alchemical theme-set, the merudaṇḍa could be linked with a piercing of the body-mountain at the top of the skull (the *brahmarandra* or fontanelle). But this so far theoretical (though likely) variation would be a later yogic parallel to Śuka's feat, for which the Buddha's famous breaking of the house-roof of the universe-body is an earlier one. More widely, cf. White 1996, 326, on the yogic-alchemical symbolism of the two Chinese mountains H'un-lun (east, with the "form of two superimposed spheres" and located in the abdomen) and K'un-lun (west, "two superimposed cones joined at their apex" and located in the head).

two peaks might "meet" or "come together," as some others have read it.[92] As the story itself has made clear during Śuka's long descent "on foot," Meru and Haimavat are separate varṣas.

Yet now, just as Śuka is about to emerge from the shattered double mountain to the applause of the hosts of heaven, we learn what the third wonder actually is. It is not what Śuka has done but what he has seen: "The two were seen, O Mahāraja; that was like a wonder." But what is the wonder? Is it that *he* saw the two mountains where one ordinarily only sees one, Himavat? Or is it that what he saw is reported, and that someone else must have seen it with him?[93] Here again we see the value of having Nārada and Mārkaṇḍeya as possible sources, for we soon learn that Vyāsa was out of range. The author comes trailing along "a bare moment, blink, wink, or twinkle"[94] behind and sees only the one "foremost of mountains" *(parvatāgram)* that his son, now "gone," had just divided. It is not certain whether Vyāsa still sees the mountain divided after this "bare moment," or whether he has just missed the division.[95] What is clear is that the mountain that the yogin sees double and shatters, and that does not obstruct his passage, is now just one mountain that obstructs the father's access to the son.[96] But which mountain is it? As if to tease us, we are not told. We would think it is Himavat, since that is the mountain Śuka approaches. But we cannot be sure, since the mountain Śuka leaves has just been *both* Himavat and Meru. Let us recall that Vyāsa not only has access to both of these mountains but hermitages on each, and keep our curiosity—that confirmed trait of Nārada and women—alive.

The "bare interval" separating father and son has, in fact, not gone unnoticed. Acclaimed while the sky fills with divine flowers, Śuka, "going up from above" *(upariṣṭād abhivrajan)*, "saw the delightful Mandākinī" in which "the delighted hosts of Apsarases bathed and

[92]Most translators, without pausing over the geographical implausibilities, have taken *saṃśliṣṭa* ("clasped together, contiguous, coherent, connected, confused") as implying some sort of (perhaps temporary?) proximity between the two mountains. See n. 90 above.

[93]Only after Śuka is through the double mountain is it indicated that the celestials have seen him "crossed beyond" and the mountain made twain, leaving it thus ambiguous what they saw while Śuka was going through.

[94]320.20c: *nimeṣāntaramātreṇa*, literally "in the gap or interval of a nimeṣa." Cf. chap. 3, n. 73, on the overlap of these conventions. Here, the combination literally gives narrative and yogic access to the stars.

[95]320.18–21. The key line is 21ab: *sa dadarśa dvidhā kṛtvā parvatāgraṃ śukaṃ gatam*, "He saw Śuka gone, having divided that foremost of mountains"; or, "He saw that Śuka had gone against the mountain peaks and split them in two" (Fitzgerald 1987, 43).

[96]We are prepared for this by one of Nārada's verses to Śuka: "When you set forth, surely no one follows behind. Only the well-done and ill-done [i.e., your karma] will follow your going" (316.35).

played. Naked, seeing Śuka empty of affect, they were unaffected" *(śūnyākāraṃ nirākārāḥ śukaṃ dṛṣṭvā vivāsasaḥ)* (320.14–17). The verbal play on *ākāra*—approximately, "affect" here—doesn't easily translate, but Śuka is empty of it *(śūnya-ākāra)* and the Apsarases are without it *(nir-ākāra)*, i.e., unaffected, when they see him.[97] The Mandākinī, in which the nymphs enjoy their water sports is of course not (or not *just*: again, it is a story of doubles) the earthly river of that name—one of the two main Himalayan tributaries of the earthly Gaṅgā—but the heavenly one, a branch of the heavenly Gaṅgā itself: the ascending Śuka now "sees" it, having shattered the double mountain and gone "up from above" the sky.[98] This is the last anyone will see of Śuka, at least on this trip. And it is important to note that he is still visible.[99] "Empty of affect," he is still a little like a parrot, a little like an innocent boy, and a little like a flash of light.[100]

And now, understanding that his son has set forth on the "supreme way" *(uttamāṃ gatim)*, along comes Vyāsa: "The father filled with affection followed along behind.[101] Then Śuka, upward from the wind,[102] having gone the course of the sky, having been brought to see his own majesty, then became all the elements."[103] All along the winds have been important to Śuka. Now he surpasses wind, that penultimate element, and becomes all the elements. Vyāsa, "of great tapas, having risen to that supreme way of great yoga" (320.20ab) now himself, lags

[97]MW, 127, includes, for *ākāra*, "expression of the face (as furnishing a clue to the disposition of mind)," which best applies to *both* Śuka and the Apsarases, while allowing a contrast between them. Cf. Bedekar, 1965, 119: finding Śuka "expressionless and vacant," the Apsarases "continued their sport undisturbed." Ganguli's "bodiless," is thus wrong, as is Shulman's "he no longer has any form" (1993, 115), and Brown's "Śuka of 'empty form' *(śūnyākāra)*," though Brown sees that *nirākāra*, which he translates as "remain unperturbed," is "a term that also suggests modesty" (1996, 163). Fitzgerald's "Naked, they looked upon Śuka as if neither he nor they had bodily forms" (1987, 43) both misconstrues the two modifiers and makes them noncontrastive. Ganguli's "felt shame" for the Apsares is the opposite of what is meant; he contradicts this translation in parentheses on the next page: "(None of them had betrayed any sign of agitation at the sight of his son)" [1884–96] 1970, 10:528–29—unless shame is not an agitation.

[98]Ganguli [1884–96] 1970, 10:528, thinks *upariṣṭād* (320.16b) implies that Śuka sees the Mandākinī below him, but, while that is possible, it is not said; it is only said that, having gone upward to the point where the gods see him *continuing* upward, he then sees the river.

[99]Contrary to several of the translations cited in n. 97 above.

[100]As earlier, seen returning from Videha, by Vyāsa, "like a flame-scattering fire of radiance like the sun's" (314.26), or as having fire's radiance *(prabhā)* in his final take-off (319.12).

[101]320.18: *pitā snehasamanvitaḥ . . . pṛṣṭhato 'nusasāra ha*.

[102]Cf. Ganguli [1884–96] 1970, 10:528, n. 1: "The Rishis knew that the height of the atmosphere is not interminable"; it could also mean "(wafted) upwards *by* the wind."

[103]320.19: *śukas tu mārutādūrdhvaṃ gatiṃ kṛtvāntarikṣagām/ darśayitvā prabhāvaṃ svaṃ sarvabhūto 'bhavat tadā*.

behind by only that "bare moment, blink, wink, or twinkle" (see n. 94) that Śuka's mokṣa has taken. But that is enough, and when Vyāsa comes to the mountain his son has sundered, Śuka is "gone." Again we see how deftly the position of author is constructed in relation to the question of sources. Says Bhīṣma, "The Ṛṣis then repeated to him [Vyāsa] that act of his son" (21cd). With this barely sufficient attribution, we get an answer to the question of who beside Śuka witnessed the third wonder, and thus also a suitably vague answer to how Bhīṣma could have gotten this missing moment of the tale. Vyāsa heard it from the witnessing celestial Ṛṣis, who could have included Nārada and Mārkaṇḍeya, who could have been among those who could have told this to Vyāsa, as well as the whole story to Bhīṣma.[104]

Vyāsa then calls out "Śuka!" in a painful long cry[105] that reverberates through the triple world, and Śuka, "having gone to all the elements, facing everywhere," answers back with the sound "Bhoḥ!" Fulfilling Śuka's last seemingly compassionate command, "the entire universe of mobile and immobile beings" then reverberates or echoes with the same sound (320.22–24). Despite his having "gone to the elements," Śuka thus answers first, *before* the world of nature he had commissioned to do so does so for him. Śuka's voice merges into the sounds of nature. One might wonder whether in describing Śuka's fresh absence by his becoming *sarvatomukhaḥ*, "facing everywhere," there is not an allusion to the sounds that come from the affectless faces of birds.[106] As if, left to his own regrets, an author first hears their calls, and . . . their echoes: "From then on and even now, on account of Śuka [the world] has uttered severally articulated sounds *(śabdān uccāritān pṛthak)* on the backs of mountains and caves" (*girigahvarapṛṣṭheṣu*; 320.25). As we have seen, Vyāsa has hermitages on the backs of Meru and Himavat. Moreover, the double mountain that Śuka has shattered, which is ultimately the firmament, remains a cave to those it obstructs. But it is also a mountain as seen from "above," which is no doubt why all the usages of *pṛṣṭha*, "back," for the mountains in this story seem to evoke or resonnate with the nākapṛṣṭha, "the back of the firmament." The nākapṛṣṭha would be a mountain from beyond as well as a cave from

[104]As we know from 12.38.7–13 (see chap. 2, § C.29 and n. 134), Bhīṣma had youthful access to other celestial Ṛṣis, and also gods.

[105]320.22ab: *tataḥ śuketi dīrghena śaikṣeṇākranditas tadā*. The construction here of the verb *ā-krand* conveys that the cry is like a painful lament.

[106]Moreover, T. P. Mahadevan (personal communication, November 2000) points out that, parallel to *sarvatomukha*, the epithet *viśvatomukha* applies to *pravachana*, sūtra-recitation—suggesting here another evocation of the parrot's connection with the Indian oral tradition; cf. n. 53 above.

within.[107] Indeed, the double mountain "a hundred yojanas crosswise in breadth and in height" that Śuka rends is ultimately, but also only by allusion, the *nākapṛṣṭha*.

As to Śuka himself, he has signed off into the most profound silence. "Having seen his majesty posed within, Śuka then, having renounced the guṇas that begin with sound, reached the supreme abode."[108] The parrot-boy has renounced sound, associated with the element space. Having renounced the guṇas in their relation through the senses to the five great elements, which he has "become" and pervaded, and the most primal of which, beyond wind, is space, Śuka has renounced the sense-substratum of space itself. Whatever space he is in, it is tuneless.[109]

But Vyāsa, his pursuit arrested, remains behind: "Having seen that glory of his son, whose tejas is unlimited, he sat down in a clearing on the mountain, so considering his son."[110] It is here, still near the celestial Gaṅgā, that Vyāsa learns the last lesson of this story.

> Then the hosts of Apsarases, playing on the banks of the Mandākinī, reaching that Ṛṣi, were all flustered, their minds confused. Having seen that best of Munis, some hid in the water, some took cover in thickets, some grabbed their clothes. Understanding the liberatedness of his son then, and also his own attachedness, the Muni became pleased and also ashamed.[111]

[107]The "back" of the mountain and the firmament can be virtually interchangeable in the *Mbh*: it is on Meru's "much-bejeweled back" (*pṛṣṭham . . . bahuratnācitam*; 1.15.9ab), "the great mountain covering the firmament with its height" (*nākam āvṛtya . . . ucchrayeṇa mahāgirim*; 7cd), that the gods gather before churning the ocean; 3.86.20: one doing tapas "on Ujjayanta, Surāṣṭra's holy mountain, . . . glories on the back of the firmament"; cf. n. 86 above. On hidden otherworldly luminosity, see 5.11.9: Nahuṣa sports on Himavat's back with his luster-consuming boon (Hiltebeitel 1977a); 5.109.1–6: on Himavat's back Candramas (the moon) was consecrated king of *vipras* (poets) and Śiva received Gaṅgā from the sky; 14.8.1–8: on Himavat's unseen glowing back, Śiva and Pārvatī do tapas in caves and Śiva plays with his hosts; 3.80.118–19: Sarasvatī "disappears into the desert's back (*marupṛṣthe*—hardly its top)" to reappear at Camasodbheda (see chap. 4 at nn. 38–39, 86).

[108]320.26: *antarhitaḥ prabhāvaṃ tu darśayitvā śukas tadā/ guṇān saṃtyajya śabdādīn padam adhyagamat param.*

[109]One is reminded of *Oṃ* as the *anāhatanāda*, the "unstruck (or unwounded) sound."

[110]320.27: *mahimānaṃ tu taṃ dṛṣṭvā putrasyāmitatejasaḥ/ niṣasāda giriprasthe* [var. *-pṛṣthe*] *putram evānucintayan*. I take *prasthe* as "clearing," following Fitzgerald 1987, 43, though it could also be "top." As with *pṛṣthe*, I avoid the translation "top," suspecting that with all the readier terms for top, something more precise is meant. As to the variant that puts Vyāsa once again "on the back of the mountain," it probably reflects a belated attempt at "precision" which we have no reason to endorse. We remain with Vyāsa in a rather uncertain mountain space somewhere this side of Śuka's fusion of Meru and Himavat.

[111]320.28–30: *tato mandākinītīre krīḍanto 'psarasāṃ gaṇāḥ/ āsādya tamṛṣiṃ sarvāḥ sambhrāntā gatacetasaḥ// jale nililyire kāścit kāścidgulmān prapedire/ vasanānyādaduḥ*

It is, of course, little more than a moment since the naked Apsarases, bathing in this same branch of the celestial Gaṅgā, were "unaffected" by the sight of Śuka "empty of affect," and other scholars have noticed that their reaction to Vyāsa is just the opposite.[112] Their shyness before Vyāsa suggests an allegory in the double ways they are "witnessed,"[113] and also anticipates (though it occurs earlier in the epic text) how lustful Vyāsa will be in siring his next three sons. Meanwhile, Vyāsa remains the lustful author who loves and pours (or has loved and poured) himself into the joys and sorrows of his text: joys that the Apsarases, perhaps more than any others, represent (it was, after all, Ghṛtācī who cooperated with him in Śuka's conception); sorrows that include not only those familiar from the "main story," but the *preceding* sorrow of the author's loss of this firstborn son, or, from another angle, of this son's exceeding his father's grasp, if not his father's text.

Now, in immediate response to Vyāsa's pleasure and shame, Śiva peremptorily[114] arrives to bring the story back to its beginnings. "Having formerly consoled *(sāntva pūrvam)*" Vyāsa with the promise of this son, he now consoles him for the loss. He answers the hanging question of whether his rephrasing of the boon from "energy of all the elements" to the "purity" thereof was merely verbal. "Your son was equal in energy[115] to fire, earth, water, wind, or space, as you formerly chose from me. He was born with such features procured by your tapas,

kāścid dṛṣṭvā taṃ munisattamam// tāṃ muktatāṃ tu vijñāya muniḥ putrasya vai tadā/ saktatāṃ ātmanaścaiva prīto 'bhūdvrīḍitaśca ha.

[112]Thus Bedekar 1965, 121: "The sage had known the uninhibitedness of his son and now realized in contrast, his own attachment to passions"; Doniger 1993b, 50: "the mirror episodes" produce "in Vyāsa an explicit ambivalence, making him both pleased [that his son was so great] and ashamed [that he himself was not]." Cf. Brown 1996, 163–64.

[113]One thinks of the Sāṃkhya image of the maiden *(prakṛti)* who stops dancing once she realizes she is being "witnessed" by puruṣa (*Sāṃkhya Kārikā* 59), and the Vedic and especially Upaniṣadic image of the two birds in the tree (*ŚvetUp* 4.4–6; cf. *ṚV* 1.164.20; *Muṇḍaka Up*. 3.1.1). On the latter, Doniger, drawing another parallel, comments: "one bird is said to be dark blue, like Kṛṣṇa, and the other green with red eyes, surely a parrot" (1993b, 56). One might substitute "Kṛṣṇa Dvaipāyana" for "Kṛṣṇa" here, but one would not want to push the allegory too hard, since the blue bird's indifference and the parrot's attachment to fruits would have to be reversed if applied to Vyāsa and Śuka.

[114]As if the immediacy of Śiva's coming is part of the story, the narrative has him "approach" without a time-marker like *tadā* or *tatas* ("then").

[115]Doniger (1993b, 40, 42, 49) keeps translating the *vīrya* that Śuka gets via the boon (310.14) as "manliness," but this can be no more than a secondary ironic meaning, if that. If Śuka has the *vīrya* of the elements, the feminine earth's *vīrya* can hardly be "manliness." Recall also that it is a *yogavīrya*, yogic energy or "effort," that Śuka bids the gods and Ṛsis to see (318.59) when he forms his final resolve. Cf. Bedekar 1965, 121, and Fitzgerald 1987, 44: "power"; Ganguli [1884–96] 1970, 10:529: "energy."

and also by my grace he was made pure."[116] As we and probably Yudhiṣṭhira suspected, the change from "energy" to "purity" was significant; indeed, it was a surplus of divine grace that supposedly exceeded the intention of the author! But it has also been the source of Vyāsa's current grief, for which Śiva now once again consoles him: Śuka "has obtained the supreme way. . . . Why do you lament him? As long as mountains stand, as long as the oceans stand, so long will be your indestructible fame along with your son's. Through my grace, O great Muni, you will always see everywhere in this world a shadow like your son himself that never goes away."[117] As Shulman observes, "[t]he father is left with three unsatisfactory substitutes": an echo, a shadow, and this fame (1993, 116). If, as would seem to be the case, the "fame" of Vyāsa is the *Mahābhārata*, Śiva would seem to be saying that it is their double fame that, by has grace, makes it what it is.[118] Vyāsa and Śuka will be strangely inseparable as a self with its shadow, but where the shadow is not that of the self but of the son. One could say that the *Mahābhārata* is then both the story Vyāsa told to Śuka before Śuka's disappearance, or better, the echo of that story, and the story Vyāsa enters into, under this lost and liberated son's shadow, which is about his further sons (Dhṛtarāṣṭra, Pāṇḍu, and Vidura), grandsons (Kauravas and Pāṇḍavas), and others down to his great-grandson (Janamejaya), who will finally be the first to hear Vyāsa's story among human beings, with Śuka, or is it his shadow?—in attendance once again.

D. The Other Side of the Mountain

Śuka's story has made the wonder of seeing the mountains a metaphor for different perspectives. Most transparently, the mountains figure forth contrasting this-worldly and other-worldly views on the moment of Śuka's breakthrough. Before this great divide, however, the varied perspectives are cosmological. It is a question not just of two but of three cosmic mountains. From the particular earthly cosmic mountain, Kailāsa, a real single mountain notable for its associations with Śiva (it is Kailāsa and its

[116] 320.33cd–34: *vīryeṇa sadṛśaḥ putras tvayā mattaḥ purā vṛtaḥ// sa tathā lakṣaṇo jātas tapasā tava sambhṛtaḥ/ mama caiva prabhāvena . . . śuciḥ.*

[117] 320.35–36: *sa gatim paramām prāpto . . . taṃ tvaṃ kim anuśocasi// yāvat sthāsyanti girayo yāvat sthāsyanti sāgarāḥ/ tāvat tavākṣayā kīrtiḥ saputrasya bhaviṣyati// chāyāṃ svaputrasadṛśīṃ sarvato 'napagāṃ sadā/ drakṣyase tvaṃ ca loke 'smin matprasādān mahāmune.*

[118] I agree with Bedekar (1965, 121) and Fitzgerald (1987, 44) that it is the fame of both Vyāsa and Śuka, and not with Ganguli ([1884–96] 1970, 10:529) and Doniger (1993b, 49), who take it to be only a matter of Śuka's fame. The *Mbh* would include the latter: it is something Śiva had foretold that Śuka "will obtain alone" (310.29).

caves that first enclose the Former Indras who are to become the heroes of the *Mahābhārata*), Śuka parts for the general earthly cosmic mountain Himavat (the Himālaya range, associated with Śiva's wife Pārvatī, seen as a totality from any point where it is visible from the north Indian plains as marking the northern horizon, where it embodies the heavenly mountain each dawn,[119] and, according to the story itself, is not exactly on earth), only to find that in the yogin's experience the earthly cosmic mountain and Meru (the unearthly cosmic mountain, the mountain by which one measures the whole universe from the standpoint of the heavens themselves)[120] flash forth at the moment one rends them as one and the same. Fully breaking through to the other side, one shatters the mountain and reaches the celestial Gaṅgā. Vyāsa has hermitages in such places and access to their "backs" and surroundings. So it is left for us to ponder what it means that Śuka breaks through the last two mountains in their conjunction, leaving his father that moment behind. Possibly it is the circulation of the Milky Way relative to the "fixed" positions of these mountains that accounts for Vyāsa's having multiple mountain hermitages in which he can find himself near the celestial Gaṅgā.[121] In any case, it is from them that he can descend into his story, which he would seem to have composed from on high, and to them that he can repeatedly return. Dare we say that Vyāsa is in the company of Ursa Major—in India usually known as the "Seven Ṛṣis," but also, and quite early, as both the Wagon and the Bear[122]—for whom there is always "the other side of the mountain"?

What kind of frame is the other side of the mountain? I take "Vyāsa's hermitage," and "the backs of the mountains" where we find it, as akin to what Derrida sees in Plato's notion of *khôra* in the *Timaeus*: a "place" but also "receptacle" symbolic of the mise en scène of writing, that which "receives so as to give place" (1998, 239), the "imprint bearer" (234), "chaos, chasm" (248). For Derrida, khôra allows one to read the reverse

[119]See chap. 4 at nn. 84–86, and discussion of Witzel 1984.

[120]See Kloetzli 1985, and discussion in chap. 4.

[121]In the *Nārāyaṇīya*, Vyāsa returns to his hermitage on Meru (see above, n. 34 and at n. 46) "having roamed constantly through the sky to the milky ocean, the abode of nectar (12.326.124). Meanwhile, this text places Nārada's hermitage on Himavat (334.2).

[122]See Witzel 1999, 13–14 and 17, n. 14, clarifying, in discussion with Achar 1999, 8, that when we "look at the Big Dipper when it appears in the early evening even today; it moves towards the north pole, surpasses it and sets in the west" (14). See *Mbh* 9.47.28–46, where Indra tells how Arundhatī, wife and companion star to Vasiṣṭha among the Seven Ṛṣis, was left behind while the Seven went to the back of Himavat (41). Brereton 1991; Parpola 1994, 222, 241–43; Witzel 1996. Curious also is a purāṇic tradition discussed by Sircar that the Great Bear takes a century crossing from one *nakṣatra* to another, and that in the reigns of Pratīpa and Parikṣit, it was in Puṣyā and in Maghā respectively (1969c, 19, 21–22).

side of Plato's allegory of the cave:[123] the latter, an account from above, from the standpoint of the "supremely real," the *agathon*, the good; an account of the source of the intelligible world of forms, paradigms, and light, below which the cave presents only the sensible world of likenesses, copies, mimesis, and shadows; a discourse on the "above" of language, where the sensible becomes intelligible and things can have their proper names and essences; the former, khôra, an account from below, a discourse on the below of language, neither mythos nor logos but exceeding and preceding both, "alogical and achronic, anachronistic too" (249), where words fail, yet from which one speaks or writes. Derrida shows that the *Timaeus* has a khôral texture: "In truth, each narrative content—fabulous, fictive, legendary, mythic, it doesn't matter for the moment—becomes in its turn the content of a different tale. Each tale is thus the *receptacle* of another. There is nothing but receptacles of narrative receptacles, or narrative receptacles of receptacles" (251). Yet the receptacle is a vertical image,[124] and in this unlike the other side of the mountain, which is a horizontal one of a series without end, a series that almost has no horizon, since what is on the other side of the mountain is always beyond the horizon.[125] With this image one moves toward the "edges of the text,"[126] where speech resorts to shadows and echoes.[127] There the author function can show (or conceal) its hidden faces: Socrates, "capable of receiving everything" (252) and also inspiring Plato to write; Vyāsa, whose "thought entire" includes everything that "is" and nothing of what "is not."

I have found some indologists allergic to "importing" "French

[123]I paraphrase Caputo 1997b, 96–97, who writes about this "almost perfect inversion."

[124]The Indian counterpart for which we could take from Geertz's "Thick Description": "Ah, Sahib, after that it is turtles all the way down" (1973, 29).

[125]Caputo 1997a, xxiv, 117–18, 129, 135, nicely calls attention to Derrida's wariness of the language of "horizons"—probably implying a critique of Gadamer's notion (1993, 306–7, 364–75) of a "fusion of horizons"—with his emphasis on deferral, the unforeseeable, and the messianic.

[126]Cf. Derrida 1998, 248: "We no longer know whence comes at times the feeling of dizziness, on what edges, up against the inside face of what wall: chaos, chasm, khōra" (248).

[127]Shulman 1993, 126–27, treating Śuka's "Bhoḥ" as a "half articulate cry" that fills all that is with "shadow/echoes" and "delineates a boundary between silence and language," recalls that it reminded A. K. Ramanujan of "the wordless 'boom' in the Marabar caves in E. M. Forster's *Passage to India*." On this image, see also above, chap. 6 after n. 5. On parroting, see above, n. 53; and cf. Feller 2000, 88–89, 98, 108, and 112–16, on an *Anuśāsana Parvan* passage (13.84) linking fire, a parrot, an aśvattha tree, and a *śamīgarbha* aśvattha (on which, see above, n. 27), from which fire comes and in which Agni hides. When the parrot reveals Agni's hiding place in the śamīgarbha, Agni curses it to be deprived of speech, but it retains speech that is indistinct, like a child's (39–41)!

thought" into the interpretation of a classical Sanskrit text such as the *Mahābhārata*. If the conviction is that the Indian past should be protected from the present or "the West," then perhaps a sinological analog will be more acceptable. I present it only as an inkling, and let the sinologists and their texts speak mostly for themselves. When Lao Tzu was born, he incarnated the Constellation of Destiny: "the Northern Bushel, that is, the Big Dipper and the Pole Star" (Schipper 1993, 120 and 237, n. 24). At birth, "his hair and beard were all white. Since he knew how to walk, he set off right away. His mother said to him, 'You! My old child! Why are you leaving without letting me look at you? Why are you going off as soon as born? I won't even know how to recognize you later!' So he turned around abruptly, his beard flying. . . . Seeing him, his mother took fright. She fainted and died on the spot" (120). But "Lao Tzu is his own mother"; they are transubstantial: in the brief moment between his birth and her apotheosis, "the Mother reveals to her child the secrets of the art of immortality, of that 'long life' which the Old Child has just experienced in her womb" (122). Having so descended into this world, when Lao Tzu sets forth to leave it, "he crossed, on his way to mount K'un-lun, the mountain pass that leads toward the West. The Guardian of the pass, a certain Yin Hsi, having probed the winds and clouds, concluded that a divine person was soon to pass through." Until then Lao Tzu "had not transmitted anything to anyone at all. He knew, however, that Yin Hsi was to become one with the Tao and therefore he stopped in the middle of the mountain pass." Asked by Yin Hsi for his teachings, Lao Tzu spoke the Five Thousand Words of the *Tao-te ching* and Yin Hsi wrote them down (183). The scene of writing is a mountain pass that the sage is crossing toward the west, the land of death, on the way to Mount K'un-lun, "the Chinese equivalent of Mount Sumeru [Meru; cf. n. 88 above]. . . . Situated in the northwest, it is encircled by 'slack water' on which not even a feather can float. Hence only winged beings are able to reach it. It touches the boundaries of the universe and stretches from the subterranean Yellow Springs to the Bushel at the center of the heavenly Vault. . . ." (Robinet 1993, 179)—that is, again, the Big Dipper and the Pole Star. A "variant" of Mount K'un-lun is "Mount Jen-niao, the Mountain of Bird-Men" (180). Mount K'un-lun "determines the position of Heaven and Earth and regulates things and symbols" (179, with citation). The terms that describe it "clearly indicate that K'un-lun is the earthly equivalent to what the Big Dipper is in Heaven—the central controller" (idem). In the Mao-Shan meditation tradition of Great Purity, the adept can take a spiritual journey that combines "entering into the mountains" with "marching on the heavenly net" up to and into the Bushel, which is further assimilated star by star to the organs of the sage's body (208, 211 and passim); or, imagining himself on Mount

K'un-lun" and seeing "the sun slowly rise above the water," he can ascend on the sun's astral rays (192). These celestial mountains are filled with rivers, hollows, and caves (183), and although I do not find their "backs" mentioned specifically, I believe it is hardly too much to say that is where Lao Tzu was headed when he dictated his text.

Vyāsa's itineraries—not only his, from birth, but those of his son—and the scenes of his composition seem similar enough, then, to those of this Chinese "hidden sage." Even though none of the *Mahābhārata*'s three frames speak of writing, I believe it is among the things they keep hidden. But Vyāsa's back-of-the-mountain hermitage does become the mise en scène of writing in a northern interpolation that in my view only makes explicit what the frame stories keep from view. In the famous story where Vyāsa dictates the *Mahābhārata* to Gaṇeśa, when the author and scribe negotiate, "Vyāsa says, 'Do not write anything that you do not understand,'" and then, "for the sake of diversion," the sage "mysteriously wove knots into the composition" to deliberately puzzle Gaṇeśa and gain some time from the ardors of composing for transcription. On the face of it, the story has turned from birds to an elephant. But Ugraśravas does not forget Śuka: "I know eight thousand verses, as does Śuka, and perhaps also Saṃjaya," he says. "Even today, O sage, no one is able to penetrate that closely woven mass of verses because of the profundity of their hidden meaning. Even the omniscient Gaṇeśa would ponder for a moment. . . ." (B. Sullivan 1990, 119–20). The eight thousand difficult verses: Ugraśravas knows them, which is perhaps why Śaunaka asked him the etymology of Jaratkāru (see chapter 4, § E). Saṃjaya, another sūta, knows them "perhaps," since Vyāsa gave him the divine eye. And Śuka. Once again, Śuka "knows" *still*. His knowledge has not vanished into the airless space of mokṣa. Perhaps that is why he will be asked to recite the *Bhāgavata Purāṇa*. Moreover, if Śuka sang the *Mahābhārata* only to Gandharvas, Rākṣasas, and Yakṣas, and if Ugraśravas sang it only to the Ṛṣis of the Naimiṣa Forest, and if Gaṇeśa, whatever he understood, only transcribed, it seems that we are to understand that the "knots" were less well understood by those, headed by Vaiśampāyana, who disseminated the epic among humans.

In effect, then, we can never find the author of the *Mahābhārata* because the other side of the mountain is an ever open expanse, and an ever receding frame. It is that "*there*" from which he and his son can come and go, a there not far from the Naimiṣa Forest, from Mount Meru, and from the Celestial Gaṅgā; a there that gives access to this world for both the father and son, but to the other world only (though, we would have to say, inconclusively) to the son, who actually shatters the mountain and obtains mokṣa, leaving it a momentary question how Vyāsa can reach what is on the other side of *that* mountain, which he surely does elsewhere, and how Śuka can return to this world, which *he* surely does elsewhere, too, even though the *Mahābhārata* tells us that he has left only his sounds and shadows on the backs of mountains and caves.[128] The outermost frame is the frame that gives the author his openings into the text and its characters' every moment, and explains his "partial" identity with the deity. No character from the "main story" of the *Mahābhārata* ever goes looking for Vyāsa. No one ever goes intentionally to even pay him a visit.[129] They wouldn't find him any more easily than we would.[130] Yet he can always find—more accurately, drop in on—his characters, and, through them, on us. A moody fellow, he treats all of them, as well as himself, and us, to his special blend of grace and cruelties. But he loves no one as much as he loves Śuka.

What do we do with these literary facts? First, I think it is simply uninteresting and probably false to explain them as the result of textual oversights or interpolations. Rather, risky as it is, we should be willing to consider doing what the story of Śuka invites us to do: to read the "main story" from the vantage point of *this* story. The main story, we are told, is a story Vyāsa tells to Śuka and his four other disciples. For one thing, the tale the father tells his son is often about father-son tales.[131] Śuka is the author's son who learns the sorrowful story from which he is allowed to escape. Or alternately, the story is the shadow and echo of what the father once told the son, who is now gone, whom he has "let go."

There are analogies in the *Rāmāyaṇa*, which has also much to say about fathers and sons: Rāma's insistence on his father's truth, and also his relation to his own sons. Indeed, the latter relation holds an interepic contrast: instead of a son hearing the story from his father, the father, Rāma, hears the story—*his* story—from his until then unknown twin sons.[132] But this is only the outcome of a deeper correspondence that

[128]Note that Śuka never says anything in the *Mbh* after his mokṣa. Only in the *BhP* does he speak as one liberated. Śuka could simply still be alive as a jīvanmukta, and Vyāsa could mourn him simply as one who no longer "affects" to be his son, but whom he occasionally meets on the circuit.

[129]Here he contrasts with Vālmīki, who is more accessible in the *Rām*.

[130]The only one who finds him at his ashram is Arjuna, and that is quite "by chance"; see chap. 2, § C.41.

[131]Writing about the Indian Oedipus, Goldman (1978) has shown that the *Mbh* is over and over about fathers and sons, real and displaced. Cf. Shulman 1993, 117–29, who, however, I think exaggerates the themes of aggression (121), punishment of the father (124), and wounding of the son (129) in the Śuka story. The Śuka story *may* leave one to imagine such themes, but only by their absence and their contrast with other father-son stories in the epic.

[132]See chap. 2 at n. 195, contrasting, instead, Arjuna's telling his story to the author with Rāma's hearing his story, via his sons.

also begins with a relation between poetry and birds.[133] Although by comparison the *Mahābhārata* virtually hides it away in its massive twelfth book, the story of Vyāsa and Śuka has its deepest resonances with the much more conspicuous and famous bird story that open's the *Vālmīki Rāmāyaṇa*.[134] As so often and, it seems, so inevitably (see chapter 1, n. 27), to rethink the *Mahābhārata* is to rethink the *Rāmāyaṇa* as well, and this book will end while doing so.

When Vālmīki hears the bereaved cry of a female *krauñca* bird whose mate he has just seen slain in the height of sexual passion by a cruel hunter, he is spontaneously inspired by the *krauñcī*'s cry of grief *(śoka)* to create the *śloka* meter as the form in which to curse the hunter—and, as Julia Leslie puts it, "[e]ncouraged by Brahmā, filled with wonder at what that dreadful moment had created, . . . chant the śloka again and again" along with "his disciples" as he composes the epic.[135] Leslie's beautiful article shows just how important it is that we understand Vālmīki to be describing the pair-bonding and exorbitant courtship displays of the sarus crane (1998, 468), "a huge, long-necked, long-legged, grey bird of considerable dignity and stature" whose "size of an adult human being" makes it "the largest of the Indian cranes, indeed the largest and arguably the most magnificent bird in India" (476). What is most moving in Leslie's reading is how this bird story puts Sītā at the center of Vālmīki's *Rāmāyaṇa*: "no minor incident," it is "the tragic episode from which the entire *Rāmāyaṇa* unfurls, the core emotion on which the epic depends. . . . The bird story presents the destruction of a loving and sexually mature couple, a dramatic evocation of the separation of Rāma and Sītā yet to come" (475–76). Moreover, "If," as Leslie continues, quoting Barbara Stoler Miller with seeming agreement, "the crane parable can be taken allegorically, it must mean that Rāvaṇa's abduction killed Rāma's trust in Sītā, separated them as if by death, and made *her*, above all, suffer the anguish of their tragedy."[136]

[133]Cf. nn. 53 and 106 above, and recall Staal's discussion of the similarities in their "refrain-like structures" between bird songs and mantras, and his point that "the names of many sāmans are inspired by birds" ([1990] 1996, 282, 292).

[134]Doniger calls attention to this analogy: "The parrot . . . is to Vyāsa's poetry what the curlews are to Vālmīki's poetry: the curlews give Vālmīki the sweet sound of sorrow, and the parrot . . . provide[s] Vyāsa with a disciple and son who can 'echo' his work in the presence of the dying king" (1993b, 56). But her worry is with Śuka's "reappearance" to recite the *BhP* before the dying King Parikṣit. Persuasively dismissing the curlew as a candidate for the krauñca, see Leslie 1998, 463. Cf. chap. 1, n. 71, and n. 52 above.

[135]Leslie 1998, 477. See *Rām* 1.2.9–14, 28, and 38.

[136]Miller 1973, 166, quoted by Leslie 1998, 476. See, also on these scenes, Shulman 1991a, 13–15, who recognizes that Rāma is brought to hear "the horror of his own gratuitous cruelty to the wife he exiled to the forest," but weights his discussion rather too singly toward the "hero-listener" (14).

It is interesting that Charlotte Vaudeville saw something of this too, but got caught up in imagining prior versions. Vaudeville notes that a passage in Ānandavardhana's *Dhvanyāloka* construes a reversal in which the krauñcī is killed rather than the krauñca. Eschewing the possibility that Ānandavardhana could have made such a change simply on his own,[137] but allowing that he (and other poetic theorists who follow him) takes the male bird's grief to parallel Rāma's celebrated but (Vaudeville thinks) textually "later" outpouring of sorrow at Sītā's abduction, Vaudeville argues that the episode "seems to refer to an early stage of development of the Rāmāyaṇa legend, in which the main heroine was Sītā."[138] Leslie does not adopt this developmental tale, and sees Ānandavardhana's change as representing only a later reading that "places Rāma at the centre" (1998, 476)—with which I would agree. But Leslie's argument has its own developmental turns. When it comes to a mainly southern verse in the *krauñca-vadha* passage that makes it absolutely clear that the birds in question are sarus cranes (474), Leslie concludes "rather sadly" but wisely "that there is no compelling reason to reinstate" it into the critically reconstituted text. She is nonetheless mindful not to suggest "either that the *Bālakāṇḍa* belongs to the earliest phase of the development of the *Rāmāyaṇa* or that the *krauñca-vadha* episode tells us the origins of the story of Rāma and Sītā" (475), such as Vaudeville imagines. This is one of my few "sadnesses" with Leslie's article—a textual one, like hers, but also with a difference. For whereas I agree that the lower criticism behind the Critical Editions of the two Sanskrit epics helps us identify additions to their "archetypes," and that attractive additions must often be seen as interpolations nonetheless, my sadness is that Leslie adopts, it seems rather diffidently, the conclusions of higher criticism regarding the *Rāmāyaṇa*'s allegedly prior and later "strata," and is willing to leave all that she finds here to a nonoriginal "phase" of the poem's "development."[139] We will never get to the bottom of this without a time machine. But within the text itself, once one removes these blinders, there is more that follows from Leslie's central point than she seems to realize.

[137]Vaudeville acknowledges that these authors "deliberately altered the meaning of the Rāmāyaṇa text" (1961-62, 126), but she joins those who want to rescue Ānandavardhana, founder of the *dhvani* school of "poetic reverberation," from "contradict[ing] Vālmīki just to impose his own views" (1961-62, 124). But that is the likeliest explanation.

[138]Vaudeville 1961-62, 125; cf. Leslie 1998, 476. Vaudeville (125) takes the description of the *Rām* as "the great story of Sītā and of the destruction of Paulastya (Rāvaṇa)" (1.4.6-7) as a basis for her argument, but must of course find this verse early and other segments late.

[139]"*Once the episode is in place*, the primary sentiment *(rasa)* of the epic becomes clear" (1998, 375 [my italics]). See further idem, 477, n. 1: "It is generally agreed" that the *Rām*'s first and last books are late.

Of course Vālmīki is moved to tell the *Rāmāyaṇa* as Sītā's story when he hears the krauñcī's wail! Sītā lived with Vālmīki in her deepest sadness after Rāma had cast her away, pregnant with their twins. Vālmīki helped her raise these boys, who are called *his* "children," "the children of the Muni."[140] For the krauñca-vadha to affect Vālmīki as it does is a direct hint (I believe the only one we get) that Sītā is living with him when he hears the krauñcī's cry, and thus that "the destruction" of this "loving and sexually mature couple" is not "a dramatic evocation of the separation of Rāma and Sītā yet to come" but of a separation that has already happened. If so, then one may also infer either that her boys are soon to be born, or, far more likely, that they are already being raised in Vālmīki's hermitage, and that they are either soon or immediately to be counted among those referred to as "all his disciples" (1.2.38): those who go on singing with Vālmīki after his pause of "wonder at what that dreadful moment had created." It is, in any case, after Rāma regains his kingdom that Vālmīki "made" *(cakāra, kṛtvā)* the entire poem, "including the future together with the last book" *(sabhaviṣyaṃ sahottaram)*, and it is to these two boys, living at this time in his hermitage "in the garb of Munis" *(muniveṣau)* and chosen for their sweet voices, intelligence, and grounding in the Veda, that he imparts "the whole *Rāmāyaṇa* poem (*kāvya*), called 'The Great Tale of Sītā *(sītāyāścaritaṃ mahat)* and The Slaying of Paulastya [Rāvaṇa]'" (1.4.1–6)[141]—and then sends them out to assemblies where, "on a certain occasion" *(kadācit)*, they are heard by the Ṛsis (12–13), and to roads and highways where, on another such occasion *(kadācit)*, they catch the eye and ear of Rāma (21). Vālmīki taught the twins their parents song, their mother's song, to astonish that "perfect man" their father. It is Vālmīki who brings the boys among his disciples to Rāma's Aśvamedha in the Naimiṣa Forest, and directs them to sing it there "at the gate of Rāma's dwelling where the action is taking place" (*rāmasya bhavanadvāri yatra karma ca vartate*; 7.84.5ab). And it is Vālmīki who brings Sītā there before Rāma, attests to her purity,[142] and tells Rāma that "she will give proof of her fidelity" (*pratyayaṃ*

[140]The phrase *munidārakau* (*dāraka* meaning "boy, child, son") is used thrice rapidly (7.84.9d, 17d, and 19b) just after Vālmīki has told them, "If Kakutstha [Rāma] should ask, 'Whose two children *(dārakau)* are you?' you may tell the lord of men so: 'Just the disciples of Vālmīki'" *(vālmīker atha śiṣyau hi brūtām evaṃ narādhipam)*.

[141]See above, n. 138, and cf. Goldman 1984, 286, on this "provocative" title, emphasizing the centrality of Sitā—a centrality now all the more striking for its mention in the context of the poem's transmission to and through her sons.

[142]7.87.14–20: Vālmīki attests that Sīta is "well-vowed, of virtuous conduct, and without sin" (14b–c), and "of pure conduct, sinless, holding her husband as a god" (20ab). Most touchingly, he says, he has understood her to be pure *(śuddha)* while meditating near a waterfall (19), suggesting her presence in his ashram.

dāsyate; 87.15c and 20d). Until this point, Rāma has led everyone to expect that he will now require Sītā to make a vast cosmically public oath (*śapatham*)[143] as the proof of her fidelity. But now he accepts Vālmīki's word as tantamount to being Sītā's word.[144] *Not* demanded to make an oath,[145] Sītā makes one nonetheless, or something comparable, in her only words of the scene, her act of truth that is presumably also what Vālmīki promised she would give as her proof of fidelity: "If I have thought with my mind of none other than Rāghava, let the goddess Mādhavī [the Earth] give me an opening . . ." (88.10). Rāma, who had rather plaintively just hoped for "affection" (*prīti*) from Sītā (88.4cd), has thus accepted the author's word as Sītā's word only to be overwhelmed with grief and horror by what her word—and the poet's—actually is. This is the human moment at which Rāma comes to realize what it means to be caught up in his own story.[146] How remarkable that in each epic, the Dharmarāja has a last question for his wife that in each case gets taken away by the poet.

If, then, the krauñca-vadha has made Sītā's and the poet's words one, that episode about birds is as much about Sītā and the poet as it is about Sītā and Rāma. Vālmīki would have heard the painful cries of both Sītā and the krauñcī. Together, they penetrate his poem,[147] and again they connect the poet's and the woman's voice.[148] Once we realize this, we

[143]Rāma summons the great Ṛṣis, Rākṣasas, monkeys, unnamed kings, and the four castes in thousands "to see the oath of Sītā" (87.1-7, quoting from 7d), and the gods from Brahmā on down come to witness just before Sītā speaks (88.5-7). Twice (88.1 and 4), in a phrase that occurs nowhere else in either epic, this failed reconciliation is said to take place "in the middle of the universe" (*jagato madhye*)—weakly translated as in the middle of "sa cour" ("his court") or "de tous vous" ("of you all"; Biardeau 1999, 1411-12), or of the "assembly" (Shastri 1970, 611). As noted above (at n. 20), the celestial Ṛṣis then return to hear the rest of the story. Shulman also normalizes the scene: Rāma only "convenes scholars and sages," after which "the sages are eager to hear the rest of the poem" (1991a, 14-15).

[144]"Surely I have proof of fidelity, O Brahman, in your stainless words. Surely proof of fidelity was formerly given by Vaidehī in the presence of the gods" (88.2c-3b).

[145]One interpolation spoils the effect, having Vālmīki close, "Let Sītā take an oath in your presence, Rāghava" (7.1361*, line 2).

[146]I find belatedly that my reading is similar in key features to that of the eighth-century playwright Bhavabhūti; see Shulman 2001, 53-56, 71, 88. See also chap. 3, n. 87: when Kṛṣṇa hears about his divine babyhood from Mārkaṇḍeya, it is an "old story" that is news only to the Pāṇḍavas. But Rāma keeps hearing of a divinity that seems always to elude him.

[147]This is not the place to discuss this imbrication, but clearly it relates to Vālmīki's troubling portrayal of Rāma around Sītā's *two* rejections by him; see Shulman 1991b, 88-95 (mostly on the first, but also 90 and n. 4 on the second); 1991a, 15 (on the second).

[148]See Biardeau's woman "just beyond voice range" (chap. 4 after n. 120); Sītā's avowal of ānṛśaṃsya as the highest dharma (chap. 5 after n. 89); Doniger's discussion of sign-exchanging heroines (chap. 6 after n. 41); and above all Suzuki's point on Homer and Helen (chap. 7, nn. 2 and 66).

also see that "playing the strata" has led to further muddles. Nārada's inspiring of Vālmīki to tell the story of Rāma, the perfect man, in the *Rāmāyaṇa*'s first sarga need not be taken as earlier or later than his inspiration by the krauñcī in sarga two, or what follows it in sarga four: Vālmīki's communication of the poem to Kuśa and Lava and their singing it to Rāma.[149] Nārada's "terse purāṇic account" (Goldman 1984, 70) inspires Vālmīki only to consider a story; it takes the krauñcī's cry to inspire him to sing an epic.[150] One points Vālmīki toward the hero; the other toward the heroine who lives in his hermitage. Nārada's prompting turns out to be another of his dark, prophetic ironies: how better to sing of perfection than inspired by the pain it caused? Imagine Nārada's coming to tell Vālmīki about Rāma's perfection while the poet was raising his children! But for these things to be true, we need not only these opening sargas of book one, but the scenes from book seven,[151] the *Rāmāyaṇa*'s last book—which Leslie likewise concedes to be "later" (1998, 477, n. 1).

The sounds of birds thus both inspire the poets and penetrate the poetics of both of the Sanskrit epics,[152] in each case with a sense of loss and an image of perfection. For what is lost is in one case the perfect man, the perfect husband, lost to dharma, and in the other the perfect boy, the perfect son, lost to mokṣa.[153] In one case it is a cry that leaves its imprint on every verse. In the other it is the cessation of sound, a silence, that can be replaced only by shadows and echoes. The education of Yudhiṣṭhira takes place in such a world as that: one that keeps him questioning and answering until the end.

[149]On this debate, see Goldman 1984, 60–63, 67–73, and above at n. 141.

[150]As noted in chap. 1, n. 71.

[151]This is not to say that one can "square" all the details of this *Uttarakāṇḍa* narrative with those in the prologue of the *Bālakāṇḍa*. One cannot do so, as noted (below n. 20) in connection with one such noncompliance, the Naimiṣa Forest location, where I suggest that poetic license might not be the worst argument.

[152]Cf. Nagy (1996b) on the nightingale's song in *Odyssey* 19.521 and in troubadour songs. Vālmīki's inspiration by the krauñci could be *poludeukēs*, "having continuity or patterning in many different ways" (39, 51), while Vyāsa's inspiration by Śuka could be *poluēkhēs*, "having many echoes" (42). And imagine my surprise during the Draupadī cult drama "Draupadī's Wedding," at Centumaṅkalam village near Tindivanam, July 2000, to hear "Vyāsa" tell how once, while doing tapas in the forest, he saw two parrots taking pleasure. When the male flew far off, a hunter killed it. Vyāsa realized this with his knowledge *(ñāṉam)* and released his *āṇmā* and *uyir* (soul and life) into the body of the dead parrot, who then returned and "joined" his mate, giving birth to Śuka Brahmarṣi with a parrot's face and a boy's body. As in *Mbh* 2.4.9b, Śuka comes to Yudhiṣṭhira's Rājasūya, where he eats a lot, making a bell ring. He was born *after* Dhṛtarāṣṭra, Pāṇḍu, and Vidura. . . .

[153]Cf. Shulman 1993, 118: "our text makes a highly original, even courageous statement, based on a refusal to look away from the human price attached to [mokṣa as] a basic cultural goal."

Abbreviations

Indian Texts

AV	*Atharva Veda*
BĀUp	*Bṛhadāraṇyaka Upaniṣad*
BD	*Bṛhaddevatā*
BhP	*Bhāgavata Purāṇa*
BhG	*Bhagavad Gītā*
BhvP	*Bhaviṣya Purāṇa*
ChUp	*Chāndogya Upaniṣad*
DBhP	*Devībhāgavata Purāṇa*
DM	*Devī Māhātmyam*
HV	*Harivaṃśa*
JB	*Jaiminīya Brāhmaṇa*
KS	*Kāṭhaka Saṃhitā*
KU	*Kaṭha Up*
Manu	*Mānava Dharmaśāstra, Laws of Manu*
Mbh	*Mahābhārata*
PB	*Pañcaviṃśa Brāhmaṇa*
Rām	*Rāmāyaṇa*
ṚV	*Ṛg Veda*
ŚB	*Śatapatha Brāhmaṇa*
ŚŚS	*Śāṅkhāyana Śrautasūtra*
VāmP	*Vāmana Purāṇa*
VDhP	*Viṣṇudharmottara Purāṇa*
VP	*Viṣṇu Purāṇa*

Other Abbreviations

ABORI	*Annals of the Bhandarkar Oriental Research Institute*
AJP	*American Journal of Philology*
AS/EA	*Asiatische Studien/ Études Asiatiques*
CE	Critical Edition
CIS	*Contributions to Indian Sociology*
CQ	*Classical Quarterly*
HR	*History of Religions*
IT	*Indologica Taurinensia*
JAOS	*Journal of the American Oriental Society*
JAS	*Journal of Asian Studies*

JBBRAS	*Journal of the Bombay Branch of the Royal Asiatic Society*
JGJRI	*Journal of the Ganganatha Jha Research Institute*
JIES	*Journal of Indo-European Studies*
JOIB	*Journal of the Oriental Institute, Baroda*
IJHS	*International Journal of Hindu Studies*
MW	Monier Monier-Williams's *Sanskrit-English Dictionary*
RSR	*Religious Studies Review*
WZKS	*Wiener Zeitschrift für die Kunde Sudasiens*
WZKSO	*Wiener Zeitschrift für die Kunde Sud- und Ostasiens*

Bibliography

Works in Sanskrit

Bhatt, G. H., and U. P. Shah, gen. eds. 1960–75. *The Vālmīki Rāmāyaṇa: Critical edition*. 7 vols. Baroda: University of Baroda.

Kinjawadekar, Ramachandra, ed. 1929–33. *Mahābhāratam with the commentary of Nīlakaṇṭha*. 6 vols. Poona: Chitrashala Press.

Śarmā, Śrīrāma. 1968. *Bhaviṣya Purāṇa*. 2 vols. Bareli: Saṃskṛti Saṃsthāna.

Shastri, J. L., ed. 1973. *Brahmāṇḍa Purāṇa*. Delhi: Motilal Banarsidass.

Sukthankar, V. S., et al., eds. 1933–70. *Mahābhārata: Critical edition*. 24 vols. with *Harivaṃśa*. Poona: Bhandarkar Oriental Research Institute.

Tokunaga, Muneo. [1991] 1994. Machine-readable text of the Mahaabhaarata based on the Poona Critical Edition. First revised version. Kyoto.

von Schroeder, Leopold, ed. [1900] 1970. *Kāṭhaka. Die saṃhitā der Kaṭha-Śākhā*. Wiesbaden: Franz Steiner Verlag.

Secondary Sources

Achar, B. N. Narahari. 1999. On exploring the Vedic sky with modern computer software. *Electronic Journal of Vedic Studies* 5, 2:3–10.

Agarwal, Purushottam. 1995. Surat, Savarkar and Draupadi: Legitimising rape as a political weapon. In Tanika Sarkar and Urvashi Butalia, eds., *Women and the Hindu right: A collection of essays*. 29–57. New Delhi: Kali for Women.

Agrawala, V. S. 1956. The *Mahābhārata*: A cultural commentary. *ABORI* 37:1–26.

Allen, N. J. 1996a. The hero's five relationships: A proto-Indo-European story. In Julia Leslie, ed., *Myth and mythmaking*. Collected Papers on South Asia No. 12. 1–20. London: Curzon.

———. 1996b. Homer's simile, Vyasa's story. *Journal of Mediterranean Studies* 6, 2:206–18.

———. 1999. Arjuna and the second function: A Dumézilian crux. *JRAS* 9, 3: 403–18.

Alles, Gregory D. 1989. Reflections on dating "Vālmīki." *JOIB* 38:217–44.

———. 1994. *The* Iliad, *the* Rāmāyaṇa, *and the work of religion: Failed persuasion and religious mystification*. University Park, PA. Pennsylvania State University Press.

Alter, Robert. 1981. *The art of biblical narrative*. New York: Basic Books.

———. 1992. *The world of biblical literature*. New York: Basic Books.

Andersen, Oe. [1987] 1999. Myth, paradigm, and "spatial form" in the *Iliad*. In Irene J. F. de Jong, ed., *Homer: Critical assessments*, Vol. 3, 427–85. London: Routledge.

Athavale, V. B. 1946. The roles of Vyāsa, Sañjaya, Vaiśampāyana and Sauti in the Kuru war narration. *JGJRI* 3, 2:121–41.

Auerbach, Erich. 1968. *Mimesis: The representation of reality in western literature*. Trans. Willard Trask. Princeton: Princeton University Press.

Austin, J. N. H. [1966] 1999. The function of digressions in the *Iliad*. In Irene J. F. de Jong, ed. *Homer: Critical assessments*, Vol. 3, 403–18. London: Routledge.

Bailey, Gregory. 1983. Suffering in the *Mahābhārata*: Draupadī and Yudhiṣṭhira. *Puruṣārtha* 7:109–29.

———. 1986. For a new study of the Vāmana Purāṇa. *IIJ* 29, 1:1–17.

———. 1987–88. Narrative coherence in the Upāsanākhaṇḍa of the Gaṇeśa Purāṇa: The interlocutory system. *Indologica Taurinensia* 14:29–45.

Bakhtin, M. M. 1981. *The dialogic imagination*. Trans. Caryl Emerson and Michael Holquist. Austin: University of Texas Press.

Bakker, Hans. 1986. *Ayodhyā*. Groningen: Egbert Forsten.

Bal, Mieke. 1978. Mise en abyme et iconicité. *Littérature* 29:16–28.

Balslev, Anindita Niyogi. 1983. *A study of time in Indian philosophy*. Weisbaden: Otto Harrassowitz.

———. 1993. Time and the Hindu experience. In Balslev and J. N. Mohanty, eds., *Religion and time*. 163–81. Leiden: E. J. Brill.

Basham, A. L. 1967. *The wonder that was India*. New York: Grove Press.

———. 1989. *The origins and development of classical Hinduism*. Kenneth G. Zysk, ed. Boston: Beacon Press.

Bedekar, V. M. 1965. The story of Śuka in the Mahābhārata and the Purāṇas: A comparative study. *Purāṇa* 7:87–127.

———. 1966. Mokṣadharma. In Sukthankar et al. 1933–70, vol. 15, pp. ccv–ccxlvii.

Belvalkar, Shripad Krishna. 1946. Mahābhārata text transmission. *ABORI* 26:106–19.

———. 1947a. Saṃjaya's "Eye divine." *ABORI* 27:310–31.

———. 1947b. *Bhīṣmaparvan*. Introduction and apparatus. In Sukthankar et al. 1933–70, vol. 7.

———. 1954, 1961, 1966. *Śāntiparvan*. Introduction and apparatus. In Sukthankar et al. 1933–70, vols. 13–16.

———. 1959. *Āśramavāsika, Mausala, Mahāprasthānika*, and *Svargārohaṇa Parvans*. Introductions and apparatus. In Sukthankar et al. 1933–70, vol. 19.

Bhaktivedanta Swami Prabhupāda, A. C., trans. 1972. *Śrīmad-Bhāgavatam. First canto. "Creation." Part one—Chapters 1-7.* New York: Bhaktivedanta Book Trust.

Bhandarkar, Ramakrishna Gopal. 1871-72. Consideration of the date of the Mahâbhârata, in connection with the correspondence from Col. Ellis. *JBBRAS* 10:81-92.

———. [1919-20] 1933a. Inaugural address at the B. O. R. Institute, delivered on the 15th of December 1918. In Narayan Bapuji Utgikar and Vasudev Gopal Paranjpe, eds., *Collected works of Sir R. G. Bhandarkar*, vol. 1. Government Oriental Series—Class B, No. 1. 516-21. Poona: Bhandarkar Oriental Research Institute.

———. [1919-20] 1933b. The Mahābhārata. In Narayan Bapuji Utgikar and Vasudev Gopal Paranjpe, eds., *Collected works of Sir R. G. Bhandarkar*, vol. 1. Government Oriental Series—Class B, No. 1. 522-26. Poona: Bhandarkar Oriental Research Institute.

———. 1929. Relations between Sanskrit, Pali, and the Prakrits and the modern vernaculars. Wilson philological lectures on Sanskrit and the derived languages, delivered in 1877. In Narayan Bapuji Utgikar, ed., *Collected works of Sir R. G. Bhandarkar*, vol. 4. Government Oriental Series—Class B, No. 4. 558-90. Poona: Bhandarkar Oriental Research Institute.

Bharadwaj, O. P. 1986. *Studies in the historical geography of ancient India.* Delhi: Sandeep.

Bhatt, G. H., ed. 1960. *The Bālakāṇḍa: The Vālmīki Rāmāyaṇa.* Bhatt and Shah 1960-75, vol. 1.

Bhattacharji, S. 1992-93. Social pressures behind the Bhārgava interpolation of the *Mahābhārata*. *ABORI* 72-73:469-82.

Bhattacharya, N. N. 1969. The Kurukṣetra war and the Pāṇḍavas. In Sircar 1969b, 37-41.

Bhattacharya, Pradip. 1995. Puranic sidelights on the Mahābhārata. *Purāṇa* 37, 2:176-90.

Biardeau, Madeleine. 1968. Some more considerations about textual criticism. *Purāṇa* 10, 2:115-23.

———. 1969. La decapitation de Reṇukā dans le mythe de Paraśurāma. In Jan C. Heesterman, ed., *Pratidānam. Indian, Iranian and Indo-European studies presented to F. B. J. Kuiper on his sixtieth birthday.* 563-72. Janua Linguarum, Series Major 34. The Hague: Mouton.

———. 1970a. Letter to the editor. *Purāṇa* 12, 1:180-81.

———. 1970b. The story of Arjuna Kārtavīrya without reconstruction. *Purāṇa* 12, 2:286-303.

———. 1976. Études de mythologie hindoue: 4. Bhakti et avatāra. *BEFEO* 63:87-237.

———. 1978. Études de mythologie hindoue: 5. Bhakti et avatāra. *BEFEO* 65:111-263.

———. 1979. Śakuntalā dans l'épopée. *IT* 7:115–25.

———. 1981. The salvation of the king in the *Mahābhārata*. *CIS* n.s. 15, 1 & 2:75–97.

———. 1984. Nala et Damayantī. Héros épiques. Part 1. *IIJ* 27:247–74.

———. 1985. Nala et Damayantī. Héros épiques. Part 2. *IIJ* 28:1–34.

———. 1989. *Histoires de poteaux. Variations védiques autour de la déesse hindoue*. Paris: École Française d'Extrême Orient.

———. 1991. Nara et Nārāyaṇa, *WZKS* 35:75–108.

———. 1993. Le Brâhmanisme ancien, ou la non-violence impossible. *Puruṣārtha* 16:125–39.

———. 1994. *Études de mythologie*, 2: *Bhakti et avatāra*. Pondicherry: Ecole Française d'Extrême Orient.

———. 1997a. Some remarks on the links between the epics, the purāṇas and their Vedic sources. In Gerhard Oberhammer, ed., *Studies in Hinduism: Vedism and Hinduism*. 69–173. Vienna: Verlag der Österreichischen Akademie der Wissenschaften.

———. 1997b. Un certain Kīcaka. In Siegfried Lienhard and Irma Piovano, eds., *Lex et litterae: Studies in honour of Professor Oscar Botto*. 35–52. Alessandria: Edizioni dell'Orso.

———. 1999. *Le Rāmāyaṇa de Vālmīki*. Paris: Gallimard.

———. CR 77-91 (1969-1983). Comptes rendus of seminars on the *Mahābhārata*. *Annuaire de l'Ecole Pratique des Hautes Etudes*, Ve section, vols. 77 (1969–70):168–73; 78 (1970–71):151–61; 79 (1971–72):139–47; 80–81 (1973–74):120–41; 82 (1973–74):89–101; 83 (1975):103–11; 84 (1975–76): 165–85; 85 (1976–77):135–67; 86 (1977–78):143–53; 87 (1978–79):145–71; 88 (1979–80):167–82; 89 (1980–81):221–50; 90 (1981–82):145–55; 91 (1982–83): 153–73.

——— and Charles Malamoud. 1976. *Le sacrifice dans l'Inde ancienne*. Paris: Presses Universitaires de France.

——— and Jean-Michel Péterfalvi. 1985. *Le Mahābhārata, Livres I à V*. Paris: Flammarion.

——— and Jean-Michel Péterfalvi. 1986. *Le Mahābhārata, Livres VI à XVIII*. Paris: Flammarion.

Bigger, Andreas. 1998. *Balarāma im Mahābhārata*. Beiträge zur Indologie 30. Wiesbaden: Otto Harrassowitz.

———. 1999a. Les pèlerinages dans le Mahābhārata. Paper prepared for an April conference in Lausanne. Personal communication.

———. 1999b. The normative redaction of the Mahābhārata: Possibilities and limitations of a working hypothesis. Paper delivered at the second Dubrovnik International Conference on the Sanskrit Epics and Purāṇas. Personal communication.

Biswas, Atreyi. 1973. *The political history of the Hūṇas in India*. Delhi: Munshiram Manoharlal.

Blackburn, Stuart H. 1989. Patterns of development for Indian oral epics. In Blackburn, Peter J. Claus, Joyce B. Flueckiger, and Susan S. Wadley, eds. *Oral epics in India*. 15–32. Berkeley: University of California Press.

Bloomfield, Maurice. 1914. On talking birds in Hindu fiction. In *Festschrift Ernst Windisch. Zum siebzigsten Geburtstag am 4. September 1914*, presented by his friends and students. 351–61. Leipzig: Otto Harrassowitz.

Bonazzoli, Giorgio. 1981. Places of purāṇic recitation according to the purāṇas. *Purāṇa* 23, 1:48–61.

Booth, Wayne C. 1983. *The rhetoric of fiction*. 2d ed. Chicago: University of Chicago Press.

Borges, Jorge Luis. 1964. *Labyrinths: Selected stories and other writings*. Donald A. Yates and James E. Irby, eds. New York: New Directions.

Bose, Buddhadeva. 1986. *The book of Yudhisthir: A study of the Mahabharat of Vyas*. Trans. Sujit Mukherjee from the Bengali *Mahabharater katha* (1974). Hyderabad: Sangam Books.

Bosworth, A. B. 1996. *Alexander and the East*. Oxford: Clarendon Press.

Boulton, J. V. 1976. Sarala Dasa: His audience, his critics, and his Mahabharata. *Image (Balasore)*, 1–24.

Brereton, Joel. 1991. Cosmographic images in the *Bṛhadāraṇyaka Upaniṣad*. *IIJ* 34:1–17.

Brockington, John L. 1981. *The sacred thread*. Edinburgh: The University Press.

———. 1984. *Righteous Rāma: The evolution of an epic*. New York: Oxford University Press.

———. 1998. *The Sanskrit epics*. Handbuch der Orientalistik, Zweite Abteilung, Indien, Vol. 12. J. Bronkhorst, ed. Leiden: E. J. Brill.

Brockington, Mary. 2000. Husband or king? Yudhiṣṭhira's dilemma in the Mahābhārata. Paper presented at XI World Sanskrit Conference, Turin. Forthcoming in *IIJ*. Personal communication.

——— and Peter Schreiner, eds. 1999. *Composing a tradition: Concepts, techniques and relationships*. Proceedings of the First Dubrovnik International Conference on the Sanskrit Epics and Purāṇas, August 1997. Zagreb: Croatian Academy of Sciences and the Arts.

Bronkhorst, Johannes. 1998a. Why is there philosophy in India? 1998 Gonda Lecture. Amsterdam: Royal Netherlands Academy of Arts and Sciences.

———. 1998b. Does the Veda have an author? A reply to Professor Stephen H. Phillips. *AS/EA* 52, 1:5–14.

Brown, C. Mackenzie. 1996. Modes of perfected living in the *Mahābhārata* and the *Purāṇas*: The different faces of Śuka the renouncer. In Andrew O. Fort and Patricia Y. Mumme, eds., *Living liberation in Hindu thought*. 157–83. Albany: State University of New York Press.

Bühler, Georg. 1904. Indian paleography from about B.C. 350 to about A.D. 1300. *IA* 33, Appendix:1–101.

Caland, Willem. 1908. *Altindische Zauberei. Darstellung der altindischen*

"Wunschopfer." Verhandlungen der Koninklijke Akademie van Wetenschappen, Afdeeling Letterkunde 10, 1. Amsterdam: Johannes Müller.

———. 1919. *Das Jaiminīya-Brāhmaṇa in Auswahl. Text, Übersetzung, Indices*. Verhandlungen der Koninklijke Akademie van Wetenschappen, Afdeeling Letterkunde 19, 4. Amsterdam: Johannes Müller.

———, trans. [1931] 1982. *Pañcaviṃśa-Brāhmaṇa: The Brāhmaṇa of twenty five chapters*. Bibliotheca Indica, No. 255. Calcutta: Asiatic Society.

———, trans. 1953. *Śāṅkhāyana-Śrautasūtra*. Nagpur: International Academy of Indian Culture.

Caputo, John D. 1997a. *The prayers and tears of Jacques Derrida: Religion without religion*. Bloomington: University of Indiana Press.

———, ed. 1997b. *Deconstruction in a nutshell: A conversation with Jacques Derrida*. New York: Fordham University Press.

Cardona, George. 1976. *Pāṇini: A survey of research*. The Hague and Paris: Mouton.

———. 1990. On attitudes towards language in ancient India. *Sino-Platonic Papers* 15:1–19.

Chadwick, H. Munro. 1912. *The heroic age*. Cambridge: Cambridge University Press.

——— and Nora Kershaw Chadwick. 1932, 1936, 1940. *The growth of literature*. 3 vols. Cambridge: Cambridge University Press.

Chakravarty, Amiya Kumar. 1969. Early history of the Śaunakas. In Sircar 1969b, 161–73.

Chatterjee, Asim Kumar. 1930. *The political history of pre-Buddhist India*. Calcutta.

Claus, Peter J., and Frank J. Korom. 1991. *Folkloristics and Indian folklore*. RRC Publications in International Folkloristics, 1. Udipi: Regional Resources Centre for Folk Performing Arts, Mahatma Gandhi College.

Collins, Alfred. 1994. Dancing with Prakṛti. Paper delivered at the Annual Meeting of the American Academy of Religion. Personal communication.

Collins, Steven. 1992. Nirvāṇa, time, and narrative. *HR* 31, 3:215–46.

Collison, Robert. 1966. *Encyclopaedias: Their history throughout the ages*. New York: Hafner Publishing Company.

Dahlmann, Joseph. 1895. *Das Mahābhārata als Epos und Rechtsbuch: Ein Problem aus Altindiens Cultur- und Literaturgeschichte*. Berlin: Felix L. Dames.

———. 1899. *Genesis des Mahābhārata*. Berlin: F. L. Dames

Dandekar, R. N. 1961. *Śalyaparvan*. Introduction and apparatus. In Sukthankar et al. 1933–70, vol. 11.

———, ed. 1966. *Anuśāsanaparvan*. Introduction and apparatus. In Sukthankar et al. 1933–70, vol. 17.

———, ed. 1990. *The Mahābhārata revisited*. New Delhi: Sahitya Akademi.

Dani, Ahmad Hasan. 1963. *Indian paleography*. Oxford: Clarendon Press.

De, S. K., ed. 1940. *Udyogaparvan*. Introduction and apparatus. In Sukthankar et al. 1933–70, vol. 6.

———, ed. 1958. *Droṇaparvan*. Introduction and apparatus. In Sukthankar et al. 1933–70, vols. 8 and 9.

Defourny, Michel. 1978. *Le mythe de Yayāti dans la littérature épique et purāṇique. Étude de mythologie hindoue*. Paris: Société d'Edition "Les Belles Lettres."

de Jong, J. W. 1975. Recent Russian publications on the Indian epic. *Adyar Library Bulletin* 39:1–42.

———. 1985. The overburdened earth in India and Greece. *JAOS* 105, 3:397–400.

Derrida, Jacques. [1976] 1994. *Of grammatology*. Trans. Gayatri Chakravorty Spivak. Delhi: Motilal Banarsidass.

———. 1991. *Given time*. 1. *Counterfeit money*. Trans. Peggy Kamuf. Chicago: University of Chicago Press.

———. 1992. Force of law: The "mystical foundation of authority." Trans. Mary Quaintance. In Drucilla Cornell, Michael Rosenfeld, and David Gray Carlson, eds., *Deconstruction and the possibility of justice*. 3–67. New York: Routledge.

———. 1995. *The gift of death*. Trans. David Wills. Chicago: University of Chicago Press.

———. 1998. *The Derrida reader: Writing performances*. Julian Wolfreys, ed. Lincoln: University of Nebraska Press.

de Santillana, Giorgio, and Hertha von Dechend. 1977. *Hamlet's mill: An essay on myth and the frame of time*. Boston: David R. Godine.

Deshpande, Madhav M. 1993a. *Sanskrit and Prakrit: Sociolinguistic issues*. Delhi: Motilal Banarsidass.

———. 1993b. The changing notion of śiṣṭa from Patañjali to Bhartṛhari. *AS/EA* 47:96–115.

Devi, Mahasweta. [1981] 1988. Draupadi. Trans. Gayatri Chakravorty Spivak, with Foreword. In Spivak 1988, 187–96, 279–99.

Dhand, Arti. 2000. "Poison, snake, the sharp edge of a razor: Yet the highest of gurus. Defining female sexuality in the *Mahābhārata*." Ph.D. dissertation. Montreal: McGill University.

Dhavalikar, M. K. 1992–93. Draupadī's garment. *ABORI* 72–73:523–26.

Doniger, Wendy, ed. 1993a. *Purāṇa perennis: Reciprocity and transformation in Hindu and Jaina texts*. Albany: State University of New York Press.

———. 1993b. Echoes of the *Mahābhārata*: Why is a parrot the narrator of the Bhāgavata Purāṇa and the Devībhāgavata Purāṇa? In Doniger 1993a, 31–58.

———. 1999. *Splitting the difference: Gender and myth in ancient Greece and India*. Chicago: University of Chicago Press. (See also O'Flaherty.)

Doniger, Wendy, trans., and Brian K. Smith, Introd. 1991. *The laws of Manu*. London and New York: Penguin.

Dubuisson, Daniel. 1978. La déesse chevelue et la reine coiffeuse. Recherches sur un thème épique de l'Inde ancienne. *JA* 166:291–310.

Dumézil, Georges. 1948. *Jupiter, Mars, Quirinus*, IV: *Explications de textes indiens et latins*. Paris: Presses Universitaires de France.

———. 1968. *Mythe et épopée*, 1: *L'Idéologie des trois fonctions dans les épopées des peuples indo-européens*. Paris: Gallimard.

———. 1969. *The destiny of the warrior*. Trans. Alf Hiltebeitel. Chicago: University of Chicago Press.

———. 1971. *Mythe et épopée*, 2: *Un héros, un sorcier, un roi*. Paris: Éditions Gallimard.

———. 1973. *The destiny of a king*. Trans. Alf Hiltebeitel. Chicago: University of Chicago Press.

Dumont, O.-E. 1927. *L'Aśvamedha: Description du sacrifice solonnel du cheval dans le culte védique d'après les textes du Yajurveda blanc*. Paris: Paul Geuthner.

Dutt, M. N. 1895–1905. *A prose English translation of the* Mahābhārata. 13 vols. Calcutta: H. C. Dass.

Dwivedi, R. K. 1977. A critical study of the changing of the social order at yugānta, or the end of the Kali age: With special reference to the *Mahābhārata*. In Lallanji Gopal, chief ed., *D. D. Kosambi commmemoration volume*. 276–97. Varanasi: Banaras Hindu University.

Edgerton, Franklin. 1944. *Sabhāparvan*. Introduction and apparatus. In Sukthankar et al. 1933–70, vol. 2.

Erdosy, George, ed. 1995. *The Indo-Aryans of ancient South Asia: Language, material culture and ethnicity*. New Delhi: Munshiram Manoharlal.

Falk, Harry. 1986. *Bruderschaft und Würfelspiel. Untersuchungen zur Entwicklungsgeschichte der vedischen Opfers*. Freiburg: Hedwig Falk.

———. 1988. Goodies for India: Literacy, orality, and Vedic culture. *Erscheinungsformen kultereller Prozesse*. Jahrbuch 1988 des Sonderforschungsbereichs "Übergänge und Spannungsfelder zwischen Mündlichket und Schriftlichkeit." 103–20. Tübingen: Gunter Narr Verlag.

———. 1993. *Schrift im alten Indien: Ein Forschungsbericht mit Anmerkungen*. Tübingen: Gunter Narr Verlag.

Falk, Nancy Auer. 1977. Draupadī and the dharma. In Rita M. Gross, ed., *Beyond androcentrism: New essays on women and religion*. 89–114. Missoula, MT: Scholars Press.

Feller, Danielle. 1999. Review of Bigger 1998. *AS/EA* 53, 3:811–14.

———. 2000. "The Sanskrit epics' representation of Vedic myths." Ph.D. dissertation. Lausanne: University of Lausanne. (See also Danielle Jatavallabhula.)

Finkelberg, Margalit. 1998. *The birth of literary fiction in ancient Greece*. Oxford: Clarendon Press.

Fitzgerald, James L. 1980. "The *mokṣa* anthology of the *Great Bhārata*. An initial survey of structural issues, themes, and rhetorical strategies." PhD dissertation. Chicago: University of Chicago.

———. 1983. The great epic of India as religious rhetoric: A fresh look at the *Mahābhārata*. *JAAR* 51, 4:611–30.

———, trans. 1987. The origin of Śuka; Śuka's flying against the mountain peaks. Personal communication.

———. 1991. India's fifth Veda: The *Mahābhārata*'s presentation of itself. In Sharma 1991, 150–70.

———. 1997. Review of Sullivan 1990. *JAOS* 117, 4:701–2.

———. 1998. Some storks and eagles eat carrion; herons and ospreys do not: Kaṅkas and kuraras (and baḍas) in the *Mahābhārata*. *JAOS* 118, 2:257–61.

———. 1999. The Rāma Jāmadagnya "thread" in the *Mahābhārata*. Paper presented at the 2d Dubrovnik International Conference on the Sanskrit Epics and Purāṇas.

———. 2000. Rāma Jāmadagnya in the MBh—what, where, why. Presented at the annual meeting of the American Oriental Society, Portland, OR.

———. Forthcoming-a. The *Mahābhārata* (draft). In Sushil Mittal and Gene Thursby, eds., *The Hindu world*. London: Routledge.

———. Forthcoming-b. The Rāma Jāmadagnya "thread" of the Mahābhārata: A new survey of of Rāma Jāmadagnya in the Pune text. In Mary Brockington, ed., *Stages and transitions*. Proceedings of the 2d Dubrovnik International Conference on the Sanskrit Epics and Purāṇas, 1999.

Flood, Gavin. 1996. *An introduction to Hinduism*. Cambridge: Cambridge University Press.

Foucault, Michel. 1979. What is an author? In Josué V. Harari, ed., *Textual Strategies: Perspectives in post-structuralist criticism*. 141–60. Ithaca: Cornell University Press.

Gadamer, Hans-Georg. 1993. *Truth and method*. 2d rev. ed. Trans. J. Weinsheimer and D. G. Marshall. New York: Continuum.

Ganguli, Kisari Mohan, trans., and Pratap Chandra Roy, publisher. [1884–96] 1970. *The Mahabharata*. New Delhi: Munshiram Manoharlal.

Geertz, Clifford. 1973. *The interpretation of cultures*. New York: Basic Books.

Gehrts, Heino. 1975. *Mahābhārata: Das Geschehen und seine Bedeutung*. Bonn: Bouvier Verlag Herbert Grundmann.

Gellrich, Jesse M. 1985. *The idea of the book in the Middle Ages: Language theory, mythology, and fiction*. Ithaca: Cornell University Press.

Gill, Christopher, trans. and ed. 1999. *Plato. The Symposium*. London: Penguin.

——— and T. P. Wiseman, eds. 1993. *Lies and fiction in the ancient world*. Austin: University of Texas Press.

Gitomer, David. 1992. King Duryodhana: The Mahābhārata discourse of sinning and virtue in epic and drama. *JAOS* 112, 2:222–32.

Gokak, V. K. 1990. Presidential address. In Dandekar 1990, 1–10.

Goldman, Robert P. 1970. Akṛtavraṇa vs. Śrīkṛṣṇa as narrators of the legend of Bhārgava Rāma: *A propos* some observations of Dr. V. S. Sukthankar. *ABORI* 53:161–73.

———. 1976a. Vālmīki and the Bhṛgu connection. *JAOS* 96, 1:97–101.

———. 1976b. India's great war. *JAS* 35, 3:463–70.

———. 1977. *Gods, priests, and warriors. The Bhṛgus of the Mahābhārata*. New York: Columbia University Press.

———. 1978. Fathers, sons, and gurus: Oedipal conflict in the Sanskrit epics. *JIP* 6:325–92.

———, trans. 1984. *The Rāmāyaṇa of Vālmīki*, vol. 1: *Bālakāṇḍa*. Princeton: Princeton University Press.

———. 1985. Karma, guilt, and buried memories: Public fantasy and private reality in traditional India. *JAOS* 105, 3:413–25.

———. 1995. Gods in hiding: The Mahābhārata's Virāṭa Parvan and the divinity of the Indian epic hero. In Narang 1995, 73–100.

——— and Sally J. Sutherland, trans. 1996. *The Rāmāyaṇa of Vālmīki*, Vol. 5: *Sundarakāṇḍa*. Princeton: Princeton University Press.

Gombach, Barbara. 2000. "Ancillary stories in the Sanskrit Mahābhārata." Ph.D. dissertation. New York: Columbia University.

Gonda, J. 1969. The meaning of Vedic *kārú*-. *JGJRI* 25:479–88.

———. 1971. The vedic Mitra and the epic Dharma. *JRAS* n.v.:120–33.

Gonzales-Reimann, Luis Arnold. 1998. "The 'Mahābhārata' and the yugas: India's great epic poem and the Hindu system of world ages." Ph.D. dissertation. Berkeley: University of California.

Gopal, Ram. 1969. Vedic sources of the Śārṅgaka legend in the *Mahābhārata*. *JGJRI* 25:397–401.

Grosz, Elizabeth. 1997. The time of violence: Deconstruction and value. Paper for Cultural Violence, Second Annual Human Sciences Conference, George Washington University, March 8.

Grünendahl, Reinhold. 1997. Zur Stellung der Nārāyaṇīya im Mahābhārata. In Schreiner 1997a, 197–240.

Gupta, Anand Swarup, ed. 1968. *The Vāmana Purāṇa with English translation*. Trans. Satyamsu Mohan Mukhopadhyaya, Abhibhushan Bhattacharya, N. C. Nath, and V. K. Verma. Varanasi: All India Kashiraj Trust.

Hacker, Paul. 1960. Zür Entwicklung der Avatāralehre. *WZKSO* 4:47–70.

Halbfass, Wilhelm. 1988. *India and Europe: An essay in understanding*. Albany: State University of New York Press.

———. 1992. *On Being and what there is: Classical Vaiśeṣika and the history of Indian ontology*. Albany: State University of New York Press.

Handelman, Susan A. 1982. *The slayers of Moses: The emergence of rabbinic interpretation in modern literary theory*. Albany: State University of New York Press.

Hazra, R. C. 1955. The Aśvamedha, the common source of origin of the purāṇa pañca-lakṣaṇa and the *Mahābhārata*. *ABORI* 36:190–203.

Heesterman, Jan. 1963. Vrātya and sacrifice. *IIJ* 6:1–37.

———. 1968/1969. On the origin of the Nāstika. *WZKSO* 12–13:171–85.

———. 1985. *The inner conflict of tradition. Essays in Indian ritual, kingship, and society*. Chicago: University of Chicago Press.

———. 1993. *The broken world of sacrifice: An essay in ancient Indian ritual*. Chicago: University of Chicago Press.

Hegarty, James M. 2000. An apprenticeship in attentiveness: Narrative patterning in the *Dyutaparvan* and the *Nalopakhyanam* of the Mahabharata. Personal communication.

Hess, Linda. 2001. Lovers' doubts: Questioning the Tulsi *Rāmāyaṇ*. In Paula Richman, ed., *Questioning Rāmāyaṇas: A South Asian narrative tradition*. 25–47. Berkeley: University of California Press.

Higonnet, Margaret R. 1994. Cassandra's question: Do women write war novels? In Higonnet, ed., *Borderwork: Feminist engagements with comparative literature*. 144–61. Ithaca: Cornell University Press.

Hiltebeitel, Alf. 1975. Comparing Indo-European "Epics" (review of Georges Dumézil's *Mythe et épopée*, vols. 2 and 3). *HR* 15:90–100.

———. 1976. The burning of the forest myth. In Bardwell L. Smith, ed., *Hinduism: New essays in the history of religions*. 208–24. Leiden: E. J. Brill.

———. [1976] 1990. *The ritual of battle. Krishna in the Mahābhārata*. Albany: State University of New York Press.

———. 1977a. Nahuṣa in the skies: A human king of heaven. *HR* 16, 4:329–350.

———. 1977b. Review of Gẹhrts 1975. *Erasmus* 29:86–92.

———. 1978. The Indus Valley "Proto-Śiva," reexamined through reflections on the goddess, the buffalo, and the symbolism of *vāhanas*. *Anthropos* 73: 677–97.

———. 1979a. Kṛṣṇa and the *Mahābhārata* (A bibliographical essay). *ABORI* 60:65–107.

———. 1979b. Ṛṣis and Rākṣasas: At home and abroad in the Indian epics. New York: American Academy of Religion annual meeting.

———. 1980a. Draupadī's garments. *IIJ* 22:97–112.

———. 1980b. Śiva, the goddess, and the disguises of the Pāṇḍavas and Draupadī. *HR* 20:147–74.

———. 1980–1981. Sītā vibhūṣitā: The jewels for her journey. *Ludwik Sternbach Commemoration Volume*. *IT* 8-9:193–200.

———. 1981. Draupadī's hair. In Madeleine Biardeau, ed., *Autour de la déesse hindoue*. *Puruṣārtha* 5:179–214.

———. 1982. Brothers, friends, and charioteers: Parallel episodes in the Irish and Indian epics. In Edgar C. Polomé, ed., *Homage to Georges Dumézil*. *JIES* Monograph, No. 3:85–112.

———. 1984. The two Kṛṣṇas on one chariot: Upaniṣadic imagery and epic mythology. *HR* 24:1–26.

———. 1985a. Two Kṛṣṇas, three Kṛṣṇas, four Kṛṣṇas, more Kṛṣṇas: Dark interactions in the *Mahābhārata*. In Arvind Sharma, ed., *Essays on the Mahābhārata, Journal of South Asian Literature* 20:71–77.

———. 1985b. Purity and auspiciousness in the Sanskrit epics. In Frédérique Appfel Marglin and John Carman, eds., *Essays on purity and auspiciousness, Journal of Developing Societies* 1:41–54.

———. 1987. Gambling. In Mircea Eliade, ed. in chief, *The encyclopedia of religion*. 5:468–74. New York: Free Press.

———. 1988. *The cult of Draupadī*, I. *Mythologies: From Gingee to Kurukṣetra*. Chicago: University of Chicago Press.

———. 1989. Kṛṣṇa at Mathurā. In Doris M. Srinivasan, gen. ed., *Mathurā: The cultural heritage*. 92–102. New Delhi: American Institute of Indian Studies.

———. 1991a. *The cult of Draupadī*, 2. *On Hindu ritual and the goddess*. Chicago: University of Chicago Press.

———. 1991b. The folklore of Draupadī: Sarees and hair. In Arjuna Appadurai, Frank Corom, and Margaret Mills, eds., *Gender, genre, and power in South Asian expressive traditions*. 395–427. Philadelphia: University of Pennsylvania Press.

———. 1993. Epic studies: Classical Hinduism in the *Mahābhārata* and the *Rāmāyaṇa*. *ABORI* 74:1–62.

———. 1995a. Dying before the *Mahābhārata* war: Martial and transsexual body-building for Aravāṉ. *JAS* 54, 2:447–73.

———. 1995b. Religious studies and Indian epic texts. *RSR* 21, 1:26–32.

———. 1998a. Conventions of the Naimiṣa Forest. *JIP* 26:161–71.

———. 1998b. Hair like snakes and mustached brides: Crossed gender in an Indian folk cult. In Barbara D. Miller and Alf Hiltebeitel, eds., *Hair: Its meaning and power in Asian cultures*. 143–76. Albany: State University of New York Press.

———. 1999a. *Rethinking India's oral and classical epics: Draupadī among Rajputs, Muslims, and Dalits*. Chicago: University of Chicago Press.

———. 1999b. Fathers of the bride, fathers of Satī: Myths, rites, and scholarly Practices. *Thamyris* 6, 1:65–92.

———. 1999c. Reconsidering Bhṛguization. In Brockington and Schreiner 1999, 155–68.

———. 1999d. Kūttāṇṭavar: The divine lives of a severed head. In Elisabeth Schömbucher and Claus Peter Zoller, eds., *Ways of dying: Death and its meaning in South Asia*. 275–310 and Pls. 9–14. Delhi: Manohar.

———. 2000a. Review of Brockington 1998. *IIJ* 43:161–69.

———. 2000b. Draupadī's question. In Kathleen Erndl and Alf Hiltebeitel, eds., *Is the goddess a feminist? The politics of South Asian goddesses*. 113–22. New York and Sheffield, England: New York University Press and Sheffield Academic Press.

———. In press-a. The primary process of the Indian epics. In Bruce Sullivan, ed., Indian literature issue. *IJHS*.

———. In press-b. Empire, invasion, and India's epics. Sushil Mittal, ed., Issue on Hinduism and religious studies. *IJHS*.

———. In press-c. Ambiguities of the Kṣatriya role model in the Sanskrit epics. In Lynn Thomas and Jacqueline Suthren Hirst, eds., *Papers from University of Cambridge Summer 1998 Conference on Creating the Future*. The Use and Abuse of Indian Role Models Today. Delhi: Curzon and Oxford University Press.

———. In press-d. Bhīṣma's sources. In Klaus Karttunen and Petteri Koskikallio, eds., Festschrift for Asko Parpola.

——— and Randy Kloetzli. Forthcoming. Time. In Sushil Mittal and Gene Thursby, eds., *The Hindu world*. London: Routledge.

Hinüber, Oskar von. 1990. *Der Beginn der Schrift und frühe Schriftlichkeit in Indien*. Akademie der Wissenschaften und der Literatur, Mainz, Abhandlungen der Geistes- und Sozialwissenschaftlichen Klasse, 1989, No. 11. Stuttgart: Franz Steiner.

Holtzmann, Adolf. 1892–95. *Das Mahābhārata und seine Theile*. 4 vols. Kiel: C. F. Haesler.

Hopkins, E. Washburn. 1898a. The Bhārata and the Great Bhārata. *AJP* 19:1–24.

———. 1898b. Parallel features in the two Sanskrit epics. *AJP* 19:138–51.

———. 1901. Yoga-technique in the great epic. *JAOS* 22:333–79.

———. [1901] 1969. *The great epic of India: Its character and origin*. Calcutta: Punthi Pustak.

Hopkins, Thomas W. 1971. *The Hindu religious tradition*. Encino, CA: Dickenson.

Inden, Ronald. 1985. The temple and the Hindu chain of being. In Jean-Claude Galey, ed., *L'espace du temple: Espaces, itinéraires, médiations. Puruṣārtha* 8:53–73.

———. 2000. Imperial purāṇas: Kashmir as Vaiṣṇava center of the world. In Inden, Jonathan Walters, and Daud Ali. *Querying the medieval: Texts and the history of practices in South Asia*. 29–98. Oxford: Oxford University Press.

Ingalls, Daniel H. H., and Daniel H. H. Ingalls, Jr. 1991. The *Mahābhārata*: Stylistic study, computer analysis, and concordance. In Sharma 1991, 19–56.

James, Henry. 1922. *The tragic muse*, vol. 1. The novels and tales of Henry James. New York Edition, vol. 7. New York: Charles Scribner's Sons.

Jamison, Stephanie. 1996. *Sacrificed wife, sacrificer's wife: Women, ritual, and hospitality in ancient India*. New York: Oxford.

Jani, A. N. 1990. The Mahābhārata as an organic growth of the oral literary tradition in ancient India. In Dandekar 1990, 71–85.

Jatavallabhula, Danielle Feller. 1999. The theft of the *soma*. In Brockington and Schreiner 1999, 199–225.

Jha, Trilokanatha. 1995. A code of conduct for robbers too! In Narang 1995, 242–43.

Kakar, Sudhir. 1991. *Shamans, mystics, and doctors: A psychological inquiry into India and its healing traditions*. Chicago: University of Chicago Press.

Kane, Pandurang Vaman. 1930–1962. *History of Darmaśāstra*. 5 vols. Poona: Bhandarkar Oriental Research Institute.

Kantawala, S. G. 1995. The legend of Aṇī Māṇḍavya. In Narang 1995, 101–9.

Karmarkar, A. P. 1938–39. Dr. V. S. Sukthankar's theory of the Bhṛguisation of the original Bhārata and the light it throws on the Dravidian problem. *ABORI* 20:21–24.

Karmarkar, R. D. 1952. The Pāriplava at the Aśvamedha. *ABORI* 33:26–40.

Karve, Irawati. 1974. *Yuganta: The end of an epoch*. New Delhi: Sangam Press.

Katre, Sadashiva L. 1960. Kṛṣṇa, Gopas, Gopīs, and Rādhā. In H. L. Hariyappa and M. M. Patkar, eds., *Professor P. K. Gode Commemoration Volume*. Pune: Oriental Book Agency.

Katre, Sumitra M. 1987. *Aṣṭādhyāyī of Pāṇini*. Austin: University of Texas Press.

Katz, Ruth Cecily. 1989. *Arjuna in the Mahabharata: Where Krishna is, there is victory*. Columbia: University of South Carolina Press.

———. 1991. The Sauptika episode in the structure of the Mahābhārata. In Sharma 1991, 13–49.

Kaveeshwar, G. W. 1972. *Chronological secrets of the Mahabharata war*. Poona: Aryabhushan Press.

Kelly, John D. 1996. What was Sanskrit for? Metadurcursive strategies in ancient India. In Jan E. M. Houben, ed., *Ideology and status of Sanskrit: Contributions to the history of the Sanskrit language*. 87–107. Leiden: E. J. Brill.

Kermode, Frank. 1967. *The sense of an ending: Studies in the theory of fiction*. London: Oxford University Press.

Kern, J. [1884] 1963. *Saddharma-puṇḍarīka or the lotus of the true law*. Sacred Books of the East, 21. New York: Dover.

Kibe, Sardar M. V. 1946. Vālmīki's āśrama located in Oudh. *JGJRI* 3, 3–4: 427–31.

Kirste, Johann. 1902. The Mahabharata question. *IA* 31:5–10.

Klaes, Norbert. 1975. *Conscience and consciousness: Ethical problems of Mahābhārata*. Bangalore: Dharmaram College.

Kloetzli, W. Randolph. 1983. *Buddhist cosmology (from single world system to Pure Land: Science and theology in the images of motion and light)*. Delhi: Motilal Banarsidass.

———. 1985. Maps of time—mythologies of descent: Scientific instruments and the purāṇic cosmograph. *HR* 25, 2:116–47.

Koskikallio, Petteri. 1994. When time turns: Yugas, ideologies, sacrifices. *Studia Orientalia* 73:253–71.

———. 1999. Baka Dālbhya: A complex character in Vedic ritual texts, epics, and purāṇas. *Studia Orientalia* 85:301–87.

Kramrisch, Stella. 1975. The Indian great goddess. *HR* 14:235–65.

Krishnaswami Aiyangar, S. 1919. The Hun problem in Indian history. *IA* 48:65–76.

Kuiper, F. B. J. 1983. *Ancient Indian cosmogony*. John Irwin, ed. New Delhi: Vikas Publishing House.

Kulkarni, S. M. 1989. An unresolved dilemma in Dyūta-Parvan: A question raised by Draupadī. In Matilal 1989, 150–56.

Kulke, Hermann, and Dietmar Rothermund. 1986. *A history of India*. London and Sydney: Croom Helm.

Kumar, Puspendra. 1995. The concept of Dharma-Rājā in the Mahābhārata. In Narang 1995, 239–41.

Laine, James W. 1989. *Visions of God: Narratives of theophany in the Mahābhārata*. Vienna: Gerold & Co.

Lakoff, George, and Mark Turner. 1989. *More than cool reason: A field guide to poetic metaphor*. Chicago: University of Chicago Press.

Lamotte, Étienne. 1988. *History of Buddhism from the origins to the Śaka era*. Trans. Sara Webb-Boin and Jean Dantinne. Publications de l'Institut Orientaliste de Louvain, 36. Louvain: Université Catholique de Louvain, Institut Orientaliste.

Larson, Gerald James, and Ram Shankar Bhattacharya. 1987. *Encyclopedia of Indian philosophies: Sāṃkhya. A dualist tradition in Indian philosophy*. Princeton: Princeton University Press.

Lath, Mukund. 1990. The concept of *ānṛśaṃsya* in the Mahābhārata. In Dandekar 1990, 113–19.

Lefeber, Rosalind, trans. 1994. *The Rāmāyaṇa of Vālmīki*, Vol. 4: *Kiṣkindhākāṇḍa*. Princeton: Princeton University Press.

Lerner, Paule. 1988. *Astrological key in Mahābhārata: The new era*. Trans. David White. Delhi: Motilal Banarsidass.

Leslie, Julia. 1998. A bird bereaved: The identity and significance of Vālmīki's *krauñca*. *JIP* 26:455–87.

Lester, Robert. 1966. *HR* Rāmānuja and Śrī-Vaiṣṇavism: The concept of prapatti or śaraṇāgati. *HR* 5, 2:266–82.

Lévi, Sylvain. 1918–19. Tato jayam udirayet. *ABORI* 1, 1:13–20.

Lévi-Strauss, Claude. 1963. *Totemism*. Boston: Beacon Press.

Lincoln, Bruce. 1994. *Authority: Construction and corrosion*. Chicago: University of Chicago Press.

Lipner, Julius. 1994. *Hindus: Their religious beliefs and practices*. London and New York: Routledge.

Lopez, Donald S., Jr. 1993. *The institution of fiction in Mahāyāna Buddhism*. In Schlomo Biderman and Ben-Ami Scharfstein, eds., *Myths and fictions*. 355–88. Leiden: E. J. Brill.

Lord, Albert B. [1960] 1974. *The singer of tales*. New York: Atheneum.

Lovejoy, Arthur O. [1936] 1960. *The great chain of being: A study in the history of an idea*. New York: Harper and Brothers.

Mabbett, I. W. 1983. The symbolism of Mount Meru. *HR* 23, 1:64–83.

Macdonell, Arthur A. [1898] 1974. *Vedic mythology*. Delhi: Motilal Banarsidass.

——— and A. B. Keith. [1912] 1967. *Vedic index of names and subjects*. 2 vols. Delhi: Motilal Banarsidass.

Malamoud, Charles. 1989. *Cuire le monde. Rite et pensée dans l'Inde ancienne.* Paris: Éditions la découverte.

———. 1996. *Cooking the world: Ritual and thought in ancient India.* Trans. David White. Delhi: Oxford University Press.

Mangels, Annette. 1994. *Zur Erzähltechnik im Mahābhārata.* Hamburg: Verlag Dr. Kovač.

Mankekar, Purnima. 1993. National texts and gendered lives: An ethnography of television viewers in a north Indian city. *American Ethnologist* 20, 3:543–63.

Masilamani-Meyer, Eveline. In press. *No house please.* Personal communication.

Matilal, Bimal Krishna, ed. 1989. *Moral dilemmas in the Mahābhārata.* Delhi: Motilal Banarsidass.

———. 1991. Kṛṣṇa: In defence of a devious divinity. In Sharma 1991, 401–18.

Mauss, Marcel. 1950. *Essai sur le don: Forme et raison de l'Échange dans les sociétés archaïques.* Part 2 of *Sociologie et anthropologie.* Paris: Presses Universitaires de France.

———. 1967. *The gift: Forms and functions of exchange in archaic societies.* Trans. Ian Cunnison. New York: Norton.

Mazumdar, B. C. 1906. Mahābhārata (Ādiparva, chap. 94). *Journal of the Royal Asiatic Society of Great Britain and Ireland* N.v.:225–26.

Mehendale, M. A. 1985. Draupadī's question. *JOIB* 35, 3–4:179–94.

———. 1990. Once again Draupadī's garments. *Bulletin of the Deccan College Research Institute* 50:285–90.

———. 1992. Has the Vedic rājasūya any relevance for the epic game of dice? In V. N. Jha, ed., *Vidyā-vratin. Professor A. M. Ghatage Felicitation Volume.* 61–67. Sri Garib Dass Oriental Series, No. 160. Delhi: Sri Satguru Publications.

———. 1995a. Is there only one version of the game of dice in the *Mahābhārata*? In Narang 1995, 33–39.

———. 1995b. *Reflections on the Mahābhārata war.* Shimla: Institute of Advanced Study.

Mehta, J. L. 1990. Dvaipāyana, poet of being and becoming. In Dandekar 1990, 101–11.

Mehta, M. 1973. The problem of the double introduction to the *Mahābhārata*. *JAOS* 93, 4:547–50.

Mehta, Mahesh M. 1971 and 1972. The *Mahābhārata*—A study of the Critical Edition [with special reference to the *Suparṇākhyāna* of the *Ādiparvan*]. *Bhāratīya Vidyā* 31:67–118 and 32:3–72.

Miller, Barbara Stoler. 1973. The original poem: *Vālmīki-Rāmāyaṇa* and Indian literary values. *Literature East and West* 17:163–73.

———. 1992. The character of authorship in the Sanskrit epics. *Journal of Oriental Research, Madras* 56–62:107–13.

Minkowski, C. Z. 1989. Janamejaya's *sattra* and ritual structure. *JAOS* 109, 3: 401–20.

———. 1991. Snakes, *sattras* and the *Mahābhārata*. In Sharma 1991, 384–400.

Mirashi, V. V. 1968. Location of the Naimiṣa Forest. *Purāṇa* 10, 1:27–34.

Mishra, Madhusudan. 1995. The new Aśvin-hymns. In Narang 1995, 48–59.

Misra, Prafulla K. 1995. Travel of Khāṇḍava Forest legend and Navaguñjara image. In Narang 1995, 144–48.

Mitchiner, John E. E. 1982. *Traditions of the seven Ṛṣis*. New Delhi: Motilal Banarsidass.

———. 1986. *The Yuga Purāṇa: Critically edited with an English translation and a detailed introduction*. Bibliotheca Indica No. 312. Calcutta: The Asiatic Society.

———. 1990. The Yuga Purāṇa: A footnote. *Bulletin of the School of Oriental and African Studies* 53, 2:320–22.

Mohanty, Jatindra Mohan. 1990. The attitude of modern creative writers towards the Mahābhārata: Oriya scene. In Dandekar 1990, 268–80.

Monier-Williams, Monier. 1863. *Indian epic poetry*. Edinburgh: Williams and Norgate.

———. [1899] 1964. *A Sanskrit-English dictionary*. Oxford: Clarendon Press.

Morgenroth, Wolfgang. 1978–79. Vishnu Sitaram Sukthankar as a student in Berlin, 1911–1914. *ABORI* 58–59:193–200.

Morson, Gary Saul. 1994. *Narrative and freedom: The shadow of time*. New Haven: Yale University Press.

Mukherjee, S. N. 1994. *Mahābhārata*: An ideal itihasa (history) of ancient India. In Lola Sharon Davidson, Mukherjee, and Z. Zlatar, eds., *The epic in history*. Sydney Studies in Society and Culture, No. 11. 1 and 6–18. Sydney: Association for Studies in Society and Culture.

Nabokov, Isabel. 2000. *Religion against the self: An ethnography of Tamil rituals*. New York: Oxford University Press.

Nagy, Gregory. 1992. Homeric questions. *Transactions of the American Philological Association* 122:17–60.

———. 1996a. *Homeric questions*. Austin: University of Texas Press.

———. 1996b. *Poetry as performance*. Cambridge: Cambridge University Press.

Narang, S. P., ed. 1995. *Modern evaluation of the Mahābhārata (Prof. P. K. Sharma felicitation volume)*. Delhi: Nag Publishers.

Narayana Rao, Velcheru. 1993. Purāṇa as Brahmanic ideology. In Doniger 1993a, 85–100.

Neusner, Jacob. 1965. *History and the Torah: Essays in Jewish history*. New York: Schocken.

———. 1979. Map without territory: Mishnah's system of sacrifice and sanctuary. *HR* 19:103–27.

Nikam, N. A., and Richard McKeon, ed. and trans. 1966. *The edicts of Asoka*. Chicago: University of Chicago Press.

Oberlies, Thomas. 1995. Arjunas Himmelsreise und die Tīrthayātrā der Pāṇḍavas. Zur Struktur der Tīrthayātrāparvan des Mahābhārata. *Acta Orientalia* n.v.:176–94.

———. 1998. Die Ratschläge der Sehers Nārada: Ritual an und unter der Oberfläche des Mahābhārata. In Hildegard L. C. Tristram, ed., *New Methods in the Research of Epic = Neue Methoden der Epenforschung*. 125–41. Tübingen: Gunter Narr Verlag.

Obeyesekere, Gananath. 1990. *The work of culture*. Chicago: University of Chicago Press.

O'Flaherty, Wendy Doniger. 1981. *The Rig Veda: An anthology*. Harmondsworth: Penguin.

———. 1984. *Dreams, illusions, and other realities*. Chicago: University of Chicago Press.

———. 1986. Horses and snakes in the *Ādi Parvan* of the *Mahābhārata*. In Margaret Case and N. Gerald Barrier, eds., *Aspects of India: Essays in honor of Edward Cameron Dimock, Jr*. 16–44. New Delhi: Manohar and American Institute of Indian Studies.

———. 1988. *Other peoples' myths: The cave of echoes*. New York: Macmillan. (See also Doniger.)

Oldenberg, Hermann. 1922. *Das Mahābhārata: Seine Entstehung, sein Inhalt, seine Form*. Göttingen: Vandenhoek und Ruprecht.

Olivelle, Patrick. 1993. *The āśrama system: The history and hermeneutics of a religious institution*. New York: Oxford University Press.

———. 1998. *The early Upaniṣads: Annotated text and translation*. New York: Oxford University Press.

Pande, G. C. 1990. The socio-cultural milieu of the Mahābhārata: An age of change. In Dandekar 1990, 121–37.

Pargiter, Frederick Eden. [1922] 1997. *Ancient Indian historical tradition*. Delhi: Motilal Banarsidass.

Parpola, Asko. 1994. *Deciphering the Indus script*. Cambridge: Cambridge University Press.

Patil, Narendranath B. 1983. *The folklore in the Mahābhārata*. Delhi: Ajanta Publications.

———. 1987. Aṇī Māṇḍavaya and criminal liability. *Vishveshvaranand Indological Journal* 35, 1–2:150–54.

Patnaik, Pathani. 1993. Sarala's Oriya Mahābhārata: "A vox populi" in Oriya literature. In K. S. Singh, ed., *The Mahābhārata in the tribal and folk traditions of India*. 171–76. Shimla: Indian Institute of Advanced Study; New Delhi: Anthropological Survey of India.

Patni, Binapani. 1995. Kṛṣṇa Dvaipāyana Vyāsa: The great compiler of the Mahābhārata. In Narang 1995, 24–29.

Patton, Laurie L. 1996. *Myth as argument: The Bṛhaddevatā as canonical commentary*. Religionsgeschichtliche Versuche und Vorarbeiten, vol. 41. Berlin and New York: Walter de Gruyter.

———. 1998. Mantras and miscarriage. Berz Lecture, George Washington University.

Peile, John. 1881. *Notes on the Nalopākhyānam or Tale of Nala*. Cambridge: Cambridge University Press.

Pinney, Thomas. 1986. *Kipling's India: Uncollected sketches 1884–88*. Houndmills: The Macmillan Press Ltd.

Pisani, Vittore. 1939. The rise of the *Mahābhārata*. In S. M. Katre and P. K. Gode, eds., *A volume of eastern and Indian studies*. 166–76. Bombay: Karnatak Publishers.

———. 1968. A note on the Anuśāsanaparvan. *ABORI* 48 and 49:59–62.

Pollock, Sheldon I. 1984a. Ātmānam mānuṣaṃ manye: Dharmākūtam on the divinity of Rāma. *JOIB* 33:505–28.

———. 1984b. The *Rāmāyaṇa* text and the Critical Edition. In Goldman 1984, 82–93.

———, trans. 1986. *The Rāmāyaṇa of Vālmīki: An epic of ancient India*, vol. 2: *Ayodhyākāṇḍa*. Robert P. Goldman, ed. Introduction and annotation by translator. Princeton: Princeton University Press.

———, trans. 1991. *The Rāmāyaṇa of Vālmīki: An epic of ancient India*, vol. 3: *Araṇyakāṇḍa*. Robert P. Goldman, ed. Introduction and annotation by translator. Princeton: Princeton University Press.

———. 1996. The Sanskrit cosmopolis, 300–1300: Transculturation, vernacularization, and the question of ideology. In Jan E. M. Houben, ed., *Ideology and status of Sanskrit: Contributions to the history of the Sanskrit language*. 197–247. Leiden: E. J. Brill.

———. 1998. The cosmopolitan vernacular. *JAS* 57, 1:6–37.

Polomé, Edgar. 1988. Draupadī and her Dumézilian interpretation. In A. Kumar et al., eds., *Studies in Indology. Prof. Rasik Vihari Joshi felicitation volume*. 59–72. New Delhi: Shree Publishing House.

Preciado-Solis, Benjamin. 1984. *The Kṛṣṇa cycle in the purāṇas: Themes and motifs in a heroic saga*. Delhi: Motilal Banarsidass.

Proudfoot, I. 1979. Interpreting Mahābhārata episodes as sources for the history of ideas. *ABORI* 60:41–63.

———. 1987. *Ahiṃsā and a Mahābhārata story: The development of the story of Tulādhāra in the Mahābhārata in connection with non-violence, cow protection, and sacrifice*. Asian Studies Monographs, new series no. 9. Canberra: Faculty of Asian Studies, Australian National University.

Puhvel, Jaan. 1987. *Comparative mythology*. Baltimore: Johns Hopkins University Press.

Pusalkar, A. D. 1943. Vishnu Sitaram Sukthankar (4 May 1887–21 January 1943). *JBBRAS* 19:89–92.

———. 1970. Social world in the *Mahābhārata*. *JGJRI* 26, 1–3:575–80.

Quint, David. 1993. *Epic and empire: Politics and generic form from Virgil to Milton*. Princeton: Princeton University Press.

Ragam, V. R. 1963. *Pilgrim's travel guide*, Part 2: *North India with Himalayan regions*. Guntur: Sri Sita Rama Nama Sankirtana Sangam.

Rajan, Chandra, trans. 1995. *Śivadāsa: The five-and-twenty tales of the genie (Vetālapañcavinśati)*. New York: Penguin.

Ramanujan, A. K. 1991. Repetition in the Mahābhārata. In Sharma 1991, 419–43.

Ray, Pratibha. 1995. *Yajnaseni: The story of Draupadī*. Trans. Pradip Bhattacharya. Calcutta: Rupa and Co.

Raychaudhuri, H. C. 1923. *The political history of ancient India, from the accession of Parikshit to the extinction of the dynasty*. Calcutta: University of Calcutta.

Redfield, James M. 1994. *Nature and culture in the Iliad: The tragedy of Hector*. Durham: Duke University Press.

Reich, Tamar Chana. 1998. "A battlefield of a text: Inner textual interpretation in the Sanskrit Mahābhārata." Ph.D. dissertation. Chicago: University of Chicago.

Renou, Louis. 1939. L'hymne aux Aśvin de l'Ādiparvan. In S. M. Katre and P. K. Gode, eds., *A volume of eastern and Indian studies presented to F. W. Thomas*. 177–87. Bombay: Karnatak Publishing House.

Richardson, Scott. 1990. *The Homeric narrator*. Nashville: Vanderbilt University Press.

Ricoeur, Paul. 1985. *Time and narrative*. Vol. 2. Chicago: University of Chicago Press.

———. 1992. *Oneself as another*. Trans. Kathleen Blamey. Chicago: University of Chicago Press.

Robinet, Isabelle. 1993. *Taoist meditation: The Mao-Shan tradition of great purity*. Trans. Julian F. Pas and Norman J. Girardot. Albany: State University of New York Press.

Ruben, Walter. 1968. Fighting against despots in old Indian literature. *ABORI* 48–49:111–18.

Salomon, Richard. 1995a. On the origin of the early Indian scripts. *JAOS* 115, 2:271–79.

———. 1995b. On drawing socio-linguistic distinctions in Old Indo-Aryan: The question of Kṣatriya Sanskrit and related problems. In Erdosy 1995, 293–306.

———. 1998. *Indian epigraphy: A guide to the study of inscriptions in Sanskrit, Prakrit, and other Indo-Aryan languages*. New York and Oxford: Oxford University Press.

Sarma, E. R. Sreekrishna. 1968. Kesin Dārbhya and the legend of his dīkṣā. *ABORI* 48–49:241–45.

Sax, William S. 1994. Playing the villains: Good guys and bad guys in a central Himalayan epic tradition. Paper presented at Madison, WI, conference on "Epics in the contemporary world." Personal communication.

———. 1995. Who's who in the Pāṇḍav Līla? In Sax, ed., *The gods at play: Līlā in South Asia*. 131–55. New York: Oxford University Press.

Saxena, Savitri. 1995. *Geographical survey of the purāṇas*. Delhi: Nag Publishers.

Scheuer, Jacques. 1982. *Śiva dans le Mahābhārata*. Bibliothèque de l'École des Haute Études, Sciences Religieuses, vol. 56. Paris: Presses Universitaires de France.

Schipper, Kristofer. 1993. *The Taoist body*. Trans. Karen C. Duval. Berkeley: University of California Press.

Schreiner, Peter, ed. 1997a. *Nārāyaṇīya-Studien*. Purāṇa Research Publications—Tubingen, Vol. 6. Wiesbaden: Harrassowitz Verlag.

———. 1997b. Introduction. In Schreiner 1997a:1–29.

———. 1998. Review of Lefeber 1994 and Goldman and Sutherland 1996. *AS/EA* 52, 1:300–5.

———. 1999. What comes first (in the *Mahābhārata*): Sāṃkhya or Yoga? *AS/EA* 53, 3:755–77.

Schwartzburg, Joseph E. [1978] 1992. *A historical atlas of South Asia*. New York: Oxford University Press.

Selvanayagam, Israel. 1992. Aśoka and Arjuna as counterfigures standing on the field of dharma: A historical-hermeneutical perspective. *HR* 32, 1:59–75.

Sen, Nabaneeta. 1966. Comparative studies in oral epic poetry and the Vālmīki Rāmāyaṇa: A report on the *Bālākaṇḍa*. *JAOS* 86:397–409.

Shah, Shalini. 1995. *The making of womanhood (gender relations in the Mahābharāta)*. Delhi: Manohar.

Shah, Umakant Premanand. 1975. *The Uttarakāṇḍa: The Vālmīki Rāmāyaṇa*. Bhatt and Shah 1960–75, vol. 7.

Sharma, Arvind, ed. 1991. *Essays on the* Mahābhārata. Leiden: E. J. Brill.

Shastri, Hari Prasad, trans. 1970. *The Ramayana of Valmiki*. Vol. III: *Yuddha Kanda*, Uttara Kanda. London: Shanti Sadan.

Shende, N. J. 1943. The authorship of the *Mahābhārata*. *ABORI* 24:67–82.

Shulman, David Dean. 1980. *Tamil temple myths: Sacrifice and divine marriage in South Indian Śaiva tradition*. Princeton: Princeton University Press.

———. 1991a. Toward a historical poetics of the Sanskrit epics. *International Folklore Review* 11:9–17.

———. 1991b. Fire and flood: The testing of Sītā in Kampaṉ's *Irāmāvatāram*. In Paula Richman, ed., *Many Rāmāyaṇas. The diversity of a narrative tradition in South Asia*. 89–113. Berkeley: University of California Press.

———. 1992. Devana and daiva. In A. W. van den Hoek, D. H. A. Kolff, and M. S. Oort, eds., *Ritual, state and history, Festschrift for Jan Heesterman*. 350–65. Leiden: E. J. Brill.

———. 1993. *The hungry god: Hindu tales of filicide and devotion*. Chicago: University of Chicago Press.

———. 1994. On being human in the Sanskrit epic: The riddle of Nala. *JIP* 22:1–29.

———. 1996. The Yakṣa's question. In Galit Hasan-Rokem and David Shulman, eds., *Untying the knot: On riddles and other enigmatic modes*. 151–68. New York: Oxford University Press.

———. 2001. Bhavabhūti on cruelty and compassion. In Paula Richman, ed., *Questioning Rāmāyaṇas: A South Asian narrative tradition*. 49–82. Berkeley: University of California Press.

Sinha, Binod Chandra. 1977. *History of the Śuṅga Dynasty*. Varanasi: Bharatiya.

Sircar, D. C. 1965. *Guhilas of Kishkindhā*. Calcutta: The Principal, Sanskrit College.

———. 1969a. *Ancient Malwa and the Vikramāditya tradition*. Delhi: Munshiram Manoharlal.

———, ed. 1969b. *The Bhārata war and purāṇic genealogies*. Calcutta: University of Calcutta Press.

———. 1969c. Myth of the great Bhārata war. In Sircar 1969b, 18–27.

Smith, Brian K. 1994. *Classifying the universe: The ancient Indian varṇa system and the origins of caste*. New York: Oxford University Press.

Smith, Frederick M. 1994. Who is in possession of the Veda? Columbia University Seminar on the Veda and Its Interpretation. Minutes by Tim Lubin.

Smith, John D. 1980. Old Indian: The two Sanskrit epics. In A. T. Hatto, ed., *Traditions of heroic and epic poetry*, 1: *The tradition*. London: Modern Humanities Press.

———. 1987. Formulaic language in the epics of India. In Bo Almqvist, Séamus Ô Catháin, and Pádraig Ô Héalaí, eds., *The heroic process: Form, function, and fantasy in folk epic*. 591–611. Dublin: Glendale Press.

———. 1989. Scapegoats of the gods: The ideology of the Indian epics. In Stuart H. Blackburn, Peter J. Claus, Joyce B. Flueckiger, and Susan S. Wadley, eds., *Oral epics in India*. 176–94. Berkeley: University of California Press.

———. 1992. The hero as gifted man: Nala in the *Mahābhārata*. In Christopher Shackle and Rupert Snell, eds., *The Indian narrative: Perspectives and patterns*. 13–32. Wiesbaden: Otto Harrassowitz.

Smith, Mary Carol. 1972. "The core of India's great epic." Ph.D. dissertation. Cambridge, MA: Harvard University.

———. 1975. The *Mahābhārata*'s core. *JAOS* 95:479–82.

———. 1992. *The warrior code of India's sacred song*. New York: Garland.

Smith, Ronald M. 1953. Temporal technique in story-telling illustrated from India. *Journal of the Bihar Research Society* 39, 3:269–92.

Smith, Vincent A. [1958] 1961. *The Oxford history of India*. Oxford: Clarendon Press.

Söhnen-Thieme, Renate. 1999. On the composition of the Dyūtaparvan in the Mahābhārata. In Brockington and Schreiner 1999, 139–54.

Sontheimer, Günther Dietz. 1981. Dasarā at Devaraguḍḍa: Ritual and play in the cult of Mailār/Khaṇḍobā. *South Asian Digest of Regional Writing* 10:1–28.

———. 1984. The Mallari/Khaṇḍobā myth as reflected in folk art and ritual. *Anthropos* 79:155–70.

Sörensen, S. [1904] 1963. *An index to the names in the Mahābhārata*. Delhi: Motilal Banarsidass.

Spivak, Gayatri Chakravorty. 1988. *In other worlds*. New York and London: Routledge.

Staal, Frits. 1983. *Agni: The Vedic ritual of the fire altar*. 2 vols. Berkeley, CA: Asian Humanities Press.

———. [1990] 1996. *Ritual and mantras: Rules without meaning*. Delhi: Motilal Banarsidass.

Strong, John S. 1983. *The legend of king Aśoka: A study and translation of the Aśokāvadāna*. Princeton: Princeton University Press.

Subramanian, M. V. 1967. *Vyasa and variations: The Mahabharata story*. Madras: Higginbothams.

Sukthankar, Vishnu S. 1930. Epic studies, 2. Further text-critical notes. *ABORI* 11:165–91.

———. 1933. *Ādiparvan*. Introduction and apparatus. In Sukthankar et al. 1933–70, vol. 1, with Prolegomena, i–cx.

———. 1936. Epic studies, 6: The Bhṛgus and the Bhārata: A text-historical study. *ABORI* 18, 1:1–76.

———. 1939. The Nala episode and the Rāmāyaṇa. In S. M. Katre and P. K. Gode, eds., *A volume of eastern and Indian studies presented to Professor F. W. Thomas*. 294–303. Bombay: Karnatak Publishing House.

———. 1942. *Āraṇyakaparvan*. Introduction and apparatus. In Sukthankar et al. 1933–70, vol. 3.

———. [1942] 1957. *On the meaning of the* Mahābhārata. Bombay: Asiatic Society of Bombay.

———. 1944. *Critical studies in the Mahābhārata*. Poona: Bhandarkar Oriental Research Institute.

Sullivan, Bruce M. 1990. *Kṛṣṇa Dvaipāyana Vyāsa and the Mahābhārata: A new interpretation*. Leiden: E. J. Brill.

———. 1995. Author and authority in the epic. In Narang 1995, 19–23.

Sullivan, William. 1996. *The secret of the Incas: Myth, astronomy, and the war against time*. New York: Crown.

Sutton, Nicholas. 1997. Aśoka and Yudhiṣṭhira: A historical setting for the ideological tensions of the *Mahābhārata*? *Religion* 27:331–41.

———. 2000. *Religious doctrines in the Mahābhārata*. Delhi: Motilal Banarsidass.

Suzuki, Mihoko. 1989. *Metamorphoses of Helen: Authority, difference, and the epic*. Ithaca: Cornell University Press.

Tadpatrikar, S. N. 1929. The Kṛṣṇa problem. *ABORI* 10:269–343.

Thakur, M. M. 1992. *Thus spake Bhīṣma*. Delhi: Motilal Banarsidass.

Thakur, U. 1969. The Hūṇas in the purāṇas. In Sircar 1969b, 174–82.

Thalmann, William G. 1984. *Conventions of form and thought in early Greek epic poetry*. Baltimore: Johns Hopkins University Press.

Thapar, Romila. 1978. *Ancient Indian social history: Some interpretations*. Delhi: Orient Longmans.

———. 1979. The historian and the epic. *ABORI* 60:199–213.

———. 1984. *From lineage to state: Social formations in the mid-first millenium B.C. in the Ganga valley*. Delhi: Oxford University Press.

———. 1991. Genealogical patterns as perceptions of the past. *Studies in history* 7, 1. n.s.:1–36.

———. 1992. *Interpreting early India*. Delhi: Oxford University Press.

Thieme, Paul. 1957. The interpretation of the learned. In A. S. Altekar, ed., *Felicitation volume presented to Professor Sripad Krishna Belvalkar*. 47–62. Benaras: M. B. Dass.

Thite, Ganesh Umakant. 1972. Animalism in ancient India. *JOIB* 21:191–209.

Thomas, Lynn. 1996. Paraśurāma and time. In Julia Leslie, ed., *Myth and myth-making*. 63–85. Richmond, Surrey: Curzon.

Tokunaga, Muneo. 1981. On the recensions of the *Bṛhaddevatā*. *JAOS* 101.3: 275–86.

Tschannerl, Volker M. 1992. *Das Lachen in der altindischen Literatur*. Frankfurt am Main: Peter Lang.

Türstig, Hans-Georg. 1985. The Indian sorcery called *abhicāra*. *WZKS* 29:69–117.

Vaidya, Chintaman Vinayak. [1905] 1966. *The Mahābhārata: A criticism*. Bombay: Bombay Book Depot and Delhi: Mehar Chand Lachhman Das.

———. [1906] 1972. *The riddle of the Rāmāyaṇa*. Delhi: Meherchand Lachhmandas.

———. 1907. *Epic India, or India as described in the Mahabharata and the Ramayana*. Bombay: Mrs Radhabai Atmaram Sagoon.

Vaidya, P. L. 1954. Introduction and apparatus. In Sukthankar et al. 1933–70, vol. 10.

van Buitenen, J. A. B. 1966. On the archaism of the *Bhāgavata Purāṇa*. In Milton Singer, ed., *Krishna: Myths, rites and attitudes*. 23–40. Chicago: University of Chicago Press.

———. 1972. On the structure of the Sabhāparvan of the Mahābhārata. In J. Ensink and P. Gaeffke, eds., *India maior: Congratulatory volume presented to J. Gonda*. 68–84. Leiden: E. J. Brill.

———. 1973, 1975, 1978. *The Mahābhārata*, vols. I: 1. *The book of beginnings;* II: 2. *The book of the assembly hall;* 3. *The book of the forest;* III: 4. *The book of Virāṭa;* 5. *The book of the effort*. Chicago: University of Chicago Press.

———. 1976. A reply to Goldman. *JAS* 35, 3:470–73.

———. 1981. *The Bhagavadgītā in the Mahābhārata: A bilingual translation*. Chicago: University of Chicago Press.

van der Veer, Peter. 1994. *Religious nationalism: Hindus and Muslims in India*. Berkeley: University of California Press.

———. 1999. Monumental texts: The critical edition of India's national heritage. In Jackie Assayag, ed., *The resources of history: Tradition, narration and nation in South Asia*. Institut Français de Pondichéry, Études thematiques, 8. 113–24. Paris and Pondicherry: École Française d'Extrême Orient.

van Nooten, Barend A. 1971. *The Mahābhārata attributed to Kṛṣṇa Dvaipāyana Vyāsa*. Twayne's World Authors Series, 131. New York: Twayne Publishers.

Vassilkov, Yaraslov. 1989–90. Draupadī in the assembly-hall, Gandharva-husbands and the origin of the Gaṇikās. *IT* 15–16:387–98.

———. 1995. The Mahābhārata's typological definition reconsidered. *IIJ* 38:249–56.

———. 1999. *Kālavāda* (the doctrine of cyclical time) in the *Mahābhārata* and the concept of heroic didactics. In Brockington and Schreiner 1999, 17–34.

Vaudeville, Charlotte. 1961–62. A further note on *krauñca-vadha* in Dhvanyāloka and Kāvyamīmāṃsā. *JOIB* 11:122–26.

Walters, Jonathan S. 2000. Buddhist history: The Sri Lankan Pāli vaṃsas and their community. In Ronald Inden, Walters, and Daud Ali, eds., *Querying the medieval: Texts and the history of practices in South Asia*. 99–164. Oxford: Oxford University Press.

Weller, F. 1936–37. Who were the Bhṛguids? *ABORI* 18:286–320.

West, M. L. 1999. The invention of Homer. *CQ* 49, 2:364–82.

White, David Gordon. 1991. *Myths of the dog-man*. Chicago: University of Chicago Press.

———. 1996. *The alchemical body: Siddha traditions in medieval India*. Chicago: University of Chicago Press.

Whitney, William Dwight. [1889] 1960. *Sanskrit grammar*. Cambridge: Harvard University Press.

Wikander, Stig. 1948. La légende des Pāṇḍava et la substructure mythique du Mahābhārata. Trans. Georges Dumézil, in Dumézil 1948.

———. 1950. Sur le fonds commun indo-iranien des épopées de la Perse et de l'Inde. *La nouvelle Clio* 1:310–29.

———. 1957. Nakula et Sahadeva. *Orientalia Suecana* 6:66–96.

———. 1960a. Från Bråvalla till Kurukshetra. *Arkhiv för Nordisk Filoligi* 75:183–93.

———. 1960b. Germanische und Indo-Iranische Eschatologie. *Kairos* 2:83–88.

———. 1978. Brávellir und Kurukshetra: Heldendichtung als Reflex germanischer und indo-iranischer Mythologie. Trans. Jörg Scherzer. *Sonderdruck aus Europäische Heldendichtung*. 63–74. Darmstadt: Wissenschaftliche Buchgesellschaft.

Willcock, M. M. 1964. Mythological paradeigma in the *Iliad*. *CQ* 14, 2:141–54.

Wilson, H. H., trans. [1840] 1972. *The Vishnu Purāṇa*. Calcutta: Punthi Pustak.

Winternitz, Moriz. 1897. Notes on the Mahābhārata, with special reference to Dahlmann's "Mahābhārata." *JRAS* n.v.:713–59.

———. 1908–22. *Geschichte der indischen Literatur*. 3 vols. Leipzig: C. F. Amelangs Verlag.

———. 1933–34. The criticial edition of the Mahābhārata: Ādiparvan. *ABORI* 1933–34:159–75.

———. 1962. *A history of Indian literature*. Trans. S. Ketkar. 2 vols. Calcutta: University of Calcutta.

Witzel, Michael. 1984. Sur le chemin du ciel. *Bulletin des études indiennes* 2:213–79.

———. 1986. JB pulpūlanī: The structure of a Brāhmaṇa tale. In M. D. Balasubrahmaniam, ed., *Dr. B. R. Sharma felicitation volume*. 189–216. Tirupati: Kendriya Sanskrit Vidyapeetha.

———. 1987a. The case of the shattered head. *Studien zur Indologie und Iranistik* 13/14:363–416.

———. 1987b. On the localization of vedic texts and schools (materials on Vedic śakhas, 7). In Gilbert Pollet, ed., *India and the ancient world: History, trade and culture before A.D. 650*. 173–213. Leuven: Departement Oriëntalistiek.

———. 1987c. On the origin of the literary device of the "frame story" in old Indian literature. In H. Falk, ed., *Hinduismus und Buddhismus: Festschrift für Ulrich Schneider*. 380–414. Freiburg: Hedwig Falk.

———. 1989a. Tracing the Vedic dialects. In Collette Caillat, ed., *Dialectes dans les littératures indo-aryennes*. Acts of the Colloque International, Paris, Sept 16–18, 1986. Publications de L'Institut de Civilisation Indienne, Series 8, Fasc. 55. 97–265. Paris: Edition-Diffusion de Bocard.

———. 1989b. Ṛgvedic history: Poets, chieftains and polities. In Collette Caillat, ed., *Dialectes dans les littératures indo-aryennes*. 307–52. Paris: Edition-Diffusion de Bocard.

———. 1995a. Early sanskritization. Origins and development of the Kuru state. Preprint from the author via Madeleine Biardeau.

———. 1995b. Early Indian history: Linguistic and textual parametres. In Erdosy 1995, 85–125.

———. 1995c. Ṛgvedic history: Poets, chieftains and polities. In Erdosy 1995, 307–52.

———. 1996. Looking for the heavenly casket. Thieme Festschrift. *Studien zur Indologie und Iranistik* 20:531–54.

———. 1997. The development of the Vedic canon and its schools: The social and political milieu. In Michael Witzel, ed., *Inside the texts—beyond the texts: New approaches to the study of the Vedas*. 257–345. Harvard Oriental Series Opera Minora, Vol. 2. Cambridge: Department of Sanskrit and Indian Studies, Harvard University.

———. 1999. The Pleiades and the Bears viewed from inside the Vedic texts. *Electronic Journal of Vedic Studies* 5, 2:10–18.

———. N.d. Partial translation of Witzel 1984. Personal communication, author.

Yardi, M. R. 1986. *The Mahābhārata: Its genesis and growth. A statistical study*. Poona: Bhandarkar Oriental Research Institute.

Zimmer, Heinrich. 1962. *Myths and symbols in Indian art and civilization*. New York: Harper.

Index

Made in the USA
Las Vegas, NV
08 November 2023

80474805R10219